W9-CZM-765

THE LIBRARY OF PHILOSOPHY AND THEOLOGY

Edited by

JOHN MCINTYRE AND IAN T. RAMSEY

HISTORICAL SELECTIONS IN THE PHILOSOPHY OF RELIGION

Already published

ESSAYS—*Philosophical and Theological*, by Rudolf Bultmann

ETHICS, by Dietrich Bonhoeffer

AN EXISTENTIALIST THEOLOGY—*A Comparison of Heidegger and Bultmann* by John Macquarrie

NEW ESSAYS IN PHILOSOPHICAL THEOLOGY, edited by Antony Flew and Alasdair MacIntyre

SUBJECT AND OBJECT IN MODERN THEOLOGY, by James Brown

MYSTERY AND PHILOSOPHY, by Michael B. Foster

METAPHYSICAL BELIEFS, edited by Alasdair MacIntyre

RELIGIOUS LANGUAGE, by Ian T. Ramsey

THE CHRISTIAN MESSAGE AND MYTH, by L. Malavez

FROM ROUSSEAU TO RITSCHL, by Karl Barth

PROBLEMS OF RELIGIOUS KNOWLEDGE, by Peter Munz

THE SCOPE OF DEMYTHOLOGIZING, by John Macquarrie

ANSELM—*Fides Quaerens Intellectum*, by Karl Barth

A DIALOGUE OF RELIGIONS, by Ninian Smart

ON THE ETERNAL IN MAN, by Max Scheler

BEING AND TIME, by Martin Heidegger

HISTORICAL SELECTIONS IN THE PHILOSOPHY OF RELIGION, edited by Ninian Smart

In preparation (the following are not necessarily titles)

THEOLOGICAL ETHICS, by H. Thielicke

PHILOSOPHY AND THEOLOGY IN THE TWENTIETH CENTURY, by John Macquarrie

HISTORICAL SELECTIONS IN THE PHILOSOPHY OF RELIGION

EDITED BY
NINIAN SMART

SCM PRESS LTD
56 BLOOMSBURY STREET
LONDON

FIRST PUBLISHED 1962

PRINTED IN GREAT BRITAIN BY
THE CAMELOT PRESS LTD
LONDON AND SOUTHAMPTON

TO CAROLINE

CONTENTS

Preface 11
Introduction 13
Acknowledgments 16

PART ONE

1 PLATO on Immortality 19
Phaedo

2 AUGUSTINE on the Existence of God and on Free Will 31
A. The Existence of God 32
De Libero Arbitrio
B. Free Will 40
De Libero Arbitrio

3 PSEUDO-DIONYSIUS on the Negative Way 50
Mystical Theology

4 ANSELM on the Ontological Argument 55
Proslogium

5 AQUINAS on Reason and Faith, the Existence of God, Analogy and on Miracles 59
A. Reason and Faith 61
Summa Theologica
B. The Existence of God 63
Summa Theologica
C. Analogy 70
Summa Theologica
D. Miracles 76
Summa Theologica

PART TWO

6 HERBERT OF CHERBURY on Reason and Faith 85
De Veritate

7 DESCARTES on the Existence of God 105
Meditations

8 SPINOZA on the Existence of God 124
Ethics

9 LOCKE on Reason and Faith 129
An Esssay concerning Human Understanding

10 LEIBNIZ on the Existence of God and on the Problem of Evil 141
A. The Existence of God 143
The Monadology
B. The Problem of Evil 146
Theodicy

11 BERKELEY on the Existence of God 156
Alciphron

12 BUTLER on Reason and Faith and on Immortality 185
A. Reason and Faith 186
Analogy of Religion
B. Immortality 192
Analogy of Religion

13 HUME on the Existence of God and on Miracles 205
A. The Existence of God 207
Dialogues on Natural Religion
B. Miracles 232
Essay on Miracles

14 KANT on the Existence of God and on Immortality 248
A. The Existence of God 250
Critique of Pure Reason
B. Immortality 271
Critique of Practical Reason

15 HEGEL on Revealed Religion 290
Encyclopaedia of the Philosophical Sciences

16 SCHLEIERMACHER on Religious Experience, Religious Language and on Miracles 306

A. Religious Experience 307

The Christian Faith

B. Religious Language 320

The Christian Faith

C. Miracles 328

The Christian Faith

17 MILL on Miracles 340

A System of Logic

18 KIERKEGAARD on Reason and Faith 345

Philosophical Fragments

19 MANSEL on the Limits of Religious Thought 361

The Limits of Religious Thought

20 JAMES on Religious Belief 378

The Will to Believe

21 ROYCE on Reason and Religion 399

Sources of Religious Insight

22 OTTO on Religious Experience 421

The Idea of the Holy

23 COOK WILSON on the Existence of God 439

Statement and Inference

24 TENNANT on the Problem of Evil 464

Philosophical Theology

Index of Names 491

Index of Subjects 495

PREFACE

THIS book is intended for those who, for whatever reason, feel impelled to investigate the philosophy of religion. It is necessary for such persons to be acquainted with the history of philosophical discussions about religion; and it is more than half a century since a book of historical selections in the philosophy of religion has been produced in Britain. The reasons for the choices which I have made will be found in the Introduction. Since many of the people who may wish to use this book will have little knowledge of philosophy, I have included prefaces about the life, work and philosophical views of the philosophers concerned, together with bibliographies and notes to the texts. But I have not tried to make everything absolutely clear (supposing it to be possible), since the main point of having selections from the writings of the important figures of the past is that the student may, initially at least, by-pass the historian and the commentator. I hope also that the book may be of some use to those who are not beginners. Philosophers and theologians may find it handy to have such a selection of original writings.

In compiling the book I have had help from a number of people. Mr John Olford suggested the idea of such a book, and successive editors of the SCM Press have been patient about my dilatoriness. I wish to thank Professor H. D. Lewis, Professor Alan Richardson, Professor Gregor Smith, Professor Paul Edwards, Professor Donald Mathers and the Rev. Howard Root for their advice. I am deeply grateful to Mr David Hamlyn for reading the MS and saving me from many errors. Acknowledgments for permission to publish copyright material are printed separately.

N. S.

INTRODUCTION

THOSE who think about theology are necessarily landed with the philosophy of religion. And those who philosophize about religion ought to know something of past philosophical theology. But it is not good just to read histories of philosophies, excellent as these occasionally are. We should treat our forebears like our contemporaries and read what they themselves have to say. This book of *Selections* may make the job easier. By 'past philosophical theology' I mean the writings about religion of philosophers in the Western tradition. It would be salutary, but alas impracticable, to include something of the Oriental theologians and philosophers, especially because they do not think according to the same presuppositions as those Westerners who claim to be guided by reason alone.

In selecting passages I have tried to bear three things in mind: the present interest of the writer, his importance in the history of philosophy and of the philosophy of religion, and the mutual relevance of the passages. There are different strands of discussion running through the book. Naturally, the supposed proofs of God's existence figure prominently, and we have Augustine, Anselm, Aquinas, Descartes, Spinoza, Leibniz, Berkeley, Hume, Kant, Kierkegaard and Cook Wilson on this. There are Pseudo-Dionysius, Aquinas, Berkeley and Schleiermacher on religious language; Augustine, Leibniz and Tennant on the problem of evil; Aquinas, Hume, Schleiermacher and Mill on miracles; Aquinas, Herbert of Cherbury, Locke, Butler, Hegel, Kierkegaard and Royce on reason and faith; Mansel and James on related topics; and Schleiermacher and Otto on religious experience. Needless to say, the topics intertwine a good deal.

I am conscious that many will quarrel with my selection of authors and passages. Part I, which is introductory (the body of the book deals with 'modern philosophers'), includes Plato, Augustine, Pseudo-Dionysius, Anselm and Aquinas. The last is represented more fully (especially in view of the marvellous compression of his arguments), for in terms of contemporary influence he belongs in a sense with the moderns. Part II includes Herbert of Cherbury, Descartes, Spinoza, Locke, Leibniz, Berkeley, Butler, Hume, Kant, Hegel, Schleiermacher, Mill, Mansel, James, Royce, Otto, Cook Wilson and Tennant. Some of these choices may be thought eccentric, notably Herbert of Cherbury, Mansel, Royce,

Cook Wilson and Tennant. Lord Herbert comes in because of his later influence on the Deists, his connections with Locke and his notable contrast to the medievals. Mansel is neglected today, but his famous Bampton Lectures express, against the background of Absolutism, a view which has contemporary echoes: the view, namely, that speculative truth about God being unattainable, we must rely for knowledge of the Unknown upon revelation. Royce is a representative of post-Hegelian Idealism, writes more clearly than most such, and gives it an original interpretation. I suspect that Cook Wilson's long essay on the proof of God's existence is the most careful and important piece of writing on this topic in this century. As for Tennant, his version of empirical theism has not gained the recognition it deserves, and though his style is somewhat opaque, the extended treatment of the problem of evil here included is an excellent complement to that of Leibniz. It is one of the best attempts to deal with this problem.

But doubtless it is the omissions that people will worry about. Only the dead are here included, but even so there are surprising gaps, some may think. Hobbes, Pascal, Bergson, C. S. Peirce, Collingwood and Oman are omitted; possibly too I should have put in Newman, Bradley and MacTaggart; and where are the Cambridge Platonists, Schopenhauer, Nietzsche? Such a list can go on multiplying. Hobbes is jostled out by others of a similar period. Pascal is hard to select from. Bergson gave way to William James. C. S. Peirce is a massive and important philosopher, but is peculiarly difficult and eccentric when writing on religion; his numerous historical references and his idiosyncratic jargon make him hard to deal with in such selections as these. Collingwood would have come in if I had been able to include a thread of passages dealing with the philosophy of history. Oman gives place, perhaps unjustly, to Tennant. But it would be tedious to outline the reasons for, and context of, all the omissions.

It will be noted that there is a fair amount of variation in the length of the passages included. Mill and Spinoza, for example, are represented briefly; the former because the passage is a rather concise reply to Hume, and the latter for a very different reason. I include something not because it stands as a reasonably self-contained essay, but simply to whet the reader's appetite for more of Spinoza's theorems. Again, Otto is on the short side, for a rather similar reason: I thought it best to present something central from his *Idea of the Holy*, even though it is not easy to chop up. By contrast, Hume is represented by a long excerpt from his *Dialogues* as well as by his *Essay on Miracles*. It was a defect of Caldecott and Mackintosh's *Selections from the Literature of Theism* that it had nothing from Hume. Schleiermacher likewise is given some prominence, not only because of his importance in the history of Protestant philosophical theology, but because he marks a turning-point in the history of philosophical theology towards an analysis of the nature of religion itself (religious concepts hitherto having for the most part been taken for granted).

Before each selection I put in a biographical note, an account of the philosophical position of the writer in question and a brief bibliography. The philosophical introductions are sometimes quite long, especially when I deal with key figures, in order that the student may get a reasonable insight into the main features of the history of European philosophy up to the beginning of this century. The revolt against Idealism, represented by such philosophers as Moore, Russell and Wittgenstein, is not described, since it belongs, in a sense, to the contemporary scene. The results of this revolt for the philosophy of religion can be seen in part in *New Essays in Philosophical Theology*, edited by Antony Flew and Alasdair MacIntyre, to which the present *Selections* can function as a companion volume.[1]

As well as the philosophical introductions, I have written notes to the text, in order that historical and technical points need not hold the student up unduly. But I have not sought, as some note-writers and commentators do, to criticize any of the arguments. This is for the reader to do for himself, or a task for the lecturer on these topics.

Further, there is a full index to supplement the cross-references in the notes. As for the texts, I have taken the liberty of altering occasional words where they are obscuringly archaic. Some of the writers' footnotes have been cut out, and the punctuation has sometimes been improved.

I hope that in these ways I have been of a little use.

[1] For the revolt against Idealism, see J. O. Urmson, *Philosophical Analysis* (Oxford, 1956) and J. Passmore, *A Hundred Years of Philosophy* (London, 1957). Another useful companion to the present volume is J. Collins, *God in Modern Philosophy* (London, 1960).

ACKNOWLEDGMENTS

I AM most grateful for the following permissions to use copyright material: to the SCM Press, London and the Westminster Press, Philadelphia, in respect of J. H. S. Burleigh's translations of *De Libero Arbitrio* taken from his *Augustine: Earlier Writings* (Library of Christian Classics VI); to the SPCK in respect of the passage here printed from C. E. Rolt's *Dionysius the Areopagite's Mystical Theology*; to Messrs Burns Oates and Washbourne in respect of four passages from the Dominican translation of Aquinas' *Summa Theologica*; to Dr Meyrick H. Carré in respect of the passage from his translation of Herbert of Cherbury's *De Veritate*; to Messrs T. & T. Clark in respect of the passages from the translation by H. R. Mackintosh, J. S. Stewart and others of Schleiermacher's *The Christian Faith*, and in respect of the chapter from Josiah Royce's *The Sources of Religious Insight*; to Princeton University Press in respect of the passage from David F. Swenson's translation of Kierkegaard's *Philosophical Fragments*; to the Oxford University Press in respect of the passages from John W. Harvey's translation of R. Otto's *The Idea of the Holy*; to the Clarendon Press, Oxford, in respect of the passage from J. Cook Wilson's *Statement and Inference*; and to the Syndics of the University Press, Cambridge, in respect of the passage from F. R. Tennant's *Philosophical Theology.*

PART ONE

I

PLATO

on IMMORTALITY

Biographical Note Born in Athens or Aegina, probably in 428–427 BC, of distinguished parentage. As a young man, he associated with Socrates, who deeply influenced him. 399, death of Socrates. Visited Italy and Sicily, ?388, where he became acquainted with members of the Pythagorean school. Invited to the court of Dionysius I of Syracuse. 388-387, returned to Athens, where he founded the Academy. Aristotle entered Academy in 367, in which year P. went again to Syracuse, to educate young Dionysius II, but soon returned to Athens. Third visit to Sicily in 361. Returned again to the Academy in 360. Died 348-347.

Principal works: *Gorgias, Meno, Euthyphro, Crito, Phaedo, Symposium, Protagoras, Republic, Phaedrus, Theaetetus, Parmenides, Sophist, Statesman, Philebus, Timaeus* and *Laws*. (There is much dispute about the ordering and dating of P.'s works: for a brief account, see F. C. Copleston, *History of Philosophy*, Vol. i, Ch. XVIII.)

Philosophical Note P.'s philosophical views can best be seen by reference to different strands of the thought of certain predecessors and contemporaries. (1) Socrates, in his questionings, tended to concentrate on moral topics and to try to discover definitions of important moral concepts, such as *courage* (in the *Laches*) and *piety* (see the *Euthyphro*). This search for definitions led P. to the view that it is through dialectic (i.e. philosophical argument) that one gains insight into the truth. (2) Heraclitus (*fl.* 504–501 BC, at Ephesus) had urged that everything is in flux: the cosmos is a constant series of changes, governed, however, by a law of rhythmic change. This suggested to P. that, if knowledge is of timeless truths, such as are yielded by dialectic, the world of shifting sense-experience does not of itself yield knowledge. (3) Parmenides (*fl.* 474, at Elea) had preached that Reality (or Being) is one, since anything other than it would be non-being, unreality, the existence of which cannot be conceived. By similar arguments he tried to show that it must be eternal, motionless, continuous, etc. This notion of an ultimate reality quite different from the world of ordinary experience influenced P. in postulating, as the proper object of knowledge, a transcendent world of Forms (or Ideas)—eternal archetypes of things and properties to be found in the observable world. (4) The Pythagorean school (founder: Pythagoras, born *c.* 580 BC in Samos) held that numbers are the ultimate constituents of things. For (*a*) it had been noticed that harmonic intervals can be expressed mathematically; (*b*) certain geometrical figures can be expressed as made up of arrangements of points (really corporeal units) which can be expressed mathematically (e.g. a straight line corresponds to 2, a right-angled triangle to 3, and so on); (*c*) advances in geometry led them to suspect that mathematics provided the key to knowledge of the world. These mathematical speculations reinforced P.'s desire to elaborate a theory of knowledge in which the highest place is given to timeless truths of a sort similar to those of deductive sciences such as geometry.

Briefly, then, P.'s metaphysical views were as follows: (i) sense-experience does not yield knowledge, but only opinion; (ii) to gain knowledge we have to transcend sense-experience—though the latter is sometimes suggestive; (iii) it is suggestive in that it points to the existence of archetypes of observable things, etc., in 'another world'; (iv) this is the world of Forms; (v) within this world of Forms there is a hierarchy, with the Form of the Good crowning the system; (vi) through mathematical studies one is led away from sense-experience and is introduced to the sphere of rigorous arguments and timeless truths; (vii) this serves as a preparation for philosophical dialectic, which leads to an insight into the nature and structure of the Forms and culminates in a vision of the Good. It will be seen, that on P.'s theory, the Forms play a number of roles. (i) They are used to show how general words have fixed meanings, for these words refer back to the archetypes of the particular and shifting things we perceive in the world; (ii) they provide a system of concepts which can, in theory, be described and so provide a structure of knowledge not unlike that of mathematics (as the most advanced science of the day it was naturally thought of as the model); (iii) they enable P. to give something of an account of the world in terms of *functions*—for the Good is placed at the top because each Form has reference to the Good inasmuch as it expresses an ideal towards which particulars strive;[1] (iv) likewise the Supreme Craftsman (see the *Timaeus*) or Demiurge imposes order and design on the world by reference to the Forms, which are here used to illuminate the purposive and orderly features of the cosmos; (v) the Good itself is the object of a kind of mystical vision. Thus the Forms play their parts as helping towards a theory of meaning, a theory of knowledge, a theory of final causes (i.e. a theory which explains features of the universe by reference to purposes or functions), a cosmology, a doctrine of the supreme religious aim.

For the Christian adaptation of P.'s doctrines, see p. 31; for the non-Christian development of Neo-Platonism, see p. 50; and for Aristotle's modifications and innovations, see p. 59.

The following passage is taken from the *Phaedo*, a report of a discussion Socrates is supposed to have had in the condemned cell. He first argues that change occurs from one opposite to another in alternation. E.g., for X to become greater it must have been smaller to start with. But the opposite of life is death. Hence just as sleeping is consequent on waking, so life is consequent on death. Again, perceptible objects can be referred to the Forms. But we do not see the Forms in this life: hence our knowledge of the Forms must be through recollection of what we have seen in a previous life. But these two arguments at most show that the span of life of the soul is greater than that of the body; something more is needed to show immortality. First, Socrates argues that by coming into contact with the Forms, the soul shows itself to be akin to the unchanging, and that by ruling the body the soul shows itself to be akin to the divine. Second, the soul is what it is by participating in (or resembling) the Form of Life. But Forms do not admit the presence of their opposites (e.g. the Hot does not admit the presence of the Cold).

[1] See also n. 5 to p. 69.

Hence the soul cannot participate in the Form of Death, and so is imperishable and therefore (though P. does not argue this) indestructible. S. also in the course of the argument replies to an argument put forward by Simmias, that the soul is the harmony of the body (i.e. the correct arrangement of bodily elements). The following passages include the second and third of the main arguments mentioned above. Cebes and Simmias, the chief interlocutors in the Dialogue, were disciples of Philolaus, a well-known later Pythagorean.

Bibliographical Note There is a complete English version of P.'s works by B. Jowett (revised, 4 vols., Oxford, 1953). The translations with 'running commentary' by F. M. Cornford of the *Republic* (Oxford, 1941), *Theaetetus* and *Sophist* (*Plato's Theory of Knowledge*, Oxford, 1935) and *Timaeus* (*Plato's Cosmology*) are admirable. The *Phaedo* is translated with introduction and notes by R. Hackforth (Cambridge, 1952). Good general introductions are A. E. Taylor, *Plato* (London, 1935), G. C. Field, *The Philosophy of Plato* (2nd edn, London, 1949) and J. Burnet, *Greek Philosophy*, Vol. i (London, 1914). More detailed works are: W. F. R. Hardie, *A Study in Plato* (Oxford, 1936), A. J. Festugière, *Contemplation et Vie selon Platon* (Paris, 1936), J. Stenzel, *Plato's Method of Dialectic* (Oxford, 1940, Eng. trans.), R. Robinson, *Plato's Earlier Dialectic* (N.Y., 1941) and W. D. Ross, *Plato's Theory of Ideas* (2nd edn, Oxford, 1953). K. Popper's *The Open Society and its Enemies*, Vol. i (3rd edn revised, London, 1957) contains an entertaining assault upon Plato, both stimulating and passionate, but see R. B. Levinson, *In Defense of Plato* (Cambridge, Mass., 1953).

IMMORTALITY

Phaedo, 72E ff.

Cebes added: Your favourite doctrine, Socrates, that knowledge is simply recollection, if true, also necessarily implies a previous time in which we have learned that which we now recollect. But this would be impossible unless our soul had been in some place before existing in the form of man; here then is another proof of the soul's immortality.

But tell me, Cebes, said Simmias, interposing, what arguments are urged in favour of this doctrine of recollection. I am not very sure at the moment that I remember them.

One excellent proof, said Cebes, is afforded by questions. If you put a question to a person in a right way he will give a true answer of himself, but how could he do this unless there were knowledge and right reason already in him? And this is most clearly shown when he is taken to a diagram or to anything of that sort.[1]

But if, said Socrates, you are still incredulous, Simmias, I would ask you

[1] P.'s doctrine of recollection is illustrated in the *Meno*, where an ignorant slave-boy is led, by questioning, to see a truth in geometry.

whether you may not agree with me when you look at the matter in another way:— I mean, if you are still incredulous as to whether knowledge is recollection?

Incredulous I am not, said Simmias; but I want to have this doctrine of recollection brought to my own recollection, and, from what Cebes has said, I am beginning to recollect and be convinced: but I should like to hear what you were going to say.

This is what I would say, he replied: We should agree if I am not mistaken that what a man recollects he must have known at some previous time.

Very true.

And what is the nature of this knowledge or recollection? I mean to ask, whether a person who, having seen or heard or in any way perceived anything, knows not only that, but has a conception of something else which is the subject, not of the same but of some other kind of knowledge, may not be fairly said to recollect that of which he has the conception?

What do you mean?

I mean what I may illustrate by the following instance:— The knowledge of a lyre is not the same as knowledge of a man?

True.

And yet what is the feeling of lovers when they recognize a lyre, or a garment, or anything else which the beloved has been in the habit of using? Do not they, from knowing the lyre, form in the mind's eye an image of the youth to whom the lyre belongs? And this is recollection. In like manner anyone who sees Simmias may recollect Cebes; and there are endless examples of the same thing.

Endless indeed, replied Simmias.

And recollection is most commonly a process of recovering that which has been already forgotten through time and inattention.

Very true, he said.

Well; and may you not also from seeing the picture of a horse or a lyre remember a man?—and from the picture of Simmias, you may be led to remember Cebes?

True.

Or you may also be led to the recollection of Simmias himself?

Quite so.

And in all these cases, the recollection may be derived from things either like or unlike?

It may be.

And when the recollection is derived from like things, then another consideration is sure to arise, namely whether the likeness in any degree falls short or not of that which is recollected.

Very true, he said.

And shall we proceed a step further and affirm that there is such a thing as equality, not of one piece of wood or stone with another, but that, over and above this, there is absolute equality? Shall we say so?

Say so, yes, replied Simmias, and swear to it, with all the confidence in life.

And do we know the nature of this absolute essence?

To be sure, he said.

And whence did we obtain our knowledge? Did we not see equalities of material things, such as pieces of wood and stones, and gather from them the idea of an equality which is different from them? For you will acknowledge that there is a difference. Or look at the matter in another way:— Do not the same pieces of wood or stone appear at one time equal and at another time unequal?

That is certain.

But are real equals ever unequal? Or is the idea of equality the same as of inequality?

Impossible, Socrates.

Then those (so-called) equals are not the same as the idea of equality?

I should say clearly not, Socrates.

And yet from these equals, although differing from the idea of equality, you conceived and attained that idea?

Very true, he said.

Which might be like or might be unlike them?

Yes.

But that makes no difference: whenever from seeing one thing you conceived another, whether like or unlike, there must surely have been an act of recollection?

Very true.

But what would you say of equal portions of wood and stone, or other material equals? And what is the impression produced by them? Are they equals in the same sense in which absolute equality is equal? Or do they fall short of this perfect equality in a measure?

Yes, he said, in a very great measure too.

And must we not allow that when I or anyone, looking at any object, observes that the thing which he sees aims at being some other thing, but falls short of and cannot be that other thing, but is inferior, he who makes this observation must have had a previous knowledge of that to which the other, although similar, was inferior?

Certainly.

And has not this been our own case in the matter of equals and of absolute equality?

Precisely.

Then we must have known equality previously to the time when we first saw the material equals and reflected that all these apparent equals strive to attain absolute equality, but fall short of it?

Very true.

And we recognize also that this absolute equality has only been known, and can only be known, through the medium of sight and touch, or of some of the other senses, which are all alike in this respect?

Yes, Socrates, as far as the argument is concerned, one of them is the same as the other.

From the senses then is derived the knowledge that all sensible things aim at an absolute equality of which they fall short?

Yes.

Then before we began to see or hear or perceive in any way we must have had a knowledge of absolute equality, or we could not have referred to that standard the equals which are derived from the senses?—for to that they all aspire and of that they fall short.

No other inference can be drawn from the previous statements.

And did we not see and hear and have the use of our other senses as soon as we were born?

Certainly.

Then we must have acquired the knowledge of equality at some previous time?

Yes.

That is to say, before we were born, I suppose?

True.

And if we acquired this knowledge before we were born, and were then having the use of it, then we also knew before we were born and at the instant of birth not only the equal or the greater or less, but all other ideas; for we are not speaking only of equality, but of beauty, goodness, justice, holiness and all which we stamp with the name of essence in the dialectical process, both when we ask and when we answer questions. Of all this we may certainly affirm that we acquired the knowledge before birth?

We may.

But if, after having acquired, we have not forgotten what in each case we acquired, then we must always have come into life having knowledge and shall always continue to know as long as life lasts—for knowing is the acquiring and retaining of knowledge and not forgetting. Is not forgetting, Simmias, just the losing of knowledge?

Quite true, Socrates.

But if the knowledge which we acquired before birth were lost by us at birth, and if afterwards by the use of the senses we recovered what we previously knew, will not the process which we call learning be a recovering of the knowledge which is natural to us, and may not this be rightly termed recollection?

Very true.

So much is clear—that when we perceive something, either by the help of sight or hearing or some other sense, from that perception we are able to obtain a notion of some other thing like or unlike which is associated with it but has been forgotten. Whence, as I was saying, one of two alternatives follows:— either we had this knowledge at birth and continued to know through life; or after birth those who are said to learn only remember—and learning is simply recollection.

Yes, that is quite true, Socrates.

And which alternative, Simmias, do you prefer? Had we the knowledge at our birth or did we recollect the things which we knew previously to our birth?

I cannot decide at the moment.

At any rate you can decide whether he who has knowledge will or will not be able to render an account of his knowledge. What do you say?

Certainly he will.

But do you think that every man is able to give an account of these very matters about which we are speaking?

Would that they could, Socrates, but I rather fear that tomorrow at this time there will no longer be anyone alive who is able to give an account of them such as ought to be given.

Then you are not of opinion, Simmias, that all men know these things?

Certainly not.

They are in process of recollecting that which they learned before?

Certainly.

But when did our souls acquire this knowledge? Not since we were born as men?

Certainly not.

And therefore previously?

Yes.

Then, Simmias, our souls must also have existed without bodies before they were in the form of man and must have had intelligence.

Unless indeed you suppose, Socrates, that these notions are given us at the very moment of birth: for this is the only time which remains.

Yes, my friend, but if so, when do we lose them? For they are not in us when we are born—that is admitted. Do we lose them at the moment of receiving them, or, if not, at what other time?

No, Socrates, I perceive that I was unconsciously talking nonsense.

Then may we not say, Simmias, that if—as we are always repeating—there is an absolute beauty and goodness and an absolute essence of all things; and if to this, which is now discovered to have existed in our former state, we refer all our sensations, and with this compare them, finding these ideas to be pre-existent and our inborn possession—then our souls must have had a prior existence, but if not, there would be no force in the argument? There is the same proof that these ideas must have existed before we were born, as that our souls existed before we were born; and if not the ideas, then not the souls.

Yes, Socrates; I am convinced that there is precisely the same necessity for the one as for the other; and the argument retreats successfully to the position that the existence of the soul before birth cannot be separated from the existence of the essences of which you speak. For there is nothing which to my mind is so patent as that beauty, goodness and the other notions of which you were just now speaking have a most real and absolute existence; and I am satisfied with the proof.

Well, but is Cebes equally satisfied? For I must convince him too.

I think, said Simmias, that Cebes is satisfied: although he is the most incredulous of mortals, yet I believe that he is sufficiently convinced of the existence of the soul before birth. But that after death the soul will continue to exist is not yet proven even to my own satisfaction. I cannot get rid of the feeling of the many to which Cebes was referring—the feeling that when the man dies the soul will be dispersed and that this may be the extinction of her. For admitting that she may have been born elsewhere, and framed out of other elements, and was in existence before entering the human body, why after having entered in and gone out again may she not herself be destroyed and come to an end?

Very true, Simmias, said Cebes; about half of what was required has been proven; to wit, that our souls existed before we were born:— that the soul will exist after death as well as before birth is the other half of which the proof is still wanting, and has to be supplied; when that is given the demonstration will be complete.

But that proof, Simmias and Cebes, has been already given, if you put the two arguments together—I mean this and the former one, in which we admitted that everything living is born of the dead. For if the soul exists before birth, and in coming to life and being born can be born only from death and dying, must she not after death continue to exist, since she has to be born again? Surely the proof which you desire has been already furnished. Still I suspect that you and Simmias would be glad to probe the argument further. Like children, you are haunted with a fear that when the soul leaves the body, the wind may really blow her away and scatter her; especially if a man should happen to die in a great storm and not when the sky is calm.

Cebes answered with a smile: Then, Socrates, you must argue us out of our fears—and yet strictly speaking, they are not our fears, but there is a child within us to whom death is a sort of hobgoblin: him too we must persuade not to be afraid when he is alone in the dark.

Socrates said: Let the voice of the charmer be applied daily until you have charmed away the fear.

And where shall we find a good charmer of our fears, Socrates, when you are gone?

Hellas, he replied, is a large place, Cebes, and has many good men, and there are barbarous races not a few: seek for him among them all, far and wide, sparing neither pains nor money; for there is no better way of spending your money. And you must seek among yourselves too; for you will not find others better able to make the search.

The search, replied Cebes, shall certainly be made. And now, if you please, let us return to the point of the argument at which we digressed.

By all means, Socrates; what else should I wish?

Very good.

Must we not, said Socrates, ask ourselves what that is which, as we imagine, is liable to be scattered, and about which we fear? And what again is that about which we have no fear? And then we may proceed further to enquire whether that which suffers dispersion is or is not of the nature of soul—our hopes and fears as to our own souls will turn upon the answers to these questions.

Very true, Cebes said.

Now the compound or composite may be supposed to be naturally capable, as of being compounded, so also of being dissolved; but that which is uncompounded, and that only, must be, if anything is, indissoluble.

Yes; I should imagine so, said Cebes.

And the uncompounded may be assumed to be the same and unchanging whereas the compound is always changing and never the same.

I agree, he said.

Then now let us return to the previous discussion. Is that idea or essence, which in the dialectical process we define as essence or true existence—whether essence of equality, beauty or anything else—are these essences, I say, liable at times to some degree of change? Or are they each of them always what they are, having the same self-existent and unchanging forms, not admitting of variation at all, or in any way, or at any time?

They must always be the same, Socrates, replied Cebes.

And what would you say about the many beautiful things—whether men or horses or garments or any other things which are named by the same names and may be called equal or beautiful,—are they all unchanging and the same always, or quite the reverse? May they not rather be described as almost always changing and hardly ever the same, either with themselves or with one another?

The latter, replied Cebes; they are always in a state of change.

And these you can touch and see and perceive with the senses, but the unchanging things you can only perceive with the mind—they are invisible and are not seen?

That is very true, he said.

Well then, added Socrates, let us suppose that there are two sorts of existences—one seen, the other unseen.

Let us suppose them.

The seen is the changing, and the unseen is the unchanging?

That may be also supposed.

And, further, is not one part of us body, another part soul?

To be sure.

And to which class is the body more alike and akin?

Clearly to the seen—no one can doubt that.

And is the soul seen or not seen?

Not by man, Socrates.

And what we mean by 'seen' and 'not seen' is that which is or is not visible to the eye of man?

Yes, to the eye of man.

And is the soul seen or not seen?

Not seen.

Unseen then?

Yes.

Then the soul is more like to the unseen and the body to the seen?

That follows necessarily, Socrates.

And were we not saying long ago that the soul when using the body as an instrument of perception, that is to say, when using the sense of sight or hearing or some other sense (for the meaning of perceiving through the body is perceiving through the senses)—were we not saying that the soul too is then dragged by the body into the region of the changeable and wanders and is confused; the world spins round her and she is like a drunkard, when she touches change?

Very true.

But when returning into herself she reflects, then she passes into the other world, the region of purity and eternity and immortality and unchangeableness, which are her kindred, and with them she ever lives, when she is by herself and is not let or hindered; then she ceases from her erring ways, and being in communion with the unchanging is unchanging. And this state of soul is called wisdom?

That is well and truly said, Socrates, he replied.

And to which class is the soul more nearly alike and akin, as far as may be inferred from this argument, as well as from the preceding one?

I think, Socrates, that in the opinion of everyone who follows the argument the soul will be infinitely more like the unchangeable—even the most stupid person will not deny that.

And the body is more like the changing?

Yes.

Yet once more consider the matter in another light: When the soul and the body are united, then nature orders the soul to rule and govern, and the body to obey and serve. Now which of these two functions is akin to the divine? And which to the mortal? Does not the divine appear to you to be that which naturally orders and rules and the mortal to be that which is subject and servant?

True.

And which does the soul resemble?

The soul resembles the divine and the body the mortal: there can be no doubt of that, Socrates.

Then reflect, Cebes: of all which has been said is not this the conclusion? —that the soul is in the very likeness of the divine and immortal and intellectual and uniform and indissoluble and unchangeable; and that the body is in the very likeness of the human and mortal and unintellectual and multiform and dissoluble and changeable. Can this, my dear Cebes, be denied?

It cannot.

But if it be true, then is not the body liable to speedy dissolution? And is not the soul almost or altogether indissoluble?

Certainly.

And do you further observe, that after a man is dead, the body or visible part of him, which is lying in the visible world, and is called a corpse, and would naturally be dissolved and decomposed and dissipated, is not dissolved or decomposed at once, but may remain for some time, nay even for a long time, if the constitution be sound at the time of death and the season of the year favourable? For the body when shrunk and embalmed, as the manner is in Egypt, may remain almost entire through infinite ages; and even in decay there are still some portions, such as the bones and ligaments, which are practically indestructible:— Do you agree?

Yes.

And is it likely that the soul, which is invisible, in passing to the place of the true Hades, which like her is invisible and pure and noble, and on her way to the good and wise God, whither, if God will, my soul is also soon to go,—that the soul, I repeat, if this be her nature and origin, will be blown away and destroyed immediately on quitting the body, as the many say? That can never be, my dear Simmias and Cebes. The truth rather is that the soul, which is pure at departing and draws after her no bodily taint, having never voluntarily during life had connection with the body, which she is ever avoiding, herself gathered into herself;—and making such abstraction her perpetual study—which means that she has been a true disciple of philosophy; and therefore has in fact been always engaged in the practice of dying? For is not philosophy the study of death?—

Certainly—

That soul, I say, herself invisible, departs to the invisible world—to the divine and immortal and rational: thither arriving, she is secure of bliss and is released from the error and folly of men, their fears and wild passions and all other human ills, and forever dwells, as they say of the initiated,[1] in company with the gods.

[1] Initiated, i.e. in the mysteries: there is a strong Orphic strand in Socrates' conception of the soul. See, on the Orphics, W. K. C. Guthrie, *Orpheus and Greek Religion* (2nd edn revised, Cambridge, 1952).

2

AUGUSTINE

on THE EXISTENCE OF GOD *and on* FREE WILL

Biographical Note Born at Tagaste in North Africa in AD 354, son of a pagan father and a Christian mother, St Monica. Educated at Madaura and Carthage, where he studied rhetoric. He broke there with Christianity and embraced Manichaeanism. Taught at Tagaste in 374, and then opened a school of rhetoric in Carthage, and lived there with a mistress, and their child, till 383, when he went to Rome. He was professor of rhetoric at Milan from 384. Hereabouts dissatisfaction with Manichaeanism and the influence of Neo-Platonism prepared the way for his acceptance of Christianity. He was converted in 386, and retired from his professorship, suffering from a lung ailment. He was baptized in 387, and returned to Africa in 388. Ordained priest, 391, and consecrated Bishop of Hippo in 396. He stayed in this post till his death in 430, during the siege of Hippo by the Vandals. Principal works: *Confessions* (AD 399), *De Libero Arbitrio* (388), *De Trinitate* (417), *De Genesi ad Litteram* (415), *De Civitate Dei* (413–26). For a full account of his works, see F. C. Copleston, *History of Philosophy*, Vol. ii, pp. 44 ff.

Philosophical Note A great deal of A.'s writing is polemical in nature, accordingly as he became involved in issues of great contemporary importance in the Church, such as the Donatist and Pelagian controversies. His own early preoccupation with the problem of evil led him likewise to attack the doctrines of Manichaeanism, while the fall of Rome to Alaric stimulated his great treatise on the nature and significance of history, *The City of God*. His various responses to these challenges led him to formulate his own position in a more systematic manner than perhaps otherwise might have been the case, and his philosophical and theological doctrines thereby had an immense influence on Christian thought down to, and even beyond, St Thomas Aquinas and the rise of medieval Aristotelianism.

In the following passages, we concentrate on two aspects of A.'s thought—his adaptation of Neo-Platonic ideas to the problem of proving God's existence, and his views on free will. A. held that, in order to explain judgments, especially mathematical and ethical ones, we must have immutable standards as opposed to the changeability of particular things. Thus he accepted something like Plato's Theory of Forms, but, like the Neo-Platonists, he placed these Forms or essences in the mind of God. A. argues that the apprehension of eternal truths implies that there is a God. In place, however, of the Platonic theory of recollection,[1] he teaches that the soul apprehends eternal truths through the illumination of the intellect by God.

The question about the existence of God arises here, in A.'s *De Libero Arbitrio*, in the course of considering the problem of evil, and in particular the question whether God ought to have given men free will. In Book II of the work, A. discusses three questions: (i) Does God exist? (ii) Are all good things from him? and (iii) Is free will a good thing? The work takes the form of a dialogue between Augustine and Evodius, bishop and friend of A.

Bibliographical Note Translations of A.'s works in W. J. Oates, *Basic Writings of St Augustine* (N.Y., 1948), M. Dods and others, *The Works of A. Augustinus* (16 vols., Edinburgh, 1871–6). Useful editions of his most famous works are *The City of God* (Modern Library, N.Y., 1950) and *Confessions* (trans. E. B. Pusey, N.Y., 1952). On his earlier theological writings, see *Augustine: Earlier Writings* (ed. and trans. J. H. S. Burleigh, London and Philadelphia, 1953). Useful introductions are A. H. Armstrong, *Introduction to Ancient Philosophy* (2nd edn, London, 1947), G. Leff, *Medieval Thought, Augustine to Ockham* (London, Pelican, 1958), F. C. Copleston, *History of Philosophy*, Vol. ii (London, 1950) and E. Portalié, *A Guide to the Thought of St Augustine* (trans.: Chicago, 1960). Also useful are E. Gilson, *The Christian Philosophy of St Augustine* (trans. L. E. M. Lynch, London, 1961), various authors, *A Monument to St Augustine* (London, 1930) and J. Burnaby, *Amor Dei* (Cambridge, 1938).

A. THE EXISTENCE OF GOD

De Libero Arbitrio, III, §28 ff.

§28.

AUG: We hold it as settled that there is such a thing as wisdom, or at least that there are wise men, and also that all men want to be happy. But where do we see this? For I have no doubt at all that you see this and that it is true. Do you see this truth in such a way that I cannot know it unless you tell me what you think? Or could I see this truth, just as you understand it, even if you did not tell me?

EVODIUS: I do not doubt that you too could see it even if I did not want you to.

A: Is not one truth which we both see with our different minds common to both of us?

E: Clearly.

A: Again, I believe you do not deny that men should strive after wisdom. You admit that that is true?

E: I have no doubt about that.

[1] See above, p. 20.

A: Here is another truth which is one and common to all who know it, though each one sees it with his own mind and not with mine or yours or any other man's. Can we deny that, since what is seen can be seen in common by all who see it?

E: We cannot deny it.

A: Again, take such propositions as these: Man ought to live justly; the worse ought to be subjected to the better; like is to be compared with like; each man should be given his due. Don't you admit that these statements are absolutely true and stable, to be shared by you and me and all who see them?

E: I agree.

A: The same would be true of these statements: The incorrupt is better than the corrupt, the eternal than the temporal, the inviolable than the violable?

E: Undeniably.

A: Could anyone claim truths of that kind as his own private truths, seeing they are unchangeably present for all to contemplate who have the capacity to contemplate them?

E: No one could claim any one of them as his own, for not only are they true but they are equally common property to all.

A: And again, who denies that the soul ought to be turned from corruption and converted to incorruption, in other words not corruption but incorruption ought to be loved? Who, confessing that that is true, does not also understand that it is unchangeably true and can be understood in common by all minds which have the capacity to understand it?

E: Most true.

A: Will anyone doubt that a life which no adversity can drive from a certain and honourable opinion is better than one which is easily broken and overwhelmed by temporal disadvantages?

E: Who can doubt it?

§29. A: I shall ask no more questions of that kind. It is sufficient that you see as I do that these rules and guiding lights of the virtues, as we may call them, are true and unchangeable, and singly or all together they stand open for the common contemplation of those who have the capacity to behold them, each with his own mind and reason. This you admit is quite certain. But I do ask whether you think these truths belong to wisdom. For I am sure you think that he who has acquired wisdom is wise.

E: I most certainly do.

A: Could the man who lives justly so live unless he saw how to apply the principles of subordinating the inferior to the superior, joining like to like, and giving to each his due?

E: He could not.

A: Would you deny that he who sees this sees wisely?

E: I would not.

A: Does not he who lives prudently choose incorruption and perceive that it is preferable to corruption?

E: Clearly.

A: If he makes what no one doubts is the right choice as to the goal towards which he should direct his mind, can it be denied that he has made a wise choice?

E: I could not deny it.

A: When he directs his mind to what he has wisely chosen, again he does it wisely?

E: Most certainly.

A: And if by no terrors or penalties can he be driven from what he has wisely chosen and towards which he has wisely directed his mind, again there is no doubt that he acts wisely?

E: There is no doubt.

A: It is therefore abundantly evident that these rules and guiding lights of virtue, as we have called them, belong to wisdom. The more a man uses them in living his life, and the more closely he follows them, the more wisely does he live and act. Everything that is wisely done cannot rightly be said to be done apart from wisdom.

E: That is perfectly true.

A: Just as the rules of numbers are true and unchangeable, and the science of numbers is unchangeably available for all who can learn it, and is common to them all, so the rules of wisdom are true and unchangeable. When you were asked about them one by one you replied that they were true and evident and open to the common contemplation of all who have the capacity to examine them.[1]

§30. E: I cannot doubt it. But I should very much like to know whether wisdom and numbers are contained within one class of things. You mentioned that they were linked together in the Holy Scriptures. Or is one of them derived from the other or contained within the other? For example, is number derived from wisdom or is it contained in wisdom? I should not dare to suggest that wisdom is derived from number or is contained in it. For I know many arithmeticians or accountants, or

[1] 'Numbers': this is an unfamiliar name for what we would now more naturally refer to as 'arithmetic', or more generally as 'mathematics'.

whatever they are to be called, who count perfectly and indeed marvellously, but somehow very few of them have wisdom, perhaps none. So wisdom strikes me as being far more worthy of respect than arithmetic.

A: You mention a matter which has often made me wonder, too. When I consider in my mind the unchangeable science of numbers and the recondite sanctuary or region, or whatever other name we are to give to the realm and abode of numbers, I find myself far removed from the corporeal sphere. I find possibly some vague idea but no words adequate to express it, and so in order to say something I return wearily to these numbers which are set before our eyes and call them by their wonted names. The same thing happens when I am thinking as carefully and intently as I can about wisdom. And so I greatly marvel that though wisdom and number are alike in being mysteriously and certainly true, and are linked together by the testimony of Scripture which I have quoted, I say I marvel greatly that number is so contemptible to the majority of men, while wisdom is precious. To be sure it may be because they are one and the same thing. On the other hand it is also written in the Scripture of Wisdom that 'she reaches from one end of the world to the other with full strength and ordereth things graciously' (Wisd. 8.1). Perhaps it is called number from its potency to reach with strength from end to end, and is properly called wisdom because it graciously ordereth all things. For both are functions of wisdom alone.[1]

§31. Wisdom has given numbers even to the smallest and most remote of things, and all bodies have their own numbers. But it has not given to bodies the power to be wise, nor even to all souls, but only to rational souls, in which, as it were, it has taken up its abode from whence it ordereth all things, even the smallest to which it has given numbers. Now we have no difficulty in judging corporeal things as things which belong to a lower order, and the numbers they bear stamped upon them we see are also lower than we are. Therefore we hold them in contempt. But when we begin to consider them from another angle we discover that they transcend our minds and abide unchangeably in the truth. And because few can be wise and many fools count, men admire wisdom and despise numbers. But learned and studious men, the further they are removed from earthly corruption, behold the more clearly in the light of truth both numbers and wisdom, and hold both to be precious. By

[1] This talk of numbers ordering things is connected with notions A. ultimately derived from the Pythagoreans (see p. 19). A. held that there are 'seminal reasons' which control the development of bodies from within, and sometimes spoke of these as numbers. The concept of 'seminal reasons' is itself a Stoic notion. See F. C. Copleston, *History of Philosophy*, Vol. ii, pp. 76–8.

comparison with truth they prize neither gold nor silver nor the other things over which men strive, indeed they even come to think of themselves as of little account.

§32. There is no need to be surprised that men think little of numbers and value wisdom highly, because counting is easier than being wise. You see how they set a higher value on gold than on the light of a candle, compared with which gold is a ridiculous thing. But a vastly inferior thing is more highly honoured because any beggar can light himself a candle, and only a few possess gold. Far be it from me to suggest that compared with numbers wisdom is inferior. Both are the same thing, but wisdom requires an eye fit to see it. From one fire light and heat are felt as if they were 'consubstantial', so to speak. They cannot be separated one from the other. And yet the heat reaches those things which are brought near to the fire, while the light is diffused far and wide. So the potency of intellect which indwells wisdom causes things nearer to it to be warm, such as rational souls. Things further away, such as bodies, it does not affect with the warmth of wisdom, but it pours over them the light of numbers. Probably you will find that obscure, but no similitude drawn from visible things can be completely adapted to explain an invisible thing so as to be understood by everybody. Only take note of this which is sufficient for the problem we have in hand, and is clear enough to humbler kinds of minds such as ours. Though it cannot be made crystal-clear to us whether number is part of wisdom or is derived from wisdom or vice versa, or whether both names can be shown to designate one thing, it is at least evident that both are true and unchangeably true.

§33. Accordingly, you will never deny that there is an unchangeable truth which contains everything that is unchangeably true. You will never be able to say that it belongs particularly to you or to me or to any man, for it is available and offers itself to be shared by all who discern things immutably true, as if it were some strange mysterious and yet public light. Who would say that what is available to be shared by all reasoning and intelligent persons can be the private property of any of them? You remember, I dare say, our recent discussion about the bodily senses.[1] Those things with which we both make contact by means of our eyes or ears, colours and sounds which you and I see or hear together, do not belong to our actual eyes or ears, but are common to both of us so that we may alike perceive them. So you would never say that those things which you and I behold in common, each with his own mind, belong to the actual mind of either of us. You would not say that what the eyes of

[1] See *De Libero Arbitrio,* III, §7.

two persons see belongs to the eyes of one or the other of them. It is a third thing towards which both direct their regard.

E: That is most clear and true.

§34. A: Do you, then, think that this truth of which we have already spoken so much and in which we behold so many things, is more excellent than our minds, or equal to our minds, or inferior? If it were inferior we should not use it as a standard of judgment, but should rather pass judgment on it, as we do on bodies which are inferior to our minds. For of them we often say not only that it *is* so or is not so, but that it *ought to be* so or not so. Similarly with our minds we know not only that it *is* thus or thus, but often also that it *ought to be* thus or thus. We judge of bodies when we say this is not so white as it ought to be, or not so square and so on. Of minds we say this one is not so capable as it ought to be, or it is not gentle enough or eager enough, according to our moral standard. All these judgments we make according to those inward rules of truth, which we discern in common. But no man passes any judgment on these rules. One may say the eternal *is* superior to the temporal, or seven and three *are* ten, but no one says these things *ought to be* so. Knowing simply that they are so one does not examine them with a view to their correction but rejoices to have discovered them. If, then, truth were the equal of our minds, it too would be mutable. Our minds sometimes see more, sometimes less, and so confess their mutability. But truth abiding steadfast in itself neither advances when we see more, nor falls short when we see less. Abiding whole and uncorrupt it rejoices with its light those who turn to it, and punishes with blindness those who turn from it. We pass judgment on our minds in accordance with truth as our standard, while we cannot in any way pass judgment on truth. For we say of our mind it understands less than it ought, or it understands exactly as it ought; and a mind approaches the proper standard of intelligence as it is brought nearer to unchangeable truth, and becomes able to cleave to it. Hence if truth is neither inferior to nor equal to our mind it must be superior and more excellent.

§35. I promised, if you remember, to show you something superior to the human mind and reason. There it is, truth itself. Embrace it if you can. Enjoy it. Delight in the Lord and he will grant you the petitions of your heart. What do you ask for more than to be happy? And what is more happy than to enjoy unshakable, unchangeable truth which is excellent above all things? Men exclaim that they are happy when they embrace the beautiful bodies, deeply longed for, of their wives or even of harlots, and shall we doubt that we are happy in the embrace of truth?

Men exclaim that they are happy when with throats parched with heat they find a fountain flowing with pure water, or being hungry, find a copious meal all ready prepared, and shall we deny that we are happy when truth is our meat and drink? We are wont to hear the voices of people proclaiming that they are happy if they lie among roses or other flowers and enjoy scented ointments, and shall we hesitate to call ourselves happy when we are inspired by truth? Many place happiness in music, vocal and instrumental, flutes and strings. When they are without music they consider themselves unhappy; when they have it, they are transported with joy. Shall we, when the harmonious and creative silence of truth steals, so to speak, noiselessly over our minds, seek the happy life elsewhere, and fail to enjoy that which is ours now and securely? Men delight in the sheen of gold and silver, gems and colours. They delight in the brightness and pleasantness of visible light as it appears in fire or in the sun, moon and stars. When no trouble or want comes to rob them of that pleasure they think themselves happy, and therefore wish to live for ever. Shall we fear to place the happy life in the light of truth?

§36. Nay, since the chief good is recognized to be truth and is possessed when truth is possessed, and truth is wisdom, in wisdom let us discern the chief good and possess it and enjoy it. He is happy indeed who enjoys the chief good. Truth points out all the things that are truly good, and intelligent men, according to their capacity, choose one or more of them in order to enjoy them. People, for example, find pleasure in looking at some object which they are glad to behold in the light of the sun. Those among them who are endowed with strong healthy eyes love to look at nothing better than the sun itself, which sheds its light upon the other things which delight weaker eyes. So a strong and vigorous mental vision may behold many true and changeless things with certain reason, but directs its regard to the truth itself whereby all things are made clear, and, cleaving to the truth and forgetting, as it were, all other things, it enjoys them all together in the truth. Whatever is pleasant in other true things is pleasant also in truth itself.

§37. Herein is our liberty, when we are subject to truth. And Truth is our God who liberates us from death, that is, from the condition of sin. For the Truth itself, speaking as Man to men, says to those who believe in him: 'If ye abide in my word ye are truly my disciples, and ye shall know the truth and the truth shall make you free' (John 8.31–2). No soul enjoys a thing with liberty unless it also enjoys it with security.

But no one is secure in the possession of goods which he can lose against his will. Truth and wisdom no one can lose unwillingly. From them there can be no spatial separation. What is called separation from truth and wisdom is a perverse will which loves lower things. No one wills anything involuntarily. Here is something which we can all enjoy equally and in common. Here there is no straitness, no deficiency. She receives all her lovers, being grudging to none, shared by all in common but chaste to each. None says to another: 'Stand back that I too may approach', or 'Remove your hand that I too may touch.' All cleave to the same wisdom. All are brought into contact with it. Nothing is consumed as in the case of food, and you cannot drink so as to prevent me from drinking too. From that common store you can convert nothing into your private possession. What you take remains unharmed for me to take also. I do not have to wait for you to breathe out what you have breathed in that I may then breathe it in. Nothing ever belongs to one man or to any group of men as a private possession. The whole is common to all at one and the same time.

§38. Truth, therefore, is less like the things we touch or taste or smell, and more like the things we hear and see. For every word is heard as a whole by all who hear it and by each one at the same time. And every sight offered to the eyes is exactly the same for all who see it, and is seen by all at the same time. But though there is similarity there is also great difference. A whole word is not spoken all at once. It is extended over a period of time, one syllable being pronounced first and another after it. Every visible sight varies with the place from which it is seen, and is nowhere seen in its totality. And certainly all these things can be taken from us whether we will or no, and there are difficulties in the way of our enjoying them. Even supposing someone could sing sweetly for ever, those who were eager to hear him would come as rivals. They would get packed closely together, and the more there were of them they would strive for seats, each one anxious to get nearer to the singer. And when they heard him no one would be able to retain permanently what was heard. They would hear nothing but transient fugitive sounds. If I wanted to look at the sun and had the power to do so without being dazzled, nevertheless it would forsake me when it set, or it might be veiled in cloud, and for many other causes I might unwillingly lose my pleasure in seeing the sun. And supposing I had the power and pleasure of eternally seeing the light and hearing music, what great advantage would I have, seeing that even beasts could share it with me? But the beauty of truth and wisdom, so long as there is a persevering will to enjoy it, does not exclude those who come by any packed crowd of hearers. It does not pass with time or change with locality. It is not interrupted by night or shut off by shadow, and is not subject to the bodily senses. To all who turn to it from the whole world, and love it, it is close at hand, everlasting, bound to no particular spot, never deficient. Externally it suggests, internally it teaches. All who behold it, it changes for the better, and by none is it changed for the worse. No one judges it, and no one without it judges aright. Hence it is evident beyond a doubt that wisdom is better than our minds, for by it alone they are made individually wise, and are made judges, not of it, but by it of all other things whatsoever.

§39. You admitted[1] for your part that if I could show you something superior to our minds you would confess that it was God, provided nothing existed that was higher still. I accepted your admission and said it would be sufficient if I demonstrated that. If there is anything more excellent than wisdom, doubtless it, rather, is God. But if there is nothing more excellent, then truth itself is God. Whether there is or is not such a higher thing, you cannot deny that God exists, and this was the question set for our discussion. If you are influenced by what we have received in faith from the holy discipline of Christ, that there is the Father of Wisdom, remember that we also received in faith that there is one equal to the eternal Father, namely Wisdom who is begotten of him. Hence there should be no further question, but we should accept it with unshakable faith. God exists and is the truest and fullest being. This I suppose we hold with undoubting faith. Now we attain it with a certain if tenuous form of knowledge. This is sufficient for the question in hand, so that we can go on to explain other pertinent questions; unless you have any opposition to offer.

B. FREE WILL

In the following passage we have a discussion of the apparent contradiction between God's foreknowledge and freedom of the will. It should be noted that, on A.'s view, the human being has been so made that it cannot be itself the good by which it is made happy, for the human is mutable. Its true happiness can only be found in what is eternal, and this is God. And thus in the exercise of free will man has the choice of turning away from the immutable Good towards changeable goods. This is a somewhat different picture from that which is presented in much of later European philosophy, where the choice is often conceived as one between obedience to the moral law (fulfilling one's duty, etc.) and one's natural inclinations. Whereas this view contrasts duty and inclination, the main contrast in A. is between a higher and a lower happiness. It should

[1] See §14, 'If . . . we could find something which you could unhesitatingly recognize not only as existing but as superior to our reason, would you have any hesitation in calling it, whatever it may be, God?' and the following passage.

be noted too that the type of predestination implied in A.'s account stems, at least in part, from his own vivid experience of God's grace: but it is interesting that his reconciliation of this with freedom of the will depends on an argument not unlike those recently employed to show the compatibility of causal determinism and free will: see, e.g., the article 'Divine Omnipotence and Human Freedom' by A. G. N. Flew in *New Essays in Philosophical Theology*, edited by Antony Flew and Alasdair MacIntyre (see above, p. 15). Here it is argued that 'what is caused' can be analysed in terms of what can be predicted in principle (i.e., if we had all the relevant facts): but to say that an act can be predicted does not entail that it is not free. For 'free', as we ordinarily use the word, means 'free from external or internal constraint' (i.e., not constrained by threats of force, etc., and not due to madness). Hence predictability and freedom are compatible, and so causal determinism and freedom are compatible.

De Libero Arbitrio, III, §1 ff.

EVODIUS: It is sufficiently evident to me that free will is to be numbered among the good things, and, indeed, not among the least of our good things. We are, therefore, compelled to confess that it has been given us by God, and that he has rightly given it to us. But now, if you think a suitable time has come, I want to learn from you whence arises the movement by which the will itself turns from the unchangeable good, which is the common property of all, to its own interests or to the interests of others or to things beneath it, and so turns to mutable goods.

AUGUSTINE: Why must you know this?

E: Because if free will is so given that it has that movement by nature, it turns of necessity to mutable goods; and no blame attaches where nature and necessity prevail.

A: Do you like or dislike that movement?

E: I dislike it.

A: So you find fault with it?

E: I do.

A: Then you find fault with a movement of the mind though it is faultless.

E: No, I do not. But I do not know whether there is any fault in abandoning the unchangeable good and turning towards the mutable goods.

A: Then you are finding fault with something which you do not know.

E: Don't insist on a verbal point. I said that I did not know whether there was any fault, but I meant to be understood really as having no doubt about it. Certainly I said I do not know, but obviously I was being ironical in suggesting that there could be any doubt about so clear a matter.

A: Just consider what is that truth you hold to be so certain that it has caused you so soon to forget what you said a moment ago. If that movement of the will exists by nature or necessity, it is in no way culpable. And yet you are so firmly convinced that it is culpable that you think fit to wax ironical about hesitation over a matter so certain. Why did you think it right to affirm, or at least to say with some hesitation, what you yourself show to be obviously false? You said: 'If free will has been given in such fashion that it has that movement by nature, then it turns to mutable things of necessity, and no fault can be found where nature and necessity rule.' But you ought to have had no doubt that it was not given in that fashion, since you do not doubt that that movement is culpable.

E: I said that the movement is culpable, and that therefore it displeases me, and that I cannot doubt that it is reprehensible. But I hold that a soul which is thereby drawn from the unchangeable good to mutable goods is not to be blamed if its nature is such that it is so moved by necessity.

§2. A: To whom belongs the movement which you admit is blameworthy?

E: I see that it is in the soul, but to whom it belongs I do not know.

A: You do not deny that the soul is moved by that motion?

E: No.

A: Do you then deny that the motion by which a stone is moved is the motion of the stone? I don't mean the motion that we give to it, or that is given to it by some other force, when it is thrown upwards, but that by which of its own accord it falls back to earth.

E: I do not deny that the motion that you refer to, by which it turns and falls downwards, is the motion of the stone, but it is its natural motion. If the motion of the soul is like that, it too is natural, and it cannot rightly be blamed for a motion that is natural. Even if it moves to its own destruction, it is compelled by the necessity of its own nature. Moreover, because we have no doubt that the soul's motion is culpable we must absolutely deny that it is natural, and therefore . . . like the motion of the stone, which is natural motion.

A: Did we achieve anything in our two previous discussions?

E: I am sure we did.

A: No doubt you remember that in the first discussion we discovered that the mind can become the slave of lust only by its own will. No superior thing and no equal thing compels it to such dishonour, because that would be unjust. And no inferior thing has the power. It remains that that must be the mind's own motion when it turns its will away from the enjoyment of the Creator to enjoyment of the creature. If that motion is accounted blameworthy—and you thought anyone who doubted that deserved to be treated ironically—it is not natural but voluntary. It is like the motion of the falling stone, in so far as it is a motion of the soul as the former is the motion of the stone. But it is dissimilar in this, that it is not in the power of a stone to arrest its downward motion, while if the soul is not willing it cannot be moved to abandon what is higher and to love what is lower. Thus the stone's motion is natural, the soul's voluntary. Hence anyone who says that a stone sins when it is carried downwards by its own weight is, I will not say more senseless than the stone but, completely mad. But we charge the soul with sin when we show that it has abandoned the higher things and prefers to enjoy lower things. What need is there, therefore, to seek the origin of the movement whereby the will turns from the unchangeable to the changeable good? We acknowledge that it is a movement of the soul, that it is voluntary and therefore culpable. And all useful learning in this matter has its object and value in teaching us to condemn and restrain that movement, and to convert our wills from falling into temporal delights to the enjoyment of the eternal good.

§3. E: I see, and in a sense grasp that what you say is true. There is nothing that I feel more certainly and more personally than that I have a will, and that it moves me to enjoy this or that. I know nothing I could call my own if the will by which I will 'yea' and 'nay' is not my own. If I use it to do evil, to whom is the evil to be attributed if not to myself? Since a good God has made me, and I can do nothing right except by willing, it is clearly evident that it was to this end that the will has been given me by God who is good. Moreover, unless the movement of the will towards this or that object is voluntary and within our power, a man would not be praiseworthy when he turns to the higher objects nor blameworthy when he turns to lower objects, using his will like a hinge. There would be no use at all in warning him to pay no attention to temporal things and to will to obtain the eternal things, or to will to live aright and to be unwilling to live an evil life. But whoever thinks that man is not to be so warned ought to be cut off from membership in the human race.

§4. That being so, I have a deep desire to know how it can be that God knows all things beforehand and that, nevertheless, we do not sin by necessity. Whoever says that anything can happen otherwise than as God has foreknown it, is attempting to destroy the divine foreknowledge with the most insensate impiety. If God foreknew that the first man would sin—and that anyone must concede who acknowledges with me that God has foreknowledge of all future events—I do not say that God did not make him, for he made him good, nor that the sin of the creature whom he made good could be prejudicial to God. On the contrary, God showed his goodness in making man, his justice in punishing his sin, and his mercy in delivering him. I do not say, therefore, that God did not make man. But this I say. Since God foreknew that man would sin, that which God foreknew must necessarily come to pass. How then is the will free when there is apparently this unavoidable necessity?

§5. A: You have knocked vigorously. May God in his mercy grant us his presence and open the door to those who knock. But I verily believe that the vast majority of men are troubled by that question for no other reason than that they do not ask it in a pious fashion. They are swifter to make excuses for their sins than to make confession of them. Some are glad to hold the opinion that there is no divine providence presiding over human affairs. They commit themselves, body and soul, to fortuitous circumstances, and deliver themselves to be carried about and tormented by lusts. They deny that there is any divine judgment, and deceive human judges when they are accused. They imagine that they are driven on by the favour of fortune. In sculpture or painting they are wont to represent Fortune as blind, either because they are better than the goddess by whom they think they are ruled, or because they confess that in their sentiments they are afflicted with that same blindness. In the case of such people it is not absurd to admit that they do everything by chance, seeing that they stumble in all that they do. But against this opinion, so full of foolish and senseless error, we have, I think, sufficiently spoken in our second disputation. Others do not venture to deny that the providence of God presides over human affairs, but they would rather indulge in the wicked error of believing that providence is weak or unjust or evil than confess their sins with suppliant piety. If all these would suffer themselves to be persuaded to believe that the goodness, justice and power of God are greater far, and far superior to any thought they can have of goodness, justice or might, if they would but take thought to themselves, they would know that they owe thanks to God, even if he had willed them to be somewhat lower in the scale of being than they actually are, and with all that is within them they would exclaim with the Psalmist: 'I have spoken: Lord have mercy upon me; heal my soul for I have sinned against thee' (Ps. 41.5). So by stages the divine mercy would bring them to wisdom. They would be neither inflated by what they discover, nor rebellious when they fail to find the truth; by learning they would become better prepared to see the truth, and by recognizing their ignorance they would become more patient in seeking it. I am quite sure that these are your views too. Now first answer a few questions I am going to put to you, and you will see how easily I can find a solution to your tremendous problem.

§6. Your trouble is this. You wonder how it can be that these two propositions are not contradictory and incompatible, namely that God has foreknowledge of all future events, and that we sin voluntarily and not by necessity. For if, you say, God foreknows that a man will sin, he must necessarily sin. But if there is necessity there is no voluntary choice in sinning, but rather fixed and unavoidable necessity. You are afraid that by that reasoning the conclusion may be reached either that God's foreknowledge of all future events must be impiously denied, or, if that cannot be denied, that sin is committed not voluntarily but by necessity. Isn't that your difficulty?

E: Exactly that.

A: You think, therefore, that all things of which God has foreknowledge happen by necessity and not voluntarily.

E: Yes, absolutely.

A: Try an experiment, and examine yourself a little, and tell me what kind of will you are going to have tomorrow. Will you want to sin or to do right?

E: I do not know.

A: Do you think God also does not know?

E: I could in no wise think that.

A: If God knows what you are going to will tomorrow, and foresees what all men are going to will in the future, not only those who are at present alive but all who will ever be, much more will he foresee what he is going to do with the just and the impious?

E: Certainly if I say that God has foreknowledge of my deeds, I should say with even greater confidence that he has foreknowledge of his own acts, and foresees with complete certainty what he is going to do.

A: Don't you see that you will have to be careful lest someone say to you that, if all things of which God has foreknowledge are done by necessity and not voluntarily, his own future acts will be done not voluntarily but by necessity?

E: When I said that all future events of which God has foreknowledge happen by necessity, I was having regard only to things which happen within his creation, and not to things which happen in God himself. Indeed, in God nothing happens. Everything is eternal.

A: God, then, is not active within his creation?

E: He determined once and for all how the order of the universe he created was going to go on, and he never changes his mind.

A: Does he never make anyone happy?

E: Indeed he does.

A: He does it precisely at the time when the man in question actually becomes happy.

E: That is so.

A: If, then, for example, you yourself are happy one year from now, you will be made happy at that time.

E: Exactly.

A: God knows today what he is going to do a year hence?

E: He eternally had that foreknowledge, but I agree that he has it now, if indeed it is to happen so.

§7. A: Now tell me, are you not God's creature? And will not your becoming happy take place within your experience?

E: Certainly I am God's creature, and if I become happy it will be within my experience.

A: If God, then, makes you happy, your happiness will come by necessity and not by the exercise of your will?

E: God's will is my necessity.

A: Will you then be happy against your will?

E: If I had the power to be happy, I should be so at once. For I wish to be happy but am not, because not I but God makes me happy.

A: The truth simply cries out against you. You could not imagine that 'having in our power' means anything else than 'being able to do what we will'. Therefore there is nothing so much in our power as is the will itself. For as soon as we will (*volumus*) immediately will (*voluntas*) is there. We can say rightly that we do not grow old voluntarily but necessarily, or that we do not die voluntarily but from necessity, and so with other similar things. But who but a raving fool would say that it is not voluntarily that we will? Therefore though God knows how we are going to will in the future, it is not proved that we do not voluntarily will anything. When you said that you did not make yourself happy, you said it as if I had denied it. What I say is that when you become happy in the future it will take place not against your will but in accordance with your willing. Therefore, though God has foreknowledge of your happiness in the future, and though nothing can happen otherwise than as he has foreknown it (for that would mean that there is no foreknowledge) we are not thereby compelled to think that you will not be happy voluntarily. That would be absurd and far from true. God's foreknowledge, which is even today quite certain that you are to be happy at a future date, does not rob you of your will to happiness when you actually attain happiness. Similarly if ever in the future you have a culpable will, it will be none the less your will because God had foreknowledge of it.

§8. Observe, pray, how blind are those who say that if God has foreknowledge of what I am going to will, since nothing can happen otherwise than as he has foreknown it, therefore I must necessarily will what he has foreknown. If so, it must be admitted that I will, not voluntarily but from necessity. Strange folly! Is there, then, no difference between things that happen according to God's foreknowledge where there is no intervention of man's will at all, and things that happen because of a will of which he has foreknowledge? I omit the equally monstrous assertion of the man I mentioned a moment ago, who says I must necessarily so will. By assuming necessity he strives to do away with will altogether. If I must necessarily will, why need I speak of willing at all? But if he puts it in another way, and says that, because he must necessarily so will, his will is not in his own power, he can be countered by the answer you gave me when I asked whether you could become happy against your will. You replied that you would be happy now if the matter were in your power, for you willed to be happy but could not achieve it. And I added that the truth cries out against you; for we cannot say we do not have the power unless we do not have what we will. If we do not have the will, we may think we will but in fact we do not. If we cannot will without willing, those who will have will, and all that is in our power we have by willing. Our will would not be will unless it were in our power. Because it is in our power, it is free. We have nothing that is free which is not in our power, and if we have something it cannot be nothing. Hence it is not necessary to deny that God has foreknowledge of all things, while at the same time our wills are our own. God has foreknowledge of our will, so that of which he has foreknowledge must come to pass. In other words, we shall exercise our wills in the future because he has foreknowledge that we shall do so; and there can be no will or voluntary action unless it be in our power. Hence God has also foreknowledge of our power to will. My power is not taken from me by God's foreknowledge. Indeed I shall be more certainly in possession of my power because he whose foreknowledge is never mistaken, foreknows that I shall have the power.

E: Now I no longer deny that whatever God has foreknown must necessarily come to pass, nor that he has foreknowledge of our sins, but in such a way that our wills remain free and within our power.

§9. A: What further difficulty do you have? Perhaps you have forgotten what we established in our first disputation, and now wish to deny that we sin voluntarily and under no compulsion from anything superior, inferior or equal to us.

E: I do not venture to deny that at all. But I must confess I do not yet see how God's foreknowledge of our sins and our freedom of will in sinning can be other than mutually contradictory. We must confess that God is just and knows all things beforehand. But I should like to know with what justice he punishes sins which must necessarily be committed; or how they are necessarily committed when he knows that they will be committed; or how the Creator is to escape having imputed to him anything that happens necessarily in his creature.

§10. A: Why do you think our free will is opposed to God's foreknowledge? Is it because it is foreknowledge simply, or because it is God's foreknowledge?

E: In the main because it is God's foreknowledge.

A: If you knew in advance that such and such a man would sin, there would be no necessity for him to sin.

E: Indeed there would, for I should have no real foreknowledge unless I knew for certain what was going to happen.

A: So it is foreknowledge generally and not God's foreknowledge specially that causes the events foreknown to happen by necessity? There would be no such thing as foreknowledge unless there was certain foreknowledge.

E: I agree. But why these questions?

A: Unless I am mistaken, you would not directly compel the man to sin, though you knew beforehand that he was going to sin. Nor does your prescience in itself compel him to sin even though he was certainly going to sin, as we must assume if you have real prescience. So there is no contradiction here. Simply you know beforehand what another is going to do with his own will. Similarly God compels no man to sin, though he sees beforehand those who are going to sin by their own will.

§11. Why then should he not justly punish sins which, though he had foreknowledge of them, he did not compel the sinner to commit? Just as you apply no compulsion to past events by having them in your memory, so God by his foreknowledge does not use compulsion in the case of future events. Just as you remember your past actions, though all that you remember were not actions of your own, so God has foreknowledge of all his own actions, but is not the agent of all that he foreknows. Of evil actions he is not the agent but the just punisher. From this you may understand with what justice God punishes sins, for he has no responsibility for the future actions of men though he knows them beforehand. If he ought not to award punishment to sinners because he knew beforehand that they would sin, he ought not to reward the righteous, because he knew equally that they would be righteous. Let us confess that it belongs to his foreknowledge to allow no future event to escape his knowledge, and that it belongs to his justice to see that no sin goes unpunished by his judgment. For sin is committed voluntarily and not by any compulsion from his foreknowledge.

§12. As to your third question how the Creator is to escape having imputed to him anything that happens necessarily in his creature, it is fitting for us to remember the rule of piety which says that we owe thanks to our Creator. That will provide us with the answer. His lavish goodness should be most justly praised even if he had made us with some lower rank in his creation. Though our soul be soiled with sins it is nevertheless loftier and better than if it were changed into invisible light. And yet light is an eminent part of creation, as you can see by considering how much God is praised for it, even by souls wholly given over to bodily sense. Wherefore, though sinful souls are censured, do not let that provoke you to say in your heart that it would have been better if they did not exist. They are censured because they are compared with what they might have been if they had not willed to sin. God, their Maker, is to be gloriously praised for the human faculties with which he has endowed them, not only because he justly subjects them to his order when they sin, but also because he made them such that, even when soiled with sin, they are not surpassed in dignity by corporeal light, for which also God is rightly praised.

3

PSEUDO-DIONYSIUS

on THE NEGATIVE WAY

Biographical Note For long the works of the unknown author from which we select the following passage were thought to have been written by Dionysius the Areopagite, converted by St Paul. St Thomas Aquinas, for example, in company with other medieval philosophers and theologians, regarded the authorship of the works as authentic. But it was bound to become obvious that the author used Neo-Platonic ideas, and so could not have been Dionysius. It is now thought that the author lived around AD 500.

The group of writings comprises: *De Divinis Nominibus*, *De Mystica Theologia*, *De Coelesti Hierarchia* and *De Eccelesiastica Hierarchia*, plus some letters.

Philosophical Note As mentioned above, Pseudo-Dionysius employed Neo-Platonist ideas. It is therefore necessary to say something briefly about Neo-Platonism, and especially about its chief exponent, Plotinus.

Plotinus (b. about AD 204 in Egypt) was a religious and philosophical teacher of the first rank. He borrowed, but transmuted, the framework of Plato's doctrines, as well as Stoic and other ideas, in order to produce a coherent account of reality which chimed in with his own mystical experience. His teachings are, briefly, as follows. (i) He describes the ultimate principle as the One, which is ineffable and incomprehensible, and which is prior to, and the source of, all existent things. But though we can say nothing in general to characterize the One, we can identify it with Goodness: it is the Good. (ii) Since the One is not a personal Being to whom we can ascribe any sort of activity, it is not the Creator. Rather, Plotinus uses the analogy of emanation. The many existent things we find in the cosmos ultimately emanate from the One. (iii) But the difference between mundane things and the One is such that intermediate principles are required to effect the transition. The first emanation is of *Nous*, Intelligence, in which exist the Forms (i.e. roughly, the Platonic Forms). This *Nous* is identified with Plato's Demiurge or Supreme Craftsman, though unlike Plato Plotinus makes the Forms inherent in the Demiurge and not archetypes external to him. As the One is called the Good, so *Nous* is Beauty. From *Nous* proceeds the World-Soul (like that of Plato's *Timaeus*). There is in this a higher and a lower aspect, the former being nearer to *Nous*, the latter being close to the world—it is called *Physis* or Nature. From the World-Soul proceed the individual souls.

It is in regard to the One that Plotinus and Neo-Platonism most influenced Pseudo-Dionysius. For the ineffability ascribed to the Godhead by Ps.-D. is reminiscent of the negative descriptions of the One. The distinction between the Affirmative Way and the Negative Way was elaborated by Proclus (AD 410–85), a later Neo-Platonist. The former Way is that whereby we ascribe to God such perfections as we find in creatures and such as are compatible with God's spiritual nature—but we attribute them to God in a pre-eminent degree. Thus Ps.-D. refers to God as the *super-essential* Beautiful, and so on, to emphasize that the content of such names as 'Beautiful' as applied to God is infinitely richer than when we use these words of creatures. Moreover, the predicates which are so ascribed apply to the manifested Godhead (God as Father, etc.) and not to the Godhead itself, which even transcends such perfections. Thus Ps.-D.'s view of the Trinity is as follows. There is (i) the Good, or undifferentiated Godhead; (ii) the manifestation of the Godhead as the Father, from whom proceed; (iii) the other Persons, considered as rays emanating eternally from the Father. The Negative Way is illustrated in the following passage.

Bibliographical Note On Neo-Platonism: E. R. Dodds, *Select Passages illustrative of Neo-Platonism* (London, 1923), A. H. Armstrong, *Introduction to Ancient Philosophy* (2nd edn, London, 1949), T. Whittaker, *The Neo-Platonists* (Cambridge, 1901), R. Inge *The Philosophy of Plotinus* (2 vols., 3rd edn, London, 1929), A. H. Armstrong, *Plotinus* (London, 1953) and E. Bréhier, *La Philosophie de Plotin* (Paris, 1928). On Pseudo-D., see E. Gilson, *History of Christian Philosophy in the Middle Ages* (Eng. trans., London, 1955), F. C. Copleston, *History of Philosophy*, Vol. ii (London, 1950) and C. E. Rolt, *On the Divine Names* and *The Mystical Theology*, trans. (London, 1920).

THE NEGATIVE WAY

Mystical Theology, Chs. II–V

Unto this Darkness which is beyond Light we pray that we may come, and attain unto vision through the loss of sight and knowledge, and that in ceasing thus to see or to know we may learn to know that which is beyond all perception and understanding (for this emptying of our faculties is true sight and knowledge), and that we may offer him that transcends all things the praises of a transcendent hymnody, which we shall do by denying or removing all things that are—like as men who, carving a statue out of marble, remove all the impediments that hinder the clear perspective of the latent image and by this mere removal display the hidden statue itself in its hidden beauty.[1] Now we must wholly distinguish this negative method from that of positive statements. For when we were making positive statements,[2] we began with the most

[1] This simile implies that there is a positive concept of God which we can attempt to express, via the Affirmative Way.

[2] I.e. in the *Divine Names*, and in the *Outlines of Divinity* (not extant). The procedure in these 'positive' writings is described in the introductory notes, above.

universal statements, and then through intermediate terms we came at last to particular titles, but now ascending upwards from particular to universal conceptions we strip off all qualities in order that we may attain a naked knowledge of that Unknowing which in all existent things is enwrapped by all objects of knowledge, and that we may begin to see that super-essential Darkness which is hidden by all the light that is in existent things.

III

Now I have in my *Outlines of Divinity* set forth these conceptions which are most proper to the affirmative method, and have shown in what sense God's holy nature is called single and in what sense trinal, what is the nature of the Fatherhood and Sonship which we attribute to it; what is meant by the articles of faith concerning the Spirit; how from the immaterial and indivisible Good the interior rays of its goodness have their being and remain immovably in that state of rest which both within their origin and within themselves is co-eternal with the act by which they spring from it; in what manner Jesus being above all essence has stooped to an essential state in which all the truths of human nature meet; and all the other revelations of Scripture whereof my *Outlines of Divinity* treat. And in the book of the *Divine Names* I have considered the meaning as concerning God of the titles Good, Existence, Life, Wisdom, Power and of the other titles which the understanding frames, and in my *Symbolical Divinity* I have considered what are the metaphorical titles drawn from the world of sense and applied to the nature of God; what are the mental or material images we form of God or the functions and instruments of activity we attribute to him; what are the places where he dwells and the robes he is adorned with; what is meant by God's anger, grief and indignation, or the divine inebriation and wrath; what is meant by God's oath and his malediction, by his slumber and awaking, and all the other inspired imagery of allegoric symbolism. And I doubt not that you have also observed how far more copious are the last terms than the first for the doctrines of God's nature and the exposition of his names could not but be briefer than the symbolic divinity. For the more we soar upwards the more our language becomes restricted to the compass of purely intellectual conceptions, even as in the present instance plunging into the Darkness which is above the intellect we shall find ourselves reduced not merely to brevity of speech but even to absolute dumbness both of speech and thought. Now in the former treatises the course of the argument, as it came down from the highest to the lowest categories, embraced an ever-widening number of conceptions which increased at each stage of the descent, but in the present treatise it mounts upwards from below towards the category of transcendence, and in proportion to its ascent it contracts its terminology, and when the whole ascent is passed it will be totally dumb, being at last wholly united with him whom words cannot describe. But why is it, you will ask, that after beginning from the highest category when one method was affirmative we begin from the lowest category when it is negative? Because, when affirming the existence of that which transcends all affirmation, we were obliged to start from that which is most akin to it, and then to make the affirmation on which the rest depended; but when pursuing the negative method, to reach that which is beyond all negation, we must start by applying our negations to those qualities which differ most from the ultimate goal. Surely it is truer to affirm that God is life and goodness than that he is air or stone, and truer to deny that drunkenness and fury can be attributed to him than to deny that we may apply to him the categories of human thought.

IV

We therefore maintain that the universal Cause transcending all things is neither impersonal nor lifeless nor without understanding: in short, that it is not a material body, and therefore does not possess outward shape or intelligible form, or quality, or quantity, or solid weight; nor has it any local existence which can be perceived by sight or touch; nor has it the power of perceiving or being perceived; nor does it suffer any vexation or disorder through the disturbance of earthly passions, or any feebleness through the tyranny of material chances, or any want of light; nor any change, or decay, or division, or deprivation, or ebb and flow, or anything else which the senses can perceive. None of these things can be either identified with it or attributed unto it.

V

Once more, ascending yet higher we maintain that it is not soul, or mind, or endowed with the faculty of imagination, conjecture, reason, or understanding; nor is it any act of reason or understanding; nor can it be described by the reason or perceived by the understanding, since it is not number, or order, or greatness, or littleness, or equality, or inequality, and since it is not immovable nor in motion, or at rest, and has no power, and is not power or light, and does not live, and is not life; nor is it personal essence, or eternity, or time; nor can it be grasped by the understanding, since it is not knowledge or truth; nor is it kingship or wisdom; nor is it one, nor is it unity, nor is it Godhead or goodness; nor is it a Spirit, as we understand the term, since it is not Sonship or Fatherhood; nor is it any other thing such as we or any other being can have knowledge of; nor does it belong to the category of non-existence or to that of existence; nor do existent beings know it as it actually is, nor does it know them as they actually are;[1] nor can reason attain to it to name it or to know it; nor is it darkness, nor is it light, or error, or truth; nor can any affirmation or negation apply to it; for while applying affirmations or negations to those orders of being that come next to it, we apply not unto it either affirmation or negation, inasmuch as it transcends all affirmation by being the perfect and unique Cause of all things, and transcends all negation by the pre-eminence of its simple and absolute nature—free from every limitation and beyond them all.

[1] It knows things in their super-essences, which are contained in itself. See above, p. 31.

4

ANSELM

on THE ONTOLOGICAL ARGUMENT

Biographical Note Born at Aosta in North Italy, in 1033. He studied in Burgundy and later at Bec. Entered the Benedictine Order, and became Prior of Bec in 1063, and Abbot in 1078. He was made Archbishop of Canterbury in 1093, succeeding his teacher Lanfranc. Died in 1109.

Principal works: *De Veritate, De Libero Arbitrio, Monologium, Proslogium* (these all probably dating from his period as Prior of Bec), and *Cur Deus Homo?* (1097).

Philosophical Note A. does not make any sharp distinction between philosophy and theology, and much of his writing concerns theology. He is chiefly remembered first for his *Cur Deus Homo?*, on the Incarnation and Atonement, and second for his presentation of the Ontological Argument, which is given below. In the *Monologium*, A. used an argument for God's existence which is found in a different form in Aquinas' Fourth Way (see below, p. 69): qualities such as goodness and greatness (see n. 2 to p. 56) are found in differing degrees in the objects which we observe; but judgments about differing degrees of goodness, etc., imply a reference to a perfect standard; so there is an absolute goodness in which all things varyingly participate. He goes on to develop a similar, though more complicated, argument about being: things possess being in virtue of a relation to one self-existent and supreme Being. But A. wanted, in accordance with the wishes of his fellow-monks, to produce an argument which would both be simple and be able to do the job which the rather complex arguments of the *Monologium* did. He thought that he had found such an argument in what came to be called the Ontological Argument.[1]

Bibliographical Note See the postscript (p. 58). A Koyré's text and translation (French) of the *Proslogium* and of the dispute with Gaunilo, *Fides Quaerens Intellectum* (Paris, 1930), is useful. See also S. F. Deane's translation of these works, the *Monologium* and the *Cur Deus Homo?* (Chicago, 1930). Interesting studies of A. are to be found in J. McIntyre, *St Anselm and his Critics* (Edinburgh, 1954), K. Barth, *Anselm: Fides Quaerens Intellectum* (Eng. trans., London, 1960) and C. C. J. Webb, *Studies in the History of Natural Theology* (Oxford, 1915).

[1] 'Ontological': concerned with the nature of what is, concerning being.

THE ONTOLOGICAL ARGUMENT

Proslogium, Chs. II f.

That God really exists, even if the foolish man said in his heart 'There is no God'.

Therefore, Lord, thou who bestowest understanding upon faith, grant me this, that I may understand (as far as thou knowest it to be expedient) that thou art, as we believe, and that thou art what we believe thee to be. Our belief is that thou art a being than which no greater can be conceived.[1] Yet it might be thought that no such being exists, for 'the foolish man hath said in his heart "There is no God" '. But surely that very man, on hearing the term, understands what he hears, and what he understands is in his understanding, even if he does not go on to understand that such a being exists. For there is a distinction between having a thing in the understanding and understanding that it is in existence. For example, when an artist prepares in his mind what he is about to create, he has the conception in his understanding, but he understands that what he has not created yet is not yet in existence. Thus even the foolish man is convinced that something than which no greater can be conceived is in his understanding, for when he hears this phrase he understands it and whatever is understood is in the understanding.

Now that than which no greater can be conceived certainly cannot just be in the understanding, for if it were only in the understanding it could then further be conceived to be in existence as well; but it then would be a greater thing.[2] Ergo, if that than which no greater can be conceived were only in the understanding, there would be something still greater than it—which is surely impossible. Something, then, indubitably exists than which no greater can be conceived, and it is both in the understanding and in reality.

Ch. III *That God cannot be thought non-existent*

Certainly, moreover, this greatest possible being exists so truly that it cannot be thought not to exist. For we can conceive that there is something which cannot be thought of as non-existent and which, therefore, is superior to anything that can be thought of as non-existent. So if that than which no greater can be conceived could be thought of as non-existent, it

[1] *Id quo nihil maius cogitari potest.*

[2] Regarding 'greater', note that A. does not use the term in a literal sense. He remarks (in the *Monologium*) 'I do not mean spatial magnitude, like a body, but greatness in goodness and value, like wisdom'.

would necessarily at the same time be both the highest object of thought and not the highest—and this is a contradiction. Therefore, so truly does something than which no greater can be conceived exist that it cannot be thought of as non-existent. And thou art this something, O Lord our God.

So truly dost thou exist, O Lord my God, that thou canst not be conceived not to exist. And rightly; for if any mind could frame the concept of something superior to thee, a creature would be transcending the creator and passing judgment on him, which is quite absurd. And indeed, everything else that exists, apart from thee alone, can be conceived to be non-existent. Thou, therefore, alone most truly of all beings hast existence. For whatever else exists, exists less truly and so has less of existence than thou.

A.'s argument was immediately answered by Gaunilo, a monk of Marmoutier (near Tours), in his *Liber pro Insipiente*. Gaunilo objected to A.'s account of atheism as being a case of verbal confusion, and argued that we might as well assert that the most beautiful possible island must exist, since we can conceive it. A. replied as follows, in his *Liber apologeticus contra Gaunilonem* (Ch. III).

I confidently affirm that if anyone has found for me something else besides the *quo maius nihil* existing either in reality or in thought alone, to which he can apply my argument, then I will not merely find that lost island for him, but I will give it to him and guarantee against its ever being lost again. We now see clearly that the *quo maius nihil* cannot be thought of as non-existent, since it exists on an assured ground of truth: indeed, otherwise it would not exist at all. Finally, if anyone says that he thinks it does not exist, I say that at the precise time when he is thinking this, he is either thinking of something than which no greater can be conceived or he is not. If he is not, then he is not thinking that that which he is not thinking of at all does not exist. And if he *is* thinking of it, surely he is thinking of something which cannot be thought not to exist. For if it could be thought of as non-existent, it could be thought to have a beginning and an end: but this is impossible. So he who is really thinking of it is thinking of something which cannot be even thought of as non-existent, or else he would be thinking what cannot be thought. It is impossible, then, to think of the non-existence of that than which no greater can be conceived.

Postscript The Ontological Argument has provoked considerable discussion, and different versions of it have been used by later philosophers, notably Descartes (see below, p. 121) and Hegel (see below, p. 290). Modern criticisms of it have centred mainly on two points: for the existence of something to be derived from the essence or definition of that thing, existence would have to be regarded as a property, but the verb 'to exist' is not on a par (logically) with verbs ascribing properties (see the paper 'Is Existence a Predicate?' by G. E. Moore, in A. G. N. Flew, *Logic and Language*, Second Series; W. C. Kneale, 'Is Existence a Predicate?', reprinted in H. Feigl and W. Sellars, *Readings in Philosophical Analysis* [N.Y., 1949], and G. Ryle, 'Mr Collingwood and the Ontological Argument', *Mind*, 1935; see also N. Malcolm, 'The Ontological Argument', *Philosophical Review*, 1960); and second, the possibility of arguing in this way presupposes that it is possible to discover truths about reality merely by taking thought, and independently of observation. This is not in line with the anti-metaphysical tendency in much contemporary philosophy, nor with the view, associated with it, that necessary propositions are true, not in virtue of ineradicable features of thought or of the world, but in virtue of linguistic conventions. Thus all necessary truths are, in effect, truths by definition, on this view. But definitions do not tell us anything about reality. By consequence, the Ontological Argument cannot tell us anything about reality, and therefore cannot show that God exists.

5

AQUINAS

on REASON AND FAITH
THE EXISTENCE OF GOD, ANALOGY
and on MIRACLES

Biographical Note Born at Roccasecca in S. Italy, 1224–5. Entered Benedictine Abbey at Monte Cassino as an oblate. When the monks were expelled from there, went to Naples University. Entered Dominican Order, 1244. His family's opposition to this move led to their detaining him forcibly for a time. 1245, went to Paris, to study under Albert the Great, whom he accompanied to Cologne, 1248–52. Lectured at Paris, 1252–9. Taught in Papal *studium curae* at Rome and elsewhere, 1259–68. Back in Paris, 1268–72. Taught at Naples, 1272–4. Died on his way to the Council of Lyons, 1274.

Principal works: *De Ente et Essentia* (1252–3), *De Veritate* (1256–9), Commentaries on various of Aristotle's works, *Summa contra Gentiles* (1259–64), *Summa Theologica* (1272–3), *Quaestiones Quodlibetales* (1256–73), *Quaestiones Disputatae* (1256-72).

Philosophical Note With the translation of many of Aristotle's works into Latin in the twelfth and thirteenth centuries, his philosophical views, despite opposition, became increasingly influential. The main tendency hitherto among Christian theologians and philosophers had been Platonic and Augustinian; and St Thomas Aquinas' great achievement was to provide a system which harmonized Aristotle with Christian theology. His original and powerful synthesis continues to be of considerable influence in contemporary philosophy, partly because of the Encyclical of Leo XIII (*Aeterni Patris*, 1879) urging Roman Catholic philosophers to draw their inspiration from Aquinas.

Aristotle, though a pupil of Plato, differed from him greatly, and especially in the following ways. First, he argued against the Platonic conception of Forms as subsisting in a separate realm. He brought them down from heaven to earth: substances (roughly: things) were now regarded as being composed of form on the one hand and matter on the other. Second, Aristotle stressed much more strongly, partly as a result of his biological studies, the notion of *purpose* in nature. Third, in line with the above two points, he elaborated a fourfold scheme of causation, distinguishing between the *formal*, *material*, *efficient* and *final* causes. Thus we can explain the existence of a thing by mentioning (*a*) the form which it takes; (*b*) the matter of which it is composed; (*c*) that which brings it about; (*d*) the purpose which it fulfils (in the case of a house, e.g., the formal cause is its design, the material is bricks, etc., the efficient is the activity of the builder, the final the purpose—to provide shelter, etc.). Of these four causes (or better, 'explanations') the material and formal causes are basic, in the sense that the final and formal causes tend to be identical, and these may be the same as the efficient cause (e.g. the idea in the mind of the builder is what determines the building). Another important element in Aristotle's metaphysics is his distinction between potentiality and actuality (*actus* in Latin: this is translated in the following selections as 'act'): e.g. the statue exists potentially in the unhewn block of stone, the sleeper is potentially awake, etc. It is easy to see how the contrast between matter and form can be presented in terms of the contrast between potentiality and actuality.

In Aristotle's system, we can distinguish at one extreme prime matter, or pure potentiality; and at the other end God, who is form, without admixture of matter, or pure act. God constitutes the first principle of change, himself unchanging. Between these two extremes is a hierarchy of substances, comprising inanimate objects, living things—up to and including man, and the celestial bodies, which describe a perfect spherical motion, are composed of a refined 'quintessential' element (see pp. 214–5), and possess souls. The earth is at the centre of the spherical universe.

In Aristotle, God is the final cause, but not the efficient cause of the world, which is eternal. St Thomas Aquinas, as will be seen below in the section on the arguments for the existence of God, argues that one can show, even if the world is eternal, that it depends for its existence upon God. Again, Aquinas goes beyond Aristotle in depicting the end of man's intellectual ascent as supernatural, viz. the knowledge of God as he is in himself. And similarly in many other particulars, Aquinas' Christian faith leads to his transmuting the naturalistic views of Aristotle. But he retains the realism, i.e. metaphysics begins with the study of concrete being.

A consequence of Aquinas' adoption of Aristotelian philosophy is that the autonomy of philosophy has to be recognized. Of course, there are some truths of sacred doctrine which cannot be yielded by philosophical reflection, but have to be taken on faith, but nevertheless there are others which are so yielded. Thus, for example, God's existence can be proved independently of any revelation. Thus we can make a distinction between revealed and natural theology (though note that they overlap as to content).

The following selections are all from the *Summa Theologica*, and consist of (1) some remarks on philosophy and sacred doctrine; (2) the proofs of the existence of God (the Five Ways); (3) a discussion of how it is possible to assert anything about God (Aquinas' theory of analogy); (4) Aquinas' doctrine regarding the possibility of miracles.

The *Summa Theologica* is divided into parts, the parts into questions, and the latter into articles. Each article consists of (1) objections against the doctrine which Aquinas is going to propose; this is then stated in (2) the body of the article; and he then proceeds to (3) replies *seriatim* to the objections.

Bibliographical Note The two *Summas* have been translated by the English Dominican Fathers (London: Burns, Oates and Washbourne, 1912 ff.). A. Pegis, *Basic Writings of St Thomas Aquinas* (2 vols., New York, 1945); Thomas Gilby, *St Thomas Aquinas, Philosophical Texts* (Oxford, 1951); and M. C. D'Arcy, *Thomas Aquinas, Selected Writings* (London, 1934 and reprints) are useful selections. Introductory works are: F. C. Copleston, *Aquinas* (London, 1955); M. C. D'Arcy,

Thomas Aquinas (2nd edn, Dublin, 1953); C. S. J. Curtis, *A Short History of Western Philosophy in the Middle Ages* (London, 1950); E. Gilson, *The Christian Philosophy of St Thomas Aquinas* (N.Y., 1956); F. C. Copleston, *A History of Philosophy*, Vol. ii (London, 1950) and Vol. iii (1953); R. L. Patterson, *The Concept of God in the Philosophy of Aquinas* (London, 1953). The following can be consulted: W. Farrell, *A Companion to the Summa (Theologica)* (4 vols., New York, 1941–2) and V. J. Bourke, *Thomistic Bibliography, 1920–40* (St Louis, 1945). E. L. Mascall, *Existence and Analogy* (London, 1949) and *He Who Is* (London, 1943) are useful expositions of a modern Thomist position.

A. REASON AND FAITH

Summa Theologica, I

QUESTION I

THE NATURE AND DOMAIN OF SACRED DOCTRINE

First Article

WHETHER, BESIDES THE PHILOSOPHICAL DISCIPLINES, ANY FURTHER DOCTRINE IS REQUIRED?

We proceed thus to the First Article:

Objection 1. It seems that, besides the philosophical disciplines, we have no need of any further doctrine. For man should not seek to know what is above reason: *Seek not the things that are too high for thee* (Ecclus. 3.22). But whatever is not above reason is sufficiently considered in the philosophical doctrines. Therefore any other doctrine besides the philosophical disciplines is superfluous.

Obj. 2. Further, doctrine can be concerned only with being, for nothing can be known, save the true, which is convertible with being.[1] But every thing that is, is considered in the philosophical disciplines—even God himself; so that there is a part of philosophy called theology, or the divine science, as is clear from Aristotle.[2] Therefore, besides the philosophical disciplines, there is no need of any further doctrine.

On the contrary, It is written (II Tim. 3.16): *All scripture of God is profitable to teach, to reprove, to correct, to instruct in justice.* Now Scripture, inspired of God, is not a part of the philosophical disciplines discovered by human

[1] A is convertible with B where not only is it the case that all A are B but also that all B are A. (Whatever is, is true; and conversely.)

[2] *Metaphysics*, V, 1.

reason. Therefore it is useful that besides the philosophical disciplines there should be another science, i.e. inspired of God.

I answer that, It was necessary for man's salvation that there should be a doctrine revealed by God, besides the philosophical disciplines investigated by human reason. First, because man is directed to God as to an end that surpasses the grasp of his reason: *The eye hath not seen, O God, besides thee, what things thou hast prepared for them that wait for thee* (Isa. 44.4). But the end must first be known by men who are to direct their intentions and actions to the end. Hence it was necessary for the salvation of man that certain truths which exceed human reason should be made known to him by divine revelation. Even as regards those truths about God which human reason can investigate, it was necessary that man be taught by a divine revelation. For the truth about God which human reason can investigate would only be known by a few, and that after a long time, and with the admixture of many errors; whereas man's whole salvation, which is in God, depends upon the knowledge of this truth. Therefore, in order that the salvation of men might be brought about more fitly and more surely, it was necessary that they be taught divine truths by divine revelation. It was therefore necessary that, besides the philosophical disciplines investigated by reason, there should be a sacred doctrine by way of revelation.

Reply Obj. 1. Although those things which are beyond man's knowledge may not be sought for by man through his reason, nevertheless, what is revealed by God must be accepted through faith. Hence the sacred text continues, *For many things are shown to thee above the understanding of man* (Ecclus. 3.25). And in such things sacred doctrine consists.

Reply Obj. 2. Sciences are diversified according to the diverse nature of their knowable objects. For the astronomer and the physicist both prove the same conclusion—that the earth, for instance, is round: the astronomer by means of mathematics (i.e. abstracting from matter), but the physicist by means of matter itself. Hence there is no reason why those things which are treated by the philosophical disciplines, so far as they can be known by the light of natural reason, may not also be treated by another science so far as they are known by the light of the divine revelation. Hence the theology included in sacred doctrine differs in genus from that theology which is part of philosophy.

B. THE EXISTENCE OF GOD

Summa Theologica, I

QUESTION II

THE EXISTENCE OF GOD
(In Three Articles)

Because the chief aim of sacred doctrine is to teach the knowledge of God not only as he is in himself, but also as the beginning of things and their last end, and especially of rational creatures, as is clear from what has been already said,[1] therefore, in our endeavour to expound this science, we shall treat: (*1*) of God; (*2*) of the rational creature's movement towards God; and (*3*) of Christ who as man is our way to God.[2]

In treating of God there will be a threefold division:

For we shall consider (*1*) what concerns the divine essence, (*2*) Whatever concerns the distinctions of Persons. (*3*) Whatever concerns the procession of creatures from him.[3]

Concerning the divine essence, we must consider:

(*1*) Whether God exists? (*2*) The manner of his existence, or, rather, what is *not* the manner of his existence. (*3*) Whatever concerns his operations—namely, his knowledge, will, power.[4]

Concerning the first, there are three points of enquiry:

(*1*) Whether the proposition *God exists* is self-evident? (*2*) Whether it is demonstrable? (*3*) Whether God exists?

First Article

WHETHER THE EXISTENCE OF GOD IS SELF-EVIDENT?

We proceed thus to the First Article:

Objection 1. It seems that the existence of God is self-evident. For those things are said to be self-evident to us the knowledge of which exists naturally in us, as we can see in regard to first principles. But as Damascene says *the knowledge of God is naturally implanted in all.*[5] Therefore the existence of God is self-evident.

[1] Q.1, a.7. [2] (*1*) is dealt with in *ST* I, (*2*) in *ST* II, (*3*) in *ST* III.

[3] (*1*) is dealt with in Q.3 and following; (*2*) in Q.27; (*3*) in Q.44.

[4] (*2*) is dealt with in Q.3 and following; (*2*) in Q.14; (*3*) in Q.14, 19 and 25 (on knowledge, will, power respectively).

[5] *De Fide Orth.*, I, 1. St John of Damascus (*c.* 675–*c.* 749) had a great influence in the West, mainly through his *De Fide Orthodoxa*.

Obj. 2. Further, those things are said to be self-evident which are known as soon as the terms are known, which the Philosopher says is true of the first principles of demonstration.[1] Thus, when the nature of a whole and of a part is known, it is at once recognized that every whole is greater than its part. But as soon as the signification of the term *God* is understood, it is at once seen that God exists. For by this name is signified that thing than which nothing greater can be conceived. But that which exists actually and mentally is greater than that which exists only mentally. Therefore, since as soon as the name *God* is understood it exists mentally, it also follows that it exists actually. Therefore the proposition *God exists* is self-evident.[2]

Obj. 3. Further, the existence of truth is self-evident. For whoever denies the existence of truth grants that truth does not exist: and, if truth does not exist, then the proposition *Truth does not exist* is true: and if there is anything true, there must be truth. But God is truth itself: *I am the way, the truth and the life* (John 14.6). Therefore *God exists* is self-evident.[3]

On the contrary, No one can mentally admit the opposite of what is self-evident, as the Philosopher states concerning the first principles of demonstration.[4] But the opposite of the proposition *God is* can be mentally admitted: *The fool said in his heart, There is no God* (Ps. 52.1). Therefore, that God exists is not self-evident.

I answer that, A thing can be self-evident in either of two ways: on the one hand, self-evident in itself, though not to us; on the other, self-evident in itself, and to us. A proposition is self-evident because the predicate is included in the essence of the subject: e.g. *Man is an animal,* for animal is contained in the essence of man.[5] If, therefore, the essence

[1] *Posterior Analytics*, I, 3. See n. 4 below.

[2] This is, of course, the Ontological Argument. See above, p. 56.

[3] Compare Augustine's argument; see above, p. 32 ff.

[4] *Metaphysics*, III, 3. The law of contradiction ('The same attribute cannot at the same time belong and not belong to the same subject and in the same respect') and the law of excluded middle ('Of one subject we must either affirm or deny any one predicate') are, according to Aristotle, instances of first principles and apply in all sciences (i.e. branches of knowledge). It is a mark of the unphilosophical man to try to *prove* such principles, for on them depends the possibility of proofs; but they can be shown to be true inasmuch as any attempt to deny them falls into absurdity. The two 'laws' mentioned above (and which are formulated in various ways), together with the law of identity ('*A* belongs to all *A*' or 'Everything is what it is'), have traditionally constituted the 'three laws of thought'. Philosophers have, however, come increasingly to feel that the term 'laws' is inappropriate, since it suggests that these principles of reasoning are like laws of nature, and so describe invariable psychological phenomena. But they are more like rules, which can remain valid even if broken, rather than laws of nature, which if 'broken' do not any longer hold universally.

[5] The essence is, briefly, that which is described in the correct definition of the thing in question. Thus, to say that the predicate is included in the essence of the subject amounts to saying that the predicate is included in the definition of the subject; e.g. the predicate 'animal' is included in the definition of 'man' in virtue of the definition of 'man' as 'rational animal'.

of the predicate and subject be known to all, the proposition will be self-evident to all; as is clear with regard to the first principles of demonstration, the terms of which are common notions that no one is ignorant of, such as being and non-being, whole and part, and the like. If, however, there are some to whom the essence of the predicate and subject is unknown, the proposition will be self-evident in itself, but not to those who do not know the meaning of the predicate and subject of the proposition. Therefore, it happens, as Boethius[1] says, that there are some notions of the mind which are common and self-evident to the learned, as that incorporeal substances are not in space. Therefore I say that this proposition, *God exists*, of itself is self-evident, for the predicate is the same as the subject, because God is his own existence as will be shown hereafter.[2] Now because we do not know the essence of God, the proposition is not self-evident to us, but needs to be demonstrated by things that are more known to us, though less known in their nature—namely, by his effects.

Reply Obj. 1. To know that God exists in a general and confused way is implanted in us by nature, inasmuch as God is man's beatitude. For man naturally desires happiness, and what is naturally desired by man is naturally known by him. This, however, is not to know absolutely that God exists; just as to know that someone is approaching is not to know that Peter is approaching, even though it is Peter who is approaching; for there are many who imagine that man's perfect good, which is happiness, consists in riches, and others in pleasures, and others in something else.

Reply Obj. 2. Perhaps not everyone who hears this name *God* understands it to signify something than which no greater can be thought, seeing that some have believed God to be a body.[3] Yet, granted that everyone understands that by this name *God* is signified something than which no greater can be thought, nevertheless, it does not therefore follow that he understands that what the name signifies exists actually, but only that it exists mentally. Nor can it be argued that it actually exists, unless it be admitted that there actually exists something than which nothing greater can be thought; and this precisely is not admitted by those who hold that God does not exist.

Reply Obj. 3. The existence of truth in general is self-evident, but the existence of a Primal Truth is not self-evident to us.

[1] See n. 4 to p. 74. [2] See *ST* Q.3, a.4.

[3] See Aristotle, *Physics*, I, 4 (187a 12), referring to early Greek philosophical theories postulating a single underlying material from which sensible appearances are derived. Anaximenes, for example, in St Augustine's words, 'attributed all the causes of things to an infinite air; he neither denied nor ignored the existence of gods, but, so far from believing that the air was made by them, he held, on the contrary, that they sprang from the air,' (*De Civitate Dei*, VIII, 3).

Second Article

WHETHER IT CAN BE DEMONSTRATED THAT GOD EXISTS?

We proceed thus to the Second Article:

Objection 1. It seems that the existence of God cannot be demonstrated. For it is an article of faith that God exists. But what is of faith cannot be demonstrated, because a demonstration produces scientific knowledge, whereas faith is of the unseen, as is clear from the Apostle (Heb. 11.1). Therefore it cannot be demonstrated that God exists.

Obj. 2. Further, essence is the middle term of demonstration. But we cannot know in what God's essence consists, but solely in what it does not consist, as Damascene says.[1] Therefore we cannot demonstrate that God exists.

Obj. 3. Further, if the existence of God were demonstrated, this could only be from his effects. But his effects are not proportioned to him, since he is infinite and his effects are finite, and between the finite and infinite there is no proportion. Therefore, since a cause cannot be demonstrated by an effect not proportioned to it, it seems that the existence of God cannot be demonstrated.

On the contrary, The Apostle says, *The invisible things of him are clearly seen, being understood by the things that are made* (Rom. 1.20). But this would not be unless the existence of God could be demonstrated through the things that are made; for the first thing we must know of anything is, whether it exists.

I answer that, Demonstration can be made in two ways: One is through the cause, and is called *propter quid,* and this is to argue from what is prior absolutely. The other is through the effect, and is called a demonstration *quia*; this is to argue from what is prior relatively only to us. When an effect is better known to us than its cause, from the effect we proceed to the knowledge of the cause. And from every effect the existence of its proper cause can be demonstrated, so long as its effects are better known to us; because, since every effect depends upon its cause, if the effect exists, the cause must pre-exist. Hence the existence of God, in so far as it is not self-evident to us, can be demonstrated from those of his effects which are known to us.

Reply Obj. 1. The existence of God and other like truths about God, which can be known by natural reason, are not articles of faith, but are preambles to the articles; for faith presupposes natural knowledge, even

[1] *De Fide Orth.*, I, 4 (*PG* 94, 800).

as grace presupposes nature and perfection the perfectible. Nevertheless, there is nothing to prevent a man, who cannot grasp a proof, from accepting, as a matter of faith, something which in itself is capable of being scientifically known and demonstrated.

Reply Obj. 2. When the existence of a cause is demonstrated from an effect, this effect takes the place of the definition of the cause in proving the cause's existence. This is especially the case in regard to God, because, in order to prove the existence of anything, it is necessary to accept as a middle term the meaning of the name, and not its essence, for the question of its essence follows from the question of its existence. Now the names given to God are derived from his effects, as will be later shown.[1] Consequently, in demonstrating the existence of God from his effects, we may take for the middle term the meaning of the name *God.*[2]

Reply Obj. 3. From effects not proportioned to the cause no perfect knowledge of that cause can be obtained. Yet from every effect the existence of the cause can be clearly demonstrated, and so we can demonstrate the existence of God from his effects; though from them we cannot know God perfectly as he is in his essence.

Third Article

WHETHER GOD EXISTS?

We proceed thus to the Third Article:

Objection 1. It seems that God does not exist; because if one of two contraries be infinite, the other would be altogether destroyed. But the name *God* means that he is infinite goodness. If, therefore, God existed, there would be no evil discoverable; but there is evil in the world. Therefore God does not exist.

Obj. 2. Further, it is superfluous to suppose that what can be accounted for by a few principles has been produced by many. But it seems that everything we see in the world can be accounted for by other principles, supposing God did not exist. For all natural things can be reduced to one principle, which is nature; and all voluntary things can be reduced to one principle, which is human reason, or will. Therefore there is no need to suppose God's existence.

On the contrary, It is said in the person of God: *I am who am* (Ex. 3.14).

I answer that, That the existence of God can be proved in five ways.

The first and more manifest way is the argument from motion. It is

[1] Q.13, a.1

[2] 'Middle term' here means middle term in a syllogism (e.g. in 'All M are P, and all S are M, so all S are P', 'M' is the middle term).

certain, and evident to our senses, that in the world some things are in motion. Now whatever is moved is moved by another, for nothing can be moved except it is in potentiality to that towards which it is moved; whereas a thing moves inasmuch as it is in act. For motion is nothing else than the reduction of something from potentiality to actuality. But nothing can be reduced from potentiality to actuality, except by something in a state of actuality. Thus that which is actually hot, as fire, makes wood, which is potentially hot, to be actually hot, and thereby moves and changes it. Now it is not possible that the same thing should be at once in actuality and potentiality in the same respect, but only in different respects. For what is actually hot cannot simultaneously be potentially hot; but it is simultaneously potentially cold. It is therefore impossible that in the same respect and in the same way a thing should be both mover and moved, i.e., that it should move itself. Therefore, whatever is moved must be moved by another. If that by which it is moved be itself moved, then this also must needs be moved by another, and that by another again. But this cannot go on to infinity, because then there would be no first mover, and, consequently, no other mover, seeing that subsequent movers move only inasmuch as they are moved by the first mover; as the staff moves only because it is moved by the hand. Therefore it is necessary to arrive at a first mover, moved by no other; and this everyone understands to be God.[1]

The second is from the nature of efficient cause. In the world of sensible things we find there is an order of efficient causes. There is no case known (neither is it, indeed, possible) in which a thing is found to be the efficient cause of itself; for so it would be prior to itself, which is impossible. Now in efficient causes it is not possible to go on to infinity, because in all efficient causes following in order, the first is the cause of the intermediate cause, and the intermediate is the cause of the ultimate cause, whether the intermediate cause be several, or one only. Now to take away the cause is to take away the effect. Therefore, if there be no first cause among efficient causes, there will be no ultimate, nor any intermediate, cause. But if in efficient causes it is possible to go on to infinity, there will be no first efficient cause, neither will there be an ultimate effect, nor any intermediate efficient causes; all of which is plainly false. Therefore it is necessary to admit a first efficient cause, to which everyone gives the name of God.[2]

The third way is taken from possibility and necessity, and runs thus. We find in nature things that are possible to be or not to be, since they

[1] See also *Summa contra Gentiles*, I, 13, and Aristotle's *Metaphysics*, XII, 6 (1071b 3ff.).

[2] This line of reasoning is suggested by Aristotle, *Metaphysics*, II, 2.

are found to be generated, and to be corrupted,[1] and consequently, it is possible for them to be and not to be. But it is impossible for these always to exist, for that which can not-be at some time is not. Therefore, if anything can not-be, then at one time there was nothing in existence. Now if this were true, even now there would be nothing in existence, because that which does not exist begins to exist only through something already existing. Therefore, if at one time nothing was in existence, it would have been impossible for anything to have begun to exist; and thus even now nothing would be in existence—which is absurd. Therefore, not all beings are merely possible, but there must exist something the existence of which is necessary. But every necessary thing either has its necessity caused by another, or not. Now it is impossible to go on to infinity in necessary things which have their necessity caused by another, as has been already proved in regard to efficient causes. Therefore we cannot but admit the existence of some being having of itself its own necessity, and not receiving it from another, but rather causing in others their necessity. This all men speak of as God.[2]

The fourth way is taken from the gradation to be found in things. Among beings there are some more and some less good, true, noble and the like. But *more* and *less* are predicated of different things according as they resemble in their different ways something which is the maximum, as a thing is said to be hotter according as it more nearly resembles that which is hottest; so that there is something which is truest, something best, something noblest, and consequently something which is uttermost being, for those things that are greatest in truth are greatest in being, as it is written in *Metaphysics*, II.[3] Now the maximum in any genus is the cause of all in that genus, as fire, which is the maximum of heat, is the cause of all hot things, as is said in the same book.[4] Therefore there must be also something which is to all beings the cause of their being, goodness, and every other perfection; and this we call God.[5]

[1] 'Generation', 'corruption'—these represent translations of the terms used by Aristotle to signify 'coming into existence' and 'going out of existence', or 'coming to be' and 'passing away'.

[2] This proof goes back through Maimonides (see below, p. 73) to Aristotle, *Metaphysics*, XII, 6 (1071b 22 ff.). The first three ways are versions of the Cosmological Argument; see below, p. 130 and pp. 143–5.

[3] 993b 30.

[4] 993b 25. Aristotle argues in this passage that what gives other things a certain character itself has that character in the highest degree, so that what makes other things true is itself most true.

[5] The argument is, though it occurs in Aristotle's *De Philosophia*, Platonic in ancestry, and is to be found substantially in St Augustine (see p. 31) and St Anselm, *Monologium*, Ch. I (see p. 55). It is an extension of one argument for the Forms (see above, p. 20), namely that ideal limits are required to explain relative predicates (e.g. the better implies a best possible).

The fifth way is taken from the governance of the world. We see that things which lack knowledge, such as natural bodies, act for an end, and this is evident from their acting always, or nearly always, in the same way, so as to obtain the best result. Hence it is plain that they achieve their end, not fortuitously, but designedly. Now whatever lacks knowledge cannot move towards an end, unless it be directed by some being endowed with knowledge and intelligence; as the arrow is directed by the archer. Therefore some intelligent being exists by whom all natural things are directed to their end; and this being we call God.[1]

Reply Obj. 1. As Augustine says: *Since God is the highest good, he would not allow any evil to exist in his works, unless his omnipotence and goodness were such as to bring good even out of evil.*[2] This is part of the infinite goodness of God, that he should allow evil to exist, and out of it produce good.

Reply Obj. 2. Since nature works for a determinate end under the direction of a higher agent, whatever is done by nature must be traced back to God as to its first cause. So likewise whatever is done voluntarily must be traced back to some higher cause other than human reason and will, since these can change and fail; for all things that are changeable and capable of defect must be traced back to an immovable and self-necessary first principle, as has been shown.

C. ANALOGY

As well as in the following passage, A. deals with analogy in the *Summa contra Gentiles* I, 34, and in the *De Veritate* 2, 11, *in corpore*.

He distinguishes two main types of analogy, namely (1) where there is a resemblance of *proportion*, and (2) a resemblance of *proportionality*. (Unfortunately in modern parlance, the former is sometimes called analogy of attribution and the latter analogy of proportion.) In the former, we attribute a predicate to two things in virtue of a relation that they have to each other. For example, wisdom can be predicated of God in virtue of the relation of creatures to God, namely their likeness to God. Since, however, perfections exist in God in a different way from the way they exist in creatures, this is neither predication in precisely the same sense, nor in a completely different sense. It is a mean between univocity and equivocity. Note that, according to A., it is improper to say that God has a likeness to creatures, but only that creatures have a likeness to God (just as we tend to say that a reproduction is like an original, but not *vice versa*). In the second type of analogy, the situation is more complex: it is founded not on a direct likeness, but on a likeness between relations—for instance, we use the term 'vision' both of the eye and the intellect, because what ordinary vision is to the eye, intellectual vision is to the mind: there is a certain resemblance between the two

[1] For further discussions of the Teleological Argument, see below, p. 206ff. See also Aristotle, *Metaphysics*, XII, 10.

[2] *Enchiridion*, XI.

relations. Thus, in application to God, we can talk about his intellectual activity, on the ground that there is a resemblance between the relation of God to his intellectual activity and the relation between man and his intellectual activity. It is clear, however, that this second type of analogy can only be used if we have first established that there is a likeness between creatures and God. Thus the first type of analogy is fundamental. The basis for asserting such a likeness, in the context of natural theology, is that God can be shown to be the cause of creatures and that perfections in creatures derive from God. For a full discussion of the doctrine of analogy, see E. L. Mascall, *Existence and Analogy* (London, 1949).

Summa Theologica, I

QUESTION XIII

THE NAMES OF GOD

Fifth Article

WHETHER WHAT IS SAID OF GOD AND OF CREATURES IS UNIVOCALLY PREDICATED OF THEM?

We proceed thus to the Fifth Article:

Objection 1. It seems that the things attributed to God and creatures are univocal.[1] For every equivocal term is reduced to the univocal, as many are reduced to one: for if the name *dog* be said equivocally of the barking dog and of the dogfish, it must be said of some univocally—viz. of all barking dogs; otherwise we proceed to infinitude. Now there are some univocal agents which agree with their effects in name and definition, as man generates man; and there are some agents which are equivocal, as the sun which causes heat, although the sun is hot only in an equivocal sense.[2] Therefore it seems that the first agent, to which all other agents are reduced, is a univocal agent: and thus what is said of God and creatures is predicated univocally.

Obj. 2. Further, no likeness is understood through equivocal names. Therefore, as creatures have a certain likeness to God, according to the text of Genesis (1.26), *Let us make man to our image and likeness*, it seems that something can be said of God and creatures univocally.

Obj. 3. Further, measure is homogeneous with the thing measured, as is said in *Metaphysics*, X.[3] But God is the first measure of all beings. Therefore is homogeneous with creatures; and thus a name may be applied univocally to God and creatures.

[1] 'Univocal', i.e. used in the same sense; 'equivocal', used in different senses.

[2] On the Aristotelian view there was a distinction between things below the moon (sublunary things) and those above. See above, p. 60.

[3] 1053a 24.

On the contrary, Whatever is predicated of various things under the same name but not in the same sense is predicated equivocally. But no name belongs to God in the same sense that it belongs to creatures; for instance, wisdom in creatures is a quality, but not in God.[1] Now a change in genus changes an essence, since the genus is part of the definition; and the same applies to other things.[2] Therefore whatever is said of God and of creatures is predicated equivocally.

Further, God is more distant from creatures than any creatures are from each other. But the distance of some creatures makes an equivocal predication of them impossible, as in the case of those things which are not in the same genus. Therefore much less can anything be predicated univocally of God and creatures; and so only equivocal predication can be applied to them.

I answer that, Univocal predication is impossible between God and creatures. The reason of this is that every effect which is not a proportioned result of the power of the efficient cause receives the similitude of the agent not in its full degree, but in a measure that falls short; so that what is divided and multiplied in the effects resides in the agent simply, and in an unvaried manner. For example, the sun by the exercise of its one power produces manifold and various forms in these sublunary things. In the same way, as was said above, all perfections existing in creatures divided and multiplied pre-exist in God unitedly. Hence, when any name expressing perfection is applied to a creature, it signifies that perfection as distinct from others according to the nature of its definition; as, for instance, by this term *wise* applied to a man, we signify some perfection distinct from a man's essence, and distinct from his power and his being, and from all similar things. But when we apply *wise* to God, we do not mean to signify anything distinct from his essence or power or being. And thus when this term *wise* is applied to man, in some degree it circumscribes and comprehends the thing signified; whereas this is not the case when it is applied to God, but it leaves the thing signified as uncomprehended and as exceeding the signification of the name. Hence it is evident that the term *wise* is not applied in the same way to God and to man. The same applies to other terms. Hence, no name is predicated univocally of God and creatures.

[1] See Q.14, a.1. On A.'s view, all divine perfections are in reality identical with one another and with the divine nature.

[2] The genus of God's wisdom differs from the genus under which human wisdom falls; but this involves the consequence that the definition of wisdom in the one case must differ from the definition of wisdom in the other case, since a definition (on the Aristotelian scheme) consists in a statement referring to the genus of the thing defined and to the characteristic distinguishing that thing from other species of the same genus. (E.g. 'Man is a rational animal'.)

Neither, on the other hand, are names applied to God and creatures in a purely equivocal sense, as some have said.[1] Because, if that were so, it follows that from creatures nothing could be known or demonstrated about God; for the reasoning would always be exposed to the fallacy of equivocation. Such a view is against the Philosopher, who proves many things about God, and also against what the Apostle says: *The invisible things of God are clearly seen being understood by the things that are made* (Rom. 1.20). Therefore it must be said that these names are said of God and creatures in an *analogous* sense, that is, according to proportion.

This can happen in two ways: either according as many things are proportioned to one (thus, for example, *healthy* is predicated of medicine and urine in relation and in proportion to health of body, of which the latter is the sign and the former the cause), or according as one thing is proportioned to another (thus *healthy* is said of medicine and an animal, since medicine is the cause of health in the animal body). And in this way some things are said of God and creatures analogically, and not in a purely equivocal nor in a purely univocal sense. For we can name God only from creatures. Hence, whatever is said of God and creatures is said according as there is some relation of the creature to God as to its principle and cause, wherein all the perfections of things pre-exist excellently. Now this mode of community is a mean between pure equivocation and simple univocation. For in analogies the idea is not, as it is in univocals, one and the same; yet it is not totally diverse as in equivocals; but the name which is thus used in a multiple sense signifies various proportions to some one thing: e.g. *healthy*, applied to urine, signifies the sign of animal health; but applied to medicine, it signifies the cause of the same health.

Reply Obj. 1. Although in predications all equivocals must be reduced to univocals, still in actions the non-univocal agent must precede the univocal agent. For the non-univocal agent is the universal cause of the whole species, as the sun is the cause of the generation of all men. But the univocal agent is not the universal efficient cause of the whole species (otherwise it would be the cause of itself, since it is contained in the species), but is a particular cause of this individual which it places under the species by way of participation. Therefore the universal cause of the whole species is not a univocal agent: and the universal cause comes before the particular cause. But this universal agent, while not univocal, nevertheless is not altogether equivocal (otherwise it could not produce its

[1] Maimonides, *Guide*, I. 59, etc. Maimonides (1135–1204), Jewish philosopher born in Spain, was a notable predecessor of Aquinas in attempting a synthesis between Aristotelianism and religious faith. His *Guide for the Perplexed* appeared in 1190.

own likeness); but it can be called an analogical agent, just as in predications all univocal names are reduced to one first non-univocal analogical name, which is *being*.[1]

Reply Obj. 2. The likeness of the creature to God is imperfect, for it does not represent the same thing even generically.[2]

Reply Obj. 3. God is not a measure proportioned to the things measured; hence it is not necessary that God and creatures should be in the same genus.

The arguments adduced in the contrary sense prove indeed that these names are not predicated univocally of God and creatures; yet they do not prove that they are predicated equivocally.

Twelfth Article

WHETHER AFFIRMATIVE PROPOSITIONS CAN BE FORMED ABOUT GOD?

We proceed thus to the Twelfth Article:

Objection 1. It seems that affirmative propositions cannot be formed about God. For Dionysius says that *negations about God are true; but affirmations are vague.*[3]

Obj. 2. Further, Boethius[4] says that *a simple form cannot be a subject.*[5] But God is most absolutely a simple form, as was shown.[6] Therefore he cannot be a subject. But everything about which an affirmative proposition is made is taken as a subject. Therefore an affirmative proposition cannot be formed about God.

Obj. 3. Further, every intellect is false which understands a thing otherwise than it is. But God has being without any composition, as was shown above.[7] Therefore, since every intellect which makes an affirmation understands something as composite, it seems that a true affirmative proposition about God cannot be made.

On the contrary, What is of faith cannot be false. But some affirmative

[1] On Aristotle's view, all predications fall under ten categories: substance, quantity, quality, relation, place, time, situation, habit, activity and passivity. The terms thus classified are held to represent different categories of being; but the sense in which a substance *is* differs from the sense in which a quality *is*, and so on.

[2] Q.4, a.3.

[3] *De Coelesti Hierarchia* II. 3. See above, p. 51.

[4] Boethius (*c.* 480–524), a Christian philosopher, holding high office under the Emperor Theodoric, though later imprisoned, dying under torture. Known chiefly for his translation of and commentary on the logical works of Aristotle and for his *Consolatio Philosophiae.*

[5] *De Trinitate* II (*PL* 64, 1250): 'subject', i.e. of a proposition.

[6] Q.3, a.7. [7] Ibid.

propositions are of faith; as that God is Three and One, and that he is omnipotent. Therefore true affirmative propositions can be formed about God.

I answer that, Affirmative propositions can be truly formed about God. To prove this we must observe that in every true affirmative proposition the predicate and the subject must signify in some way the same thing in reality, and diverse things in idea. And this appears to be the case both in propositions which have an accidental predicate and in those which have a substantial predicate.[1] For it is manifest that *man* and *white* are the same in subject, and diverse in idea; for the idea of man is one thing, and that of whiteness is another. The same applies when I say *Man is an animal*, since the same thing which is man is truly animal; for in the same *suppositum*[2] there is both a sensible nature by reason of which he is called animal, and the rational nature by reason of which he is called man; hence, here again, predicate and subject are the same as to the *suppositum*, but diverse as to idea. But in propositions where the thing is predicated of itself,[3] the same rule in some way applies, inasmuch as the intellect considers as the *suppositum* what it places in the subject; and what it places in the predicate it considers as the nature of the form existing in the *suppositum*, according to the saying that *predicates are taken formally, and subjects materially*. To this diversity in idea corresponds the plurality of predicate and subject, while the intellect signifies the identity of the thing by the composition itself.

God, however, as considered in himself, is altogether one and simple, yet our intellect knows him according to diverse conceptions because it cannot see him as he is in himself. Nevertheless, although it understands him under diverse conceptions, it yet knows that absolutely one and the same reality corresponds to its conceptions. Therefore the plurality of predicate and subject represents the plurality of idea; and the intellect represents the unity by composition.

Reply Obj. 1. Dionysius says that affirmations about God are vague or, according to another translation, *incongruous*, inasmuch as no name can be applied to God according to its mode of signification, as was said above.

Reply Obj. 2. Our intellect cannot apprehend simple subsisting forms as they really are in themselves; but it apprehends them after the manner of composite things in which there is something taken as subject and

[1] I.e. propositions where the predicate stands for an accident (i.e. a property which is not included in, or a necessary adjunct to, the essence of the thing), and propositions where the predicate stands for the substance.

[2] *Suppositum*: entity referred to.

[3] I.e. tautological propositions (e.g. 'The man is a man').

something that is inherent. Therefore it apprehends the simple form as a subject and attributes something else to it.

Reply Obj. 3. This proposition, *The intellect understanding anything otherwise than it is, is false*, can be taken in two senses, according as this adverb *otherwise* modifies the verb *to understand* from the standpoint of the thing understood, or from the standpoint of the one who understands. Taken as referring to the thing understood, the proposition is true, and the meaning is: Any intellect which understands that a thing is otherwise than it is, is false. But this does not hold in the present case, because our intellect, in forming a proposition about God, does not affirm he is composite, but that he is simple. But taken as referring to the one who understands, the proposition is false. For our intellect understands in one way, and things are in another. Thus it is clear that our intellect understands material things below itself in an immaterial way; not that it understands them to be immaterial things: but its way of understanding is immaterial. Likewise, when it understands simple things above itself, it understands them according to its own way, which is composite; yet not so as to understand composite things. And thus our intellect is not false in composing a judgment concerning God.

D. MIRACLES

Summa Theologica, I

QUESTION CV

THE MOVEMENT OF GOD IN CREATURES

Fifth Article

WHETHER GOD WORKS IN EVERY AGENT?

We proceed thus to the Fifth Article:

Objection 1. It would seem that God does not work in every agent. For we must not attribute any insufficiency to God. If therefore God works in every agent, he works sufficiently in each one. Hence it would be superfluous for the created agent to work at all.

Obj. 2. Further, the same work cannot proceed at the same time from two sources, just as neither can one and the same movement belong to two moveable things. Therefore if the creature's operation is from God operating in the creature, it cannot at the same time proceed from the creature; and so no creature works at all.

Obj. 3. Further, the maker is the cause of the operation of the thing made, as giving it the form whereby it operates. Therefore, if God is the cause of the operation of the things made by him, this would be inasmuch as he gives them the power of operating. But this is in the beginning, when he makes them. Thus it seems that God does not operate any further in the operating creature.

On the contrary, It is written (Isa. 26.12): *Lord, thou hast wrought all our works in us.*

I answer that, Some have understood God to work in every agent in such a way that no created power has any effect in things, but that God alone is the immediate cause of everything wrought; for instance, that it is not fire that gives heat, but God in the fire, and so forth. But this is impossible. First, because the order of cause and effect would be taken away from created things, and this would imply a lack of power in the creator; for it is due to the power of the cause, that it bestows active power on its effect. Secondly, because the operative powers which are seen to exist in things would be bestowed on things to no purpose, if things produced nothing through them. Indeed, all things created would seem, in a way, to be purposeless, if they lacked an operation proper to them; since the purpose of everything is its operation. For the less perfect is always for the sake of the more perfect. Consequently, just as the matter is for the sake of the form, so the form which is the first act is for the sake of its operation, which is the second act;[1] and thus operation is the end of the creature. We must therefore understand that God works in things in such a manner that things have also their proper operation.

In order to make this clear, we must observe that of the four causes[2] matter is not a principle of action, but the subject that receives the effect of action. On the other hand, the end, the agent and the form are principles of action, but in a certain order. For the first principle of action is the end which moves the agent, the second is the agent, and the third is the form of that which the agent applies to action (although the agent also acts through its own form). This may be clearly seen in things made by art. For the craftsman is moved to action by the end, which is the thing wrought, for instance a chest or a bed, and he applies to action the axe which cuts because it is sharp.

Thus then does God work in every agent, according to these three things. First, as an end. For since every operation is for the sake of some good, real or apparent, and since nothing is good, either really or apparently, except in so far as it participates in a likeness to the highest good,

[1] See above, in the introductory philosophical note. The form stands to the matter as act(uality) to potentiality; but the operation of a thing is the actualization of the potentiality of that thing. The distinction between actuality and potentiality is relative, and may be made at different levels.

[2] See above, p. 59.

which is God, it follows that God himself is the cause of every operation as its end. Again, it is to be observed that where there are several agents in order, the second always acts in virtue of the first; for the first agent moves the second to act. And thus all agents act in virtue of God himself; and so he is the cause of action in every agent. Thirdly, we must observe that God not only moves things to operate, as it were applying their forms and powers to operation, just as the workman applies the axe to cutting (who nevertheless did not himself give the axe its form), but he also gives created agents their forms and preserves them in being. Therefore he is the cause of action not only by giving the form which is the principle of action, as the generator is said to be the cause of movement in things heavy and light, but also as conserving the forms and powers of things; just as the sun is said to be the cause of the manifestation of colours, inasmuch as it gives and conserves the light by which colours are made manifest. And since the form of a thing is within the thing, and all the more so, as it approaches nearer to the first and universal cause; and because in all things God himself is properly the cause of universal being which is innermost in all things:— it follows that God works intimately in all things. For this reason in Holy Scripture the operations of nature are attributed to God in operating in nature, according to Job 10.11: *Thou hast clothed me with skin and flesh: thou hast put me together with bones and sinews.*

Reply Obj. 1. God works sufficiently in things as a first cause, but it does not follow from this that the operation of secondary agents is superfluous.

Reply Obj. 2. One action does not proceed from two agents of the same orders. But nothing hinders the same action from proceeding from a primary and a secondary agent.[1]

Reply Obj. 3. God not only gives things their forms, but he also conserves them in being, and applies them to act, and is moreover the end of every action, as was explained above.

Sixth Article

WHETHER GOD CAN DO ANYTHING OUTSIDE THE ESTABLISHED ORDER OF NATURE?

We proceed thus to the Sixth Article:

Objection 1. It would seem that God cannot do anything outside the established order of nature. For Augustine says: *God, the maker and creator*

[1] E.g. God is the primary efficient cause, in that he is the cause of the whole series of efficient causes; but the immediate (secondary) cause of an event can still be described as the cause.

of each nature, does nothing against nature.[1] But that which is outside the natural order seems to be against nature. Therefore God can do nothing outside the natural order.

Obj. 2. Further, as the order of justice is from God, so is the order of nature. But God cannot do anything outside the order of justice, for then he would do something unjust. Therefore he cannot do anything outside the order of nature.

Obj. 3. Further, God established the order of nature. Therefore, if God does anything outside the order of nature, it would seem that he is changeable; which cannot be said.

On the contrary, Augustine says: *God sometimes does things which are contrary to the wonted course of nature.*[2]

I answer that, From each cause there results a certain order to its effects, since every cause is a principle; and so, according to the multiplicity of causes, there results a multiplicity of orders, subject one to the other, just as cause is subject to cause. Hence, a higher cause is not subject to a cause of a lower order, but conversely. An example of this may be seen in human affairs. On the father of a family depends the order of the household; which order is contained in the order of the city; which order again depends on the ruler of the city; while this last depends on that of the king, by whom the whole kingdom is ordered.

If, therefore, we consider the order of things according as it depends on the first cause, God cannot do anything against this order; for if he did so, he would act against his foreknowledge, or his will, or his goodness. But if we consider the order of things according as it depends on any secondary cause, thus God can do something outside such order. For he is not subject to the order of secondary causes, but, on the contrary, this order is subject to him, as proceeding from him, not by natural necessity, but by the choice of his own will; for he could have created another order of things. Therefore God can do something outside this order created by him, when he chooses,—for instance, by producing the effects of secondary causes without them, or by producing certain effects to which secondary causes do not extend. So Augustine says: *God acts against the wonted course of nature, but by no means does he act against the supreme law; because he does not act against himself.*[3]

Reply Obj. 1. In natural things something may happen outside this natural order, in two ways. It may happen by the action of an agent which did not give them their natural inclination, as, for example, when a man moves a heavy body upwards, which does not owe to him its natural inclination to move downwards. Now this would be against nature. It

[1] *Contra Faust.*, XXVI, 3 (*PL* 42, 480). [2] Ibid., 3 (*PL* 42, 481). [3] Ibid.

may also happen by the action of the agent on whom the natural inclination depends, and this is not against nature, as is clear in the ebb and flow of the tide, which is not against nature, although it is against the natural movement of water, which is moved downward; for it is owing to the influence of a heavenly body, on which the natural inclination of lower bodies depends. Therefore, since the order of nature is given to things by God, if he does anything outside this order, it is not against nature. Hence Augustine says: *That is natural to each thing which is caused by him from whom is all limit, number and order in nature.*[1]

Reply Obj. 2. The order of justice arises by relation to the first cause, which is the rule of all justice; and that is why God can do nothing against such an order.

Reply Obj. 3. God fixed a certain order in things in such a way that at the same time he reserved to himself whatever he intended to do otherwise than by a particular cause. So when he acts outside this order, he does not change.

Seventh Article

WHETHER WHATEVER GOD DOES OUTSIDE THE NATURAL ORDER IS MIRACULOUS?

We proceed thus to the Seventh Article:

Objection 1. It would seem that not everything which God does outside the natural order of things is miraculous. For the creation of the world and of souls, and the justification of the unrighteous, are done by God outside the natural order; for these effects are not accomplished by the action of any natural cause. Yet these things are not called miracles. Therefore not everything that God does outside the natural order is a miracle.

Obj. 2. Further, a miracle is *something difficult, which seldom occurs, surpassing the faculty of nature, and going so far beyond our hopes as to compel our astonishment.*[2] But some things outside the order of nature are not arduous, for they occur in small things, such as the recovery of some precious stone or the healing of the sick. Nor are they of rare occurrence, since they happen frequently; as when the sick were placed in the streets, to be healed by the shadow of Peter (Acts 5.15). Nor do they surpass the ability of nature; as when people are cured of a fever. Nor are they beyond our hopes, since we all hope for the resurrection of the dead, which nevertheless will be outside the course of nature. Therefore not all things that are outside the course of nature are miraculous.

[1] *Contra Faust.*, ibid. [2] *De Util. Cred.*, XVI (*PL* 42, 90).

Obj. 3. Further, the term *miracle* is derived from admiration,[1] which arises when an effect is manifest, whereas its cause is hidden; as when a man sees an eclipse without knowing its cause, as the Philosopher says in the beginning of his *Metaphysics*.[2] Now the cause of a manifest effect may be known to one, but unknown to others. Hence a thing is wonderful to one man, and not at all to others; as an eclipse is to a rustic, but not to an astronomer. Now a miracle is so called as being full of wonder, in other words, as having a cause absolutely hidden from all. This cause is God. Therefore those things which God does outside the causes which we know are called miracles.

Reply Obj. 1. Creation, and the justification of the unrighteous, though done by God alone, are not, properly speaking, miracles, because they are not of a nature to proceed from any other cause; so they do not occur outside the order of nature, since they do not belong to the capacity of nature.

Reply Obj. 2. An arduous thing is called a miracle, not because of the excellence of the thing wherein it is done, but because it surpasses the ability of nature. So, too, a thing called unusual, not because it does not often happen, but because it is outside the usual natural course of things. Furthermore, a thing is said to be above the ability of nature, not only by reason of the substance of the thing done, but also because of the manner and order in which it is done. Again, a miracle is said to go beyond the hope *of nature*, not above the hope *of grace*, which hope comes from faith, whereby we believe in the future resurrection.

Reply Obj. 3. The knowledge of the Apostles, although not manifest in itself, yet was made manifest in its effect, from which it was shown to be wonderful.

[1] I.e. from the verb *miror*, 'to wonder at'.

[2] Aristotle, *Metaphysics* 982b 16.

PART TWO

6

HERBERT OF CHERBURY

on REASON AND FAITH

Biographical Note Edward Herbert born 1583, at Eyton, Shropshire; brother of George Herbert, the poet. Entered the University of Oxford at age of 12, and while still at Oxford married his cousin. Went to Court, and upon the accession of James I was made Knight of the Bath and later appointed Sherriff of Montgomeryshire. 1608, travelled to France, and went on to the Low Countries, where he joined the army of the Prince of Orange. In 1614, after a time back at Court and on his country estate, H. went back to the Continent, travelling in France, Germany and Italy. In 1617, he returned to the family seat at Montgomery Castle, and during the enforced leisure of illness began planning and writing the *De Veritate*. 1618, appointed Ambassador to France. *De Veritate* published in 1624, despite H.'s diffidence about it (but the experience of hearing a loud but gentle noise from a clear sky overcame his doubts). After being recalled by James I, he could find no responsible appointment, though he was created Baron Cherbury. Nor was he in favour under Charles I; and even when summoned to York in 1640 for a council of war, his views were unpopular, and he largely retired from public affairs, the remainder of his life being spent in literary work. Died in 1648.

Principal works: *De Veritate* (1624), *Religio Laici* (1645), *De Religione Gentium* and *Autobiography* (both published posthumously).

Philosophical Note Lord Herbert of Cherbury is chiefly remembered as being the father of Deism, though perhaps the description is not in one sense very accurate, since those who, in the eighteenth century, revived Herbert's ideas went far beyond him in their religious scepticism (for example, the denial of immortality). Moreover, the Deistic tendency to picture the universe as a machine which, having been produced by God, is then left to tick over is not apparent in H.'s writings (for the picture was largely the product of reflection upon Newtonian physics). Nevertheless, H., by his attempt to base religion upon certain Common Notions implicit in man's reason, gave new impetus to natural theology and to the desire to found religion upon the principles of reason alone. The Common Notions of which he spoke are central to his theory of knowledge, and require elucidation.

H. wished to give an account of knowledge which would both assist in making a decision between the welter of different theological and metaphysical views consequent upon the Reformation and provide an alternative to Scholastic logic and epistemology. H. rejected the fashionable scepticism which led (if one took the left-hand turn) to religious disbelief or (if one took the right hand turn) to the uncritical leap of faith (for the philosophical sceptic, such as Montaigne,[1] could argue that since there is no certain knowledge yielded either by perception or demonstration, one cannot object to religious doctrines on the ground that they cannot be established through perception or demonstration). H. repudiated the Scholastic view of the passivity of the mind in perception and the principle that there is nothing in the intellect which was not previously in the senses. 'Let us have done', he wrote, 'with the theory which asserts that the mind is a clean sheet, as though we derived our capacity for dealing with objects from the objects themselves.' H.'s theory of knowledge is based on a correspondence theory of truth, i.e. a theory which asserts that truth consists in the correspondence of judgments on the one hand to objects on the other. But if so, the criteria of truth are criteria of whether this relation of correspondence holds: but the terms of the relation cannot themselves provide the criteria. Hence, there must be something outside either the faculties of perception (etc.) or things themselves which will provide the tests of truth. H. finds this in the intellect, which apprehends certain truths quite independently of perception, but through Natural Instinct implanted in all men. These truths, which H. calls Common Notions, are self-evident and can be used as touchstones for the trustworthiness of the faculties. (Under the title of 'innate ideas' they were laboriously attacked by Locke: see below, p. 129). They are to be known by the following marks: they are *a priori*,[2] independent (i.e. not mutually derivable), universal (to be found everywhere among men), certain, necessary to our preservation (in that we could, by comprehending them as a whole, understand the divine purpose), and directly apprehended. The following discussion deals specifically with the Common Notions implicit in religion.

Bibliographical Note The *De Veritate* is translated by M. H. Carré (Bristol, 1937). W. R. Sorley's article, 'The Philosophy of Herbert of Cherbury' in *Mind* (1894) may be found useful. On Deism, see *A Critical History of Free Thought* by A. S. Farrer (Bampton Lectures, 1862), J. M. Robertson, *Short History of Free Thought* (London, 1906) and articles in Hastings' *Encyclopaedia of Religion and Ethics* and *Encyclopaedia Britannica*.

REASON AND FAITH

De Veritate, Chs. IX f.

COMMON NOTIONS CONCERNING RELIGION

Before I proceed to discuss revelation, I think that certain assumptions which underlie our notions of revelation ought to be examined. Every religion which proclaims a revelation is not good, nor is every doctrine which is taught under its authority always essential or even valuable. Some doctrines due to revelation may be, some of them ought to be, abandoned. In this connection the teaching of Common Notions is important; indeed, without them it is impossible to establish any standard

[1] Montaigne (1533–92) argued in this way in his *Apology for Raimonde of Sebonde*.

[2] *A priori*: knowable prior to (without recourse to) any particular observations, as opposed to that which is *a posteriori*.

of discrimination in revelation or even in religion. Theories based upon implicit faith, though widely held not only in our own part of the world but also in the most distant regions, are here irrelevant. Instances of such beliefs are: that human reason must be discarded, to make room for Faith; that the Church, which is infallible, has the right to prescribe the method of divine worship, and in consequence must be obeyed in every detail; that no one ought to place such confidence in his private judgment as to dare to question the sacred authority of priests and preachers of God's word; that their utterances, though they may elude human grasp, contain so much truth that we should rather lay them to heart than debate them; that to God all the things of which they speak and much more are possible. Now these arguments and many other similar ones, according to differences of age and country, may be equally used to establish a false religion as to support a true one. Anything that springs from the productive, not to say seductive seed of Faith will yield a plentiful crop. What pompous charlatan can fail to impress his ragged flock with such ideas? Is there any fantastic cult which may not be proclaimed under such auspices? How can any age escape deception, especially when the cunning authorities declare their inventions to be heaven-born, though in reality they habitually confuse and mix the truth with falsehood? If we do not advance towards truth upon a foundation of Common Notions, assigning every element its true value, how can we hope to reach any but futile conclusions? Indeed, however those who endeavour to base their beliefs upon the disordered and licentious codes of superstititon may protest, their behaviour is precisely similar to people who with the purpose of blinding the eyes of the wayfarer with least trouble to themselves offer with singular courtesy to act as guides on the journey. But the actual facts are otherwise. The supreme Judge requires every individual to render an account of his actions in the light, not of another's belief, but of his own. So we must establish the fundamental principles of religion by means of universal wisdom, so that whatever has been added to it by the genuine dictates of Faith may rest on that foundation as a roof is supported on a house. Accordingly we ought not to accept any kind of religion lightly, without first enquiring into the sources of its prestige. And the Reader will find all these considerations depend upon Common Notions. Can anyone, I beg to ask, read the huge mass of books composed with such immense display of learning, without feeling scorn for these age-long impostures and fables, save in so far as they point the way to holiness? What man could yield unquestioning faith to a body which, disguised under the name of the Church, wastes its time over a multitude of rites, ceremonies and vanities, which fights in so many parts of the world under different banners, if he were not led to perceive, by the aid of conscience, some marks of worship, piety, penance, reward and punishment? Who, finally, would attend to the living voice of the preacher if he did not refer all his deeds and words to the Sovereign Deity? It would take too long to deal with every instance. It is sufficient to make clear that we cannot establish any of them without the Common Notions. I value these so highly that I would say that the book, religion and prophet which adheres most closely to them is the best. The system of Notions, so far at least as it concerns theology, has been clearly accepted at all times by every normal person, and does not require any further justification. And, first of all, the teaching of Common Notions, or true Catholic Church, which has never erred, nor ever will err and in which alone the glory of Divine Universal Providence is displayed asserts that

There is a Supreme God.

No general agreement exists concerning the gods, but there is universal recognition of God. Every religion in the past, every religion in the future, did and will acknowledge some sovereign deity among the gods. Thus to the Romans this supreme power is Optimus Maximus;[1] to the Greeks he is *ὁ ἐπὶ πᾶσαι Θεός, αὐτοφυὴς, παντοκράτωρ, ἀρχὴ πάντων τε τελευτή;*[2] to the Jews he is יהוה, Jehovah; to the Mahomedans, Allah; to the Indians of the West, Pachama Viracocha,[3] etc. The Eastern Indians[4] have similar names for him. Accordingly that which is everywhere accepted as the supreme manifestation of deity, by whatever name it may be called, I term God. I pass on to consider his attributes, using the same method. And in the first place I find that he is blessed. Secondly, he is the end to which all things move. Thirdly, he is the cause of all things, at least in so far as they are good. From which follows, according to his providence that, in the fourth place, he is the means by which all things are produced; for how could we pass from the beginning to the end but by the means provided? We need not be deterred by the type of philosophers who have refused to grant the medium any share of providence. Since circumstances seldom fall out in accordance with their wishes, they make a desperate attempt to abolish particular providence, as though the course of events were ordained by themselves and not by the divine will. We must realize that writers of this kind are only wrangling about the means by which divine providence acts; they are not, I think, disputing providence itself. Meanwhile the utmost agreement exists concerning

[1] That is, Jupiter Optimus Maximus.

[2] 'The God over all, self-existent, almighty, the beginning and the end of all.'

[3] Who figures in an Inca Creation legend.

[4] That is, the Indians of India. H. knew nothing of agnostic Buddhism or Jainism.

universal providence, or nature. But every religion believes that the Deity can hear and answer prayers; and we are bound to assume a special providence—to omit other sources of proof—from the universal testimony of the sense of divine assistance in times of distress. In the fifth place, he is eternal. For we are taught by a Common Notion that what is first is eternal. In the sixth place, a Common Notion tells us that the Deity is good, since the cause of all good is supremely good. In the seventh place, he is just; a Common Notion, experience and history bear witness at every point that the world is ruled under his providence with absolute justice. For as I have often observed, Common Notions, which solve the most difficult questions of philosophy and theology, teach us that all things are governed with righteousness and justice, though their causes may be hidden from us. In the eighth place, he is wise; for marks of his wisdom do not only appear in the attributes of which I have spoken, but are manifest daily in his works.

In addition to these qualities there are certain attributes, such as infinity, omnipotence and liberty, concerning which I find there is much difference of opinion. But his infinity is proved by the infinity of position or space. For the supreme God penetrates all things, according to the teaching of Common Notions. His omnipotence follows from his infinity, for it is certain that there is nothing which is beyond the power of the infinite. His omnipotence proves his liberty, since no man in his senses has ever doubted that he who can do everything is absolutely free. I think, however, that those who feel otherwise must be approached from a different angle. And here there is a Common Notion that what exists in us in a limited degree is found absolutely in God. If he is so far beyond our capacity as to be illimitable he will be infinite. If he has created all things without using any existent matter he will be omnipotent. And finally if he is the author of our liberty he will be supremely free. The ancient Schools were wrong in holding that men were free while God was fettered to the first Sphere.[1] The divine attributes prove these points as effectively when taken separately as when taken together. On the attributes and their synonyms the Schools may be usefully consulted, and I find that in general they discuss them very fairly. It is true that I have found that the names which they have given these attributes are conflicting and often inappropriate. Thus the pagans confuse the attribute of infinity with that of unity, and invent a number of gods. Even if you suppose with some that under the names of Apollo, Mars and Ceres, various aspects of divine providence were recognized, you cannot deny that the fables which

[1] Referring to the series of concentric spheres constituting the heavens: see above, p. 60.

the ancients invented under these names have always been thought foolish, since no one has ever doubted (so far as I am aware) the evils of their creed. As for the attributes which are rejected in our discussion, they are those which make the Deity strange, physical, composite, particular, or capable of condemning men for his own pleasure. Such a God is nothing but an idol of the imagination, and exists nowhere else. I pass now to the second Common Notion of theology.

This Sovereign Deity ought to be worshipped.

While there is no general agreement concerning the worship of gods, sacred beings, saints and angels, yet the Common Notion or universal consent tells us that adoration ought to be reserved for the one God. Hence divine religion—and no race, however savage, has existed without some expression of it—is found established among all nations, not only on account of the benefits which they received from general providence, but also in recognition of their dependence upon grace, or particular providence. Hence, too, men have been convinced, as I have observed above, that they can not only supplicate that heavenly power but prevail upon him, by means of the faculties implanted in every normal man. Hence, finally, what is a more important indication, this power was consulted by the seers in order to interpret the future and they undertook no important action without referring to it. So far the peoples were surely guided by the teaching of natural instinct. The all-wise cause of the universe does not suffer itself to be enclosed within its own sphere, but it bestows general grace on all and special grace on those whom it has chosen. Since everyone can experience this in himself, would it not be unjust to refuse the same power to God? God does not suffer us to beseech him in vain, as the universal experience of divine assistance proves, to pass over all other arguments. Although I find that the doctrine of special providence, or grace, was only grudgingly acknowledged by the ancients, as may be gathered from their surviving works, yet since the worship of the divine power was recognized in every age, and carried with it this doctrine of grace or special providence, I assert that this doctrine is a Common Notion. From this source spring supplications, prayers, sacrifices, acts of thanksgiving; to this end were built shrines, sanctuaries, and finally for this purpose appeared priests, prophets, seers, pontiffs, the whole order of ministers. And even if their activity has been equally evident in human affairs as in the affairs of God, since they have often been a crafty and deceitful tribe, prone to avarice, and often ineffective, this is because they have introduced much under the pretext of religion which has no bearing on religion. In this way with extraordinary skill they have confused sacred matters with profane, truth with falsehood, possibility with probability, lawful worship with licentious ceremonies and senseless superstitions; with the result, I make bold to say, that they have corrupted, defiled and prostituted the pure name of religion. However necessary the priests were, whenever they brought contempt upon themselves, the fear of God and the respect due to sacred things diminished in proportion. Accordingly we must give them the honour which is due to them. I obtain, then, proof of this external aspect of divine worship in any type of religion from every age, country and race. It is therefore a Common Notion. It is no objection that temples or regions sacred to the gods are not found among savages. For in their own fashion they consulted oracles and undertook no serious task without propitiating their deity. I am aware that an author of reputation has said that in one remote region no religious practice can be observed. But this statement has been rejected by a later writer who pointed out that the author was ignorant of the language of that country. However, if anyone denies the assertion we must reply that the same religious faculties which anyone can experience in himself exist in every normal human being, though appear in different forms and may be expressed without any external ceremony or ritual. And in postulating this principle I draw the conclusion that religion is the ultimate difference of man. I am not deterred by the fact that irreligious men exist, and even some who appear to be atheists. In reality they are not atheists; but because they have noticed that some people apply false and shocking attributes to God, they have preferred not to believe in a God of such a character. When he is endowed with true attributes so far from not believing in him they would pray that such a God might exist, if there were no such being. If, however, you still maintain that irreligious persons and even atheists can be found (which I do not believe), reflect that there may be not a few madmen and fools included among those who maintain that rationality is the final difference of man. Otherwise there would hardly have been such endless disputes about religion, nor such a multitude of martyrs; for there is no church which does not boast of its legendary heroes, men who for the sake of religion have not only adopted lives of the utmost austerity, but have endured death itself. Such conflicts would not have occurred if there had not been men so stubborn and unreasonable that they were incapable of distinguishing truth from probability, possibility and falsity.

I pass now to aspects of worship which are universally recognized. Those which can be referred to the analogy between man and God, between man and things, and between things themselves, I include under the right conformation of the faculties. I say then that

The connection of virtue and piety, defined in this work as the right conformation

of the faculties, is and always has been held to be, the most important part of religious practice.

There is no general agreement concerning rites, ceremonies, traditions, whether written or unwritten, or concerning revelation; but there is the greatest possible consensus of opinion concerning the right conformation of the faculties. The way in which this right conformation of the faculties may be established I have discussed at length above, and the reader is invited to refer to that passage.[1] There he will learn how conscience guided by Common Notions produces virtue combined with piety, how from this there springs true hope, from such true hope, faith, from true faith, love, from true love, joy, and from true joy, blessedness. Thus we now see that no faculty which leads to piety, purity of life, holiness and virtue, is not included under this heading. If I am to make some survey of these faculties, in respect of a person's years and the degree of wisdom which it has pleased God to give him, I would say that children recognize and seek God in their own way in the form of happiness, and acknowledge him in the spontaneous gratitude which they accord their benefactors. No trait, therefore, is so excellent as gratitude, nothing so base as ingratitude. And when gratitude is expressed by more mature persons and the Common Notions gradually reveal their objects more clearly, religion becomes enriched and appears in a greater variety of ways, though no practice emerges which is more admirable than this gratitude. With the advantage of age, piety and holiness of life take deeper root within the conscience, and give birth to a profound love and faith in God. Very often, too, vanities and superstitions and even vices and crimes spring up and multiply together with these virtues, like tares and weeds which grow from the decaying seed of wheat. Though they blossom more slowly, they mature quickly, unless they are uprooted in good time. I assign this growth to those factors which compose the body. Accordingly while our animal nature actually comes into being later, it reaches its completion in us before the reasoning element. This will not surprise those who notice that the animals attain their maturity in three years. Whether this fact is to be traced to their fallen state or to some other cause I will not stay to discuss. It may seem paradoxical that moral virtue which is so strict and severe is and always has been esteemed by men in every age and place and respected in every land, in spite of the fact that it conflicts with our physical and, I may say, agreeable feelings. But the reason for this is as follows. Since nature unceasingly labours to deliver the soul from its physical burden, so nature itself instils men with its secret conviction that virtue constitutes the most effective means by which our mind may be

[1] See *De Veritate*, Ch. VI: in particular see pp. 188 ff. of Carré's translation.

gradually separated and released from the body, and enter into its lawful realm. And though many arguments could be cited to the same purpose, I know no more convincing proof than the fact that it is only virtue that has the power to draw our soul from the delights which engulf it, and even to restore it to its native region, so that freed from the foul embrace of vice, and finally from the fear of death itself, it can apply itself to its proper function and attain inward everlasting joy.

The minds of men have always been filled with horror for their wickedness. Their vices and crimes have been obvious to them. They must be expiated by repentance.

There is no general agreement concerning the various rites or mysteries which the priests have devised for the expiation of sin. Among the Romans, ceremonies of purification, cleansing, atonement, among the Greeks, rites of expiation and purging, and in nearly all races, sacrifices, even of human victims, a cruel and abominable device of the priests, were instituted for this purpose. Among the Egyptians and all the human races observances of a similar kind prevailed. I have referred to many of them in my book *On the Religion of the Gentiles*[1] and also in my work, not yet published, *On the Causes of Errors*.[2] Among the Mahommedans Ramadan is held twice each year after the manner of our Forty Days. But above all other races the Eastern Indians display the most energy in exercises of this kind. At a certain sacred period of the year they gather in the forests, and taking a piece of sharp rock or stone, let forth a quantity of blood, until their spirits are on the point of leaving them, protesting at the same time that the root-causes of their sins had lain hidden in their blood and that by allowing it to gush forth they atone for their sins. But we pass over such rites, some of which may well appear ridiculous. General agreement among religions, the nature of divine goodness, and above all, conscience tell us that our crimes may be washed away by true penitence, and that we can be restored to new union with God. For this inner witness condemns wickedness while at the same time it can wipe out the stain of it by genuine repentance, as the inner form of apprehension under proper conditions proves. I do not wish to consider here whether any other more appropriate means exists by which the divine justice may be appeased, since I have undertaken in this work only to rely on truths which are not open to dispute but are derived from the evidence of immediate perception and admitted by the whole world. This alone I assert, whatever may be said to the contrary, that unless wickedness can be abolished by penitence and faith in God, and unless the divine goodness can satisfy the divine justice (and no further appeal can be invoked), then there does not exist,

[1] His *De Religione Gentilium.*

[2] The *De Causis Errorum,* which was added as an appendix to the *De Veritate.*

nor ever has existed any universal source to which the wretched mass of men, crushed beneath the burden of sin, can turn to obtain grace and inward peace. If this were the case, God has created and condemned certain men, in fact the larger part of the human race, not only without their desire, but without their knowledge. This idea is so dreadful and consorts so ill with the providence and goodness, and even the justice of God, that it is more charitable to suppose that the whole human race has always possessed in repentance the opportunity of becoming reconciled with God. And as long as men did not cut themselves off from it their damnation would not have been due to the benevolent will of God, but to their own sins, nor could God have been charged with blame if they failed to find salvation. All the teaching of the greatest preachers concerning eternal salvation coincides on this issue, since every means of redress is useless except penitence and becomes, as they tell us, empty and futile. Accordingly they hold it to be of such importance in relation to the divine goodness that they consider that when no readier way presents itself the entire secret of salvation may be revealed in this process. Some critics of nature or of divine universal providence object that it is not always within our power to experience remorse. I have myself pointed out that wisdom is always within our grasp. But these critics fail to notice the distinction which I have made above, between voluntary and involuntary actions, nor do they recognize that some movements cannot be prevented, and others cannot be provoked into action. Man does not remember, or keep awake, or sleep, just as he desires. Some of these activities like many other inner movements admit of degrees and exceptions. But to declare that God has cut us off from the means by which we can return to him, provided that we play our part to the utmost of our ability, is a blasphemy so great that those who indulge in it seek to destroy not merely human goodness, but also the goodness of God. They must abandon these ideas, and their ideas and utterances, at least concerning the secret judgments of God, must be guarded. For they cannot deny that if not from general providence, yet from particular providence or grace, may flow the means by which God's favour may be won. We realize what we owe to grace when we reflect that by it our works are accomplished, by it they are made acceptable to God. I think that it is chiefly by this means that God's mercy meets the demands of his goodness. For in the mutual relationship which exists between us, when our goods are seized by plunder or theft, the common laws of nations or universal consent requires that in addition to repentance there should be restoration. Now, if anyone with perverted curiosity asks me why we possess the liberty to commit sin and crime, I can only answer that it is due to the secret judgments of God. If he persists in asking what can be known within the moderate limits of the human faculties, I must reply that man is a finite animal, and therefore cannot do anything which is absolutely good or even absolutely bad. Yet the nature of each is modified in every action, so that the action shares to some extent in both, though it is named according to the element which has the larger share. Anyone who desires further discussion on this problem may refer to what I have said on an earlier page.[1] I have now briefly examined the principal Common Notions about the way of God which refer to the journey of life. I pass on to treat of the state of the future life. And this I shall comprise in a single proposition.

There is reward or punishment after this life.

The rewards that are eternal have been variously placed in heaven, in the stars, in the Elysian fields, or in contemplation. Punishment has been thought to lie in metempsychosis, in hell (which some describe as filled with fire, but the Chinese imagine pervaded with smoke), or in some infernal regions, or regions of the middle air, or in temporary or everlasting death. But all religion, law, philosophy and, what is more, conscience, teach openly or implicitly that punishment or reward awaits us after this life. Religion teaches us this explicitly when it uses the terms which I have mentioned. It teaches the same doctrine indirectly by establishing the immortality of the soul or by proving that God avenges crimes which are committed with impunity in this life. In this sense there is no nation, however barbarous, which has not and will not recognize the existence of punishments and rewards. That reward and punishment exist is, then, a Common Notion, though there is the greatest difference of opinion as to their nature, quality, extent and mode. It is no objection that the soul perishes with the body, as some people assert. For they refer this very fact to punishment for sin, or else they mean only that part of the soul with which they have been familiar, namely, the physical senses; or finally they must be ignored since they talk sheer nonsense; for there is nothing in the faculties of the mind to suggest such ideas. That the soul could be immortal if God willed it is clearly a Common Notion in that among the most distant races, seething with every type of superstition, there exists a general conviction that purity of life and courage of mind promote happiness. It is on this account that they are said to honour the bones of those who have died bravely in battle. But I do not trouble myself about such matters, since I am not concerned with superstitions and sacred rites; it is not what a large number of men assert, but what all men of normal mind believe, that I find important. Scanning the vast array of absurd fictions I am content to discover a tiny Common Notion. And this is of the utmost

[1] See Carré's translation, pp. 191 ff.

importance, since when the general mass of men have rejected a whole range of beliefs which it has found valueless, it proceeds to acquire new beliefs by this method, until the point is reached where faith can be applied.

It follows from these considerations that the dogmas which recognize a sovereign deity, enjoin us to worship him, command us to live a holy life, lead us to repent our sins, and warn us of future recompense or punishment, proceed from God and are inscribed within us in the form of Common Notions. But those dogmas which postulate a plurality of gods, which do not forbid crimes and sins, which rail against penitence, and which express doubts about the eternal state of the soul, cannot be considered either Common Notions or truths. Accordingly every religion, if we consider it comprehensively, is not good; nor can we admit that salvation is open to men in every religion. For how could anyone who believes more than is necessary, but who does less than he ought, be saved? But I am convinced that in every religion, and indeed in every individual conscience, either through grace or nature, sufficient means are granted to men to win God's good will; while all additional and peculiar features which are found at any period must be referred to their inventors. It is not sufficient that they should be old if they have once been new. Ideas which are superfluous or even false may be not only novel but ancient, and truths which are only seized by a few cannot be essential to all. The truth which belongs to revelation occupies a special place here; and no faith in it is in any way disparaged by the principles which I have described. On the contrary, whatever it adds to them I hold to be valuable. The fundamental principles of revelation itself are here established, so that it is possible to reduce all disputes to the question 'On what faculty does the argument depend?' Accordingly so far from these views conflicting with ordinary beliefs or depending on new principles, I have asserted nothing but the symbol of Common Notions and what has been universally accepted by every religion, age and country. I do not deny that sacred ceremonies can form part of religion; on the contrary I find that some ceremonies are included in every religion and serve to embellish it; so far they are valuable. But when they are made by the priests the essential elements of divine worship, then religion, and we who practise it, are the victims of imposture. Rites must be kept within bounds. We can only accept them on the understanding that religion is chaste and only requires such ornaments as render a matron more venerable and respected. When she paints and dyes herself, her appearance is too suggestive of the harlot.

Such, then, are the Common Notions of which the true Catholic or universal church is built. For the church which is built of clay or stone or living rock or even of marble cannot be claimed to be the infallible church. The true Catholic church is not supported on the inextricable confusion of oral and written tradition to which men have given their allegiance. Still less is it that which fights beneath any one particular standard, or is comprised in one organization so as to embrace only a restricted portion of the earth, or a single period of history. The only Catholic and uniform church is the doctrine of Common Notions which comprehends all places and all men. This church alone reveals divine universal providence, or the wisdom of nature. This church alone explains why God is appealed to as the common Father. And it is only through this church that salvation is possible. The adoration which has been bestowed on every particular church belongs to it. Every church, as I have pointed out above, is the more exposed to error the further it is separated from it. Anyone who courts uncertain doctrines in place of the sure truths of divine providence, and forges new articles of faith, forsakes this church. If, however, anyone receives some truth by revelation, which I think can occur both in the waking state and in sleep, he must use it as occasion warrants, remembering that unless he is entrusted with a message of interest to all, he should reserve it to himself. For it is not likely that what is not evident to the faculties of all, can have any bearing on the whole human race. I have often observed that we can take much on faith with true piety, and we need not abandon any belief as long as it does not conflict with the divine attributes. It is not the case therefore, as some critics may point out, that after examining the means by which divine universal providence acts and admitting that it is universal in its operation, I then restrict it to its own kingdom. I desire that every feature which redounds to the glory of God may be added to the characteristics which have been mentioned. For my part I accept with earnest faith and gratitude all that preceding ages have uttered in praise of God's goodness and mercy. I agree with the majority of mankind that all that they tell us not merely could have come to pass but actually did so. But I maintain that the principles of faith are to be found in the truths of divine universal providence, since I cannot see that in any other way the harmony of nature or general providence, with grace or particular providence can be preserved. This does not exclude the right of the church to decide all matters which concern external worship, or ecclesiastical organization, or the publication for future generations of the records of earlier times, and especially those events which confirm the true attributes of God. For when these Catholic truths are received into the recesses of the soul they rest on a foundation of indubitable faith, and anything which remains can and ought to be believed with piety upon the authority of the church; provided that is, that all contradictions are avoided or recognized, and only those doctrines are impressed on men's minds which promote universal peace and concord, and make for purity of life. Whether these means are sufficient to prepare us for eternal salvation I leave in the hands of God. I, at least, do not seek to pry into the secret judgments of God. I am content to have shown that the human mind informed by the Common Notions has been able in every age and place to apprehend these principles. If we set aside superstitions and legends, the mind takes its stand on my five articles, and upon nothing else. To deny this would be to allow less sense to men than to sheep; for they at least when they are let into the pastures avoid those herbs which are harmful and only eat those which are good for them. Whether indeed human wisdom has undertaken this examination in any age or place, or whether, even if it has done so, all who have rejected the inferior and trifling portions of religion, or possibly have accepted a mystical interpretation of them on the authority of their priests, equally enjoy the supreme happiness, I have not attempted to discuss. I firmly maintain, however, that it is and always has been possible for all men to reach the truths I have described. But whether they have been manifest, or whether, even when they are manifest they are immediately accepted, I am so far from wishing to discuss that all matters of this nature which depend upon the secret counsels of God, I leave to be inferred from the divine wisdom and goodness. But if anyone calls them in dispute, I am prepared stoutly to defend them. For by no other method could the existence of divine universal providence, the highest attribute of God, be proved by the principles of common reason. If we abandon these principles —and as I have often pointed out nature or the common providence of the world does not operate beyond the means at its disposal—and if we give way to wicked blasphemies, terrible crimes, and finally to impenitence, to which we are sacramentally bound; if we defile the purity of religion with foolish superstitions and degrading legends; it would be wholly unjust to blame the Supreme Goodness for our sins. It would be like accusing a host who provides a feast set out with a splendid profusion of dishes, of encouraging drunkenness, gluttony and licence. For what is sufficient is due to God, excess is due to us. Why then, as I have said elsewhere, following the law of common reason, can we not apply the same rule to the perfect sphere of the religion of God that we apply to any circle? If anything is added to it, or taken from it, its shape is destroyed, and its perfection ruined. I do not, however, wish to decide too hastily on this question. I would, indeed, firmly maintain that it is impossible to remove any feature from religion. But whether anything can be suitably added to the orb of religion, as is possible with a circle, I am not so certain; though the shape of a visible circle is continuous, so that no part of it is hidden. The fair form of divine universal providence ought to stand forth in all its beauty and not lurk behind a mask. Whatever feature is added to this circular shape should fitly and exactly correspond in a form which is harmonious and congruent both with its centre and its circumference. The chief reason for this is that no other genuine and almighty God can be accepted but he who directs universal providence to those ends which essentially concern the salvation of the soul. But since no other pattern of that providence can be found than that which lies open to the whole human race in these articles, and in these alone, we ought to consider whether it is possible to conceive of any stricter or purer religion, or of any means by which it is possible for a man to become more virtuous or more just, than is contained in these Catholic articles. Accordingly if the priests have agreed to emphasize for the sake of universal peace not merely these principles (since dogmas are permissible in matters of faith) but have further resolved to add those parts of beliefs in historical events which display great mercy towards the human race, a procedure with which I am in full accord, yet they should not suffer elements to be introduced which disparage the work of universal providence or confine it within strict or narrow limits. But neither must they allow features to be introduced which, through too hasty a desire for forgiveness, soften or destroy the austere outline of religion; otherwise men may relapse more quickly and with less foresight into sin. I humbly recommend these considerations to the judgment of the priests, with the hope that they may abandon their mysteries and direct themselves to accomplishing their function towards God and his interests in accordance with the most sacred maxims given us to that end, and so exert themselves on behalf of the people. Anyone may add for himself, their substance, quality, quantity, mode, etc., to these articles.[1] I shall now discuss what may be derived from revelation.

X

ON REVELATION

Revealed truth exists; and it would be unjust to ignore it. But its nature is quite distinct from the truth discussed above, in that the truth as I have defined it is based upon our faculties, while the truth of revelation depends upon the authority of him who reveals it. We must, then, proceed with great care in discerning what actually is revealed. Since there may be

[1] For H.'s system of categories, see *De Veritate*, Ch. VIII.

false revelations, I think it is hardly sufficient to apprehend what is revealed except through our faculties. But I believe that we can trust revelation when the following conditions occur. The first is that we must employ prayers, vows, faith and every faculty which can be used to invoke particular and general providence. The second is that revelation must be given directly to some person; for what is received from others as revelation must be accounted not revelation but tradition or history. And since the truth of history or of tradition depends upon him who recounts it, its foundations lie outside us, and in consequence it is, so far as we are concerned, mere possibility. The third condition is that revelation must recommend some course of action which is good; in this way genuine revelations may be distinguished from false and wicked temptations. The fourth condition is that the breath of the divine Spirit must be immediately felt, for in this way we can distinguish the inner efforts of the faculties of truth from revelations which come from without us. When, therefore, what comes to us surpasses human understanding and all the preceding conditions are present and we feel the divine guidance in our activities, we must recognize with reverence the good will of God. We cannot indeed prescribe the way in which true revelation must be conveyed to us; it is beyond our power to formulate laws for events which are supernatural. We must, then, regard revelation as divine, whether it comes during sleep or when we are awake, in ecstasy, in speaking, in reading, or in any other way, whenever the conditions which I have enumerated occur. But we must take great care to avoid deception, for men who are depressed, superstitious or ignorant of causes are always liable to it. I shall discuss this question more fully, with God's help, in the treatise *On the Causes of Error*.[1] As for the means of revelation it is generally held that revelations are most frequently made with the medium of spirits which have been recognized in all ages as a special order of beings, invisible, impalpable, free of physical substance, endowed with rapid movement, and variously called angels, demons, intelligences and geniuses.[2] Some doubt, however, exists concerning their nature. Some people imagine them to be good, others think they are evil, so that we can reasonably leave their real character an open question. But this need not disturb us, as long as the preceding conditions are present, for otherwise no announcement of this kind can possibly come from God. But if we can only place confidence in revelation when it is given under the conditions which I have laid down, what are we to think of those revelations which are solemnly asserted by the priests

[1] See n. 2 to p. 93.

[2] 'Geniuses' is here, of course, not used in the modern sense, but with the Latin meaning, as in *genius loci*, the spirit or tutelary deity of a place.

to have occurred in former ages? Must we place greater faith in them? In spite of such a body of authority the ordinary layman may fairly demand from his priest the following criteria, in addition to those already enumerated. Firstly, that it be proved beyond all doubt that a revelation has been given to the priest. Secondly, that the revelation should have proceeded from the supreme God, speaking with his own voice, as he is said formerly to have done, or through the agency of some good angel. Thirdly, that the revelation or oracle or utterance should have been accurately expressed and reported by the priest; or when it had to be written down and transmitted to posterity through the priest's script, it should have been possible fully to correct and restore it in the light of the transcription, in case any addition, omission or alteration had been made in the succeeding centuries. Fourthly, the revelation should concern later ages so closely that it necessarily becomes an article of faith; particularly since nearly all such points depend upon confidence in a single witness. A priest should offer satisfactory credentials on all these points before the layman can yield implicit trust in his revelation. If the priest should fail in this, the cautious layman may not arrive at any conclusion by means of the alleged revelation which he could not have gathered apart from it; such as ideas of a better life, and similar notions which, as I have shown above, are written in our hearts.

So much concerning revelation in its narrower sense, whether given to us personally or to others. Though the layman plays his own part in this discussion, it will not be permissible for him to draw any conclusion contrary to those dogmas which have been fully sanctioned by the true Catholic church, and published to the glory of the supreme God. If revelation is taken in a more general sense, it includes whatever is required of God's grace. In this sense the succour sent from heaven to lost souls at times of affliction in response to their prayers is revelation. So, too, are those intimate divine apprehensions concerning faith, good works and repentance. Movements of conscience and prayerful impulses have their beginning and end in revelation. In a word every original impulse of pity and joy which springs in our hearts is a revelation. More strictly, however, the only revelations are those which are recognized by the inner perception to lie beyond the scope of general providence. For this reason if we did not possess a supernatural and miraculous sense we should be obliged to hold that God confined himself to his universal providence, and disclosed himself only through those faculties of faith and prayer which are implanted in every normal human being. These considerations, therefore, serve to distinguish what is due to universal providence, what to special providence, and what are genuine revelations. The learned, who imagine that they are competent in the ways of grace, cannot suppose that I fail to acknowledge it, when they read what I have written. I do not hesitate to repeat that our actions are perfected and brought to completion only by grace. Yet under the guidance of the inner consciousness I maintain that the principles of good actions spring from Common Notions, or the divine wisdom within us. Accordingly I think it is certain that no human being can so deafen his conscience as to lose his power of distinguishing, in any particular case, between good and evil. Thus when evil has been done owing to a failure to perceive the distinction, and the inward consciousness causes the sinner profound trouble of mind, and fills him with disgust; when he comes to repent his misdeeds so as to turn from them with horror, and bends all his endeavours to change his ways; when he directs himself with vows and prayers towards God, before whom his conscience forthwith displays its guilt, and decides upon a better manner of life; in all this it is clear that nothing falls outside the sphere of common grace. So far, then, the universal providence of God applies. But when in a moment of intense faith we make a special appeal to God, and feel within us his saving power and a sense of marvellous deliverance, I do not doubt that the mind is touched by grace, or particular providence, and that since some new aspect of God is revealed, we pass beyond the normal level of experience. I maintain in short that what crowns and brings to fruition the principle of actions which are due to the wisdom of nature or common providence, and what makes these actions pleasing to God, belong to grace. In this way I think the respective provinces of nature or common providence and of grace or particular providence may be satisfactorily established. And on these we can decide between revelations in the more general and in the restricted senses.

Now though I consider all the articles of faith shine by their own glory, so that unless they receive their authority from some personal revelation they are subject to examination in the same ways as other judgments; yet since there is no means which God in his great goodness may not employ, it is no less important to examine the instrument through which the revelation is transmitted than the nature of the mode of perception which is used. And this I have discussed above. What anyone may hope to derive from the mighty works of religion I leave to be inferred from what I have said. I make no claim to interpret oracles. It is sufficient if the reader is able and indeed feels it his duty to embrace with faith and thankfulness all sacred utterances and acts in any age or place which are throughout history cited as miraculous; especially when no obvious contradiction is to be found in them. Before I pass on to discuss probability[1] I wish to consider whether the precepts contained in the Decalogue are Common Notions, since their injunctions are implicit in every kind of law and religion. I have often observed that the universal providence which governs empires does not fail to operate in matters of necessity. We cannot believe, then, that whatever the diverse sources of these commands are, and though many of them have come to be mixed with elements which have little relation to piety and justice, yet they cannot be thought without sacrilege to have been established apart from Common Notions. It is of no importance whether sacred priests or legislators promulgated these laws, since the wisest men of antiquity taught that the observance of them was sanctioned not only by the civil code but also by religion. They are therefore Common Notions. But since we may easily fall into error in the process of giving an account of them, it is reasonable to suppose that God himself has granted us some indication of them in his mercy, and in a special divine way. So, firstly, the highest respect is due to God, according to a Common Notion; and lest men should suppose that persons distinguished for holiness of life deserve some special form of worship, he commands that he only should be worshipped. Secondly, since men were able to form some image, which could arouse reverence and veneration, he forbade all kinds of symbols and images. Thirdly, since this supreme goodness may be treated lightly and with contempt, and so come to be slandered in frivolous deed or word, God does not allow us to use his name in vain. Fourthly, for fear that men should be destroyed by labour and toil, or on the other hand should enjoy too much leisure (for leisure is of God and is a Common Notion) he ordered that six days should be given to work and care, the seventh to rest and the worship of God. Fifthly, lest men might look upon their relation to their parents as a kind of first cause, and should therefore accord them divine worship, he has taught us what benefit we may hope for from honouring our parents. Sixthly, lest men should injure themselves or others except under the need of self-preservation, he has forbidden murder. Seventhly, lest men should suppose that in love anything may be permitted, he does not allow adultery. Eighthly, he has forbidden theft, lest men should seize another's property to increase their own goods. Ninthly, he prohibits false witness, so that truth may stand secure. And finally, lest men should think they can encroach on the rights of others, which they all hold according to their deserts, he enjoins on each contentedness of heart. These commandments, therefore, constitute a summary of Common Notions. But since it is easy to add to them, we must faithfully believe that God has given us fore-warning

[1] In Ch. XI, not included here.

of them by revelation or particular providence; and this I believe more readily since though our parents lived in earlier ages under conditions in which the law of nature was inviolate, yet because in process of time their hearts became corrupt, it is reasonable to suppose that God prescribed the foregoing rules as guides to a better life.

7

DESCARTES

on THE EXISTENCE OF GOD

Biographical Note Born at La Haye in Touraine, 1596. Entered College of La Flèche, 1606, where he continued until 1614. Obtained Baccalauréat and Licence in Civil and Common Law at Poitiers, 1616. After a period in Paris, left France for Holland, 1618, and took service as gentleman volunteer in army of Prince Maurice of Nassau. Resigned from army service, 1619, toured northern, eastern and central Europe. Returned to France, 1622; travelled in Italy, 1623–5. Probably in Paris, 1626–8. Went to and remained in Holland (during which period he worked on *Le Monde*), except for three short visits to France, 1628–49. (1633, Galileo is condemned: D. withholds publication of *Le Monde*.) Published *Discours de la Méthode*, together with works on optics, meteorology and geometry, 1637. 1641, *Meditations*. 1644, *Principia Philosophiae* (including the substance of *Le Monde*). Died in Stockholm, 1650, after brief period as private instructor to Queen Christine of Sweden.

Principal works: those mentioned above, together with *Dioptrique* and *La Géométrie* (1637) and *Les Passions de l'Âme* (1639).

Philosophical Note D., apart from being famous as a philosopher (he is commonly called 'the father of modern philosophy') was a brilliant innovator in other fields, notably mathematics and physical science, and it is necessary to view his philosophical achievements in the setting of these others. The heliocentric theory of Copernicus (1543), Kepler's work on planetary motion (1609), the investigations into the laws of motion and the use of the telescope by Galileo (1564–1642), the discovery of the circulation of the blood by William Harvey (1578–1657)—these and other advances in science were opening up exciting new fields for speculation. Moreover, this was an age when a brilliant explorer like D. could contribute to many different branches of learning: thus D. did notable work in philosophy, mathematics, physics, optics, meteorology, physiology and embryology—a breadth of originality which would be quite impossible today. In 1619, at the age of 22, he discovered the principle of analytical geometry, which he considered to be a key to nature: for in unifying geometry and algebra it promised to be a powerful instrument for the mathematical exploration of natural phenomena. He attempted this in the field of physics by his celebrated theory of vortices, which, though it had a brief period of great success, was completely outmoded by Newtonian physics (Newton's *Principia*, 1687). On D.'s view, matter is simply extension, and the universe is a plenum entirely filled with matter and without any void. This being so, the apparent differences in the properties of the various bits of matter cannot be explained by appeal to any intrinsic differences, but are simply the effect of motion. As D. said: 'Give me matter and motion and I will construct the universe.' Though motion in itself *qua* motion proceeds rectilinearly, in actual fact and given that there is no void such rectilinear motion is impossible: rather, motion occurs in circuits in which there is the simultaneous displacement of different bits of matter by each other. In three-dimensional space these motions take the form of vortices. D. explains on these principles how three different kinds of element arise. Motion causes different bits of matter to get ground down into minute spherical particles, which constitute the vast majority of all matter. But this grinding down also gives off fragments of no fixed shape which, moving round the spherical particles, fill the gaps between them completely and form a virtually perfect fluid. At the centre of each vortex they collect in more or less pure form to constitute such large bodies as the sun and the stars. Finally, certain large pieces of matter possessing an initial relatively slow motion have not been so easily divided in the way which has occurred to the spherical particles and larger portions join together to form the planets and comets. It is to be noted that despite the eventual failure of Cartesian vortical theory, it had certain points of philosophical interest. (i) The identification of matter and extension is an attempt to provide a theory in which a thoroughly mathematical treatment of physics is possible. (ii) The explanation of physical events in terms of extension and motion involves a transcending of the data of sense-perception: the 'real' physical world is rather different from the world as it appears to us. This bifurcation of the two 'worlds' led D. to distinguish between what were later called by Locke 'primary' and 'secondary' qualities (see below, p. 130 and n. 2 to p. 114). D. gave a theological interpretation to his physical theory: the laws of motion are imposed and inscrutably decreed by God. And further, God is not merely creator but conserver of the universe. For time, D. held, is not continuous but is made up of durationless instants—mainly because, contrary to the common view that a cause precedes its effect, he believed that they are simultaneous (this was chiefly to explain how vortical motion was possible). Thus, since each separate instant is independent, so to speak, of every other, the cause-effect relationship does not bridge the gap between one instant and another, so that sequences of events have to be interpreted as God's continuous creative action. Finally, a word about D.'s views on physiology: bodies are as much part of matter as anything else, and their actions can be explained in physical and mechanistic terms. Thus organisms are automata, except that humans have minds or rational faculties distinguishing them from animals. But D.'s dualism between mind and body, joined only at the pineal gland, left him somewhat at a loss as to the effect of the one on the other, and it was left to later Cartesians to work out a theory of *occasionalism*, according to which there is no real interaction between mind and body, but the stimulation of, e.g., the optic nerve by light rays is not the *cause* of my sensation, but the *occasion for God to cause* the sensation in me.

In the *Meditations concerning First Philosophy*, D. employs his famous 'method of doubt'—i.e. he scrutinizes all his beliefs so that he may reject those which are doubtful. In constructing a system of knowledge on absolutely certain premises, from which the rest of the propositions taken to be true can be deduced, D. follows the procedure (at least as he regarded it) of mathematics. Just as science must become mathematical, so metaphysics—which on his view the foundation on which physics and the other sciences are to be built—requires equal rigour.

In *Meditation* I he shows why we can doubt the existence of all things and of material objects in particular. Such doubt might not at first appear useful, but it is very much so, D. claims, since it delivers us from all kinds of prejudice and makes available an easy method of accustoming the mind to become independent of the senses (compare what was said above about the transcendence of sense-experience in science). In *Meditation* II, he argues that there is one truth which we cannot doubt, viz. that the doubter exists: *cogito ergo sum.* Having thus established that there is one indubitable truth, that a thinking substance exists, D. goes on, in *Meditation* III, to provide a causal argument for the existence of God. By establishing the existence of a God who is not a deceiver, D. will then be in a position to be confident about the rule that what is apprehended clearly and distinctly (see p. 108) is true, and to put the previously dubitable truths—such as that external objects exist—on a surer footing.

Bibliographical Note There are useful selections of Descartes' philosophical writings by P. T. Geach and G. E. M. Anscombe (London, 1954) and N. Kemp Smith (London, 1952). The complete edition of his works, *Œuvres de Descartes,* edited by C. Adam and P. Tannery, was published in Paris during the years 1897–1913. Other reading is: A. Boyce Gibson, *The Philosophy of Descartes* (London, 1932); S. V. Keeling, *Descartes* (London, 1934); J. Maritain, *The Dream of Descartes* (N.Y., 1944) and *Three Reformers: Luther, Descartes, Rousseau* (N.Y., 1937); and N. Kemp Smith, *New Studies in the Philosophy of Descartes* (London, 1952).

THE EXISTENCE OF GOD

MEDITATION III

OF GOD: THAT HE EXISTS

I shall now shut my eyes, stop up my ears and turn away my senses from their objects; I will even efface from my consciousness all images of corporal things—or at least, since this can hardly be done, I shall look on them as empty and false; and thus, holding converse only with myself and closely examining my nature, I shall try to gain by degrees a more intimate and familiar knowledge of myself. I am a thinking thing, i.e. a being who doubts, affirms, denies, and knows a few things, and is ignorant of many, who loves, hates, wills, refuses, who also imagines and perceives;[1] for, as I remarked earlier, although the things which I sense or imagine are perhaps nothing at all apart from me and in themselves, I am nevertheless sure that those modes of thinking which I call sensations and imaginations do, in so far as they are modes of thinking, exist in me.

[1] D. includes under the head of 'thinking' (*penser*) a good deal more than is usually suggested by the term. See also n. 1 to p. 114

In these brief remarks I think that I have summed up all that I really know, or at least all that I am so far aware that I know. Now, as I am trying to extend my knowledge more widely, I shall be circumspect and consider carefully whether I can still discover anything further in me which I have not up to now noticed. I am certain that I am a thinking thing; but do I not therefore also know what is needed to make me certain of something? In this initial knowledge, there is doubtless nothing that makes me certain of its truth except the clear and distinct perception of what I affirm. This would not indeed be enough to make me sure that what I affirm is true if it could ever be that anything which I clearly and distinctly perceive should prove false; and so it seems to me that I may now take as a general rule that everything which I apprehend really clearly and distinctly is true.

Nevertheless, I previously accepted and admitted many things as quite certain and obvious which I afterwards found doubtful. What, then, were they? They were the earth, the sky, the stars and all the other things which I used to perceive through the senses. But what was it that I clearly perceived in them? Nothing more than that the ideas and thoughts of those things were present to my mind. And even now I do not deny that these ideas are found in my mind. But there was something else which I used to affirm, and which, from the habit of believing it, I thought I clearly perceived—namely, the existence of objects external to me from which these ideas came and to which they were absolutely similar. This was where I was wrong; or at any rate, even if my opinion happened to be true, it was not based on any knowledge which I had.

But when I considered any simple and easy matter in arithmetic and geometry, as, for example, that two added to three makes five and so on, did I not at least intuit them with enough clarity to guarantee their truth? Indeed, my later judgment that these things might be doubted was due simply to the thought which occurred to me that a God might have given me such a nature that I would be deceived even about those things that seemed to me most evidently true. But every time this notion of the sovereign power of a God presents itself to my mind, I am forced to concede that it is easy for him, if he wishes to, to cause me to make a mistake, even in matters where I think I apprehend with the eye of the mind with the greatest possible lucidity; while on the other hand, every time I direct my attention to things which I think I apprehend quite clearly, I am so convinced of their truth that I find it natural to come out with expressions such as these: 'Let anyone deceive me who can, but no one will ever be able to bring it about that I do not exist as long as I am conscious that I do, or at any future time make it true that I have never existed it now being true that I do exist, or make two and three more or less than five and so on, in matters where I recognize an obvious contradiction and which I see clearly could not be otherwise than as I conceive them.'

And certainly, since I have no reason to believe that God is a deceiver and since I have not even considered those reasons by which the existence of a God is established, the ground for doubt resting only on this supposition is very slight and, one might say, metaphysical. But so that I can remove it completely, I must investigate as to whether there is a God, as soon as an opportunity of doing so presents itself; and if I find that there is a God I must also investigate as to whether he can be a deceiver. For without the knowledge of these two truths I do not see that I can be certain of anything. And in order that I may be able to examine this without interrupting the order of meditation I have proposed to myself, which is to pass by degrees from the notions I find first in my mind to those I shall discover afterwards, it is necessary first to divide all my thoughts into certain classes and to consider in which of these classes there is, strictly, truth or error.

Among my thoughts some are, as it were, images of things and to these alone properly belongs the name 'idea'—as when I think of a man, a chimera, the sky, an angel or God. Others again have different forms—as when I wish or fear or affirm or deny. In these cases I always, it is true, apprehend something as the object of my thought, but I also embrace, in this act of thought, something more than the idea I have of the object: and of this class of thoughts, some are called volitions or emotions, and others judgments.[1]

Now, in regard to ideas, if these are considered only in themselves and are not referred to any object beyond them, they cannot properly speaking be false: for whether I imagine a goat or a chimera it is no less true that I imagine the one than the other. Nor need we fear that falsity may exist in the will or emotions: for although I may desire objects that are wrong or even ones that never existed, it is still true that I desire them. Thus there

[1] On D.'s view there is a close relation between volitions or acts of will and judgments. In *Meditation* IV in discussing the problem of how errors occur, seeing that 'everything in me is derived from God and he has not given me any ability to make mistakes', D. says that the understanding does not by itself assert or deny anything, but merely conceives the ideas of things which I may assert or deny. Assertion and denial involve an act of will; and errors arise because the will has a greater range than the understanding, so that 'I do not restrain it within the same limits but extend it even to those things which I do not understand. Being by its nature indifferent about such matters, it very easily is diverted from the true and the good and chooses the false and evil. And thus it occurs that I make mistakes and that I sin.' Thus there is a close parallelism between judgment and moral choice, and in this way D. avoids the apparent difficulty arising from the two statements (i) God's workmanship is perfect; and (ii) men make mistakes.

only remain our judgments, in which we must take very good care that we are not deceived. But the chief and most common error that arises here consists in judging that the ideas which are in us are similar or conformed to the things that are outside us. For certainly, if I only considered the ideas themselves as certain modes or ways in which I think, without referring them to anything beyond, they would hardly offer any occasion for error.

Among these ideas, some seem to me to be innate,[1] others to be foreign to me and to come from outside, and the rest to be made and invented by myself. For when I conceive what is called a thing or a truth or a thought, it seems to me that I get the power to do so from no other source than my own nature. Next, if I hear a noise, see the sun or feel heat, I have all along reckoned that these sensations proceeded from some objects existing outside of myself; finally, it seems to me that sirens, hippogriffs, and so on are inventions of my own mind. But perhaps I may come to be persuaded that all these ideas are of the type I call 'foreign' and which come from outside, or perhaps that they are all innate or that they are all inventions; for I have not yet clearly found their true origin. What I must principally do here is to consider, with reference to those that appear to come from objects outside me, what grounds there are for thinking them similar to these objects.

The first of these grounds is that it appears to me that I am so taught by nature; and the second, that I am aware that these ideas are not dependent on my will and therefore not on myself, for they frequently occur to me against my will—for example, at present, whether I will it or not, I feel heat; and I am therefore convinced that this sensation or idea of heat is produced in me by something different from myself, namely by the heat of the fire by which I am sitting. I see nothing more reasonable than to suppose that this object imprints on me its own likeness rather than anything else.

I must consider now whether these reasons are strong and convincing enough. When I speak of being taught by nature in this matter, I mean by the word 'nature' merely a certain spontaneous inclination impelling me to believe that the resemblance mentioned exists, and not the light of nature which makes me know that it is true.[2] But these two things are very different; for what the light of nature shows to be true cannot be at all doubtful—as for example that I exist because I doubt and other such truths. There is no way in which this could be doubted inasmuch as I

[1] With regard to the theory that such general ideas are innate, see p. 86.

[2] 'Light of nature': *lumen naturalis, lumière naturelle.* This was a concept commonly accepted in D.'s time—the light of nature is a faculty, given to him by God, whereby a man can immediately apprehend intellectual truths.

possess no other faculty with which to distinguish truth from falsity that could teach me that what the light of nature shows to be true is false and which is as trustworthy as the light of nature. But as for inclinations, which also appear to me to be natural, I have noticed that in questions of choosing between right and wrong actions they frequently led me to choose the bad; and I do not see that I have any better ground for following them in what relates to truth and falsity.

As for the second reason, that because these ideas do not depend on my will they must arise from objects outside, I find this no more convincing than the first. For just as those natural inclinations which I have just dealt with are found in me, despite the fact that they are not always in harmony with my will, so similarly it may be that there is some faculty or power within me which I have not really noticed and which is capable of producing ideas without the help of any external objects. (Indeed I have always supposed that during sleep they are formed by some such power without the help of anything external.) Finally, even if I were to concede that they came from external objects it does not necessarily follow that they must be similar to them. On the contrary, I have often noticed in many cases that there was a considerable difference between the object and the idea. Thus, for example, I find in my mind two quite different ideas of the sun: one has its origin in the senses and must be placed in the class of 'foreign' ideas—according to this idea the sun is extremely small; while the other is derived from astronomical considerations, that is it is elicited from certain innate ideas or formed by myself in some other way—according to it the sun seems to me to be many times larger than the whole earth. These two ideas cannot certainly both resemble the same sun existing outside me, and reason teaches me that the one which seems to have emanated directly from the sun is the more unlike it. These points are sufficient to show that it has not been by a sure and considered judgment, but only by a blind and rash impulse, that I have believed in the existence of things different from myself which, through the organs of sense or by whatever other means it may be, conveyed the ideas or images of themselves into my mind and imprinted on me their likenesses.

But there is still another route by which to find out whether, of the objects whose ideas are in my mind, there are any that exist outside me. If ideas are considered only in so far as they are modes of thought, I do not notice any difference or inequality among them, and all of them seem to proceed from myself in the same manner. But if they are considered as images, of which some represent one thing and some another, it is clear that they differ greatly among themselves. For without doubt, those that represent substances are something more, and contain in themselves—so to speak—more objective reality, or rather participate by representation in a higher degree of being or perfection, than those which represent only modes or accidents.[1] Furthermore, that by which I conceive a supreme God, eternal, infinite, immutable, omniscient, omnipotent and the creator of all things existing outside himself—this idea, I claim, certainly contains in itself more objective reality than those ideas by which finite substances are represented.

Now it is evident, by the light of nature, that there must be at least as much reality in the efficient and total cause as in its effect. For where can the effect derive its reality from if not from its cause? And how could this cause communicate this reality to the effect unless it possessed it in itself? Hence it follows not merely that what exists cannot be produced by that which does not exist, but also that the more perfect—i.e. that which contains in itself more reality—cannot be the effect of the less perfect. This is not only evidently true in regard to effects which have what philosophers call actual or formal reality, but also in regard to ideas, where one considers only what is called objective reality.[2] For example a stone which does not yet exist cannot now begin to exist unless it is produced by something which possesses in itself formally or eminently all that enters into its composition (i.e. which contains in itself the same properties that are in a stone or others that are superior to them): similarly, heat cannot be produced in a thing that was previously devoid of it, except by a cause that is of an order, degree or kind at least as perfect as heat. And so on. But further, even the idea of heat or of a stone cannot exist in me unless it has been put there by something which contains in itself at least as much reality as I conceive there is in heat or a stone. For even though the cause of it does not transfer to my idea anything of its actual or formal reality, we must not for this reason suppose that such a cause is any less real; and we have to recognize that the nature of an idea, since it is a work of the mind, is such that it needs no other formal reality than that which it derives from our thought or mind, of which it is only a

[1] Regarding 'objective reality', see below. Regarding 'modes': D. writes in his *Principia Philosophiae*, i, Prop. 56, 'We have understood by modes the same as what we elsewhere designate attributes or qualities. But when we consider substance as affected or varied by them, we use the term *modes*.' That is, modes are opposed to properties necessarily characterizing a substance, e.g. (re bodies) extension: see above, n. 1 to p. 75.

[2] 'Objective': unfortunately this term has reversed its meaning since D.'s day. D. means it roughly in the sense of the modern 'subjective'—that which is 'objective' is an object of the mind. 'Formal', in the present passage, as the phrase 'actual or formal' indicates, means roughly what the modern 'objective' means, when we talk about the objective properties of a material object, etc. The equivalence of 'formal' and 'actual' arises out of the Aristotelian and Scholastic equation of matter with potentiality and form with actuality. See above, p. 60.

mode (i.e. a way or manner of thinking). But in order that an idea may contain one particular objective reality rather than another, it must surely derive it from some cause in which is to be found at least as much formal reality as the idea does objective reality. For if we suppose that there is found in an idea anything which is not in its cause, it must have derived this from nothing. But however imperfect may be this mode of being by which a thing exists objectively or through representation by its idea in the understanding, certainly we cannot for all that deny that this mode and manner of existing is nothing and consequently must assert that the idea cannot owe its origin to nothing. Nor must it be supposed that since the reality which is considered in these ideas is only objective, the same reality is not present formally or actually in the causes of these ideas, but that it is sufficient that it should be objectively present in them. For just as the mode of existing objectively belongs to ideas by their special nature, so also the mode of existing formally belongs to the causes of these ideas—or at the very least to their first and principal causes—by their special nature. And even though it might happen that an idea gives rise to an idea, this cannot continue indefinitely: we must eventually reach a first idea, the cause of which is, as it were, the archetype in which all the reality or perfection that is found objectively or by representation in these ideas is contained formally and actually. I am thus taught clearly by the light of nature that ideas exist in me as pictures or images, which can indeed easily fall short of the perfection of the objects from which they are taken, but can never contain anything greater or more perfect.

The longer and the more carefully I examine these matters, the more clearly and distinctly I know that they are true. But what conclusion shall I draw from all this? Just this: that if the objective reality or perfection of any one of my ideas be such as clearly to convince me that this same reality or perfection does not exist in me, either formally or eminently, and if, as follows from this, I myself cannot be the cause of it, it necessarily follows that I am not alone in the world, but that there is some other being which exists as the cause of that idea. On the other hand, if I can find no such idea in myself, I shall have no argument sufficiently strong to convince me that there is some other being besides myself. For after a most careful search I have up to now been unable to find any other possible one.

Among all these ideas which exist in me, besides that which represents me to myself (about which there can be no difficulty here), there is another which represents a God, others corporeal and inanimate things, others angels, others animals and still others which represent men like myself. As for the ideas which represent other men, or angels, or animals, I can easily imagine that they were formed by the mixture and combination of my other ideas—of myself, of corporeal objects and of God—even though there were outside me no other men in the world, nor animals nor angels. And as for the ideas of corporeal objects, I have never recognized anything in them so great or so excellent that it seems impossible that they could originate from myself. For if I consider these ideas closely and scrutinize them individually in the same way that I examined the idea of wax yesterday,[1] I find that there is very little in them that I can clearly and distinctly conceive—namely, size (i.e. extension in length, width and depth), shape (which results from the limitation of extension), location (which bodies of different shape preserve with reference to each other) and motion (i.e. the change of location); to these may be added substance, duration and number. But as for light, colours, sounds, odours, tastes, heat, cold and the other qualities yielded by the sense of touch—they occur in my mind with so much obscurity and confusion that I do not know whether they are true or false: i.e. whether the ideas I have of these qualities are really the ideas of real objects or whether they only represent imaginary beings which are incapable of independent existence.[2] For although I pointed out before that it is only in judgments that formal falsity (i.e. falsity properly so-called) can occur, there may nevertheless be found in ideas a certain material falsity, which arises when they represent that which is nothing as though it were something. Thus, for example, the ideas I have of cold and heat are so far from being clear and distinct that I am unable to gather from them whether cold is only a privation of heat or vice versa; or whether they are or are not real qualities. And since, ideas being as it were images, there cannot be any which do not seem to represent some object, the idea which represents cold as something real and positive will not improperly be said to be false if it turn out that cold is nothing but a privation of heat. And similarly in other cases. To ideas

[1] In *Meditation* II D. tries to show that perceiving is, strictly, nothing else but thinking (in this way he attempts to rebut the suggestion that we have a clearer understanding of corporeal things than of our own intellect: for it would on his view be paradoxical if we were clearer about what is doubtful than about that which exists indubitably). He takes the example of a piece of wax: after being subjected to heat all its perceptible properties seem to change (it was hard, now is soft; was cold, now is warm; had a sweet smell, now is odourless . . ., etc.). The wax in itself seems therefore to be simply something extended, flexible and movable: but the infinite possible variations in extension and motion cannot be comprehended by my imagination. Therefore I grasp the nature of the wax neither by my senses nor by my imagination, but through my understanding.

[2] D.'s distinction between the elements which can be clearly conceived such as extension, etc. (those which, be it noted, are capable of mathematical treatment) and those which cannot, foreshadows Locke's distinction between primary and secondary qualities (*An Essay concerning Human Understanding*, Bk II, Ch. VIII, 9 ff.). For a criticism of the distinction, see Berkeley's *Principles of Human Knowledge*, II.9; also see his *Alciphron*, below, p. 168. And for a full discussion of these points, G. J. Warnock, *Berkeley* (London, Pelican, 1953) pp. 92–101, 151–60.

of this sort, indeed, I need not assign any other source than myself. For if they are false—i.e. if they represent objects which do not exist—the light of nature teaches me that they proceed from nothing: i.e. they occur in me merely because there is something imperfect in my nature. If on the other hand these ideas are true, they nevertheless exhibit to me so little reality that I cannot even clearly distinguish the object represented from the non-existent, and so I do not see even so why I should not be the author of them.

As for those ideas of corporeal things that are clear and distinct, there are some which, it appears to me, might have been derived from the idea I have of myself—like those of substance, duration, number and so on. For when I think that a stone is a substance (i.e. a thing capable of existing by itself) and that I myself am also a substance, even though I understand that I am a thinking and non-extended thing[1] while a stone on the contrary is extended and does not think, these two ideas still seem to have this in common, that they both represent substances. Similarly, when I think of myself as now existing and recall in addition that I existed some time back, and when I am aware of various thoughts whose number I recognize, I then acquire the ideas of duration and number, which I can afterwards apply to any other objects I wish. As for the other qualities that go to make up the ideas of corporeal objects—namely, extension, shape, location and motion—it is true that they do not formally belong to me, since I am only a thinking thing; but since they are only particular modes of substance (i.e. the garments, as it were, in which corporeal substance appears to us) and since I am myself a substance, it seems that they might be contained in my nature eminently.

There only remains, then, the idea of God, and we must consider whether there is anything in it which could not have originated in myself. By the word 'God' I mean an infinite substance, eternal, immutable, independent, omniscient, omnipotent, and by which I myself and everything else that exists (if anything else *does* exist) were created. But these properties are so great and so excellent that the more attentively I consider them the less I feel convinced that the idea I have of them owes its origin to myself alone. And thus we must necessarily conclude from all that I have previously said that God exists: for though the idea of substance is in my mind for the simple reason that I myself am a substance, I could not have the idea of an *infinite* substance, seeing that I am a finite being, unless it were given me by some substance which is in reality infinite.

[1] In ordinary language 'I' is used to refer to something which *is* extended (as in 'I am six feet tall', etc.). But D. has, in the *Cogito*, merely exhibited that a thinking substance indubitably exists, and the existence of his own body is as much in doubt as the existence of external objects. There is thus a sharp mind-body dualism in D.'s theory.

And I must not suppose that I do not apprehend the infinite by a real idea, but only by the negation of the finite, in the same way that I comprehend rest and darkness by the negation of motion and light. For on the contrary I clearly recognize that there is more reality in the infinite substance than in the finite and therefore that in some way my notion of the infinite is prior to that of the finite, i.e. that of God is prior to that of myself. For how could I know that I doubt, desire or that something is lacking in me and that I am not wholly perfect, if I possessed no idea of a being more perfect than myself by comparison with which I recognize the deficiencies of my nature?

And it cannot be said that this idea of God is perhaps materially false and consequently that it might have arisen from nothing (i.e. that it might exist in me as a result of my imperfection) as I previously asserted about the ideas of heat, cold and so on. For on the contrary, this idea is very clear and distinct and contains in itself more objective reality than any other so there can be no other which is in itself more true or which is less open to the suspicion of falsity.

This idea, I say, of a supremely perfect and infinite being is in the highest degree true. For although maybe we may imagine that such a being does not exist, we cannot nevertheless suppose that this idea represents nothing real in the way we can about the idea of cold. It is also extremely clear and distinct, since everything which my mind conceives clearly and distinctly as real and true and as containing any perfection is entirely contained in this idea. This is true despite the fact that I do not comprehend the infinite and that there may be an infinite number of things in God which I cannot comprehend nor perhaps even reach by thought in any way, for it is the nature of the infinite that I, who am finite, cannot comprehend it. It is enough that I correctly understand this and judge that all qualities which I conceive clearly and in which I know there is some perfection and perhaps also an infinite number of properties of which I am ignorant, are formally or eminently contained in God, so that the idea which I have of God is seen to be the most true, clear and distinct of all the ideas which I have in my mind.

But maybe I am something more than I suppose myself to be. Maybe all the perfections which I attribute to God exist in some way potentially in me, although they are not yet actualized and do not yet show themselves in actuality. Indeed, I am already aware that my knowledge is being increased and perfected by degrees, and I see nothing to prevent it from gradually increasing in this way to infinity nor any reason why, after such increase and attainment of perfection, I should not be able to acquire all the other perfections of the Divine nature; nor finally why the power I have of acquiring those perfections, if it really does exist in me now, should not be sufficient to give rise to the ideas of them. Yet, on examining the matter more closely, I find that it cannot be so. For, in the first place, though it may be true that my knowledge daily acquires new degrees of perfection, and though there may be potentially in my nature much that is not yet in it actually, still all these excellences do not approach anywhere near the idea I have of the Deity, in whom there exists no perfection merely *potentially* and in whom everything is actual and real. It is even a most certain and unmistakable token of the imperfection of my knowledge that it can grow little by little and increase by degrees. Further, even if my knowledge increased more and more, I am not nevertheless induced for this reason to think that it will ever be actually infinite, since it can never reach that point beyond which it will be incapable of further increase. But I conceive God as actually infinite, so that nothing can be added to the supreme perfection which he already possesses. Finally, I know very well that what is objective in an idea can never be produced by a being which is merely potential and which, strictly speaking, is nothing, but only by a formal or actual being.[1]

And certainly there is nothing in all that I have just said which is not easily known by the light of nature to all those who will examine it carefully. But when I allow my attention to relax a bit, my mind's vision is obscured, as though it were blinded by the images of perceptible objects, and I do not readily recall the reason why the idea of a being more perfect than myself must necessarily have proceeded from a being which is *in reality* more perfect. Hence I am here eager to inquire further as to whether I, who possess this idea of God, could exist supposing no God existed. From whom could I, in that case, derive my existence? Maybe from myself or from my parents or from some other causes less perfect than God. For anything more perfect or even equal to God cannot be conceived or imagined. But if I were independent of anything else and were myself the author of my own existence, I should have no doubts, I should desire nothing and finally I should lack no perfection: for I would have bestowed upon myself every perfection of which I possess the idea and would thus be God. It must not be supposed either that what is now lacking in me is perhaps more difficult to acquire than that which I already possess, for, on the contrary, it is quite clear that it was a matter of much greater difficulty that I, a thinking being, should arise from nothing, than it would be for me to gain the insight into and knowledge of many things

[1] This is a special application of the Scholastic principle (see above, p. 68) that nothing can be brought from potentiality into actuality except through something which is already in actuality.

of which I am ignorant and which are merely the accidents of a thinking substance; and certainly if I had given myself the greater perfection of which I have just spoken (i.e. if I were author of my own existence), I would not at least have denied myself things that can be more easily obtained (such as that infinite variety of pieces of knowledge which I at present lack). I surely would not even have denied myself any property which I recognize to be contained in the idea of God, for none of them seems to me more difficult to create or acquire. And if there were any that happened to be more difficult to acquire, they would certainly appear so to me (on the assumption that I am the source of the other things that I possess) because I would see in them a limitation of my power, since I would not be able to acquire them. And even if I were to suppose that I have always been as I am now, I still could not evade the force of this argument. For it would not follow that no author of my existence need then be sought. For the whole duration of my life can be divided into an infinite number of parts, each of which is in no way dependent on any other; and so it does not follow that because I existed a short time ago I must now exist, unless at this moment some cause creates me anew, as it were—or, more properly, conserves me.[1] In reality, it is quite clear and evident to all those who will attentively consider the nature of time that a substance, to be conserved at every moment of its duration, needs the same power and the same action that would be required to create it if it did not exist. So it is obviously a ruling of the light of nature that conservation and creation differ merely in respect of our way of thinking and not in reality. All, then, that is needed here is that I should question myself to find out whether I possess any power by means of which I can bring it about that I, who now exist, shall exist a moment from now. For since I am merely a thinking being (or at least since this is the only part of me that so far has been in question), then if such a power were in me, I would certainly be aware of it and recognize it. But I am aware of no such power, and thereby I quite evidently recognize that I am dependent upon some other being different from myself.

But maybe the being on whom I am dependent is not God: maybe I have been produced by my parents or by some causes less perfect than God. But this cannot be. For, as I have already said, it is quite evident that there must be at least as much reality in the cause as in its effect; and since I am a being that thinks and that has some idea of God, whatever turns out to be the cause of my existence must be admitted to be likewise a thinking being which has in itself the idea of all the perfections which I attribute to the divine nature of God. Thus we can go on to ask

[1] See the introductory philosophical note regarding the non-continuousness of time.

whether this cause derives its origin and its existence from itself or from some other entity. If it is self-existent, it follows, from the reasons given above, that this cause must be God himself; for since it possesses the perfection of self-existence, it must similarly without doubt have the power of actually possessing every perfection of which it has the idea, i.e. all those which I apprehend as being in God. But if it owes its existence to a cause other than itself, we can ask again, in the same way, whether this second cause exists of itself or through something else—and so on until we eventually reach an ultimate cause, which will be God. And it is quite obvious that in this matter there can be no infinite regress of causes, seeing that the question we are asking is not so much as to the cause which has in the past produced me as to that which conserves me in the present.

Nor can it be supposed that several partial causes came together to produce me, and that from one of them I got the idea of one of the perfections which I attribute to God, and from another the idea of some other perfection, and so on, so that each of these perfections is really to be found somewhere or other in the universe but nowhere are they all joined together and assembled in one entity, i.e. God. For on the contrary, the unity, simplicity or inseparability of all the properties of God is one of the chief perfections which I apprehend to be in him. And certainly this idea of all the perfections of God would certainly not be put into my mind by any cause from which I did not similarly derive the ideas of all the other perfections: for no power could enable me to apprehend these qualities as joined together and inseparable without at the same time giving me knowledge of what they are and of the mode in which they exist.

Finally, regarding my parents, from whom it seems that I derive my birth, even if all that I could ever have believed about them were true, it does not nevertheless follow that I am conserved by them, nor even that they made and produced me in so far as I am a thinking being (there being no relation between the bodily activity by which I have been accustomed to believe I was engendered and the production of a thinking substance). The most that they can have contributed to my origin is that they implanted certain modifications in the matter in which I have hitherto considered that I, i.e. my mind—which is what I have up to now taken myself really to be—, is enclosed. Thus there can be no further question regarding my parents, and we must necessarily conclude from the mere fact that I exist and that I have an idea of an absolutely perfect being, i.e. of God, that his existence is most obviously demonstrated.

The only job left is to consider how I got this idea from God. I have not acquired it through the senses, nor has it ever occurred to me unexpectedly, as the ideas of perceptible objects usually do when these objects are presented or seem to be presented to my external sense-organs. Nor is it only a product or fiction of my mind, for it is not in my power to add to it or subtract from it. So the only alternative remaining is that it is born and produced with me from the moment when I was created, just as is the idea of myself. Surely I ought not to find it strange that God, in creating me, put this idea in my nature in much the same way as a craftsman imprints his mark on his work. Nor is it necessary that this mark be something different from the work itself: seeing that God is my creator, it is highly probable that he in some way fashioned me in his own image and likeness, and that I apprehend this likeness, in which is contained the idea of God, by the same faculty by which I apprehend myself—in other words, when I direct my mind attentively upon myself, not only do I know that I am an imperfect, incomplete being, dependent on some other being, and striving and inspiring incessantly to become something better and greater than I now am; but also and at the same time I recognize that the being upon which I depend possesses in itself all these great qualities to which I aspire and the ideas of which I find in my mind, and possesses them, moreover, not indefinitely or just potentially, but really, i.e. actually and infinitely,[1] and so I perceive that it is God. The whole force of this argument which I have used here to prove the existence of God, consists in this: that I recognize that it is impossible that my nature should be what it is, namely that I should have in me the idea of God, if God did not in reality exist—a God, I say, the idea of whom is in my mind, i.e. a being possessing all those lofty perfections which, however much they may transcend my powers of comprehension, I am yet in some degree able to apprehend, and who is subject to no defects and has no share in any of those qualities which involve imperfection. And from all this it is quite evident that he cannot be a deceiver, for the light of nature teaches us that deception must always be the consequence of some deficiency.

But before I examine this conclusion more carefully and pass on to the consideration of other truths that may be deduced from it, it seems fitting to pause a while to contemplate this all-perfect God, to ponder at leisure his wonderful attributes, to behold, admire and adore the unsurpassable beauty of this inexhaustible light, so far at least as the power of my mind permits, dazzled as it is by the sight. For just as by faith we believe that the

[1] D. makes a distinction between the infinite and the indefinite. Extension, for example, is indefinitely extended and indefinitely divisible; while the term 'infinite' is reserved for God alone. In employing the expression 'indefinite' for the mathematical infinite, D. shrugged off the problem of the infinitesimal then exercising Fermat and Roberval, contemporary mathematicians, and later mastered by Newton and Leibniz in the discovery of the calculus. See N. Kemp Smith, *New Studies in the Philosophy of Descartes*, pp. 171 ff. and 334 ff.

supreme joy of the next life consists simply in this contemplation of the Divine majesty, so even now we learn from experience that a similar contemplation, though incomparably less perfect, is the source of the highest satisfaction of which we are capable in this life.

In *Meditation* IV, D., in order to be able to go on to use the existence of God as a stepping-stone to his ultimate validation of the previously dubitable claims to knowledge about the external world, has to meet the difficulty that in spite of our knowledge of this first principle we nevertheless are liable frequently to make mistakes. He therefore has a discussion of truth and falsity (see n. 1 to p. 109), and concludes that error can be avoided by only accepting that which can be apprehended clearly and distinctly (see pp. 107 ff.), the non-deceitfulness of God being a guarantee of the correctness of this criterion. In *Meditation* V D. considers the clear and distinct ideas we have about material objects, viz. those that represent the 'mathematical' properties of matter (number, shape, notion, etc.: see above, pp. 106, 130); and a further, simpler argument for God's existence is introduced: this is a variant of the Ontological Argument, though D. does not mention Anselm. Part of *Meditation* V follows.

Now, if as soon as I am able to find an idea of something in my thought it follows that whatever I apprehend clearly and distinctly is truly pertaining to that object, may I not derive from this an argument by which the existence of God can demonstratively be proved? It is certain that I find in my mind the idea of a God, of a supremely perfect being, no less than that of any shape or number whatsoever. And I know that an actual and eternal existence belongs to his nature no less clearly and distinctly than I know that all I can demonstrate about some number or shape actually belongs to the nature of that shape or number. Thus, even if everything that I concluded in the preceding Meditations were perchance false, the existence of God ought not to have for me a lesser degree of certainty than that which I have up to now been ascribing to mathematical truths.[1]

This, on first hearing, is not immediately obvious and seems to be a piece of sophistry. For, as I have been accustomed to make a distinction in all other matters between existence and essence, I am easily convinced that the existence of God can be separated from his essence, and therefore that God can be conceived as not existing. But on close inspection I find that it is obvious that we can no more separate the existence of God from his essence than we can separate from the essence of a rectilinear triangle the fact that the sum of its three angles equals two right angles,

[1] But note that even mathematical truths are doubtful in some degree until it has been established that a non-deceiving God exists. Similarly, the Ontological Argument here propounded is not a self-sufficient independent argument, as D. recognized: 'That consideration of the efficient cause is the first and principal, indeed the *only* means of proving the existence of God, is, I think, obvious to everyone' (*Reply to Objections*, IV).

or from the idea of a mountain the idea of a valley. Thus it is just as self-contradictory to conceive of a God—a supremely perfect being—who lacks existence as it is to conceive of a mountain without a valley.

But (it may be objected) even though I cannot conceive of a God without existence, any more than of a mountain without a valley, nevertheless, just as from the mere fact that I cannot conceive of a mountain without a valley it does not follow that there *is* a mountain anywhere in the world, so neither does it follow that because I think of God as existing he does in fact exist. My thought imposes no necessity upon things. Just as I can at will imagine a winged horse, even though no horses have wings, so I could perhaps ascribe existence to God, even though there were no God.

But this is quite wrong, and the objection rests upon a fallacy. For from the fact that I cannot conceive a mountain without a valley it does not follow that there is a mountain or valley anywhere in the world, but only that mountain and valley, whether they exist or not, are inseparable from each other. Whereas from the fact alone that I cannot think of God except as existing, it follows that existence is inseparable from him, and therefore that he really exists. Not that this is brought about by my thinking it so, or that my thought imposes any necessity on things; on the contrary, the necessity which is in the thing itself—i.e. the necessity of the existence of God—determines me to have this thought: for it is not in my power to conceive of a God without existence—i.e. of a supremely perfect being without complete perfection—in the way in which I am free to imagine a horse either with or without wings.

And it must not be objected here that it is only necessary that I grant that God exists *after* I have supposed that he possesses all kinds of perfections, since existence is one of them; but that my prior supposition is *not* necessary. For instance, it is not necessary to suppose that all four-sided figures can be inscribed in a circle, but if we suppose I do have this idea, we have to grant that a rhombus can be so inscribed (since it is a four-side figure)—a conclusion which is obviously false. This objection is, I say, invalid. It is not necessary that I should at any time have a thought of God; yet each time I may be concerned to entertain the thought of a first and supreme being, and to derive, so to speak, the idea of God from the storehouse of my mind, it is necessary that I attribute to him all kinds of perfections, even though I may not then enumerate them all nor think of any one of them in particular. And this necessity is sufficient to cause me very properly to conclude afterwards, as soon as I come to recognize that existence is a perfection, that this first, supreme being really exists—just as, while it is not at any time necessary for me to be imagining a triangle, yet whatever I wish to consider a rectilinear figure having three sides, it is absolutely necessary that I attribute to it everything that generates the conclusion that its three angles are not greater than two right angles—even if maybe I do not then direct my attention to this matter in particular. But when I wish to decide what figures can be inscribed in a circle, it is in no way necessary that I think that all four-sided figures are of this number: on the contrary, I cannot even pretend that this is the case, so long as I refuse to accept anything which cannot be clearly and distinctly apprehended. Consequently there is an immense difference between false assumptions, such as this one, and the true ideas which are innate in me, of which the first and chief is the idea of God. For indeed I discern on many grounds that this idea is not imaginary, depending simply upon my thought, but is the image of a true and changeless nature. For first, I cannot conceive any other being except God to whose essence existence necessarily belongs. Another reason is that I cannot possibly conceive in the same way of two or more such as he. Again, assuming one such God now exists, I perceive clearly that he must have existed from all eternity and will exist to all eternity. And a final reason is that I apprehend many other properties in God, none of which I can either diminish or change at all.

Thus, whatever proof or argument I use, I must always come back to this conclusion: that it is only the things that I conceive clearly and distinctly which have the power to convince me completely. And although some of the things which I conceive in this way are obvious to everyone, while others of them are only recognized after close and careful investigation, nevertheless, once they have been discovered, none of them can be reckoned less certain than the others. Thus, for example, take a right-angled triangle: that the square of the hypotenuse is equal to the squares of the other two sides is not so readily apparent as that the hypotenuse lies opposite the largest angle; nevertheless, after this fact has once been recognized we are as much convinced of its truth as of the other's. As regards God, if my mind were not overlaid by so many prejudices, and distracted by the constant presence on all sides of images of perceptible objects, there would certainly be nothing that I would recognize sooner or more clearly than God. For is there anything clearer and more obvious in itself than that there is a God, that is to say a supreme and perfect being, in whom alone essence includes necessary or eternal existence? And although, in order thoroughly to grasp this truth, I have had to make a great mental effort, I now nevertheless not only feel as sure of it as of all that I hold most certain, but further I have come to recognize that the certainty of all other truths is so utterly dependent on it that without this knowledge nothing at all can be perfectly known.

8

SPINOZA

on THE EXISTENCE OF GOD

Biographical Note Born in Amsterdam in 1632, of Portuguese Jewish descent, his father being a merchant. An early acquaintance with the works of Maimonides,[1] Descartes and others probably contributed to his religious unorthodoxy, for which reason, in 1656, he was expelled from the synagogue. He tutored for a time, but thereafter eked out a modest legacy by grinding optical lenses. In 1660, moved to Rijnsberg outside Leyden, where he wrote a 'geometrical' version of Descartes' *Principia Philosophiae*, with an appendix, *Metaphysical Thoughts*. In 1663, moved to Voorburg, where he wrote the *Tractatus Theologico-Politicus* (published 1670). In 1673, offered chair of philosophy at Heidelberg, but preferred to carry on his work privately. From 1670, lived in the Hague, till his death in 1677, which year saw the publication of the *Opera Posthuma*, including the *Ethics* (completed in 1675) and *Political Treatise*.

Principal works: as above.

Philosophical Note S.'s *Ethics*, his principal metaphysical work, is, like his version of Descartes, set out in geometrical fashion, beginning with definitions and axioms and proceeding to establish in a supposedly rigorous way a number of propositions or theorems. S. did not suppose that philosophy could be as rigorous as geometry, however; but the method lends clarity and consistency to metaphysics. Moreover, there is this analogy between philosophy and mathematics—that the test of truth is coherence or consistency rather than (as empiricists tend to think) the correspondence of a proposition with what is given in experience. Like Leibniz, S., as a radical rationalist, thought that all truths about nature could be known *a priori* if we were in a position to survey the whole system of interconnections. What appears contingent in perception is, then, necessary when seen in a wider whole. Thus the relation between cause and effect, for example, is, properly speaking, that between a ground and its consequent: in this sense mathematics provides a good model for the sciences. It follows from S.'s view of truth that nature must be regarded as a single system. Moreover, any causal interaction between things must arise from the inner nature of those things (for every feature of the universe is necessary); but this implies that they are not strictly separate things, dovetailing their effects in a comprehensive manner (though this came to be the doctrine of Leibniz: see below, pp. 141–2), but parts of a single thing or substance. In other words, there can only be one substance, and this S. called 'God or Nature' (*Deus sive Natura*). Nevertheless, S. recognized, like Descartes,

[1] See n. 1 to p. 73.

the distinction between Thought and Extension. Yet it would be repugnant to suppose, like Descartes, that they are two independent substances. They must be different Attributes of the one absolute and infinite Substance. The latter is infinite, for any limitation implies that there is something to limit it, i.e. some other substance; but it has already been seen that there can only be one. This infinite substance is *causa sui*, so that if we regard it as a free cause we can call it *Natura Naturans*; but regarding it as the system as being self-created, it is called *Natura Naturata* (it is the latter that corresponds to what people ordinarily think of as Nature). Likewise Nature, though a single Substance, can be conceived under the distinction between Thought and Extension, which are Infinite Attributes of God or Nature, mental and physical events being respectively modifications of these Attributes. Unlike Descartes and his followers, who found the causal relation between mind and body puzzling (which puzzle led to the doctrine of occasionalism: see p. 106 and p. 142), S. held that a mental event and its corresponding physical event are a single occurrence, and thus no question of causal interaction arises. The idea and the bodily change which it reflects are two different ways in which Nature expresses itself, under the two Attributes.

Considered under the Attribute of Extension, Nature is a system of changes explicable in terms of what he calls Motion-and-Rest (rest being, despite the Aristotelians, a special case of motion), an intrinsic property of Nature, and not put into the system (as according to Descartes) by God. Since there can be nothing external to the system to bring about a change in the total quantity of Motion-and-Rest (or energy), this remains constant. Individual changes are, then, changes within an unchanging whole. But although S. insists on the unity of Nature, he allows a certain individuality to particular things, through the concept of *conatus*, the tendency of a thing to maintain itself, so that S. has a place for sub-systems within the embracing system of Nature, and this modifies his general atomistic theory of physics. In such ways, S. provides a theoretical basis for physics and biology which is much more consistent and rational than Descartes'—since the latter had to regard physical laws as inscrutably decreed by God and organisms as mere automata.

Nature considered under the Attribute of Thought has an important bearing on S.'s ethics and religion. For the power or perfection of a finite mode such as a human being is proportional to its causal activeness: the human is more perfect as his ideas are not externally caused, but follow each other in logical sequence. And the human being is free in so far as he clearly understands the causes of his own mental and physical states (S. insists on causal determinism in regard to human beings, like everything else in Nature, and hence repudiates the notion of moral goodness and badness as ordinarily understood); such clear understanding presupposes an understanding of wider aspects of Nature. But this understanding induces in us neutrality in our feelings about ourselves and others, for we see ourselves and them as links in a causal system. In that, through correct thinking, we are no longer externally affected, there is no hindrance to our happiness. The wiser, then, the happier; and through greater knowledge of Nature we find increased knowledge of (by definition) God, and ultimately an intuitive knowledge of God or Nature as an eternal whole. In this sense a person's mind may be said to be eternal.

In the sphere of religion as understood by the orthodox, S. is notable for his defence (in the *Tractatus Theologico-Politicus*) of freedom of conscience in matters of belief, and for his elaboration of methods of Biblical criticism, three centuries in advance of his times. He does not hold that there is a separate province for revelation or faith as an independent source of metaphysical truth; rather, revelation is the working out, by men of powerful imagination, of truths which ultimately must stand the test of reasoning. Indeed, some aspects of traditional religion, chiefly the dualism between God and the created world, are repugnant to S.'s metaphysical system.

Bibliographical Note There are translations of the *Ethics* by R. H. M. Elwes (London, 1883), W. H. White (London, 1883), A. Boyle (London, Everyman, 1910). *Correspondence*, ed. and tr. A. Wolf (London, 1928). His political works have been ed. and tr. by A. G. Wernham (Oxford, 1958). The following are useful accounts and criticisms of S.: H. H. Joachim, *A Study of Spinoza's Ethics* (Oxford, 1901); H. A. Wolfson, *The Philosophy of Spinoza* (Cambridge, Mass., 1928); L. Roth, *Spinoza, Descartes and Maimonides* (Oxford, 1924). Stuart Hampshire, *Spinoza* (London, Pelican, 1951), is splendid. Also worth looking at is H. F. Hallett, *Aeternitas, A Spinozistic Study* (London, 1928).

THE EXISTENCE OF GOD

Ethics, Part I, Prop. XI

Prop. XI—*God, or Substance constituted of an infinity of attributes, each of which expresses an eternal and infinite essence, exists necessarily.*

Demonstr. 1.—If you deny this, conceive, if it be possible, that God does not exist. Then (by Ax.7[1]) the essence of God would not involve existence. But this (by Prop. VII[2]) is absurd. God therefore exists necessarily. Q.E.D.

Demonstr. 2.—A cause or reason must be assigned for the existence or non-existence of each individual thing. For example, if a triangle exists, there must be a reason or cause for its existence. If it does not exist, there must likewise be a reason or cause which prevents or which annuls its existence. Now this cause or reason must be found either in the nature of the thing, or outside of and beyond it. For example, the reason why a square circle does not exist is indicated by the nature of the thing itself, and no less because the idea of such a thing involves a contradiction. But, on the contrary, the reason why substance exists is because it follows from

[1] Namely: When a thing can be conceived as non-existent, its essence does not involve existence.

[2] Namely: Existence belongs to the nature of substance. S. argues this on the ground that one substance cannot be produced by any other (Prop. VI), and therefore must be its own cause. Prop. VI is mainly established on the reasoning that there cannot be two substances with the same attribute (for we distinguish them as two on the ground of diversity of attributes), whereas they would require to have something in common if one were the cause of the other (by Prop. III). This Prop. (III) is affirmed because if A is the cause of B, the concept of B must be included in A.

its very nature, which involves existence (see Prop. VII). But the reason of the existence or non-existence of a circle or triangle does not follow from the nature of either, but from the universal order of corporeal or material nature, from which it must follow either that the triangle already necessarily exists or that it was impossible for it ever to exist. This is self-evident. It follows from this that a thing exists necessarily when there is no cause or reason to prevent or annul its existence. If therefore no cause can be assigned that would prevent or destroy the existence of God, it is absolutely to be concluded that God exists necessarily. But if any such cause or reason could be given, it would have to be found either in the nature of God or out of it; that is, it would have to be found in another substance of a different nature; for to imagine it in a substance of the same nature would be to concede the existence of God. But a substance of another nature could have nothing in common with God (Prop. II[1]) and so could neither be the cause of God's existence nor destroy it. Since, therefore, there cannot be found outside or extraneous to God any cause or reason which abrogates or destroys the divine existence, such cause or reason does not exist, or else it must be found in God—which involves a manifest contradiction. But it is absurd to affirm a contradiction in the absolutely infinite and consummately perfect Being. Therefore as there is neither in God nor out of God any cause or reason that can abrogate or destroy the divine existence, it follows that God exists necessarily. Q.E.D.

Demonstr. 3.—Not to be able to exist implies impotence; and on the contrary to be able to exist implies power. (This is obvious.) If therefore that which exists necessarily comprised finite beings only, it would follow that finite beings were more powerful than the absolutely infinite Being, which (obviously) is absurd. Therefore either nothing exists or else the absolutely infinite Being exists necessarily. But we exist either in ourselves, or in something else which exists necessarily (see Ax.1[2] and Prop. VII). Therefore an absolutely infinite Being, that is (by Def.6[3]) God, exists necessarily. Q.E.D. Scholium—In this last demonstration I desired to show the existence of God *a posteriori*, in order that the demonstration might be more easily perceived, and not because the existence of God does not also follow *a priori* from the very same grounds. For as ability to exist is power, it follows that the more of reality the nature of anything possesses the more power it has of itself to exist; and consequently the absolutely

[1] Namely: Between two substances which have different attributes there is nothing in common.

[2] Whatever it is in itself or in some other thing.

[3] Namely: I understand by God the Absolutely Infinite Being; that is to say, substance constituted by an infinity of attributes, each of which expresses an eternal and infinite essence.

infinite Being, or God, has an absolutely infinite power of existence, and therefore exists absolutely, or necessarily. And yet some, perchance, may not readily perceive the clearness of this demonstration, because they are accustomed to contemplate those things only that result from external causes; and because they see that that which grows quickly—that is to say, which exists easily—perishes just as quickly and easily; whilst on the contrary those things which they judge to be formed with more difficulty—that is, which exist not so readily or easily—they conceive to have more endurance. To free these persons from such prejudices I do not think there is need to show here for what reason the homely adage 'Soon ripe, soon rotten' is true, nor yet to consider whether in respect to nature at large all things exist with equal facility or otherwise. It will suffice merely to remark that I do not speak here of things produced by external causes, but of substance only, which (by Prop. VI) can be produced by no external cause. For things that are produced by external causes, whether they are composed of many or of few parts, owe all that they have of perfection or reality to the virtue of the cause which produced them,[1] so that their existence depends on the perfection of the external cause alone and does not arise from the things themselves. On the contrary, whatever perfection substance may have is due to no external cause. Wherefore its existence must follow from its own nature and consequently is nothing else than its very essence. Perfection, therefore, does not destroy the existence of a thing, but affirms it; imperfection, on the contrary, destroys it; so that there is not anything of whose existence we can be more certain than of the existence of the absolutely infinite and perfect Being, to wit, God. For inasmuch as the essence of God excludes all imperfection and involves all perfection absolutely, every cause for doubt of God's existence disappears and we have the highest possible certitude of it—which I believe will be clear to everyone who gives the subject even a moderate degree of attention.

[1] See n. 2 to p. 144.

9

LOCKE

on REASON AND FAITH

Biographical Note Born 1632 in Somerset, son of a lawyer. Educated Westminster School and Christ Church, Oxford. B.A., 1656, M.A., 1658. Elected to Senior Studentship at Christ Church, 1659. Became interested in medicine (eventually awarded degree of Doctor of Medicine, 1674). Went as secretary to diplomatic mission to Brandenburg, 1665. Returned to Oxford that year and became acquainted with Lord Ashley (later Earl of Shaftesbury), whose employment he entered as medical adviser, political secretary and son's tutor, 1667. 1675–9, extended stay in France: meets Cartesian philosophers. 1679, re-enters Shaftesbury's service. After latter's fall and death, flees to Holland, 1683. Returns to England, 1689: appearance of Latin version of *A Letter concerning Toleration*. 1690, *Two Treatises on Civil Government; Essay concerning Human Understanding*. Died at Oates in Essex, 1704.

Principal works: those mentioned above, together with *The Reasonableness of Christianity* (1695), and *A Discourse of Miracles* (1706).

Philosophical Note In his famous *Essay*, L. is chiefly concerned with what has come to be called 'epistemology' or 'the theory of knowledge', i.e. a philosophical investigation of the kinds of evidence and warrant we have for claims to knowledge. He combats the theory that there are 'innate ideas', i.e. that certain kinds of knowledge, such as the so-called 'laws of thought' (e.g. the law of contradiction: 'It is impossible for the same thing both to be and not to be') and moral principles are contained in the mind prior to any experience. (It is somewhat unclear whom he was attacking: probably the followers of Descartes, but Locke specifically mentions only Lord Herbert of Cherbury, see above, p. 86.) On the contrary, L. holds, the mind at birth is like 'a white paper, void of all characters, without any ideas', and all knowledge comes through experience. It is in this sense that L. can be classified as an empiricist. Experience he divides into two sorts: sensation (i.e. perception) and reflection (i.e. introspection or experience of the workings of the mind itself); and it is in terms of the ideas yielded by these two sources that he attempts his inquiry into the 'origin, certainty and extent of *human knowledge*, together with the grounds and degrees of *belief*, *opinion* and *assent*' (Intro. 2). It follows from this position that it is impossible to have any sure knowledge of any reality supposed to underly what is given in experience: thus the concept of substance is an uncertain supposition of something we know not what. Nevertheless, he believed that there were arguments establishing certainly the existence of God (see below). An important aspect of Locke's account of experience is his distinction between primary and secondary qualities. The former are those, like figure, number, motion, rest and bulk, which are capable of quantitative and mathematical treatment; while the latter, such as colours, smells, etc., are the qualities produced in the mind by the primary qualities in things. The distinction was criticized by Berkeley (see below, p. 156), but arises out of L.'s hope of providing a philosophical basis for the new and expanding experimental sciences.

The present excerpt from L.'s *Essay* illustrates the importance he attached to reason as a check on religious revelation, this at least partly because of his distrust of 'enthusiasm' (see below, p. 136) which he considered to be a cause of religious bigotry. He had ample experience in his own lifetime of the effects of intolerance, and his views on the intellectual bases of religious belief (expressed fully in his *The Reasonableness of Christianity*) were of a piece with his liberal political attitude (as expressed, in his *A Letter concerning Toleration*, dealing specifically with religious toleration, and in his *Treatises*). It may be noted that in Bk IV, Ch. X, L. uses a variant of the Cosmological Argument (see pp. 67–9) to show that there is an 'eternal, most powerful and most knowing Being, which whether anyone please to call *God* it matters not'.

Bibliographical Note There are three useful editions of Locke's *Essay*, the abridged edn, edited by R. Wilburn (London, Everyman, 1947), that of A. S. Pringle-Pattison (Oxford, 1924) and the edn with critical introduction and notes by A. C. Fraser (Oxford, 1894). His *The Reasonableness of Christianity* and *A Discourse of Miracles* are edited and abridged by I. T. Ramsey (London, 1958). *The Second Treatise concerning Civil Government* and *A Letter concerning Toleration* are edited by J. W. Gough (Oxford, 1950). A good introduction is R. I. Aaron, *John Locke* (Oxford, 2nd edn, 1955), and also useful is D. J. O'Connor, *John Locke* (London, Pelican, 1952). M. Cranston, *John Locke, A Biography* (London, 1957), is excellent. Other works to consult are H. MacLachlan, *The Religious Opinions of Milton, Locke and Newton* (Manchester, 1941) and J. W. Yolton, *John Locke and the Way of Ideas* (Oxford, 1956).

REASON AND FAITH

An Essay concerning Human Understanding, Book IV, Chs. XVIII f.

1. OF FAITH AND REASON, AND THEIR DISTINCT PROVINCES

1. It has been above shown: (1) That we are of necessity ignorant, and want knowledge of all sorts, where we want ideas.[1] (2) That we are

[1] L. defines 'idea' as 'whatever it is which the mind can be employed about in thinking' (Intro. 8). On his view, all ideas have the common function of being signs of that with which we cannot be directly acquainted: this is perhaps the excuse for his use of the word to cover so many things—for 'idea', as he employs it, refers to sense-data (i.e. what we are immediately aware of: patches of colour, smells, pains, etc.), complexes of sense-data (complex ideas, e.g. what I am aware of when I look at, smell, etc., a tree), memory

ignorant, and want rational knowledge, where we want proofs. (3) That we want certain knowledge and certainty, as far as we want clear and determined specific ideas. (4) That we want probability to direct our assent in matters where we have neither knowledge of our own nor testimony of other men to bottom our reason upon.

From these things thus premised, I think we may come to lay down the measures and boundaries between *faith and reason*: the want whereof may possibly have been the cause, if not of great disorders, yet at least of great disputes, and perhaps mistakes, in the world. For till it be resolved how far we are to be guided by reason, and how far by faith, we shall in vain dispute and endeavour to convince one another in matters of religion.

2. I find every sect, as far as reason will help them, make use of it gladly: and where it fails them, they cry out. It is a matter of faith and above reason. And I do not see how they can argue with anyone, or ever convince an objector who makes use of the same plea, without setting down strict boundaries between faith and reason; which ought to be the first point established in all questions where faith has anything to do.

Reason, therefore, here, as contradistinguished to *faith*, I take to be the discovery of the certainty or probability of such propositions or truths, which the mind arrives at by deduction made from such ideas as it has got by the use of its natural faculties; viz. by sensation or reflection.

Faith, on the other side, is the assent to any proposition, not thus made out by the deductions of reason, but upon the credit of the proposer, as coming from God, in some extraordinary way of communication. This way of discovering truths to men we call *revelation*.

3. First, then, I say, that *no man inspired by God can by any revelation communicate to others any new simple ideas*[1] *which they had not before from sensation or reflection*. For whatever impressions he himself may have from the immediate hand of God, this revelation, if it be of new simple ideas, cannot be conveyed to another, either by words or any other signs. For words, seen or heard, recall to our thoughts those ideas only which to us they have been wont to be signs of, but cannot introduce any perfectly new and formerly unknown simple ideas.

Thus whatever things were discovered to St Paul, when he was rapt up into the third heaven; whatever new ideas his mind received, all the description he can make to others of that place, is only this, that there

images and other 'mental pictures', general properties (such as sweetness, gratitude, etc.), concepts (the meanings of words, etc.). See D. J. O'Connor, *John Locke*, p. 33 ff. for an excellent discussion of L'.s ambiguities here.

[1] Simple ideas of sensation and reflection are those which cannot be further analysed but are of one uniform appearance or conception (Bk II, Ch. II, 1); complex ideas are combinations of these (Bk II, Ch. XII, 1).

are such things, 'as eye hath not seen, nor ear heard, nor hath it entered into the heart of man to conceive'. And supposing God should discover to anyone, supernaturally, a species of creatures inhabiting, for example, Jupiter or Saturn (for that it is possible there may be such, nobody can deny), which had six senses; and imprint on his mind the ideas conveyed to theirs by that sixth sense: he could no more, by words, produce in the minds of other men those ideas imprinted by that sixth sense, than one of us could convey the idea of any colour, by the sound of words, into a man who, having the other four senses perfect, had always totally lacked the fifth, of seeing. For our simple ideas, then, which are the foundation and sole matter of all our notions and knowledge, we must depend wholly on our reason, I mean our natural faculties; and can by no means receive them, or any of them from traditional revelation. I say, *traditional revelation*, in distinction to *original revelation*. By the one, I mean that first impression which is made immediately by God on the mind of any man, to which we cannot set any bounds; and by the other, those impressions delivered over to others in words, and the ordinary ways of conveying our conceptions one to another.

4. Secondly, I say that *the same truths may be discovered and conveyed down from revelation, which are discoverable to us by reason, and by those ideas we naturally may have*. So God might, by revelation, manifest the truth of any proposition in Euclid; as well as men, by the natural use of their faculties, come to make the discovery themselves. In all things of this kind there is little need or use of revelation, God having furnished us with natural and surer means to arrive at the knowledge of them. For whatever truth we come to the clear discovery of, from the knowledge and contemplation of our own ideas, will always be more certain to us than those which are conveyed to us by *traditional revelation*. For the knowledge we have that this revelation came at first from God can never be so sure as the knowledge we have from the clear and distinct perception of the agreement or disagreement of our own ideas:[1] e.g. if it were revealed some ages since that the three angles of a triangle were equal to two right angles, I might assent to the truth of that proposition, upon the credit of the tradition that it was revealed: but that would never amount to so great a certainty as the knowledge of it upon . . . comparing and measuring my own ideas of two right angles and the three angles of a triangle. The like holds in matters of fact knowable by our senses; e.g. the history of the deluge is conveyed to us by writings which had their origin from revelation: and yet nobody, I think, will say he has as certain and clear a knowledge of the flood as

[1] L. defines knowledge as 'the perception of connexion of and agreement or disagreement and repugnancy of any of our ideas' (Bk IV, Ch. I, 2).

Noah, that saw it; or that he himself would have had, had he been alive and seen it. For he has no greater an assurance than that of his senses, that it is written in the book supposed written by Moses inspired: but he has not so great an assurance that Moses wrote that book as if he had seen Moses write it. So that the assurance of its being a revelation is less still than the assurance of his senses.

5. In propositions, then, whose certainty is built upon the clear perception of the agreement or disagreement of our ideas, attained either by immediate intuition, as in self-evident propositions,[1] or by evident deductions of reason in demonstrations, we need not the assistance of revelation, as necessary to gain our assent, and introduce them into our minds. Because the natural ways of knowledge could settle them there, or had done it already—which is the greatest assurance we can possibly have of anything, unless where God immediately reveals it to us: and there too our assurance can be no greater than our knowledge . . . that it *is* a revelation from God.

Since no evidence of our faculties, by which we receive revelations, can exceed, if equal, the certainty of our intuitive knowledge, we can never receive for a truth anything that is directly contrary to our clear and distinct knowledge; e.g. the ideas of one body and one place do so clearly agree and the mind has so evident a perception of their agreement, that we can never assent to a proposition that affirms the same body to be in two distant places at once, however it should pretend to the authority of a divine revelation: since the evidence, first, that we deceive not ourselves in ascribing it to God [and], secondly, that we understood it right can never

[1] L. distinguishes between intuition and demonstration as follows: intuitive knowledge is of such truths as 'White is not black', 'Three is greater than two', 'A circle is not a triangle', etc. Such kinds of truths, he says (Bk IV, Ch. II, 1) are perceived by the mind 'at the first sight of the ideas together, by bare intuition, without the intervention of any other idea; and this kind of knowledge is the clearest and most certain that human frailty is capable of.' All certainty depends ultimately on such intuitions. Demonstration is where two ideas are seen to agree or disagree by means of a proof, where intervening ideas are used to show this agreement or disagreement. For example, if idea A agrees with B, B with C and C with D, B and C are the intervening ideas which can be used to show that A and D agree. Since demonstration involves steps of an argument, there is room for error and hence it is less certain than intuition. Intuition and demonstration, L. says, 'are the degrees of our *knowledge*; whatever comes short of these . . . is but *faith* or *opinion* . . . at least in all general truths. There is, indeed, another perception of the mind, employed about *the particular existence of finite things outside us*, which going beyond bare probability, and yet not reaching either to either of the foregoing degrees of certainty, passes under the name of *knowledge*.' (Bk IV, Ch. II, 14.) This last L. calls *sensitive* knowledge. Thus there are three degrees of knowledge: intuitive, demonstrative and sensitive or perceptual, in descending order of certainty. Note that L. shares with Descartes and other rationalist philosophers a preference for mathematics as providing the paradigm of knowledge—this perhaps is not surprising in an age of astonishing mathematical advances: e.g. the discovery of co-ordinate geometry (Fermat and Descartes: see above, p. 106) and the calculus (Leibniz and Newton: see below, p. 141 and n. 1 to p. 120). For later advances in mathematics, see n. 1 to p. 388.

be so great as the evidence of our own intuitive knowledge, whereby we discern it to be impossible for the same body to be in two places at once. And therefore *no proposition can be received for divine revelation, or obtain the assent due to all such, if it be contradictory to our clear intuitive knowledge.* Because this would be to subvert the principles and foundations of all knowledge, evidence and assent whatsoever: and there would be left no difference between truth and falsehood, no measures of credible and incredible in the world, if doubtful propositions . . . take precedence over self-evident [ones]; and what we certainly know give way to what we may possibly be mistaken in. Faith can never convince us of anything that contradicts our knowledge. Because, though faith be founded on the testimony of God (who cannot lie) revealing any proposition to us, yet we cannot have an assurance of the truth of its being a divine revelation greater than our own knowledge, since the whole strength of the certainty depends on our knowledge that God revealed it—which, in this case, where the proposition supposed revealed contradicts our knowledge or reason, will always have this objection hanging on to it, viz. that we cannot . . . conceive as coming from God, the bountiful Author of our being, that which, if received for true, must overturn all the principles and foundations of knowledge he has given us; render all our faculties useless; wholly destroy the most excellent part of his workmanship, our understandings; and put a man in a condition wherein he will have less light . . . than the beast that perishes.

6. Thus far a man has use of reason, and ought to hearken to it, even in immediate and original revelation, where it is supposed to be made to himself. But to all those who pretend not to immediate revelation, but are required to pay obedience and to receive the truths revealed to others, which by the tradition of writings or by word of mouth are conveyed down to them, reason has a great deal more to do, and is that which alone can induce us to receive them. For matters of faith, being only divine revelation, have to do with no propositions but those which are supposed to be divinely revealed. So that I do not see how those who make revelation alone the sole object of faith can say that it is a matter of faith, and not of reason, to believe that such-and-such a proposition, to be found in such-and-such a book, is of divine inspiration, unless it be revealed that that proposition, or all in that book, was communicated by divine inspiration. Without such a revelation, the believing or not believing that proposition or book to be of divine authority can never be [a] matter of faith, but [a] matter of reason. In all things, therefore, where we have clear evidence from our ideas, and those principles of knowledge I have above mentioned, reason is the proper judge, and revelation, though it

may in consenting with it confirm its dictates, yet cannot in such cases invalidate its decrees.

7. But thirdly, there being many things wherein we have very imperfect notions or none at all, and other things of whose past, present and future existence, by the natural use of our faculties, we can have no knowledge at all, these, as being beyond the discovery of our natural faculties and *above reason*, are, when revealed, *the proper matter of faith*. Thus, that part of the angels rebelled against God and thereby lost their first happy state, and that the dead shall rise and live again—these and the like, being beyond the discovery of reason, are purely matters of faith, with which reason has directly nothing to do.

8. But since God, in giving us the light of reason, has not thereby tied up his own hand from affording us, when he thinks fit, the light of revelation in any of those matters wherein our natural faculties are able to give a probable determination, *revelation*, where God has been pleased to give it, *must carry it against the probable conjectures of reason*. Because the mind, not being certain of the truth of that [which] it does not evidently know, but only yielding to the probability that appears in it, is bound to give up its assent to such a testimony, which, it is satisfied, comes from one who cannot err and will not deceive. But yet it still belongs to reason to judge of the truth of its being revelation and of the signification of the words wherein it is delivered. Indeed, if anything shall be thought revelation which is contrary to the plain principles of reason and the evident knowledge the mind has of its own clear and distinct ideas, there reason must be hearkened to, as a matter within its province.

9. First, whatever proposition is revealed, of whose truth our mind, by its natural faculties and notions, cannot judge, that is purely [a] matter of faith and above reason.

Secondly, all propositions whereof the mind, by the use of its natural faculties, can come to determine and judge, from naturally acquired ideas, are matters of reason: with this difference still that, in those concerning which it has but an uncertain evidence and so is persuaded of their truth upon only probable grounds which still admit a possibility of the contrary to be true, without doing violence to the certain evidence of its own knowledge and overturning the principles of all reason—in such probable propositions, I say, an evident revelation ought to determine our assent, even against probability.

10. Whatever God has revealed is certainly true: no doubt can be made of it. This is the proper object of faith: but whether it be a *divine* revelation or no, reason must judge, which can never permit the mind to reject a greater evidence to embrace what is less evident nor allow it to entertain

probability in opposition to knowledge and certainty. There can be no evidence that any traditional revelation is of divine origin, in the words we receive it and in the sense we understand it, so clear and so certain as that of the principles of reason: and therefore *nothing that is contrary to and inconsistent with the clear and self-evident dictates of reason has a right to be urged or assented to as a matter of faith, wherein reason has nothing to do*. Whatsoever is divine revelation ought to overrule all our opinions, prejudices and interest and has a right to be received with full assent. Such a submission as this, of our reason to faith, takes not away the landmarks of knowledge: this shakes not the foundations of reason, but leaves us that use of our faculties for which they were given us.

11. If the provinces of faith and reason are not kept distinct by these boundaries, there will, in matters of religion, be no room for reason at all, and those extravagant opinions and ceremonies that are to be found in the several religions of the world will not deserve to be blamed. For, to this crying up of faith in *opposition* to reason we may, I think, in good measure ascribe those absurdities that fill almost all the religions which possess and divide mankind.

2. OF ENTHUSIASM (Ch. XIX)

1. He that would seriously set upon the search of truth ought in the first place to prepare his mind with a love of it. For he that loves it not will not take much pains to get it nor be much concerned when he misses it. There is nobody in the commonwealth of learning who does not profess himself a lover of truth and there is not a rational creature that would not take it amiss to be thought otherwise of. And yet for all this one may truly say that there are very few lovers of truth for truth's sake, even amongst those who persuade themselves that they are so. How a man may know whether he be so in earnest is worth enquiry: and I think there is one unerring mark of it, viz. the not entertaining any proposition with greater assurance than the proofs it is built upon will warrant. Whatsoever credit or authority we give to any proposition more than it receives from the principles and proofs it supports itself upon is owing to our inclinations that way, and is so far a derogation from the love of truth as such which, as it can receive no evidence from our passions or interests, so it should receive no tincture from them.

2. The assuming an authority of dictating to others and a forwardness to prescribe their opinions is a constant concomitant of this bias and corruption of our judgments. For how almost can it be otherwise but that he should be ready to impose on another's belief, who has already imposed

on his own? Who can reasonably expect arguments and conviction from him in dealing with others, whose understanding is not accustomed to them in dealing with himself?—[and] who does violence to his own faculties, tyrannizes over his own mind and usurps the prerogative that belongs to truth alone, which is to command assent by only its own authority, i.e. by and in proportion to that evidence which it carries with it.

3. Upon this occasion I shall take the liberty to consider *a third ground of assent*, which with some men has the same authority, and is as confidently relied on, as either faith or reason; I mean *enthusiasm*,[1] which, laying aside reason, would set up revelation without it. Whereby in effect it takes away both reason and revelation and substitutes in the room of them the ungrounded fancies of a man's own brain, and assumes them for a foundation both of opinion and conduct.

4. *Reason* is *natural revelation*, whereby the eternal Father of light and fountain of all knowledge communicates to mankind that portion of truth which he has laid within the reach of their natural faculties: *revelation* is *natural reason enlarged* by a new set of discoveries communicated by God immediately; which reason vouches the truth of, by the testimony and proofs it gives that they come from God. So that he that takes away reason to make way for revelation puts out the light of both and does much the same as if he would persuade a man to put out his eyes, the better to receive the remote light of an invisible star by a telescope.

5. Immediate revelation being a much easier way for men to establish their opinions and regulate their conduct than the tedious and not always successful labour of strict reasoning, it is no wonder that some have been very apt to pretend to revelation and to persuade themselves that they are under the peculiar guidance of heaven in their actions and opinions, especially in those of them which they cannot account for by the ordinary methods of knowledge and principles of reason. Hence we see that, in all ages, men in whom melancholy has mixed with devotion or whose conceit of themselves has raised them into an opinion of a greater familiarity with God and a nearer admittance to his favour than is afforded to others have often flattered themselves with a persuasion of an immediate intercourse with the Deity and frequent communications from the Divine Spirit.

6. Their minds being thus prepared, whatever groundless opinion comes to settle itself strongly upon their fancies is an illumination from the Spirit of God and presently of divine authority: and whatsoever odd action

[1] 'Enthusiasm': this is used in the seventeenth-century sense, pejoratively, meaning religious fanaticism on the basis of inner experience. It was a term commonly applied to the Anabaptists, and at a later period to the Puritans.

they find in themselves a strong inclination to do . . . is concluded to be a call or direction from heaven and must be obeyed: it is a commission from above and they cannot err in executing it.

7. This I take to be properly *enthusiasm*, which, though founded neither on reason nor divine revelation, but rising from the conceits of a warmed or overweening brain, works yet, where it once gets footing, more powerfully on the persuasions and actions of men than either of those two or both together, men being most forwardly obedient to the impulses they receive from themselves; and the whole man is sure to act more vigorously where the whole man is concerned by a natural motion. For strong conceit, like a new principle, carries all easily with it, when got above common sense, and freed from all restraint of reason and check of reflection it is heightened into a divine authority, in concurrence with our own temper and inclination.

8. Though the odd opinions and extravagant actions enthusiasm has run men into were enough to warn them against this wrong principle, so apt to misguide them both in their belief and conduct, yet the love of something extraordinary, the ease and glory it is to be inspired and be above the common and natural ways of knowledge so flatters many men's laziness, ignorance and vanity that . . . once they are got into this way of immediate revelation, of illumination without search and of certainty without proof and without examination, it is a hard matter to get them out of it. Reason is lost upon them—they are above it: they see the light diffused into their understandings and cannot be mistaken; it is clear and visible there, like the light of bright sunshine, shows itself and needs no other proof but its own evidence; they feel the hand of God moving them within, and the impulses of the Spirit, and cannot be mistaken in what they feel. This light from heaven is strong, clear and pure, carries its own demonstration with it; and we may as naturally take a glow-worm to assist us to discover the sun as to examine the celestial ray by our dim candle, reason.

9. This is the way of talking of these men: they are sure, because they are sure: and their persuasions are right because they are strong in them.

10. But to examine a little soberly this internal light and this feeling on which they build so much. These men have, they say, clear light and they see; they have awakened sense, and they feel: this cannot, they are sure, be disputed them. For when a man says he sees or feels, nobody can deny him that he does so. But here let me ask: This seeing, is it perception of the truth of the proposition, or of this, that it is a revelation from God? This feeling, is it a perception of an inclination or fancy to do something, or of the Spirit of God moving that inclination? These are two very

different perceptions and must be carefully distinguished, if we would not impose upon ourselves. I may perceive the truth of a proposition and yet not perceive that it is an immediate revelation from God. I may perceive the truth of a proposition in Euclid without its being, or my perceiving it to be, a revelation: nay I may perceive I came not by this knowledge in a natural way and so may conclude it [is] revealed, without perceiving that it is a revelation of God. Because there be spirits which, without being divinely commissioned, may excite those ideas in me and lay them in such order before my mind that I perceive their connection. So that the knowledge of any proposition coming into my mind, I know not how, is not a perception that it is from God. Much less is a strong persuasion that it is true a perception that it is from God, or so much as true. But however it be called light and seeing, I suppose it is at most but belief and assurance, and the proposition taken for revelation is not such as they *know* to be true, but *take* to be true. For where a proposition is known to be true, revelation is needless, and it is hard to conceive how there can be revelation to anyone of what he knows already. If therefore it be a proposition which they are persuaded, but do not know, to be true, whatever they may call it, it is not seeing, but believing. For these are two ways whereby truth comes into the mind, wholly distinct, so that one is not the other. What I see, I know to be so, by the evidence of the thing itself: what I believe I take to be so upon the testimony of another. But the testimony I must know to be given, or else what ground have I of believing? I must see that it is God that reveals this to me, or else I see nothing. The question then here is: How do I know that it is God who is the revealer of this to me; that this impression is made upon my mind by his Holy Spirit; and that therefore I ought to obey it? If I know not this, how great soever the assurance is that I am possessed with, it is groundless; whatever light I pretend to, it is but *enthusiasm*. For whether the proposition supposed to be revealed be in itself evidently true or visibly probable or, by the natural ways of knowledge, uncertain, the proposition that must be well grounded and manifested to be true is this: that God is the revealer of it, and that what I take to be a revelation is certainly put into my mind by him and is not an illusion dropped in by some other spirit or raised by my own fancy. For, if I mistake not, these men receive it for true because they presume God revealed it. Does it not, then, behove them to examine upon what grounds they presume it to be a revelation from God? or else all their confidence is mere presumption, and this light they are so dazzled with is nothing but an *ignis fatuus* that constantly leads them round in this circle: *It is a revelation because they firmly believe it; and they believe it because it is a revelation.*

11. In all that is of divine revelation there is need of no other proof than that it is an inspiration from God, for he can neither deceive nor be deceived. But how shall it be known that any proposition in our minds is a truth infused by God, a truth that is revealed to us by him, which he declares to us and therefore we ought to believe? Here it is that enthusiasm fails of the evidence it pretends to. For men thus possessed boast of a light whereby they say they are enlightened and brought into the knowledge of this or that truth. The light they speak of is but a strong, though ungrounded, persuasion of their own minds that it is a truth. For rational grounds from proofs that it is a truth, they must acknowledge to have none; for then it is not received as a revelation, but upon the ordinary grounds that other truths are received: and if they believe it to be true because it is a revelation and have no other reason for its being a revelation except that they are fully persuaded, without any other reason, that it is true, then they believe it to be a revelation only because they strongly believe it to be a revelation—which is a very unsafe ground to proceed on, either in our tenets or actions. . . .

13. Light, true light, in the mind is or can be nothing else but the evidence of the truth of any proposition; and if it be not a self-evident proposition, all the light it has or can have is from the clearness and validity of those proofs upon which it is received. To talk of any other light in the understanding is to put ourselves in the dark or in the power of the Prince of Darkness and, by our own consent, to give ourselves up to delusion, to believe a lie.

14. He therefore that will not give himself up to all the extravagance of delusion and error must bring this guide of his *light within* to the trial. God when he makes the prophet does not unmake the man. He leaves all his faculties in the natural state, to enable him to judge of his inspirations whether they be of divine origin or no. When he illuminates the mind with supernatural light he does not extinguish that which is natural. If he would have us assent to the truth of any proposition he either evidences that truth by the usual methods of natural reason or else makes it known to be a truth which he would have us assent to by his own authority, and convinces us that it is from him by some marks which reason cannot be mistaken in. *Reason must be our last judge and guide in everything.* I do not mean that we must consult reason and examine whether a proposition revealed from God can be made out by natural principles, and if it cannot, that then we may reject it: but consult it we must and by it examine whether it be a revelation from God or no: and if reason finds it to be revealed from God, reason then declares for it as much as for any other truth and makes it one of her dictates.

10

LEIBNIZ

on THE EXISTENCE OF GOD *and on* THE PROBLEM OF EVIL

Biographical Note Gottfried Wilhelm Leibniz was born at Leipzig in 1646, son of Professor of Moral Philosophy. Entered Leipzig University, 1661. Became Doctor of Laws at Altdorf, Nuremburg, 1666. 1667, entered service of Elector-Archbishop of Mainz. Diplomatic mission to Paris, 1672. Short visit to London, 1673. Returned to Paris, studied geometry there under Huygens. 1676, formulates his discovery of calculus (previously and independently discovered by Newton, though L.'s way of presenting it has since been universally adopted). 1676, librarian to the Duke of Brunswick, settled in Hanover. Largely instrumental, with Sophia-Charlotte, later Queen of Prussia, in establishing Berlin Academy, of which he was elected President, 1700. Continued quietly in Hanover, where he died, 1716, largely forgotten.

Principal works: *De Arte Combinatoria* (1666), *Systema Theologicum* (1686), *Theodicy* (1710), *Principles of Nature and Grace* (1718), *Monadology* (1720).

Philosophical Note L.'s philosophical system rests largely on two points: first, a view about the nature of individuality, and second, a view about the existence of individuals. Under the former head, L. believed that in a true proposition the predicate is ordinarily included in the subject (thus the proposition is, in Kant's terminology, analytic: see n. 2 to p. 253, but L. recognized that since the analysis of propositions about matters of fact is infinitely complex, we cannot see directly that these propositions are analytic) and that this principle applies not merely to general propositions, but also to propositions about individuals. It follows therefore that all those truths which may be asserted about Adam are contained in the essential notion of Adam. Thus all true statements ascribing properties to or describing events concerning Adam are necessarily true. Under the second head, L. saw that though the above doctrine applies to subject-predicate statements of an ordinary sort, it would not apply to statements about the existence of individuals: to account for why these individuals exist in the world rather than others, it is necessary to go beyond the principle of contradiction, which merely shows what is impossible and possible, given the notions of different individuals. To account for existence, then, it is necessary to introduce a further principle, which L. calls the *principle of sufficient reason* (see p. 143). In accordance with this, the Author of the world chooses, out of an infinite number of possible universes, this particular one.

It will be seen that L.'s view implies that an individual's career and properties are entirely determined internally and do not depend upon the action of other individuals. Nevertheless, the world *appears* to contain interaction: and L. attempts to account for this by supposing that there is a pre-established harmony, such that the internal development of one corresponds with that of every other. The individuals (or *monads*, i.e. units, as L. calls them) are, because of their complete independence, described colourfully as 'windowless'—there is no window by which anything could pass in or out. By reason of the harmony, it may be said that each monad represents, from its own point of view, the state of the whole universe, and therefore L. called each passing state of a monad a *perception*. But of course not all individual entities in fact are conscious, and L. makes a distinction between unconscious perceptions and those which are conscious or *apperceived*.

This somewhat peculiar way of talking about the monads becomes more intelligible when it is noted that L. held that a real individual must be indivisible and simple and therefore cannot have extension. In view of this and of the fact that individuals must in some way be capable of change, L. considered that they must in some manner resemble souls—for souls have both the property of being simple and indivisible and that of being capable of variety and change. Hence, though he did not ascribe to all monads consciousness, he viewed them as like souls.

The application of these metaphysical views of physics resulted in L.'s differing profoundly from the Cartesians. It is clear that he cannot accept the view that the essence of matter is extension, nor that the fundamental concept in explaining change is motion. Rather, force—a character contained in things and presupposed by the notions of motion and solidity—is the basic concept in dynamics.

In regard to the union of body and soul, L. tries to account for this by using the idea of the pre-established harmony, and thus adopts a theory reminiscent of occasionalism (see above, p. 106). Changes in the mind which are apparently caused by bodily events (e.g. the pain apparently consequent upon the sting of a wasp) are to be explained by reference to the internal nature of the mind, which is geared, so to speak, to predetermined bodily events. The theory, L. holds, is consistent with free will—for the soul's actions are caused by itself alone—and with immortality—for bodily dissolution will not in any way touch the soul. L.'s theory is deterministic in so far as all changes, including mental ones, are completely explained through previous states: but though minds are automata, they are not *material* mechanisms like bodies.

The *Monadology*, from which the first selection is taken, is a short epitome of L.'s metaphysics, written in 1714, not long before L.'s death. The first sections explain his theory of monads and of perceptions.

Bibliographical Note There are translations of L.'s principal works in G. M. Duncan, *The Philosophical Works of L.* (New Haven, Conn., 1890), R. Latta, *The Monadology and other philosophical works* (Oxford, 1898), G. R. Montgomery, *Discourse on Metaphysics, Correspondence with Arnauld, The Monadology* (Chicago, 1902), E. M. Huggard, *Theodicy* (London, 1952), P. Lucas and L. Grint, *Discourse on Metaphysics* (Manchester, 1957), and H. G. Alexander, *The Leibniz-Clarke Correspondence* (Manchester, 1956). R. Saw, *Leibniz* (London, Pelican, 1954) is a useful introduction. See also B. Russell, *A Critical Exposition of the Philosophy of Leibniz* (new edn, London, 1937) and H. W. B. Joseph, *Lectures on the Philosophy of Leibniz* (Oxford, 1949).

A. THE EXISTENCE OF GOD

The Monadology, §29 ff.

29. But it is the knowledge of necessary and eternal truths which distinguishes us from mere animals and provides us with *reason* and the sciences, raising us to a knowledge of ourselves and of God. And it is this that is called the rational soul or mind.

30. It is also through the knowledge of necessary truths and abstracting from them that we attain to *acts of reflection*, making us think of what is termed the *self* and observes that this or that is within us: and in this way, thinking of ourselves we think of being, of substance, simple and compound, of the immaterial and of God himself, and conceive that what is limited in us is in him without any limits. These reflective acts provide the main objects of our reasonings.

31. The latter are based on *two great principles*, that of contradiction, in virtue of which we judge to be *false* that which involves a contradiction, and *true* that which is opposed to or contradicts that which is false.

32. And that of *sufficient reason*, in virtue of which we hold that no state of affairs can be real or existent, and no proposition can be true, unless there is a sufficient reason why it should be so and not otherwise—even though such reasons cannot usually be known to us.

33. Further, there are two kinds of *truths*: truths of *reasoning* and truths of *fact*. The former are necessary and their opposite is impossible, while the latter are contingent and their opposite is possible. When a truth is necessary, its reason can be found through analysis, by resolving it into simpler ideas and truths until we arrive at those which are primary.

34. Thus in mathematics speculative *theorems* and practical *canons* are reduced by analysis to *definitions*, *axioms* and *postulates*.

35. In brief, there are *simple ideas*, definitions of which cannot be given; then there are axioms and postulates, or *primary principles*, which cannot be proved and indeed need no proof: they are *identical propositions*, whose opposites contain an explicit contradiction.

36. But a *sufficient reason* must also be found in regard to *contingent truths* or *truths of fact*, i.e. for the series of things scattered through the whole universe: for here the process of analysis into particular reasons might go into infinite detail, because of the huge variety of things in nature and the infinite division of bodies. There is an infinite number of shapes and motions, past and present, which go to make up the efficient cause of my present writing; and there is an infinite number of minute tendencies and

dispositions of my soul, past and present, which go to make up its final cause.[1]

37. And since all this detail in turn involves other prior and more detailed contingent things, each of which requires a similar analysis to explain it, we are no further forward; and the sufficient or ultimate reason must lie outside the series of particular contingent things, however infinite this may be.

38. Thus the ultimate reason of things must lie in a necessary substance in which the detailed variety of changes exists merely eminently,[2] as in its source: and this substance we call *God.*

39. Now since this substance is a sufficient reason for all this variety of particulars which is, moreover, connected throughout, *there is only one God and this God is sufficient.*

40. We may further conclude that since this supreme substance, which is unique, universal and necessary, has nothing outside it which is independent of it and which is a simple series of possible being, it must be incapable of any limitation and must contain the greatest possible reality.

41. It follows from this that God is absolutely perfect, for perfection is nothing but amount of positive reality, in the strictest sense, leaving out of account the limits or bounds in things which are limited. And where there are no bounds, i.e. in God, perfection is absolutely infinite.

42. It follows also that created beings derive their perfections from the influence of God, but that their imperfections stem from their own nature, which is incapable of existing without limits. For it is in this that they are distinguished from God.

43. Similarly, the source of not only existences but also of essences, in so far as they are real, i.e. the source of what is real in the possible, lies in God. For the understanding of God is the region of eternal truths and of the ideas on which they depend; and, further, without him there would be nothing real in the possibilities of things: not only would nothing exist, but nothing would be possible.

44. For if there is a reality in essences or possibilities, or rather in eternal truths, this reality must be founded on something existent and actual, and consequently upon the existence of a necessary being in whom essence involves existence, i.e. it is enough for him to be possible in order that he should be actual.

[1] See above, p. 60.

[2] According to Scholastic philosophy, a perfection which exists in an effect must exist in the cause (a principle used by Descartes in his causal argument for God's existence—see above, p. 107). This covers two cases, (1) where the cause and effect are of the same kind; (2) where the cause is of a different and superior kind. In the latter case, the perfection is said to exist more excellently or *eminently* in the cause.

45. Thus God alone (or the necessary being) has this privilege, that he must exist necessarily if he is possible. And since nothing could prevent the possibility of that which has no limitations, no negation and consequently no contradiction, God's possibility is sufficient to establish his existence *a priori*.[1] We have proved it also by the reality of eternal truths; and also a little while back (paras. 36–9) we proved it *a posteriori*, since there exist contingent beings which can only have their ultimate or sufficient reason in a necessary being which has the reason for its existence in itself.

46. However, we must not imagine, as some do, that because eternal truths depend upon God they are therefore arbitrary and depend upon his will—as Descartes seems to have held and thereafter M. Poiret.[2] This is only true of contingent truths, whose principle is *fitness* or the choice of the *best*, whereas necessary truths depend solely on his understanding and are its internal object.

47. Thus God alone is the primary unity or original simple substance, from which all monads, created or derived, are produced and are generated, as it were, by continual effulgences of the Divinity from instant to instant, limited by the receptivity of the creature, which is essentially limited.

48. In God there is *power*, which is the source of everything, *knowledge*, which contains the detailed variety of ideas, and lastly *will*, which produces changes and things according to the principle of what is best. . . .

53. Now since there is an infinite number of possible universes contained in God's ideas, and since only one of these can exist, there must be a sufficient reason for the choice which God makes, leading him to prefer one to another.

54. And this reason can only be discovered in the *fitness*, or in the degrees of perfection, which these universes possess, for each possible thing can legitimately aspire to existence in proportion to the amount of perfection which it contains in germ.

55. It is this, then, which causes the existence of the Best, namely that his wisdom makes it known to him, his goodness makes him choose it and his power makes him produce it.

The above passages give a brief expression of L.'s arguments for the existence of a necessary being and of his view that this is the best of all possible worlds. The following extended passage forms the whole of L.'s own summary of the arguments in the *Theodicy*, published in 1710 and concerned with the problem of evil. The

[1] For the meaning of *a priori*, see n. 2 to p. 86.

[2] Pierre Poiret (1646–1719) was a French Protestant and contemplative, who interpreted mysticism in terms of Cartesianism.

summary itself constitutes part of the whole *Theodicy*, which includes (i) an introductory discourse on the conformity of faith with reason; (ii) the main part of the work, containing three essays, the first on the nature of evil in general, the second on moral evil and the third on physical evil; (iii) the summary here given; (iv) an examination of Hobbes' work *Questions concerning Liberty, Necessity and Chance*; (v) comments on a work by King on *The Origin of Evil*; (vi) a more extended summary. The *Theodicy* was written in memory of Queen Sophia-Charlotte of Prussia and arose out of conversations with her on the problems of freedom and evil, occasioned by certain objections to L.'s position which she found in Bayle's *Dictionary* (Pierre Bayle [1647–1706]; his *Dictionnaire historique et critique* was designed to criticize philosophical and theological views in such a way as to show that dogmatism was untenable).

B. THE PROBLEM OF EVIL

Theodicy, Summary of the Argument, first paragraph omitted

I. *Objection*. Whoever does not choose the best is lacking either in power or in knowledge or in goodness.

God did not choose the best in creating this world.

Therefore God was lacking either in power or in knowledge or in goodness.

Answer. I deny the minor premiss, i.e. the second premiss of this syllogism; and our opponent proves it by this:

Prosyllogism. Whoever makes things in which there is evil, but which could have been made without any evil or need not have been made at all, does not choose the best.

God made a world in which there is evil; a world, I say, which could have been made without any evil or need not have been made at all.

Therefore God did not choose the best.

Answer. I grant the minor premiss of this prosyllogism; for it must be confessed that there is evil in this world which God has created, and that it was possible to make a world without any evil or even not to create a world at all, for its creation depended upon the free will of God. But I deny the major, i.e. the first of the two premisses of the prosyllogism, and I could content myself with asking for its proof; but in order to make the matter clearer I wish to justify this denial by showing that the best course is not always that which seeks to avoid evil, since it is possible that the evil is accompanied by a greater good. For instance, an army general would prefer a great victory and a slight wound to a state of affairs without either. We have proved this more fully in the main work by examples taken from mathematics and elsewhere, making it clear that an imperfection in a part may be necessary for a greater perfection in the whole.

In this I have followed the view of St Augustine, who said a hundred times that God has allowed evil in order to bring about good, i.e. a greater good, and that of Thomas Aquinas (in *libr.*II, *sent.*, *dist.* 32, *qu.* I, *art.* i), that the permitting of evil tends to the good of the universe. I have shown that the older writers called Adam's fall *felix culpa*, a fortunate sin, because it had been redeemed with great advantage through the incarnation of the Son of God, who has given to the universe something nobler than anything that otherwise would have occurred among creatures. And for the clearer understanding of the matter I added, following many good authors, that it was in accord with order and the general good that God should allow certain creatures the opportunity for exercising their freedom, even when he foresaw that they would opt for evils: for God could so easily rectify the matter. For it was not proper that in order to counteract sin God should always act in an extraordinary manner. To refute this objection, therefore, it is sufficient to show that a world which contains evil may be better than one without evil. But I have gone even further in the main work and have even proved that this world must in reality be better than any other possible world.

II. *Objection.* If there is more evil than good in intelligent creatures, there is more evil than good in the whole of God's work.

Now there is more evil than good in intelligent creatures.

Therefore there is more evil than good in the whole of God's work.

Answer. I deny the major and the minor of this hypothetical syllogism. As to the major: I do not admit it at all, since this alleged deduction from a part to the whole (from intelligent creatures to all creatures) presupposes tacitly and without proof that creatures destitute of reason cannot be compared with or taken into account with those which possess it. But why should it not be that the surplus of good in the non-intelligent creatures which fill the world compensate for and even incomparably exceed the surplus of evil in rational creatures? True, the value of the latter is greater; but by way of compensation the others are incomparably the more numerous; and it may be that the proportion of number and quantity exceeds that of quality and value.

As to the minor: I cannot admit this either, namely that there is more evil than good in intelligent creatures. One need not even concede that there is more evil than good in intelligent creatures. There is no need even to admit that there is more evil than good in the human race, since it is possible—and in fact very probable—that the glory and perfection of the blessed is incomparably greater than the misery and imperfection of the damned and that here the excellence of the total good in the smaller number outweighs the total evil in the greater number. The blessed draw near to the Divinity by means of a Divine Mediator, as far as can belong to these creatures, and make such progress in good as is impossible for the damned to make in evil, however close they may get to the nature of demons. God is infinite and the devil is limited; the good can and does go on *ad infinitum*, while evil is bounded. It is therefore possible and indeed is probable that in the comparison between the blessed and the damned the opposite of what I said might occur regarding the comparison between intelligent and non-intelligent creatures takes place: namely, it is possible that in the comparison between the happy and the unhappy the proportion in degree exceeds the numerical proportion—while in the comparison between intelligent and non-intelligent creatures the numerical proportion exceeds that of value. One has the right to assume that a thing is possible so long as its impossibility is not proved; and indeed what I have put forward here goes beyond mere assumption.

But secondly, should one concede that there is more evil than good in the human race, one still has good grounds for not admitting that there is more evil than good in all intelligent creatures. For there is an inconceivable number of spirits and perhaps other rational beings as well. And an opponent could not prove that in the whole City of God, composed as much of spirits as of rational animals without number and of an infinity of different kinds, evil exceeds good. And although in order to answer an objection there is no need to prove that a thing is, when its mere possibility suffices, yet in this work I have not failed to show that it is a consequence of the supreme perfection of the Sovereign of the universe that the kingdom of God should be the most perfect of all states or governments possible, and that consequently what little of evil there is is required for the consummation of the vast good to be found there.

III. *Objection*. If it is always impossible not to sin, it is always unjust to punish.

Now it is always impossible not to sin; or in other words all sin is necessary.

Therefore it is always unjust to punish. The minor of this syllogism is proved thus:

1. *Prosyllogism*. All that is predetermined is necessary.

Every event is predetermined.

Therefore every sin (and consequently sin also) is predetermined.

And this second minor is proved thus:

2. *Prosyllogism*. That which is future, that which is foreseen, that which is involved in causes, is predetermined.

Every event is of this sort.

Therefore every event is predetermined.

Answer. I admit in a certain sense the conclusion of the second prosyllogism, which is the minor premiss of the first. But I shall deny the major of the first prosyllogism, namely that everything predetermined is necessary, taking 'necessity'—say the necessity to sin or the impossibility of not sinning or of not doing some action—in the sense which is relevant here, that is, as an essential and absolute necessity which destroys the morality of an action and the justice of punishments. For if anyone meant a different necessity or impossibility (that is, a mere moral or hypothetical necessity—this will be explained shortly), it is clear that we would deny him the major given in the objection. I might content myself with this answer and ask for the proof of the proposition denied; but again I wish to explain my procedure in the present work in order better to elucidate the matter and to throw more light on the whole topic, by explaining what the necessity is which must be rejected and what the determination is which must be allowed. That *necessity* which is in conflict with morality and which ought to be rejected and which would make punishment useless is an insuperable necessity which would make all opposition vain, even if we should wish with all our heart to avoid the necessary action and should make all possible efforts to that end. Now it is obvious that this is not applicable to voluntary actions, for we would not do them did we not choose to. Their prevision and predetermination are not absolute, but presuppose will: if it is certain that we shall perform the actions it is no less certain that we shall choose to perform them. These voluntary actions and their consequences will not take place *no matter what* we do or whether we desire them or not, but *because of* what we shall do and of what we shall choose to do, which leads to them. And this is involved in prevision and predetermination and forms their ground. And the necessity of such an event is called conditional or hypothetical, or the necessity of consequence, because it presupposes the will and other requisite conditions; whereas the necessity which destroys morality and makes punishment unjust and reward useless is found in those things which will be whatever we may do and whatever we may wish to do: in a word, it exists in that which is essential. This is what is called absolute necessity. Thus it is pointless, as regards what is absolutely necessary, to issue prohibitions or commands, to propose penalties or prizes, to praise or blame: for it will happen none the less.[1] On the other hand, as regards voluntary actions and that which

[1] A similar view of the distinction between morally free and other acts is described above (p. 41). But Kant (see p. 271) was later to argue that the distinction is merely juridical and that morality presupposes a stronger sense of 'freedom', in which moral acts are not predetermined by prior causes. There therefore seems to be a conflict between the presupposition of scientific enquiry that every event has a cause and moral thinking.

depends upon them, precepts armed with the power of punishment and reward are frequently useful and are included in the train of causes that make an action happen. It is for this reason that not only pains and effort but also prayer are effective, God having had even these prayers in view before he arranged things and having made proper allowance for them. This is why the precept *Ora et labora* ('Pray and work') still holds good. Thus not only those who (under empty pretext that events are necessary) maintain that the pains which affairs demand may be neglected, but also those who argue against prayer fall into what the Ancients even then called the *lazy fallacy*. Thus the predetermination of events by causes is precisely that which contributes to morality and does not destroy it, and the causes incline the will without compelling it. For this reason the determination in question is not a necessitation: it is certain (to someone who is omniscient) that the effect will follow this inclination of the will, but the effect does not follow by necessary consequence, i.e. in such a way that the contrary implies self-contradiction. It is by such an internal inclination, also, that the will is determined, without there being any necessity. Suppose that one has the greatest possible craving (for example, a great thirst), it will be conceded that the soul can find some reason for resisting it—even if it is only that of displaying its power. Thus although one may never be in a perfect state of equilibrium and there may always be a preponderance of inclination for the action taken, nevertheless this preponderance never renders the decision taken absolutely unnecessary.

IV. *Objection*. Whoever can prevent sin in another and does not do so but instead contributes to it although he is well aware of it is accessory to it.

God can prevent the sin of intelligent creatures; but he does not do so and instead contributes to it by his concurrence and by the opportunities he creates although he is well aware of it.

Therefore God is accessory to sin.

Answer. I deny the major premiss of this syllogism. For it is possible that one could prevent sin and yet ought not to, because one could not do so without committing a sin, or (as regards God) without acting in an unreasonable manner. I have given examples of this and applied them to God.[1] It may also be that we contribute to evil and even open the way for it in doing some things that we are obliged to do. And when one does one's duty or (in the case of God) when, after full deliberation, one performs that which reason demands, one is not responsible for the consequences, even when one foresees them. We do not desire these evils, but we are willing to allow them for the sake of a greater good, which we cannot reasonably help preferring to other considerations. This is a case of *consequent*

[1] See *Theodicy*, ii. §§158–67.

will, resulting from acts of *antecedent* will, in which one wills the good. I know that some people, in talking of the antecedent and consequent will of God, have meant by the antecedent that which wills that all men should be saved and by the consequent that which wills, in consequence of persistent sin, that some should be damned. But these are merely examples of a more general idea, and it may be said for the same reason that God, by his antecedent will, wills that men should not sin and that, by his consequent, or final and decreeing, will (that which is always followed by its effect) he wills to allow them to sin, this permission being a result of superior reasons. One is indeed justified in asserting in general that the antecedent will of God tends to the production of good and the prevention of evil, each taken in itself and as if in isolation (*particulariter et secundum quid*: Thomas Aquinas, I, *qu.* 19, *art.* 6[1]), according to the measure of the degree of each good and each evil; but that the consequent, or final and total, will tends towards the production of as many goods as can be put together, whose combination becomes thereby determined, and involves also the permission of some evils and the exclusion of some goods, as is demanded by the best possible plan of the universe. Arminius, in his *Anti-Perkinsus*,[2] has explained very well that the will of God can be called consequent not merely in relation to the action of the creature considered beforehand in the divine understanding, but also in relation to other prior acts of divine will. But the consideration of the passage cited from Thomas Aquinas and that from Scotus (I, *dist.* 46, *qu.* 11)[3] is enough to show that they make this distinction as I have made it here. Nevertheless if anybody objects to this use of the terms, he can substitute 'deliberating will' for 'antecedent will' and 'final' or 'decreeing' for 'consequent'. For I do not want to dispute about words.

V. *Objection*. Whoever produces all that is real in a thing is its cause.
God produces all that is real in sin.
Therefore God is the cause of sin.

Answer. I might content myself with denying the major premiss or the minor, since the term 'real' admits of interpretations which would make these propositions false. But in order to give a clearer explanation, I shall make a distinction. 'Real' refers either to that which is positive only or it

[1] The reference given is to the *Summa Theologica*.

[2] Jacobus Arminius (1560–1609), Dutch Reformed Church theologian, was an opponent of Calvinism, arguing that divine omnipotence is compatible with human free will. His *Anti-Perkinsus* (1598) was a reply to the work on predestination published by William Perkins (1558–1602), the Cambridge theologian and Puritan, in that year.

[3] Duns Scotus (*c.* 1264–1308), the Scottish theologian and philosopher, differed from St Thomas Aquinas principally over the concept of natural law, which he held to flow from God's will and therefore to be capable of change. See C. R. S. Harris, *Duns Scotus* (2 vols., Oxford, 1927).

includes also privative beings:[1] in the former case, I deny the major and concede the minor; in the latter case, I do the opposite. I might have limited myself to this but I have chosen to go further and explain the reason for this distinction. I have been very glad therefore to point out that every purely positive or absolute reality is a perfection, and that imperfection comes from limitation, i.e. from the privative—for to limit is to bar progress or the greatest possible progress. Now God is the cause of all perfections and so of all realities when they are considered as purely positive. But limitations or privations result from the original imperfection of creatures, which restricts their receptivity. It is with them as with a loaded boat, which the river carries along at a higher or lower speed in proportion to the weight it bears: thus its speed comes from the river, but the retardation which restricts the speed comes from the load. Thus in the *Theodicy* we have shown how the creature, in causing sin, is a deficient cause; how errors and evil inclinations spring from privation; and how privation is effective in an accidental way;[2] and I have justified the view of St Augustine (*lib.* I, *ad Simpl.*, *qu.* 2), who explains, for instance, how God makes the soul obdurate, not by giving it something evil, but because the effect of the good he imprints on it is restricted by the soul's resistance, so that he does not give it all the good needed to overcome its evil. *Nec* (he says) *ab illo erogatur aliquid quo homo fit deterior, sed tantum quo fit melior non erogatur.*[3] But if God had wished to do more, he would have had to make either other natures for creatures or fresh miracles to change their natures, things which the best plan could not allow. It is as if the current of the river needs to be faster than the slope admits or that boats should be loaded less heavily if they had to be made to move at a greater speed. So the limitation or original imperfection of creatures requires that even the best plan of the universe cannot admit more good and cannot be free of certain evils—these, though, being of such a kind as to conduce to a greater good. There are some disorders in the parts which marvellously enhance the beauty of the whole—just as some dissonances, appropriately used, render harmony more beautiful. But this depends on what has already been said in answer to the first objection.

VI. *Objection.* Whoever punishes those who have done as well as it is in their power to do is unjust.

God does this.

[1] *Privation* is, in Aristotelian and medieval philosophy, the absence of what is natural (e.g., blindness is a privation of sight): one solution, therefore, of the problem of evil is to declare that evil has no positive reality, but is merely the absence of good. See p. 465.

[2] For the technical notion of an accident, see n. 1 to p. 75.

[3] 'It is not that anything is bestowed by him whereby a man becomes worse, but only that something whereby he becomes better is not bestowed.'

Therefore God is unjust.

Answer. I deny the minor premiss of this argument. And I believe that God always gives sufficient help and grace to those who have a good will, that is, to those who do not reject this grace by a new sin. Thus I do not concede the damnation of infants who have died without baptism or outside the Church, nor the damnation of adults who have acted in accordance with the light which God has given them. And I believe that if *anyone has followed the light he has been given,* he will assuredly receive greater light when he needs it, as the late Herr Hülsemann,[1] well known as a profound theologian of Leipzig, has somewhere remarked; and if such a man had failed to receive light during his life, he will at least receive it in the hour of death.

VII. *Objection.* Whoever gives only to some and not to all the means of producing effectively in them a good will and final saving faith has not sufficient goodness.

God does so.

Therefore God has not sufficient goodness.

Answer. I deny the major premiss. It is true that God could overcome the greatest resistance in the human heart, and indeed he sometimes does so—either by inner grace or by outer circumstances that can have a great effect upon souls; but he does not always do this. What is the cause of this distinction, some may ask, and why does his goodness appear limited? The reason is that it would not have been, as I have already pointed out in my answer to the first objection, proper always to act in an extraordinary manner and to upset the connexion of things. The reasons for this connexion, by which one person is placed in more favourable circumstances than is another, are concealed in the depths of God's wisdom: they depend upon the universal harmony. The best plan of the universe, which God could not fail to choose, required it. One concludes thus from the event itself: since God made the world, it was not possible to do better. Such management, far from being contrary to goodness, has rather sprung from supreme goodness itself. This objection with its solution might have been inferred from what was said regarding the first objection, but it seemed advantageous to point it out separately.

VIII. *Objection.* Whoever cannot fail to choose the best is not free.

God cannot fail to choose the best.

Therefore God is not free.

I deny the major premiss of this argument. Rather it is true freedom, and the most perfect, to be able to use one's free will for the best and always to exercise this power without being diverted either by external

[1] (1602–61), Lutheran theologian.

force or by inward passions—the first of which causes slavery of the body, the second slavery of the soul. There is nothing less servile and more in accord with the highest degree of freedom than to be always attracted towards the good, and always by one's own inclination, without either constraint or displeasure. And to object that God therefore needed external things is only a piece of sophistry. He created them freely; but when he had set before him an end, that of exercising his goodness, his wisdom determined him to choose the means best fitted for attaining this end. To call this a *need* is to take the term in an unusual sense, one which frees it of all imperfection, just as when we speak of the wrath of God.

Seneca[1] says somewhere that God commanded only once but that he obeys always, because he obeys laws which he willed to prescribe to himself: *semel jussit, semper paret*. But he might better have said that God always commands and that he is always obeyed; for in willing he always follows the tendency of his own nature, and all other things always follow his will. And as this will is always the same one cannot say that he obeys only that will which he previously had. Nevertheless, though his will is always infallible and always tends towards the best, the evil or the lesser good which he rejects does not cease to be possible in itself; or else the necessity of the good would be geometrical (so to speak) or metaphysical and quite absolute: the contingency of things would be destroyed and there would be no choice.[2] But necessity of this sort, which does not destroy the possibility of the contrary, has the name only by analogy: it becomes effective not through the pure essence of things, but through that which is outside them and above them, that is, by the will of God. This necessity is called moral, because, for the wise, what is necessary and what ought to be are equivalent; and when it always has its effect, as it really has in the perfectly wise one, that is, in God, it may be said to be a happy necessity. The nearer creatures get to it the nearer they get to perfect happiness. Also, this kind of necessity is not that which we try to avoid and which destroys morality, rewards and praise. For that which it brings to pass does not occur whatever one may do and whatever one may will, but because one desires it. And a will such that it is natural for it to choose well deserves praise so much the more; moreover it carries its own reward with it—supreme happiness. And as this constitution of the divine nature gives complete satisfaction to the one who possesses it, it is similarly the best and the most desirable for the creatures who are all dependent upon God. If the will of God did not have as its rule the principle of the best, it would

[1] Roman writer (*c.* 3 BC–AD 65), sometime tutor and adviser to Nero. An eclectic Stoic in philosophy, his elevated tone and trust in Providence caused him to be mistaken for a Christian in the early Middle Ages.

[2] For L.'s view on 'the contingency of things', see p. 141.

either tend towards evil, which would be the worst case, or else it would in some way be indifferent to good and evil and would be guided by chance: but a will which would permit itself to be guided always by chance would not be any better for the government of the universe than the chance concourse of particles, without there being any divinity there. And even if God were to abandon himself to chance only in some cases and in a certain way (as he would do if he did not always work entirely for the best and if he were capable of preferring a lesser good to a greater one, that is, an evil to a good—for that which prevents a greater good is evil), he would be just as imperfect as the object of his choice. He would not deserve absolute confidence; he would act without reason in such a case; and the government of the world would be like certain games, equally divided between reason and chance. All this proves that the objection here made against the choice of the best perverts the notions of *free* and *necessary*, and represents the best to us even as evil: but this is either malicious or absurd.

II

BERKELEY

on THE EXISTENCE OF GOD

Biographical Note Born in 1685, near Kilkenny in Ireland, and educated at Kilkenny College and at Trinity College Dublin, taking his degree in 1704. Elected a Fellow of Trinity College Dublin in 1707, and ordained that year. In 1709 he published his first major work, *An Essay towards a New Theory of Vision*, and in 1710 the *Treatise concerning the Principles of Human Knowledge*. Between 1713 and 1721 he was in England and abroad. In 1724 he was made Dean of Derry, and for the next few years devoted himself to the project of setting up a missionary college in Bermuda for the evangelization of America. In 1728 he set sail for America in this connection, and during his time in Rhode Island composed *Alciphron*, published in 1732. He was made Bishop of Cloyne in 1734. In 1744 appeared his strange work, *Siris*. Moved to Oxford in 1752, and died there in 1753.

Principal works: those mentioned above, together with *Dialogues between Hylas and Philonous* (1713).

Philosophical Note Berkeley's metaphysical position can best be understood by recalling Locke's views on substance and on primary and secondary qualities (see above, p. 130). Through his insistence that knowledge must come through sense-experience, Locke was left in the position where, in line with common sense, he affirmed the existence of an unknown something as underlying ideas given in perception, and yet where, in the nature of the case, no sense-experience of this underlying substratum could be had. B. takes Locke's empiricism a stage further, by affirming that matter must be analysed entirely in terms of sense-experience, so that, for matter, *esse est percipi*—to be is to be perceived. Likewise, he rejected Locke's distinction between primary and secondary qualities, the former being, according to B., as mind-dependent as the latter. Thus, for B., the concept of a mathematically describable material world independent of perceptions must be abandoned. Nevertheless, such radical empiricism creates a major problem. Do material objects (given this new analysis) continue to exist if no one is actually perceiving them? B. attempted to resolve this difficulty by introducing God as the perpetual perceiver, who through his continued existence and perception guarantees the existence of otherwise unperceived objects. Further, we notice that one perception suggests another: for example, when I see a tree I expect that if I go close enough to it I shall have certain tactile sensations—though there is no *a priori* reason why the two sorts of perception should go together—so that perception is like a language, where one sign suggests another arbitrarily linked to it (e.g. the sound 'horse' suggests to us the appearance of such an animal). Nature, then, is a system of symbolism. But since there is no *a priori* reason why it should be thus systematic, B. sees in this fact evidence that nature as a system has been ordered by God. Hence, God speaks to us through perception in a sort of language. Moreover, we notice that we do not (normally) control our perceptions: we ourselves do not create the phenomena which we perceive. This indicates that there is a Power other than ourselves in the universe. But since matter does not exist by itself, as it were, but is dependent upon a perceiving spirit, phenomena must depend upon a Power whose nature is Spirit. In such ways, B. believed that a radical and consistent analysis of knowledge in terms of experience must inevitably lead to theism.

The following dialogue illustrates B.'s conception of perception as a divinely ordered language.

Bibliographical Note A new critical edition of B.'s works, ed. A. A. Luce and T. E. Jessop, has been published in 9 vols. (London, 1948–56). Useful selections are those by T. E. Jessop (London, 1952), A. C. Fraser (Oxford, 6th edn, 1910), and A. D. Lindsay (Everyman, London, 1910). In *British Empirical Philosophers*, ed. A. J. Ayer and R. Winch (London, 1952), some selections from B. are to be found. Useful are A. A. Luce, *Berkeley's Immaterialism* (London, 1945) and *Life of George Berkeley* (1949). G. J. Warnock, *Berkeley* (London, Pelican, 1953) is a stimulating introduction, and E. A. Sillem, *George Berkeley and the Proofs for the Existence of God* (London, 1949) should be consulted.

THE EXISTENCE OF GOD

Alciphron, or the Minute Philosopher, 4th Dialogue

DIVINE VISUAL LANGUAGE

1. Early the next morning, as I looked out of my window, I saw Alciphron walking in the garden with all the signs of a man in deep thought. Upon which I went down to him.

Alciphron, said I, this early and profound meditation puts me in no small fright.

How so?

Because I should be sorry to be convinced there was no God. The thought of *anarchy in Nature* is to me more shocking than in civil life: inasmuch as natural concerns are more important than civil, and the basis of all others.

I grant, replied *Alciphron*, that some inconvenience may possibly follow from disproving a God: but as to what you say of fright and shocking, all that is nothing but mere prejudice. Men frame an idea or chimera in their own minds, and then fall down and worship it. Notions govern mankind: but of all notions that of God's governing the world has taken the deepest root and spread the farthest: it is therefore in philosophy an heroical achievement to dispossess this imaginary monarch of his government, and banish all those fears and spectres which the light of reason can alone dispel:

> Non radii solis, non lucida tela diei
> Discutiunt, sed naturae species ratioque.[1]

My part, said I, shall be to stand by, as I have hitherto done, and take notes of all that passes during this memorable event; while a minute philosopher,[2] not six feet high, attempts to dethrone the monarch of the universe.

Alas! replied *Alciphron*, arguments are not to be measured by feet and inches. One man may see more than a million; and a short argument, managed by a free-thinker, may be sufficient to overthrow the most gigantic chimera.

As we were engaged in this discourse, Crito and Euphranor joined us.

I find you have been beforehand with us today, said *Crito* to Alciphron, and taken the advantage of solitude and early hours, while Euphranor and I were asleep in our beds. We may, therefore, expect to see Atheism placed in the best light, and supported by the strongest arguments.

2. *Alc.* The being of a God is a subject upon which there has been a world of commonplace, which it is needless to repeat. Give me leave therefore to lay down certain rules and limitations, in order to shorten our present conference. For, as the end of debating is to persuade, all those things foreign to this end should be left out of our debate.

First then, let me tell you I am not to be persuaded by metaphysical arguments; such, for instance, as are drawn from the idea of an all-perfect being,[3] or from the absurdity of an infinite progression of causes.[4] This sort of arguments I have always found dry and jejune: and, as they are not suited to my way of thinking they may perhaps puzzle, but never will convince me. Secondly, I am not to be persuaded by the authority either of past or present ages, of mankind in general, or of particular wise men which passes for little or nothing with a man of sound argument and free thought. Thirdly, all proofs drawn from utility or convenience are foreign to the purpose. They may prove indeed the usefulness of the

[1] Lucretius, *De Rerum Natura*, vs. 147, 148. 'Neither the rays of the sun nor the bright shafts of the day dispel (sc. such gloomy terrors), but the law-like aspect of nature.' Lucretius (*c.* 99–*c.* 55 BC) expounded Epicurus' (see p. 227) rationalistic system.

[2] 'Minute philosophers': a phrase used for agnostic empiricists.

[3] E.g. the argument used by Anselm and Descartes: see above, p. 121.

[4] That is, the Cosmological Argument: see above, p. 130.

notion, but not the existence of the thing. Whatever legislators or statesmen may think, truth and convenience are very different things to the rigorous eye of a philosopher.

And now, that I may not seem partial, I will limit myself also not to object, in the first place, from anything that may seem irregular or unaccountable in the works of nature, against a cause of infinite power and wisdom; because I already know the answer you will make, to wit, that no one can judge of the symmetry and use of the parts of an infinite machine, which are all relative to each other, and to the whole, without being able to comprehend the entire machine, or the whole universe. And, in the second place, I shall engage myself not to object against the justice and providence of a Supreme Being from the evil that befalls good men, and the prosperity which is often the portion of wicked men in the life; because, I know that, instead of admitting this to be an objection against a Deity, you would make it an argument for a future state, in which there shall be such a retribution of rewards and punishments as may vindicate the Divine attributes, and set all things right in the end. Now, these answers, though they should be admitted for good ones, are in truth no proofs of the being of God, but only solutions of certain difficulties which might be objected, supposing it already proved by proper arguments. Thus much I thought fit to premise, in order to save time and trouble both to you and myself.

Cri. I think that as the proper end of our conference ought to be supposed the discovery and defence of truth, so truth may be justified, not only by persuading its adversaries, but, where that cannot be done, by shewing them to be unreasonable. Arguments, therefore, which carry light have their effect, even against an opponent who shuts his eyes, because they shew him to be obstinate and prejudiced. Besides, this distinction between arguments that puzzle and that convince is least of all observed by minute philosophers, and need not therefore be observed by others in their favour.—But perhaps, Euphranor may be willing to encounter you on your own terms, in which case I have nothing further to say.

3. *Euph.* Alciphron acts like a skilful general, who is bent upon gaining the advantage of the ground, and alluring the enemy out of their trenches. We who believe a God, are entrenched within tradition, custom, authority and law. And, nevertheless, instead of attempting to force us, he proposes that we should voluntarily abandon these intrenchments and make the attack; when we may act on the defensive with much security and ease, leaving him the trouble to dispossess us of what we need not resign. Those reasons (continued he, addressing himself to Alciphron) which you have

mustered up in this morning's meditation, if they do not weaken, must establish our belief of a God; for the utmost is to be expected from so great a master in his profession, when he set his strength to a point.

Alc. I hold the confused notion of a Deity, or some invisible power, to be of all prejudices the most unconquerable. When half a dozen ingenious men are got together over a glass of wine, by a cheerful fire, in a room well-lighted, we banish with ease all the spectres of fancy and education, and are very clear in our decisions. But, as I was taking a solitary walk before it was broad daylight in yonder grove, methought the point was not quite so clear; nor could I readily recollect the force of those arguments which used to appear so conclusive at other times. I had I know not what awe upon my mind, and seemed haunted by a sort of panic, which I cannot otherwise account for than by supposing it the effect of prejudice: for, you must know, that I, like the rest of the world, was once upon a time catechized and tutored into the belief of a God or Spirit. There is no surer mark of prejudice than the believing a thing without reason. What necessity then can there be that I should set myself the difficult task of proving a negative, when it is sufficient to observe that there is no proof of the affirmative, and that the admitting it without proof is unreasonable? Prove therefore your opinion; or, if you cannot, you may indeed remain in possession of it, but you will only be possessed of a prejudice.

Euph. O Alciphron, to content you *we* must prove, it seems, and we must prove upon your own terms. But, in the first place, let us see what sort of proof you expect.

Alc. Perhaps I may not expect it, but I will tell you what sort of proof I would have: and that is, in short—such proof as every man of sense requires of a matter of fact, or the existence of any other particular thing. For instance, should a man ask why I believe there is a king of Great Britain? I might answer—Because I had seen him. Or a king of Spain? Because I had seen those who saw him. But as for this King of kings, I neither saw him myself, or any one else that ever did see him. Surely, if there be such a thing as God, it is very strange that he should leave himself without a witness; that men should still dispute his being; and that there should be no one evident, sensible, plain proof of it, without recourse to philosophy or metaphysics. A matter of fact is not to be proved by notions, but by facts.[1] This is clear and full to the point. You see what I would be at. Upon these principles I defy superstition.

Euph. You believe then as far as you can see?

Alc. That is my rule of faith.

[1] See also Hume, *Inquiry*, IV, pt I. See also p. 58.

Euph. How! will you not believe the existence of things which you hear, unless you also see them?

Alc. I will not say so neither. When I insisted on *seeing*, I would be understood to mean perceiving in general. Outward objects make very different impressions upon the animal spirits, all of which are comprised under the common name of *sense*. And whatever we can perceive by *any* sense we may be sure of.

4. *Euph.* What! do you believe then that there are such things as animal spirits?

Alc. Doubtless.

Euph. By what sense do you perceive them?

Alc. I do not perceive them immediately by any of my senses. I am nevertheless persuaded of their existence, because I can collect it from their effects and operations. They are the messengers which, running to and fro in the nerves, preserve a communication between the soul and outward objects.

Euph. You admit then the being of a soul?

Alc. Provided I do not admit an immaterial substance, I see no inconvenience in admitting there may be such a thing as a soul. And this may be no more than a thin fine texture of subtle parts or spirits residing in the brain.

Euph. I do not ask about its nature. I only ask whether you admit that there is a principle of thought and action, and whether *it* be perceivable by sense.

Alc. I grant that there is such a principle, and that it is not the object of sense itself, but inferred from appearances which are perceived by sense.

Euph. If I understand you rightly, from animal functions and motions you infer the existence of animal spirits, and from reasonable acts you infer the existence of a reasonable soul. Is it not so?

Alc. It is.

Euph. It should seem, therefore, that the being of things imperceptible to sense may be collected from effects and signs, or sensible tokens.

Alc. It may.

Euph. Tell me, Alciphron, is not the soul that which makes the principal distinction between a real person and a shadow, a living man and a carcass?

Alc. I grant it is.

Euph. I cannot, therefore, know that *you*, for instance, are a distinct thinking individual, or a real living man, by surer or other signs than those from which it can be inferred that you have a soul.

Alc. You cannot.

Euph. Pray tell me, are not all acts immediately and properly perceived by sense reducible to motion?

Alc. They are.

Euph. From motions, therefore, you infer a mover or cause; and from reasonable motions (or such as appear calculated for a reasonable end) a rational cause, soul or spirit?

Alc. Even so.

5. *Euph.* The soul of man actuates but a small body, an insignificant particle, in respect of the great masses of Nature, the elements, and heavenly bodies, and System of the World. And the wisdom that appears in those motions which are the effect of human reason is incomparably less than that which discovers itself in the structure and use of organized natural bodies, animal or vegetable. A man with his hand can make no machine so admirable as the hand itself; nor can any of those motions by which we trace out human reason approach the skill and contrivance of those wonderful motions of the heart, and brain, and other vital parts, which do not depend on the will of man.

Alc. All this is true.

Euph. Doth it not follow, then, that from natural motions, independent of man's will, may be inferred both power and wisdom incomparably greater than that of the human soul?

Alc. It should seem so.

Euph. Further, is there not in natural productions and effects a visible unity of counsel and design? Are not the rules fixed and immovable? Do not the same laws of motion obtain throughout? The same in China and here, the same two thousand years ago and at this day?

Alc. All this I do not deny.

Euph. Is there not also a connexion or relation between animals and vegetables, between both and the elements, between the elements and heavenly bodies; so that, from their mutual respects, influences, subordinations, and uses they may be collected to be parts of one whole, conspiring to one and the same end, and fulfilling the same design?

Alc. Supposing all this to be true.

Euph. Will it not then follow that this vastly great, or infinite, power and wisdom must be supposed in one and the same Agent, Spirit, or Mind; and that we have at least as clear, full, and immediate certainty of the being of this infinitely wise and powerful Spirit, as of any one human soul whatsoever besides our own?

Alc. Let me consider; I suspect we proceed too hastily. What! Do you pretend you can have the same assurance of the being of a God that you can have of mine, whom you actually *see* before you and talk to you?

Euph. The very same, if not greater.

Alc. How do you make this appear?

Euph. By the person Alciphron is meant an individual thinking thing, and not the hair, skin, or visible surface, or any part of the outward form, colour, or shape of Alciphron.

Alc. This I grant.

Euph. And, in granting this, you grant that, in a strict sense, I do not see Alciphron, i.e. that individual thinking thing, but only such visible signs and tokens as suggest and infer the being of that invisible thinking principle or soul. Even so, in the self-same manner, it seems to me that, though I cannot with eyes of flesh behold the invisible God, yet I do in the strictest sense behold and perceive by all my senses such signs and tokens, such effects and operations, as suggest, indicate, and demonstrate an invisible God—as certainly, and with the same evidence, at least, as any other signs, perceived by sense, do suggest to me the existence of your soul, spirit, or thinking principle; which I am convinced of only by a few signs or effects, and the motions of one small organized body: whereas I do at all times and in all places perceive sensible signs which evince the being of God. The point, therefore, doubted or denied by you at the beginning, now seems manifestly to follow from the premises. Throughout this whole enquiry, have we not considered every step with care, and made not the least advance without clear evidence? You and I examined and assented singly to each foregoing proposition: what shall we do then with the conclusion? For my part, if you do not help me out, I find myself under an absolute necessity of admitting it for true. You must therefore be content henceforward to bear the blame, if I live and die in the belief of a God.

6. *Alc.* It must be confessed, I do not readily find an answer. There seems to be some foundation for what you say. But, on the other hand, if the point was so clear as you pretend, I cannot conceive how so many sagacious men of our sect should be so much in the dark as not to know or believe one syllable of it.

Euph. O Alciphron, it is not our present business to account for the oversights, or vindicate the honour, of those great men the free-thinkers, when their very existence is in danger of being called in question.

Alc. How so?

Euph. Be pleased to recollect the concessions you have made, and then shew me, if the arguments for a Deity be not conclusive, by what better arguments you can prove the existence of that thinking thing which in strictness constitutes the free-thinker.

As soon as Euphranor had uttered these words, Alciphron stopped short, and stood in a posture of meditation, while the rest of us continued our walk and took two or three turns, after which he joined us again with a smiling countenance, like one who had made some discovery.

I have found, said he, what may clear up the point in dispute, and give Euphranor entire satisfaction; I would say an argument which will prove the existence of a free-thinker, the like whereof cannot be applied to prove the existence of God. You must know then that your notion of our perceiving the existence of God, as certainly and immediately as we do that of a human person, I could by no means digest; though I must own it puzzled me, till I had considered the matter. At the first methought a particular structure, shape, or motion was a most certain proof of a thinking reasonable soul. But a little attention satisfied me that these things have no necessary connexion with reason, knowledge, and wisdom; and that, allowing them to be certain proofs of a living soul, they cannot be so of a thinking and reasonable one. Upon second thoughts, therefore, and a minute examination of this point, I have found that nothing so much convinces me of the existence of another person as *his speaking to me*. It is my hearing you talk that, in strict and philosophical truth, is to me the best argument for your being. And this is a peculiar argument, inapplicable to your purpose; for, you will not, I suppose pretend that God speaks to man in the same clear and sensible manner as one man does to another?

7. *Euph.* How! is then the impression of sound so much more evident than that of other senses? Or, if it be, is the voice of man louder than that of thunder?

Alc. Alas! you mistake the point. What I mean is not the sound of speech merely as such, but the arbitrary use of sensible signs, which have no similitude or necessary connexion with the things signified;—so as by the apposite management of them to suggest and exhibit to my mind an endless variety of things, differing in nature, time, and place; thereby informing me, entertaining me, and directing me how to act, not only with regard to things near and present, but also with regard to things distant and future. No matter whether these signs are pronounced or written; whether they enter by the eye or ear; they have the same use, and are equally proofs of an intelligent, thinking designing cause.

Euph. But what if it should appear that God really speaks to man; would this content you?

Alc. I am for admitting no inward speech, no holy instincts, or suggestions of light or spirit. All that, you must know, passes with men of sense for nothing. If you do not make it plain to me that God speaks to men by outward sensible signs, of such sort and in such manner as I have defined, you do nothing.

Euph. But if it shall appear plainly that God speaks to men by the intervention and use of arbitrary, outward, sensible signs, having no resemblance or necessary connexion with the things they stand for and suggest: if it shall appear that, by innumerable combinations of these signs, an endless variety of things is discovered and made known to us; and that we are thereby instructed or informed in their different natures; that we are taught and admonished what to shun, and what to pursue; and are directed how to regulate our motions, and how to act with respect to things distant from us, as well in time as place,—will this content you?

Alc. It is the very thing I would have you make out; for therein consists the force and use and nature of language.

Euph. Look, Alciphron, do you not see the castle upon yonder hill?

Alc. I do.

Euph. Is it not at a great distance from you?

Alc. It is.

Euph. Tell me, Alciphron, is not distance a line turned endwise to the eye?

Alc. Doubtless.

Euph. And can a line, in that situation, project more than one single point on the bottom of the eye?

Alc. It cannot.

Euph. Therefore the appearance of a long and of a short distance is of the same magnitude, or rather of no magnitude at all—being in all cases one single point.

Alc. It seems so.

Euph. Should it not follow from hence that distance is not immediately perceived by the eye?

Alc. It should.

Euph. Must it not then be perceived by the mediation of some other thing?

Alc. It must.

Euph. To discover what this is, let us examine what alteration there may be in the appearance of the same object placed at different distances from the eye. Now, I find by experience that when an object is removed still farther and farther off in a direct line from the eye, its visible appearance still grows lesser and fainter; and this change of appearance, being proportional and universal, seems to me to be that by which we apprehend the various degrees of distance.

Alc. I have nothing to object to this.

Euph. But littleness or faintness, in their own nature, seem to have no necessary connexion with greater length of distance?

Alc. I admit this to be true.

Euph. Will it not follow then that they could never suggest it but from experience?

Alc. It will.

Euph. That is to say—we perceive distance, not immediately, but by mediation of a sign, which has no likeness to it, or necessary connexion with it, but only suggests it from repeated experience—as words do things.

Alc. Hold, Euphranor: now I think of it, the writers in optics tell us of an angle made by the two optic axes, where they meet in the visible point or object; which angle, the obtuser it is the nearer it shows the object to be, and by how much the acuter, by so much the farther off; and this from a necessary demonstrable connexion.

Euph. The mind then finds out the distance of things by geometry?

Alc. It does.

Euph. Should it not follow, therefore, that nobody could see but those who had learned geometry, and knew something of lines and angles?

Alc. There is a sort of natural geometry which is got without learning.

Euph. Pray inform me, Alciphron, in order to frame a proof of any kind, or deduce one point from another, is it not necessary that I perceive the connexion of the terms in the premises, and the connexion of the premises with the conclusion; and in general to know one thing by means of another, must I not first know that other thing? When I perceive your meaning by your words, must I not first perceive the words themselves? And must I not know the premises before I infer the conclusion?

Alc. All this is true.

Euph. Whoever, therefore, collects a nearer distance from a wider angle, or a farther distance from an acuter angle, must first perceive the angles themselves. And he who does not perceive those angles can infer nothing from them. Is it so or not?

Alc. It is as you say.

Euph. Ask now the first man you meet whether he perceives or knows anything of those optic angles? Or whether he ever thinks about them, or makes any inferences from them, either by natural or artificial geometry? What answer do you think he would make?

Alc. To speak the truth, I believe his answer would be that he knew nothing of these matters.

Euph. It cannot therefore be that men judge of distance by angles: nor consequently can there be any force in the argument you drew from thence, to prove that distance is perceived by means of something that has a necessary connexion with it.

Alc. I agree with you.

Euph. To me it seems that a man may know whether he perceives a thing or no; and if he perceives it, whether it be immediately or mediately: and if mediately, whether by means of something like or unlike, necessarily or arbitrarily connected with it.

Alc. It seems so.

Euph. And is it not certain that distance is perceived only by experience, if it be neither perceived immediately by itself, nor by means of any image, nor of any lines and angles which are like it, or have a necessary connexion with it?

Alc. It is.

Euph. Does it not seem to follow from what has been said and allowed by you that before all experience a man would not imagine the things he saw were at any distance from him?

Alc. How? Let me see.

Euph. The littleness or faintness in appearance, or any other idea or sensation not necessarily connected with or resembling distance, can no more suggest different degrees of distance, or any distance at all, to the mind which has not experienced a connexion of the things signifying and signified, than words can suggest notions before a man has learned the language.

Alc. I allow this to be true.

Euph. Will it not thence follow that a man born blind, and made to see, would, upon first receiving his sight, take the things he saw not to be at any distance from him, but in his eye, or rather in his mind?

Alc. I must own it seems so. And yet, on the other hand, I can hardly persuade myself that, if I were in such a state, I should think those objects which I *now* see at so great distance to be at no distance at all.

Euph. It seems then that you now think the objects of sight are at a distance from you?

Alc. Doubtless I do. Can anyone question but yonder castle is at a great distance?

Euph. Tell me, Alciphron, can you discern the doors, windows and battlements of that same castle?

Alc. I cannot. At this distance it seems only a small round tower.

Euph. But I, who have been at it, know that it is no small round tower, but a large square building with battlements and turrets, which it seems you do not see.

Alc. What will you infer from this?

Euph. I would infer that the very object which you strictly and properly perceive by sight is not that thing which is several miles distant.

Alc. Why so?

Euph. Because a little round object is one thing, and a great square object is another. Is it not?

Alc. I cannot deny it.

Euph. Tell me, is not the visible appearance alone the proper object of sight?

Alc. It is.

Euph. What think you now (said *Euphranor*, pointing towards the heavens) of the visible appearance of yonder planet? It is not a round luminous flat, no bigger than a sixpence?

Alc. What then?

Euph. Tell me then what you think of the planet itself. Do you not conceive it to be a vast opaque globe, with several unequal risings and valleys?

Alc. I do.

Euph. How can you therefore conclude that the proper object of your sight exists at a distance?

Alc. I confess I know not.

Euph. For your further conviction, do but consider that crimson cloud. Think you that if you were in the very place where it is you would perceive anything like what you now see?

Alc. By no means. I should perceive only a dark mist.

Euph. Is it not plain, therefore, that neither the castle, the planet nor the cloud which you see here are those real ones which you suppose exist at a distance?

Alc. What am I to think then? Do we see anything at all, or is it altogether fancy and illusion?

Euph. Upon the whole it seems the proper objects of sight are light and colours, with their several shades and degrees; all which, being infinitely diversified and combined, do form a language wonderfully adapted to suggest and exhibit to us the distances, figures, situations, dimensions and various qualities of tangible objects—not by similitude, nor yet by inference of necessary connexion, but by the arbitrary imposition of Providence, just as words suggest the things signified by them.

Alc. How? Do we not, strictly speaking, perceive by sight such things as trees, houses, men, rivers and the like?

Euph. We do indeed perceive or apprehend those things by the faculty of sight. But will it follow from thence that they are the proper and immediate objects of sight, any more than that all those things are the proper and immediate objects of hearing which are signified by the help of words or sounds?

Alc. You would have us think, then, that light, shades and colours, variously combined, answer to the several articulations of sound in language; and that, by means thereof, all sorts of objects are suggested to the mind through the eye, in the same manner as they are suggested by words or sounds through the ear: that is, neither from necessary deduction to the judgment, nor from similitude to the fancy, but purely and solely from experience, custom and habit.

Euph. I would not have you think anything more than the nature of things obliges you to think, nor submit in the least to my judgment, but only to the force of truth—which is an imposition that I suppose the freest thinkers will not pretend to be exempt from.

Alc. You have led me, it seems, step by step, till I am got I know not where. But I shall try to get out again, if not by the way I came, yet by some other of my own finding.

Here *Alciphron* having made a short pause, proceeded as follows:

Answer me, Euphranor: should it not follow from these principles that a man born blind, and made to see, would at first sight not only not perceive their distance, but also not so much as know the very things themselves which he saw, for instance, men or trees?—which surely to suppose must be absurd.

Euph. I grant, in consequence of those principles, which both you and I have admitted, that such a one would never think of men, trees or any other objects that he had been accustomed to perceive by touch, upon having his mind filled with new sensations of light and colours, whose various combinations he does not yet understand, or know the meaning of; no more than a Chinese, upon first hearing the words *man* and *tree* would think of the things signified by them. In both cases there must be time and experience, by repeated acts, to acquire a habit of knowing the connexion between the signs and things signified; that is to say, of understanding the language, whether of the eyes or of the ears. And I conceive no absurdity in all this.

Alc. I see, therefore, in strict philosophical truth, that rock only in the same sense that I may be said to hear it, when the word *rock* is pronounced.

Euph. In the very same.

Alc. How comes it to pass then that everyone shall say he sees, for instance, a rock or a house, when those things are before his eyes; but nobody will say he hears a rock or a house, but only the words or sounds themselves, by which those things are said to be signified or suggested but not heard? Besides, if vision be only a language speaking to the eyes, it may be asked: when did men learn this language? To acquire the knowledge of so many signs as go to the making up a language is a work of some difficulty. But will any man say he has spent time, or been at pains, to learn this Language of Vision?

Euph. No wonder; we cannot assign a time beyond our remotest memory. If we have been all practising this language, ever since our first entrance into the world: if the Author of Nature constantly speaks to the eyes of all mankind, even in their earliest infancy, whenever the eyes are open in the light, whether alone or in company: it does not seem to me at all strange that men should not be aware they had ever learned a language begun so early and practised so constantly, as this of Vision. And if we also consider that it is the same throughout the whole world and not, like other languages, differing in different places, it will not seem unaccountable that men should mistake the connexion between the proper objects of sight and the things signified by them to be founded in necessary relation or likeness; or that they should even take them for the same things. Hence it seems easy to conceive why men who do not think should confound in this language of vision the signs with the things signified, otherwise than they are wont to do in the various particular languages formed by the several nations of men.

It may also be worth while to observe that signs, being little considered in themselves for their own sake, but only in their relative capacity and for the sake of those things whereof they are signs, it comes to pass that the mind overlooks them so as to carry its attention immediately to the things signified. Thus for example in reading we run over the characters with the slightest regard and pass on to the meaning. Hence it is frequent for men to say they see words and notions and things in reading a book—whereas in strictness they see only the characters which suggest words, notions and things. And, by parity of reason, may we not suppose that men, not resting in, but overlooking the immediate and proper objects of sight, as in their own nature of small moment, carry their attention onward to the very things signified, and talk as if they saw the secondary objects?—which in truth and strictness are not *seen*, but only *suggested* and *apprehended* by means of the proper objects of sight, which alone are seen.

Alc. To speak my mind freely, this dissertation grows tedious, and runs into points too dry and minute for a gentleman's attention.

I thought, said *Crito*, we had been told that minute philosophers love to consider things closely and minutely.

Alc. That is true; but in so polite an age who would be a mere philosopher? There is a certain scholastic accuracy which ill suits the freedom and ease of a well-bred man. But, to cut short this chicane, I propound it fairly to your own conscience whether you really think that God himself speaks every day and in every place to the eyes of all men.

Euph. That is really and in truth my opinion; and it should be yours too if you are consistent with yourself and abide by your own definition of language—since you cannot deny that the great Mover and Author of nature constantly explains himself to the eyes of men by the sensible intervention of arbitrary signs, which have no similitude or connexion with the things signified; so as, by compounding and disposing them, to suggest and exhibit an endless variety of objects differing in nature, time and place; thereby informing and directing men to act with respect to things distant and future, as well as near and present. In consequence, I say, of your own sentiments and concessions, you have as much reason to think the Universal Agent or God speaks to your eyes as you can have for thinking any particular person speaks to your ears.

Alc. I cannot help thinking that some fallacy runs throughout this whole ratiocination, though perhaps I may not readily point it out. Hold! Let me see. In language the signs are arbitrary, are they not?

Euph. They are.

Alc. And consequently they do not always suggest real matters of fact. Whereas this Natural Language, as you call it, or these visible signs, do always suggest things in the same uniform way and have the same constant regular connexion with matters of fact—and therefore according to the definition premised it can be no language. How do you solve this objection?

Euph. You may solve it yourself by the help of a picture or looking-glass.

Alc. You are in the right. I see there is nothing in it. I know not what else to say to this opinion, more than that it is so odd and contrary to my way of thinking that I shall never assent to it.

Euph. Be pleased to recollect your own lectures upon prejudice and apply them in the present case. Perhaps they may help you to follow where reason leads and to suspect notions which are strongly riveted without having been ever examined.

Alc. I disdain the suspicion of prejudice. And I do not speak only for myself. I know a club of most ingenious men, the freest from prejudice of any men alive, who abhor the notion of a God, and I doubt not would be very able to untie this knot.

Upon which words of Alciphron, I, who had acted the part of an indifferent stander-by, observed to him that it misbecame his character and repeated professions to own an attachment to the judgment or build upon the abilities of other men, however ingenious soever; and that this proceeding might encourage his adversaries to have recourse to authority, in which perhaps they would find their account more than he.

Oh, said *Crito*, I have often observed the conduct of minute philosophers. When one of them has got a ring of disciples round him, his method is to exclaim against prejudice and recommend thinking and reasoning, giving to understand that he himself is a man of deep researches and close argument, one who examines impartially, and concludes warily. The same man in other company, if he chance to be pressed with reason, shall laugh at logic and assume the lazy supine airs of a fine gentleman, a wit, a *railleur*, to avoid the dryness of a regular and exact enquiry. This double face of the minute philosopher is of no small use to propagate and maintain his notions. Though to me it seems a plain case that if a fine gentleman will shake off authority and appeal from religion to reason, unto reason he must go: and if he cannot go without leading-strings, surely he had better be led by the authority of the public than by that of any knot of minute philosophers.

Alc. Gentlemen, this discourse is very irksome and needless. For my part I am a friend to enquiry. I am willing reason should have its full and free scope. I build on no man's authority. For my part I have no interest in denying a God. Any man may believe or not believe a God, as he pleases, for me. But, after all, Euphranor must allow me to stare a little at his conclusions.

Euph. The conclusions are yours as much as mine, for you were led to them by your own concessions.

You, it seems, stare to find that God is not far from every one of us; and that in him we live and move and have our being. You, who in beginning of this morning's conference thought it strange that God should leave himself without a witness, do now think it strange the witness should be so full and clear.

Alc. I must own I do. I was aware indeed of a certain metaphysical hypothesis of our seeing all things in God by the union of the human soul with the intelligible substance of the Deity, which neither I nor anyone else could make sense of.[1] But I never imagined it could be pretended that

[1] A reference to the views of the French philosopher Malebranche (1638–1715). Since, according to Malebranche, one cannot have any idea of God, for every idea is limited and finite, the only knowledge of God is that which he has of himself, and in so far as human beings have a vision of God, this consists in the presence in the soul of the divine Word. Since God contains the ideas of all the things he has created, we thereby see all things in God.

we saw God with our fleshly eyes as plain as we see any human person whatsoever, and that he daily speaks to our senses in a manifest and clear dialect.

Cri. As for that metaphysical hypothesis I can make no more of it than you. But I think it plain this Optic Language has a necessary connexion with knowledge, wisdom and goodness. It is equivalent to a constant creation betokening an immediate act of power and providence. It cannot be accounted for by mechanical principles, by atoms, attractions or effluvia. The instantaneous production and reproduction of so many signs, combined, dissolved, transposed, diversified and adapted to such an endless variety of purposes, ever shifting with the occasions and suited to them, being utterly inexplicable and unaccountable by the laws of motion, by chance, by fate or the like blind principles, does set forth and testify the immediate operation of a spirit or thinking being—and not merely of a spirit, which every motion or gravitation may possibly infer, but of one wise, good and provident Spirit which directs and rules and governs the world. Some philosophers, being convinced of the wisdom and power of the Creator, from the make and contrivance of organized bodies and orderly system of the world, did nevertheless imagine that he left this system with all its parts and contents well adjusted and put in motion, as an artist leaves a clock, to go thenceforward of itself for a certain period.[1] But this Visual Language proves, not a Creator merely, but a provident Governor, actually and intimately present, and attentive to all our interests and motions, who watches over our conduct and takes care of our minutest actions and designs throughout the whole course of our lives, informing, admonishing and directing incessantly, in a most evident and sensible manner. This is truly wonderful.

Euph. And is it not so that men should be encompassed by such a wonder without reflecting on it?

Something there is of divine and admirable in this Language, addressed to our eyes, that may well awaken the mind and deserve its utmost attention:— it is learned with so little pains: it expresses the differences of things so clearly and aptly: it instructs with such facility and despatch, by one glance of the eye conveying a greater variety of advices, and a more distinct knowledge of things, than could be got by a discourse of several hours. And, while it informs, it amuses and entertains the mind with such singular pleasure and delight. It is of such excellent use in giving a stability and permanency to human discourse, in recording sounds and bestowing life on dead languages, enabling us to converse with men of remote ages and countries. And it answers so apposite to the uses and

[1] A reference to Leibniz's doctrine of the pre-established harmony: see above, p. 142.

necessities of mankind, informing us more distinctly of those objects whose nearness and magnitude qualify them to be of greatest detriment or benefit to our bodies, and less exactly in proportion as their littleness or distance makes them of less concern to us.

Alc. And yet these strange things affect men but little.

Euph. But they are not strange, they are familiar; and that makes them be overlooked. Things which rarely happen strike; whereas frequency lessens the admiration of things, though in themselves ever so admirable. Hence a common man, who is used to think and make reflections, would probably be more convinced of the being of a God by one single sentence heard once in his life from the sky than by all the experience he has had of this Visual Language, contrived with such exquisite skill, so constantly addressed to his eyes, and so plainly declaring the nearness, wisdom and providence of him with whom we have to do.

Alc. After all, I cannot satisfy myself how men should be so little surprised or amazed about this visual faculty, if it was really of a nature so surprising and amazing.

Euph. But let us suppose a nation of men blind from their infancy, among whom a stranger arrives, the only man who can see in all the country; let us suppose this stranger travelling with some of the natives, and that one while he foretells to them that, in case they walk straight forward, in half an hour they shall meet men or cattle, or come to a house; that, if they turn to the right and proceed, they shall in a few minutes be in danger of falling down a precipice; that, shaping their course to the left, they will in such a time arrive at a river, a wood or a mountain. What think you? Must they not be infinitely surprised that one who had never been in their country before should know it so much better than themselves? And would not those predictions seem to them as unaccountable and incredible as prophecy to a minute philosopher?

Alc. I cannot deny it.

Euph. But it seems to require intense thought to be able to unravel a prejudice that has been so long forming; to get over the vulgar errors or ideas common to both senses; and so to distinguish between the objects of sight and touch, which have grown (if I may so say), blended together in our fancy, as to be able to suppose ourselves exactly in the state that one of those men would be in, if he were made to see. And yet this I believe is possible and might seem worth the pains of a little thinking, especially to those men whose proper employment and profession it is to think, and unravel prejudices, and confute mistakes.

Alc. I frankly own I cannot find my way out of this maze, and should gladly be set right by those who see better than myself.

Cri. The pursuing this subject in their own thoughts would possibly open a new scene to those speculative gentlemen of the minute philosophy. It puts me in mind of a passage in the Psalmist, where he represents God to be covered with light as with a garment, and would methinks be no ill comment on that ancient notion of some eastern sages—that God had light for his body, and truth for his soul.

This conversation lasted till a servant came to tell us the tea was ready: upon which we walked in and found Lysicles at the tea-table.

As soon as we sat down, I am glad, said *Alciphron*, that I have here found my second, a fresh man to maintain our common cause, which, I doubt, Lysicles will think has suffered by his absence.

Lys. Why so?

Alc. I have been drawn into some concessions you will not like.

Lys. Let me know what they are.

Alc. Why, that there is such a thing as a God, and that his existence is very certain.

Lys. Bless me! How came you to entertain so wild a notion?

Alc. You know we profess to follow reason wherever it leads. And in short I have been reasoned into it.

Lys. Reasoned! You should say amused with words, bewildered with sophistry.

Euph. Have you a mind to hear the same reasoning that led Alciphron and me step by step that we may examine whether it be sophistry or no?

Lys. As to that I am very easy. I guess all that can be said on that head. It shall be my business to help my friend out, whatever arguments drew him in.

Euph. Will you admit the premises and deny the conclusions?

Lys. What if I admit the conclusion?

Euph. How! Will you grant there is a God?

Lys. Perhaps I may.

Euph. Then we are agreed.

Lys. Perhaps not.

Euph. O Lysicles, you are a subtle adversary. I know not what you would be at.

Lys. You must know then that at bottom the being of a God is a point in itself of small consequence, and a man may make this concession without yielding much. The great point is what sense the word *God* is to be taken in. The very Epicureans[1] allowed the being of gods; but then they were

[1] See n. 1 to p. 227.

indolent gods, unconcerned with human affairs. Hobbes[1] allowed a corporeal god: and Spinoza[2] held the universe to be God. And yet nobody doubts they were staunch free-thinkers. I could wish indeed the word 'God' were quite omitted; because in most minds it is coupled with a sort of superstitious awe, the very root of all religion. I shall not, nevertheless, be much disturbed, though the *name* be retained, and the being of a God allowed in any sense but in that of a Mind which knows all things and beholds human actions, like some judge or magistrate, with infinite observation and intelligence. The belief of a God in this sense fills a man's mind with scruples, lays him under constraints and embitters his very being: but in another sense it may be attended with no great ill consequence. This I know was the opinion of our great Diagoras,[3] who told me he would never have been at the pains to find out a demonstration that there was no God, if the received notion of God had been the same with that of some Fathers and Schoolmen.

Euph. Pray what was that?

Lys. You must know, Diagoras, as a man of much reading and enquiry, had discovered that once upon a time the most profound and speculative divines, finding it impossible to reconcile the attributes of God—taken in the common sense, or in any known sense—with human reason, and the appearance of things, taught that the words *knowledge*, *wisdom*, *goodness* and such like, when spoken of the Deity, must be understood in quite a different sense from what they signify in the vulgar acceptation, or from anything that we can form a notion of or conceive. Hence, whatever objections might be made against the attributes of God they easily solved—by denying those attributes belonged to God in this or that or any known particular sense or notion; which was the same thing as to deny they belonged to him at all. And thus, denying the attributes of God, they in effect denied his being, though perhaps they were not aware of it.

Suppose, for instance, a man should object that future contingencies were inconsistent with the foreknowledge of God, because it is repugnant that certain knowledge should be of an uncertain thing, it was a ready and easy answer to say that this may be true with respect to knowledge taken in the common sense or in any sense that we can possibly form the notion of; but that there would not appear the same inconsistency between the contingent nature of things and divine foreknowledge, taken to signify somewhat that we know nothing of, which in God supplies the place of what we understand by 'knowledge'; from which it differs not in quantity

[1] Hobbes (1588–1679) expounded, in his *Leviathan*, primarily a political treatise, a system of radical materialism.

[2] See above, p. 124.

[3] A fictional friend of Lysicles.

or degree of perfection, but altogether and in kind, as light does from sound;—and even more, since these agree in that they are both sensations; whereas knowledge in God has no sort of resemblance or agreement with any notion that man can frame of knowledge. The like may be said of all the other attributes, which indeed may by this means be equally reconciled with everything or with nothing. But all men who think must needs see this is cutting knots and not untying them. For how are things reconciled with the divine attributes when these attributes themselves are in every intelligible sense denied; and consequently the very notion of God taken away and nothing left but the name, without any meaning annexed to it? In short, the belief that there is an unknown subject of attributes absolutely unknown is a very innocent doctrine; which the acute Diagoras well saw, and was therefore wonderful delighted with this system.

For, said he, if this could once make its way and obtain in the world, there would be an end to all natural and rational religion, which is the basis both of the Jewish and the Christian: for he who comes to God or enters himself in the Church of God must first believe that there is a *God in some intelligible sense*; and not only that there is *Something in general, without any proper notion, though never so inadequate, of any of its qualities or attributes*: for this may be fate or chaos or plastic nature or anything else as well as God. Nor will it avail to say: There is something in this unknown being *analogous* to knowledge and goodness; that is to say, which produces those effects which we could not conceive to be produced by men, in any degree, without knowledge and goodness. For this is in fact to give up the point in dispute between theists and atheists—the question having always been not whether there was a Principle (which point was allowed by all philosophers, as well before as since Anaxagoras[1]), but whether this principle was a *νοῦς*, a thinking intelligent being—that is to say whether that order and beauty and use visible in natural effects could be produced by anything but a Mind or Intelligence, in the proper sense of the word? And whether there must not be true, real and proper knowledge in the First Cause? We will, therefore, acknowledge that all those natural effects which are vulgarly ascribed to knowledge and wisdom proceed from a being in which there is, properly speaking, no knowledge or wisdom at all, but only something else, which in reality is the cause of those things which men, for want of knowing better, ascribe to what they call knowledge and wisdom and understanding. You wonder perhaps to hear a man of

[1] Anaxagoras (b. about 500 BC), a pre-Socratic Greek philosopher, held that the cosmos was a system of infinitely small elements, combined in changing ways under the direction of Noûs or Intelligence.

pleasure, who diverts himself as I do, philosophize at this rate. But you should consider that much is to be got by conversing with ingenious men, which is a short way to knowledge, that saves a man the drudgery of reading and thinking. And now we have granted to you that there is a God in this indefinite sense, I would fain see what use you can make of this concession. You cannot argue from unknown attributes or, which is the same thing, from attributes in an unknown sense. You cannot prove that God is to be loved for his goodness or feared for his justice or respected for his knowledge: all which consequences, we own, would follow from those attributes admitted in an intelligible sense. But we deny that those or any other consequences can be drawn from attributes admitted in no particular sense or in a sense which none of us understand. Since, therefore, nothing can be inferred from such an account of God, about conscience or worship or religion, you may even make the best of it. And, not to be singular, we will use the name too, and so at once there is an end of atheism.

Euph. This account of a Deity is new to me. I do not like it, and therefore shall leave it to be maintained by those who do.

Cri. It is not new to me. I remember not long since to have heard a minute philosopher triumph upon this very point; which put me on enquiring what foundation there was for it in the Fathers or Schoolmen. And for aught that I can find, it owes its origin to those writings which have been published under the name of Dionysius the Areopagite.[1] The author of which, it must be owned, has written upon the divine attributes in a very singular style. In his treatise *De Hierarchia Coelesti* he says that God is something above all essence and life, *ὑπὲρ πᾶσαν οὐσίαν καὶ ζωήν*; and again in his treatise *De Divinis Nominibus*, that he is above all wisdom and understanding, *ὑπὲρ πᾶσαν σοφίαν καί σύνεσιν*, ineffable and innominable, *ἄρρητος καὶ ἀνώνυμος*; the wisdom of God he terms as unreasonable, unintelligent and foolish wisdom, *τὴν ἄλογον καὶ ἄνουν καὶ μωρὰν σοφίαν*. But then the reason he gives for expressing himself in this strange manner is that the divine wisdom is the cause of all reason, wisdom and understanding, and therein are contained the treasures of all wisdom and knowledge. He calls God *ὑπέρσοφος* and *ὑπέρζως*; as if 'wisdom' and 'life' were words not worthy to express the divine perfections: and he adds that the attributes 'unintelligent' and 'unperceiving' must be ascribed to the Divinity, not *κατ' ἔλλειψιν*, by way of defect, but *καθ' ὑπεροχήν*, by way of eminency—which he explains by our giving the name of darkness to light inaccessible. And notwithstanding the harshness of his expressions in some places, he affirms over and over in others that God knows all things; not that he is beholden

[1] See above, p. 50.

to creatures for his knowledge, but by knowing himself, from whom they all derive their being and in whom they are contained as in their cause. It was late before these writings appear to have been known in the world; and although they obtained credit during the age of the Schoolmen, yet, since critical learning has been cultivated, they have lost that credit, and are at this day given up for spurious, as containing several evident marks of a much later date than the age of Dionysius. Upon the whole, although this method of growing in expression and dwindling in notion, of clearing up doubts by nonsense and avoiding difficulties by running into affected contradictions, may perhaps proceed from a well-meant zeal, yet it appears not to be according to knowledge; and instead of reconciling atheists to the truth has, I doubt, a tendency to confirm them in their own persuasion. It should seem, therefore, very weak and rash in a Christian to adopt this harsh language of an apocryphal writer preferably to that of the Holy Scriptures. I remember, indeed, to have read of a certain philosopher who lived some centuries ago that used to say: If these supposed works of Dionysius had been known to the primitive Fathers they would have furnished them admirable weapons against the heretics and would have saved a world of pains. But the event since this discovery has by no means confirmed his opinion.

It must be owned, the celebrated Picus of Mirandula,[1] among his nine hundred conclusions (which that prince, being very young, proposed to maintain by public disputation at Rome) has this for one—to wit that it is more improper to say of God 'He is an intellect or intelligent being' than to say of a reasonable soul that it is an angel: which doctrine, it seems, was not relished. And Picus, when he comes to defend it, supports himself altogether by the example and authority of Dionysius, and in effect explains it away into a mere verbal difference—affirming that neither Dionysius nor himself ever meant to deprive God of knowledge or to deny that he knows all things; but that, as reason is of a kind peculiar to man, so by intellection he understands a kind or manner of knowing peculiar to angels; and that the knowledge which is in God is more above the intellection of angels than angel is above man. He adds that, as his tenet consists with admitting the most perfect knowledge in God, so he would by no means be understood to exclude from the Deity intellection itself, taken in the common or general sense, but only that peculiar sort of intellection proper to angels, which he thinks ought not to be attributed to God any more than human reason. Picus, therefore, though he speaks

[1] Picus (better known as Pico della Mirandola) (1463–94), Count of Mirandola, was much under the influence, during his time in Florence, of a group of Platonists, including Ficino, and attempted a synthesis of Plato's and Aristotle's thought, together with a mass of arcane material. See N. A. Robb, *Neoplatonism of the Italian Renaissance* (London, 1935).

as the apocryphal Dionysius, yet, when he explains himself, it is evident he speaks like other men. And although the aforementioned books on the *Celestial Hierarchy* and the *Divine Names*, being attributed to a saint and martyr of the apostolic age, were respected by the Schoolmen, yet it is certain they rejected or softened his harsh expressions, and explained away or reduced his doctrine to the received notions taken from Holy Scripture and the light of nature.

Thomas Aquinas[1] expresses his sense of this point in the following manner. All perfections, says he, derived from God to the creatures are in a certain higher sense or (as the Schoolmen term it) *eminently* in God. Whenever, therefore, a name borrowed from any perfection in the creature is attributed to God, we must exclude from its signification everything that belongs to the imperfect manner wherein that attribute is found in the creature. Whence he concludes that knowledge in God is not a habit but a pure act.[2] And again, the same Doctor observes that our intellect gets its notions of all sorts of perfections from the creatures and that as it apprehends those perfections so it signifies them by names. Therefore, says he, in attributing these names to God we are to consider two things: first, the perfections themselves, as goodness, life and the like, which are properly in God; and secondly, the manner, which is peculiar to the creature, and cannot strictly and properly speaking be said to agree to the Creator.

And although Suarez,[3] with other Schoolmen, teaches that the mind of man conceives knowledge and will to be in God as faculties or operations, by analogy only to created beings, yet he gives it plainly as his opinion that when knowledge is said not to be properly in God it must be understood in a sense including imperfections, such as discursive knowledge or the like imperfect kind found in the creatures: and that none of those imperfections in the knowledge of men or angels belonging to the formal notion of knowledge, or to knowledge as such, it will not thence follow that knowledge, in its proper formal sense, may not be attributed to God. And of knowledge taken in general for the clear evident understanding of all truth, he expressly affirms that it is in God and that this was never denied by any philosopher who believed a God. It was, indeed, a current opinion in the schools that even *being* itself could be attributed analogically to God and the creatures. That is, they held that God, the supreme, independent, self-originate cause and source of all beings, must

[1] See n. 2 to p. 144.

[2] See Aquinas' *Summa Theologica*, Q. 15, art. 1. 'Habit' here corresponds to the modern 'disposition'. See G. Ryle, *Concept of Mind* (London, 1949) p. 43 ff.

[3] Suarez (1548–1617), Jesuit philosopher and theologian, and commentator on Aquinas.

not be supposed to *exist* in the same sense as created beings; not that he exists less truly, properly or formally than they, but only because he exists in a more eminent and perfect manner.

But to prevent any man's being led, by mistaking the scholastic use of the terms *analogy* and *analogical*, into an opinion that we cannot frame in any degree a true and proper notion of attributes applied by analogy or, in the school phrase, predicated analogically, it may not be amiss to enquire into the true sense and meaning of those words. Everyone knows that *analogy* is a Greek word used by mathematicians to signify a similitude of proportions. For instance, when we observe that 2 is to 6 as 3 is to 9, this similitude or equality of proportion is termed 'analogy'. And although proportion strictly signifies the habitude or relation of one quantity to another, yet in a looser and translated sense it has been applied to signify every other habitude; and consequently the term 'analogy' comes to signify all similitude of relations or habitudes whatsoever. Hence the Schoolmen tell us there is analogy between intellect and sight—forasmuch as intellect is to the mind what sight is to the body,—and that he who governs the state is analogous to him who steers a ship. Hence a prince is analogically styled a pilot, being to the state as a pilot is to his vessel.

For the further clearing of this point it is to be observed that a twofold analogy is distinguished by the Schoolmen—metaphorical and proper. Of the first kind there are frequent instances in Holy Scripture, attributing human parts and passions to God. When he is represented as having a finger, an eye or an ear; when he is said to repent, to be angry or grieved —everyone sees that analogy is metaphorical. Because those parts and passions, taken in the proper signification, must in every degree, necessarily and from the formal nature of the thing, include imperfection. When therefore it is said 'The finger of God appears in this or that event', men of common sense mean no more than that it is as truly ascribed to God as the works wrought by human fingers are to man—and so of the rest. But the case is different when wisdom and knowledge are attributed to God. Passions and senses, as such, imply defect; but in knowledge simply, or as such, there is no defect. Knowledge, therefore, in the proper formal meaning of the word, may be attributed to God *proportionately*, that is, preserving a proportion to the infinite nature of God. We may say, therefore, that as God is infinitely above man, so is the knowledge of God infinitely above the knowledge of man, and that is what Cajetan[1] calls *analogia proprie facta*. And after this same analogy we must understand all those attributes to belong to the Deity which in themselves simply, and as such, denote perfection. We may therefore consistently with what has

[1] (1469–1534), Cardinal and commentator on the *Summa Theologica*.

been premised affirm that all sorts of perfection which we can conceive in a finite spirit are in God, but without any of that alloy which is found in the creatures. This doctrine, therefore, of analogical perfections in God, or our knowing God by analogy, seems very much misunderstood and misapplied by those who would infer from thence that we cannot frame any direct or proper notion, though never so inadequate, of knowledge or wisdom, as they are in the Deity; or understood any more of them than one born blind can of light and colours.

And now gentlemen, it may be expected I should ask your pardon for having dwelt so long on a point of metaphysics and introduced such unpolished and unfashionable writers as the Schoolmen into good company; but as Lysicles gave the occasion, I leave him to answer for it.

Lys. I never dreamt of this dry dissertation. But if I have been the occasion of discussing these scholastic points, by my unluckily mentioning the Schoolmen, it was my first fault of the kind and I promise it shall be the last. The meddling with crabbed authors of any sort is none of my taste. I grant one meets now and then with a good notion in what we call dry writers, such a one for example as this I was speaking of, which I must own struck my fancy. But then, for these we have such as Prodicus or Diagoras, who look into obsolete books and save the rest of us that trouble.

Cri. So you pin your faith upon them?

Lys. It is only for some odd opinions and matters of fact and critical points. Besides, we know the men to whom we give credit; they are judicious and honest and have no end to serve but the truth. And I am confident some author or other has maintained the forementioned notion in some sense as Diagoras related it.

Cri. That may be. But it never was a received notion and never will, so long as men believe a God: the same argument that proves a First Cause proving an Intelligent Cause—intelligent, I say in the proper sense, wise and good in the true and formal acceptation of the words. Otherwise, it is evident that every syllogism brought to prove those attributes or, which is the same thing, to prove the being of a God, will be found to consist in four terms and consequently can conclude nothing.[1] But for your part, Alciphron, you have been fully convinced that God is a thinking intelligent being, in the same sense as other spirits, though not in the same imperfect manner or degree.

Alc. And yet I am not without my scruples: for with knowledge you

[1] The fallacy of four terms consists in a syllogistic argument which contains an ambiguity, so that there are in effect four terms instead of three. E.g. 'All humans are rational beings; no rational being would use the fallacy of four terms; ergo no human being would use the fallacy of four terms.'

infer wisdom, and with wisdom goodness. But how is it possible to conceive God so good and man so wicked? It may perhaps with some colour be alleged that a little soft shadowing of evil sets off the bright and luminous parts of creation and so contributes to the beauty of the whole piece; but for blots so large and so black it is impossible to account by that principle. That there should be so much vice and so little virtue upon earth and that the laws of God's kingdom should be so ill observed by his subjects is what can never be reconciled with that surpassing wisdom and goodness of the supreme Monarch.

Euph. Tell me, Alciphron, would you argue that a state was well administered or judge of the manners of its citizens by the disorders committed in the jail or dungeon?

Alc. I would not.

Euph. And for aught we know this spot, with the few sinners on it, bears no greater proportion to the universe of intelligences than a dungeon does to a kingdom. It seems we are led, not only by revelation, but by common sense, observing and inferring from the analogy of visible things, to conclude there are innumerable orders of intelligent beings more happy and more perfect than man; whose life is but a span, and whose place, this earthly globe, is but a point in respect of the whole system of God's creation. We are dazzled, indeed, with the glory and grandeur of things here below, because we know no better. But I am apt to think, if we knew what it was to be an angel for one hour, we should return to this world, though it were to sit on the brightest throne in it, with vastly more loathing and reluctance than we would now descend into a loathsome dungeon or sepulchre.

Cri. To me it seems natural that such a weak, passionate and short-sighted creature as man should be ever liable to scruples of one kind or other. But as this same creature is apt to be over-positive in judging and over-hasty in concluding, it falls out that these difficulties and scruples about God's conduct are made objections to his being. And so men come to argue from their own defects against the divine perfections. And, as the views and humours of men are different and often opposite, you may sometimes see them deduce the same atheistical conclusions from contrary premises. I knew an instance of this in two minute philosophers of my acquaintance, who used to argue each from his own temper against a Providence. One of them, a man of a choleric and vindictive spirit, said he could not believe a Providence because London was not swallowed up or consumed by fire from heaven—the streets being, as he said, full of people who show no other belief or worship of God but perpetually praying that he would damn, rot, sink and confound them. The other, being of an indolent, easy temper, concluded there could be no such thing as Providence; for that a being of consummate wisdom must needs employ himself better than in minding the prayers and actions and little interests of mankind.

Alc. After all, if God have no passions, how can it be true that vengeance is his? Or how can he be said to be jealous of his glory?

Cri. We believe that God executes vengeance without revenge and is jealous without weakness, just as the mind of man sees without eyes and apprehends without hands.

Alc. To put a period upon this discourse, we will grant there is a God in this dispassionate sense; but what then? What has this to do with religion or divine worship? To what purpose are all these prayers and praises and thanksgivings and singing of praises, which the foolish vulgar call serving God? What sense or use or end is there in all these things?

Cri. We worship God, we praise and pray to him, not because we think that he is proud of our worship or fond of our praise or prayers and affected with them as mankind are, or that all our service can contribute in the least degree to his happiness or good, but because it is good for *us* to be so disposed towards God, because it is just and right and suitable to the nature of things and becoming the relation we stand in to our supreme Lord and Governor.

Alc. If it be good for us to worship God, it should seem that the Christian religion, which pretends to each man the knowledge and worship of God, was of some use and benefit to mankind.

Cri. Doubtless.

Alc. If this can be made appear, I shall own myself very much mistaken.

Cri. It is now near dinner-time. Wherefore, if you please, we will put an end to this conversation for the present.

12

BUTLER

on REASON AND FAITH *and on* IMMORTALITY

Biographical Note Joseph Butler, born in 1692 at Wantage, Berks., son of a Presbyterian shopkeeper. Educated at an academy at Tewkesbury (intending to become a Dissenting minister); and at Oriel College, Oxford (after ceasing to be a Nonconformist). B.A., 1718, and ordained. Appointed preacher at the Rolls Chapel. 1722, appointed to rectory of Haughton, near Darlington: and to the rectory of Stanhope in Weardale, 1725. After being chaplain to Lord Chancellor Talbot, was made Clerk of the Closet to Queen Caroline, 1736. Consecrated Bishop of Bristol, 1738. 1750, translated to diocese of Durham. 1752, died at Bath.

Principal works: *Fifteen Sermons* (1726), *Analogy of Religion* (1736), *Six Sermons preached upon public occasions* (1748).

Philosophical Note Perhaps the chief interest which B. has for philosophers today lies in his ethical writings. In these he depicts human nature as a kind of hierarchy, rising up from the various passions to two main principles, those of benevolence and self-love, and crowned by conscience. To be benevolent and reflectively self-loving leads, on the whole, to virtue. Since these two principles are directed towards happiness, respectively of others and of oneself, B.'s theory so far is Utilitarian (see below, p. 340), but the principles must submit themselves to the natural and supreme authority of conscience, which is able to pronounce moral judgments which tell us what actions are intrinsically good or evil. B.'s stress on the importance of cool self-love is partly due to his desire to rebut unrealistically altruistic accounts of morality, and holds that in great measure virtue and happiness come together. Nevertheless, this coincidence is not universal, as far as this life is concerned, but, there being a good God, virtue may 'combat with greater advantage hereafter, and prevail completely, and enjoy its consequent rewards, in some future states'.

His principal theological work, the *Analogy of Religion*, has as its chief aim (which is explained more fully in the passage which follows) that of showing that the natural constitution of the world is analogous to and of a piece with revealed religion, and this creates the presumption that they both proceed from the same source. Consequently, objections which are urged against religion will apply to our understanding of nature, where they would certainly be false. B. here is mainly arguing against the Deists (see above, p. 85), who attempted to base religion upon natural theology alone, without recourse to the Christian revelation, and whose conclusions often seemed to imply that God, apart from his initial creativity, has no further intimate concern with life within the cosmos. It is noteworthy that B. emphasizes the importance of probability as a guide to judgment, and in this respect differs markedly from those who, as he says, form their 'notions of the constitution and government of the world upon reasoning, without foundations for the principles which they assume'.

Bibliographical Note There are editions of B.'s works by J. H. Bernard (2 vols., London, 1900) and W. E. Gladstone (2 vols., Oxford, 1896, with suppl. vol.). An excellent introduction to his ethical theory is A. Duncan-Jones' *Butler's Moral Philosophy* (London, Pelican, 1952). See also C. D. Broad, *Five Types of Ethical Theory* (London, 1930). On the religious controversy, see L. Stephen, *History of English Thought in the Eighteenth Century* (Vol. 1, 1876) and W. A. Spooner, *Bishop Butler* (1901).

A. REASON AND FAITH

Analogy of Religion, Introduction

Probable evidence is essentially distinguished from demonstrative by this —that it admits of degrees, and of all variety of them, from the highest moral certainty to the very lowest presumption. We cannot, indeed, say a thing is probably true upon very slight presumption for it, because, as there may be probabilities on both sides of a question, there may be some against it; and though there be not, yet a slight presumption does not beget that degree of conviction which is implied in saying a thing is probably true. But that the slightest possible presumption is of the nature of a probability appears from hence, that such low presumption, often repeated, will amount even to moral certainty. Thus a man's having observed the ebb and flow of the tide today affords some sort of presumption, though the lowest imaginable, that it may happen again tomorrow; but the observation of this event for so many days and months and ages together gives us a full assurance that it will.

That which chiefly constitutes *probability* is expressed in the word *likely* —that is, like some truth or true event; like it, in itself, in its evidence, in some more or fewer of its circumstances. For when we determine a thing to be probably true, suppose that an event has or will come to pass, it is from the mind's remarking in it a likeness to some other event which we have observed has come to pass. And this observation forms, in numberless daily instances, a presumption, opinion or full conviction that such an event has or will come to pass, according as the observation is that the like event has sometimes, most commonly or always come to pass at like distances of time or place, or upon like occasions. Hence arises the belief that a child, if it lives twenty years, will grow up to the stature and strength of a man; that food will contribute to the preservation of its life, and the want of it for such a number of days be its certain destruction. So likewise the rule and measure of our hopes and fears concerning the success of our pursuits; our expectations that others will act so and so in such circumstances; and our judgment that such actions proceed from such principles:—all these rely upon our having observed the like to what we hope, fear, expect, judge—I say upon our having observed the like, either with respect to others or ourselves. And thus whereas the prince[1] who had always lived in a warm climate naturally concluded, in the way of analogy, that there was no such thing as water's becoming hard, because he had always observed it to be a fluid and yielding, we on the contrary, from analogy, conclude that there is no presumption at all against this, that it is supposable there may be frost in England any given day in January next, probable that there will on some day of the month, and that there is a moral certainty—i.e. ground for an expectation without any doubt of it—in some part or other of the winter.

Probable evidence, in its very nature, affords but an imperfect kind of information and is to be considered as relative only to beings of limited capacities; for nothing which is the possible object of knowledge, whether past, present or future, can be probable to an infinite intelligence, since it cannot but be discerned absolutely as it is in itself, certainly true or certainly false; but to us probability is the very guide of life.

From these things it follows that in questions of difficulty or such as are thought so, where more satisfactory evidence cannot be had or is not seen, if the result of the examination be that there appears upon the whole even the lowest presumption on one side and none on the other, or a greater presumption on one side, though in the lowest degree greater, this determines the question, even in matters of speculation; and in matters of practice will lay us under an absolute and formal obligation, in point of prudence and of interest, to act upon that presumption or low probability —though it be so low as to leave the mind in very great doubt which is the truth. For surely a man is as really bound in prudence to do what upon the whole appears, according to the best of his judgment, to be for his happiness as what he certainly knows to be so. Nay, further, in questions of great consequence a reasonable man will think it concerns him to remark lower probabilities and presumptions than these, such as amount to no more than showing one side of a question to be as supposable and credible as the other; nay, such as but amount to much less even than this. For numberless instances might be mentioned respecting the common pursuits

[1] The reference is to the story of an Indian prince: for a similar example, see Hume's *Essay on Miracles* (below, p. 235) and also Locke's *Essay*, I. vi. 13.

of life where a man would be thought in a literal sense distracted who would not act, and with great application too, not only upon an even chance, but upon much less, and where the probability or chance was greatly against his succeeding.[1]

It is not my design to enquire farther into the nature, the foundation and measure of probability, or whence it proceeds that *likeness* should beget that presumption, opinion or full conviction which the human mind is formed to receive from it and which it does necessarily produce in everyone, or to guard against the errors to which reasoning from analogy is liable. This belongs to the subject of logic, and is a part of that subject which has not yet been thoroughly considered.[2] Indeed I shall not take upon me to say how far the extent, compass and force of analogical reasoning can be reduced to general heads and rules and the whole be formed into a system. But though so little in this way has been attempted by those who have treated of our intellectual powers and the exercise of them, this does not hinder but that we may be, as we unquestionably are, assured that analogy is of weight, in various degrees, towards determining our judgment and our practice. Nor does it in any wise cease to be of weight in those cases because persons, either given to dispute or who require things to be stated with greater exactness than our faculties appear to admit of in practical matters, may find other cases in which 'tis not easy to say whether it be or be not of any weight, or instances of seeming analogies which are really of none. It is enough to the present purpose to observe that this general way of arguing is evidently natural, just and conclusive. For there is no man can make a question but that the sun will rise tomorrow and be seen, where it is seen at all, in the figure of a circle and not in that of a square.

Hence, namely from analogical reasoning, Origen[3] has, with singular sagacity, observed that 'he who believes the Scripture to have proceeded from him who is the Author of Nature may well expect to find the same sort of difficulties in it as are found in the constitution of nature'. And, in like way of reflection, it may be added that he who denies the Scriptures to have been from God upon account of these difficulties may, for the very same reason, deny the world to have been formed by him. On the other hand, if there be an analogy or likeness between that system of things and dispensation of Providence which experience, together with reason, informs us of—that is, the known course of nature—this is a presumption that they have both the same author and cause, at least so far as to answer

[1] See the *Analogy of Religion*, Pt II, Ch. vi.
[2] For brief accounts of the development of inductive logic, see W. Kneale, *Probability and Induction* (Oxford, 1949), Pt II, and G. H. von Wright, *The Logical Problem of Induction* (Helsinki, 1941), Ch. ii. See below also, p. 340f.
[3] (*c.* 185–*c.* 254), Alexandrian theologian and mystic.

objections against the former's being from God, drawn from anything which is analogical or similar to what is in the latter, which is acknowledged to be from him; for an Author of Nature is here supposed.

Forming our notions of the constitution and government of the world upon reasoning without foundation for the principles which we assume, whether from the attributes of God or anything else, is building a world upon hypothesis like Descartes. Forming our notions upon reasoning from principles which are certain, but applied to cases to which we have no ground to apply them (like those who explain the structure of the human body and the nature of diseases and medicines, from mere mathematics, without sufficient data), is an error much akin to the former; since what is assumed, in order to make the reasoning applicable, is *hypothesis*. But it must be allowed just to join abstract reasonings with the observation of facts, and argue from such facts as are known to others that are like them; from that part of the divine government over intelligent creatures which comes under our view to that larger and more general government over them which is beyond it; and from what is present to collect what is likely, credible or not incredible will be hereafter.

This method, then, of concluding and determining being practical—and what, if we will act at all, we cannot but act upon in the common pursuits of life—being evidently conclusive, in various degrees, proportionable to the degree and exactness of the whole analogy or likeness; and having so great authority for its introduction into the subject of religion, even revealed; my design is to apply it to the subject in general, both natural and revealed, taken for proved that there is an intelligent Author of Nature and natural governor of the world. For as there is no presumption against this prior to the proof of it, so it has been often proved with accumulated evidence, from this argument of analogy and final causes, from abstract reasonings, from the most ancient tradition and testimony and from the general consent of mankind. Nor does it appear, so far as I can find, to be denied by the generality of those who profess themselves dissatisfied by the evidence of religion.

As there are some who instead of thus attending to what is in fact the constitution of nature form their notions of God's government upon hypothesis, so there are others who indulge themselves in vain and idle speculations how the world might possibly have been framed otherwise than it is; and upon supposition that things might, in imagining that they should, have been disposed and carried on after a better model than what appears in the present disposition and conduct of them. Suppose, now, a person of such a turn of mind to go on with his reveries till he had at length fixed upon some particular plan of nature as appearing to him the best. One shall scarce be thought guilty of detraction against human understanding if one should say, even beforehand, that the plan which this speculative person would fix upon, though he were the wisest of the sons of men, probably would not be the very best even according to his own notions of *best*—whether he thought that to be so which afforded occasions and motives for the exercise of the greatest virtue, or which was productive of the greatest happiness, or that these two were necessarily connected, and run up into one and the same plan. However, it may not be amiss once for all to see what would be the amount of these emendations and imaginary improvements upon the system of nature or how far they would mislead us. And it seems there could be no stopping till we came to such conclusions as these:— That all creatures should at first be made as perfect and as happy as they were ever capable of being: that nothing, to be sure, of hazard or danger should be put upon them to do—some indolent persons would perhaps think nothing at all: or certainly, that effectual care should be taken that they should, whether necessarily or not, yet eventually and in fact, always do what was right and most conducive to happiness, which would be thought easy for infinite power to effect; either by not giving them any principles which would endanger their going wrong, or by laying the right motive of action in every instance before their minds continually in so strong a manner as would never fail of inducing them to act conformably to it: and that the whole method of government by punishments should be rejected as absurd—as an awkward roundabout method of carrying things on—nay, as contrary to a principal purpose for which it would be supposed creatures were made, namely happiness.

Now without considering what is to be said in particular to the several parts of this train of folly and extravagance, what has been above intimated is a full direct general answer to it—namely that we may see beforehand that we have not faculties for this kind of speculation. For though it be admitted that from the first principles of our nature we unavoidably judge or determine some ends to be absolutely in themselves preferable to others and that the ends now mentioned are, or, if they run up into one, that this one is, absolutely the best—and consequently that we must conclude the ultimate end designed, in the constitution of nature and conduct of providence, is the most virtue and happiness possible—yet we are far from being able to judge what particular disposition of things would be most friendly and assistant to virtue, or what means might be absolutely necessary to produce the most happiness in a system of such extent as our own world may be, taking in all that is past and to come, though we should suppose it detached from the whole of things. Indeed we are so far from being able to judge of this that we are not judges what may be the necessary means of raising and conducting one person to the highest perfection and happiness of his nature. Nay, even in the little affairs of the present life we find men of different educations and ranks are not competent judges of the conduct of each other. Our whole nature leads us to ascribe all moral perfection to God, and to deny all imperfection of him. And this will for ever be a practical proof of his moral character, to such as will consider what a practical proof is, because it is the voice of God speaking in us. And from hence we conclude virtue must be the happiness, and vice the misery, of every creature; and that regularity and order and right cannot but prevail finally in a universe under his government. But we are in no sort judges what are the necessary means of accomplishing this end.

Let us then, instead of that idle and not very innocent employment of forming imaginary models of a world and schemes of governing, turn our thoughts to what we experience to be the conduct of nature with respect to intelligent creatures: which may be resolved into general laws or rules of administration, in the same way as many of the laws of nature, respecting inanimate matter, may be collected from experiments. And let us compare the known constitution and course of things with what is said to be the moral system of nature, the acknowledged dispensations of Providence, or that government which we find ourselves under, with what religion teaches us to believe and expect, and see whether they are not analogous and of a piece. And upon such a comparison it will, I think, be found that they are very much so—that both may be traced up to the same general laws and resolved into the same principles of divine conduct.

The analogy here proposed to be considered is of pretty large extent and consists of several parts; in some more, in others less, exact. In some few instances, perhaps, it may amount to a real practical proof, in others not so; yet in these there is a confirmation of what is proved otherways. It will undeniably show, what too many need to have shown to them, that the system of religion, both natural and revealed, considered only as a system and prior to the proof of it, is not a subject of ridicule, unless that of nature be so too. And it will afford an answer to almost all objections against the system both of natural and revealed religion, though not perhaps in so great a degree, yet in a very considerable degree, an answer to the objections against the evidence of it: for objections against a proof and objections against what is said to be proved, the reader will observe, are different things.

B. IMMORTALITY

Analogy of Religion, Part I, Ch. I

Strange difficulties have been raised by some concerning personal identity, or the sameness of living agents, implied in the notion of our existing now and hereafter or in any two successive moments.[1] . . . But without regard to any of them here let us consider what the analogy of nature, and the several changes which we have undergone and those which we know we may undergo without being destroyed, suggest as to the effect which death may or may not have upon us; and whether it be not from thence probable that we may survive this change and exist in a future state of life and perception.

I. From our being born into the present world in the helpless imperfect state of infancy and having arrived from thence to mature age, we find it to be a general law of nature in our own species that the same creatures, the same individuals, should exist in degrees of life and perception, with capacities of action, enjoyment and suffering in one period of their being greatly different from those appointed them in another period of it. And in other creatures the same law holds. For the difference of their capacities and states of life at their birth (to go no higher) and in maturity—the change of worms into flies and the vast enlargement of their locomotive powers by such change; and birds and insects bursting the shell, their habitation, and by this means entering into a new world, furnished with new accommodations for them, and finding a new sphere of action assigned them: these are instances of this general law of nature. Thus all the various and wonderful transformations of animals are to be taken into consideration here. But the states of life in which we ourselves existed formerly, in the womb and in our infancy, are almost as different from our present, in mature age, as it is possible to conceive any two states or degrees of life can be. Therefore, that we are to exist hereafter in a state as different (suppose) from our present as this is from our former is but according to

[1] B. refers in particular to Locke's views on the problem of personal identity, which he criticizes in a Dissertation appended to the *Analogy*. Locke had argued that personal identity lies in the identity of consciousness, for when we ascribe two acts at different times to the same person, it is implied that he who does the later act remembers or could remember the earlier act, and personal identity does not appear to consist in identity of matter, since in living creatures the variation of great parcels of matter does not alter the identity. For this and other arguments see *An Essay concerning Human Understanding*, Bk II, Ch. xxvii. B. replies tellingly that remembering itself presupposes the idea of personal identity (for to remember an action involves remembering that it is *my* action). Consequently an attempt to define personal identity in terms of memory or consciousness will be circular, and therefore useless.

the analogy of nature—according to a natural order or appointments of the very same kind as what we have already experienced.

II. We know we are endued with capacities of action, of happiness and misery, for we are conscious of acting, of enjoying pleasure and suffering pain. Now, that we have these powers and capacities before death is a presumption that we shall retain them through and after death, indeed a probability of it sufficient to act upon, unless there be some positive reason to think that death is the destruction of those living powers—because there is in every case a probability that all things will continue as we experience they are, in all respects except those in which we have some reason to think they will be altered. This is that kind of presumption or probability from analogy, expressed in the very word *continuance*, which seems our only natural reason for believing the course of the world will continue tomorrow as it has done so far as our experience or knowledge of history can carry us back. Nay, it seems our only reason for believing that any one substance now existing will continue to exist a moment longer—the self-existent substance only excepted. Thus, if men were assured that the unknown event, death, was not the destruction of our faculties of perception and of action, there would be no apprehension that any other power or event unconnected with this of death would destroy their faculties just at the instant of each creature's death—and therefore no doubt but that they would remain after it; which shows the high probability that our living powers will continue after death, unless there be some ground to think that death is their destruction.* For if it would be in a manner certain that we should survive death, provided it were certain that death would not be our destruction, it must be highly probable that we shall survive it if there be no ground to think death will be our destruction.

Now though I think it must be acknowledged that prior to the natural and moral proofs of a future life commonly insisted upon, there would arise a general confused suspicion that in the great shock and alteration which we shall undergo by death we (that is, our living powers) might be wholly destroyed; yet even prior to these proofs there is really no particular distinct ground or reason for this apprehension at all, so far as I can find.

* *Destruction of living powers* is a manner of expression unavoidably ambiguous, and may suggest either *the destruction of a living being so as that the same living being shall be incapable of ever perceiving or acting again at all* or *the destruction of those means and instruments by which it is capable of its present life, of its present state of perception and action.* It is here used in the former sense. When it is used in the latter, the epithet *present* is added. The loss of a man's eye is a destruction of living powers in the latter sense. But we have no reason to think the destruction of living powers in the former sense to be possible. We have no more reason to think a being, endued with living powers, ever loses them during its whole existence than to believe that a stone ever acquires them.

If there be, it must arise either from *the reason of the thing* or from *the analogy of Nature*.

But we cannot argue from *the reason of the thing* that death is the destruction of living agents, because we know not at all what death is in itself, but only some of its effects, such as the dissolution of flesh, skin and bones. And these effects do in no wise appear to imply the destruction of a living agent. And besides, as we are greatly in the dark upon what the exercise of our living powers depends, so we are wholly ignorant what the powers themselves depend upon—the powers themselves as distinguished not only from their actual exercise but also from the present capacity of exercising them, and as opposed to their destruction: for sleep or . . . a swoon shows us not only that these powers exist when they are not exercised but shows also that they exist when there is no present capacity of exercising them, or that the capacities of exercising them for the present, as well as the actual exercise of them, may be suspended and yet the powers themselves remain undestroyed. Since, then, we know not at all upon what the existence of our living powers depends, this shows farther there can no probability be collected from the reason of the thing that death will be their destruction; because their existence may depend upon something in no degree affected by death—upon something quite out of the reach of this king of terrors—so that there is nothing more certain than that *the reason of the thing* shows us no connection between death and the destruction of living agents. Nor can we find anything throughout the whole *analogy of Nature* to afford us even the slightest presumption that animals ever lose their living powers, much less, if it were possible, that they lose them by death; for we have no faculties wherewith to trace any beyond or through it, so as to see what becomes of them. This event removes them from our view. It destroys the *perceptible* proof which we had before their death of their being possessed of living powers, but does not appear to afford the least reason to believe that they are then, or by that event, deprived of them.

And our knowing that they were possessed of these powers, up to the very period to which we have faculties capable of tracing them, is itself a probability of their retaining them beyond it. And this is confirmed, and a sensible credibility is given to it, by observing the very great and astonishing changes which we have experienced; so great that our existence in another state of life, of perception and of action will be but according to a method of providential conduct the like to which has been already exercised even with regard to ourselves according to a course of nature the like to which we have already gone through.

However, as one cannot but be greatly sensible how difficult it is to silence imagination enough to make the voice of reason even distinctly heard in this case, as we are accustomed from our youth up to indulge that forward delusive faculty ever obtruding beyond its sphere—of some assistance indeed to apprehension, but the author of all error, as we plainly lose ourselves in gross and crude conceptions of things, taking for granted that we are acquainted with what, indeed, we are wholly ignorant of—it may be proper to consider the imaginary presumptions that death will be our destruction, arising from these kinds of early and lasting prejudices, and to show how little they can really amount to, even though we cannot wholly divest ourselves of them. And:

I. All presumption of death's being the destruction of living beings must go upon supposition that they are compounded and so dissoluble; but since consciousness is a single and indivisible power it should seem that the subject in which it resides must be so too. For were the motion of any particle of matter absolutely one and indivisible so that it should imply a contradiction to suppose part of this motion to exist and part not to exist—that is, part of this matter to move and part to be at rest—then its power of motion would be indivisible and so also would the subject in which the power inheres, namely the particle of matter; for if this could be divided into two, one part might be moved and the other at rest, which is contrary to the supposition. In like manner it has been argued,[1] and, for anything appearing to the contrary, justly, that since the perception or consciousness which we have of our own existence is indivisible, so as that it is a contradiction to suppose one part of it should be here and the other there, the perceptive power or the power of consciousness is indivisible too, and consequently the subject in which it resides, that is, the conscious being. Now upon supposition that the living agent each man calls himself is thus a single being, which there is at least no more difficulty in conceiving than in conceiving it to be a compound, and of which there is the proof now mentioned, it follows that our organized bodies are no more ourselves or part of ourselves than any other matter around us. And it is as easy to conceive how matter, which is no part of ourselves, may be appropriated to us in the manner which our present bodies are, as how we can receive impressions from and have power over any matter. It is as easy to conceive that we may exist out of bodies as in them; that we might have animated bodies of any other organs and senses wholly different from these now given us and that we may hereafter animate these same or new bodies variously modified and organized; as to conceive how we can animate

[1] Samuel Clarke (1675–1729), English theologian and philosopher, whose Boyle Lectures, *A Discourse concerning the Being and Attributes of God*, includes an extended criticism of Locke's empiricism. In 1717 was published his famous correspondence with Leibniz regarding Newtonian ideas concerning space and time.

such bodies as our present. And lastly, the dissolution of all these several organized bodies, supposing ourselves to have successively animated them, would have no more conceivable tendency to destroy the living beings, ourselves, or deprive us of living faculties, the faculties of perception and action, than the dissolution of any foreign matter, which we are capable of receiving impressions from and making use of for the common occasions of life.

II. The simplicity and absolute oneness of a living agent cannot, indeed, from the nature of the thing, be properly proved by experimental observations; but as these *fall in* with the supposition of its unity, so they plainly lead us to *conclude* certainly that our gross organized bodies, with which we perceive the objects of sense, and with which we act, are no part of ourselves, and therefore show us that we have no reason to believe their destruction to be ours, even without determining whether our living substances be material or immaterial. For we see by experience that men may lose their limbs, their organs of sense and even the greatest part of these bodies, and yet remain the same living agents. And persons can trace up the existence of themselves to a time when the bulk of their bodies was extremely small in comparison with what it is in mature age; and we cannot but think that they might then have lost a considerable part of that small body, and yet have remained the same living agents, as they may now lose great part of their present body and remain so. And it is certain that the bodies of all animals are in a constant flux from that never-ceasing attrition which there is in every part of them. Now things of this kind unavoidably teach us to distinguish between these living agents, ourselves, and large quantities of matter in which we are very closely interested: since these may be alienated and actually are in a daily course of succession and changing their owners, whilst we are assured that each living agent remains one and the same permanent being. And this general observation leads us on to the following ones:

First, that we have no way of determining by experience what is the certain bulk of the living being each man calls himself; and yet, till it be determined that it is larger in bulk than the solid elementary particles of matter, which there is no ground to think any natural power can dissolve, there is no sort of reason to think death to be the dissolution of it, of the living being, even though it should not be absolutely indissoluble.

Secondly, from our being so nearly related to and interested in certain systems of matter, suppose our flesh and bones, and afterwards ceasing to be at all related to them—the living agents, ourselves, remaining all this while undestroyed, notwithstanding such alienation, and consequently these systems of matter not being ourselves—it follows further that we have no ground to conclude any other, suppose *internal systems* of matter to be the living agents, ourselves, because we can have no ground to conclude this but from our relation to and interest in such systems of matter; and therefore we can have no reason to conclude what befalls those systems of matter at death to be the destruction of the living agents. We have already, several times over, lost a great part, or perhaps the whole, of our body, according to certain common established laws of nature, yet we remain the same living agents: when we shall lose as great a part, or the whole, by another common established law of nature, death, why may we not also remain the same? That the alienation has been gradual in one case and in the other will be more at once, does not prove anything to the contrary. We have passed undestroyed through those many and great revolutions of matter, so peculiarly appropriated to ourselves; why should we imagine death will be so fatal to us? Nor can it be objected that what is thus alienated or lost is no part of our original solid body, but only adventitious matter, because we may lose entire limbs which must have contained many solid parts and vessels of the original body; or if this be not admitted, we have no proof that any of these solid parts are dissolved or alienated by death—though, by the way, we are very closely related to that extraneous and adventitious matter whilst it continues united to and distending the several parts of our solid body. But, after all, the relation a person bears to those parts of his body to which he is the most closely related—what does it appear to amount to but this, that the living agent and those parts of the body mutually affect each other? And the same thing, the same thing in kind, though not in degree, may be said of *all foreign* matter which gives us ideas and which we have any power over. From these observations, the whole ground of the imagination is removed that the dissolution of any matter is the destruction of a living agent, from the interest he once had in such matter.

Thirdly, if we consider our body somewhat more distinctly, as made up of organs and instruments of perception and motion, it will bring us to the same conclusion. Thus the common optical experiments show, and even the observation how sight is assisted by glasses shows, that we see with our eyes in the same sense as we see with glasses. Nor is there any reason to believe that we see with them in any other sense—any other, I mean, which would lead us to think the eye itself a percipient. The like is to be said of hearing; and our feeling distant solid matter by means of something in our hand, seems an instance of the like kind, as to the subject we are considering. All these are instances of foreign matter, or such as is no part of our body, being instrumental in preparing objects for and conveying them to the perceiving power, in a manner similar or like to the manner in which our organs of sense prepare and convey them. Both are, in a like way, instruments of our receiving such ideas from external objects, as the Author of Nature appointed those external objects to be the occasions of exciting in us. However, glasses are evidently instances of this: namely, of matter which is no part of our body preparing objects for and conveying them towards the perceiving power, in like manner as our bodily organs do. And if we see with our eyes only in the same manner as we do with glasses, the like may be justly concluded by analogy of all our other senses. It is not intended, by anything here said, to affirm that the whole apparatus of vision or of perception by any other of our senses can be traced, through all its steps, quite up to the living power of seeing, of perceiving; but that so far as it can be traced by experimental observations, so far it appears that our organs of sense prepare and convey on objects in order to their being perceived, in like manner as foreign matter does, without affording any shadow of appearance that they themselves perceive. And that we have no reason to think our organs of sense percipients is confirmed by instances of persons losing some of them, the living beings themselves, their former occupiers, remaining unimpaired. It is confirmed also by the experience of dreams; by which we find we are at present possessed of a latent, and what would otherwise be an unimagined, unknown power of perceiving sensible objects in as strong and lively a manner without our external organs of sense as with them.

So also with regard to our power of moving or directing motion by will or choice: upon the destruction of a limb, this active power remains, as it evidently seems, unlessened, so that the living being who has suffered this loss would be capable of moving as before it had another limb to move with. It can walk by the help of an artificial leg, just as it can make use of a pole or a lever to reach towards itself and to move things beyond the length and power of its natural arm: and this last it does in the same manner as it reaches and moves with its natural arm things nearer and of less weight. Nor is there so much as any appearance of our limbs being endued with a power of moving or directing themselves; though they are adapted, like the several parts of a machine, to be the instruments of motion to each other, and some parts of the same limb to be instruments of motion to other parts of it.

Thus a man determines that he will look at such an object through a microscope; or, being lame, suppose that he will walk to such a place with a staff a week hence. His eyes and feet no more determine in these cases than the microscope and staff. Nor is there any ground to think they any more put the determination in practice, or that his eyes are the seers or his feet the movers, in any other sense than as the microscope and the staff are. Upon the whole, then, our organs of sense and our limbs are certainly instruments which the living persons, ourselves, make use of to perceive and move with—there is not any probability that they are any more, nor, consequently, that we have any other kind of relation to them, than what we may have to any other foreign matter formed into instruments of perception and motion, suppose into a microscope or a staff (I say any other kind of relation, for I am not speaking of the degree of it); nor consequently is there any probability that the alienation or dissolution of these instruments is the destruction of the perceiving and moving agent.

And thus our finding that the dissolution of matter in which living beings were most closely interested is not their dissolution and that the destruction of several of the organs and instruments of perception and of motion belonging to them is not their destruction shows, demonstratively, that there is no ground to think that the dissolution of any other matter or destruction of any other organs and instruments will be the dissolution or destruction of living agents from the like kind of relation. And we have no reason to think we stand in any other kind of relation to anything which we find dissolved by death.

But it is said these observations are equally applicable to brutes; and it is thought an insuperable difficulty that they should be immortal and by consequence capable of everlasting happiness. Now this manner of expression is both invidious and weak; but the thing intended by it is really no difficulty at all, either in the way of natural or moral consideration. For (1) suppose the invidious thing, designed in such a manner of expression, were really implied, as it is not in the least, in the natural immortality of brutes—namely, that they must arrive at great attainments and become rational and moral agents—even this would be no difficulty, since we know not what latent powers and capacities they may be endued with. There was once, prior to experience, as great presumption against human creatures as there is against brute creatures arriving at that degree of understanding which we have in mature age—for we can trace up our own existence to the same origin as theirs. And we find it to be a general law of nature that creatures, endued with capacities of virtue and religion, should be placed in a condition of being in which they are altogether without the use of them for a considerable length of their duration, as in infancy and childhood. And a great part of the human species go out of the present world before they come to the exercise of these capacities in any degree at all. But then (2), the natural immortality of brutes does not in the least imply that they are endued with any latent capacities of a rational or moral nature; and the economy of the universe might require that there should be living creatures without any capacities of this kind. And all difficulties as to the manner how they are disposed of are so apparently and wholly founded on our ignorance that 'tis wonderful they should be insisted upon by any but such as are weak enough to think they are acquainted with the whole system of things. There is, then, absolutely nothing at all in this objection which is so rhetorically urged, against the greatest part of the natural proof or presumptions of the immortality of human minds, for 'tis less applicable to the following observation, which is more peculiar to mankind:

III. That as 'tis evident our *present* powers and capacities of reason, memory and affection do not depend upon our gross body in the manner in which perception by our organs of sense does, so they do not appear to depend upon it at all in any such manner as to give ground to think that the dissolution of this body will be the destruction of these our *present* powers of reflection as it will of our powers of sensation, or to give ground to conclude even that it will be so much as a suspension of the former.

Human creatures exist at present in two states of life and perception different from each other, each of which has its own peculiar laws and its own peculiar enjoyments and sufferings. When any of our senses are affected or appetites gratified with the objects of them we may be said to exist or live in a state of sensation. When none of our senses are affected and yet we perceive and reason and act we may be said to exist or live in a state of reflection. Now it is by no means certain that anything which is dissolved by death is in any way necessary to the living being in this state of reflection, after ideas are gained; for though from our present constitution and condition of being our external organs are necessary for conveying in ideas to our reflecting powers, as carriages and levers and scaffolds are in architecture, yet when these ideas are brought in we are capable of reflecting in the most intense degree and of enjoying the greatest pleasure and feeling the greatest pain by means of that reflection, without any assistance from our senses, and without any at all which we know of from that body which will be dissolved by death. It does not appear, then, that the relation of this gross body to the reflecting being is in any degree necessary to thinking—to our intellectual enjoyments and sufferings—nor consequently that the dissolution or alienation of the former by death will be the destruction of those present powers which render us capable of this state of reflection. Further, there are instances of mortal diseases which do not at all affect our present intellectual powers; and this affords a presumption that those diseases will not destroy these present powers. Indeed, from the observations made above it appears that there is no presumption, from their mutually affecting each other, that the dissolution of the body is the destruction of the living agent. And by the same reasoning it must appear too that there is no presumption, from their mutually affecting each other, that the dissolution of the body is the destruction of our present reflecting powers; but instances of their not affecting each other afford a presumption to the contrary. Instances of mortal diseases not impairing our present reflecting powers evidently turn our thoughts even from imagining such diseases to be the destruction of them. Several things, indeed, greatly affect all our living powers and at length suspend the exercise of them—as for instance drowsiness, increasing till it ends in sound sleep; and from hence we might have imagined it would destroy them, till we found by experience the weakness of this way of judging. But in the diseases now mentioned there is not so much as this shadow of probability to lead us to any such conclusion as to the reflecting powers which we have at present; for in these diseases persons, the moment before death, appear to be in the highest vigour of life—they reveal apprehension, memory, reason, all entire, with the utmost force of affection, sense of a character, of shame and honour, and the highest mental enjoyments and sufferings, even to the last gasp; and these surely prove even greater vigour of life than bodily strength does. Now what pretence is there for thinking that a progressive disease, when arrived to such a degree, I mean that degree which is mortal, will destroy those powers which were not impaired, which were not affected by it, during its whole progress quite up to that degree? And if death by diseases of this kind is not the destruction of our present reflecting powers, 'twill scarce be thought that death by any other means is.

It is obvious that this general observation may be carried on farther: and there appears so little connection between our bodily powers of sensation and our present powers of reflection that there is no reason to conclude that death, which destroys the former, does so much as suspend the exercise of the latter or interrupt our *continuing* to exist in the like state of reflection which we do now. For suspension of reason, memory and the affections which they excite is no part of the idea of death nor is implied in our notion of it. And our daily experiencing these powers to be exercised without any assistance that we know of from those bodies which will be dissolved by death, and our finding that our exercise of them is so lively to the last—these feelings afford a sensible apprehension that death may not perhaps be so much as a discontinuance of the exercise of these powers nor of the enjoyments and sufferings which it implies;* so that our

* There are three distinct questions relating to a future life here considered: Whether death be the destruction of living agents? if not, Whether it be the destruction of their *present* powers of reflection, as it certainly is the destruction of their present powers of sensation? and if not, Whether it be the suspension or discontinuance of the exercise of these present reflecting powers? Now if there be no reason to believe the last there will be, if that were possible, less for the next, and still less for the first.

post-humous life, whatever there may be in it additional to our present, yet may not be entirely beginning anew, but going on. Death may, in some sort and in some respects, answer to our birth, which is not a suspension of the faculties which we had before it or a total change of the state of life in which we existed when in the womb, but a continuation of both, with such and such great alterations.

Nay, for aught we know of ourselves, of our present life and of death, death may immediately in the natural course of things put us into a higher and more enlarged state of life as our birth does: a state in which our capacities and sphere of perception and of action may be much greater than at present. For, as our relation to our external organs of sense renders us capable of existing in our present state of sensation, so it may be the only natural hindrance to our existing, immediately and of course, in a higher state of reflection. The truth is, reason does not at all show us in what state death naturally leaves us. But were we sure that it would suspend all our perceptive and active powers, yet the suspension of a power and the destruction of it are effects so totally different in kind—as we experience from sleep and a swoon—that we cannot in any wise argue from one to the other or conclude, even to the lowest degree of probability, that the same kind of force which is sufficient to suspend our faculties, though it be increased ever so much, will be sufficient to destroy them.

These observations together may be sufficient to show how little presumption there is that death is the destruction of human creatures. However, there is the shadow of analogy, which may lead us to imagine it is—the supposed likeness which is observed between the decay of vegetables and of living creatures. And this likeness is indeed sufficient to afford the poets very apt illusions to the flowers of the field, in their pictures of the frailty of our present life. But in reason, the analogy is so far from holding that there appears no ground even for the comparison as to the present question, because one of the two subjects compared is wholly void of that which is the principal and chief thing in the other, the power of perception and of action, and which is the only thing we are enquiring about the continuance of; so that the destruction of a vegetable is an event not similar or analogous to the destruction of a living agent.

But if, as was above intimated, leaving off the delusive custom of substituting imagination in the room of experience, we would confine ourselves to what we do know and understand; if we would argue only from that and from that form of expectation; it would appear at first sight that as no probability of living beings ever ceasing to be so can be concluded from the reason of the thing, so none can be collected from the analogy of

Nature, because we cannot trace any living beings beyond death. But as we are conscious that we are endued with capacities of perception and of action and are living persons, what we are to go upon is that we shall continue so till we foresee some accident or event which will endanger those capacities or be likely to destroy us, which death does in no wise appear to be.

And thus, when we go out of this world we may pass into new scenes and a new state of life and action just as naturally as we came into the present. And this new state may naturally be a social one. And the advantages of it, advantages of every kind, may naturally be bestowed, according to some fixed general laws of wisdom, upon every one in proportion to the degrees of his virtue. And though the advantages of that future natural state should not be bestowed, as these of the present in some measure are, by the will of the society, but entirely by his more immediate action upon whom the whole frame of nature depends, yet this distribution may be just as natural as their being distributed here by the instrumentality of men. And indeed though one were to allow any confused undetermined sense which people please to put upon the word *natural*, it would be a shortness of thought scarce credible to imagine, that no system or course of things can be so, but only what we see at present: especially whilst the probability of a future life or the natural immortality of the soul is admitted upon the evidence of reason; because this is really both admitting and denying at once a state of being different from the present to be natural. But the only distinct meaning of that word is *stated*, *fixed* or *settled*; since what is natural as much requires and presupposes an intelligent agent to render it so—that is, to affect it continually or at stated times—as what is supernatural or miraculous does to affect it once. And from hence it must follow that people's notion of what is natural will be enlarged in proportion to their greater knowledge of the works of God and the dispensations of his Providence. Nor is there any absurdity in supposing that there may be beings in the universe whose capacities and knowledge and views may be so extensive as that the whole Christian dispensation may to them appear natural—that is, analogous or conformable to God's dealings with other parts of his creation—as natural as the visible known course of things appears to us; for there seems scarce any other possible sense to be put upon the word but that only in which it is here used, similar, stated or uniform.

The credibility of a future life which has here been insisted upon, how little soever it may satisfy our curiosity, seems to answer all the purposes of religion in like manner as a demonstrative proof. Indeed a proof, even a demonstrative one, of a future life, would not be a proof of religion.

For that we live hereafter is just as reconcilable with the scheme of atheism and as well to be accounted for by it as that we are now alive is; and therefore nothing can be more absurd than to argue from that scheme that there can be no future state. But as religion implies a future state, any presumption against such a state is a presumption against religion. And the foregoing observations remove all presumptions of this sort and prove, to a very considerable degree of probability, one fundamental doctrine of religion which, if believed, would greatly open and dispose the mind seriously to attend to the general evidence of the whole.

13

HUME

on THE EXISTENCE OF GOD *and on* MIRACLES

Biographical Note David Hume was the third child of a Scots country gentleman, with an estate near Berwick. Born in Edinburgh, 1711. Educated at Edinburgh University, at which he matriculated in 1723. Finished there in 1725 or 1726, and lived at home for a time. After an unsuccessful venture into business in Bristol, 1734, he went to France, staying chiefly at La Flèche in Anjou (see above, p. 105), during which time he wrote the *Treatise of Human Nature*. Returned to England in 1737; and the work was published in 1739–40. He went back to the family home and continued there until 1745, when he served for a year as tutor to the Marquis of Annandale. He held an appointment on the staff of General St Clair, a distant relative, for two years in the first instance, and then later in Vienna and Turin, returning to Scotland in 1749. Removed to Edinburgh in 1751 and was elected Keeper of the Advocates' Library in 1752. An appointment in the embassy gave him three years in Paris, 1763–6. After a time in London he returned to Edinburgh, where he died in 1776.

Principal philosophical works: *Treatise of Human Nature* (1739–40), *Essays Moral and Political* (1741–2), *Philosophical Essays concerning Human Understanding* (1748), *An Enquiry concerning the Principles of Morals* (1751) and *Dialogues concerning Natural Religion* (published posthumously).

Philosophical Note H. is usually classed with Locke and Berkeley as one of the three great British empiricists. His principle that all knowledge is based upon impressions (i.e. perceptions) and ideas (the copies of impressions, i.e. the images given in memory and imagination) entailed that there is no 'external world' distinct from perceptions. But perhaps the most important part of his theory is his criticism of the notion of *causation* (it was this which stimulated Kant's enquiries, since it appeared to cut away the basis of Newtonian science). H. contended, briefly, that the necessary connection ascribed to the relation of cause and effect is merely a habit of our own minds; for an investigation of causes shows that all that is given in experience is that two perceptions (one of the cause, the other of the effect) are constantly conjoined—i.e. the cause is constantly found to precede and be contiguous with the effect. But if there is no necessary connection between cause and effect, then causal inferences appear to have no rational ground, but are simply produced by habit. It is mainly for two reasons, then, that H. is characterized as a sceptic: first, for his rejection of a reality independent of perceptions; and second, for his view that there is no rational ground for asserting that the future will be like the past.

In his *Natural History of Religion*, H. deals with the origin of religion in human nature, while in the *Dialogues* he is concerned with the foundation of religion in reason: that is, in the one work he investigates the causes of religious belief, in the other with the reasons for religious belief. Thus the *Dialogues* are more strictly philosophical in nature than the other work. But it is useful, as background to the following selections, to note the main points made by H. in the earlier work. Man is, he says, at first a barbarous creature, so much concerned to fulfil his many wants that he has no leisure for rational enquiry. The traditional stories about divinities serve to satisfy such questions as he is inclined to raise. However, it being thought that gods are open to influence through gifts and adulation, each generation successively, pressed by fears and hardships, increases its flattery in describing the gods—'till at last they arrive at infinity itself, beyond which there is no further progress'. Thus it is by chance that religion and philosophy (which recognizes that nature bespeaks an intelligent Author) come to coincide. Despite the philosophical superiority of monotheism, however, certain advantages still lie with polytheism. For the concept of a single and universal God calls forth furious and implacable religious zeal, while idolatry is tolerant. Again, where the gods are but little superior to men, there is a greater tendency to emulate them, while the idea of an infinitely good and great Being merely tends to inspire abasement. H. also adds a harsh stricture upon Christianity, in that whereas in pagan religions there was a fair division of labour between philosophy and religion—the former catering for the educated, the latter for the ignorant—, in Christianity philosophy is made into a handmaid of theology and reason in this way is restricted and perverted. These and other unfavourable contrasts between monotheism and polytheism are hardly perhaps the sort of comments which are legitimate in a work which is in intention descriptive; but they give some indication of the attitude of H. towards traditional religion.

The *Dialogues*, published after H.'s death, present some difficulty in interpretation, since it is not quite clear which, if any, of the disputants represents H.'s own opinion. It is true that one of the three speakers, Demea—who is the representative of orthodoxy and is somewhat impatient of philosophical criticisms of religion—certainly does not express H.'s views. But whether H. speaks through Philo—the extreme sceptic—or Cleanthes—whose scepticism is very moderate and who propounds a fairly straightforward empiricist position with regard to the truth of religion—is disputable. For references to writings bearing on this issue and for a convincing attempt to show that it is Philo who chiefly represents H. in the discussion, see N. Kemp Smith, Hume's *Dialogues concerning Natural Religion*, Ch. V.

The uncertainty about H.'s own position on the matters discussed in the *Dialogues* is partly also due to the fact that the argument between the three disputants and the comments thereon are reported by a fourth character, the young Pamphilus: when, therefore, in the concluding paragraph, Pamphilus says that Cleanthes' position is preferable to that of Philo, this need by no means be taken as an expression of the author's own judgment.

Summary of Preceding Argument. In Part I, the discussion opens with some remarks about Pamphilus' education. It is Cleanthes' statement that natural theology is the last subject in the curriculum which leads Philo to ask why the principles of religion should be taught so late on—and this triggers off the general discussion on the evidence of God's existence. Cleanthes declares that, whatever *general* scepticism we may profess, we accept evidence on particular matters; and he claims that the *a posteriori* argument, from design, is incontrovertible. He then proceeds to state his version of the argument.

Bibliographical Note The following editions are useful: L. A. Selby-Bigge, *Enquiries concerning the Human Understanding and concerning the Principles of Morals* (2nd edn, Oxford, 1902), and *Treatise of Human Nature* (reprint, Oxford, 1955), N. K. Smith, *Dialogues on Natural Religion* (London, 1935), H. E. Root, *Natural History of Religion*; and selections illustrating his Theory of Knowledge (D. C. Yalden-Thomas, 1951), and Theory of Politics (F. Watkins, 1951). Accounts of H.'s philosophy are given in: J. A. Passmore, *Hume's Intentions* (London, 1952), D. G. C. Macnabb, *David Hume* (Oxford, 1951), A. H. Basson, *David Hume* (London, Pelican, 1959), N. K. Smith, *Philosophy of David Hume* (London, 1941). On particular aspects, see H. H. Price, *Hume's Theory of the External World* (Oxford, 1940) and A. E. Taylor, 'David Hume and the Miraculous', *Philosophical Studies* (London, 1934).

A. THE EXISTENCE OF GOD

Dialogues on Natural Religion, Parts II (opening paragraphs omitted)–V

Not to lose time in circumlocutions, said *Cleanthes*, addressing himself to Demea, much less in replying to the pious declamations of Philo, I shall briefly explain how I conceive this matter. Look round the world: contemplate the whole and every part of it: you will find it to be nothing but one great machine, subdivided into an infinite number of lesser machines, which again admit of subdivisions, to a degree beyond what human senses and faculties can trace and explain. All these various machines, and even their most minute parts, are adjusted to each other with an accuracy which ravishes into admiration all men who have ever contemplated them. The curious adapting of means to ends, throughout all nature, resembles exactly, though it much exceeds, the productions of human contrivance; of human design, thought, wisdom and intelligence. Since therefore the effects resemble each other we are led to infer, by all the rules of analogy, that the causes also resemble, and that the Author of nature is somewhat similar to the mind of man, though possessed of much larger faculties, proportioned to the grandeur of the work, which he has executed. By this argument *a posteriori*[1] and by this argument alone, we do prove at once the existence of a Deity and his similarity to human mind and intelligence.

I shall be so free, Cleanthes, said *Demea*, as to tell you that from the beginning I could not approve of your conclusion concerning the similarity of the Deity to men; still less can I approve of the means by which

[1] I.e., an argument which starts with observed facts. See n. 2 to p. 86.

you endeavour to establish it. What! No demonstration of the being of a God! No abstract arguments! No proofs *a priori*! Are these, which have hitherto been so much insisted upon by philosophers, all fallacy, all sophism? Can we reach no farther in this subject than experience and probability? I will not say that this is betraying the cause of a Deity: but surely, by this affected candour, you give advantage to atheists, which they never could obtain by the mere dint of argument and reasoning.

What I chiefly scruple in this subject, said *Philo*, is not so much that all religious arguments are by Cleanthes reduced to experience, as that they appear not to be even the most certain and irrefragable of that inferior kind. That a stone will fall, that fire will burn, that the earth has solidity, we have observed a thousand and a thousand times, and when any new instance of this nature is presented we draw without hesitation the accustomed inference. The exact similarity of the cases gives us a perfect assurance of a similar event, and a stronger evidence is never desired nor sought after. But wherever you depart, in the least, from the similarity of the cases, you diminish proportionally the evidence, and may at last bring it to a very weak *analogy* which is confessedly liable to error and uncertainty. After having experienced the circulation of blood in human creatures, we make no doubt that it takes place in Titius and Maevius: but from its circulation in frogs and fishes, it is only a presumption, though a strong one, from analogy, that it takes place in men and other animals. The analogical reasoning is much weaker when we infer the circulation of the sap in vegetables from our experience that the blood circulates in animals, and those who hastily followed that imperfect analogy are found, by more accurate experiments, to have been mistaken.

If we see a house, Cleanthes, we conclude, with the greatest certainty, that it had an architect or builder, because this is precisely that species of effect which we have experienced to proceed from that species of cause. But surely you will not affirm that the universe bears such a resemblance to a house that we can with the same certainty infer a similar cause, or that the analogy is here entire or perfect. The dissimilitude is so striking that the utmost you can here pretend to is a guess, a conjecture, a presumption concerning a similar cause; and how that pretension will be received in the world I leave you to consider.

It would surely be very ill received, replied *Cleanthes*, and I should be deservedly blamed and detested, did I allow that the proofs of a Deity amounted to no more than a guess or conjecture. But is the whole adjustment of means to ends in a house and in the universe so slight a resemblance? The economy of final causes?[1] The order, proportion and

[1] 'Economy': 'management', 'system'.

arrangement of every part? Steps of a stair are plainly contrived that human legs may use them in mounting, and this inference is certain and infallible. Human legs are also contrived for walking and mounting; and this inference, I allow, is not altogether so certain, because of the dissimilarity which you remark; but does it therefore deserve the name only of presumption or conjecture?

Good God! cried *Demea*, interrupting him, where are we? Zealous defenders of religion allow that the proofs of a Deity fall short of perfect evidence! And you, Philo, on whose assistance I depended in proving the adorable mysteriousness of the divine nature, do you assent to all these extravagant opinions of Cleanthes? For what other name can I give them? Or why spare my censure, when such principles are advanced, supported by such an authority, before so young a man as Pamphilus?

You seem not to apprehend, replied *Philo*, that I argue with Cleanthes in his own way, and by showing him the dangerous consequences of his tenets hope at last to reduce him to our opinion. But what sticks most with you, I observe, is the representation which Cleanthes has made of the argument *a posteriori*, and finding that that argument is likely to escape your hold and vanish into air, you think it so disguised that you can scarcely believe it to be set in its true light. Now, however much I may dissent in other respects from the dangerous principles of Cleanthes I must allow that he has fairly represented that argument, and I shall endeavour so to state the matter to you that you will entertain no farther scruples with regard to it.

Were a man to abstract from every thing which he knows or has seen he would be altogether incapable, merely from his own ideas, to determine what kind of scene the universe must be, or to give the preference to one state or situation of things above another. For as nothing which he clearly conceives could be esteemed impossible or implying a contradiction, every chimera of his fancy would be upon an equal footing; nor could he assign any just reason why he adheres to one idea or system and rejects the others which are equally possible.

Again: after he opens his eyes and contemplates the world as it really is it would be impossible for him, at first, to assign the cause of any one event, much less of the whole of things or of the universe. He might set his fancy a-rambling and she might bring him in an infinite variety of reports and representations. These would all be possible; but being all equally possible, he would never of himself give a satisfactory account for his preferring one of them to the rest.

Now according to this method of reasoning, Demea, it follows (and is indeed tacitly allowed by Cleanthes himself) that order, arrangement or the adjustment of final causes[1] is not, of itself, any proof of design, but only so far as it has been experienced to proceed from that principle. For aught we can know *a priori*, matter may contain the source or spring of order originally, within itself, as well as mind does; and there is no more difficulty in conceiving that the several elements from an internal unknown cause may fall into the most exquisite arrangement than to conceive that their ideas, in the great, universal mind, from a like internal, unknown cause, fall into that arrangement. The equal possibility of both these suppositions is allowed. By experience we find (according to Cleanthes) that there is a difference between them. Throw several pieces of steel together, without shape or form; they will never arrange themselves so as to compose a watch; stone, and mortar, and wood, without an architect, never erect a house. But the ideas in a human mind, we see, by an unknown, inexplicable economy, arrange themselves so as to form the plan of a watch or house. Experience, therefore, proves that there is an original principle of order in mind, not in matter. From similar effects we infer similar causes. The adjustment of means to ends is alike in the universe, as in a machine of human contrivance. The causes, therefore, must be resembling.

I was from the beginning scandalized, I must own, with this resemblance, which is asserted, between the Deity and human creatures and must conceive it to imply such a degradation of the supreme Being as no sound theist could endure. With your assistance, therefore, I shall endeavour to defend what you justly call the adorable mysteriousness of the divine nature, and shall refute this reasoning of Cleanthes, provided he allows that I have made a fair representation of it.

When Cleanthes has assented, *Philo*, after a short pause, proceeded in the following manner.

That all inferences, Cleanthes, concerning fact, are founded on experience and that all experimental reasonings are founded on the supposition that similar causes prove similar effects, and similar effects similar causes, I shall not at present much dispute with you. But observe, I entreat you, with what extreme caution all just reasoners proceed in the transferring of experiments to similar cases. Unless the cases be exactly similar they repose no perfect confidence in applying their past observation to any particular phenomenon. Every alteration of circumstances occasions a doubt concerning the event, and it requires new experiments to prove certainly that the new circumstances are of no moment or importance. A change in bulk, situation, arrangement, age, disposition of the air or surrounding bodies—any of these particulars may be attended

[1] See above, p. 59.

with the most unexpected consequences. And unless the objects be quite familiar to us, it is the highest temerity to expect with assurance, after any of these changes, an event similar to that which before fell under our observation. The slow and deliberate steps of philosophers[1] here, if anywhere, are distinguished from the precipitate march of the vulgar, who, hurried by the smallest similitude, are incapable of all discernments or consideration.

But can you think, Cleanthes, that your usual phlegm and philosophy have been preserved in so wide a step as you have taken, when you compared to the universe houses, ships, furniture, machines, and from their similarity in some circumstances inferred a similarity in their causes? Thought, design, intelligence, such as we discover in men and other animals, is no more than one of the springs and principles of the universe, as well as heat or cold, attraction or repulsion, and a hundred others which fall under daily observation. It is an active cause by which some particular parts of nature, we find, produce alterations on other parts. But can a conclusion, with any propriety, be transferred from parts to the whole? Does not the great disproportion bar all comparison and inference? From observing the growth of a hair can we learn anything concerning the generation of a man? Would the manner of a leaf's blowing, even though perfectly known, afford us any instruction concerning the vegetation of a tree?[2]

But allowing that we were to take the *operations* of one part of nature upon another for the foundation of our judgment concerning the *origin* of the whole (which can never be admitted) yet why select so minute, so weak, so bounded a principle as the reason and designof animals as found to be upon this planet? What peculiar privilege has this little agitation of the brain which we call thought, that we must thus make it the model of the whole universe? Our partiality in our own favour does indeed present it on all occasions; but sound philosophy ought carefully to guard against so natural an illusion.

So far from admitting, continued *Philo*, that the operations of a part can afford us any just conclusion concerning the origin of the whole, I will not allow any one part to form a rule for another part if the latter be very remote from the former. Is there any reasonable ground to conclude that the inhabitants of other planets possess thought, intelligence, reason or any thing similar to these faculties in men? When nature has so extremely diversified her manner of operation in this small globe, can we

[1] 'Philosopher' is here used in its earlier, more general sense, as when physics is called—even today in Scottish universities—'natural philosophy'. Thus 'scientist' might be an apt translation here.

[2] 'Vegetation'—i.e. manner of growth.

imagine that she incessantly copies herself throughout so immense a universe? And if thought, as we may well suppose, be confined merely to this narrow corner, and has even there so limited a sphere of action, with what propriety can we assign it for the original cause of all things? The narrow views of a peasant who makes his domestic economy the rule for the government of kingdoms is in comparison a pardonable sophism.

But were we ever so much assured that a thought and reason resembling the human were to be found throughout the whole universe and were its activity elsewhere vastly greater and more commanding than it appears in this globe, yet I cannot see why the operations of a world, constituted, arranged, adjusted, can with any propriety be extended to a world which is in its embryo-state and is advancing towards that constitution and arrangement. By observation we know something of the economy, action and nourishment of a finished animal, but we must transfer with great caution that observation to the growth of a foetus in the womb, and still more, to the formation an animalcule in the loins of its male parent.[1] Nature, we find, even from our limited experience, possesses an infinite number of springs and principles which incessantly discover themselves on every change of her position and situation. And what new and unknown principles would actuate her in so new and unknown a situation as that of the formation of a universe, we cannot without the utmost temerity pretend to determine.

A very small part of this great system, during a very short time, is very imperfectly discovered to us: and do we thence pronounce decisively concerning the origin of the whole?

Admirable conclusion! Stone, wood, brick, iron, brass have not at this time, in this minute globe of earth, an order or arrangement without human art or contrivance; therefore the universe could not originally attain its order and arrangement without something similar to human art. But is a part of nature a rule for another part very wide of the former? Is it a rule for the whole? Is a very small part a rule for the universe? Is nature in one situation a certain rule for nature in another situation, vastly different from the former?

And can you blame me, Cleanthes, if I here imitate the prudent reserve of Simonides,[2] who, according to the noted story, being asked by Hiero *What God was?* desired a day to think of it, and then two days more, and after that manner continually prolonged the term, without ever

[1] 'Animalcule': a term used by seventeenth- and eighteenth-century biologists to refer to the preformed germ of man (and other animals) supposed to reside in the spermatozoon.

[2] Simonides of Ceos (*c.* 556–*c.* 468 BC), the famous Greek lyric poet, ended his days at the court of Hiero I, ruler of Syracuse from 478–67. For the story, see Cicero, *De Natura Deorum* i. 22.

bringing in his definition or description? Could you even blame me if I had answered at first that I did not know and was sensible that this subject lay vastly beyond the reach of my faculties? You might cry out 'Sceptic' and 'Raillier' as much as you pleased; but having found in so many other subjects much more familiar the imperfections and even contradictions of human reason, I never should expect any success from its feeble conjectures in a subject so sublime and so remote from the sphere of our observation. When two *species* of objects have always been observed to be joined together, I can *infer*, by custom, the existence of one wherever I *see* the existence of the other:[1] and this I call an argument from experience. But how this argument can have place, where the objects, as in the present case, are single, individual, without parallel, or specific resemblance, may be difficult to explain. And will any man tell me with a serious countenance, that an orderly universe must arise from some thought and art like the human, because we have experience of it? To ascertain this reasoning, it were requisite that we had experience of the origin of worlds; and it is not sufficient surely that we have seen ships and cities arise from human art and contrivance——

Philo was proceeding in this vehement manner, somewhat between jest and earnest as it appeared to me, when he observed some signs of impatience in Cleanthes and then immediately stopped short. What I had to suggest, said *Cleanthes*, is only that you would not abuse terms or make use of popular expressions to subvert philosophical reasonings. You know that the vulgar often distinguish reason from experience even where the question only relates to matters of fact and existence, though it is found that when that *reason* is properly analysed it is nothing but a species of experience. To prove by experience the existence of the universe from mind is not more contrary to common speech than to prove the motion of the earth from the same principle. And a caviller might raise all the same objections to the Copernican system which you have urged against my

[1] Hume's analysis of causation led him into a curious reliance on *custom*. He argued that the causal relation is not *logical*, i.e. 'A is the cause of B' cannot be deduced from the idea of A. But on the other hand, no general assertion that As cause Bs can be established simply by experience. For what we call the causal relation is simply the constant conjunction of A and B in a regular order of succession (in time) and contiguity. But even when experience has informed us of the constant conjunction of two objects it is impossible for us to satisfy ourselves by reason why we should extend that experience beyond the particular instances we have observed. (We cannot rely on the principle of the Uniformity of Nature—that the future will resemble the past—, since this is neither a logical truth, i.e. it is not such that its denial is self-contradictory, nor is it confirmable by induction, i.e. proceeding from observation, since inductive reasoning presupposes the principle.) Thus H.'s analysis of causation leads him to say that causal inference depends upon custom: having observed a constant conjunction, custom established the principle that like objects placed in like circumstances will always produce like effects. (See Hume's *Treatise*, Bk I, Pt III.) It was H.'s problem and his attempted solution of it that woke Kant from his 'dogmatic slumber': see p. 248.

reasonings. Have you other earths, might he say, which you have seen to move——

Yes! cried Philo, interrupting him, we have other earths. Is not the moon another earth, which we see to turn round its centre? Is not Venus another earth, where we observe the same phenomenon? Are not the revolutions of the sun also a confirmation, from analogy, of the same theory? All the planets, are they not earths, which revolve about the sun? Are not the satellites moons, which move round Jupiter and Saturn, and along with the primary planets, round the sun? These analogies and resemblances, with others which I have not mentioned, are the sole proofs of the Copernican system. And to you it belongs to consider whether you have any analogies of the same kind to support your theory.

In reality, Cleanthes, continued he, the modern system of astronomy is now so much received by all enquirers and has become so essential a part even of our earliest education that we are not commonly very scrupulous in examining the reasons upon which it is founded. It is now become a matter of mere curiosity to study the first writers on that subject who had the full force of prejudice to encounter and were obliged to turn their arguments on every side, in order to render them popular and convincing. But if we peruse Galileo's famous Dialogues concerning the system of the world[1] we shall find that that great genius, one of the sublimest that ever existed, first bent all his endeavours to prove that there was no foundation for the distinction commonly made between elementary and celestial substances.[2] The schools, proceeding from the illusions of sense, had carried this distinction very far, and had established the latter substances to be ingenerable, incorruptible, unalterable, impassible, and had assigned all the opposite qualities to the former. But Galileo, beginning with the moon, proved its similarity in every particular to the earth—its convex figure, its natural darkness when not illuminated, its density, its distinction into solid and liquid, the variations of its phases, the mutual illuminations of the earth and moon, their mutual eclipses, the inequalities of the lunar surface, etc. After many instances of this kind with regard to all the planets, men plainly saw that these bodies became proper objects of experience, and the similarity of their nature enabled us to extend the same arguments and phenomena from one to the other.

In this cautious proceeding of the astronomers you may read your own condemnation, Cleanthes; or rather you may see that the subject in which you are engaged exceeds all human reason and enquiry. Can you pretend

[1] Galileo (1564–1642) published his *Dialogue concerning the Two Chief Systems of the World, the Ptolemaic and the Copernican,* dedicated to the Pope, in 1632.

[2] See above, p. 60.

to show any such similarity between the fabrication of a house and the generation of a universe? Have you ever seen nature in any such situation as resembles the first arrangement of the elements? Have worlds ever been formed under your eye? And have you had leisure to observe the whole progress of the phenomenon, from the first appearance of order to its final consummation? If you have, then cite your experience and deliver your theory.

PART III

Now the most absurd argument, replied *Cleanthes*, in the hands of a man of ingenuity and invention may acquire an air of probability! Are you not aware, Philo, that it became necessary for Copernicus and his first disciples to prove the similarity of the terrestrial and celestial matter because several philosophers,[1] blinded by old systems, and supported by some perceptual appearances, had denied this similarity? but that it is by no means necessary that theists should prove the similarity of the works of nature to those of art, because this similarity is self-evident and undeniable? The same matter, a like form—what more is requisite to show an analogy between their causes and to ascertain the origin of all things from a divine purpose and intention? Your objections, I must freely tell you, are no better than the abstruse cavils of those philosophers who denied motion, and ought to be refuted in the same manner, by illustrations, examples and instances, rather than by serious argument and philosophy.

Suppose, therefore, that an articulate voice were heard in the clouds, much louder and more melodious than any which human art could ever reach. Suppose that this voice were extended in the same instant over all nations and spoke to each nation in its own language and dialect. Suppose that the words delivered not only contain a just sense and meaning, but convey some instruction altogether worthy of a benevolent Being superior to mankind. Could you possibly hesitate a moment concerning the cause of this voice? And must you not instantly ascribe it to some design or purpose? Yet I cannot see but all the same objections (if they merit that appellation) which lie against the system of theism may also be produced against this inference.

Might you not say that all conclusions concerning facts were founded on experience, that when we hear an articulate voice in the dark and thence infer a man, it is only the resemblance of the effects which leads us to conclude that there is a like resemblance in the cause; but that this extraordinary voice, by its loudness, extent and flexibility to all languages,

[1] See above, p. 60.

bears so little analogy to any human voice that we have no reason to suppose any analogy in their causes; and consequently that a rational, wise, coherent speech proceeded you knew not whence from some accidental whistling of the winds, not from any divine reason or intelligence? You see clearly your own objections in these cavils; and I hope too you see clearly that they cannot possibly have more force in the one case than in the other.

But to bring the case still nearer the present one of the universe, I shall make two suppositions, which imply not any absurdity or impossibility.[1] Suppose that there is a natural, universal, invariable language common to every individual of the human race, and that books are natural productions which perpetuate themselves in the same manner as animals and vegetables, by descent and propagation. Several expressions of our passions contain a universal language; all brute animals have a natural speech which, however limited, is very intelligible to their own species. And as there are infinitely fewer parts and less contrivance in the finest composition of eloquence than in the coarsest organized body, the propagation of an Iliad or Aeneid is an easier supposition than that of any plant or animal.

Suppose, therefore, that you enter into your library, thus peopled by natural volumes, containing the most refined reason and exquisite beauty: could you possibly open one of them and doubt that its original cause bore the strongest analogy to mind and intelligence? When it reasons and discourses, when it expostulates, argues and enforces its views and topics, when it collects, disposes and adorns every consideration suited to the subject—could you persist in asserting that all this, at the bottom, had really no meaning and that the first formation of this volume in the loins of its original parent proceeded not from thought and design? Your obstinacy, I know, reaches not that degree of firmness: even your sceptical play and wantonness would be abashed at so glaring an absurdity.

But if there be any difference, Philo, between this supposed case and the real one of the universe, it is all to the advantage of the latter. The anatomy of an animal affords many stronger instances of design than the perusal of Livy and Tacitus. And any objection which you start in the former case, by carrying me back to so unusual and extraordinary a scene as the first formation of worlds, the same objection has place on the

[1] I.e. there is no *logical* absurdity in these suppositions. To suppose that books grow like vegetables is perhaps in an ordinary sense absurd, for it runs counter to a pretty complex set of well established facts and so is unrealistic (whereas to suppose that lemons were red would not be in this way absurd). Nevertheless, the supposition which Cleanthes makes about the books is possible, since it is not self-contradictory, and so is not *logically* absurd. Since much of philosophy is concerned with what is logically possible or impossible, the use of (sometimes fanciful) examples plays a big part in philosophical investigations.

supposition of our vegetating library. Choose then your party, Philo, without ambiguity or evasion: assert either that a rational volume is no proof of a rational cause, or admit of a similar cause to all the works of nature.

Let me here observe too, continued *Cleanthes*, that this religious argument, instead of being weakened by that scepticism so much affected by you, rather acquires force from it and becomes more firm and undisputed. To exclude all argument or reasoning of every kind is either affectation or madness. The declared profession of every reasonable sceptic is only to reject abstruse, remote and refined arguments, to adhere to common sense and the plain instincts of nature, and to assent, wherever any reasons strike him with so full a force that he cannot, without the greatest violence, prevent it. Now the arguments for natural religion are plainly of this kind, and nothing but the most perverse, obstinate metaphysics can reject them. Consider, anatomize the eye: survey its structure and contrivance; and tell me from your own feeling if the idea of a contriver does not immediately flow in upon you with a force like that of sensation. The most obvious conclusion, surely, is in favour of design, and it requires time, reflection and study to summon up those frivolous, though abstruse, objections which can support infidelity. Who can behold the male and female of each species, the correspondence of their parts and instincts, their passions and whole course of life before and after generation, but must be aware that the propagation of the species is intended by nature? Millions and millions of such instances present themselves through every part of the universe, and no language can convey a more intelligible, irresistible meaning than the curious adjustment of final causes. To what degree therefore of blind dogmatism must one have attained to reject such natural and such convincing arguments?

Some beauties in writing we may meet with which seem contrary to rules and which gain the affections and animate the imagination in opposition to all the precepts of criticism and to the authority of the established masters of art. And if the argument of theism be, as you pretend, contradictory to the principles of logic, its universal, its irresistible influence proves clearly that there may be arguments of a like irregular nature. Whatever cavils may be urged, an orderly world, as well as coherent, articulate speech, will still be received as an incontestable proof of design and intention.

It sometimes happens, I own, that the religious arguments have not their due influence on an ignorant savage and barbarian, not because they are obscure and difficult, but because he never asks himself any question with regard to them. Whence arises the curious structure of an animal? From the copulation of its parents. And these whence? From *their* parents. A few removes set the objects at such a distance that to him they are lost in darkness and confusion, nor is he actuated by any curiosity to trace them farther. But this is neither dogmatism nor scepticism, but stupidity—a state of mind very different from your sifting, inquisitive disposition, my ingenious friend. You can trace causes from effects, you can compare the most distant and remote objects, and your greatest errors proceed not from barrenness of thought and invention but from too luxuriant a fertility which suppresses your natural good sense by a profusion of unnecessary scruples and objections.

Here I could observe, Hermippus,[1] that Philo was a little embarrassed and confounded, but while he hesitated in delivering an answer, luckily for him *Demea* broke in upon the discourse and saved his countenance.

Your instance, Cleanthes, said he, drawn from books and language, being familiar, has, I confess, so much more force on that account; but is there not some danger too in this very circumstance, and may it not render us presumptuous by making us imagine we comprehend the Deity and have some adequate idea of his nature and attributes? When I read a volume, I enter into the mind and intention of the author: I become him, in a manner, for the instant, and have an immediate feeling and conception of those ideas which revolved in his imagination while employed in that composition. But so near an approach we never surely can make to the Deity. His ways are not our ways. His attributes are perfect, but incomprehensible. And this volume of nature contains a great and inexplicable riddle, more than any intelligible discourse or reasoning.

The ancient platonists, you know, were the most religious and devout of all the pagan philosophers, yet many of them, particularly Plotinus, expressly declare that intellect or understanding is not to be ascribed to the Deity and that our most perfect worship of him consists not in acts of veneration, reverence, gratitude or love, but in a certain mysterious self-annihilation or total extinction of all our faculties.[2] These ideas are, perhaps, too far stretched; but still it must be acknowledged that by representing the Deity as so intelligible and comprehensible and so similar to the human mind we are guilty of the grossest and most narrow partiality and make ourselves the model of the whole universe.

All the sentiments of the human mind—gratitude, resentment, love, friendship, approbation, blame, pity, emulation, envy—have a plain

[1] The person to whom Pamphilus, the narrator, is describing the discussion.
[2] See above, p. 50.

reference to the state and situation of man, and are calculated for preserving the existence and promoting the activity of such a being in such circumstances. It seems therefore unreasonable to transfer such sentiments to a supreme existence, or to suppose him actuated by them; and the phenomena, besides, of the universe will not support us in such a theory. All our *ideas*, derived from the senses, are confessedly false and delusive and cannot therefore be supposed to have a place in a supreme intelligence. And as the ideas of internal sentiment, added to those of the external senses, compose the whole furniture of human understanding, we may conclude that none of the *materials* of thought are in any respect similar in the human and in the divine intelligence. Now, as to the *manner* of thinking: how can we make any comparison between them or suppose them in any wise resembling? Our thought is fluctuating, uncertain, fleeting, successive and compounded; and were we to remove these circumstances we absolutely annihilate its essence, and it would, in such a case, be an abuse of terms to apply to it the name of thought or reason. At least, if it appear more pious and respectful, as it really is, still to retain these terms when we mention the supreme Being, we ought to acknowledge that their meaning, in that case, is totally incomprehensible, and that the infirmities of our nature do not permit us to reach any ideas which in the least correspond to the ineffable sublimity of the divine attributes.

PART IV

It seems strange to me, said *Cleanthes*, that you, Demea, who are so sincere in the cause of religion should still maintain the mysterious, incomprehensible nature of the Deity and should insist so strenuously that he has no manner of likeness or resemblance to human creatures. The Deity, I can readily allow, possesses many powers and attributes of which we can have no comprehension, but if our ideas, so far as they go, be not just and adequate and correspondent to his real nature, I know not what there is in this subject worth insisting on. Is the name, without any meaning, of such mighty importance? Or how do you mystics, who maintain the absolute incomprehensibility of the Deity, differ from sceptics or atheists, who assert that the first cause of All is unknown and unintelligible? Their temerity must be very great if, after rejecting the production by a mind—I mean a mind resembling the human (for I know of no other)—, they pretend to assign, with certainty, any other specific, intelligible cause. And their conscience must be very scrupulous indeed if they refuse to call the universal unknown cause a God or Deity, and to bestow on him as many sublime eulogies and unmeaning epithets as you shall please to require of them.

Who could imagine, replied *Demea*, that Cleanthes, the calm, philosophical Cleanthes, would attempt to refute his antagonists by affixing a nick-name to them and like the common bigots and inquisitors of the age, have recourse to invective and declamation instead of reasoning? Or does he not perceive that these points are easily retorted, and that *anthropomorphite* is an appellation as invidious, and implies as dangerous consequences, as the epithet of *mystic*, with which he has honoured us? In reality, Cleanthes, consider what it is you assert, when you represent the Deity as similar to a human mind or understanding. What is the soul of man? A composition of various faculties, passions, sentiments, ideas, united indeed into one self or person, but still distinct from each other. When it reasons, the ideas which are parts of its discourse arrange themselves in a certain form or order, which is not preserved entire for a moment, but immediately gives place to another arrangement. New opinions, new passions, new affections, new feelings arise, which continually diversify the mental scene and produce in it the greatest variety and most rapid succession imaginable. How is this compatible with that perfect immutability and simplicity which all true theists ascribe to the Deity? By the same act, say they, he sees past, present and future: his love and his hatred, his mercy and his justice are one individual operation: he is entire in every instant of duration. No succession, no change, no acquisition, no diminution. What he is implies not in it any shadow of distinction or diversity. And what he is, this moment, he ever has been and ever will be, without any new judgment, sentiment or operation. He stands fixed in one simple, perfect state; nor can you ever say, with any propriety, that this act of his is different from that other, or that this judgment or idea has been lately formed and will give place, by succession, to any different judgment or idea.

I can readily allow, said *Cleanthes*, that those who maintain the perfect simplicity of the supreme Being, to the extent in which you have explained it, are complete *mystics* and chargeable with all the consequences which I have drawn from their opinion. They are, in a word, atheists without knowing it. For though it be allowed that the Deity possesses attributes of which we have no comprehension, yet we ought never to ascribe to him any attributes which are absolutely incompatible with that intelligent nature essential to him. A mind whose acts and sentiments and ideas are not distinct and successive, one that is wholly simple and totally immutable, is a mind which has no thought, no reason, no will, no sentiment, no love, no hatred—or in a word is no mind at all. It is an abuse of terms to give it that appellation and we may as well speak of limited extension without shape or of number without composition.

Pray consider, said *Philo*, whom you are at present inveighing against. You are honouring with the appellation of atheist all sound, orthodox divines almost who have treated of this subject; and you will at last be yourself found, according to your reckoning, the only sound theist in the world. But if idolaters be atheists, as I think may justly be asserted, and Christian theologians the same, what becomes of the argument, so much celebrated, from the universal consent of mankind?

But because I know you are not much swayed by names and authorities I shall endeavour to show you a little more distinctly the inconveniences of that anthropomorphism which you have embraced, and shall prove that there is no ground to suppose a plan of the world to be formed in the divine mind, consisting of distinct ideas, differently arranged, in the same manner as an architect forms in his head the plan of a house which he intends to execute.

It is not easy, I own, to see what is gained by this supposition, whether we judge of the matter by *reason* or by *experience*. We are still obliged to mount higher in order to find the cause of this cause which you had assigned as satisfactory and conclusive.

If *reason* (I mean abstract reason, derived from enquiries *a priori*) be not alike mute with regard to all questions concerning cause and effect, this sentence at least it will venture to pronounce: that a mental world or universe of ideas requires a cause as much as does a material world or universe of objects, and if similar in its arrangement, must require a similar cause. For what is there in this subject which should occasion a different conclusion or inference? In an abstract view they are entirely alike, and no difficulty attends the one supposition which is not common to both of them?

Again, when we will needs force *experience* to pronounce some sentence, even on these subjects which lie beyond her sphere, neither can she perceive any material difference between these two kinds of worlds, but finds them to be governed by similar principles and to depend upon an equal variety of causes in their operations. We have specimens in miniature of both of them. Our own mind resembles the one, a vegetable or mineral body the other. Let experience therefore judge from these samples. Nothing seems more delicate with regard to its causes than thought, and as these causes never operate in two persons after the same manner, so we never find two persons who think exactly alike. Nor indeed does the same person think exactly alike at any two different periods of time. A difference of age, of the disposition of his body, of weather, of food, of company, of books, of passions—any of these particulars or others more minute are sufficient to alter the curious machinery of thought and communicate to it very different movements and operations. As far as we can judge, vegetables and animal bodies are not more delicate in their motions nor depend upon a greater variety or more curious adjustment of springs and principles.

How therefore shall we satisfy ourselves concerning the cause of that Being whom you suppose the Author of nature, or, according to your system of anthropomorphism, the ideal world into which you trace the material? Have we not the same reason to trace that ideal world into another ideal world or new intelligent principle? But if we stop and go no farther, why go so far? Why not stop at the material world? How can we satisfy ourselves without going on *ad infinitum*? And after all, what satisfaction is there in that infinite progression? Let us remember the story of the Indian philosopher and his elephant.[1] It was never more applicable than to the present subject. If the material world rests upon a similar ideal world, this ideal world must rest upon some other—and so on without end. It were better, therefore, never to look beyond the present material world. By supposing it to contain the principle of its order within itself, we really assert it to be God; and the sooner we arrive at that divine Being so much the better. When you go one step beyond the mundane system you only excite an inquisitive humour which it is impossible ever to satisfy.

To say the the different ideas which compose the reason of the supreme Being fall into order of themselves and by their own nature is really to talk without any precise meaning. If it has a meaning, I would fain know why it is not as good sense to say that the parts of the material world fall into order of themselves and by their own nature? Can the one opinion be intelligible while the other is not so?

We have, indeed, ideas which fall into order of themselves and without any *known* cause. But, I am sure, we have a much larger experience of matter which does the same; as in all instances of generation, where the accurate analysis of the cause exceeds all human comprehension. We have also experience of particular systems of thought and matter which have no order—of the first, in madness; of the second, in corruption. Why then should we think that order is more essential to one than the other? And if it requires a cause in both, what do we gain by your system, in tracing the universe of objects into a similar universe of ideas? The first step which we make leads us on for ever. It were, therefore, wise in us to limit all our

[1] A reference to the mythological account of the world as being held up by an elephant, and the elephant in turn by tortoises, and the tortoises . . . ?

enquiries to the present, without looking farther. No satisfaction can ever be attained by those speculations, which so far exceed the narrow bounds of human understanding.

It was usual with the Peripatetics,[1] you know, Cleanthes, when the cause of any phenomenon was demanded, to have recourse to their *faculties* or *occult qualities* and to say, for instance, that bread nourished by its nutritive faculty, and senna purged by its purgative (faculty): but it has been discovered that this subterfuge was nothing but the disguise of ignorance and that these philosophers, though less ingenuous, really said the same thing as the sceptics or the vulgar, who fairly confessed that they knew not the cause of these phenomena. In like manner, when it is asked what cause produces order in the ideas of the supreme Being, can any other reason be assigned by you anthropomorphites than that it is a *rational* faculty and that such is the nature of the Deity? But why a similar answer will not be equally satisfactory in accounting for the order of the world, without having recourse to any such intelligent Creator as you insist on, may be difficult to determine. It is only to say that *such* is the nature of material objects and that they are all originally possessed of a *faculty* of order and proportion. These are only more learned and elaborate ways of confessing our ignorance, nor has the one hypothesis any real advantage above the other, except in its greater conformity to vulgar prejudices.

You have displayed this argument with great emphasis, replied *Cleanthes*: you seem not aware how easy it is to answer it. Even in common life, if I assign a cause for any event, is it any objection, Philo, that I cannot assign the cause of that cause and answer every new question which may incessantly be started? And what philosophers could possibly submit to so rigid a rule?—philosophers who confess ultimate causes to be totally unknown and are aware that the most refined principles into which they trace phenomena are still as inexplicable as these phenomena are themselves to the vulgar. The order and arrangement of nature, the curious adjustment of final causes, the plain use and intention of every part and organ—all these bespeak in the clearest language an intelligent cause or Author. The heavens and the earth join in the same testimony; the whole chorus of nature raises one hymn to the praises of its Creator; you alone, or almost alone, disturb this general harmony. You start abstruse doubts, cavils and objections: you ask me what is the cause of this cause? I know not; I care not; that concerns not me. I have found a Deity, and here I stop my enquiry. Let those go farther who are wiser and more enterprising.

I pretend to be neither, replied *Philo*, and for that very reason I should

[1] That is, the followers of Aristotle.

never perhaps have attempted to go so far—especially when I am aware that I must at last be contented to sit down with the same answer, which, without farther trouble, might have satisfied me from the beginning. If I am still to remain in utter ignorance of causes and can absolutely give an explication of nothing, I shall never esteem it any advantage to shove off for a moment a difficulty which, you acknowledge, must immediately, in its full force, recur upon me. Naturalists indeed very justly explain particular effects by more general causes, though these general themselves should remain in the end totally inexplicable, but they never surely thought it satisfactory to explain a particular effect by a particular cause which was no more to be accounted for than the effect itself. An ideal system,[1] arranged of itself without a precedent design, is not a whit more explicable than a material one which attains its order in a like manner, nor is there any more difficulty in the latter supposition than in the former.

PART V

But to show you still more inconveniences, continued *Philo*, in your anthropomorphism, please to take a new survey of your principles. *Like effects prove like causes.* This is the experimental argument; and this you say is the sole theological argument. Now it is certain that the liker the effects are which are seen and the liker the causes which are inferred, the stronger is the argument. Every departure on either side diminishes the probability and renders the experiment less conclusive. You cannot doubt of this principle, neither ought you to reject its principles.

All the new discoveries in astronomy which prove the immense grandeur and magnificence of the works of nature are so many additional arguments for a Deity, according to the true system of theism: but according to your hypothesis of experimental theism they become so many objections, by removing the effect still farther from all resemblance to the effects of human art and contrivance. For if Lucretius, even following the old system of the world, could exclaim

> Quis regere immensi summam, quis habere profundi
> Indu manu validas potis est moderanter habenas?
> Quis pariter caelos omnes convertere? et omnes
> Ignibus aetheriis terras suffire feraces?
> Omnibus inve locis esse omni tempore praesto?[2]

[1] I.e. a system of ideas.

[2] *De Rerum Natura* II. 1095: 'Who can rule the whole, hold in his hand with controlling power the strong reins of the deep? Who can at one time make all the heavens roll, and heat with ethereal fires the fertile lands? Or be present in all places at all times?' See p. 158.

If Cicero esteemed this reasoning so natural as to put it into the mouth of his Epicurean. 'Quibus enim oculis animi intueri potuit vester Plato fabricam illam tanti operis, qua construi a Deo atque aedificari mundum facit? quae molitio? quae ferramenta? qui vectes? quae machinae? qui ministri tanti muneris fuerunt? quemadmodum autem oboedire et parere voluntati architecti aer, ignis, aqua, terra potuerunt?'[1] If this argument, I say, had any force in former ages, how much greater must it have at present when the bounds of nature are so infinitely enlarged and such a magnificent scene is opened to us? It is still more unreasonable to form our idea of so unlimited a cause from our experience of the narrow productions of human design and invention.

The discoveries by microscopes, as they open a new universe in miniature, are still objections, according to you, arguments, according to me.[2] The farther we push our researches of this kind we are still led to infer the universal cause of All to be vastly different from mankind or from any object of human experience and observation.

And what say you to the discoveries in anatomy, chemistry, botany? . . . These surely are no objections, replied *Cleanthes*: they only discover new instances of art and contrivance. It is still the image of mind reflected on us from innumerable objects. Add: a mind *like the human*, said *Philo*. I know of no other, replied *Cleanthes*. And the liker the better, insisted *Philo*. To be sure, said *Cleanthes*.

Now Cleanthes, said *Philo* with an air of alacrity and triumph, mark the consequences. *First*, by this method of reasoning you renounce all claim to infinity in any of the attributes of Deity. For as the cause ought only to be proportioned to the effect, and the effect—so far as it falls under your cognizance—is not infinite: what pretensions have we, upon your suppositions, to ascribe that attribute to the divine Being? You will still insist that, by removing him so much from all similarity to human creatures, we give into the most arbitrary hypothesis and at the same time weaken all proofs of his existence.

Secondly, you have no reason, on your theory, for ascribing perfection to the Deity, even in his finite capacity, or of supposing him free from

[1] *De Natura Deorum* I.8: 'For what spiritual eyes could your Plato have used to behold the immense task of construction by which he represents the universe as having been put together and built by God? What engineering method was used? What tools, levers, machines, workmen, were employed? How came it that air, fire, water and earth could submit to and obey the will of the architect?' Cicero's *De Natura Deorum*, written in 45 BC, sets out the doctrines of the three principal Greek schools of philosophy at that time—the Epicurean, Stoic and Academic (Platonic). In the present passage, Velleius, who is the representative in the dialogue of Epicureanism, is addressing Cotta, the representative of the Academics (so called after Plato's Academy): hence the phrase 'your Plato'.

[2] The microscope was probably invented around AD 1600 by a father and son named Janssen. Galileo produced a similar instrument. See above, p. 105.

every error, mistake or incoherence in his undertakings. There are many inexplicable difficulties in the works of nature which, if we allow a perfect Author to be proved *a priori*, are easily solved, and become only seeming difficulties from the narrow capacity of man, who cannot trace infinite relations. But according to your method of reasoning, these difficulties become all real, and perhaps will be insisted on as new instances of the likeness to human art and contrivance. At least you must acknowledge that it is impossible for us to tell, from our limited views, whether this system contains any great faults or deserves any praise if compared to other possible—or even real—systems. Could a peasant, if the Aeneid were read to him, pronounce that poem to be absolutely faultless, or even assign to it its proper rank among the productions of human wit—he, who had never seen any other production?

But were this world ever so perfect a production, it must still remain uncertain whether all the excellencies of the work can justly be ascribed to the workman. If we survey a ship, what an exalted idea must we form of the ingenuity of the carpenter who framed so complicated, useful and beautiful a machine? And what surprise must we entertain when we find him a stupid mechanic, who imitated others and copied an art which, through a long succession of ages, after multiplied trials, mistakes, corrections, deliberations and controversies, had been gradually improving? Many worlds might have been botched and bungled, throughout an eternity, ere this system was struck out: much labour lost: many fruitless trials made: and a slow but continued improvement carried on during infinite ages in the art of world-making. In such subjects, who can determine where the truth—nay, who can determine where the probability—lies, amidst a great number of hypotheses which may be proposed and a still greater number which may be imagined?

And what shadow of an argument, continued Philo, can you produce, from your hypothesis, to prove the unity of the Deity? A great number of men join in building a house or ship, in rearing a city, in framing a commonwealth: why may not several Deities combine in contriving and framing a world? This is only so much greater similarity to human affairs. By sharing the work among several, we may so much farther limit the attributes of each and get rid of that extensive power and knowledge which must be supposed in one Deity, and which, according to you, can only serve to weaken the proof of his existence. And if such foolish, such vicious creatures as men can yet often unite in framing and executing one plan, how much more those Deities or Demons, whom we may suppose several degrees more perfect?

To multiply causes without necessity is indeed contrary to true philosophy: but this principle applies not to the present case. Were one Deity antecedently proved by your theory, who were possessed of every attribute requisite to the production of the universe, it would be needless, I own, though not absurd, to suppose any other Deity existent. But while it is still a question whether all these attributes are united in one subject or dispersed among several independent Beings: by what phenomena in nature can we pretend to decide the controversy? Where we see a body raised in a scale we are sure that there is in the opposite scale, however concealed from sight, some counterpoising weight equal to it; but it is still allowed to doubt whether that weight would be an aggregate of several distinct bodies or one uniformed united mass. And if the weight requisite very much exceeds any thing which we have ever seen conjoined in any single body, the former supposition becomes still more probable and natural. An intelligent Being of such vast power and capacity as is necessary to produce the universe, or, to speak in the language of ancient philosophy, so prodigious an animal, exceeds all analogy and even comprehension.

But farther, Cleanthes, men are mortal and renew their species by generation; and this is common to all living creatures. The two great sexes of male and female, says Milton, animate the world. Why must this circumstance, so universal, so essential, be excluded from those numerous and limited Deities? Behold then the theogony of ancient times brought back upon us.

And why not become a perfect anthropomorphite? Why not assert the Deity or Deities to be corporeal and to have an eye, a nose, mouth ears, etc.? Epicurus[1] maintained that no man had ever seen reason but in a human figure: therefore the gods must have a human figure. And this argument, which is deservedly so much ridiculed by Cicero,[2] becomes—according to you—solid and philosophical.

In a word, Cleanthes, a man who follows your hypothesis is able, perhaps, to assert or conjecture that the universe sometime arose from something like design: but beyond that position he cannot ascertain one single circumstance and is left afterwards to fix every point of this theology by the utmost licence of fancy and hypothesis. The world, for aught he knows, is very faulty and imperfect, compared to a superior standard, and was only the first rude essay of some infant Deity who afterwards abandoned it, ashamed of his lame performance; it is the work only of some dependent, inferior Deity and is the object of derision to his superiors; it is the production of old age and dotage in some superannuated Deity, and ever since his death has run on at adventures, from the first impulse

[1] (341–270 BC), founder of the Epicurean school, who considerd pleasure to be the highest good, to be obtained through moderation and virtue.

[2] In *De Natura Deorum* I. 43 ff.

and active force which it received from him—you justly give signs of horror, Demea, at these strange suppositions, but these—and a thousand more of the same kind—are Cleanthes' suppositions, not mine. From the moment the attributes of the Deity are supposed finite, all these have place. And I cannot for my part think that so wild and unsettled a system of theology is in any respect preferable to none at all.

These suppositions I absolutely disown, cried *Cleanthes*; they strike me, however, with no horror, especially when proposed in that rambling way in which they drop from you. On the contrary, they give me pleasure when I see that by the utmost indulgence of your imagination you never get rid of the hypothesis of design in the universe, but are obliged at every turn to have recourse to it. To this concession I adhere steadily, and this I regard as a sufficient foundation for religion.

In Part VI Philo replies to Cleanthes with the objection that there *is* an alternative hypothesis to that of design, viz. that the universe is itself an animal,—for it is more like an organism than an artifact. Cleanthes replies with two points: (i) the universe has no organs of sense, seat of thought, etc.—and so is more like a vegetable than an animal; (ii) the hypothesis implies the eternity of the world, which is inconsistent with the recent origin of the arts and sciences. But Philo proceeds to back up his position with the general thesis (repeated later in Part IX, see below) that there is an eternal principle of order inherent in the world. 'Were the inmost essence of things laid open to us, we should then discover a scene of which at present we can have no idea. Instead of admiring the order of natural beings, we should clearly see that it was absolutely impossible for them in the smallest article ever to admit of any other disposition.' Philo continues his criticism of Cleanthes' assumption that thought is the only source of order, in Parts VII and VIII.

Part IX is a digression, in that it deals with a version by Demea, of the *a priori* argument for God's existence.

PART IX

But if so many difficulties attend the argument *a posteriori*, said *Demea*, had we not better adhere to that simple and sublime argument *a priori* which, by offering to us infallible demonstration, cuts off at once all doubt and difficulty? By this argument too we may prove the *infinity* of the divine attributes, which, I am afraid, can never be ascertained with certainty from any other line of argument. For how can an effect which is finite—or for aught we know may be so—, how can such an effect, I say, prove an infinite cause? The unity too of the divine nature it is very difficult, if not absolutely impossible, to deduce merely from contemplating the works of nature; nor will the uniformity alone of the plan, even were it allowed, give us any assurance of that attribute. Whereas the argument *a priori*——

You seem to reason, Demea, interposed *Cleanthes*, as if those advantages and conveniences in the abstract argument were full proofs of its solidity. But it is first proper, in my opinion, to determine what argument of this nature you choose to insist on, and we shall afterwards, from itself, better than from its *useful* consequences, endeavour to determine what value we ought to put upon it.

The argument, replied *Demea*, which I would insist on is the common one. Whatever exists must have a cause or reason for its existence, it being absolutely impossible for any thing to produce itself or be the cause of its own existence. In mounting up, therefore, from effects to causes we must either go on in tracing an infinite succession without any ultimate cause at all, or must at last have recourse to some ultimate cause that is *necessarily* existent. Now that the first supposition is absurd may be thus proved. In the infinite chain or succession of causes and effects, each single effect is determined to exist by the power and efficacy of that cause which immediately preceded; but the whole chain or succession, taken together, is not determined or caused by any thing. And yet it is evident that it requires a cause or reason, as much as any particular object which begins to exist in time. The question is still reasonable why this particular succession of causes existed from eternity and not any other succession or no succession at all. If there be no necessarily existent Being, any supposition which can be formed is equally possible; nor is there any more absurdity in nothing's having existed from eternity than there is in that succession of causes which constitutes the universe. What was it then which determined something to exist rather than nothing, and bestowed being on a particular possibility, exclusive of the rest? *External causes*, there are supposed to be none. *Chance* is a word without meaning. Was it *nothing*? But that can never produce any thing. We must therefore have recourse to a necessarily existent Being, who carries the *reason* of his existence in himself and who cannot be supposed not to exist without an express contradiction. There is consequently such a Being; that is, there is a Deity.

I shall not leave it to Philo, said *Cleanthes* (though I know that the starting objections is his chief delight), to point out the weakness of this metaphysical reasoning. It seems to me so obviously ill-grounded and at the same time of so little consequence to the cause of true piety and religion that I shall myself venture to show the fallacy of it.

I shall begin with observing that there is an evident absurdity in pretending to demonstrate a matter of fact or to prove it by any arguments *a priori*. Nothing is demonstrable unless the contrary implies a contradiction.[1] Nothing that is distinctly conceivable implies a contradiction. Whatever we can conceive as existent we can also conceive as non-existent. There is no Being, therefore, whose non-existence implies a contradiction. Consequently there is no Being whose existence is demonstrable. I propose this argument as entirely decisive and am willing to rest the whole controversy upon it.

It is pretended that the Deity is a necessarily existent Being, and this necessity of his existence is attempted to be explained by asserting that if we knew his whole essence or nature we should perceive it to be as impossible for him not to exist as for twice two not to be four. But it is evident that this can never happen while our faculties remain the same as at present. It will still be possible for us, at any time, to conceive the non-existence of what we formerly conceived to exist, nor can the mind ever lie under a necessity of supposing any object to remain always in being, in the same manner as we lie under the necessity of always conceiving twice two to be four. The words, therefore, *necessary existence*, have no meaning; or which is the same thing, none that is consistent.

But farther: why may not the material universe be the necessarily existent Being, according to this pretended explication of necessity? We dare not affirm that we know all the qualities of matter, and for aught we can determine it may contain some qualities which, were they known, would make its non-existence appear as great a contradiction as that twice two is five. I find only one argument employed to prove that the material world is not the necessarily existent Being; and this argument is derived from the contingency both of the matter and the form of the world. 'Any particle of matter', it is said, 'may be *conceived* to be annihilated and any form may be *conceived* to be altered. Such an annihilation or alteration, therefore, is not impossible.' But it seems a great partiality not to perceive that the same argument extends equally to the Deity, so far as we have any conception of him, and that the mind can at least imagine him to be non-existent or his attributes to be altered. It must be some unknown, inconceivable qualities which can make his non-existence appear impossible or his attributes unalterable; and no reason can be assigned why these qualities may not belong to matter. As they are altogether unknown and inconceivable they can never be proved incompatible with it.

Add to this that in tracing an eternal succession of objects it seems absurd to enquire for a general cause or first Author. How can anything

[1] 'Demonstrable' is here being used in a strict sense. Cleanthes is saying that the existence of a thing cannot be demonstrated the way a mathematical theorem can be demonstrated (see next paragraph). With regard to the concept *existence* see p. 58 and p. 141.

that exists from eternity have a cause, since that relation implies priority in time and a beginning of existence?

In such a chain too, or succession of objects, each part is caused by that which preceded it and causes that which succeeds it. Where then is the difficulty? But the *whole*, you say, wants a cause. I answer that the uniting of these parts into a whole, like the uniting of several distinct counties into one kingdom, or several distinct members into one body, is performed merely by an arbitrary act of the mind and has no influence on the nature of things. Did I show you the particular causes of each individual in a collection of twenty particles of matter, I should think it very unreasonable should you afterwards ask me what was the cause of the whole twenty. This is sufficiently explained in explaining the cause of the part.

Though the reasonings which you have urged, Cleanthes, may well excuse me, said *Philo*, from starting any farther difficulties, yet I cannot forbear insisting still upon another topic. It is observed by arithmeticians that the products of 9 compose always either 9 or some lesser product of nine if you add together all the digits of which any of the former products is composed. Thus, of 18, 27, 36, which are products of 9, you make 9 by adding 1 to 8, 2 to 7, 3 to 6. Thus 369 is a product also of 9; and if you add 3, 6 and 9, you make 18, a lesser product of 9. To a superficial observer, so wonderful a regularity may be admired as the effect either of chance or design; but a skilful algebraist immediately concludes it to be the work of necessity and demonstrates that it must for ever result from the nature of these numbers. Is it not probable, I ask, that the whole economy of the universe is conducted by a like necessity, though no human algebra can furnish a key which solves the difficulty? And instead of admiring the order of natural beings, may it not happen that, could we penetrate into the intimate nature of bodies, we should clearly see why it was absolutely impossible they could ever admit of any other disposition? So dangerous is it to introduce this idea of necessity into the present question! And so naturally does it afford an inference directly opposite to the religious hypothesis!

But dropping all these abstractions, continued Philo, and confining ourselves to more familiar topics, I shall venture to add an observation that the argument *a priori* has seldom been found convincing except to people of a metaphysical head, who have accustomed themselves to abstract reasoning and who, finding from mathematics that the understanding frequently leads to truth through obscurity and contrary to first appearances, have transferred the same habit of thinking to subjects where it ought not to have place. Other people, even of good sense and the best inclined to religion, feel always some deficiency in such arguments, though they are not perhaps able to explain distinctly where it lies. A certain proof that men ever did, and ever will, derive their religion from other sources than from this species of reasoning.

B. MIRACLES

Hume's *Essay on Miracles* was published in 1748, in his *Philosophical Essays concerning Human Understanding*.

PART I

There is, in Dr Tillotson's[1] writings, an argument against the *real presence*, which is as concise, and elegant, and strong, as any argument can possibly be supposed against a doctrine so little worthy of a serious refutation. It is acknowledged on all hands, says that learned prelate, that the authority, either of the Scripture or of tradition, is founded merely on the testimony of the Apostles, who were eyewitnesses to those miracles of our Saviour, by which he proved his divine mission. Our evidence, then, for the truth of the *Christian* religion, is less than the evidence for the truth of our senses; because, even in the first authors of our religion, it was not greater; and it is evident it must diminish in passing from them to their disciples; nor can anyone rest such confidence in their testimony as in the immediate object of his senses. But a weaker evidence can never destroy a stronger; and therefore, were the doctrine of the real presence ever so clearly revealed in Scripture, it were directly contrary to the rules of just reasoning to give our assent to it. It contradicts sense, though both the Scripture and tradition, on which it is supposed to be built, carry not such evidence with them as sense, when they are considered merely as external evidences, and are not brought home to every one's breast by the immediate operation of the Holy Spirit.

Nothing is so convenient as a decisive argument of this kind, which must at least *silence* the most arrogant bigotry and superstitions, and free us from their impertinent solicitations. I flatter myself that I have discovered an argument of a like nature, which, if just, will, with the wise and learned, be an everlasting check to all kinds of superstitious delusion, and consequently will be useful as long as the world endures; for so long, I presume, will the accounts of miracles and prodigies be found in all history, sacred and profane.

Though experience be our only guide in reasoning concerning matters of

[1] John Tillotson (1630–94), Archbishop of Canterbury, held Zwinglian views about the Eucharist.

fact it must be acknowledged, that this guide is not altogether infallible, but in some cases is apt to lead us into errors. One who in our climate should expect better weather in any week of June than in one of December, would reason justly and conformably to experience; but it is certain that he may happen, in the event, to find himself mistaken. However, we may observe that, in such a case, he would have no cause to complain of experience, because it commonly informs us beforehand of the uncertainty, by that contrariety of events which we may learn from a diligent observation. All effects follow not with like certainty from their supposed causes. Some events are found, in all countries and all ages, to have been constantly conjoined together: others are found to have been more variable, and sometimes to disappoint our expectations; so that in our reasonings concerning matters of fact, there are all imaginable degrees of assurance, from the highest certainty to the lowest species of moral evidence.

A wise man, therefore, proportions his belief to the evidence. In such conclusions as are founded on an infallible experience, he expects the event with the last degree of assurance, and regards his past experience as a full *proof* of the future existence of that event. In other cases he proceeds with more caution: he weighs the opposite experiments; he considers which side is supported by the greater number of experiments; to that side he inclines with doubt and hesitation; and when at last he fixes his judgment, the evidence exceeds not what we properly call *probability*. All probability, then, supposes an opposition of experiments and observations, where the one side is found to overbalance the other, and to produce a degree of evidence proportioned to the superiority. A hundred instances or experiments on one side, and fifty on another, afford a doubtful expectation of any event; though a hundred uniform experiments, with only one that is contradictory, reasonably beget a pretty strong degree of assurance. In all cases, we must balance the opposite experiments, where they are opposite, and deduct the smaller number from the greater, in order to know the exact force of the superior evidence.[1]

To apply these principles to a particular instance; we may observe, that there is no species of reasoning more common, more useful, and even necessary to human life, than that which is derived from the testimony of men, and the reports of eyewitnesses and spectators. This species of reasoning, perhaps, one may deny to be founded on the relation of cause and effect. I shall not dispute about a word. It will be sufficient to observe, that our assurance in any argument of this kind is derived from no other principle than our observation of the veracity of human testimony, and of the usual conformity of facts to the report of witnesses. It being a general

[1] Compare below, p. 384.

maxim that no objects have any discoverable connection together, and that all the inferences which we can draw from one to another, are founded merely on our experience of their constant and regular conjunction, it is evident that we ought not to make an exception to this maxim in favour of human testimony, whose connection with any event seems, in itself, as little necessary as any other. Were not the memory tenacious to a degree; had not men commonly an inclination to truth and a principle of probity; were they not sensible to sham when detected in a falsehood: were not these, I say, discovered by *experience* to be qualities inherent in human nature, we should never repose the least confidence in human testimony. A man delirious, or noted for falsehood and villainy, has no manner of authority with us.

And as the evidence derived from witnesses and human testimony is founded on past experience, so it varies with the experience, and is regarded either as a *proof* or a *probability*, according as the conjunction between any particular kind of report, and any kind of object, has been found to be constant or variable. There are a number of circumstances to be taken into consideration in all judgments of this kind; and the ultimate standard by which we determine all disputes that may arise concerning them, is always derived from experience and observation. Where this experience is not entirely uniform on any side, it is attended with an unavoidable contrariety in our judgments, and with the same opposition and mutual destruction of argument as in every other kind of evidence. We frequently hesitate concerning the reports of others. We balance the opposite circumstances which cause any doubt or uncertainty; and when we discover a superiority on any side, we incline to it, but still with a diminution of assurance, in proportion to the force of its antagonist.

This contrariety of evidence, in the present case, may be derived from several different causes; from the opposition of contrary testimony; from the character or number of the witnesses; from the manner of their delivering their testimony; or from the union of all these circumstances. We entertain a suspicion concerning any matter of fact when the witnesses contradict each other; when they are but few or of a doubtful character; when they have an interest in what they affirm; when they deliver their testimony with hesitation, or, on the contrary, with too violent asseverations. There are many other particulars of the same kind, which may diminish or destroy the force of any argument derived from human testimony.

Suppose, for instance, that the fact which the testimony endeavours to establish partakes of the extraordinary and the marvellous, in that case, the evidence resulting from the testimony admits of a diminution, greater or less, in proportion as the fact is more or less unusual. The reason why we place any credit in witnesses and historians, is not derived from any *connection* which we perceive *a priori* between testimony and reality, but because we are accustomed to find a conformity between them. But when the fact attested is such a one as has seldom fallen under our observation, here is a contest of two opposite experiences, of which the one destroys the other as far as its force goes, and the superior can only operate on the mind by the force which remains. The very same principle of experience, which gives us a certain degree of assurance in the testimony of witnesses, gives us also, in this case, another degree of assurance against the fact which they endeavour to establish; from which contradiction there necessarily arises a counterpoise, and mutual destruction of belief and authority.

I should not believe such a story were it told me by Cato, was a proverbial saying in Rome, even during the lifetime of that philosophical patriot.[1] The incredibility of a fact, it was allowed, might invalidate so great an authority.

The Indian prince, who refused to believe the first relations concerning the effects of frost, reasoned justly; and it naturally required very strong testimony to engage his assent to facts that arose from a state of nature with which he was unacquainted, and which bore so little analogy to those events of which he had had constant and uniform experience. Though they were not contrary to his experience, they were not conformable to it.*

But in order to increase the probability against the testimony of witnesses, let us suppose that the fact which they affirm, instead of being only marvellous, is really miraculous; and suppose also, that the testimony, considered apart and in itself, amount to an entire proof, in that case there is proof against proof, of which the strongest must prevail, but still with a diminution of its force, in proportion to that of its antagonist.

A miracle is a violation of the laws of nature; and as a firm and

[1] Plutarch, *Life of C.* Cato (95–46 BC), opponent of Julius Ceasar, was known for his integrity.

* No Indian, it is evident, could have experience that water did not freeze in cold climates. This is placing nature in a situation quite unknown to him; and it is impossible for him to tell *a priori* what will result from it. It is making a new experiment, the consequence of which is always uncertain. One may sometimes conjecture from analogy what will follow; but still this is but conjecture. And it must be confessed, that, in the present case of freezing, the event follows contrary to the rules of analogy, and is such as a rational Indian would not look for. The operations of cold upon water are not gradual, according to the degrees of cold; but whenever it comes to the freezing point, the water passes in a moment, from the utmost liquidity to perfect hardness. Such an event, therefore, may be denominated *extraordinary*, and requires a pretty strong testimony, to render it credible to people in a warm climate: but still it is not *miraculous*, not contrary to uniform experience of the course of nature in cases where all the circumstances are the same. The inhabitants of Sumatra have always seen water fluid in their own climate, and the freezing of their rivers ought to be deemed a prodigy: but they never saw water in Muscovy during the winter; and therefore they cannot reasonably be positive what would there be the consequence.

unalterable experience has established these laws, the proof against a miracle from the very nature of the fact, is as entire as any argument from experience can possibly be imagined. Why is it more than probable that all men must die; that lead cannot, of itself, remain suspended in the air; that fire consumes wood, and is extinguished by water; unless it be that these events are found agreeable to the laws of nature, and there is required a violation of these laws, or, in other words, a miracle to prevent them? Nothing is esteemed a miracle, if it ever happen in the common course of nature. It is no miracle that a man, seemingly in good health, should die on a sudden; because such a kind of death, though more unusual than any other, has yet been frequently observed to happen. But it is a miracle that a dead man should come to life; because that has never been observed in any age or country. There must, therefore, be an uniform experience against every miraculous event, otherwise the event would not merit that appellation. And as an uniform experience amounts to a proof, there is here a direct and full *proof*, from the nature of the fact, against the existence of any miracle; nor can such a proof be destroyed, or the miracle rendered credible, but by an opposite proof, which is superior.*

The plain consequence is (and it is a general maxim worthy of our attention), 'That no testimony is sufficient to establish a miracle, unless the testimony be of such a kind, that its falsehood would be more miraculous than the fact which it endeavours to establish: and even in that case there is a mutual destruction of arguments, and the superior only gives us an assurance suitable to that degree of force which remains after deducting the inferior.' When anyone tells me that he saw a dead man restored to life, I immediately consider with myself whether it be more probable that this person should either deceive or be deceived, or that the fact which he relates should really have happened. I weigh the one miracle against the other; and according to the superiority which I discover, I pronounce my

* Sometimes an event may not, *in itself, seem* to be contrary to the law of nature, and yet, if it were real, it might, by reason of some circumstances, be denominated as a miracle; because, in *fact*, it is contrary to these laws. Thus if a person, claiming a divine authority, should command a sick person to be well, a healthful man to fall down dead, the clouds to pour rain, the winds to blow; in short, should order many natural events, which immediately follow upon his command; these might justly be esteemed miracles, because they are really, in this case, contrary to the laws of nature. For if any suspicion remain, that the event and command concurred by accident, there is no miracle and no transgression of the laws of nature. If this suspicion be removed, there is evidently a miracle, and a transgression of these laws; because nothing can be more contrary to the laws of nature than that the voice or command of a man should have such an influence. A miracle may be accurately defined, *a transgression of a law of nature by a particular volition of the Deity, or by the interposition of some invisible agent*. A miracle may either be discovered by men or not. This alters not its nature and essence. The raising of a house or ship into the air is a visible miracle. The raising of a feather, when the wind wants ever so little of a force requisite for that purpose, is as real a miracle, thought not so sensible with regard to us.

decision, and always reject the greater miracle. If the falsehood of his testimony would be more miraculous than the event which he relates, then, and not till then, can he pretend to command my belief or opinion.

PART II

In the foregoing reasoning we have supposed, that the testimony upon which a miracle is founded, may possibly amount to entire proof, and that the falsehood of that testimony would be a real prodigy: but it is easy to show that we have been a great deal too liberal in our concession, and that there never was a miraculous event established on so full an evidence.

For, *first*, there is not to be found, in all history, any miracle attested by a sufficient number of men, of such unquestioned good sense, education and learning, as to secure us against all delusion in themselves; of such undoubted integrity, as to place them beyond all suspicion of any design to deceive others; of such credit and reputation in the eyes of mankind, as to have a great deal to lose in case of their being detected in any falsehood; and at the same time attesting facts, performed in such a public manner, and in so celebrated a part of the world, as to render the detection unavoidable: all which circumstances are requisite to give us a full assurance in the testimony of men.

Secondly, we may observe in human nature a principle which, if strictly examined, will be found to diminish extremely the assurance, which we might, from human testimony, have in any kind of prodigy. The maxim, by which we commonly conduct ourselves in our reasonings, is, that the objects, of which we have no experience, resemble those of which we have; that what we have found to be most usual is always most probable; and that where there is an opposition of arguments, we ought to give the preference to such as are founded on the greatest number of past observations. But though, in proceeding by this rule, we readily reject any fact which is unusual and incredible in an ordinary degree; yet in advancing further, the mind observes not always the same rule; but when anything is affirmed utterly absurd and miraculous, it rather the more readily admits of such a fact, upon account of that very circumstance which ought to destroy all its authority. The passion of *surprise* and *wonder*, arising from miracles, being an agreeable emotion, gives a sensible tendency towards the belief of those events from which it is derived. And this goes so far, that even those who cannot enjoy this pleasure immediately, nor can believe those miraculous events of which they are informed, yet love to partake the satisfaction at second hand, or by rebound, and place a pride and delight in exciting the admiration of others.

With what greediness are the miraculous accounts of travellers received, their descriptions of sea and land monsters, their relations of wonderful adventures, strange men, and uncouth manners? But if the spirit of religion join itself to the love of wonder, there is an end of common sense; and human testimony, in these circumstances, loses all pretensions to authority. A religionist may be an enthusiast, and imagine he sees what has no reality: he may know his narrative to be false, and yet persevere in it, with the best intentions in the world, for the sake of promoting so holy a cause: or even where this delusion has not place, vanity, excited by so strong a temptation, operates on him more powerfully than on the rest of mankind in any other circumstances; and self-interest with equal force. His auditors may not have, and commonly have not, sufficient judgment to canvass his evidence: what judgments they have they renounce by principle in these sublime and mysterious subjects: or if they were ever so willing to employ it, passion and a heated imagination disturb the regularity of its operations. Their credulity increases his impudence; and his impudence overpowers their credulity.

Eloquence, when at its highest pitch, leaves little room for reason or reflection; but addressing itself entirely to the fancy or the affections, captivates the willing hearers, and subdues their understanding. Happily, this pitch it seldom attains. But what a Tully[1] or a Demosthenes[2] could scarcely effect over a Roman or Athenian audience, every *Capuchin*, every itinerant or stationary teacher, can perform over the generality of mankind, and in a higher degree, by touching such gross and vulgar passions.

The many instances of forged miracles and prophecies and supernatural events, which, in all ages, have either been detected by contrary evidence, or which detect themselves by their absurdity, prove sufficiently the strong propensity of mankind to the extraordinary and marvellous, and ought reasonably to beget a suspicion against all relations of this kind. This is our natural way of thinking, even with regard to the most common and most credible events. For instance, there is no kind of report which arises so easily, and spreads so quickly, especially in country places and provincial towns, as those concerning marriages; insomuch that two young persons of equal condition never see each other twice, but the whole neighbourhood immediately join them together. The pleasure of telling a piece of news so interesting, of propagating it, and of being the first reporters of it, spreads the intelligence; and this is so well known, that no man of sense gives attention to these reports till he find them confirmed by some greater evidence. Do not the same passions, and others still stronger,

[1] I.e., Cicero (Marcus Tullius Cicero).

[2] (*c.* 383–322 BC), orator and statesman.

incline the generality of mankind to believe and report, with the greatest vehemence and assurance, all religious miracles?

Thirdly, it forms a strong presumption against all supernatural and miraculous relations, that they are observed chiefly to abound among ignorant and barbarous nations; or if a civilized people has ever given admission to any of them, that people will be found to have received them from ignorant and barbarous ancestors, who transmitted them with that inviolable sanction and authority which always attend received opinions. When we peruse the first histories of all nations, we are apt to imagine ourselves transported into some new world, where the whole frame of nature is disjointed, and every element performs its operations in a different manner from what it does at present. Battles, revolutions, pestilence, famine, and death, are never the effect of those natural causes which we experience. Prodigies, omens, oracles, judgments, quite obscure the few natural events that are intermingled with them. But as the former grow thinner every page, in proportion as we advance nearer the enlightened ages, we soon learn that there is nothing mysterious or supernatural in the case, but that all proceeds from the usual propensity of mankind towards the marvellous, and that though this inclination may at intervals receive a check from sense and learning, it can never be thoroughly extirpated from human nature.

It is strange, a judicious reader is apt to say, upon the perusal of these wonderful historians, *that such prodigious events never happen in our days*! But it is nothing strange, I hope, that men should lie in all ages. You must surely have seen instances enough of that frailty. You have yourself heard many such marvellous relations stated, which, being treated with scorn by all the wise and judicious, have at last been abandoned even by the vulgar. Be assured, that those renowned lies, which have spread and flourished to such a monstrous height, arose from like beginnings; but being sown in a more proper soil, shot up at last into prodigies almost equal to those which they relate.

It was a wise policy in that false prophet Alexander,[1] who, though now forgotten, was once so famous, to lay the first scene of his impostures in Paphlagonia, where, as Lucian tells us, the people were extremely ignorant and stupid, and ready to swallow even the grossest delusion. People at a distance, who are weak enough to think the matter at all worthy enquiry, have no opportunity of receiving better information. The stories come magnified to them by a hundred circumstances. Fools are industrious in propagating the impostures; while the wise and learned are

[1] Alexander of Abonuteichos, contemporary of Lucian (see below, n. * to p. 240), claimed to be a manifestation of Asclepius.

contented, in general, to deride its absurdity, without informing themselves of the particular facts by which it may be distinctly refuted. And thus the imposter above mentioned was enabled to proceed, from his ignorant Paphlagonians, to the enlisting of votaries, even among the Grecian philosophers, and men of the most eminent rank and distinction in Rome: nay, could engage the attention of that sage emperor Marcus Aurelius,[1] so far as to make him trust the success of a military expedition to his delusive prophecies.

The advantages are so great, of starting an imposture among an ignorant people, that even though the delusion should be too gross to impose on the generality of them (*which, though seldom, is sometimes the case*), it has a much better chance for succeeding in remote countries, than if the first scene had been laid in a city renowned for arts and knowledge. The most ignorant and barbarous of these barbarians carry the report abroad. None of their countrymen have a large correspondence, or sufficient credit and authority to contradict and beat down the delusion. Men's inclination to the marvellous has full opportunity to display itself. And thus a story, which is universally exploded in the place where it was first started, shall pass for certain at a thousand miles distance. But, had Alexander fixed his residence at Athens, the philosophers at that renowned mart of learning had immediately spread, throughout the whole Roman Empire, their sense of the matter; which, being supported by so great authority, and displayed by all the force of reason and eloquence, had entirely opened the eyes of mankind. It is true, Lucian, passing by chance through Paphlagonia, had an opportunity of performing this good office. But, though much to be wished, it does not always happen that every Alexander meets with a Lucian, ready to expose and detect his impostures.*

I may add, as a *fourth* reason, which diminishes the authority of prodigies, that there is no testimony for any, even those which have not been expressly detected, that is not opposed by an infinite number of witnesses; so that not only the miracle destroys the credit of testimony, but the testimony destroys itself. To make this the better understood, let us consider, that in matters of religion, whatever is different is contrary; and that it is impossible the religions of ancient Rome, of Turkey, of Siam, and of

[1] Marcus Aurelius, Emperor (AD 161–80) and author of the famous *Meditations*, a devotional work expressing the consolations of Stoicism.

* It may perhaps be objected that I proceed rashly, and form my notions of Alexander merely from the account given of him by Lucian, a professed enemy. It were indeed to be wished that some of the accounts published by his followers and accomplices had remained. The opposition and contrast betwixt the character and conduct of the same man as drawn by a friend or an enemy, is as strong, even in common life, much more in these religious matters, as that betwixt any two men in the world; betwixt Alexander and St Paul, for instance. [Lucian (*c.* 115–*c.* 200 AD)—satirist and science-fiction writer.]

China, should all of them be established on any solid foundation. Every miracle, therefore, pretended to have been wrought in any of these religions (and all of them abound in miracles), as its direct scope is to establish the particular system to which it is attributed, so has it the same force, though more indirectly, to overthrow every other system. In destroying a rival system, it likewise destroys the credit of those miracles on which that system was established, so that all the prodigies of different religions are to be regarded as contrary facts, and the evidences of these prodigies, whether weak or strong, as opposite to each other. According to this method of reasoning, when we believe any miracle of Mahomet or his successors, we have for our warrant the testimony of a few barbarous Arabians: and on the other hand, we are to regard the authority of Titus Livius,[1] Plutarch,[2] Tacitus,[3] and in short, of all the authors and witnesses, Grecian, Chinese and Roman Catholic, who have related any miracle in their particular religion; I say, we are to regard their testimony in the same light as if they had mentioned the Mahometan miracle, and had in express terms contradicted it with the same certainty as they have for the miracle they relate. This argument may appear over subtile and refined, but is not in reality different from the reasoning of a judge, who supposes that the credit of two witnesses, maintaining a crime against any one, is destroyed by the testimony of two others, who affirm him to have been two hundred leagues distant at the same instant when the crime is said to have been committed.

One of the best attested miracles in all profane history, is that which Tacitus reports of Vespasian,[4] who cured a blind man in Alexandria by means of his spittle, and a lame man by the mere touch of his foot, in obedience to a vision of the god Serapis, who had enjoined them to have recourse to the Emperor for these miraculous cures. The story may be seen in that fine historian; where every circumstance seems to add weight to the testimony, and might be displayed at large with all the force of argument and eloquence, if any one were now concerned to enforce the evidence of that exploded and idolatrous superstition. The gravity, solidity, age, and probity, of so great an Emperor, who, through the whole course of his life conversed in a familiar manner with his friends and courtiers, and never affected those extraordinary airs of divinity assumed by Alexander and Demetrius:[5] the historian, a contemporary writer,

[1] Livy, the Roman historian (3rd century BC).
[2] Plutarch (*c.* 46–*c.* 120 AD), Greek biographer and moralist.
[3] Tacitus (*c.* 55–*c.* 117 AD), Roman historian.
[4] Vespasian, Emperor from AD 70–79, first of the Flavian line.
[5] Alexander the Great (356–23 BC); and Demetrius Poliorketes ('The Besieger'), successor of Alexander and ruler of Macedonia (277–39 BC), founder of the Antigonid dynasty.

noted for candour and veracity, and withal, the greatest and most penetrating genius perhaps of all antiquity; and so free from any tendency to credulity, that he even lies under the contrary imputation of atheism and profaneness: the persons, from whose authority he related the miracle, of established character for judgment and veracity, as we may well presume; eyewitnesses of the fact, and confirming their testimony, after the Flavian family was despoiled of the empire, and could no longer give any reward as the price of a lie. *Utrumque, qui interfuere, nunc quoque memorant, postquam nullum mendacio pretium.*[1] To which, if we add the public nature of the facts, as related, it will appear that no evidence can well be supposed stronger for so gross and so palpable a falsehood.

There is also a memorable story related by Cardinal de Retz,[2] which may well deserve our consideration. When that intriguing politian fled into Spain to avoid the persecution of his enemies, he passed through Saragossa, the capital of Arragon, where he was shown, in the cathedral, a man who had served seven years as a door-keeper, and was well known to everybody in town that had ever paid his devotions at that church. He had been seen for so long a time wanting a leg, but recovered that limb by the rubbing of holy oil upon the stump; and the Cardinal assures us that he saw him with two legs. This miracle was vouched by all the canons of the church; and the whole company in town were appealed to for the confirmation of the fact; whom the Cardinal found, by their zealous devotion, to be thorough believers of the miracle. Here the relater was also contemporary to the supposed prodigy, of an incredulous and libertine character, as well as of great genius; the miracle of so *singular* a nature as could scarcely admit of a counterfeit, and the witnesses very numerous, and all of them in a manner, spectators of the fact to which they gave their testimony. And what adds mightily to the force of the evidence, and may double our surprise on this occasion, is, that the Cardinal himself, who relates the story, seems not to give any credit to it, and consequently cannot be suspected of any concurrence in the holy fraud. He considered justly, that it was not requisite, in order to reject a fact of this nature, to be able accurately to disprove the testimony, and to trace its falsehood through all the circumstances of knavery and credulity which produced it. He knew that, as this was commonly altogether impossible at any small distance of time and place, so was it extremely difficult, even where one was immediately present, by reason of the bigotry, ignorance, cunning and roguery of a great part of mankind. He

1 'Now those who were present relate each event, now that there is no reward for lying.'

2 Cardinal de Retz (1614–79), rival of Mazarin and, for a time, confidante of Louis XIV; he wrote famous *Memoirs*.

therefore concluded, like a just reasoner, that such an evidence carried falsehood upon the very face of it, and that a miracle, supported by any human testimony, was more properly a subject of derision than of argument. . . .[1]

Is the consequence just, because some human testimony has the utmost force and authority in some cases, when it relates the battles of Philippi or Pharsalia for instance, that therefore all kinds of testimony must, in all cases, have equal force and authority? Suppose that the Cæsarean or Pompeian factions had, each of them, claimed the victory in these battles, and that the historians of each party had uniformly ascribed the advantage to their own side, how could mankind, at this distance, have been able to determine between them? The contrariety is equally strong between the miracles related by Herodotus[2] or Plutarch, and those delivered by Mariana,[3] Bede[4] or any monkish historian.

The wise lend a very academic faith to every report which favours the passion of the reporter, whether it magnifies his country, his family or himself, or in any other way strikes in with his natural inclinations and propensities. But what greater temptation than to appear a missionary, a prophet, an ambassador from heaven? Who would not encounter many dangers and difficulties in order to obtain so sublime a character? Or if, by the help of vanity and a heated imagination, a man has first made a convert of himself, and entered seriously into the delusion, who ever scruples to make use of pious frauds in support of so holy and meritorious a cause?

The smallest spark may here kindle into the greatest flame, because the materials are always prepared for it. The *avidum genus auricularum*,[5] the gazing populace, receive greedily, without examination, whatever soothes superstition and promotes wonder.

How many stories of this nature have, in all ages, been detected and exploded in their infancy? How many more have been celebrated for a time, and have afterwards sunk into neglect and oblivion? Where such reports, therefore, fly about, the solution of the phenomenon is obvious; and we judge in conformity to regular experience and observation, when we account for it by the known and natural principles of credulity and delusion. And shall we, rather than have recourse to so natural a solution,

[1] A paragraph and note, with similar examples, is omitted.

[2] (*c.* 480–*c.* 425 BC), the 'father of history'.

[3] (1536–1623), Spanish Jesuit historian.

[4] (*c.* 672–735), Northumbrian historian and exegete.

[5] A reference to the line from Lucretius (see above, n. 1 to p. 158), *De Rerum Natura*, IV. 593–4: '. . . *ut omne / humanum genus est avidum nimis auricularum*': 'as the whole of mankind has too greedy ears.'

allow of a miraculous violation of the most established laws of nature?

I need not mention the difficulty of detecting a falsehood in any private or even public history, at the place where it is said to happen; much more when the scene is removed to ever so small a distance. Even a court of judicature, with all the authority, accuracy and judgment, which they can employ, find themselves often at a loss to distinguish between truth and falsehood in the most recent actions. But the matter never comes to any issue, if trusted to the common method of altercation and debate, and flying rumours, especially when men's passions have taken part on either side.

In the infancy of new religions, the wise and learned commonly esteem the matter too inconsiderable to deserve their attention or regard. And when afterwards they would willingly detect the cheat, in order to undeceive the undeluded multitude, the season is now past, and the records and witnesses, which might clear up the matter, have perished beyond recovery.

No means of detection remain but those which must be drawn from the very testimony itself of the reporters: and these, though always sufficient with the judicious and knowing, are commonly too fine to fall under the comprehension of the vulgar.

Upon the whole, then, it appears, that no testimony for any kind of miracle has ever amounted to a probability, much less to a proof; and that, even supposing it amounted to a proof, it would be opposed by another proof, derived from the very nature of the fact which it would endeavour to establish. It is experience only which gives authority to human testimony; and it is the same experience which assures us of the laws of nature. When, therefore, these two kinds of experience are contrary, we have nothing to do but to subtract the one from the other, with that assurance which arises from the remainder. But according to the principle here explained, this subtraction with regard to all popular religions amounts to an entire annihilation; and therefore we may establish it as a maxim, that no human testimony can have such force as to prove a miracle, and make it a just foundation for any such system of religion.

I beg the limitations here made may be remarked, when I say, that a miracle can never be proved so as to be the foundation of a system of religions. For I own, that otherwise there may possibly be miracles, or violations of the usual course of nature, of such a kind as to admit of proof from human testimony; though perhaps it will be impossible to find any such in all the records of history. Thus, suppose all authors, in all languages, agree, that, from the 1st of January, 1600, there was a total darkness over the whole earth for eight days: suppose that the tradition of this extraordinary event is still strong and lively among the people: suppose that all travellers who return from foreign countries bring us accounts of the same tradition, without the least variation or contradiction: it is evident that our present philosophers, instead of doubting the fact, ought to receive it as certain, and ought to search for the causes whence it might be derived. The decay, corruption and dissolution of nature, is an event rendered probable by so many analogies, that any phenomenon, which seems to have a tendency towards that catastrophe, comes within the reach of human testimony, if that testimony be very extensive and uniform.

But suppose that all the historians who treat of England should agree, that on the 1st of January, 1600, Queen Elizabeth died; that both before and after her death, she was seen by her physicians and the whole court, as is usual with persons of her rank; that her successor was acknowledged and proclaimed by the Parliament; and that, after being interred for a month, she again appeared, resumed the throne and governed England for three years: I must confess that I should be surprised at the concurrence of so many odd circumstances, but should not have the least inclination to believe so miraculous an event. I should not doubt of her pretended death, and of those other public circumstances that followed it: I should only assert it to have been pretended, and that it neither was, nor possibly could be, real. You would in vain object to me the difficulty, and almost impossibility of deceiving the world in an affair of such consequence; the wisdom and solid judgment of that renowned Queen; with the little or no advantage which she could reap from so poor an artifice: all this might astonish me; but I would still reply, that the knavery and folly of men are such common phenomena, that I should rather believe the most extraordinary events to arise from their concurrence, than admit of so signal a violation of the laws of nature.

But should this miracle be ascribed to any new system of religion; men, in all ages, have been so much imposed on by ridiculous stories of that kind, that this very circumstance would be a full proof of a cheat, and sufficient, with all men of sense, not only to make them reject the fact, but even reject it without further examination. Though the being to whom the miracle is ascribed, be in this case Almighty, it does not, upon that account, become a whit more probable; since it is impossible for us to know the attributes or actions of such a Being, otherwise than from the experience which we have of his productions in the usual course of nature. This still reduces us to past observation, and obliges us to compare the instances of the violation of truth in the testimony of men, with those of the violation of the laws of nature by miracles, in order to judge which of them is most likely and probable. As the violations of truth are more common in the testimony concerning religious miracles than in that concerning any other matter of fact; this must diminish very much the authority of the former testimony, and make us form a general resolution never to lend any attention to it, with whatever specious pretence it may be covered.

Lord Bacon seems to have embraced the same principles of reasoning. 'We ought,' says he, 'to make a collection or particular history of all monsters and prodigious births or productions; and, in a word, of every thing new, rare and extraordinary in nature. But this must be done with the most severe scrutiny, lest we depart from truth. Above all, every relation must be considered as suspicious which depends in any degree upon religion, as the prodigies of Livy: and no less so everything that is to be found in the writers on natural magic or alchemy, or such authors who seem all of them to have an unconquerable appetite for falsehood and fable.'[1]

I am the better pleased with the method of reasoning here delivered, as I think it may serve to confound those dangerous friends, or disguised enemies to the *Christian religion*, who have undertaken to defend it by the principles of human reason. Our most holy religion is founded on *Faith*, not on reason; and it is a sure method of exposing it to put it to such a trial as it is by no means fitted to endure. To make this more evident, let us examine those miracles related in Scripture; and, not to lose ourselves in too wide a field, let us confine ourselves to such as we find in the *Pentateuch*, which we shall examine, according to the principles of these pretended Christians, not as the word or testimony of God himself, but as the production of a mere human writer and historian. Here, then, we are first to consider a book, presented to us by a barbarous and ignorant people, written in an age when they were still more barbarous, and, in all probability, long after the facts which it relates, corroborated by no concurring testimony, and resembling those fabulous accounts which every nation gives of its origin. Upon reading this book, we find it full of prodigies and miracles. It gives an account of a state of the world and of human nature entirely different from the present: of our fall from that state: of the age of man, extended to near a thousand years: of the destruction of the world by a deluge: of the arbitrary choice of one people as the favourites of heaven; and that people the countrymen of the author: of their deliverance from bondage by prodigies the most astonishing imaginable: I desire

[1] *Novum Organum*, Bk II, aphorism 29. Francis Bacon (1561–1626) was chiefly interested, as a philosopher, in the basis of the experimental sciences, and in his *Novum Organum* gives an account of the nature of induction (see n. 1 to p. 188).

anyone to lay his hand upon his heart, and, after a serious consideration, declare whether he thinks that the falsehood of such a book, supported by such a testimony, would be more extraordinary and miraculous than all the miracles it relates; which is, however, necessary to make it be received, according to the measures of probability above established.

What we have said of miracles, may be applied without any variation to prophecies; and, indeed, all prophecies are real miracles, and as such, only can be admitted as proofs of any revelation. If it did not exceed the capacity of human nature to foretell future events, it would be absurd to employ any prophecy as an argument for a divine mission or authority from heaven. So that, upon the whole, we may conclude, that the *Christian Religion* not only was at first attended with miracles, but even at this day cannot be believed by any reasonable person without one. Mere reason is insufficient to convince us of its veracity: and whoever is moved by *Faith* to assent to it, is conscious of a continued miracle in his own person, which subverts all the principles of his understanding, and gives him a determination to believe what is most contrary to custom and experience.

14

KANT

on THE EXISTENCE OF GOD *and on* IMMORTALITY

Biographical Note Born in 1724 at Königsberg, son of a saddler. Educated at the Collegium Fridericianum and at Königsberg University, after which he was a private tutor for a few years. 1755, appointed Privatdozent at Königsberg University and in 1770 as Professor of Logic and Metaphysics. 1775–81, worked on the *Critique of Pure Reason*; and subsequently the other two *Critiques*. Failing health induced him to resign his position in 1801. Died, 1804.

Principal works: *Critique of Pure Reason* (1781), *Prolegomena to every future Metaphysics* (1873), *Critique of Practical Reason* (1787), *Critique of Judgment* (1790), *Religion within the Limits of Pure Reason* (1793), *Groundwork of the Metaphysic of Morals* (1785).

Philosophical Note K. had been brought up philosophically in the rationalist tradition, and until in the 1770s when he broke with it was an adherent of the metaphysical position of Christian Wolff (1697–1754). The latter had systematized and adapted the teachings of Leibniz. All knowledge, he held, could become (or already was) 'scientific', i.e. complete, systematic, *a priori* and certain—and thus the capacity of the understanding to apprehend the nature of things as they really are, whether or not they could be experienced, was not questioned. This philosophical position was dogmatic (as opposed to K.'s later 'critical' philosophy) in the sense that it involved speculation without a previous inquiry into the scope and limits of knowledge. K., on his own testimony, was roused from his 'dogmatic slumber' by Hume. The latter's empiricism offered a serious challenge to the *a priori* approach of the rationalists, but at the same time his analysis of causation appeared to cut away the basis of science. Another reason for K.'s rejection of dogmatic metaphysics was his discovery of the Antinomies—namely, that certain pairs of contradictory propositions (e.g. 'The world has, as to space and time, a beginning or limit' and 'The world is, as to space and time, infinite'—see *Prolegomena*, §§50, 52) can equally rigorously be proved true, on the supposition that our intellectual concepts genuinely apply to reality. Finally, the universal causal determination of events, which the scientific investigation of nature seems to presuppose, is in conflict, K. held, with the requirement of morality that some actions are free: and thus the rationalist view that laws such as that of universal causation can be extended to apply, not merely to sense-experience, but also to ultimate reality seems to remove the possibility of human freedom (see, regarding Leibniz, above, p. 50). These motives impelled K. to break with dogmatic metaphysics, and to attempt to solve two fundamental problems: first, as to how mathematics and the natural sciences can be defended against Hume's scepticism; and second, to expose the illusions of speculative metaphysics and to substitute in its place metaphysics as a science (a science which will exhibit systematically the whole body of philosophical knowledge, will avoid the Antinomies and will satisfy the needs of theoretical reason without destroying freedom).

A main way in which K. attempted to deal with these problems was through his so-called 'Copernican revolution'. Just as Copernicus had explained the peculiar motions of celestial bodies as appearances resulting from the fact that we are on a moving earth, so K. explained the position and extension of things in space and their succession in time as resulting from the peculiar constitution of our faculty of perception. Mathematics applies to the world because space and time are contributed, so to speak, not by things in themselves but by the mind: the form in which we see things is such that they appear in space and time. Similarly, the understanding (which is 'the faculty of cognition by means of concepts', applied to particular things given in experience) contains certain *a priori* concepts, —notably that of *causality*,—(what K. calls the 'categories'), without the use of which we cannot have scientific understanding of what we perceive. But, it must be noted, these categories cannot be used to apply to what is entirely outside all possible experience: it is the attempt of speculative metaphysicians to do this which leads to the Antinomies. Nevertheless, reason does not remain content to apply the categories to experience, but tries to transcend it: for instance, the sequence of causes and effects is traced back to a first cause (God). Thus are generated certain unifying concepts, which K. (reminiscently of Plato) calls 'Ideas', viz. God, the world (as a whole, lying beyond any finite sum of experiences) and the soul. K. holds that these Ideas have a merely regulative function, i.e. their purpose is to guide enquiry, but are not constitutive notions, i.e. they are not applicable to experience and thus do not stand for anything existing objectively. They serve the purpose of giving the greatest unity and breadth to our enquiries: thus it is useful to think *as if* there were a first cause as a constant spur to retracing the links in the chain of causes we find in the world. K. calls the Ideas 'transcendental' (as opposed to 'transcendent') to signalize that they are *a priori* conditions of making knowledge possible (as opposed to the usual concepts of speculative metaphysics which are transcendent in that they are used to apply outside the limits of possible experience). Briefly then: mathematics is possible because space and time are supplied, so to speak, by the mind; natural science is possible because the understanding legislates for nature by applying the categories to phenomena; and metaphysics is possible in that the elaboration of *a priori* concepts yields certain useful Ideas, though it is not possible as a speculative attempt to produce any knowledge of that which transcends experience. However, a somewhat different account of the Idea of God is given by Kant later in the *Critique of Practical Reason* (see below, pp. 284–9).

In the following passage, K. is chiefly concerned to show the invalidity of the traditional arguments for the existence of God, which he reduces to three forms, the ontological, cosmological and teleological arguments, which he discusses successively. In the previous sections of the first *Critique* he had criticized Rational Psychology, i.e. the attempt to establish speculatively the existence of such a permanent substance, and Rational Cosmology, i.e. the attempt to prove *a priori* propositions about the cosmos, the sum total of things in space and time. He now goes on to deal with Rational Theology, the attempt to establish in a speculative fashion the existence of God. In the first section, which gives an account of the general nature of the theistic arguments, K. examines the different concepts of a *necessary being* and of the *ens realissimum* (Being which contains in itself all reality), holding that all the proofs are based on the supposed connection between them. The investigation as to whether this connection exists is therefore a necessary preliminary to the detailed treatment of the arguments. For it is, for instance, insufficient to show that a necessary being exists: what is needed, in addition, if God's existence is to be proved, is a proof that the necessary being is the infinitely perfect being (the *ens realissimum*).

It should be noted that K. is particularly anxious to show the invalidity of the Ontological Argument, as it contains in a nutshell the claim of speculative metaphysics that pure thought can yield knowledge about reality.

Bibliographical Note There are translations of *The Critique of Pure Reason* by N. K. Smith (London, 1929) and J. Meiklejohn (London, 1881); for the *Critique of Practical Reason*, see the translations of T. K. Abbot (6th edn, London 1909) and Lewis W. Beck (Chicago, 1948); for the *Critique of Judgment*, see J. C. Meredith (Oxford, 1952); the *Groundwork*, H. J. Paton, *The Moral Law* (3rd edn, London, 1956); the *Prolegomena*, P. G. Lucas (Manchester, 1953); C. C. J. Webb, *Kant's Philosophy of Religion* (Oxford, 1926); and *Religion within the Limits of Reason Alone*, trans. with introduction and notes by Theodore M. Green and Hoyt A. Hudson (Harper Torch Books, N.Y., 1960). S. Körner's *Kant* (London, Pelican, 1955) is an excellent introduction. See also: H. J. Paton, *Kant's Metaphysic of Experience*, 2 vols. (London, 1936), T. D. Weldon, *Introduction to Kant's Critique of Pure Reason* (Oxford, 1945), H. J. Paton, *The Categorical Imperative* (London, 1947) and H. W. Cassirer, *A Commentary on Kant's Critique of Judgment* (London, 1938).

A. THE EXISTENCE OF GOD

Critique of Pure Reason, Transcendental Dialectic, Bk II, Ch. iii, last part of §3 *et seq.*

There are only three ways of proving the existence of a Deity on the grounds of speculative reason.

All the paths leading to this end either begin with determinate experience and the special constitution of the world of sense-experience and rise, in accordance with the laws of causality, from it to the highest cause existing apart from the world; or they begin with a purely indeterminate experience, i.e. some empirical existent; or abstraction is made of all experience and the existence of a supreme cause is inferred from *a priori* concepts alone. The first is the *physico-theological* argument,[1] the second is the *cosmological* argument and the third is the *ontological* argument. There are no more, and more there cannot be.

I shall show that it is as unsuccessful on the one path, the empirical, as on the other, the transcendental, and that it stretches its wings in vain, to

[1] I.e. the Teleological Argument.

soar beyond the world of sense-experience by the mere power of speculative thought. As to the order in which we must discuss these arguments, it will be exactly the reverse of that in which reason, in the progress of its development, reaches them—the order in which they are arranged above. For it will be made obvious to the reader that although experience presents the occasion and starting-point, it is the transcendental Idea of reason which guides it in its pilgrimage and is the goal of all its efforts. I shall therefore begin with the transcendental argument and afterwards enquire what additional strength has accrued to this mode of proof from the addition of the empirical element.

Of the Impossibility of an Ontological Proof of the Existence of God.[1]

It is clear from what has been said that the concept of an absolutely necessary being is a mere Idea, the objective reality of which is far from being established by the mere fact that it is a need of reason. On the contrary, this Idea serves merely to indicate a certain unattainable perfection, and limits the operations rather than, by the presentation of new objects, extends the sphere of the understanding. But we are met at the very threshold by a strange anomaly: for the inference from a given existence in general to an absolutely necessary existence seems to be correct and unavoidable, while the conditions of the *understanding* refuse to help us in forming any conception of such a being.

Philosophers have always talked of an *absolutely necessary* being and yet nevertheless have declined to take the pains of conceiving whether—and how—a being of this nature is even thinkable, not to mention whether its existence is actually demonstrable. A verbal definition of the concept is certainly easy enough: it is something the non-existence of which is inconceivable. But does this definition throw any light on the conditions rendering it impossible to conceive the non-existence of a thing—conditions which we wish to ascertain in order that we may find out whether we think anything in the concept of such a being or not? For the mere fact that I discard, by means of the word 'Unconditioned', all the conditions which the understanding customarily requires in order to regard anything as necessary is very far from making it clear whether by means of the concept of the unconditionally necessary I think of something or really nothing at all.

Nay more: many have tried to explain this chance concept, now become so current, by examples which seem to render any enquiry concerning its intelligibility quite superfluous. Every geometrical proposition—e.g. 'A triangle has three angles'—, it was said, is absolutely

[1] K. gives the argument in the form taught by Wolff (see above, p. 248).

necessary; and people spoke in this way of an object which lay outside the sphere of our understanding as if it were perfectly obvious what the concept of such a being meant.

All the examples adduced have been drawn, without exception, from *judgments*[1] and not from *things*. But the unconditioned necessity of a judgment does not amount to the absolute necessity of a thing. On the contrary the absolute necessity of a judgment is only a conditioned necessity of a thing, or of the predicate in a judgment. The proposition mentioned above does not assert that the three angles necessarily exist, but, upon the condition that a triangle exists, three angles must necessarily exist, in it. And this logical necessity has been thus a source of the greatest delusions. Having formed an *a priori* concept of a thing, the content of which was made to include existence, we believed ourselves safe in concluding that because existence belongs necessarily to the object of this concept (i.e. under the condition that I posit this thing as given), the existence of the thing is also posited necessarily, and that it is therefore absolutely necessary—merely because its existence has been included in the concept.

If, in an identical judgment,[2] I negate the predicate in thought and retain the subject, a contradiction results; and hence I say that the former belongs necessarily to the latter. But if I suppress both subject and predicate in thought, no contradiction arises; for there *is nothing* at all and hence no means of constructing a contradiction. To suppose the existence of a triangle and not that of its three angles is self-contradictory; but to suppose the non-existence of both triangle and angles is perfectly admissible. Similarly with the concept of an absolutely necessary being. Annihilate its existence in thought and you annihilate the thing itself, with all its predicates: how then can there be room for a contradiction? Externally, there is nothing to give rise to a contradiction, for a thing cannot be necessary externally; nor internally, for by the annihilation or suppression of the thing itself its internal properties are annihilated. God is omnipotent—this is a necessary judgment. His omnipotence cannot be denied, once the existence of a Deity has been posited—the existence, that is, of an infinite being, the two concepts being identical. But when you say 'God does not exist', neither omnipotence nor any other predicate is affirmed; they must all vanish with the subject, and in this judgment there cannot be the slightest self-contradiction.[3]

[1] I.e. propositional judgments (the judgment that P, etc.).

[2] I.e., a judgment where subject and predicate are the same.

[3] K.'s point here is briefly: Necessary judgments are such that if S exists, P exists, and it is self-contradictory to assert that S exists and not P. But if we deny that S exists, there is no contradiction in supposing that P does not exist. If 'God exists' entails 'God necessarily exists', it still does not follow that 'God does not exist' is self-contradictory, for supposing God does not exist, there is no application for the predicate 'necessarily existent'.

You have thus seen that when the predicate of a judgment is annihilated in thought along with the subject no internal contradiction can arise, whatever the predicate may be. There is no way of avoiding the conclusion—you find yourselves forced to say 'There are certain subjects which cannot be annihilated in thought'. But this is nothing more than saying 'There exist subjects which are absolutely necessary'—which is the very hypothesis you are called on to establish. For I find myself unable to form the slightest idea of a thing which, when annihilated in thought with all its predicates, leaves behind it a contradiction. And contradiction is the only criterion of impossibility, in the sphere of pure *a priori* concepts.

Against these general considerations, the correctness of which no one can dispute, one argument is employed which is thought to furnish a satisfactory demonstration of the point. It is asserted that there is one and only one concept in which the non-being or annihilation of the object is self-contradictory, namely the concept of an *ens realissimum*. It possesses, you say, all reality and you feel yourselves justified in granting the possibility of such a being. (This I am willing to grant for the moment, although the existence of a concept which is not self-contradictory is far from being enough to show the possibility of the object.*) Now the notion of all reality includes that of existence: the notion, therefore, of existence is contained in the concept of this possible thing. If this thing is annihilated in thought, the internal possibility of the thing is annihilated too, which is self-contradictory.

I answer: It is absurd to introduce into the concept of a thing, which is to be conceived solely with reference to its possibility,[1] the concept of its existence, disguised under whatever term. Once this is granted, you will have apparently won the day—but in fact will have asserted nothing but an empty tautology. I ask: Is the proposition that *this or that thing* (which I am granting to be possible) *exists* an analytic or synthetic proposition?[2] If the former, no addition is made to the subject

* A concept is always possible, provided it is not self-contradictory. This is the logical criterion of possibility, distinguishing the object referred to by such a concept from the *nihil negativum*. [Provided a concept is genuine, it is capable of referring to an object. Thus 'There are unicorns' expresses a logical possibility, in that 'unicorn' is not self-contradictory. But if unicorns are non-existent, they are clearly non-existent in a different sense from the way squircles (see next note) are non-existent. That unicorns do not exist is a matter of empirical fact: that there are no squircles is a logical truth.]

[1] The only thing which would prevent an alleged concept from really being one is self-contradiction. Thus I might invent the term 'squircle', to mean: 'square circle'. There would, however, be no real concept *squircle* since its definition is self-contradictory. See K.'s note above.

[2] K. regarded all judgments as being capable of division into a subject and a predicate: thus in the judgment 'This cat is yellow' the predicate 'yellow' is ascribed to the subject 'this cat'. Now either the predicate is already included, so to speak, in the concept of the subject or it is not. If it is, as in the proposition 'Bachelors are unmarried' (for *being*

of your thought by the assertion of its existence: but then the concept in your minds is identical with the thing itself, or you have supposed the existence of the thing to be possible and then inferred its existence from its internal possibility[1]—which is only a miserable tautology. The word *reality* in the concept of the thing and the word *existence* in the concept of the predicate will not get you out of your difficulty. For suppose you were to call all positing of a thing *reality*, you have thereby posited the thing with all its predicates in the concept of the subject and assumed its actual existence: and this you merely repeat in the predicate. But if you concede, as every reasonable person must, that every existential proposition is synthetic, how can it be maintained that the predicate of existence cannot be denied without self-contradiction—a property which characterizes analytic propositions alone?

I should have a reasonable hope of putting an end for ever to this sophistical method of argumentation, by a strict definition of the concept of existence, were I not taught by my own experience that the illusion which arises from confounding a logical with a real predicate (one which helps in the determination of the thing) resists almost all efforts at explanation and illustration. A logical predicate may be anything you please—even the subject may be predicated of itself—; for logic has no reference to the content of a judgment. But the determination of a concept is a predicate which adds to and expands the concept. It must not therefore be contained in the predicate.

Being is evidently not a real predicate, i.e. a concept of something which is added to the concept of some other thing. It is merely the positing of a thing or of certain elements in it. Logically, it is merely the copula of a judgment. The proposition 'God is omnipotent' contains two concepts, which have a certain object or content; but the word 'is' is no additional predicate—it merely indicates the relation of the predicate to the subject. Now if I take the subject (God) with all its predicates (omnipotence being one) and say 'God is' or 'There is a God', I add no new predicate to the concept of God: I merely posit or affirm the existence of the subject with all its predicates—I posit the *object* in relation to my *concept*. The content of both is the same; and no addition is made to the concept, which expresses merely the possibility of the object it refers to, by my thinking of the object—in the expression 'it *is*'—as absolutely given and existing. Thus the real contains no more than the possible. A hundred real

unmarried is part of what is meant by *being a bachelor*), we have an analytic proposition. If it is not, as in the proposition 'Bachelors like comfort' (for 'X is a bachelor' is consistent with 'X does not like comfort' and therefore does not entail 'X likes comfort'), we have a synthetic proposition (see *Prolegomena* §2).

[1] I.e. its internal consistency—its non-self-contradictoriness.

dollars contain no more than a hundred possible dollars. For since the latter words[1] indicate the concept and the former[2] the object, then on the supposition that the content of the former was greater than the content of the latter, my concept would not express the whole object and would hence be an inadequate concept of it. Still, when I am counting my wealth there may be said to be more in a hundred real dollars than in a hundred possible dollars—i.e. in the mere concept of them. For the real object—the dollars—is not analytically contained in my concept, but forms a synthetic addition to my concept (which is merely a determination of my mental state), although this objective reality—the existence—apart from my concept does not by the least amount increase the aforementioned hundred dollars.[3]

By whatever kind and number of predicates, even to the complete determination of it, I may conceive a thing, I do not augment in the slightest the object of my concept by adding the statement: 'This thing exists.' Otherwise there would exist something not exactly the same as, but something more than, that which was thought of in my concept, and I could not assert that the precise object of my concept had real existence. If I think of a thing as containing all modes of reality save one, the mode of reality which is absent is not added to the concept of the thing by the assertion that it exists; on the contrary, the thing exists—if it exists at all—with the same defect as that thought of in its concept; otherwise, not that which was thought of, but something else, exists.[4] Now if I conceive a being as the highest reality, without defect or imperfection, the question still remains whether this being exists or not. For although no element is lacking in the possible real content of my concept, there is a defect in relation to my mental state, i.e. I am ignorant as to whether the knowledge indicated by the concept is possible *a posteriori*. And here the reason for the present difficulty becomes clear. If the question concerned an object of sense-experience merely, it would be impossible for me to confuse the concept with the existence of the thing. For the concept merely enables me to conceive of an object as according with the general conditions of experience; while the existence of the object allows me to

[1] Namely, 'a hundred possible dollars'.

[2] 'A hundred real dollars'.

[3] That is, 'exists' is not an ordinary predicate (compare the common modern view, for references to which see above, p. 58), though all existential judgments are synthetic, since though 'exists' does not add to the content of the concept of the subject, it expresses something not given by the mere concept.

[4] Perhaps a simpler way of putting K.'s point is this: a concept is a specification to which there may or may not be some object corresponding. But to say that an object does correspond to the specification does not add to the specification: for if it did, it would be a new specification. (Moreover, there is the question: Does any object correspond to this new specification?—and so on.)

think of it as contained in the sphere of actual experience. At the same time, this connexion with the world of experience does not in the least augment the concept, although a possible perception has been added to the experience of the mind. But if we conceive existence by the pure category alone, it is not surprising that we should find ourselves incapable of providing any criterion sufficient to distinguish it from mere possibility.

Whatever may be the content of our concept of an object, it is necessary to go beyond it if we wish to predicate existence of the object. In the case of perceptible objects, this is done by their connexion according to empirical laws with some one of my perceptions; but there is no means of having knowledge of the objects of pure thought, because this must happen purely *a priori*. But all our knowledge of existence (either immediately by perception or by inferences connecting some object with a perception) belongs entirely to the sphere of experience—which is in perfect unity with itself; and though an existence out of this sphere cannot be pronounced absolutely to be impossible, it is a hypothesis whose truth we have no means of determining.

The notion of a Supreme Being is in many ways a highly useful Idea; but for the very reason that it is an Idea, it is unable to expand our knowledge regarding the existence of things. It is not even adequate to instructing us as to the possibility of a being which we do not know to exist. The analytic test of possibility, which consists in the absence of contradiction in propositions, cannot be denied it. But the connexion of real properties in a thing is a synthesis, about the possibility of which an *a priori* judgment cannot be formed, since these realities are not presented to us specifically. And even if this were to occur, a judgment would still not be possible, since the criterion of the possibility of pieces of synthetic knowledge must be looked for in the world of experience, to which the thing an Idea is supposed to refer cannot belong. Thus the celebrated Leibniz has failed completely to establish on *a priori* grounds the possibility of this sublime ideal being.[1]

The celebrated ontological or Cartesian argument[2] for the existence of a Supreme Being is therefore inadequate; and we can as much hope to increase our stock of knowledge by the aid of mere Ideas as the merchant to augment his wealth by the addition of noughts to his cash account.

Of the Impossibility of a Cosmological Proof of the Existence of God

It was by no means a natural way to proceed, but on the contrary an invention wholly due to scholastic subtlety, to try to get from a mere Idea

[1] For L.'s argument, see above, p. 145.

[2] 'Cartesian' because of Descartes' use of this form of argument; see above, p. 121.

a proof of the existence of an object corresponding to it. Such a course would never have been pursued had it not been for that need of reason which demands that it should suppose that a necessary being exists as a basis for the empirical regress and that, since this necessity must be unconditioned and *a priori*, reason is bound to come upon a concept which will satisfy, if possible, this demand and enable us to attain to the *a priori* knowledge of such an object. This concept was thought to be found in the Idea of an *ens realissimum*, and thus this Idea was used for reaching a better defined knowledge of a necessary being regarding the existence of which we were convinced or persuaded on other grounds. Thus reason was seduced from her natural course; and instead of ending with the concept of an *ens realissimum* an attempt was made to begin with it, for the purpose of inferring from it that idea of a necessary existence which it is in fact brought in to complete. Thus arose the unhappy ontological argument, which neither satisfies the healthy common sense of man nor bears the scientific scrutiny of the philosopher.

The *cosmological argument*, which we are now going to investigate, retains the connexion between absolute necessity and the highest reality; but instead of reasoning from the highest reality to a necessary existence, like the preceding argument, it infers from the given unconditioned necessity of some being its unlimited reality. The path it takes, whether rational or sophistical, is at least a natural one, and not only goes far to convince the common understanding but also shows itself worthy of respect from the speculative intellect. At the same time, it contains in outline all the arguments used in natural theology—arguments which always have been and will still remain in use and authority. However these may be adorned and whatever embellishments of rhetoric and sentiment may clothe them, they are at bottom identical with the arguments which we are about to discuss now. This proof, called by Leibniz the *argumentum a contingentia mundi*,[1] I shall now lay before the reader and subject to strict examination.

It is framed as follows: If something exists, an absolutely necessary being must likewise exist. Now I, at least, exist. Therefore, there exists an absolutely necessary being. The minor premiss contains an experience,[2]

[1] As K. states the argument it has two stages: (I) If any contingent being exists, a necessary being exists; some contingent being exists; so a necessary being exists: (II) Every necessary being is also an *ens realissimum* (an infinitely perfect being), for the *ens realissimum* contains in itself all reality, and no other being contains the conditions of its own existence. K. argues that stage II involves the use of the Ontological Argument. But see below, n. 1 to p. 260.

[2] I.e. it refers to an object given in experience. The minor premiss does not, of course, have to take the form given it here by K.: any sort of object will do; all that is needed is that some existential proposition is true.

the major reasons from a general experience to the existence of a necessary being.* Thus this argument really begins at experience and is not completely *a priori* or ontological. The object of all possible experience being the world (cosmos), it is called the *cosmological* proof. It contains no reference to any specific property of perceptible objects by which this world of sense-experience might be distinguished from other possible worlds, and in this respect it differs from the physico-theological proof, which is based upon the consideration of the specific constitution of our sensuous world.

The proof goes on as follows:—A necessary being can be determined in only one way, i.e. by only one of all possible predicates; so it must be *completely* determined in and by its concept. But there is only a single concept of a thing possible which completely determines the thing *a priori*, namely the concept of the *ens realissimum*. It follows that the concept of the *ens realissimum* is the only one by and in which we can think of a necessary being.

In this cosmological argument are assembled so many fallacious propositions that speculative reason seems to have exerted in it all her dialectical skill to induce a transcendental illusion of the most extreme kind. We shall postpone our investigation of this argument for the moment and confine ourselves to exposing the manœuvre by which it imposes on us an old argument in new dress, and appeals to the agreement of two witnesses, the one possessing the credentials of pure reason, and the other possessing those of empiricism:—whereas in fact it is only the former who has changed his dress and voice in order to pass himself off as an additional witness. So that it may have a secure foundation, it bases its conclusions upon experience, and thus seems to be quite distinct from the ontological argument, which places its confidence entirely in pure *a priori* concepts. But this experience aids reason in merely making one step—to the existence of a necessary being. What the properties of this being are cannot be learned from experience, and therefore reason abandons it altogether and pursues its enquiries in the realm of pure concepts, in order to discover what the properties of an absolutely necessary being ought to be, i.e. what among all possible things contains the conditions (*requisita*) of absolute necessity. Reason believes that it has found those requisites in the concept of an *ens realissimum*, and there alone, and so concludes: The *ens realissimum* is an absolutely necessary being. But it is clear that reason has

* This inference is too well known to warrant more detailed discussion. It is based on the spurious transcendental law of causality that everything which is *contingent* has a cause which, if itself contingent, must have a cause . . . and so on, till the series of subordinated causes must end with an absolutely necessary cause, without which it would not possess completeness.

here presupposed that the concept of an *ens realissimum* is perfectly adequate to the concept of a being of absolute necessity, i.e. that we may infer the existence of the latter from that of the former—a proposition which formed the basis of the ontological argument, contrary to the wish and professions of its inventors. For the existence of an absolutely necessary being is given in concepts alone. But if I say 'The concept of the *ens realissimum* is a concept of this sort and in fact the only concept which is adequate to our idea of a necessary being', then I am obliged to concede that the latter may be inferred from the former. Thus it is properly the ontological argument which figures in the cosmological and constitutes the whole power of the latter—while the spurious basis in experience has been of no further use than to guide us to the concept of absolute necessity, being completely insufficient to demonstrate the presence of this attribute in any determinate existent or thing. For when we propose to ourselves a purpose of this kind we must abandon the realm of experience and rise to that of pure concepts, which we investigate with the aim of finding out whether any one of them contains the conditions of the possibility of an absolutely necessary being. But if the possibility of such a being is demonstrated in this way, its existence is also proved; for we may then say that among all possible beings there is one which possesses the atrribute of necessity—in other words, this being possesses an absolutely necessary existence.

All illusions in an argument are more easily detected when they are presented in the formal manner employed by the schools,[1] which we now proceed to do.

If the proposition 'Every absolutely necessary being is also an *ens realissimum*' is correct (and it is this which constitutes the crucial point of the cosmological argument), it must, like all affirmative judgments, be capable of conversion, the *conversio per accidens* at least.[2] It follows that some *entia realissima* are absolutely necessary beings. But no *ens realissimum* is in any respect different from another, and what is valid of some is valid of all. In this present case, therefore, I may use simple conversion and assert 'Every *ens realissimum* is a necessary being'. But as this proposition is determined *a priori* by the concepts contained in it, the mere concept of an

[1] I.e. the formalized way of setting out arguments in accordance with the rules of traditional (Aristotelian) logic.

[2] The affirmative propositions recognized in traditional logic are of the form 'All S are P' or 'Some S are P'. From 'All S are P' one can infer 'Some P are S' (this is called *conversio per accidens*). Arguing from 'All S are P' to 'All P are S' is, unless some other premiss is given, fallacious (known as the fallacy of simple conversion) (e.g. you cannot argue from 'All lions are man-eaters' to 'All man-eaters are lions'). In the present case, K. argues from 'All S are P' to 'Some P are S', and then, given the premiss that what is true of some P is true of all P, to 'All P are S'. But there is an ambiguity about the word 'all'.

ens realissimum must possess the additional attribute of absolute necessity. But this is exactly what was maintained in the ontological argument, and not recognized by the cosmological, although it constituted the real basis of its disguised and illusory reasoning.[1]

Thus the second method used by speculative reason of demonstrating the existence of a Supreme Being is not only like the first illusory and inadequate, but possesses the added blemish of an *ignoratio elenchi*[2]—professing to guide us by a new route to the desired goal, but bringing us back, after a short circuit, to the old path which we had left at its call.

I mentioned above that this cosmological argument contains a whole nest of dialectical assumptions which transcendental criticism[3] does not find it hard to expose and explode. I shall merely enumerate these, leaving it to the reader, who must by now be well practised in such matters, to examine the fallacies residing therein.

The following fallacies, for example, are to be found in this mode of proof:—(1) The transcendental principle 'Everything that is contingent must have a cause'—a principle which is without significance except in the world of sense-experience. For the purely intellectual concept of the contingent cannot produce any synthetic proposition, like that of causality,[4] which is itself without significance or distinguishing characteristic

[1] K. has been criticized by Thomists for making a mistake here. For the word 'all' is ambiguous: 'All lions are man-eaters' would normally be taken to imply that there are lions, but 'All trespassers will be prosecuted' does not imply that there are or will be any (the notice is put up with the purpose of ensuring that there are or will be *no* trespassers) —it means 'If anyone is a trespasser, he will be prosecuted'. It does not imply 'Someone is a trespasser'. Now the conversion of 'All S are P' to 'Some P are S' only works with the first sense of 'all'. K. would therefore have to reformulate his criticism; for the conversion he proposes will only be valid if it is true that some necessary being(s) exist(s). This has been, supposedly, proved in the first part of the cosmological argument, and it is therefore incorrect to assert that this is only a piece of 'dressing up' which conceals the real nature of the argument as being a version of the Ontological Argument. Nevertheless, it may still be held that one criticism of the Ontological Argument, namely that it involves claiming that there is one existential proposition at least which is necessarily true, applies to the Cosmological Argument inasmuch as it employs the notion of a necessary being. For these points and references to the Thomist criticisms, see J. J. C. Smart, 'The Existence of God' in *New Essays in Philosophical Theology*, ed. Flew and MacIntyre (London, 1955), pp. 37 ff.

[2] The fallacy of arguing to the wrong point.

[3] *Transcendental criticism*: i.e. the critical investigation of transcendental arguments, viz. arguments not proceeding on empirical principles. In K.'s system, there are certainly transcendental presuppositions: but these do not constitute a separate and peculiar body of propositions which tell us about the nature of reality lying beyond all possible experience, but are merely preconditions of our knowing and understanding anything. Thus the Ideas, for instance, do not stand for anything objective, such as might be given in experience; but merely serve to guide our enquiries. See p. 249.

[4] The judgment 'Every change has a cause' is, K. holds, both synthetic (see n. 2 to p. 253) and *a priori* (for it a necessary presupposition of scientific thinking). But it is fallacious to use it beyond the limits of possible experience, and so beyond science.

except in the phenomenal world. But in the present instance it is used to help us beyond the limits of its sphere. (2) From the impossibility of an infinite ascending series of causes in the world of sense-experience a first cause is inferred;—a conclusion which the principles of the employment of reason do not justify even in the sphere of experience and still less when an attempt is made to go beyond the limits of this sphere. (3) Reason permits itself to be satisfied on inadequate grounds with regard to the completion of the series. It removes all conditions (without which, however, no conception of necessity can take place); and since thereafter it is beyond our capacity to form any other concept, it accepts this as a completion of the concept it desires to form of the series. (4) The logical possibility of a concept of the whole of reality (the criterion of this possibility being the absence of contradiction) is confused with the transcendental, which requires a principle to determine the practicability of such a synthesis—a principle which again refers us to the world of experience. And so on.

The aim of the cosmological argument is to escape the need to prove the existence of a necessary being *a priori* from mere concepts—a proof which must be ontological and of which we feel ourselves quite incapable. With this aim, we reason from actual existence, an experience in general, to an absolutely necessary condition of that existence. It is in this case unnecessary to prove its possibility. For after having established that it exists, the question of its possibility is superfluous. Now when we wish to define more strictly the nature of this necessary being, we do not look out for some being the concept of which would enable us to comprehend the necessity of its being—for if we could do this an empirical presupposition would be unnecessary: no, we try to find merely the negative condition (*conditio sine qua non*), without which a being would not be absolutely necessary. Now this would be perfectly admissible in every sort of reasoning from a consequence to its ground; but in the present instance it happens unfortunately that the condition of absolute necessity can be found in but a single being, the concept of which must consequently contain all that is requisite for demonstrating the presence of absolute necessity and thus entitle me to infer this absolute necessity *a priori*. That is, it must be possible to argue in the other direction and say: 'The thing to which the concept of the highest reality belongs is absolutely necessary.' But if I cannot argue in this way, and I cannot, unless I believe in the adequacy of the ontological argument, I find unsurmountable obstacles in my new path; and I am really no further on than the point from which I started. The concept of a Supreme Being satisfies all questions *a priori* concerning the internal determinations of a thing, and is for this reason an Ideal without equal or parallel,[1] the general concept of it indicating that it is at the same time an *ens individuum* among all possible things. But the concept does not satisfy the question about its existence—which was the purpose of all our enquiries; and even though the existence of a necessary being were conceded, we should find it impossible to answer the question 'What of all things in the world must be considered as necessary?'

It is certainly legitimate to *admit* the existence of an all-sufficient being—a cause of all possible effects—for the purpose of enabling reason to bring unity to its mode and grounds of explanation with regard to phenomena. But to claim that such a being *necessarily exists* is no longer the enunciation of an allowable hypothesis, but the boldest assertion of an apodeictic certainty:[2] for the knowledge of that which is absolutely necessary must itself possess that character.

The purpose of the transcendental Ideal formed by the mind is either to discover a concept which will harmonize with the idea of absolute necessity or a concept which will contain that idea. If the one is possible, so is the other; for reason recognizes only one thing as absolutely necessary, namely that which is necessary from its concept. But both attempts are equally beyond our capacity: we find it impossible to *satisfy* the understanding on this point, and as impossible to persuade it to remain at rest in relation to this incapacity.

Unconditioned necessity, which, as the ultimate support and prop of all existing things, is an unavoidable requirement of the mind, is an abyss on the verge of which human reason trembles in dismay. Even the idea of eternity, terrible and sublime, as depicted by Haller,[3] does not impress upon the mental vision such a feeling of awe and terror, for although it *measures* the duration of things it does not *support* them. We cannot bear the thought—nor can we get rid of it—that a being which we regard as the greatest of all possible existences should *say to himself* 'I am from eternity to eternity; beside me there is nothing, save that which exists by my will; *but whence then am I?*' Here all sinks away from under us; and the greatest, like the smallest, perfection hovers without prop or footing in the presence of the speculative reason, which finds it as easy to part with the one as the other.

Many physical powers, which evidence their existence by their effects, are absolutely inscrutable in their nature: they elude all our powers of

[1] K. calls the concept of God not just an Idea but also an Ideal, since it implies not merely (like the other Ideas) completion, but also personality as the bearer of all possible perfections.

[2] 'Apodeictic': demonstrative. The expression goes back to Aristotle; see *Posterior Analytics*, 91b 33 ff.

[3] Berchtold Haller (1492–1536), Protestant Reformer, from Berne.

observation. The transcendental object which constitutes the basis of phenomena and, in connexion with it, the reason why our faculty of perception possesses this rather than that particular kind of conditions are and must ever stay hidden from our mental vision; the fact exists, the reason for the fact we cannot see. But an Ideal of pure reason cannot be called mysterious or *inscrutable*, because the only credential for its reality is the need of it which is felt by reason for the purpose of giving completeness to the world of synthetic unity. An Ideal is not even given as a thinkable *object*, and so cannot be inscrutable; on the contrary, it must, as a mere Idea, be based on the constitution of reason itself, and on this account must be capable of explanation and solution. For the very essence of reason lies in its capacity to give an account of all our concepts, opinions and assertions—upon objective grounds, or, when they happen to be illusory and fallacious, upon subjective ones.

Detection and Explanation of the Dialectical Illusion in all Transcendental Arguments for the Existence of a Necessary Being

Both of the above arguments are transcendental: in other words, they do not proceed on empirical principles. For although the cosmological argument professed to lay a foundation of experience for its edifice of reasoning, it did not base its procedure on the peculiar constitution of experience, but on pure principles of reason—in relation to an existence given by empirical consciousness, but utterly abandoning its guidance in order to support its assertions entirely upon pure concepts. Now what is the cause, in these transcendental arguments, for the dialectical, but natural, illusion that links the concepts of necessity and supreme reality and hypostatizes that which cannot be anything but an idea? What is the cause of this unavoidable step made by reason of admitting that some one among all existing things must be necessary, while it recoils from the existence of such a being as from an abyss? And how does reason go on to explain this anomaly to itself, and from the wavering state of timid and reluctant approval—always withdrawn again—arrive at a calm and settled insight into its cause?

It is a very remarkable thing that, supposing that something exists, I cannot escape the inference that something exists necessarily. Upon this perfectly natural (though not on that account reasonable) inference the cosmological argument rests. But whatever concept I form of a thing, I find that I cannot conceive the existence of the thing as absolutely necessary and that nothing hinders me (whatever the thing or being may be) from conceiving its non-existence. I may thus be forced to admit that all existing things have a necessary basis while I cannot conceive any single or individual thing as necessary. In other words, I can never *complete* the regress through the conditions of existence without conceding the existence of a necessary being; yet on the other hand I cannot make a *beginning* from this being.

If I must conceive something as existing necessarily as the basis of existing things and yet am not allowed to conceive anything in particular as in itself necessary, the inevitable conclusion is that necessity and contingency are not properties of things themselves—or else an internal contradiction would result—; but merely subjective principles of reason—the one requiring us to search for a necessary ground for everything that exists, i.e. to be satisfied with no other explanation than that which is complete *a priori*, the other forbidding us ever to hope to attain this completeness, i.e. to consider no entity in the empirical world as unconditioned. In this way of viewing them, both principles, in this purely heuristic and regulative[1] character, and as concerning merely the formal interest of reason, are quite consistent with each other. The one asserts: 'You must philosophize about nature as if there existed a necessary prime basis of all existing things, solely in order to bring systematic unity to your knowledge by pursuing an Idea of this character—a foundation which is arbitrarily granted to be ultimate'; while the other warns you to regard no individual determination concerning the existence of things as such an ultimate basis, i.e. as absolutely necessary, but always to keep open the way for further progress in deduction and to treat every determination as determined by some other. But if all that we perceive must be considered as conditionally necessary, it is impossible that anything which is given empirically should be absolutely necessary.

It follows from this that you must accept the absolutely necessary as *outside* and beyond the world, inasmuch as it is useful only as a principle of the highest possible unity in experience, and you cannot find any such necessary existent in the *world*, the second rule requiring you to regard all empirical causes of unity as themselves deduced.

The ancient philosophers considered all the forms of nature as contingent, while matter was thought by them—in accordance with the judgment of the common reason of mankind—as primary and necessary. But if they considered matter, not relatively, as the substratum of phenomena, but absolutely and *in itself*, as an independent existent, this idea of absolute necessity would straight away have disappeared. For there is nothing absolutely connecting reason with such an existent; on the contrary, it can annihilate it in thought, always and without self-contradiction. But the Idea of absolute necessity lay in thought alone. A

[1] See p. 249.

regulative principle must therefore have been at the basis of this opinion. In fact, extension and impenetrability, which jointly constitute our concept of matter, form the supreme empirical principle of the unity of phenomena, and this principle, in so far as it is empirically unconditioned, has the character of a regulative principle. But since every determination of matter which constitutes what is real in it, including impenetrability, is an effect which must have a cause and for this reason is always derivative, the notion of matter cannot harmonize with the Idea of a necessary being in its character of being the principle of all derived unity. For every one of its real properties, being derived from something, must be only conditionally necessary[1] and can therefore be annihilated in thought; hence the whole of existent matter can be annihilated or suppressed in this way. If this were not so, we would have discovered in the world of phenomena the highest ground or condition of unity—which is impossible, according to the second regulative principle. It follows that matter and, in general, all that is part of the world of sense-experience, cannot be a necessary primal being nor even a principle of empirical unity, but that this principle or being must be assigned to an area external to the world. And in this way we can proceed with perfect confidence to deduce the phenomena of the world and their existence from other phenomena just as if there were no necessary being; and we can at the same time strive without ceasing towards the attainment of completeness in our deduction just as if such a being, the supreme condition of all existence, were presupposed by the mind.

These remarks will have made it clear to the reader that the Ideal of the Supreme Being, far from being an assertion of the existence of a being necessary in itself, is no more than the *regulative principle* of reason which requires us to look on all connexions obtaining between phenomena as if they had their origin in an all-sufficient necessary cause. Upon this the rule of systematic and necessary unity in the explanation of phenomena is based. At the same time, we cannot help regarding this formal principle, by a surreptitious transcendental transition, as constitutive and so hypostatize this unity. It is exactly the same with our notion of space. Space is the primary condition of all forms, which properly are so many different limitations of it; and thus, though it is only a principle of the capacity to perceive, we cannot help looking on it as an absolutely necessary and self-subsistent being—as an object given *a priori* in itself. In the same way, it is quite natural that since the systematic unity of nature cannot be established as a principle for the empirical employment

[1] A conditional necessity is one where the necessity exists only given some condition: given A it is necessary that B.

of reason, unless it is based on the Idea of an *ens realissimum*, as the supreme cause, we should regard this Idea as a real object and this object, in its character as supreme condition, as absolutely necessary. In this way a *regulative principle* is naturally transformed into a *constitutive* one. This interchange becomes evident when I consider this supreme being which, relative to the world, was absolutely (unconditionally) necessary, as a thing *per se*. In this case, I find it impossible to represent this necessity in or by any concept, and it exists merely in my own mind as the formal condition of thought, but not as the material or hypostatic condition of existence.

Of the Impossibility of a Physico-Theological Proof (Ch. III, §6)

If then neither a pure concept nor the general experience of an existing being can provide a sufficient foundation for the proof of the existence of the Deity, we can try by the only remaining method—that of basing our argument on a *determinate experience* of the phenomena of the present world, their constitution and disposition, and find out whether we can in this way reach a sound conviction of the existence of a Supreme Being.[1] This argument we shall call the *physico-theological* argument. If it is shown to be inadequate, reason cannot give us any satisfactory proof of the existence of a being corresponding to our transcendental Ideal.

It is clear from the points that have been made in the preceding sections that an answer to this question will be far from difficult and unconvincing. For how can any experience be commensurate with an Idea? The very essence of an Idea consists in the fact that no experience can ever be found to match it or equal it. The transcendental Idea of a necessary and all-sufficient Being is so immeasurably great, so high above everything empirical, which is conditioned, that we hope in vain to discover materials in the sphere of experience sufficiently ample for our concept; and we look in vain for the unconditioned among things that are conditioned, while examples and even guidance are denied us by the laws of empirical synthesis.

If the Supreme Being constitutes a link in the chain of empirical conditions, it must be a member of the empirical series, and like the lower members which it precedes it must have its origin in some higher member of the series. But if on the other hand we disengage it from the chain and

[1] The Teleological Argument is based on determinate experience, unlike the Cosmological Argument, inasmuch as it appeals to particular experiences of a certain sort, viz. experiences of order and design, while the latter argument included as its *a posteriori* premises the proposition 'Something exists' and any sort of experience would be sufficient to confirm the truth of this.

conceive it as an intelligible being which is apart from the series of natural causes, then how will reason bridge the gulf that separates the latter from the former? All laws concerning the regress from effects to causes, all synthetic additions to our knowledge, relate solely to possible experience and the objects of the perceptible world and apart from them are without significance.

The world around us opens before our gaze so magnificent a spectacle of order, variety, beauty and adaptation to ends that whether we pursue our observations into the infinity of space in the one direction or into its infinite divisions on the other, whether we look at the world in its greatest or in its smallest manifestations,—even after we have reached the highest peak of knowledge which our frail minds can rise to—we find that language loses its force when confronted by such inconceivable wonders and that number loses its power to calculate; and our notion of the whole dissolves into an amazement with no way of expressing it—all the more eloquent that it is dumb. Everywhere around us we see a chain of causes and effects, of means and ends, of death and birth; and since nothing has entered of its own accord into the condition in which we find it, we are constantly referred to some other thing, which in turn suggests the same enquiry concerning *its* cause, and thus the universe must sink into the abyss of nothingness unless we concede that, besides this infinite chain of contingencies, there exists something primary and self-subsistent—something which, as the cause of the world of phenomena, ensures its continuation and preservation.

What magnitude shall we attribute to this highest cause? We are ignorant of the content of the world; still less can we calculate its magnitude by comparison with the sphere of the possible. But this supreme cause is a necessity of the human mind, and what is to prevent us from attributing to it such a degree of perfection as to put it above the sphere of *all* that is possible? This we can easily do, though only by the aid of the faint outline of an abstract concept, by representing this being to ourselves as containing in itself, as an individual substance, all possible perfection—a concept which satisfies that requirement of reason which demands parsimony in principles,[1] which is free from contradiction, which even contributes to extending the use of reason in experience through the guidance afforded by this Idea to order and system, and which in no respect conflicts with any law of experience.

This argument always deserves to be mentioned with respect. It is the oldest, clearest and most in accord with the common reason of mankind.

[1] It being a formal advantage if, other things being equal, the number of principles used in an explanatory system is smaller than that employed in an alternative system.

It animates the study of nature, as it itself derives its existence and ever draws new strength from that source. It introduces aims and ends into a sphere in which our observation could not by itself have found them and extends our knowledge of nature by directing our attention to a unity whose principle lies beyond nature. This knowledge of nature reacts in turn upon this Idea, its cause; and thus our belief in a Divine author of the universe rises to the strength of an irresistible conviction.

For these reasons it would be quite hopeless to try to rob this argument of the authority in which it has always been held. The mind, continuously elevated by these considerations, which, though empirical, are so remarkably powerful and always increasing in force, will not allow itself to be depressed by the doubts suggested by subtle speculation; it tears itself away from this state of uncertainty as soon as it casts a glance at the wonderful forms of nature and the majesty of the universe, and so rises from height to height until it has risen to the supreme and unconditioned author of all.

But though we have no objection to make to the reasonableness and usefulness of this procedure, but rather ought to commend and encourage it, we cannot approve of the claims made by this argument to demonstrative certainty and to a reception on its own merits, apart from favour and support by other arguments. Nor can it harm the cause of morality to try to lower the tone of the arrogant sophist and to teach him the modesty and moderation which are the attributes of a belief that brings calm and contentment to the mind, without prescribing to it an unworthy subjection. I hold, then, that the physico-theological argument is inadequate by itself to prove the existence of a Supreme Being, that it must entrust this to the ontological argument—to which it functions as merely an introduction—, and that consequently this latter argument contains the *only possible ground of proof* possessed by speculative reason for the existence of this being.

The chief steps in the physico-theological argument are as follows:—(1) We observe in the world obvious signs of an arrangement full of purpose, executed with great wisdom, and existing in a whole which is indescribably various and limitlessly extended. (2) This arrangement of means and ends is entirely alien to the things existing in the world—it belongs to them merely as a contingent attribute: in other words, the nature of different things could not by itself, whatever means were used, tend harmoniously towards certain purposes, were they not selected and directed for these purposes by a rational and disposing principle, in accordance with certain fundamental ideas. (3) There exists, therefore, a sublime and wise cause (or several), which is not just a blind, omnipotent nature which produces the beings and events which fill the world in unconscious *fecundity*, but a *free* and intelligent cause of the world. (4) The unity of this cause may be inferred from the unity of the mutual relation existing between the parts of the world, like portions of an artistic edifice—an inference which all our observation encourages and which all our principles of analogy support.

In the above argument, it is inferred from the analogy of certain products of nature to those of human skill, when it compels nature to obey its purposes—as in the case of a house, a ship or a watch—, that the same kind of causality (namely, understanding and will) resides in nature. It is also asserted that the internal possibility of this freely-acting nature (which is the source of all art and perhaps also of human reason) is derivable from another, and superhuman, art—a conclusion which would perhaps be found incapable of surviving the test of subtle transcendental criticism. But at present we shall not object to either of these opinions. We shall only point out that it must be confessed that, if we are to discuss the subject of cause at all, we cannot proceed more securely than with the guidance of the analogy obtaining between nature and such products of design—these being the only products whose causes and modes of origination are completely known to us. Reason would not be able to satisfy her own needs if she passed from a causality which she does know to obscure and indemonstrable principles of explanation which she does not know.

According to the physico-theological argument, the connexion and harmony existing in the world are evidence of the contingency of the form merely, but not of the matter, that is, of the substance of the world. To establish the truth of the latter claim,[1] it would be necessary to show that everything is in itself incapable of this harmony and order, unless they were, even as regards their *substance*, the product of a supreme wisdom. But this would require very different grounds of proof from those presented by the analogy with human art. This proof can, then, at most demonstrate the existence of an *architect of the world* whose efforts are limited by the capacities of the material with which he works, but not of a *creator of the world*, to whom all things are subject. Thus this argument is quite inadequate for the task in front of us, a demonstration of the existence of an all-sufficient being. If we wish to prove the contingency of matter, we must have recourse to a transcendental argument—and this was what the physico-theological argument was constructed expressly to avoid.

We infer, from the order and design visible in the universe, as a disposition of a thoroughly contingent kind, the existence of a cause

[1] I.e. the claim that the harmony and connection existing in the world are evidence that the *matter* of the world is contingent (or dependent on some prior cause).

proportionate to it. The concept of this cause must contain certain *determinate* qualities and it must therefore be regarded as the concept of a being which possesses all power, wisdom and so on—in a word, all perfection; the concept, that is, of an all-sufficient being. For the predicates of *very great*, *astonishing* or immeasurable power and excellence give us no determinate concept of the thing, nor do they tell us what the thing may be in itself. They merely indicate the relation obtaining between the magnitude of the object and the observer, who compares it with himself and with his own capacity to comprehend, and are mere expressions of praise and reverence by which the object is either magnified or the observing subject depreciated in relation to the object. Where we have to deal with the magnitude (of the perfection) of a thing, we can find no determinate concept except that which embraces all possible perfection or completeness, and it is only the total (*omnitudo*) of reality which is completely determined in and through its concept alone.

Now it cannot be expected that anyone will be rash enough to assert that he has a perfect insight into the relation which the magnitude of the world he contemplates bears (in its extent as well as its content) to omnipotence, into that of the order of the world to the supreme wisdom and into that of the unity of the world to the absolute unity of a Supreme Being.[1] Physico-theology is therefore unable to present a determinate concept of a supreme cause of the world and is therefore insufficient as a principle of theology—a theology which itself is to be the basis of religion.

The attainment of absolute totality is utterly impossible on the path of empiricism. And yet this is the path taken in the physico-theological argument. What means shall we use to bridge the abyss?

After elevating ourselves to admiration of the magnitude of the power, wisdom and other attributes of the author of the universe, and finding that we can go on no farther, we leave the argument on empirical grounds and proceed to infer the contingency of the world from the order and conformity to purposes that are observable in it. From this contingency we infer, by the help of transcendental concepts alone, the existence of something which is absolutely necessary; and still advancing, we proceed from the concept of the absolute necessity of the first cause to the completely determined or determining concept thereof—the concept of an all-embracing reality. In this way the physico-theological argument, failing in its task, falls back in its embarrassment to the cosmological argument; and since this is just the ontological argument in disguise it achieves its aim solely by the aid of pure reason, although it at first

[1] No one, that is, will be rash enough to claim that he is certain that the world could not have existed without an *omnipotent* author of the highest wisdom and absolute unity.

pretended to have no connexion with this faculty and to base its entire procedure upon experience alone.

The physico-theologians have therefore no reason to look upon the transcendental mode of argument with such contempt and to disdain it with the clear-sighted conceit of observers of nature as the brain-cobweb of obscure speculators. For if they reflect upon and examine their own arguments, they will see that, after following for some time the path of nature and experience and finding themselves no nearer their goal, they suddenly leave this path and pass into the region of pure possibility, where they hope to reach, on the wings of Ideas, what had eluded their empirical investigations. Gaining, as they imagine, a firm footing after this vast leap, they extend their determinate conception (which they have come to possess they know not how) over the whole sphere of creation, and explain their Ideal, which is entirely a product of pure reason, by examples drawn from experience—though in a degree miserably unworthy of the grandeur of the object, while they refuse to acknowledge that they have arrived at this cognition or hypothesis by a very different road from that of experience.

Thus the physico-theological is based on the cosmological argument, and this in turn on the ontological proof of the existence of a Supreme Being; and since besides these three there is no other path open to speculative reason, the ontological proof, based on the pure concepts of reason, is the only possible one if any proof of a proposition so far transcending the empirical exercise of the understanding is possible at all.

B. IMMORTALITY

Introductory Note As has been explained above (p. 249), K. had concluded that the Idea of God has, in its theoretical employment, a merely regulative function. Nevertheless, the theoretical use of reason is not the only one. Central to human experience is moral action, and here reason has a practical use, which indeed appears to conflict with the presuppositions of scientific enquiry. For the latter imply causal determinism, whereas morality presupposes that moral actions are free: 'ought' implies 'can', since only where I am free to do X or to refrain from doing X can I be said to have a duty regarding X. One task, then, that K. sets himself in the *Critique of Practical Reason* is the resolution of this conflict. But further it is necessary to analyse the notion of moral duty itself. The principles by which we guide our actions K. called 'maxims', and his task is to discover what count as moral maxims. Broadly, these involve that they should be in accordance with the moral law and that I should be acting *for the sake of* the moral law. But in particular, there is a test for distinguishing whether they are indeed in accordance with the moral law. This test is the Categorical Imperative, which K. distinguishes from hypothetical imperatives. The latter are of the form 'If you want happiness or to achieve some specific purpose, do such-and-such'. Strictly, they are assertions in hypothetical form about the course of nature. But the moral law is unconditional, and is formulated as the Categorical Imperative (K. gave different forms of this) to the following effect: 'Act only on that maxim through which at the same time you can will that it should become a universal law.' A maxim which passes this test is moral, and unconditional, for its contradictory would if universalized involve self-contradiction. For example, if I steal on the principle that in this particular instance it is all right, and then suppose that everyone were to act on a like principle, the institution of property would collapse and thereby the point of stealing would itself vanish. Thus the essence of morality is universalizability. K. has provided a rational basis for moral action. It follows from his position that I cannot, on the grounds of any inclinations or impulses which I may have, morally make an exception for myself. This situation creates a continual conflict between the demands of the moral law and my own nature. How then do I ever succeed in obeying the moral law? K. gave some sort of answer to this in terms of a feeling of reverence for the moral law arising from a recognition of the way it overrides my sensuous nature. But essentially K. is prevented from any psychological account of how it is that I exercise my free will in obeying the moral law, for causal determinism applies quite as much to my introspectible psychological states as to the external world. Nevertheless, since moral action implies freedom, K. must give some sort of explanation, and this he does by using his distinction between *phenomena* and *noumena*. In the *Critique of Pure Reason*, he was obliged to hold that although we cannot apply the categories beyond what is given in experience, i.e. beyond phenomena, nevertheless we are committed to saying that there are unknowable things-in-themselves outside me which (so to speak) give rise to my experience. The concept of such intelligible entities or *noumena* is allowable, according to K., since it does not give rise to any contradictions. Using this distinction, then, K. holds that the self as having free will is a *noumenon*; and this is compatible with holding that as *phenomenon* he is causally determined. In these ways, then, K. established that morality is autonomous—it is not to be subsumed (because of the Categorical Imperative) under prudence—even prudence which is given a religious content through the idea of salvation—nor is to be engulfed by science.

But problems remain, driving us to make further postulates. The postulate of freedom of the will is insufficient for a complete theory of morality, for it is implicit in the moral law that our duty is to attain holiness, or complete adequacy of the will to the moral law. But in view of the conflict between the law and one's empirical nature, one is incapable of achieving this at any moment of one's life. Thus holiness must imply that there is an infinite progress, and this implies immortality. But this second postulate in turn must be supplemented by a third; for it is also implied in morality that we ought to promote the highest good, the *summum bonum*. But this itself involves that happiness should be commensurate to virtue—the perfectly good man ought to be perfectly happy (this being in contrast to the kind of state of affairs found in the empirical world). This requirement can only, according to K., be met if there be a God who exists to ensure the matching of goodness and happiness. Thus God, merely a regulative Idea in the *Critique of Pure Reason*, reappears as an Idea having practical content. The argument outlined in this paragraph is elaborated in the passage which follows.

It is to be noted (and this is brought out further in K.'s *Religion within the Limits of Reason Alone*) that the practical objectivity of God in no way infringes the autonomy of ethics. Morality does not require God as a ground: it is not in any way *derived* from religion, even if morality is conceived as God's command. Indeed, the relation of dependence works the other way round. Religion, if anything, is a consequence of morality. K. therefore held that there can only be one true religion, although creeds differ. It is not surprising that in reaction against the Kantian position, others such as Schleiermacher (see below, p. 306) and Otto (see below, p. 421) should have used the quasi-Kantian idea of the 'autonomy' of religion, in trying to show that religious concepts are *sui generis* and of value even apart from their bearing on theoretical knowledge and morality.

Critique of Practical Reason, Book II, Chs. II–V

Of the Dialectic of Pure Reason in Defining the Conception of the 'Summum Bonum'

The concept of the *summum* itself contains an ambiguity which might occasion needless disputes if we did not attend to it. The *summum* may mean either the supreme (*supremum*) or the perfect (*consummatum*). The former is that condition which is itself unconditioned, i.e. not subordinate to any other (*originarium*); the second is that whole which is not a part of a greater whole of the same kind (*perfectissimum*). It has been shown in the Analytic[1] that *virtue* (as worthiness to be happy) is the *supreme condition* of all that can appear to us desirable, and consequently of all our pursuit of happiness, and is therefore the *supreme* good. But it does not follow that it is the whole and perfect good as the object of the desires of rational finite beings; for this requires happiness also, and that not merely in the partial eyes of the person who makes himself an end, but even in the judgment of an impartial reason, which regards persons in general as ends in themselves. For to need happiness, to deserve it and yet at the same time not to participate in it cannot be consistent with the perfect volition of a rational being possessed at the same time of all power, if, for the sake of experiment, we conceive such a being. Now inasmuch as virtue and happiness together constitute the possession of the *summum bonum* in a person, and the distribution of happiness in exact proportion to morality (which is the worth of the person and his worthiness to be happy) constitutes the *summum bonum* of a possible world; hence this *summum bonum* expresses the whole, the perfect good, in which, however, virtue as the condition is always the supreme good, since it has no condition above it; whereas happiness, while it is pleasant to the possessor of it, is not of itself absolutely

[1] See *Critique of Practical Reason*, Bk I, Ch. II.

and in all respects good, but always presupposes morally right behaviour as its condition.

When two elements are *necessarily* united in one concept they must be connected as reason and consequence, and this either so that their unity is considered as *analytic* (logical connexion),[1] or as *synthetic* (real connexion)[1]—the former following the law of identity,[2] the latter that of causality. The connexion of virtue and happiness may therefore be understood in two ways: either the endeavour to be virtuous and the rational pursuit of happiness are not two distinct actions, but absolutely identical, in which case no maxim need be made the principle of the former, other than what serves for the latter; or the connexion consists in this, that virtue produces happiness as something distinct from the consciousness of virtue, as a cause produces an effect.

The ancient Greek schools were, properly speaking, only two, and in determining the concept of the *summum bonum* these followed in fact one and the same method, inasmuch as they did not allow virtue and happiness to be regarded as two distinct elements of the *summum bonum*, and consequently sought the unity of the principle by the rule of identity; but they differed as to which of the two was to be taken as the fundamental notion. The Epicurean[3] said: To be conscious that one's maxims lead to happiness is virtue; the Stoic[4] said: To be conscious of one's virtue is happiness. With the former, *prudence* was equivalent to morality; with the latter, who chose a higher designation for virtue, morality alone was true wisdom.

While we must admire the men who in such early times tried all imaginable ways of extending the domain of philosophy, we must at the same time lament that their acuteness was unfortunately misapplied in trying to trace out identity between two extremely heterogeneous notions, those of happiness and virtue. But it agreed with the dialectical spirit of their times (and subtle minds are even now sometimes misled in the same way) to get rid of irreconcilable differences in principle by seeking to change them into a mere contest about words, and thus apparently working out the identity of the notion under different names—and this usually occurs in cases where the combination of heterogeneous principles lies so deep or so high, or would require so complete a transformation of the doctrines assumed in the rest of the philosophical system, that men are afraid to penetrate deeply into the real difference, and prefer treating it as a difference in matters of form.

While both schools sought to trace out the identity of the practical

[1] See n. 2 to p. 253. [2] See n. 4 to p. 64. [3] See n. 1 to p. 227.

[4] See H. D. Hicks, *Stoic and Epicurean* (1910).

principles of virtue and happiness, they were not agreed as to the way in which they tried to force this identity, but were separated infinitely from one another—the one placing the principle on the side of sense, the other on that of reason: the one in the consciousness of sensible[1] wants, the other in independence of practical reason from all sensible grounds of determination. According to the Epicurean the notion of virtue was already involved in the maxim that one should promote one's own happiness; according to the Stoics on the other hand the feeling of happiness was already contained in the consciousness of virtue. Now whatever is contained in another notion is identical with part of the containing notion, but not with the whole, and moreover two wholes may be specifically distinct, although they consist of the same parts, namely if the parts are united into a whole in totally different ways. The Stoic maintained that virtue was the *whole summum bonum* and happiness only the consciousness of possessing it, as making part of the state of the subject. The Epicurean maintained that happiness was the *whole summum bonum* and virtue only the form of the maxim for its pursuit, viz. the rational use of the means for attaining it.

Now it is clear from the Analytic that the maxims of virtue and those of private happiness are quite heterogeneous as to their supreme practical principle; and although they belong to one *summum bonum* which together they make possible, yet they are so far from coinciding that they restrict and check one another very much in the same subject. Thus the question 'How is the *summum bonum* practically possible?' still remains an unsolved problem, notwithstanding all the *attempts at coalition* that have hitherto been made. The Analytic has, however, shown what it is that makes the problem difficult to solve—namely, that happiness and morality are two specifically *distinct elements of the summum bonum*, and therefore their combination *cannot* be *analytically* cognized (as if the man that seeks his own happiness should find by mere analysis of his concept that in so acting he is virtuous, or as if the man that follows virtue should in the consciousness of such conduct find that he is already happy *ipso facto*), but must be a *synthesis* of concepts. Now since this combination is recognized as *a priori*, and therefore as practically necessary, and consequently not as derived from experience, so that the possibility of the *summum bonum* does not rest on any empirical principle, it follows that the deduction of this concept must be transcendental.[2] It is *a priori* (morally) necessary to *produce the summum bonum by freedom of will*: therefore the condition of its possibility must rest solely on *a priori* principles of cognition.

[1] 'Sense' here means 'sensible nature', i.e. one's capacity to have sensations, etc.

[2] See above, p. 249. 'Deduction' here means 'validation'.

I. *The Antinomy of Practical Reason*

In the *summum bonum* which is practical for us, i.e. to be realized by our will, virtue and happiness are thought as necessarily combined, so that the one cannot be assumed by pure practical reason without the other also being attached to it. Now this combination (like every other) is either *analytic* or *synthetic*. It has been shown that it cannot be analytic; it must then be synthetic, and, more particularly, must be conceived as the connexion of cause and effect, since it concerns a practical good, i.e. one that is possible by means of action. Consequently, either the desire of happiness must be the motive to maxims of virtue, or the maxim of virtue must be the efficient cause of happiness. The first is *absolutely* impossible, because (as was proved in the Analytic) maxims which place the determining principle of the will in the desire of personal happiness are not moral at all, and no virtue can be founded on them. But the second is *also* impossible, because the practical connexion of causes and effects in the world, as the result of the determination of the will does not depend upon the moral dispositions of the will, but on the knowledge of the laws of nature and the physical power to use them for one's purposes; consequently we cannot expect in the world by the most punctilious observance of the moral laws any necessary connexion of happiness with virtue adequate to the *summum bonum*. Now as the promotion of this *summum bonum*, the concept of which contains this connexion, is *a priori* a necessary object of our will, and inseparably attached to the moral law, the impossibility of the former must prove the falsity of the latter. If then the supreme good is not possible by practical rules, then the moral law also which commands us to promote it is directed to vain imaginary ends and must consequently be false.

II. *Critical Solution of the Antinomy of Practical Reason*

The antinomy of pure speculative reason[1] exhibits a similar conflict between freedom and physical necessity in the causality of events in the world. It was solved by showing that there is no real contradiction when the events and even the world in which they occur are regarded (as they ought to be) merely as appearances—since one and the same acting being, *as an appearance* (even to his own inner sense), has a causality in the world of sense that always conforms to the mechanism of nature, but with respect to the same events, so far as the acting person regards himself at the same time as a noumenon[2] (as pure intelligence in an existence not dependent on the condition of time), he can contain a principle by which

[1] See above, p. 248. [2] See above, p. 272.

that causality acting according to laws of nature is determined, but which is itself free from all laws of nature.

It is just the same with the foregoing antinomy of pure practical reason. The first of the two propositions—that the endeavour after happiness produces a virtuous mind—is *absolutely false*. But the second—that a virtuous mind necessarily produces happiness—is *not absolutely* false, but only in so far as virtue is considered as a form of causality in the sensible world, and consequently only if I suppose existence in it to be the only sort of existence of a rational being; it is then only *conditionally* false. But as I am not only justified in thinking that I exist also as a noumenon in a world of the understanding, but even have in the moral law a purely intellectual determining principle of my causality (in the sensible world) if not immediate yet mediate (viz. through an intelligent author of nature), and moreover necessary; while in a system of nature which is merely an object of the senses this combination could never occur except contingently, and therefore could not suffice for the *summum bonum*.

Thus, notwithstanding this seeming conflict of practical reason with itself, the *summum bonum*, which is the necessary supreme end of a will morally determined, is a true object thereof; for it is practically possible, and the maxims of the will which as regards this matter refer to it have objective reality, which at first was threatened by the antinomy that appeared in the connexion of morality with happiness by a general law; but this was merely from a misconception, because the relation between appearances was taken for a relation of the things in themselves[1] to these appearances.

When we find ourselves obliged to go so far, namely to the connexion with an intelligible world, to find the possibility of the *summum bonum*, which reason points out to all rational beings as the goal of all their moral wishes, it must seem strange that, nevertheless, the philosophers both of ancient and modern times have been able to find happiness in accurate proportion to virtue even in *this life* (in the sensible world), or have persuaded themselves that they were conscious thereof. For Epicurus[2] as well as the Stoics extolled above everything the happiness that springs from the consciousness of living virtuously; and the former was not so base in his practical precepts as one might infer from the principles of the theory, which he used for explanation and not for action, or as they were interpreted by many who were misled by his using the term 'pleasure' for contentment; on the contrary, he reckoned the most disinterested practice of good amongst the ways of enjoying the most intimate delight, and his scheme of pleasure (by which he meant constant cheerfulness of mind)

[1] See p. 272. [2] See above, n. 1 to p. 227.

included the moderation and control of the inclinations, such as the strictest moral philosopher might require. He differed from the Stoics chiefly in making this pleasure the motive, which they very rightly refused to do. For, on the one hand, the virtuous Epicurus, like many well-intentioned men of his day, who do not reflect deeply enough on their principles, fell into the error of presupposing the virtuous *disposition* in the persons for whom he wished to provide the springs to virtue (and indeed the upright man cannot be happy if he is not first conscious of his uprightness; since with such a character the reproach that his habit of thought would oblige him to make against himself in case of transgression, and his moral self-condemnation would rob him of all enjoyment of the pleasantness which his condition might otherwise contain). But the question is: How is such a disposition possible in the first instance, and such a habit of thought in estimating the worth of one's existence, since prior to it there can be in the subject no feeling at all for moral worth? If a man is virtuous without being aware of his integrity in every action, he will certainly not enjoy life, however favourable fortune may be to him in its physical circumstances; but can we make him virtuous in the first instance, in other words, before he esteems the moral worth of his existence so highly, by praising to him the peace of mind that would result from the consciousness of an integrity for which he has no sense?

On the other hand, however, there is here an occasion of a *vitium subreptionis*, and as it were of an optical illusion, in the selfconsciousness of what one *does* as distinguished from what one *feels*, an illusion which even the most experienced cannot altogether avoid. The moral disposition of the mind is necessarily combined with a consciousness that the will is determined *directly by the law*. Now the consciousness of a determination of the faculty of desire is always the source of a satisfaction in the resulting action; but this pleasure, this satisfaction in oneself, is not the determining principle of the action; on the contrary, the determination of the will directly by reason is the source of the feeling of pleasure, and this remains a pure practical, not sensible, determination of the faculty of desire. Now as this determination has exactly the same effect within in impelling to activity that a feeling of the pleasure to be expected from the desired action would have had, we easily look on what we ourselves do as something which we merely passively feel, and take the moral spring for a sensible impulse, just as it happens in the so-called illusion of the senses (in this case the inner sense[1]). It is a sublime thing in human nature to be determined to actions immediately by a purely rational law; sublime even

[1] Inner sense, as opposed to outer sense (the capacity to see, hear, etc.); the capacity to have feelings.

is the illusion that regards the subjective side of this capacity of intellectual determination as something sensible, and the effect of a special sensible feeling (for an intellectual feeling would be a contradiction). It is also of great importance to attend to this property of our personality, and as much as possible to cultivate the effect of reasoning on this feeling. But we must beware lest by falsely extolling this moral determining principle as a spring, making its course lie in particular feelings of pleasure (which are in fact only results), we degrade and disfigure the true genuine spring, the law itself, by putting as it were a false foil upon it. Respect, not pleasure or enjoyment of happiness, is something for which it is not possible that reason should have any *antecedent* feeling as its foundation, for this would always be sensible and pathological; and consciousness of immediate obligation of the will by the law is by no means analogous to the feeling of pleasure, although in relation to the faculty of desire it produces the same effect, but from different sources: it is only by this mode of conception, however, that we can attain what we are seeking, namely that actions be done not merely in accordance with duty (as a result of pleasant feelings), but from duty, which must be the true end of all moral cultivation.

Have we not, however, a word which does not express enjoyment, as happiness does, but indicates a satisfaction in one's existence, an analogue of the happiness which must necessarily accompany the consciousness of virtue? Yes: this word is *self-contentment*, which in its proper signification always designates only a negative satisfaction in one's existence, in which one is conscious of needing nothing. Freedom and the consciousness of it as a faculty of following the moral law with unyielding resolution is *independence of inclinations*, at least as motives determining (though not as *affecting*) our desire, and so far as I am conscious of this freedom in following my moral maxims, it is the only source of an unaltered contentment which is necessarily connected with it and rests on no special feeling. This may be called intellectual contentment. The sensible contentment, (improperly so-called) which rests on the satisfaction of the inclinations, however delicate they may be imagined to be, can never be adequate to the conception of it. For the inclinations change, they grow with the indulgence shown them, and always leave behind them a still greater void than we had thought to fill. Hence they are always *burdensome* to a rational being, and although he cannot lay them aside, they wrest from him the wish to be rid of them. Even an inclination to what is right (e.g. to beneficence), though it may much facilitate the efficacy of the *moral* maxims, cannot produce any. For in these all must be directed to the conception of the law as a determining principle, if the action is to contain *morality* and not just *legality*. Inclination is blind and slavish whether it be of a good sort or not, and when morality is in question, reason must not play the part merely of guardian to inclination, but, disregarding it altogether, must attend simply to its own interest as pure practical reason. This very feeling of compassion and tender sympathy, if it precedes the deliberation on the question of duty and becomes a determining principle, is even annoying to right-thinking persons, brings their deliberate maxims into confusion and makes them wish to be delivered from it and to be subject to law-giving reason alone.

From this we can understand how the consciousness of this faculty of a pure practical reason produces by action (virtue) a consciousness of mastery over one's inclinations, and therefore of independence of them and consequently also of the discontent that always accompanies them, and thus a negative satisfaction with one's state, i.e. *contentment*, which is primarily contentment with one's own person. Freedom itself becomes in this way (namely indirectly) capable of an enjoyment which cannot be called happiness, because it does not depend on the positive concurrence of a feeling, nor is it, strictly speaking, *bliss*, since it does not include complete independence of inclinations and wants, but it resembles bliss in so far as the determination of one's will at least can hold itself free from their influence; and thus, at least in origin, this enjoyment is analogous to the self-sufficiency which we can ascribe only to the Supreme Being.

From this solution of the antinomy of pure practical reason it follows that in practical principles we may at least conceive as possible a natural and necessary connexion between the consciousness of morality and the expectation of a proportionate happiness as its result, though it does not follow that we can know or perceive this connexion; that, on the other hand, principles of the pursuit of happiness cannot possibly produce morality; and that therefore morality is the *supreme* good (as the first condition of the *summum bonum*), while happiness constitutes its second element, but only in such a way that it is the morally conditioned but necessary consequence of the former. Only with this subordination is the *summum bonum* the whole object of pure practical reason, which must necessarily conceive it as possible, since it commands us to contribute to the utmost of our power to its realization. But since the possibility of such connexion of the conditioned with its condition belongs wholly to the suprasensual relation of things, and cannot be given according to the laws of the world of sense, although the practical consequences of the idea belong to the world of sense, namely the actions that aim at realizing the *summum bonum*, we will therefore endeavour to set forth the grounds of that possibility—first in respect of what is immediately in our power, and then secondly in that which is not in our power, but which reason presents to us as the supplement of our impotence, for the realization of the *summum bonum* (which by practical principles is necessary).

III

Of the Primacy of Pure Practical Reason in its Union with the Speculative Reason

By primacy between two or more things connected by reason, I understand the prerogative belonging to one, of being the first determining principle in the connexion with all the rest. In a narrower practical sense it means the prerogative of the interest of one in so far as the interest of the other is subordinated to it, while it is not put second to any other. To every faculty of the mind we can attribute an interest, that is a principle that contains the condition on which alone the former is called into exercise. Reason, as the faculty of principles, determines the interest of all the powers of mind and is determined by its own. The interest of its speculative employment consists in the *cognition* of the object pushed to the highest *a priori* principles: that of its practical employment, in the determination of the *will* in respect of the final and complete end. As to what is necessary for the possibility of any employment of reason at all, namely that its principles and affirmations should not contradict one another, this constitutes no part of its interest; it is only its development, not mere consistency in itself, that is reckoned as its interest.

If practical reason could not assume or think as given anything further than what speculative reason of itself could offer it from its own interest, the latter would have the primacy. But supposing that it had of its original *a priori* principles with which certain theoretical positions are inseparably connected, while these were withdrawn from any possible insight of speculative reason (which, however, they must not contradict), then the question is which interest is the superior (not which must give way, for they are not necessarily conflicting)—whether speculative reason, which knows nothing of all that the practical offers for its acceptance, should take up these propositions, and (although they transcend it) try to unite them with its own concepts as a foreign possession handed over to it; or whether it is justified in obstinacy following its own separate interest, and according to the canonic of Epicurus rejecting as vain subtlety everything that cannot accredit its objective reality by manifest examples to be shown in experience, even though it should be never so much interwoven with the interest of the practical (pure) use of reason, and in itself not contradictory to the theoretical, merely because it infringes on the interest of the speculative reason to this extent, that it removes the bounds which the latter had set to itself, and gives it up to every nonsense or delusion of imagination?

In fact, so far as practical reason is taken as dependent on pathological conditions—that is, as merely regulating the inclinations under the sensible principles of happiness—we could not require speculative reason to take its principles from such a source. Mohammed's paradise, or the absorption into the Deity of the theosophists and mystics, would press their monstrosities on the reason according to the taste of each, and one might as well have no reason as surrender it in such fashion to all sorts of dreams. But if pure reason of itself can be practical and is actually so, as the consciousness of the moral law proves, then it is still only one and the same reason which, whether in a theoretical or a practical point of view, judges according to *a priori* principles; and then it is clear that although it is in the first point of view incompetent to establish certain propositions positively, which, however, do not contradict it, then as soon as these propositions are *inseparably* attached *to the practical interest* of pure reason, then it must accept them, though it be as something offered to it from a foreign source, something that has not grown on its own ground, but yet is sufficiently authenticated. And it must try to compare and connect them with everything that it has in its power as speculative reason. It must remember, however, that these are not additions to its insight, but yet are extensions of its employment in another, namely a practical, aspect; and this is not in the least opposed to its interest, which consists in the restriction of wild speculation.

Thus, when pure speculative and pure practical reason are combined in one cognition, the latter has the *primacy*, provided namely that this combination is not *contingent* and arbitrary, but founded *a priori* on reason itself and therefore *necessary*. For without this subordination there would arise a conflict of reason with itself—since if they were merely co-ordinate, the former would close its boundaries strictly and admit nothing from the latter into its domain, while the latter would extend its bounds over everything, and when its needs required would seek to embrace the former within them. Nor could we reverse the order and require pure practical reason to be subordinate to the speculative, since all interest is ultimately practical, and even that of speculative reason is conditional, and it is only in the practical employment of reason that it is complete.

IV

The Immortality of the Soul as a Postulate of Pure Practical Reason

The realization of the *summum bonum* in the world is the necessary object of a will determinable by the moral law. But in this will the *perfect accordance* of the mind with the moral law is the supreme condition of the *summum bonum.* This then must be possible, as well as its object, since it is contained in the command to promote the latter. Now the perfect accordance of the will with the moral law is *holiness*, a perfection of which no rational being of the sensible world is capable at any moment of his existence. Since, nevertheless, it is required as practically necessary, it can only be found in a *progress in infinitum* towards that perfect accordance, and on the principles of pure practical reason it is necessary to assume such a practical progress as the real object of our will.

Now this endless progress is only possible on the supposition of an *endless* duration of the *existence* and personality of the same rational being (which is called the immortality of the soul). The *summum bonum*, then, practically is only possible on the supposition of the immortality of the soul; consequently, this immortality, being inseparably connected with the moral law, is a postulate of pure practical reason (by which I mean a *theoretical* proposition, not demonstrable as such, but which is an inseparable result of an unconditioned *a priori practical* law).

This principle of the moral destination of our nature, namely that it is only in an endless progress that we can attain perfect accordance with the moral law, is of the greatest use, not merely for the present purpose of supplementing the impotence of speculative reason, but also with respect to religion. In default of it, either the moral law is quite degraded from its *holiness*, being made out to be *indulgent*, and comformable to our convenience; or else men strain their notions of their vocation and their expectation to an unattainable goal, hoping to acquire complete holiness of will, and so they lose themselves in fanatical *theosophic* dreams, which wholly contradict self-knowledge. In both cases the unceasing *effort* to obey punctually and thoroughly a strict and inflexible command of reason, which yet is not ideal but real, is only hindered. For a rational but finite being the only thing possible is an endless progress from the lower to higher degrees of moral perfection. The *Infinite* Being, to whom the condition of time is nothing, sees in this to us endless succession a whole of accordance with the moral law; and the holiness which his command inexorably requires, in order to be true to his justice in the share which he assigns to each in the *summum bonum*, is to be found in a single intellectual intuition of the whole existence of rational beings. All that can be expected of the creature in respect of the hope of this participation would be the consciousness of his tried character, by which, from the progress he has hitherto made from the worse to the morally better, and the immutability of purpose which has thus become known to him, he may hope for a further unbroken continuance of the same, however long his existence may last, even beyond this life—and thus he may hope, not indeed here, nor at any imaginable point of his future existence, but only in the endlessness of his duration (which God alone can survey) to be perfectly adequate to his will (without indulgence or excuse, which do not harmonize with justice).

V

The Existence of God as a Postulate of Pure Practical Reason

In the foregoing analysis the moral law led to a practical problem which is prescribed by pure reason alone, without the aid of any sensible motives, namely that of the necessary completeness of the first and principal element of the *summum bonum*, viz. morality: and as this can only be perfectly solved in eternity, to the postulate of *immortality*. The same law must also lead us to affirm the possibility of the second element of the *summum bonum*, viz. happiness proportioned to that morality, and this on grounds as disinterested as before, and solely from impartial reason; that is, it must lead to the supposition of the existence of a cause adequate to this effect; in other words it must postulate the *existence of God*, as the necessary condition of the possibility of the *summum bonum* (an object of the will which is necessarily connected with the moral legislation of pure reason). We proceed to exhibit this connexion in a convincing manner.

Happiness is the condition of a rational being in the world with whom *everything goes according to his wish and will*; it rests therefore on the harmony of physical nature with his whole end and likewise with the essential determining principle of his will. Now the moral law as a law of freedom commands by determining principles which ought to be quite independent of nature and of its harmony with our faculty of desire (as springs). But the acting rational being in the world is not the cause of the world and of nature itself. There is not the least ground, therefore, in the moral law for a necessary connexion between morality and proportionate happiness in a being that belongs to the world as part of it, and therefore dependent on it, and which for that reason cannot by his will be a cause of this nature, nor by his own power make it thoroughly harmonize, as far as happiness is concerned, with his practical principles. Nevertheless, in the practical problem of pure reason, i.e. the necessary pursuit of the *summum bonum*, such a connexion is postulated as necessary: we ought to endeavour to promote the *summum bonum*, which therefore must be possible. Accordingly, the existence of a cause of all nature, distinct from nature itself, and containing the principle of this connexion, namely of the exact harmony of happiness with morality, is also *postulated*. Now this supreme cause must contain the principle of the harmony of nature, not merely with a law of the will of rational beings, but with the concept of this *law*, in so far as they make it the *supreme determining principle of the will*, and consequently not merely with the form of morals but with their morality as their motive, that is, with their moral character. Therefore the *summum bonum* is possible only on the supposition of a supreme Being having a causality corresponding to moral character. Now a being that is capable of acting on the concept of laws is an *intelligence* (a rational being), and the causality of such a being according to this concept of laws is his *will*; therefore the supreme cause of nature, which must be presupposed as a condition of the *summum bonum* is a being which is the cause of nature by *intelligence* and *will*, consequently its author, that is God. It follows that the postulate of the possibility of the *highest derived good* (the best world) is likewise the postulate of the reality of the *highest original good*, that is to say, of the existence of God. Now it was seen to be a duty for us to promote the *summum bonum*; consequently it is not merely allowable, but it is a necessity connected with duty as a requisite, that we should presuppose the possibility of this *summum bonum*; and as this is possible only on condition of the existence of God, it inseparably connects the supposition of this with duty; that is, it is morally necessary to assume the existence of God.

It must be remarked here that this moral necessity is *subjective*, that is it is a want, and not *objective*, that is itself a duty—for there cannot be a duty to suppose the existence of anything (since this concerns only the theoretical employment of reason). Moreover, it is not meant by this that it is necessary to suppose the existence of God *as a basis of all obligation in general* (for this rests, as has been sufficiently proved, simply on the autonomy of reason itself). What belongs to duty here is only the endeavour to realize and promote the *summum bonum* in the world, the possibility of which can therefore be postulated; and as our reason finds it not conceivable except on the supposition of a supreme intelligence, the admission of this existence is therefore connected with the consciousness of our duty, although the admission itself belongs to the domain of speculative reason. Considered in respect of this alone, as a principle of explanation, it may be called a *hypothesis*, but in reference to the intelligibility of an object given to us by the moral law (the *summum bonum*), and consequently of a requirement for practical purposes, it may be called *faith*, that is to say a pure *rational faith*, since pure reason (both in its theoretical and its practical use) is the sole source from which it springs.

From this *deduction* it is now intelligible why the Greek schools could never attain the solution of their problem of the practical possibility of the *summum bonum*, because they made the rule of the use which the will of man makes of his freedom the sole and sufficient ground of this possibility, thinking that they had no need for that purpose of the existence of God. No doubt they were so far right that they established the principle of morals of itself independently of this postulate, from the relation of reason only to the will, and consequently made it the *supreme* practical condition of the *summum bonum*; but it was not therefore the *whole* condition of its possibility. The Epicureans had indeed assumed as the supreme principle of morality a wholly false one, namely that of happiness, and had substituted for a law a maxim of arbitrary choice according to every man's inclination. They proceeded, however, *consistently* enough in this: that they degraded their *summum bonum* likewise just in proportion to the meanness of their fundamental principle, and looked for no greater happiness than can be attained by human prudence (including temperance and moderation of the inclinations), and this as we know would be scanty enough and would be very different according to circumstances; not to mention the exceptions that their maxims must perpetually admit and which make them incapable of being laws. The Stoics, on the contrary, had chosen their supreme practical principle quite rightly, making virtue the condition of the *summum bonum*; but when they represented the degree of virtue required by its pure law as fully attainable in this life, they not only strained the moral powers of the man whom they called *the wise* beyond all the limits of his nature, and assumed a thing that contradicts all our knowledge of men, but also and principally they would not allow the second element of the *summum bonum*, namely happiness, to be properly a special object of human desire, but made their wise man—like a divinity in his consciousness of the excellence of his person—wholly independent of nature (as regards his own contentment). They exposed him indeed to the evils of life, but made him not subject to them (at the same time representing him also as free from moral evil). They thus in fact left out the second element of the *summum bonum*, namely personal happiness, placing it solely in action and satisfaction with one's own personal worth, thus including it in the consciousness of being morally minded, in which they might have been sufficiently refuted by the voice of their own nature.

The doctrine of Christianity, even if we do not yet consider it as a religious doctrine, gives, touching this point, a concept of the *summum bonum* (the kingdom of God), which alone satisfies the strictest demand of practical reason. The moral law is holy (unyielding) and demands holiness of morals, although all the moral perfection to which man can attain is still only virtue—that is, a rightful disposition arising from *respect* for the law, implying consciousness of a constant propensity to transgression, or at least a want of purity, that is, a mixture of many spurious (not moral) motives of obedience to the law, consequently a self-esteem combined with humility. In respect then of the holiness which the Christian law requires, this leaves the creature nothing but a progress *in infinitum*, but for that very reason it justifies him in hoping for an endless duration of his existence. The *worth* of a character *perfectly* accordant with the moral law is infinite, since the only restriction on all possible happiness in the judgment of a wise and all-powerful distributor of it is the absence of conformity of rational beings to their duty. But the moral law of itself does not *promise* any happiness, for according to our conceptions of an order of nature in general, this is not necessarily connected to obedience to the law. Now Christian morality supplies this defect (of the second indispensable element of the *summum bonum*) by representing the world in which rational beings devote themselves with all their soul to the moral law as a *kingdom of God*, in which nature and morality are brought into a harmony foreign to each of itself, by a holy Author who makes the derived *summum bonum* possible. *Holiness* of life is prescribed to them as a rule even in this life, while the welfare proportioned to it, namely *bliss*, is represented as attainable only in an eternity; because the former must always be the pattern of their conduct in every state, and progress towards it is already possible and necessary in this life,—while the latter, under the name of happiness, cannot be attained at all in this world (so far as our own power is concerned) and therefore is made simply an object of hope. Nevertheless the Christian principle of morality itself is not theological (so as to be heteronomy) but is autonomy of pure practical reason, since it does not make the knowledge of God and his will the foundation of these laws, but only of the attainment of the *summum bonum*, on condition of following these laws, and it does not even place the proper *spring* of this obedience in the desired results, but solely in the concept of duty, as that of which the faithful observance alone constitutes the worthiness to obtain those happy consequences.

In this manner the moral laws lead through the concept of the *summum bonum* as the object and final end of pure practical reason to *religion*, that is, to the *recognition of all duties as divine command, not as sanctions, that is to say arbitrary ordinances of a foreign will and contingent in themselves*, but as essential *laws* of every free will in itself, which nevertheless must be regarded as commands of the Supreme Being, because it is only from a morally perfect (holy and good) and at the same time all-powerful will, and consequently only through harmony with this will, that we can hope to attain the *summum bonum* which the moral law makes it our duty to take as the object of our endeavours. Here again, then, all remains disinterested and founded merely on duty; neither fear nor hope being made the fundamental springs, which if taken as principles would destroy the whole moral worth of actions. The moral law commands me to make the highest possible good in a world the ultimate object of all my conduct. But I cannot hope to effect this otherwise than by the harmony of my will with that of a holy and good Author of the world; and although the conception of the *summum bonum* as a whole, in which the greatest happiness is conceived as combined in the most exact proportion with the highest degree of moral perfection (possible in creatures), includes *my own happiness*, yet it is not this that is the determining principle of the will which is enjoined to promote the *summum bonum*, but the moral law, which on the contrary limits by strict conditions my unbounded desire of happiness.

Hence also morality is not properly the doctrine how we should *make* ourselves happy, but how we should become *worthy* of happiness. It is only when religion is added that there also comes in the hope of participating some day in happiness in proportion as we have endeavoured to be not unworthy of it.

A man is *worthy* to possess a thing or a state when his possession of it is in harmony with the *summum bonum*. We can now easily see that all worthiness depends on moral conduct, since in the conception of the *summum bonum* this constitutes the condition of the rest (which belongs to one's state), namely the participation in happiness. Now it follows from this that *morality* should never be treated as a *doctrine of happiness*, that is, an instruction how to become happy; for it has to do simply with the rational condition (*conditio sine qua non*) of happiness, not with the means of attaining it. But when morality has been completely expounded (which merely imposes duties instead of providing rules for selfish desires), then first, after the moral desire to promote the *summum bonum* (to bring the kingdom of God to us) has been awakened, a desire founded on a law, and which could not previously arise in any selfish mind, and when for the behoof of this desire the step to religion has been taken, then this ethical doctrine may be also called a doctrine of happiness, because the *hope* of happiness first begins with religion only.

We can also see from this that when we ask what is *God's ultimate end* in creating the world, we must not name that *happiness* of the rational beings in it, but the *summum bonum*, which adds a further condition to that wish of such beings—namely the condition of being worthy of happiness, that is, the *morality* of these same rational beings, a condition which alone contains the rule by which only they can hope to share in the former at the hand of a *wise* Author. For as *wisdom* theoretically considered signifies *the knowledge of the summum bonum*, and practically *the accordance of the will with the summum bonum*, we cannot attribute to a supreme independent wisdom an end based merely on *goodness*. For we cannot conceive the action of this goodness (in respect of the happiness of rational beings) as suitable to the highest original good, except under the restrictive conditions of the harmony with the holiness of the will. Therefore those who placed the end of creation in the glory of God (provided that this is not conceived anthropomorphically as a desire to be praised) have perhaps hit upon the best expression. For nothing glorifies God more than that which is the most estimable thing in the world—respect for his command, the observance of the holy duty that his law imposes on us,—when there is added thereto his glorious plan of crowning such a beautiful order of things with corresponding happiness. If the latter (to speak humanly) makes him worthy of love, by the *former* he is an object of adoration. Even men can never acquire respect by benevolence alone, though they may gain love, so that the greatest beneficence only procures them honour when it is regulated by worthiness.

That in the order of ends, man (and with him every rational being) is *an end in himself*, that is, that he can never be used merely as a means by any (not even by God), without being at the same time an end also himself, that therefore *humanity* in our person must be *holy* to ourselves, this follows now of itself because he is the *subject of the moral law*, in other words of that which is holy in itself, and on account of which alone anything can be termed holy. For this moral law is founded on the autonomy of his will, as a free will which by its universal laws must necessarily be able to agree with that to which it is to submit itself.

15

HEGEL

on REVEALED RELIGION

Biographical Note Born in Stuttgart in 1770, son of an under-official in the service of the Duke of Württemburg. Studied philosophy and theology at Tübingen, 1788–93. Thereafter he was private tutor at Bern from 1793–96 and at Frankfurt from 1797–1801. From this year he lectured at Jena and was Schelling's collaborator in the editing of the *Kritisches Journal der Philosophie*. In 1806, moved to Bamberg, and from 1808–16 was Rector of the Aegidien Gymnasium at Nuremberg. 1816, became professor of philosophy at Heidelberg, and two years later was invited to become Fichte's successor in the chair at Berlin. Died, 1831.

Principal works: *De Orbitis Planetarum* (1801), *Phenomenology of Spirit* (1806), *Logic* (1812–16), *Encyclopaedia of the Philosophical Sciences* (1817), *Philosophy of Right* (1821), and lectures on *Aesthetics*, *Philosophy of Religion*, *Philosophy of History* and *History of Philosophy*.

Philosophical Note Kant's philosophy became transmuted in his successors. Fichte (1762–1814), for instance, criticized Kant's doctrines of 'things-in-themselves' (see above, p. 272); and this prepared the way for holding that everything in experience is the product of the self. But since *a priori* knowledge does not depend on the particular nature of the individual, knowledge, and indeed all experience, as structured, belongs to and is the product of an Absolute Self. Schelling (1775–1854) distinguished between the manifestation of the Absolute in mind and its manifestation in experience, and in consequence regarded it as something indefinite underlying both these forms of manifestation. H. criticized Schelling's view, since it makes the Absolute too static and abstract: if we are to take rationalism seriously the Absolute must show itself concretely. H. criticized Kant, furthermore, on the ground that he treated the principles through which we understand reality—such principles as space, time and causality—as though they were ingredients simply added to experience by the mind. But how do they give us a genuine apprehension of reality? Again, to take rationalism seriously, it must be held (as H. said) that what is real is rational and what is rational is real. Nevertheless, a solution is needed to Kant's problem: for the merely regulative function of the Ideas of reason is, according to Kant, a consequence of the contradictions with which we are landed if we treat concepts such as God, the world and the soul as though they applied directly to experience. H. deals with the problem by affirming boldly that contradiction is implicit in the nature of things and in the manner in which we think. The understanding, whereby we attempt to gain a systematic grasp of reality, involves giving a sharpness and definition to our concepts; but the deployment of these concepts leads to contradictions—for while the concepts in their originally fluid and vague form can apply to experience and, in a sense, live together, the process of sharpening and refining them gives them a kind of mutual independence which must issue in collisions. Thus partial abstractions must be complemented by their opposites, a process which H. calls the dialectic. The contradictions are overcome in a higher stage, that of reason, but not facilely by removing them, but by seeing them as a necessary feature of thought and reality. Thus the attempt by Schelling to postulate an underlying Absolute reconciling the apparent contradictions between mind and nature is an offence against the true method of dialectic.

Kant's failure, according to H., can be put another way: by saying that his critical philosophy gives no account of itself. On a genuinely rationalist account, philosophy must show how its own development is a necessary, dialectical evolution (so that, *inter alia*, philosophy is also the history of philosophy). Thus there is a real sense in which knowledge is self-consciousness. But self-consciousness requires others (I cannot be aware of myself save through recognizing persons and things 'outside' me); so nature and a multiplicity of selves are a necessary condition of the increasing self-awareness of Absolute Mind. (This is a notion which H. partly derived from Fichte.) Knowledge, therefore, necessarily has a social context, and H. was able to apply the idea of the dialectic to history. A 'thesis' is affirmed, then the 'antithesis', and then both are taken up into a higher 'synthesis' (e.g. Judaism and Classical culture are taken up into Christianity). Later, of course, the doctrine was adapted by Marx and interpreted in terms of the class struggle. The dialectic, then, is both an historical and a logical process.

Although the idea of a transcendent being is foreign to H.'s system, there are ways in which H.'s view of religion was given a Christian interpretation. Religion is distinguished from philosophy as being an attitude expressed in symbolic rather than conceptual form, even though both are directed to the same object, namely the Absolute. At the religious level, Absolute Mind manifests itself pictorially by means of 'representations': if these were removed religion would become speculative philosophy—and it is part of the dialectic that religion tends to transcend itself in precisely this manner. The self-communication of the Absolute through such representations is God's self-consciousness in man (here the immanentism of H.'s view comes out) and reaches its highest expression in Christ, whose self-denial expresses the principle that only through the dialectical process, i.e. by first denying itself, can the Absolute Mind reveal itself.

The following selection follows upon a passage describing the nature of art, which, according to H., prepares the way for the insights of religion and philosophy by showing how the non-spiritual can be taken up into Spirit through the suffusing of material presented to the senses with an inner meaning. The symbolic forms of art are, however, incomplete, and demand a higher expression, viz. in the representations of religion.

Bibliographical Note The following translations may be found useful: W. Wallace, *Logic* (2 vols., 1893), *Philosophy of Mind* (1894), J. B. Baillie, *The Phenomenology of Mind* (rev. 2nd edn, 1949) and W. H. Johnston and L. G. Struthers, *Science of Logic* (2 vols., 1929). Important critical works are: J. M. E. McTaggart, *Studies in the Hegelian Dialectic* (Cambridge, 1922), W. T. Stace, *The Philosophy of*

Hegel (London, 1924) and J. N. Findlay, *Hegel: A Reinterpretation* (London, 1958). Also *Hegel Selections*, ed. J. Loewenberg (N.Y., 1929) is a handy collection of passages from Hegel.

REVEALED RELIGION

Encyclopaedia of the Philosophical Sciences, §564 ff.

564. It lies essentially in the notion of religion,—the religion i.e. whose content is absolute mind[1]—that it be *revealed*, and, what is more, revealed *by God*. Knowledge (the principle by which the substance is mind) is a self-determining principle, as infinite self-realizing form,—it therefore is manifestation out and out. The spirit is only spirit in so far as it is for the spirit, and in the absolute religion it is the absolute spirit which manifests no longer abstract elements of its being but itself.

The old conception—due to a one-sided survey of human life—of Nemesis, which made the divinity and its action in the world only a levelling power, dashing to pieces everything high and great,—was confronted by Plato and Aristotle with the doctrine that God is not *envious*. The same answer may be given to the modern assertions that man cannot ascertain God. These assertions (and more than assertions they are not) are the more illogical, because made within a religion which is expressly called the revealed; for according to them it would rather be the religion in which nothing of God was revealed, in which he had not revealed himself, and those belonging to it would be the heathen 'who know not God'. If the word of God is taken in earnest in religion at all, it is from him, the theme and centre of religion, that the method of divine knowledge may and must begin: and if self-revelation is refused him, then the only thing left to constitute his nature would be to ascribe envy to him. But clearly if the word Mind is to have a meaning, it implies the revelation of him.

If we recollect how intricate is the knowledge of the divine Mind for those who are not content with the homely pictures of faith but proceed to thought,—at first only 'rationalizing' reflection, but afterwards, as in duty bound, to speculative comprehension, it may almost create surprise that so many, and especially theologians whose vocation it is to deal with these Ideas, have tried to get off their task by gladly accepting anything offered them for this behoof. And nothing serves better to shirk it than to adopt the conclusion that man knows nothing of God. To know what God as spirit is—to apprehend this accurately and distinctly in thoughts—requires

[1] Or 'Spirit' (*Geist*).

careful and thorough speculation. It includes, in its forefront, the propositions: God is God only so far as he knows himself: his self-knowledge is, further, his self-consciousness in man, and man's knowledge of God, which proceed to man's self-knowledge in God. . . .

565. When the immediacy and sensuousness of shape and knowledge is superseded, God is, in point of content, the essential and actual spirit of nature and spirit, while in point of form he is, first of all, presented to consciousness as mental representation.[1] This quasi-pictorial representation gives to the elements of his content, on the one hand, a separate being, making them presuppositions towards each other, and phenomena which succeed each other; their relationship it makes a series of events according to finite reflective categories. But, on the other hand, such a form of finite representationalism is also overcome and superseded in the faith which realizes one spirit and in the devotion of worship.

566. In this separating, the form parts from the content: and in the form the different functions of the notion part off into special spheres or media, in each of which the absolute spirit exhibits itself; (α) as eternal content, abiding self-centred, even in its manifestation; (β) as distinction of the eternal essence from its manifestation, which difference becomes the phenomenal world into which the content enters; (γ) as infinite return, and reconciliation with the eternal being, of the world it gave away—the withdrawal of the eternal from the phenomenal into the unity of its fullness.

567. (α) Under the 'moment' of *Universality*,[2]—the sphere of pure thought or the abstract medium of essence,—it is therefore the absolute spirit, which is at first the presupposed principle, not however staying aloof and inert, but (as underlying and essential power under the reflective category of causality) creator of heaven and earth: but yet in this

[1] See above, p. 291.

[2] The sense of this extremely difficult passage is, briefly, as follows. Thought proceeds through universals, a bringing together of diverse particulars under common notions. This capacity to universalize is, however, both a characteristic of individual selves and what they have in common—it is the working of Absolute Mind or Spirit immanently in individual selves. But as has been pointed out above (see p. 291), knowledge through universals presupposes nature and a multiplicity of selves, and universals which could be applied to no experiential content would be empty. Hence Absolute Mind 'creates' particulars: nature on the one hand, finite selves on the other. In creating this 'opposition' to itself, it thereby creates evil (ignorance, etc.); but this is overcome when individual self-consciousness sees itself as an embodiment of the Absolute. This dialectic is reflected pictorially in the Christian doctrine of the Trinity. The Father stands for Absolute Mind as universal; this implies its opposite, the finite self set over against it, regarding it as an Other; but the two 'moments' or phases of the Absolute are reconciled, when Christ throws off his finite independence of the Absolute, and shows the unity between the universal and the individual. This mediation brings about the indwelling of Absolute Spirit in conscious selves. Thus Christianity is a pictorial and historical way of representing the inner dialectic of the Absolute.

eternal sphere rather only begetting himself as his *son*, with whom, though different, he still remains in original identity,—just as, again, this differentiation of him from the universal essence eternally supersedes itself, and, through this mediating of a self-superseding mediation, the first substance is essentially as *concrete individuality* and subjectivity,—is the *Spirit.*

568. (β) Under the 'moment' of *particularity*, or of judgment, it is this concrete eternal being which is presupposed: its movement is the creation of the phenomenal world. The eternal 'moment' of mediation—of the only Son—divides itself to become the antithesis of two separate worlds. On one hand is heaven and earth, the elemental and the concrete nature, —on the other hand, standing in action and reaction with such nature, the spirit, which therefore is finite. That spirit, as the extreme of inherent negativity, completes its independence till it becomes wickedness, and is that extreme through its connexion with the confronting nature and through its own naturalness thereby investing it. Yet, amid that naturalness, it is, when it thinks, directed towards the Eternal, though for that reason, only standing to it in an external connexion.

569. (γ) Under the 'moment' of *individuality* as such,—of subjectivity and the notion itself, in which the contrast of universal and particular has sunk to its identical ground, the place of presupposition (1) is taken by the *universal* substance, as actualized out of its abstraction into an *individual* self-consciousness. This individual, who as such is identified with the essence,—(in the Eternal sphere he is called the Son)—is transplanted into the world of time, and in him wickedness is implicitly overcome. Further, this immediate, and thus sensuous, existence of the absolutely concrete is represented as putting himself in judgment and expiring in the pain of *negativity*, in which he, as infinite subjectivity, keeps himself unchanged, and thus, as absolute return from that negativity and as universal unity of universal and individual essentiality, has realized his being as the Idea of the spirit, eternal, but alive and present in the world.

570. (2) This objective totality of the divine man who is the Idea of the spirit is the implicit presupposition for the *finite* immediacy of the single subject. For such subject therefore it is at first an Other, an object of contemplating vision,—but the vision of implicit truth, through which witness of the spirit in him, he, on account of his immediate nature, at first characterized himself as nought and wicked. But, secondly, after the example of his truth, by means of the faith in the unity (in that example implicitly accomplished) of universal and individual essence, he is also the movement to throw off his immediacy, his natural man and self-will, to close himself in unity with that example (who is his implicit life)

in the pain of negativity, and thus to know himself made one with the essential Being. Thus the Being of Beings (3) through this mediation brings about his own indwelling in self-consciousness, and is the actual presence of the essential and self-subsisting spirit who is all in all.

571. These three syllogisms,[1] constituting the one syllogism of the absolute self-mediation of spirit, are the revelation of that spirit whose life is set out as a cycle of concrete shapes in pictorial thought. From this its separation into parts, with a temporal and external sequence, the unfolding of the mediation contracts itself in the result,—where the spirit closes in unity with itself,—not merely to the simplicity of faith and devotional feeling but even to thought. In the immanent simplicity of thought the unfolding still has its expansion, yet is all the whole known as an indivisible coherence of the universal, simple, and eternal spirit in itself. In this form of truth, truth is the object of *philosophy*.

If the result—the realized Spirit in which all mediation has superseded itself—is taken in a merely formal, contentless sense, so that the spirit is not also at the same time known as *implicitly* existent and objectively self-unfolding;—then that infinite subjectivity is the merely formal self-consciousness, knowing itself in itself as absolute,—Irony. Irony, which can make every objective reality nought and vain, is itself the emptiness and vanity, which from itself, and therefore by chance and its own good pleasure, gives itself direction and content, remains master over it, is not bound by it,—and, with the assertion that it stands on the very summit of religion and philosophy, falls rather back into the vanity of wilfulness. It is only in proportion as the pure infinite form, the self-centred manifestation, throws off the one-sidedness of subjectivity in which it is the vanity of thought, that it is the free thought which has its infinite characteristic at the same time as essential and actual content, and has that content as an object in which it is also free. Thinking, so far, is only the formal aspect of the absolute content.

PHILOSOPHY

572. This science is the unity of Art and Religion. Whereas the vision-method of Art, external in point of form, is but subjective production and shivers the substantial content into many separate shapes, and whereas Religion, with its separation into parts, opens it out in mental picture, and mediates what is thus opened out; Philosophy not merely keeps them together to make a total, but even unifies them into the simple spiritual vision, and then in that raises them to self-consciousness thought. Such

[1] On H.'s use of the term 'syllogism', see n. 1 to p. 389.

consciousness is thus the intelligible unity (cognized by thought) of art and religion, in which the diverse elements in the content are cognized as necessary, and this necessary as free.

573. Philosophy thus characterizes itself as a cognition of the necessity in the content of the absolute picture-idea, as also of the necessity in the two forms—on one hand, immediate vision and its poetry, and the objective and external revelation presupposed by representation,—on the other hand, first the subjective retreat inwards, then the subjective movement of faith and its final identification with the presupposed object. This cognition is thus the *recognition* of this content and its form; it is the liberation from the one-sidedness of the forms, elevation of them unto the absolute form which determines itself to content, remains identical with it, and is in that the cognition of that essential and actual necessity. This movement, which philosophy is, finds itself already accomplished, when at the close it seizes its own notion,—i.e. only *looks* back on its knowledge.

Here might seem to be the place to treat in a definite exposition of the reciprocal relations of philosophy and religion. The whole question turns entirely on the difference of the forms of speculative thought from the forms of mental representation and 'reflecting' intellect. But it is the whole cycle of philosophy, and of logic in particular, which has not merely taught and made known this difference, but also criticized it, or rather has let its nature develop and judge itself by these very categories. It is only by an insight into the value of these forms that the true and needful conviction can be gained, that the content of religion and philosophy is the same—leaving out, of course, the further details of external nature and finite mind which fall outside the range of religion. But religion is the truth *for all men*: faith rests on the witness of the spirit, which as witnessing is the spirit in man. This witness—the underlying essence in all humanity—takes, when driven to expound itself, its first definite form under those acquired habits of thought which his secular consciousness and intellect otherwise employs. In this way the truth becomes liable to the terms and conditions of finitude in general. This does not prevent the spirit, even in employing sensuous ideas and finite categories of thought, from retaining its content (which as religion is essentially speculative) with a tenacity which does violence to them, and acts *inconsistently* towards them. By this inconsistency it corrects their defects.[1] Nothing easier therefore for the

[1] On H.'s view, the contradictions arising from the understanding (see above, p. 291) and brought out in the dialectic are 'overcome' by the reason, the faculty of speculative thought. Speculative thought then preserves the contradictions in a higher unity; likewise religion represents speculative truth pictorially, and in doing so preserves contradictions. 'Rationalism' is content to remain at the level of understanding, with its sharp definition of concepts, as though contradictions can be simply avoided.

'Rationalist' than to point out contradictions in the exposition of the faith, and then to prepare triumphs for its principle of formal identity. If the spirit yields to this finite reflection, which has usurped the title of reason and philosophy ('Rationalism')—it strips religious truth of its infinity and makes it in reality nought. Religion in that case is completely in the right in guarding herself against such reason and philosophy and treating them as enemies. But it is another thing when religion sets herself against comprehending reason, and against philosophy in general, and specially against a philosophy of which the doctrine is speculative, and so religious. Such an opposition proceeds from failure to appreciate the difference indicated and the value of spiritual form in general, and particularly of the logical form; or, to be more precise still, from failure to note the distinction of the content—which may be in both the same—from these forms. It is on the ground of form that philosophy has been reproached and accused by the religious party; just as conversely its speculative content has brought the same charges upon it from a self-styled philosophy—and from a pithless orthodoxy. It had too little of God in it for the former; too much for the latter.

The charge of *Atheism*, which used often to be brought against philosophy (that it has *too* little of God), has grown rare: the more widespread grows the charge of Pantheism, that it has *too much* of him:—so much so, that it is treated not so much as an imputation, but as a proved fact, or a sheer fact which needs no proof. Piety, in particular, which with its pious airs of superiority fancies itself free to dispense with proof, goes hand in hand with empty rationalism—(which means to be so much opposed to it, though both repose really on the same habit of mind)—in the wanton assertion, almost as if it merely mentioned a notorious fact, that Philosophy is the All-one doctrine, or Pantheism. It must be said that it was more to the credit of piety and theology when they accused a philosophical system (e.g. Spinozism) of Atheism than of Pantheism, though the former imputation at the first glance looks more cruel and insidious. The imputation of Atheism presupposes a definite idea of a full and real God, and arises because the popular idea does not detect in the philosophical notion the peculiar form to which it is attached. Philosophy indeed can recognize its own forms in the categories of religious consciousness, and even its own teaching in the doctrine of religion—which therefore it does not disparage. But the converse is not true: the religious consciousness does not apply the criticism of thought to itself, does not comprehend itself, and is therefore, as it stands, exclusive. To impute Pantheism instead of Atheism to Philosophy is part of the modern habit of mind—of the new piety and new theology. For them philosophy has too much of God:—

so much so, that, if we believe them, it asserts that God is everything and everything is God. This new theology, which makes religion only a subjective feeling and denies the knowledge of the divine nature, thus retains nothing more than a God in general without objective characteristics. Without interest of its own for the concrete, fulfilled notion of God, it treats it only as an interest which *others* once had, and hence treats what belongs to the doctrine of God's concrete nature as something merely historical. The indeterminate God is to be found in all religions; every kind of piety—that of the Hindu to asses, cows,—or to dalailamas,[1]—that of the Egyptians to the ox—is always adoration of an object which, with all its absurdities, also contains the generic abstract God in general. If this theory needs no more than such a God, so as to find God in everything called religion, it must at least find such a God recognized even in philosophy, and can no longer accuse it of Atheism. The mitigation of the reproach of Atheism into that of Pantheism has its ground therefore in the superficial idea to which this mildness has attentuated and emptied God. As that popular idea clings to its abstract universality, from which all definite quality is excluded, all such definiteness is only the non-divine, the secularity of things, thus left standing in fixed undisturbed substantiality. On such a presupposition, even after philosophy has maintained God's absolute universality, and the consequent untruth of the being of external things, the hearer clings as he did before to his belief that secular things still keep their being, and form all that is definite in the divine universality. He thus changes that universality into what he called the pantheistic:—*Everything is*—(empirical things, without distinction, whether higher or lower in the scale, *are*)—all possess substantiality; and so—thus he understands philosophy—each and every secular thing is God. It is only his own stupidity, and the falsifications due to such a misconception, which generate the imagination and the allegation of such pantheism.

But if those who give out that a certain philosophy is Pantheism, are unable and unwilling to see this—for it is just to see the notion that they refuse—they should before everything have verified the alleged fact that *any one philosopher, or any one man*, had really ascribed substantial or objective and inherent reality to all things and regarded them as God:—that such an idea had ever come into the hand of anybody but themselves. This allegation I will further elucidate in this exoteric discussion: and the only way to do so is to set down the evidence. If we want to take so-called Pantheism in its most poetical, most sublime, or if you will its grossest shape, we must, as is well known, consult the oriental poets: and the most copious delineations of it are found in Hindu literature. Amongst

[1] A reference to Tibetan Buddhism.

the abundant resources open to our disposal on this topic, I select—as the most authentic statement accessible—the *Bhagavad-Gita*,[1] and amongst its effusions, prolix and reiterative *ad nauseam*, some of the most telling passages. In the 10th Lesson Krishna says of himself:—'I am the self, seated in the hearts of all beings. . . . I am the beginning and the middle and the end also of all beings. . . . I am the beaming sun amongst the shining ones, and the moon among the lunar mansions. . . . Amongst the Vedas[2] I am the Sāma-Veda: I am mind amongst the senses: I am consciousness in living beings. And I am Śankara (Śiva) among the Rudras . . . Meru among the high-topped mountains, . . . the Himalaya among the firmly-fixed (mountains). . . . Among beasts I am the Lord of beasts. . . . Among letters I am the letter A: . . . I am the spring among the seasons. . . . I am also that which is the seed of all things: there is nothing moveable or immoveable which can exist without me.'

Even in these totally sensuous delineations, Krishna (and we must not suppose there is, besides Krishna, still God, or a God besides; as he said before he was Śiva or Indra, so it is afterwards said that Brahma too is in him) makes himself out to be—not everything, but only—the most excellent of everything. Everywhere there is a distinction drawn between external unessential existences and one essential amongst them, which he is. Even when, at the beginning of the passage, he is said to be the beginning, middle and end of living things, this totality is distinguished from the living things themselves as single existences. Even such a picture which extends deity far and wide in its existence cannot be called pantheism: we must rather say that in the infinitely multiple empirical world, everything is reduced to a limited number of essential existences, to a polytheism. But even what has been quoted shows that these very substantialities of the externally-existent do not retain the independence entitling them to be named Gods; even Śiva, Indra, etc., melt into the one Krishna.

This reduction is more expressly made in the following scene (7th Lesson). Krishna says: 'I am the producer and the destroyer of the whole universe. There is nothing else higher than myself; all this is woven upon me, like the number of pearls upon a thread. I am the taste in water; . . . I am the light of the sun and the moon; I am "Om" in all the Vedas. . . . I am life in all beings. . . . I am the discernment of the discerning ones. . . . I am also the strength of the strong.' Then he adds: 'The whole universe deluded by these three states of mind developed from the qualities (sc.

[1] The *Bhagavad-Gītā* ('Song of the Lord'), one of the most impressive scriptures of Hinduism, describes how God (in the form of Krishna) appears to Arjuna just before a battle. It constitutes one book of the immense Indian epic, the *Mahābhārata*.

[2] The original scriptures of Hinduism, being collections of hymns, etc., the Sāma-Veda being one such collection.

goodness, passion, darkness) does not know me who am beyond them and inexhaustible: for this delusion of mine,' (even the Māyā[1] is *his*, nothing independent), 'developed from the qualities is divine and difficult to transcend. Those cross beyond this delusion who resort to me alone.' Then the picture gathers itself up in a simple expression 'At the end of many lives, the man possessed of knowledge approaches me, (believing) that Vasudeva is everything. Such a high-souled mind is very hard to find. Those who are deprived of knowledge by various desires approach other divinities. . . . Whichever form of deity one worships with faith, from it he obtains the beneficial things he desires really given by me. But the fruit thus obtained by those of little judgment is perishable. . . . The undiscerning ones, not knowing my transcendent and inexhaustible essence, than which there is nothing higher, think me who am unperceived to have become perceptible.'

This 'All' which Krishna calls himself, is not, any more than the Eleatic One,[2] and the Spinozan Substance,[3] the Every-thing. This everything, rather, the infinitely-manifold sensuous manifold of the finite is in all these pictures, but defined as the 'accidental', without essential being of its very own, but having its truth in the substance, the One which, as different from that accidental, is alone the divine and God. Hinduism, however, has the higher conception of Brahma, the pure unity of thought in itself, where the empirical everything of the world, as also those proximate substantialities, called Gods, vanish. On that account Colebrooke[4] and many others have described the Hindu religion as at bottom a Monotheism. That this description is not incorrect is clear from these short citations. But so little concrete is this divine unity—spiritual as its idea of God is—so powerless its grip, so to speak—that Hinduism, with a monstrous inconsistency, is also the maddest of polytheisms. But the idolatry of the wretched Hindu, when he adores the ape, or other creatures, is still a long way from that wretched fancy of a Pantheism, to which everything is God, and God everything. Hindu monotheism moreover is itself an example how little comes of mere monotheism, if the Idea of God is not deeply determinate in itself. For that unity, if it be intrinsically abstract and therefore empty, tends of itself to let whatever is concrete, outside it —be it as a lot of Gods or as secular, empirical individuals—keep its independence. That pantheism indeed—on the shallow conception of it

[1] *Māyā*, a word of many meanings in Sanskrit: 'creative power', 'illusion', or the illusion created by God through his creative power.

[2] Eleatic, i.e. Parmenidean: see above, p. 19.

[3] See above, p. 124.

[4] H. T. Colebrooke (1765–1837), the first great European Sanskrit scholar.

—might with a show of logic as well be called a monotheism; for if God, as it says, is identical with the world, then as there is only one world there would be in that pantheism only one God. Perhaps the empty numerical unity must be predicated of the world: but such abstract predication of it has no further special interest; on the contrary, a mere numerical unity just means that its *content* is an infinite multiplicity and variety of finitudes. But it is that delusion with the empty unity, which alone made possible and induces the wrong idea of pantheism. It is only the picture—floating in the indefinite blue—of the world as *one thing*, *the all*, that could ever be considered capable of combining with God: only on that assumption could philosophy be supposed to teach that God is the world: for if the world were taken as it is, as everything, as the endless lot of empirical existence, then it would hardly have been even held possible to suppose a pantheism which asserted of such stuff that it is God.

But to go back again to the question of fact. If we want to see the consciousness of the One—not as with the Hindus split between the featureless unity of abstract thought, on one hand, and on the other, the long-winded weary story of its particular detail, but—in its finest purity and sublimity, we must consult the Mohommedans. If e.g. in the excellent Jelaleddīn-Rūmī[1] in particular, we find the unity of the soul with the One set forth, and that unity described as love, this spiritual unity is an exaltation above the finite and vulgar, a transfiguration of the natural and the spiritual, in which the externalism and transitoriness of immediate nature, and of empirical secular spirit, is discarded and absorbed.

I refrain from accumulating further examples of the religious and poetic conceptions which it is customary to call pantheistic. Of the philosophies to which that name is given, the Eleatic, or Spinozist, it has been remarked earlier that so far are they from identifying God with the world and making him finite, that in these systems this 'everything' has no truth, and that we should rather call them monotheistic, or, in relation to the popular idea of the world, acosmical. They are most accurately called systems which apprehend the Absolute only as substance. Of the oriental, especially the Mohammedan, modes of envisaging God, we may rather say that they represent the Absolute as the utterly universal genus which dwells in the species or existences, but dwells so potently that these existences have no actual reality. The fault of all these modes of thought and systems is that they stop short of defining substance as subject and as mind.

These systems and modes of pictorial conception originate from the

[1] Jalāl-ad-dīn Rūmī, Persian Sufi poet (1207–73), whose *Masnavi yi ma'navi* is a compendium, illustrated by allegories, of Sufi doctrines.

one need common to all philosophies and all religions of getting an idea of God, and, secondly, of the relationship of God and the World. (In philosophy it is specially made out that the determination of God's nature determines his relations with the world.) The 'reflective' understanding begins by rejecting all systems and modes of conception which, whether they spring from heart, imagination or speculation, express the inter-connexion of God and the world: and in order to have God pure in faith or consciousness, he is as essence parted from appearance, as infinite from the finite. But, after this partition, the conviction arises also that the appearance has a relation to the essence, the finite to the infinite, and so on: and thus arises the question of reflection as to the nature of this relation. It is in the reflective form that the whole difficulty of the affair lies, and that causes this relation to be called incomprehensible by the agnostic. The close of philosophy is not the place, even in a general exoteric discussion, to waste a word on what a 'notion' means.[1] But as the view taken of this relation is closely connected with the view taken of philosophy generally and with all imputations against it, we may still add the remark that though philosophy certainly has to do with unity in general, it is not, however, with abstract unity, mere identity and the empty absolute, but with concrete unity (the notion), and that in its whole course it has to do with nothing else;—that each step in its advance is a peculiar term or phase of this concrete unity, and that the deepest and last expression of unity is the unity of absolute mind itself. Would-be judges and critics of philosophy might be recommended to familiarize themselves with these phases of unity and to take the trouble to get acquainted with them, at least to know so much that of these terms there are a great many, and that amongst them there is great variety. But they show so little acquaintance with them—and still less take trouble about it—that when they hear of unity—and relation *ipso facto* implies unity—they rather stick fast at quite abstract indeterminate unity, and lose sight of the chief point of interest—the special mode in which the unity is qualified. Hence all they can say about philosophy is that dry identity is its principle and result, and that it is the system of identity. Sticking fast to the indigested thought of identity, they have laid hands on, not the concrete unity, the notion and content of philosophy, but rather its reverse. In the philosophical field they proceed, as in the physical field the physicist;

[1] H.'s doctrine of the notion (*begriff*) briefly is as follows. Any unification of the multiplicity of the particulars given in experience comes from the capacity of the conscious self to universalize—to bring together different individuals through a concept or notion. Thus 'notion' essentially stands for the thinking being of the individual person; but this, of course, is (on H.'s view) something common to all conscious selves; so that 'notion' stands, in a sense, for the Absolute (see above, p. 291 and n. 2 to p. 293).

who also is well aware that he has before him a variety of sensuous properties and matters—or usually matters alone (for the properties get transformed into matters also for the physicist)—and that these matters (elements) *also* stand in *relation* to one another. But the question is, Of what kind is this relation? Every peculiarity and the whole difference of natural things, inorganic and living, depend solely on the different modes of this unity. But instead of ascertaining these different modes, the ordinary physicist (chemist included) takes up only one, the most external and the worst, viz. *composition*, and applies only it in the whole range of natural structures, which he thus renders for ever inexplicable.

The aforesaid shallow pantheism is an equally obvious inference from this shallow identity. All that those who employ this invention of their own to accuse philosophy gather from the study of God's *relation* to the world is that the one, but only the one, factor of this category of relation—and that the factor of indeterminateness—is identity. Thereupon they stick fast in this half-perception, and assert—falsely as a fact—that philosophy teaches the identity of God and the world. And as in their judgment either of the two,—the world as much as God—has the same solid substantiality as the other, they infer that in the philosophic Idea God is *composed* of God and the world. Such then is the idea they form of pantheism, and which they ascribe to philosophy. Unaccustomed in their own thinking and apprehending of thoughts to go beyond such categories, they import them into philosophy, where they are utterly unknown; they thus infect it with the disease against which they subsequently raise an outcry. If any difficulty emerge in comprehending God's relation to the world, they at once and very easily escape it by admitting that this relation contains for them an inexplicable contradiction; and that hence, they must stop at the vague conception of such relation, perhaps under the more familiar names of, e.g., omnipresence, providence, etc. Faith in their use of the term means no more than a refusal to define the conception, or to enter on a closer discussion of the problem. That men and classes of untrained intellect are satisfied with such indefiniteness, is what one expects; but when a trained intellect and an interest for reflective study is satisfied, in matters admitted to be of superior, if not even of supreme interest, with indefinite ideas, it is hard to decide whether the thinker is really in earnest with the subject. But if those who cling to this crude 'rationalism' were in earnest, e.g. with God's onmipresence, so far as to realize their faith thereon in a definite mental idea, in what difficulties would they be involved by their belief in the true reality of the things of sense! They would hardly like, as Epicurus does, to let God dwell in the interspaces of things, i.e. in the pores of the physicists,—said pores being the negative, something supposed to exist *beside* the material reality. This very 'Beside' would give their pantheism its spatiality,—their everything, conceived as the mutual exclusion of parts in space. But in ascribing to God, in his relation to the world, an action on and in the space thus filled on the world and in it, they would endlessly split up the divine actuality into infinite materiality. They would really thus have the misconception they call pantheism or all-one-doctrine, only as the necessary sequel of their misconceptions of God and the world. But to put that sort of thing, this stale gossip of oneness or identity, on the shoulders of philosophy, shows such recklessness about justice and truth that it can only be explained through the difficulty of getting into the head thoughts of notions, i.e., not abstract unity, but the many-shaped modes specified. If statements as to facts are put forward, and the facts in question are thoughts and notions, it is indispensable to get hold of their meaning. But even the fulfilment of this requirement has been rendered superfluous, now that it has long been a foregone conclusion that philosophy is pantheism, a system of identity, an all-one-doctrine, and that the person therefore who might be unaware of this fact is treated either as merely unaware of a matter of common notoriety, or as prevaricating for a purpose. On account of this chorus of assertions, then, I have believed myself obliged to speak at more length and exoterically on the outward and inward truth of this alleged fact: for exoteric discussion is the only method available in dealing with the external apprehension of notions as mere facts—by which notions are perverted into their opposite. The esoteric study of God and identity, as of cognitions and notions, is philosophy itself.

574. This notion of philosophy is the self-thinking Idea, the truth aware of itself,—the logical system, but with the signification that it is universality approved and certified in concrete content as in its actuality. In this way the science has gone back to its beginning: its result is the logical system but as a spiritual principle: out of the presupposing judgment, in which the notion was only implicit and the beginning an immediate,—and thus out of the *appearance* which it had there—it has risen to its pure principle and thus also unto its proper medium.

575. It is this appearing which originally gives the motive of the further development. The first appearance is formed by the syllogism, which is based on the logical system as starting-point, with Nature for the middle term which couples the Mind with it. The logical principle turns to Nature and Nature to Mind. Nature, standing between the Mind and its essence, sunders itself, not indeed to extremes of finite abstraction, nor itself to something away from them and independent,—which, as other than they, only serves as a link between them: for the

syllogism is *in the Idea* and Nature is essentially defined as a transition-point and negative factor, and as implicitly the Idea. Still the mediation of the notion has the external form of *transition*, and the science of Nature presents itself as the course of necessity, so that it is only in the one extreme that the liberty of the notion is explicit as a self-amalgamation.

576. In the second syllogism this appearance is so far superseded, that the syllogism is the standpoint of the Mind itself, which—as the mediating agent in the process—presupposes Nature and couples it with the logical principle. It is the syllogism where Mind reflects on itself in the Idea: philosophy appears as a subjective cognition, of which liberty is the aim, and which is itself the way to produce it.

577. The third syllogism is the Idea of philosophy, which has self-knowing reason, the absolutely-universal, for its middle term: a middle, which divides itself into Mind and Nature, making the former its presupposition, as process of the Idea's subjective activity, and the latter its universal extreme, as process of the objectively and implicitly existing Idea. The self-judging of the Idea into its two appearances characterizes both as its (the self-knowing reason's) manifestations: and in it there is a unification of the two aspects:—it is the nature of the fact, the notion, which causes the movement and development, yet this same movement is equally the action of cognition. The eternal Idea, in full fruition of its essence, eternally sets itself to work, engenders and enjoys itself as absolute Mind.

16

SCHLEIERMACHER

on RELIGIOUS EXPERIENCE, RELIGIOUS LANGUAGE *and on* MIRACLES

Biographical Note Born in Breslau, in 1768, son of an army chaplain in Silesia. From 1873 onwards he was educated at a Moravian school and college at Niesky and Barby respectively. In 1787 entered the University of Halle, obtaining his licentiate in 1790. Acted as tutor in a nobleman's house in West Prussia for a time, and in 1794 was ordained. 1796, became chaplain to the Charité Hospital in Berlin; and here he was able to spend much of his time in philosophical and theological study, while his circle of friends included F. Schlegel and others of the Romantic movement. His famous *Speeches on Religion* appeared in 1799, and in 1800 the *Monologen*. In 1802 became pastor in Stolpe in Pomerania. In 1804, returned to Halle as Professor of Theology. Owing to the suspension of the University by Napoleon he left in 1806, and after Jena went to Berlin as a pastor. Appointed Professor of Theology in the new University of Berlin in 1810. In 1821 appeared his *Christliche Glaube*, setting forth a new and systematic Protestant theology. Died in 1834.

Principal works: those mentioned above, together with *Grundlineen einer Kritik der bisherigen Sittenlehre* (1803).

Philosophical Note S. lived at an eventful time, both philosophically and politically. The Enlightenment, the chief philosophical representative of which was Kant, was giving way to the Romantic movement, partly a protest against the foregoing rationalism in religion and morality. The Romantics found in the beauties and intricacies of nature and in the feelings of human beings a richness which they considered to be neglected by their predecessors. S. was deeply influenced by this movement, though he thought that the new aesthetic interests were incomplete by themselves, and needed religion to fulfil themselves. But he was at one with the Romantics in criticizing the concept of 'religion within the limits of reason alone'. Changes in the philosophical situation were, moreover, reinforced by the excitement and insecurity accruing upon the French Revolution and the Napoleonic wars.

S.'s most famous work, the *Speeches on Religion*, attempted to show afresh the inner nature of religion, given that the rationalist accounts of it largely missed the point. S. in this provided a turning-point in the history of philosophical theology; unlike the usual procedure of his predecessors, which is to take religious concepts for granted, and argue pro and con on the basis of them, S.'s primary concern is to give an account of the special nature of religious ideas as distinguished from others. In line with other Romantics, he is impressed by the significance of human feelings and intuitions, and by the undoubted fact that the religious people are not merely concerned with a First Cause or a source of morality. Religion is independent of knowledge (in the rationalist sense) and action. S. came to formulate the essential feeling or intuition at the heart of religion as the 'feeling of absolute dependence' (there is some ambiguity, however, in the use of 'feeling'—sometimes it stands for experience and sometimes for feeling in a narrower sense). Or, as he says in the *Speeches*, 'The contemplation of the pious is the immediate consciousness of the universal existence of all finite things in and through the Infinite, and of all temporal things in and through the Eternal'. Thus S. bids people look within themselves for the essential religious intuition. This enabled him to claim that the highest capacity of human nature is realized in religion—it is in this way that religion completes and fulfils humanism and Romanticism. Also, the interpretation of faith in terms of experience expresses S.'s reaction against not merely rationalistic religion but also formalism and dogmatism within the Church. Doctrines cannot be treated as external propositions, but gain their significance from the way in which they express the apprehension of truth gained by the individual and the community. S. is strong in his insistence that it is for each individual to appropriate the truth for himself, and thus foreshadows the Existentialist movement, as well as giving a powerful impetus to the sympathetic investigation of the comparative study of religions. But his description of religion has been criticized by biblical theologians such as Barth, on the ground that it leaves largely out of account the scriptural sources of Christian faith.

His *Christian Faith*, written much later than his powerful and revolutionary *Speeches*, contains S.'s mature elaboration of a systematic philosophical theology on the basis of his original insights. It is perhaps Protestantism's nearest rival to the *Summa Theologica*.

Bibliographical Note There are translations of the *Speeches* by J. Oman (London, 1893; Harper Torchbooks, N.Y., 1958), of the *Monologen* by H. L. Friess (Chicago, 1926) and *The Christian Faith* by H. R. Mackintosh, J. S. Stewart and others (Edinburgh, 1928). Accounts and criticisms of S. are found in G. Cross, *The Theology of Schleiermacher* (Chicago, 1911); W. B. Selbie, *The Great Christian Theologies* (London, 1913); J. A. Chapman, *An Introduction to Schleiermacher* (London, 1932); R. B. Brandt, *The Philosophy of Schleiermacher* (N.Y., 1941) and K. Barth, *From Rousseau to Ritschl* (London, 1959) and *Theology and Church* (London, 1962).

A. RELIGIOUS EXPERIENCE

The Christian Faith, I, §4 f.

§4. *The common element in all howsoever diverse expressions of piety, by which these are conjointly distinguished from all other feelings, or, in other words, the self-identical essence of piety, is this: the consciousness of being absolutely dependent, or, which is the same thing, of being in relation with God.*

1. In any actual state of consciousness, no matter whether it merely accompanies a thought or action or occupies a moment for itself, we are never simply conscious of our selves in their unchanging identity, but are always at the same time conscious of a changing determination of them. The ego in itself can be represented objectively; but every consciousness of self is at the same time the consciousness of a variable state of being. But in this distinction of the latter from the former, it is implied that the variable does not proceed purely from the self-identical, for in that case it could not be distinguished from it. Thus in every self-consciousness there are two elements, which we might call respectively a self-caused element and a non-self-caused element; or a being and a having-by-some-means-come-to-be. The latter of these presupposes for every self-consciousness another factor besides the ego, a factor which is the course of the particular determination, and without which the self-consciousness would not be precisely what it is. But this other is not objectively presented in the immediate self-consciousness with which alone we are here concerned. For though, of course, the double constitution of self-consciousness causes us always to look objectively for an other to which we can trace the origin of our particular state, yet this search is a separate act with which we are not at present concerned. In self-consciousness there are only two elements: the one expresses the existence of the subject for itself, the other its co-existence with an other.

Now to these two elements, as they exist together in the temporal self-consciousness, correspond in the subject its *receptivity* and its (spontaneous) *activity*. If we could think away the co-existence with an other, but otherwise think ourselves as we are, then a self-consciousness which predominantly expressed an affective condition of receptivity would be impossible, and any self-consciousness could then express only activity—an activity, however, which, not being directed to any object, would be merely an urge outwards, an indefinite 'agility' without form or colour. But as we never do exist except along with an other, so even in every outward-tending self-consciousness the element of receptivity, in some way or other affected, is the primary one; and even the self-consciousness which accompanies an action (acts of knowing included), while it predominately expresses spontaneous movement and activity, is always related (though the relation is often a quite indefinite one) to a prior moment of affective reciprocity, through which the original 'agility' received its direction. To these propositions assent can be unconditionally demanded; and no one will deny them who is capable of a little introspection and can find interest in the real subject of our present enquiries.

2. The common element in all those determinations of self-consciousness

which predominately express a receptivity affected from some outside quarter is the *feeling of dependence*. On the other hand, the common element in all those determinations which predominately express spontaneous movement and activity is the *feeling of freedom*. The former is the case not only because it is by an influence from some other quarter that we have come to such a state, but particularly because we could not so become except by means of an other. The latter is the case because in these instances an other is determined by us, and without our spontaneous activity could not be so determined. These two definitions may, indeed, seem to be incomplete, inasmuch as there is also a mobility of the subject which is not connected with an other at all, but which seems to be subject to the same antithesis as that just explained. But when we become such-and-such from within outwards, for ourselves, without any other being involved, that is the simple situation of the temporal development of a being which remains essentially self-identical, and it is only very improperly that this can be referred to the concept 'freedom'. And when we cannot ourselves, from within outwards, become such-and-such, this only indicates the limits which belong to the nature of the subject itself as regards spontaneous activity, and this could only very improperly be called 'dependence'.

Further, this antithesis must on no account be confused with the antithesis between gloomy or depressing and elevating or joyful feelings, of which we shall speak later. For a feeling of dependence may be elevating, if the 'having become such-and-such' which it expresses is complete; and similarly a feeling of freedom may be dejecting, if the moment of predominating receptivity to which the action can be traced was of a dejecting nature, or again if the manner and method of the activity prove to be a disadvantageous combination.

Let us now think of the feeling of dependence and the feeling of freedom as *one*, in the sense that not only the subject but the corresponding other is the same in both. Then the total self-consciousness made up of both together is one of *reciprocity* between the subject and the corresponding other. Now let us suppose the totality of all moments of feeling, of both kinds, as one whole: then the corresponding other is also to be supposed as a totality or as one, and then that term 'reciprocity' is the right one for our self-consciousness in general, inasmuch as it expresses our connexion with everything which either appeals to our receptivity or is subjected to our activity. And this is true not only when we particularize this other and ascribe to each of its elements a different degree of relation to the twofold consciousness within us, but also when we think of the total 'outside' as one, and moreover (since it contains other receptivities and activities to which we have a relation) as one together with ourselves, that is, *as a world.* Accordingly our self-consciousness of our existence in the world or of our co-existence with the world, is a series in which the feeling of freedom and the feeling of dependence are divided. But neither an absolute feeling of dependence, i.e. without any feeling of freedom in relation to the co-determinant, nor an absolute feeling of freedom, i.e. without any feeling of dependence in relation to the co-determinant, is to be found in this whole realm. If we consider our relations to Nature, or those which exist in human society, there we shall find a large number of objects in regard to which freedom and dependence maintain very much of an equipoise: these constitute the field of equal reciprocity. There are other objects which exercise a far greater influence upon our receptivity than our activity exercises upon them, and also *vice versa*, so that one of the two may diminish until it is imperceptible. But neither of the two members will ever completely disappear. The feeling of dependence predominates in the relation of children to their parents, or of citizens to their fatherland; and yet individuals can, without losing their relationship, exercise upon their fatherland not only a directive influence, but even a counter-influence. And the dependence of children on their parents, which very soon comes to be felt as a gradually diminishing and fading quantity, is never from the start free from the admixture of an element of spontaneous activity towards the parents: just as even in the most absolute autocracy the ruler is not without some slight feeling of dependence. It is the same in the case of Nature: towards all the forces of Nature—even, we may say, towards the heavenly bodies—we ourselves do, in the same sense in which they influence us, exercise a counter-influence, however minute. So that our whole self-consciousness in relation to the world or its individual parts remains enclosed within these limits.

3. There can, accordingly, be for us no such thing as a feeling of absolute freedom. He who asserts that he has such a feeling is either deceiving himself or separating things which essentially belong together. For if the feeling of freedom expresses a forth-going activity, this activity must have an object which has been somehow given to us, and this could not have taken place without an influence of the object upon our receptivity. Therefore in every such case there is involved a feeling of dependence which goes along with the feeling of freedom, and thus limits it. The contrary could only be possible if the object altogether came into existence through our activity, which is never the case absolutely, but only relatively. But if, on the other hand, the feeling of freedom expresses only an inward movement of activity, not only is every such individual movement bound up with the state of our stimulated receptivity at the moment, but,

further, the totality of our free inward movements, considered as a unity, cannot be represented as a feeling of absolute freedom, because our whole existence does not present itself to our consciousness as having proceeded from our own spontaneous activity. Therefore in any temporal existence a feeling of absolute freedom can have no place. As regards the feeling of absolute dependence which, on the other hand, our proposition does postulate: for just the same reason, this feeling cannot arise from the influence of an object which has in some way to be *given* to us; for upon such an object there would always be a counter-influence, and even a voluntary renunciation of this would always involve a feeling of freedom. Hence a feeling of absolute dependence, strictly speaking, cannot exist in a single moment as such, because such a moment is always determined, as regards its total content, by what is *given*, and thus by objects towards which we have a feeling of freedom. But the self-consciousness which accompanies all our activity and therefore, since that is never zero, accompanies our whole existence, and negatives absolute freedom, is itself precisely a consciousness of absolute dependence; for it is the consciousness that the whole of our spontaneous activity comes from a source outside of us in just the same sense in which anything towards which we should have a feeling of absolute freedom must have proceeded entirely from ourselves. But without any feeling of freedom a feeling of absolute dependence would not be possible.

4. As regards the identification of absolute dependence with 'relation to God' in our proposition: this is to be understood in the sense that the *Whence* of our receptive and active existence, as implied in this self-consciousness, is to be designated by the word 'God', and that this is for us the really original signification of that word. In this connexion we have first of all to remind ourselves that, as we have seen in the foregoing discussion, this 'Whence' is not the world, in the sense of the totality of temporal existence, and still less is it any single part of the world. For we have a feeling of freedom (though, indeed, a limited one) in relation to the world, since we are complementary parts of it, and also since we are continually exercising an influence on its individual parts; and, moreover, there is the possibility of our exercising influence on all its parts; and while this does permit a limited feeling of dependence, it excludes the absolute feeling. In the next place, we have to note that our proposition is intended to oppose the view that this feeling of dependence is itself conditioned by some previous knowledge about God. And this may indeed be the more necessary since many people claim to be in the sure possession of a concept of God, altogether a matter of conception and original, i.e. independent of any feeling; and in the strength of this higher self-consciousness,

which indeed may come pretty near to being a feeling of absolute freedom, they put far from them, as something almost infra-human, that very feeling which for us is the basic type of all piety. Now our proposition is in no wise intended to dispute the existence of such an original knowledge, but simply to set it aside as something with which, in a system of Christian doctrine, we could never have any concern, because plainly enough it has itself nothing to do directly with piety. If, however, word and idea are always originally one, and the term 'God' therefore presupposes an idea, then we shall simply say that this idea, which is nothing more than the expression of the feeling of absolute dependence, is the most direct reflection upon it and the most original idea with which we are here concerned, and is quite independent of that original knowledge (properly so called), and conditioned only by our feeling of absolute dependence. So that in the first instance God signifies for us simply that which is the co-determinant in this feeling and to which we trace our being in such a state; and any further content of the idea must be evolved out of this fundamental import assigned to it. Now this is just what is principally meant by the formula which says that to feel oneself absolutely dependent and to be conscious of being in relation with God are one and the same thing; and the reason is that absolute dependence is the fundamental relation which must include all others in itself. This last expression includes the God-consciousness in the self-consciousness in such a way that, quite in accordance with the above analysis, the two cannot be separated from each other. The feeling of absolute dependence becomes a clear self-consciousness only as this idea comes simultaneously into being. In this sense it can indeed be said that God is given to us in feeling in an original way; and if we speak of an original revelation of God to man or in man, the meaning will always be just this, that, along with the absolute dependence which characterizes not only man but all temporal existence, there is given to man also the immediate self-consciousness of it, which becomes a consciousness of God. In whatever measure this actually takes place during the course of a personality through time, in just that measure do we ascribe piety to the individual. On the other hand, any possibility of God being in any way *given* is entirely excluded, because anything that is outwardly given must be given as an object exposed to our counter-influence, however slight this may be. The transference of the idea of God to any perceptible object, unless one is all the time conscious that it is a piece of purely arbitrary symbolism, is always a corruption, whether it be a temporary transference, i.e. a theophany, or a constitutive transference, in which God is represented as permanently a particular perceptible existence.

§5. *What we have thus described constitutes the highest grade of human self-consciousness; but in its actual occurrence it is never separated from the lower, and through its combination therewith in a single moment it participates in the antithesis of the pleasant and the unpleasant.*

1. The relation between these two forms of self-consciousness, namely the feeling of absolute dependence and the self-consciousness which, as expressing the connexion with perceptible finite existence, splits up into a partial feeling of dependence and a partial feeling of freedom, will best be seen if we bring in yet a third form. If we go back to the first obscure period of the life of man, we find there, all over, the animal life almost solely predominating, and the spiritual life as yet entirely in the background; and so we must regard the state of his consciousness as closely akin to that of the lower animals. It is true, indeed, that the animal state is to us really entirely strange and unknown. But there is general agreement that, on the one hand, the lower animals have no knowledge, properly so called, nor any self-consciousness which combines the different moments into a stable unity, and that, on the other hand, they are nevertheless not entirely devoid of consciousness. Now we can hardly do justice to this state of affairs except by postulating a consciousness of such a sort that in it the objective and the introversive, or feeling and perception, are not really distinct from each other, but remain in a state of unresolved confusion. The consciousness of children obviously approximates to this form, especially before they learn to speak. From that time on, this condition tends more and more to disappear, confining itself to those dreamy moments which form the transition between sleep and waking; while in our wideawake hours feeling and perception are clearly distinct from each other, and thus make up the whole wealth of man's sensible life, in the widest sense of the term. In that term we include (speaking simply of the consciousness, and leaving out action proper), on the one hand, the gradual accumulation of perceptions which constitute the whole field of experience in the widest sense of the word, and, on the other hand, all determinations of self-consciousness which develop from our relations to nature and to man, including those which we described above (§4.2) as coming nearest to the feeling of absolute dependence; so that by the word 'sensible' we understand the social and moral feelings no less than the self-regarding, since they all together have their place in that realm of the particular which is subject to the above-mentioned antithesis. The former division (i.e the accumulation of perceptions) which belongs to the objective consciousness, we pass over, as it does not concern us here. But in the whole of the latter class, consisting of feelings which we have designated

sensible, the corresponding co-determinant to which we trace the constitution of the present state belongs to the realm of reciprocal action; so that, whether we are at the moment more conscious of dependence or of freedom, we take up towards it, in a sense, an attitude of equal co-ordination, and indeed set ourselves as individuals (or as comprised within a large individual as, e.g., in our patriotic feelings) over against it as another individual. Now it is in this respect that these feelings are most definitely distinguished from the feeling of absolute dependence. For while the latter from its very nature negatives absolute freedom (§4.3), though it does it under the form of self-consciousness, this is not the consciousness of ourselves as individuals of a particular description, but simply of ourselves as individual finite existence in general; so that we do not set ourselves over against any other individual being, but, on the contrary, all antithesis between one individual and another is in this case done away. Hence there seems to be no objection to our distinguishing three grades of self-consciousness: the confused animal grade, in which the antithesis cannot arise, as the lowest; the sensible self-consciousness, which rests entirely upon the antithesis, as the middle; and the feeling of absolute dependence, in which the antithesis again disappears and the subject unites and identifies itself with everything which, in the middle grade, was set over against it, as the highest.

2. If there did exist a feeling of absolute freedom, in it also the above antithesis would be done away. Only, such a subject could never stand in any relation with other similarly constituted subjects, but whatever is given to it must be given as purely susceptible or passive material. And since, for this reason alone, such a feeling is never found in man, the only immediate self-consciousness in man on that grade is the feeling of absolute dependence which we have described. For every moment which is made up of a partial feeling of dependence places us in a position of co-ordinate antithesis to a similar other. But now there remains the question whether there exists any other self-consciousness, not immediate but accompanying some kind of knowledge or action as such, which can be ranked along with that which we have described. Let us then conceive, as the act or state of an individual, a highest kind of knowledge in which all subordinate knowledge is comprised. This, indeed, in its province is likewise elevated above all antithesis. But its province is that of the objective consciousness. However, it will of course be accompanied by an immediate self-consciousness expressive of certainty or conviction. But since this concerns the relation of the subject as knower to the known as object, even this self-consciousness which accompanies the highest knowledge remains in the realm of the antithesis. In the same way, let us

conceive a highest kind of action, in the form of a resolve which covers the whole field of spontaneous activity, so that all subsequent resolves are developed out of it, as individual parts, which were already contained in it. This also in its province stands above all antithesis, and it is likewise accompanied by a self-consciousness. But this also concerns the relation of the subject as agent to that which may be the object of its action, and thus has its place within the antithesis. And since obviously this must be equally true of every self-consciousness which accompanies any particular knowledge or action, it follows that there is no other self-consciousness which is elevated above the antithesis, and that this character belongs exclusively to the feeling of absolute dependence.

3. While the lowest or animal grade of consciousness gradually disappears as the middle grade develops, the highest cannot develop at all so long as the lowest is present; but, on the other hand, the middle grade must persist undiminished even when the highest has reached its perfect development. The highest self-consciousness is in no wise dependent on outwardly given objects which may affect us at one moment and not at another. As a consciousness of absolute dependence it is quite simple, and remains self-identical while all other states are changing. Therefore, in itself it cannot possibly be at one moment thus and at another moment otherwise, nor can it by intermission be present at one moment and absent at another. Either it is not there at all, or, so long as it is there, it is continuously there and always self-identical. Now if it were impossible for it to co-exist with the consciousness of the second grade (as it cannot with that of the third), then either it could never make an appearance in time, but would always remain in the concealment in which it lay during the predominance of the lowest grade, or it must drive out the second and exist alone, and, indeed, in ever-unchanging identity. Now this latter supposition is controverted by all experience, and indeed is manifestly impossible unless our ideation and action are to be entirely stripped of self-consciousness, which would irrevocably destroy the coherence of our existence for our own minds. It is impossible to claim a constancy for the highest self-consciousness except on the supposition that the sensible self-consciousness is always conjoined with it. Of course, this conjunction cannot be regarded as a fusion of the two: that would be entirely opposed to the conception of both of them which we have established. It means rather a co-existence of the two in the same moment, which, of course, unless the ego is to be split up, involves a reciprocal relation of the two. It is impossible for anyone to be in some moments exclusively conscious of his relations within the realm of the antithesis, and in other moments of his absolute dependence in itself and in a general way; for it is as a person

determined for this moment in a particular manner within the realm of the antithesis that he is conscious of his absolute dependence. This relatedness of the sensibly determined to the higher self-consciousness in the unity of the moment is the consummating point of the self-consciousness. For to the man who once recognizes what piety is, and appropriates it as a requirement of his being, every moment of a merely sensible self-consciousness is a defective and imperfect state. But even if the feeling of absolute dependence in general were the entire content of a moment of self-consciousness, this also would be an imperfect state; for it would lack the definiteness and clearness which spring from its being related to the determination of the sensible self-consciousness. This consummation, however, since it consists in the two elements being related to each other, may be described in two different ways. Described from below it is as follows: when the sensible self-consciousness has quite expelled the animal confusion, then there is disclosed a higher tendency over against the antithesis, and the expression of this tendency in the self-consciousness is the feeling of absolute dependence. And the more the subject, in each moment of sensible self-consciousness, with his partial freedom and partial dependence, takes at the same time the attitude of absolute dependence, the more religious is he. Described from above it is as follows: the tendency which we have described, as an original and innate tendency of the human soul, strives from the very beginning to break through into consciousness. But it is unable to do so as long as the antithesis remains dissolved in the animal confusion. Subsequently, however, it asserts itself. And the more it contributes to every moment of sensibly determined self-consciousness without the omission of any, so that the man, while he always feels himself partially free and partially dependent in relation to other finite existence, feels himself at the same time to be also (along with everything towards which he had that former feeling) absolutely dependent—the more religious is he.

4. The sensibly determined self-consciousness splits up of itself, in accordance with its nature, into a series of moments that differ in their content, because our activity exercised upon other beings is a temporal one, and their influence upon us is likewise temporal. The feeling of absolute dependence, on the other hand, being in itself always self-identical, would not evoke a series of thus distinguishable moments; and if it did not enter into relation with such a series in the manner described above, either it could never become an actual consciousness in time at all, or else it must accompany the sensible self-consciousness monotonously without any relation to the manifold rising and falling variations of the latter. But, as a matter of fact, our religious consciousness does not take

either of these forms, but conforms to the description we have given above. That is to say: being related as a constituent factor to a given moment of consciousness which consists of a partial feeling of freedom and a partial feeling of dependence it thereby becomes a particular religious emotion, and being in another moment related to a different datum, it becomes a different religious emotion; yet so that the essential element, namely the feeling of absolute dependence, is the same in both, and thus throughout the whole series, and the difference arises simply from the fact that it becomes a different moment when it goes along with a different determination of the sensible self-consciousness. It remains always, however, a moment of the higher power; whereas, where there is no piety at all, the sensible self-consciousness breaks up (as was likewise described) into a series of moments of the lower power, while in the period of animal confusion there does not even take place a definite separation and antithesis of the moments for the subject.

It is the same with the second part of our proposition. That is to say: the sensible self-consciousness splits up also, of itself and from its very nature, into the antithesis of the pleasant and unpleasant, or of pleasure and pain. This does not mean that the partial feeling of freedom is always pleasure, and the partial feeling of dependence always pain, as seems to be assumed by those who wrongly think that the feeling of absolute dependence has, of its very nature, a depressing effect. For the child can have a feeling of perfect well-being in the consciousness of dependence on its parents, and so also (thank God) can the subject in his relation to the government; and other people, even parents and governments, can feel miserable in the consciousness of their freedom. So that each may equally well be either pleasure or pain, according to whether life is furthered or hindered by it. The higher self-consciousness, on the other hand, bears within it no such antithesis. Its first appearance means, of course, an enhancement of life, if a comparison arises with the isolated sensible self-consciousness. But if, without any such reference, we think of it in its own self-identity, its effect is simply as unchanging identity of life, which excludes any such antithesis. This state we speak of under the name of the blessedness of the finite being as the highest summit of his perfection. But our religious consciousness, as we actually find it, is not of that character, but is subject to variation, some pious emotions approximating more to joy, and others to sorrow. Thus this antithesis refers simply to the manner in which the two grades of self-consciousness are related to each other in the unity of the moment. And thus it is by no means the case that the pleasant and the unpleasant, which exist in the sensible feeling, impart the same character to the feeling of absolute dependence. On the contrary, we often find, united in one and the same moment (as a clear sign that the two grades are not fused into each other or neutralized by each other so as to become a third) a sorrow of the lower and a joy of the higher self-consciousness; as, e.g., whenever with a feeling of suffering there is combined a trust in God. But the antithesis attaches to the higher self-consciousness, because it is the nature of the latter to become temporal, to manifest itself in time, by entering into relation with the sensible self-consciousness so as to constitute a moment. That is to say: as the emergence of this higher self-consciousness at all means an enhancement of life, so whenever it emerges *with ease*, to enter into relation with a sensible determination, whether pleasant or unpleasant, this means an easy progress of that higher life, and bears, by comparison, the stamp of joy. And as the disappearance of the higher consciousness, if it could be perceived, would mean a diminution of life, so whenever it emerges *with difficulty*, this approximates to an absence of it, and can only be felt as an inhibition of the higher life.

Now this alternation undeniably forms the feeling-content of every religious life, so that it seemed superfluous to illustrate these formulae by examples. But we may now go on to ask how this usual course of the religious life is related to that which we have at an earlier point described, if only problematically, as the highest development of it. Suppose that the opposite characters are both continuously being strongly imprinted upon the individual religious emotions, so that both alternately rise to a passionate level: this gives to the religious life an instability which we cannot regard as of the highest worth. But suppose that the difficulties gradually disappear, so that facility of religious emotions becomes a permanent state; and that gradually the higher grade of feeling comes to preponderate over the lower, so that in the immediate self-consciousness the sensible determination asserts itself rather as an opportunity for the appearance of the feeling of absolute dependence than as containing the antithesis, which is therefore transferred into the realm of mere perception;[1] then this fact, that the antithesis has almost disappeared again from the higher grade of life, indisputably means that the latter has attained its richest content of feeling.

5. From the above it follows directly that (and in what sense) an uninterrupted sequence of religious emotions can be required of us, as indeed Scripture actually requires it; and it is confirmed every time a religious soul laments over a moment of his life which is quite empty of the consciousness of God (since no one laments the absence of anything which is recognized to be impossible). Of course, it goes without saying in this

[1] That is, transferred from the realm of feeling to that of perception.

connexion that the feeling of absolute dependence, when it unites with a sensibly determined self-consciousness, and thus becomes an emotion, must vary as regards strength. Indeed, there will naturally be moments in which a man is not definitely and directly conscious of such a feeling at all. And yet, indirectly, it can be shown that in these moments the feeling was not dead; as, e.g. when such a moment is followed by another in which the feeling strongly asserts itself, while the second is not felt to be of a different character from the first or a definite departure from it, but to be linked up with it tranquilly as a continuation of its essentially unchanged identity (which is not the case when the preceding moment was one from which the feeling was definitely excluded). Also, of course, the different formations assumed by the sensible self-consciousness in virtue of the highly manifold minglings of the feeling of freedom and the feeling of dependence, differ in the degree in which they evoke or encourage the appearance of the higher self-consciousness; and in the case of those which do it in a lesser degree, a weaker appearance of the higher need not be felt as an inhibition of the higher life. But there is no determination of the immediate sensible self-consciousness which is incompatible with the higher; so that there is no kind of necessity for either of the two ever to be interrupted, except when the confused state of consciousness gains ground, and both retire behind it.

Postscript. If thus the direct inward expression of the feeling of absolute dependence is the consciousness of God, and that feeling, whenever it attains to a certain clearness, is accompanied by such an expression, but is also combined with, and related to, a sensible self-consciousness: then the God-consciousness which has in this way arisen will, in all its particular formations, carry with it such determinations as belong to the realm of the antithesis in which the sensible self-consciousness moves. And this is the source of all those anthropomorphic elements which are inevitable in this realm in utterances about God, and which form such a cardinal point in the ever-recurring controversy between those who accept that fundamental assumption and those who deny it. For those who rejoice in the possession of an original of the Supreme Being derived from some other quarter, but who have no experience of piety, will not tolerate the statement that the expression of that feeling posits the action of the very same thing which is expressed in their original idea. They assert that the God of feeling is a mere fiction, an idol, and they may perhaps even hint that such a fancy is more tenable in the form of polytheism. And those who will not admit either a conception of God or a feeling which represents him, base their position on the contention that the representation of God which is put together out of such utterances, in which God appears as human, destroys itself. Meanwhile, religious men know that it is only in speech that they cannot avoid the anthropomorphic: in their immediate consciousness they keep the object separate from its mode of representation, and they endeavour to show their opponents that without this integration of feeling no certainty is possible even for the strongest forms of objective consciousness or of transitive action, and that, to be consistent, they must limit themselves entirely to the lower grade of life.

B. RELIGIOUS LANGUAGE

The Christian Faith, I, §15 ff.

§15. *Christian doctrines are accounts of the Christian religious affections set forth in speech.*

1. All religious emotions, to whatever type and level of religion they belong, have this in common with all other modifications of the affective self-consciousness, that as soon as they have reached a certain stage and a certain definiteness they manifest themselves outwardly by mimicry in the most direct and spontaneous way, by means of facial features and movements of voice and gesture, which we regard as their expression. Thus we definitely distinguish the expression of devoutness from that of a sensuous gladness or sadness, by the analogy of each man's knowledge of himself. Indeed, we can even conceive that, for the purpose of maintaining the religious affections and securing their repetition and propagation (especially if they were common to a number of people), the elements of that natural expression of them might be put together into sacred signs and symbolical acts, without the thought having perceptibly come in between at all. But we can scarcely conceive such a low development of the human spirit, such a defective culture, and such a meagre use of speech, that each person would not, according to the level of reflection on which he stands, become in his various mental states likewise an object to himself, in order to comprehend them in idea and retain them in the form of thought. Now this endeavour has always directed itself particularly to the religious emotions; and this, considered in its own inward meaning, is what our proposition means by an account of the religious affections. But while thought cannot proceed even inwardly without the use of speech, nevertheless there are, so long as it remains merely inward, fugitive elements in this procedure, which do indeed in some measure indicate the object, but not in such a way that either the formation or the synthesis of concepts (in however wide a sense we take the

word 'concept') is sufficiently definite for communication. It is only when this procedure has reached such a point of cultivation as to be able to represent itself outwardly in definite speech, that it produces a real doctrine,[1] by means of which the utterances of the religious consciousness come into circulation more surely and with a wider range than is possible through the direct expression. But no matter whether the expression is natural or figurative, whether it indicates its object directly or only by comparison and delimitation, it is still a doctrine.

2. Now Christianity everywhere presupposes that consciousness has reached this stage of development. The whole work of the Redeemer himself was conditioned by the communicability of his self-consciousness by means of speech, and similarly Christianity has always and everywhere spread itself solely by preaching. Every proposition which can be an element of the Christian preaching (κήρυγμα) is also a doctrine, because it bears witness to the determination of the religious self-consciousness as inward certainty. And every Christian doctrine is also part of the Christian preaching, because every such doctrine expresses as a certainty the approximation to the state of blessedness which is to be effected through the means ordained by Christ. But this preaching very soon split up into three different types of speech, which provide as many different forms of doctrine: the poetic, the rhetorical (which is directed partly outwards, as combative and commendatory, and partly inwards, as rather disciplinary and challenging), and finally the descriptively didactic. But the relation of communication through speech to communication through symbolic action varies very much according to time and place, the former having always retreated into the background in the Eastern Church (for when the letter of doctrine has become fixed and unalterable, it is in its effect much nearer to symbolic action than to free speech), and having become ever more prominent in the Western Church. And in the realm of speech it is just the same with these three modes of communication. The relation in which they stand to each other, the general degree of richness, and the amount of living intercourse in which they unfold themselves, as they nourish themselves on one another—these things testify not so much to the degree or level of piety as rather to the character of the communion or fellowship and its ripeness for reflection and contemplation. Thus this communication is, on the one hand, something different from the piety itself, though the latter cannot, any more than anything else which is human, be conceived entirely separated from all communication. But, on the other hand, the doctrines in all their forms have their ultimate ground so exclusively in the emotions of the

[1] *Glaubenssatz.*

religious self-consciousness, that where these do not exist the doctrines cannot arise.

§16. *Dogmatic propositions are doctrines of the descriptively didactic type, in which the highest possible degree of definiteness is aimed at.*

1. The poetic expression is always based originally upon a moment of exaltation which has come purely from within, a moment of enthusiasm or inspiration; the rhetorical upon a moment whose exaltation has come from without, a moment of stimulated interest which issues in a particular definite result. The former is purely descriptive, and sets up in general outlines images and forms which each hearer completes for himself in his own peculiar way. The rhetorical is purely stimulative, and has, in its nature, to do for the most part with such elements of speech as, admitting of degrees of signification, can be taken in a wider or narrower sense, content if at the decisive moment they can accomplish the highest, even though they should exhaust themselves thereby and subsequently appear to lose somewhat of their force. Thus both of these forms possess a different perfection from the logical or dialectical perfection described in our proposition. But, nevertheless, we can think of both as being primary and original in every religious communion, and thus in the Christian Church, in so far as we ascribe to everyone in it a share in the vocation of preaching. For when anyone finds himself in a state of unusually exalted religious self-consciousness, he will feel himself called to poetic description, that which proceeds from this state most directly. And, on the other hand, when anyone finds himself particularly challenged by insistent or favourable outward circumstances to attempt an act of preaching, the rhetorical form of expression will be the most natural to him for obtaining from the given circumstances the greatest possible advantage. But let us conceive of the comprehension and appropriation of what is given in a direct way in these two forms, as being now also wedded to language and thereby made communicable: then this cannot again take the poetic form, nor yet the rhetorical; but, being independent of that which was the important element in those two forms, and expressing as it does a consciousness which remains self-identical, it becomes, less as preaching than as confession (ὁμολογία), precisely that third form—the didactic—which, with its descriptive instruction, remains distinct from the two others, and is made up of the two put together, as a derivative and secondary form.

2. But let us confine ourselves to Christianity, and think of its distinctive beginning, namely the self-proclamation of Christ, who, as subject of the divine revelation, could not contain in himself any distinction of stronger and weaker emotion, but could only partake in such a diversity through

his common life with others. Then we shall not be able to take either the poetic or the rhetorical form of expression as the predominating, or even as the really primary and original, form of his self-proclamation. These have only a subordinate place in parabolic and prophetic discourses. The essential thing in his self-proclamation was that he had to bear witness regarding his ever unvarying self-consciousness out of the depths of its self-repose, and consequently not in poetic but in strictly reflective form; and thus had to set himself forth, while at the same time communicating his alone true objective consciousness of the condition and constitution of men in general, thus instructing by description or representation, the instruction sometimes being subordinate to the description, and sometimes *vice versa*. But this descriptively didactic mode of expression used by Christ is not included in our proposition, and such utterances of the Redeemer will hardly be set up anywhere as dogmatic propositions; they will only, as it were, provide the text for them. For in such essential parts of the self-proclamation of Christ the definiteness was absolute, and it is only the perfection of the apprehension and appropriation which reproduces these, that can be characterized by the endeavour after the greatest possible definiteness. Subordinate to these, however, there do appear genuinely dogmatic propositions in the discourses of Christ, namely at those points at which he had to start from the partly erroneous and partly confused ideas current among his contemporaries.

3. As regards the poetic and rhetorical forms of expression, it follows directly from what we have said, that they may fall into apparent contradiction both with themselves and with each other, even when the self-consciousness which is indicated by different forms of expression is in itself one and the same. And a solution will only be possible, in the first place, when it is possible in interpreting expressions that are apparently contradictory to take one's bearings from the original utterances of Christ (a thing which can in very few cases be done directly), and, in the second place, when the descriptively didactic expression, which has grown out of those three original forms put together, is entirely or largely free from these apparent contradictions. This, however, will not be possible of achievement so long as the descriptively didactic expression itself keeps vacillating between the emotional and the didactic, in its presentation to the catechumens or the community, and approaches sometimes more to the rhetorical and sometimes more to the figurative. It will only be possible in proportion as the aim indicated in our proposition underlies the further development of the expression and its more definite separation from the rhetorical and the poetic, both of which processes are bound up with the need of settling the conflict. Now, of

course, this demand, that the figurative expression be either exchanged for a literal one or transformed into such by being explained, and that definite limits be imposed on the corresponding element in the rhetorical expressions, is unmistakably the interest which science has in the formation of language; and it is mainly with the formation of religious language that we are here concerned. Hence dogmatic propositions develop to any considerable extent and gain recognition only in such religious communions as have reached a degree of culture in which science[1] is organized as something distinct both from art and from business, and only in proportion as friends of science are found and have influence within the communion itself, so that the dialectical function is brought to bear on the utterances of the religious self-consciousness, and guides the expression of them. Such a union with organized knowledge has had a place in Christianity ever since the earliest ages of the Church, and therefore in no other religious communion has the form of the dogmatic proposition evolved in such strict separation from the other forms, or developed in such fulness.

Postscript. This account of the origin of dogmatic propositions, as having arisen solely out of logically ordered reflection upon the immediate utterances of the religious self-consciousness, finds its confirmation in the whole of history. The earliest specimens of preaching preserved for us in the New Testament scriptures already contain such propositions; and on closer consideration we can see in all of them, in the first place, their derivation from the original self-proclamation of Christ, and, in the second place, their affinity to figurative and rhetorical elements which, for permanent circulation, had to approximate more to the strictness of a formula. Similarly in later periods it is clear that the figurative language, which is always poetic in its nature, had the most decided influence upon the dogmatic language, and always preceded its development, and also that the majority of the dogmatic definitions were called forth by contradictions to which the rhetorical expressions had led.

But when the transformation of the original expressions into dogmatic propositions is ascribed to the logical or dialectical interest, this is to be understood as applying only to the form. A proposition which had originally proceeded from the speculative activity, however akin it might be to our propositions in content, would not be a dogmatic proposition. The purely scientific activity, whose task is the contemplation of existence, must, if it is to come to anything, either begin or end with the Supreme Being; and so there may be forms of philosophy containing propositions of speculative import about the Supreme Being which, in spite of the fact

[1] 'Science' here means 'organized knowledge', and does not merely comprise science in the modern sense.

that they arose out of the purely scientific interest, are, when taken individually, difficult to distinguish from the corresponding propositions which arose purely out of reflection upon the religious emotions, but have been worked out dialectically. But when they are considered in their connexions, these two indubitably show differences of the most definite kind. For dogmatic propositions never make their original appearance except in trains of thought which have received their impulse from religious moods of mind; whereas, not only do speculative propositions about the Supreme Being appear for the most part in purely logical or natural-scientific[1] trains of thought, but even when they come in as ethical presuppositions and corollaries, they show an unmistakable leaning towards one or other of those two directions. Moreover, in the dogmatic developments of the earliest centuries, if we discount the quite unecclesiastical Gnostic schools, the influence of speculation upon the content of dogmatic propositions may be placed at zero. At a later time, certainly, when the classical organization of knowledge had fallen in ruins, and the conglomerate-philosophy of the Middle Ages took shape within the Christian Church, and at the same time came to exercise its influence upon the formation of dogmatic language, a confusion of the speculative with the dogmatic, and consequently a mingling of the two, was almost inevitable. But this was for both an imperfect condition, from which philosophy freed itself by means of the avowal, growing ever gradually louder, that at that time it had stood under the tutelage of ecclesiastical faith, and therefore under an alien law. Having, however, since then made so many fresh starts in its own proper development, it was able to escape the wearisome task of enquiring exactly as to what kind of speculative propositions were at that time taken to be dogmatic, and *vice versa*. For the Christian Church, however, which is not in a position ever and anon to begin the development of its doctrine over again from the start, this separation is of the greatest importance, in order to secure that speculative matter (by which neither the poetic and rhetorical nor the popular expression can consent to be guided) may not continue to be offered to it as dogmatic. The Evangelical (Protestant) Church in particular is unanimous in feeling that the distinctive form of its dogmatic propositions does not depend on any form of school of philosophy, and has not proceeded at all from a speculative interest, but simply from the interest of satisfying the immediate self-consciousness solely through the means ordained by Christ, in their genuine and uncorrupted form. Thus it can consistently adopt as dogmatic propositions of its own no propositions except such as can show their derivation. Our dogmatic theology will not, however, stand on its

[1] Natural science, as distinguished from other branches of organized knowledge.

own proper ground and soil with the same assurance with which philosophy has so long stood upon its own, until the separation of the two types of proposition is so complete that, e.g. so extraordinary a question as whether the same proposition can be true in philosophy and false in Christian theology, and *vice versa*, can no longer be asked, for the simple reason that a proposition cannot appear in the one context precisely as it appears in the other: however similar it sounds, a difference must always be assumed. But we are still very far from this goal, so long as people take pains to base or deduce dogmatic propositions in the speculative manner, or even set themselves to work up the products of speculative activity and the results of the study of religious affections into a single whole.

§17. *Dogmatic propositions have a twofold value—an ecclesiastical and a scientific; and their degree of perfection is determined by both of these and their relation to each other.*

1. The ecclesiastical value of a dogmatic proposition consists in its reference to the religious emotions themselves. Every such emotion, regarded singly, is indeed for description an infinite, and all dogmatic concepts, as well as all concepts of psychology, would have to be used to describe one moment of life. But just as in such a moment the religious strain may be the dominant one, so again in every such strain some one relation of the higher self-consciousness stands out as determinative; and it is to this strain, uniformly for all analogous moments of religious emotion, that the dogmatic propositions refer. Thus, in all completely expressed dogmatic propositions, the reference to Christ as Redeemer must appear with the same measure of prominence which it has in the religious consciousness itself. Naturally, however, this is not equally strongly the case in all religious moments, any more than in the life of any civic state the distinctive character of its constitution can appear equally strongly in all moments. Accordingly, the less strongly the reference to Christ is expressed in a dogmatic proposition, as, e.g., in the religious emotion mediated by our relation to the external world, the more easily may it resemble a doctrinal proposition of another religious communion, in cases where the distinctive character of that communion too remains for the most part in the background. Now if this occurs even within the Christian Church itself, in respect of the various modifications of the Christian consciousness for all alike, then it actually holds good in a larger circle, but it is not calculated to show up differences, which are thus indirectly marked as unimportant or in process of disappearing. If, on the other hand, it has respect only to one of these different modifications, then it

holds good only within this smaller compass. Sometimes the former kind of dogma may seem colourless, and the latter be the right kind; at other times the latter may be factious or sectarian, and the former be the right kind. But such differences in dogmatic propositions dealing with the same subject, which do not represent any differences at all in the immediate religious self-consciousness, are of no significance for their ecclesiastical value.

2. The scientific value of a dogmatic proposition depends in the first place upon the definiteness of the concepts which appear in it, and of their connexion with each other. For the more definite these become, the more does the proposition pass out of the indefinite realm of the poetic and rhetorical, and the more certain will it be that the proposition cannot enter into apparent contradiction with other dogmatic propositions belonging to the same form of religious consciousness. But in forming its concepts Dogmatics has not succeeded—indeed, one might say that from the nature of the subject it cannot succeed—in everywhere substituting the exact expression for the figurative; and thus the scientific value of dogmatic propositions depends, from this side, for the most part simply upon the highest possible degree of precision and definiteness in explaining the figurative expressions which occur. And we can the more readily leave it at that, since, even if the exact expression could throughout be substituted for the figurative, the latter is the original, and therefore the identity of the two would have to be shown, which would come to the same thing in the end. In the second place, the scientific value of a dogmatic proposition consists in its fruitfulness, that is to say, its many-sidedness in pointing us towards other kindred ones; and not so much in a heuristic way (since no dogmatic proposition is based upon another, and each one can only be discovered from contemplation of the Christian self-consciousness) as in a critical way, because it can then be the more easily tested how well one dogmatic proposition harmonizes with others. For it is undeniable that, of a number of dogmatic expressions which are supposed to refer to the same fact of the Christian consciousness, that one will deserve the preference which opens up and enters into combination with the largest range of other expressions referring to kindred facts. And when we find a realm or system of dogmatic language which is closely bound together and forms a self-contained whole, that is an account of the facts which we may presume to be correct.

A proposition which lacks the first of these two properties, and which thus belongs entirely to the poetic or the rhetorical realm of language, has not got to the length of being a dogmatic proposition. A proposition which, as regards the second of the two properties, goes beyond the principle we have set up, and seeks to establish anything objectively without going back to the higher self-consciousness, would not be a religious doctrine at all, and would simply not belong to our field.

3. Now since every doctrine of the faith has, as such, an ecclesiastical value, and since these doctrines become dogmatic when they acquire a scientific value, dogmatic propositions are the more perfect the more their scientific character gives them an outstanding ecclesiastical value, and also the more their scientific content bears traces of having proceeded from the ecclesiastical interest.

C. MIRACLES

The Christian Faith, I, §46 f.

§46. *The religious self-consciousness, by means of which we place all that affects or influences us in absolute dependence on God, coincides entirely with the view that all such things are conditioned and determined by the interdependence of nature.*

1. It is not in the least meant that the pious self-consciousness is realized with every stimulation of the sensuous consciousness, any more than every perception causes us actually to visualize the interrelatedness of nature. But whenever objective consciousness reaches this degree of clarity we assume afresh the interdependence of nature as universal and as determining everything which has not led to our consciousness of it; and in the same way we recognize in the moments when the pious self-consciousness is present that those in which it is lacking are really imperfect states, and we postulate the feeling of absolute dependence as valid for everything without exception, because we apply it to our own existence in so far as we are a part of the world.

But neither is our proposition meant to fall short of the conception of preservation, although in accordance with the nature of self-consciousness it is limited to what affects us; and, indeed, only the movements and changes of things stimulate us directly, not the things themselves or their inner being. For every impulse directed towards perception and knowledge which yet has the qualities, essence and being of things as its object, begins with a stimulation of self-consciousness which thus accompanies the process of apprehending; and, consequently, the being and nature of things belongs to that which affect us. Within this range our proposition admits no distinction; in each and every situation we ought to be conscious of, and sympathetically experience, absolute dependence on God just as we conceive each and every thing as completely conditioned by the interdependence of nature.

But we find the opposite idea to this very widely spread. Namely, the idea that these two views do not coincide, but that each excludes the other as its contradictory. It is said that the more clearly we conceive anything to be entirely conditioned by the interdependence of nature, the less can we arrive at the feeling of its absolute dependence upon God; and, conversely, the more vivid this latter feeling is the more indefinitely must we leave its interrelatedness with nature an open question. But it is obvious that, from our standpoint, and in consistency with what we have already said, we cannot admit such a contradiction between the two ideas. For otherwise (since everything would present itself to us as always in the system of nature), as our knowledge of the world grew perfect, the development of the pious self-consciousness in ordinary life would cease; which is quite contrary to our presupposition that piety is of the essence of human nature. And on the other hand, conversely, the love of religion would be opposed to all love of research and all widening of our knowledge of nature; which would entirely contradict the principle that the observation of creation leads to the consciousness of God. And besides, prior to the completion of both tendencies the most competent naturalist would have to be the least religious of men, and *vice versa*. Now, as the human soul is just as necessarily predisposed towards a knowledge of the world as towards a consciousness of God, it can only be a false wisdom which would put religion aside, and a misconceived religion of love of which the progress of knowledge is to be arrested.

The only apparent ground for this assertion is the fact that, as a rule, the more strongly the objective consciousness predominates at any given moment, the more at that identical moment the consciousness of self is repressed and *vice versa*, because in the one case, through absorption in ourselves, we lose consciousness of the object affecting us, just as in the other case we are entirely merged in the object. But this in no way prevents the one activity, after having satisfied itself, from stimulating and passing over into the other. We are clearly quite wrong if we allege, as a general experience, that the incomprehensible as such is more conducive to the awakening of the religious feeling than that which is understood. The favourite example is the great natural phenomena, produced by elemental forces; but in point of fact the religious feeling is not destroyed even by the completest confidence with which we accept this or that hypothetical explanation of these phenomena. The reason why these manifestations so readily arouse religious feeling lies rather in the immensity of their operations both in the promotion and destruction of human life and works of skill, and thus in the awakening of the consciousness of the limitation of our activity by universal forces. But this precisely is the most complete recognition of the universal interrelatedness of nature, and thus it turns out in fact to be the other way round, a support for our thesis. It is certainly, however, an expedient often adopted by human indolence to attribute what is not understood to the supernatural immediately; but this does not at all belong to the tendency to piety. Since the Supreme Being here takes the place of the system of nature, we find ourselves tending rather to knowledge; besides, in that case not everything but only the incomprehensible would be placed in absolute dependence upon God. Starting from this men have imagined evil and destructive supernatural powers in the same way as they have gone back to a highest good Power; which makes it immediately evident that this kind of linking up (with the supernatural) has not arisen in the interests of religion, for such a setting of one over against the other would inevitably destroy the unity and completeness of the relation of dependence.

As furthermore we regard everything stimulating us as an object of the pious consciousness, it follows that not even the least and most unimportant thing should be excluded from the relation of absolute dependence. But here it should be remarked that frequently, on the one hand, an undue value is placed on expressly tracing back the least detail of this relation; while on the other hand, we often oppose such a relation. The first mistake appears in the view that, because the greatest events often arise from small, the smallest detail must be expressly ordained by God. For it appears to be only an empty, and by no means trustworthy, play of the fantasy, when we so often hear people describing great events as arising from small causes, and thereby drawing our attention away from the universal relatedness in which the true causes really lie hidden. A clear judgment can only be formed on the principle of the similarity of cause and effect in the domain of history and of nature, and it is only under definite conditions that individual changes with their causes can be severed from the universal interrelatedness and taken separately. But as soon as the pious feeling combines with such a view, thought has no choice but to recur to the universal interdependence of nature; otherwise an isolated and separate activity would be ascribed in too human fashion to God. The second point, i.e. that the application of absolute dependence to the smallest matters is felt to be objectionable, has its origin in the fear that religion might be drawn into blasphemy, if, say, our free choices in little things were to be traced back to divine appointment: for instance, the point which foot shall be put forward first, or chance in matters of no serious importance such as winning or losing in sports and contests. Still, the incongruity here does not lie in the object, but in our way of thinking about it: that is, in the isolation of single events, because in cases of the first kind the apparent free choice is sometimes only an individual instance of a general situation, from which many similar events follow, and sometimes it is the expression of a more general law by which many similar events are controlled; while in cases of the second kind, the issue can always be regarded as submission to a universal will. Neither of these can be regarded as insignificant, and thus no reason can be found against treating both as subsumed under absolute dependence on God.

2. If we now examine our proposition purely in itself, it must be directly evident in its wider scope to everyone who accepts it as a general principle of experience that the feeling of absolute dependence can be aroused through stimulations of our sensuous self-consciousness. For that feeling is most complete when we identify ourselves in our self-consciousness with the whole world and feel ourselves in the same way as not less dependent. This identification can only succeed in so far as in thought we unite everything that in experience is scattered and isolated, and by means of this unifying association conceive of everything as one. For the most complete and universal interdependence of nature is posited in this 'All-One' of finite being, and if we also feel ourselves to be absolutely dependent, then there will be a complete coincidence of the two ideas—namely the unqualified conviction that everything is grounded and established in the universality of the nature-system, and the inner certainty of the absolute dependence of all finite being upon God. From this follows, on the one hand, the possibility of pious self-consciousness in every moment of the objective consciousness, and on the other the possibility of complete world-consciousness. For with regard to the latter, where a pious feeling is actually existent, there the interdependence of nature is always posited; and therefore the effort to extend the idea of the latter and perfect it in a world-representation will not be detrimental to the former, but can be effected just in so far as the tendency towards knowlege is predominant. And as regards the former, wherever there is an objective idea, there is always a stimulated self-consciousness; and from this the pious self-consciousness can develop without prejudice to the objective idea (with its world-conception, which is more or less clearly co-posited), in proportion as the tendency in each towards feeling is dominant. Now if we conceive both tendencies as fully developed in a given man, then each would with perfect ease call forth the other, so that every thought, as part of the whole world-conception, would become in him the purest religious feeling, and every pious feeling as evoked by a part of the world, would become a complete world-conception. On the contrary, if the one did not call forth the other, but in some way limited it, then the more completely the one developed, the more it would destroy the other. It has

always been acknowledged by the strictest dogmaticians that divine preservation, as the absolute dependence of all events and changes on God, and natural causation, as the complete determination of all events by the universal nexus, are one and the same thing simply from different points of view, the one being neither separated from the other nor limited by it. If anyone should detect in this an appearance of pantheism he ought to bear in mind that so long as philosophy does not put forward a generally accepted formula to express the relation of God and the world, even in the province of Dogmatics, directly we begin to speak not of the origin of the world but of its co-existence with God and its relatedness to God, we cannot avoid an oscillation between formulas, on the one hand, which approach to the identification of the two, and formulas, on the other, which go near to putting them in opposition to one another. Moreover, in order not to confuse ourselves in this way, we ought to observe more carefully the difference between a universal and an individual cause. For in the totality of finite being only a particular and partial causality is given to each individual, since each is dependent not on one another but on all the others; the universal causality attaches only to that on which the totality of this partial causality is itself dependent.

Postscript. In Dogmatics the analytical method originating with the Scholastics has led to a division of our simple proposition in a number of different ways into many elements and sections, and it will not make much difference which of these divisions we select in order to show its relation to our statement. Some have divided the conception of preservation, which is expressed in our proposition as referring both to the whole and the parts, into the following: the *general*, which is related to the whole world as a unity; the *special*, which is concerned with species; and the *most special*, which is concerned with individuals (*generalis*, *specialis* and *specialissima*). This classification does not appear to be made in the interest of religion (from which everything should start), for the simple reason that it leads to a question which is purely one for natural science, i.e. whether there is anything in the world which cannot be brought under the idea of a species. But supposing this question must be answered in the affirmative and the division be made complete, nevertheless universal preservation must include everything, and the division thus becomes quite superfluous to us, since our fundamental feeling rests solely on the finiteness of being as such. But a further purpose of this division may be surmised, if we take into account the addition usually made to the third member of it—namely that God sustains individual things in their existence and their powers as long as he wills.[1] For in that case the species, as reproductions of

[1] See *Summa Theologica* Q. 104, art. 1.

individual things, are in a sense immortal, but the individual is mortal; and the wish arose to establish a difference between the preservation of what endures and of what is mortal.

For those, however, who accept a beginning and an end of the world there is absolutely no reason to differentiate between the world and individual things. But in any case the proposition must cover equally the beginning and the end; and we know fairly certainly of our earth that there have been species on it which are no longer extant and that the present species have not always existed; so that our propositions must be stretched to embrace these also. It really affirms nothing except that the temporality or the duration of the finite is to be conceived solely in absolute dependence upon God. But since the duration of individual as well as of universal things is simply an expression for the degree of their power as each coexists with all the rest, it follows that the addition taken in itself contains nothing which our statement had not expressed already. But the way in which the addition is framed might easily give rise to the idea that the sustaining will of God began or ended at some particular time, and in anticipation of this it must be said that God, in sustaining as in creating, must remain apart from all means and occasions of time.

Another similar division is to discriminate between the work of God as *preserving* and as *co-operating*; but the distinction is not made in the same way by all teachers of doctrine, for some connect the expression 'preservation' only with matter and form, and 'co-operation' with powers and actions; others again connect preservation with existence and powers of things, and co-operation only with activity. The fact, however, that the expression 'co-operation' contains a hidden meaning should not be overlooked, as if there is in the finite an activity in and for itself and thus independent of the sustaining divine activity. This tendency must be entirely avoided and not merely covered over by indefiniteness. If, however, such a distinction ought not to be drawn, and if the powers of things are something as little separated from the divine sustaining activity as their being itself (the latter we only divide into matter and form by an abstraction which has no place here), then the difference between preservation and co-operation rests also on a similar abstraction. For being posited for itself can only exist where there is also power, just as power always exists only in activity; thus a preservation which did not include the placing of all the activities of any finite being in absolute dependence on God would be just as empty without preservation. And in the same way, if we conceived co-operation without conceiving that the existence of a thing in its whole duration was dependent on God, then this thing might be independent of God even at its first moment of existence, and this would be equivalent to conceiving preservation in such a way that it did not include creation and positing it without creation. It should be added here that even theologians who have treated the subject quite correctly on the whole have allowed themselves to be led into describing co-operation as something more immediate than preservation, so that deeds, as distinct from the preservation of powers, proceed from a divine activity. The result of this would be, if we took it seriously, to reduce the preservation of power to nothing, for in the system of nature power is always dependent on the activity of the rest of things. Thus we can only say that, in the region of absolute dependence on God, everything is equally direct and equally indirect, some in one relation and some in another.

Some combine the idea of divine *government* immediately with these two ideas. But if by that is meant the fulfilment of divine decrees or the guidance of all things to divine ends, and if it be taken as signifying anything else than that everything can happen and has happened only as God originally willed and always wills, by means of the powers distributed and preserved in the world—this is already included in our proposition, and we cannot consider it here. For here we are concerned in general with the description of the feeling of absolute dependence, and must set completely aside a view which is based upon the distinction between means and end without reference to the question whether this distinction can exist for God. On the one hand, for our Christian consciousness it could only be the Kingdom of God, established by means of redemption (i.e. something quite foreign to our present purpose), to which everything else is related as its goal: and on the other, if our self-consciousness is to represent finite existence in general, and end and means are related to one another as that which is posited for its own sake and that not posited for its own sake, or more exactly as what is willed by God and what is not willed by God, then we must take up into our religious self-consciousness an antithesis of which our present discussion knows nothing. The only thing then that this conception (divine government) could suggest to us at this point would be that so far as the divine preservation relates, as co-operation, to powers and activities taken separately, we require a counterpart to it to cover the passive state of finite things; but since these are just as essential parts for the attainment of the divine purpose, their absolute dependence is included in the conception of government. Even this is, however, superfluous so far as we are concerned. For since preservation has as its object the being of things, and in this, so far as they are centres of power, the antithesis of self-activity and susceptibility is included, the passive states are already subsumed under absolute dependence; and particularly when they also belong to that which affects our self-consciousness, whether in the form of perception or of sympathy, they are included in our general proposition. But, in addition, the passive states of one thing are only the result of the active states of others; while, on the other hand, the way in which the active states emerge successively and the strength which they display depends not only on each thing's peculiar mode of existence, but also on its concurrence with other things, hence on the influence of others and on its own passive states. From this we may think that perhaps we should differentiate better if we said that what proceeds from the intrinsic characteristics of each individual thing and what proceeds from its co-existence with all other things are both alike to be placed in absolute dependence upon God. But even this would be an abstraction without importance for our religious self-consciousness, for which the two are not distinguished from one another as stimulating objects; and thus we should do better to include everything which stimulates our consciousness together in the idea of finite being which is only relatively individual and is conditioned in its individuality by the universal co-existence. And this is wholly identical with what our proposition denotes by the term interdependence of nature.

§47. *It can never be necessary in the interest of religion so to interpret a fact that its dependence on God absolutely excludes its being conditioned by the system of nature.*

1. This proposition is so much a direct consequence of what went before that there would be no reason to make an express statement of it, but that ideas which have still a circulation in the Christian Church must be considered in their appropriate place in any Dogmatic. Now there is a general idea that the miracles which are interwoven with the beginnings of Christianity or at least in some form are reported in the Scriptures should be regarded as events of the kind described: and yet if the idea itself is inadmissible it cannot be applied to this or that particular fact. It is in this way that theologians from of old have generally treated the question. We have not to pass judgment here on its inherent possibility, but only on the relation of the theory to the feeling of absolute dependence. If, then, this relation is what our proposition declares it to be, we must in our field try, as far as possible, to interpret every event with reference to the interdependence of nature and without detriment to that principle.

Now some have represented miracle in this sense as essential to the perfect manifestation of the divine omnipotence. But it is difficult to conceive, on the one side, how omnipotence is shown to be greater in the suspension of the interdependence of nature than in its original immutable course which was no less divinely ordered. For, indeed, the capacity to make a change in what has been ordained is only a merit in the ordainer, if a change is necessary, which again can only be the result of some imperfection in him or in his work. If such an interference be postulated as one of the privileges of the Supreme Being, it would first have to be assumed that there is something not ordained by him which could offer him resistance and thus invade him and his work; and such an idea would entirely destroy our fundamental feeling. We must remember, on the other hand, that where such a conception of miracles is commonly found, namely, in conditions where there is least knowledge of nature, there, too, the fundamental feeling appears to be weakest and most ineffectual. But where a knowledge of nature is most widely spread, and therefore this conception seldom occurs, more is found of that reverence for God which is the expression of our fundamental feeling. It follows from this that the most perfect representation of omnipotence would be a view of the world which made no use of such an idea.

Other teachers defend the conception in a more acute but scarcely more tenable way, by saying that God was partly in need of miracles that he might compensate for the effects of free causes in the course of nature, and partly that he might generally have reasons for remaining in direct contact with the world. The latter argument presupposes, for one thing, a wholly lifeless view of the divine preservation, and for another, an opposition in general between the mediate and immediate activities of God which cannot be conceived without bringing the Supreme Being within the sphere of limitation. The former sounds almost as if free causes were not themselves objects of divine preservation, and (since preservation includes in itself the idea of creation) had not come into being and been maintained in absolute dependence upon God. But if, on the contrary, they are in this condition there can be just as little necessity for God to counteract their influences as to counteract the influences which a blind natural force exercises in the domain of another natural force. But none of us understands by 'the world' which is the object of the divine preservation a nature-mechanism alone, but rather the interaction of the nature-mechanism and of free agents, so that in the former the latter are taken into account just as in the latter the former are reckoned.

Moreover, the biblical miracles, on account of which the whole theory has been devised, are much too isolated and too restricted in content for any theory to be based on them which should assign them the function of restoring in the nature-mechanism what free agents had altered. That one great miracle, the mission of Christ, has, of course, the aim of restoration, but it is the restoration of what free causes have altered in their own province, not in that of the nature-mechanism or in the course of things originally ordained by God. Nor does the interest of religion require that the free cause which performs the function of restoration in the sphere of phenomena should have a different relation to the order of nature from that of other free causes.

Two other reasons may be put forward why an absolute suspension of the interrelatedness of nature by miracles may be held to be in the interests of religion. And it cannot be denied that it is mostly for these reasons, even though they may have never been formulated as actual church doctrine, that this conception of miracle has maintained its practical hold over many Christians. The first is that of answer to prayer; for prayer seems really to be heard only when because of it an event happens which would not otherwise have happened: thus there seems to be the suspension of an effect which, according to the interrelatedness of nature, should have followed. The other is that of regeneration, which, represented as a new creation, in part requires some such suspension and in part introduces a principle not comprised in the system of nature. Neither subject can be discussed in this place; but it may suffice to remark in relation to the first, which more concerns piety in general, that our statement places prayer, too, under divine preservation, so that prayer and its fulfilment or refusal are only part of the original divine plan, and consequently the idea that otherwise something else might have happened is wholly meaningless. With regard to the second we need only refer here to what was said above. If the revelation of God in Christ is not necessarily something absolutely supernatural, Christian piety cannot be held bound in advance to regard as absolutely supernatural anything that goes along with this revelation or flows from it.

2. The more accurate definitions by which the acceptance of such miracles is brought into connexion with the propositions and concepts which indicate the complete dependence of the system of nature on God shows very clearly how little that idea is demanded by our religious emotions. For the more they try definitely to fix an absolute miracle, the further off they are from making it the expression of a religious emotion, and, instead of genuine dogmatic material, something of quite a different character comes in. Speaking generally, the question can most easily be considered if we start from the point that the event in which a miracle occurs is connected with all finite causes, and therefore every absolute miracle would destroy the whole system of nature. There are, therefore, two ways of looking at such a miracle—a positive way when we consider the whole future, and a negative way when we consider it as affecting in some sense the whole of the past. Since, that is, that which

would have happened by reason of the totality of finite causes in accordance with the natural order does not happen, an effect has been hindered from happening, and certainly not through the influence of other normally counteracting finite causes given in the natural order, but in spite of the fact that all active causes are combining to produce that very effect. Everything, therefore, which had ever contributed to this will, to a certain degree, be annihilated, and instead of introducing a single supernatural power into the system of nature as we intended, we must completely abrogate the conception of nature.

From the positive point of view we must consider that some event follows which is not to be explained by the totality of finite causes. But as this event now enters into the interrelatedness of nature as an active member, throughout the whole future everything will be different from what it would have been had this single miracle not occurred. Thus every miracle not only suspends the entire continuity of the original order for all future time, but every later miracle annuls all earlier ones, in so far as they have become part of the continuity of active causes. But now, in order to describe the origin of the effect, we have to allow for the entrance of a divine activity apart from natural causes. Yet at whatever point we admit the entrance of this particular divine activity, which must always seem like magic, in each case there will always appear a number of possibilities according to which the same result could have been attained by natural causes if they had been opportunely directed towards this end. In this way we shall be driven to hold either that miracles have a purely epideictic tendency in view of which God purposely did not so order the system of nature that his whole will should be accomplished in it (a view against which we directed our earlier discussion of the relation between omnipotence and this conception of miracle), or if the totality of finite causes could not have been so directed, then what can be explained by the order of nature can never rightly evoke in us the feeling of the absolute dependence of all finite being.

Now, if others think it would be easier to establish this conception of miracles by first dividing the divine co-operation into ordinary and extraordinary (which, however, is only ostensibly different from the unordered), and then attributing the former to the natural and the latter to the supernatural, so that the negative aspect of a miracle would be the withdrawal of the ordinary co-operation, but the positive aspect the entrance of the extraordinary, this means, on the one hand, that the ordinary co-operation is no longer ordinary if it can be withdrawn, and is not to be definitely distinguished from the extraordinary; only that we call that which occurs more frequently the ordinary, and what seldom occurs the extraordinary, a relation which might equally well be reversed. On the other hand, the miracle is effected in the first instance by finite causes, even if by means of extraordinary divine co-operation; but since thereby something comes into existence which according to its natural character would not have come into existence, it follows that in this case either they are not causes, and the expression 'co-operation' is inaccurate, or they have become something different from what they were formerly. In that case, every such extraordinary co-operation is really a creation, on which afterwards the re-establishment of actual things in their original state must follow as a further creation cancelling the former one. Moreover, it should be recognized with regard to these explanations that the one corresponds more closely to the one class of biblical miracle and the other to the other class, and therefore the different characteristics of these events have had an important influence on the development of these different formulae. If, however, anyone finds it difficult to accept this view, yet it must be admitted that although the older theologians on the whole still maintain this conception of miracle, the younger ones do not maintain its exclusive validity, but also admit the legitimacy of another hypothesis —namely, that God has prepared miracles in nature itself in some way incomprehensible to us; and this, in the interests of religion itself, we must admit to be pure gain.

3. On the whole, therefore, as regards the miraculous, the general interests of science, more particularly of natural science, and the interests of religion seem to meet at the same point, i.e. that we should abandon the idea of the absolutely supernatural because no single instance of it can be known by us, and we are nowhere required to recognize it. Moreover, we should admit, in general, that since our knowledge of created nature is continually growing, we have not the least right to maintain that anything is impossible; and also we should allow, in particular (by far the greater number of New Testament miracles being of this kind), that we can neither define the limits of the reciprocal relations of the body and mind nor assert that they are, always and everywhere, entirely the same without the possibility of extension or deviation. In this way, everything—even the most wonderful thing that happens or has happened—is a problem for scientific research; but, at the same time, when it in any way stimulates the pious feeling, whether through its purpose or in some other way, that is not in the least prejudiced by the conceivable possibility of its being understood in the future. Moreover, we free ourselves entirely from a difficult and highly precarious task with which Dogmatics has so long laboured in vain, i.e. the discovery of definite signs which shall enable us to distinguish between the false and diabolical miracle and the divine and true.

17

MILL

on MIRACLES

Biographical Note Born 1806, in London, son of James Mill, the philosopher and friend of Bentham. He was educated at home on Benthamite principles, till 1820, when he was sent to the Continent for a year. During the next six years he studied Benthamism extensively. Entered the India Office in 1823, later rising to be Head of his Department; from this post he resigned in 1858, because of the Indian Mutiny. Meanwhile, he engaged in intense philosophical and political activity. The death of Bentham (1832) and of his father (1836) left him the leading exponent of Utilitarianism, though he was more eclectic and conservative than the Radicals in Parliament. In 1865 he was elected M.P. for Westminster, holding this seat till 1868. Thereafter, lived mostly at Avignon. He died in 1873.

Principal works: *A System of Logic* (1843), *On Liberty* (1859), *Representative Government* (1861), *Utilitarianism* (1863), *Examination of Sir William Hamilton's Philosophy*[1] (1865), *Autobiography* (1873), *Three Essays on Religion* (posthumous, 1874).

Philosophical Note M. is chiefly remembered for his ethical writings, in which, following but modifying Bentham (1747–1832), he elaborated the theory known as Utilitarianism. According to this a good action or moral rule is one which conduces to the greatest happiness of the greatest number. This principle provides a means of testing moral judgments which is in marked contrast to that enunciated by Kant (see above, p. 272). But both Kant and M. agree upon the autonomy of ethics, in so far as each provides a test of morality not requiring reference to supernatural authority or to God as the source of moral values. M. applied Utilitarian principles to political theory, since above all he regarded his moral theory as providing a rationale for social reform, and was a strong advocate of individualism.

His great work in the non-ethical parts of philosophy is undoubtedly his *Logic*, in which he explores, from an empiricist standpoint, the logic of induction and scientific method. Scientific investigation, he held, aims at discovering causal relations between phenomena, and M. formulated five methods of detecting them. The main one is the method of difference: given that a phenomenon occurs on one occasion and not upon another, where all the circumstances are the same except that one occurs on the former occasion but not on the latter, then this extra

[1] See below, p. 361.

circumstance must be the cause, or part of the cause, of the phenomenon. M. supplements his account of induction with a theory about the use of deductive methods in science, for, where phenomena are complicated, we have to deduce the cause of a complex effect from the laws concerning its separate causes. In such ways M. hoped to give a general account of scientific procedure complementing the traditional formalization of deductive logic.

M.'s views on religion are mainly to be found in his *Essays on Religion*. In the third and last of these, on 'Theism', he argues that the arguments and evidences for God's existence are sufficiently weak to make scepticism (or, as we now should say, agnosticism) the right attitude. Nevertheless he was impressed by the appeal which Christianity had for so many of the best minds, and thought that belief in God as an ideal (an imaginary ideal) was a worthwhile inspiration to moral goodness.

The following passage expresses, from the standpoint of scientific method as he understood it, his criticism of Hume on miracles (see above, pp. 232–47), and his evaluation of the grounds for believing in supernatural intervention on particular occasions.

Bibliographical Note J. Plamenatz, *The English Utilitarians* (London, 1949), R. P. Anschutz, *The Philosophy of J. S. Mill* (Oxford, 1953) and K. Britton, *John Stuart Mill* (London, Pelican, 1953) are useful general works.

MIRACLES

A System of Logic, Book III, Ch. XXV

OF THE GROUNDS OF DISBELIEF

§2. It is to be remarked in the first place that the positive evidence produced in support of an assertion which is nevertheless rejected on the score of impossibility or improbability is never such as amounts to full proof. It is always grounded on some approximate generalization. The fact may have been asserted by a hundred witnesses; but there are many exceptions to the universality of the generalization that what a hundred witnesses affirm is true. We may seem to ourselves to have actually seen the fact; but that we really see what we think we see is by no means an universal truth; our organs may have been in a morbid state, or we may have inferred something and imagined that we perceived it. The evidence, then, in the affirmative being never more than an approximate generalization, all will depend on what the evidence in the negative is. If that also rests on an approximate generalization, it is a case for comparison of probabilities. If the approximate generalizations leading to the affirmative are, when added together, less strong, or in other words, farther from being universal, than the approximate generalizations which support the negative side of the question, the proposition is said to be improbable and is to be disbelieved provisionally. If, however, an alleged fact be in contradiction, not to any number of approximate generalizations, but to a completed generalization grounded on a rigorous induction, it is said to be impossible and is to be disbelieved totally.

This last principle, simple and evident as it appears, is the doctrine which, on the occasion of an attempt to apply it to the question of miracles, excited so violent a controversy. Hume's celebrated doctrine,[1] that nothing is credible which is contradictory to experience or at variance with laws of nature, is merely this plain and harmless proposition, that whatever is contrary to a complete induction[2] is incredible. That such a maxim as this should either be accounted a dangerous heresy or mistaken for a great and recondite truth speaks ill for the state of philosophical speculation on such subjects.

But does not (it may be asked) the very statement of the proposition imply a contradiction? An alleged fact, according to this theory, is not to be believed if it contradict a complete induction. But it is essential to the completeness of an induction that it shall not contradict any known fact. Is it not then a *petitio principii*[3] to say that the fact ought to be disbelieved because the induction opposed to it is incomplete? How can we have a right to declare the induction complete while facts, supported by credible evidence, present themselves in opposition to it?

I answer: we have that right whenever the scientific canons of induction give it to us; that is, whenever the induction *can* be complete. We have it, for example, in a case of causation in which there has been an *experimentum crucis*. If an antecedent A, superadded to a set of antecedents in all other respects unaltered, is followed by an effect B which did not exist before, A is in that instance at least the cause of B or an indispensable part of its cause; and if A be tried again with many totally different sets of antecedents and B still follows, then it is the whole cause. If these observations or experiments have been repeated so often and by so many persons as to exclude all supposition of error in the observer, a law of nature is established; and so long as this law is received as such, the assertion that on any particular occasion A took place and yet B did not follow, *without any counteracting cause*, must be disbelieved. Such an assertion is not to be credited on any less evidence than what would suffice to overturn the law. The general truths that whatever has a beginning has a cause and that when none but the same causes exist the same effects follow rest

[1] See above, p. 236.

[2] By a 'complete induction' M. means an inductive argument where, in order to show that all A are B, one enumerates all instances of A, showing them to be B.

[3] I.e., a circular argument.

on the strongest inductive evidence possible; the proposition that things affirmed by even a crowd of respectable witnesses are true is but an approximate generalization; and—even if we fancy we actually saw or felt the fact which is in contradiction to the law—what a human being can see is no more than a set of appearances; from which the real nature of the phenomenon is merely an inference, and in this inference approximate generalizations usually have a large share. If, therefore, we make our election to hold by the law, no quantity of evidence whatever ought to persuade us that there has occurred anything in contradiction to it. If, indeed, the evidence produced is such that it is more likely that the set of observations and experiments on which the law rests should have been inaccurately performed or incorrectly interpreted, than that the evidence in question should be false, we may believe the evidence; but then we must abandon the law. And since the law was received on what seemed a complete induction, it can only be rejected on evidence equivalent; namely as being inconsistent not with any number of approximate generalizations, but with some other and better established law of nature. This extreme case of a conflict between two supposed laws of nature has probably never actually occurred where, in the process of investigating both the laws, the true canons of scientific induction have been kept in view; but if it did occur, it must terminate in the total rejection of one of the supposed laws. It would prove that there must be a flaw in the logical process by which either one or the other was established; and if there be so, that supposed general truth is no truth at all. We cannot admit a proposition as a law of nature and yet believe a fact in real contradiction to it. We must disbelieve the alleged fact or believe that we were mistaken in admitting the supposed law.

But in order that any alleged fact should be contradictory to a law of causation, the allegation must be not simply that the cause existed without being followed by the effect, for that would be no uncommon occurrence, but that this happened in the absence of any adequate counteracting cause. Now in the case of an alleged miracle, the assertion is the exact opposite of this. It is that the effected was defeated, not in the absence, but in consequence of a counteracting cause, namely a direct interposition of an act of the will of some being who has power over nature; and in particular of a Being whose will being assumed to have endowed all the causes with the powers by which they produce their effects, may well be supposed able to counteract them. A miracle, as was justly remarked by Brown,[1] is no contradiction to the law of cause and effect; it is a new effect,

[1] In his *Inquiry into the Relation of Cause and Effect*, notes A and F. Thomas Brown (1778–1820) was a Scottish metaphysician and doctor. After practising medicine, he was appointed Professor of Moral Philosophy in Edinburgh in 1810.

supposed to be produced by the introduction of a new cause. Of the adequacy of that cause, if present, there can be no doubt; and the only antecedent improbability which can be ascribed to the miracle is the improbability that any such cause existed.

All, therefore, which Hume has made out, and this he must be considered to have made out, is that (at least in the imperfect state of our knowledge of natural agencies, which leaves it always possible that some of the physical antecedents may have been hidden from us) no evidence can prove a miracle to anyone who did not previously believe the existence of a being or beings with supernatural power, or who believes himself to have full proof that the character of the Being whom he recognizes is inconsistent with his having seen fit to interfere on the occasion in question.

If we do not already believe in supernatural agencies, no miracle can prove to us their existence. The miracle itself, considered merely as an extraordinary fact, may be satisfactorily certified by our senses or by testimony; but nothing can ever prove that it is a miracle: there is still another hypothesis—that of its being the result of some unknown natural cause; and this possibility cannot be so completely shut out as to leave no alternative but that of admitting the existence and intervention of a Being superior to nature. Those, however, who already believe in such a Being, have two hypotheses to choose from, a supernatural and an unknown natural agency; and they have to judge which of the two is the most probable in the particular case. In forming this judgment an important element of the question will be the conformity of the result to the laws of the supposed agent, that is, to the character of the Deity as they conceive it. But, with the knowledge which we now possess of the general uniformity of the course of nature, religion, following in the wake of science, has been compelled to acknowledge the government of the universe as being on the whole carried out by general laws, and not by special interpositions. To whoever holds this belief, there is a general presumption against any supposition of divine agency not operating through general laws, or, in other words, there is an antecedent improbability in every miracle which, in order to outweigh it, requires an extraordinary strength of antecedent probability derived from the special circumstances of the case.

18

KIERKEGAARD

on REASON AND FAITH

Biographical Note Born in 1813, son of a Copenhagen merchant. After a lonely and rigorous childhood, he entered the University in 1830, to study theology, in accordance with his father's wishes. Instead, however, he devoted himself to the study of philosophy and literature, and to a gay time (concealing his melancholic disposition), so that he did not graduate till 1840, when he entered a seminary—without, however, being ordained. An emotional crisis precipitated the breaking of his engagement to Regina Olsen. From this time onwards he showed prodigious literary activity. In 1854, launched a bitter attack on the Danish Church as having betrayed Christ. Died, 1855.

Principal works: *Either-Or* (1843), *Philosophical Fragments* (1844), *The Concept of Dread* (1844), *Concluding Unscientific Postscript* (1846), *Sickness unto Death* (1849) *Christian Discourses* (1850), *Training in Christianity* (1850).

Philosophical Note K., a highly personal writer whose passion and psychological penetration distinguish him from many more orthodox philosophers, was preoccupied with the problem of finding the true meaning of Christianity. He was repelled by Hegelian metaphysics, partly because its apparent pantheism distorted the Christian message, and partly because it failed to bring out the personal predicament of man 'existing before God'. This revolt against Hegelian Idealism, with its emphasis upon reason, marks K. as the father of modern Existentialism, and K.'s views have had a considerable impact, especially upon theologians, in this century.

K. distinguishes three stages or levels of life: the aesthetic, the ethical and the religious. In the first (here K.'s descriptions are influenced by Romanticism[1]) a person adopts the attitude of spectator; under this head, K. included both scepticism and metaphysical speculation, for they are both ways of evading ethical commitment (the latter, as exemplified in Hegelianism, tries to solve the problems of life in a mechanical fashion, without facing up to the essential predicament of free man in a necessitated Nature). One goes beyond the aesthetic stage in accepting one's status as an ethical agent. But this stage also leads to despair if one does not go beyond it, for considered by itself it implies personal self-sufficiency: yet the individual cannot be master over his whole destiny, since this is partly determined by his own nature and by external circumstances. Thus the ethical stage must lead to self-acceptance, the recognition of my sin and shortcoming. But this

[1] See above, p. 306.

self-acceptance is only possible at the third, the religious, stage, where in dependence upon God I gain his acceptance. Thus the best freedom I can attain is through dependence upon God.

Dependence upon God implies a commitment. One cannot apprehend God, as metaphysics supposes, by mere reasoning; nor is simple knowledge of history (e.g. the history of Christ) sufficient. The former point is relevant to his dictum that 'truth is subjectivity'. Here K. is, of course, thinking of truth in the sense of 'ultimate truth' (about God, the nature of man, etc.). In his violent reaction against the attempt to describe such ultimate truth through concepts or essences, K. stresses the vital point that the apprehension of God is a person-to-person affair: it is not 'objective' in the sense that it is like conceptual or scientific knowledge (indeed, K. saw in attempts to describe men in an objective scientific manner a danger of distortion and dehumanization). Because ultimate truth (or God) cannot be found through concepts or essences, K.'s teaching can be described as existentialist (existence comes before essence, not, as rationalists hold, *vice versa*). Philosophy's real task, therefore, is to show its own limitations: once one sees the barrenness of speculation one will be in a better position to make the 'leap of faith'. Thus K., though he repudiates the Hegelian dialectic, has a dialectical method of his own. One needs to go through the stage of metaphysical and theological speculation, only to see its inadequacy. The truth that is subjectivity must lie beyond formulations and creeds.

In *Philosophical Fragments* K. uses the example of Socrates to illustrate the nature of the philosophical predicament. The doctrine of reminiscence or recollection[1] presupposes, as philosophy must always presuppose, an affinity between the human mind and ultimate truth. Yet if the Forms are always to be found in the soul, the seeker for truth already has it, and the moment of discovery or recollection is impossible or without significance. But according to Christianity the link between the human mind and ultimate truth has been broken; so that time, implying the possibility of a real moment of discovery and encounter, has profound significance. But though man has fallen into this predicament of being cut off from the truth through freedom, he cannot thereby restore it. Only God can be his Teacher by recreating the soul, and by removing, through the Incarnation, the obstacles preventing men from accepting what God has to offer. There is the possibility, then, that God may break in upon the human soul in a moment of eternal significance. But the truth thereby apprehended is far removed from that which metaphysics attempts to discover. In the passage given below, K. proceeds, with great acuteness, to examine the claims of metaphysics.

Bibliographical Note K.'s principal works have been translated by D. F. Swenson and others (Princeton and London, 1936 ff.); see also R. Bretall, *A Kierkegaard Anthology* (Princeton, 1947). For introductions to his thought, see E. L. Allen, *Kierkegaard* (London, 1935), R. Thomte, *Kierkegaard's Philosophy of Religion* (Princeton, 1948), T. H. Croxall, *Glimpses and Impressions of Kierkegaard* (London, 1958), J. Hohlenberg, *Soren Kierkegaard* (Eng. trans., London, 1954), J. H. Thomas, *Subjectivity and Paradox* (London, 1957), D. Roberts, *Existentialism and Religious Belief* (N.Y., 1957), and H. Diem, *Kierkegaard's Dialectic of Existence* (Edinburgh, 1959).

[1] See above, p. 20.

REASON AND FAITH

Philosophical Fragments, Ch. III

THE ABSOLUTE PARADOX: A METAPHYSICAL CROTCHET

In spite of the fact that Socrates studied with all diligence to acquire a knowledge of human nature and to understand himself, and in spite of the fame accorded him through the centuries as one who beyond all other men had an insight into the human heart, he has himself admitted that the reason for his shrinking from reflection upon the nature of such beings as Pegasus and the Gorgons was that he, the life-long student of human nature, had not yet been able to make up his mind whether he was a stranger monster than Typhon,[1] or a creature of a gentler and simpler sort, partaking of something divine (*Phaedrus*, 229E). This seems to be a paradox. However, one should not think slightingly of the paradoxical; for the paradox is the source of the thinker's passion, and the thinker without a paradox is like a lover without feeling: a paltry mediocrity. But the highest pitch of every passion is always to will its own downfall; and so it is also the supreme passion of the Reason to seek a collision, though this collision must in one way or another prove its own undoing. The supreme paradox of all thought is the attempt to discover something that thought cannot think. This passion is at bottom present in all thinking, even in the thinking of the individual, in so far as in thinking he participates in something transcending himself. But habit dulls our sensibilities, and prevents us from perceiving it. So for example the scientists tell us that our walking is a constant falling. But a sedate and proper gentleman who walks to his office in the morning and back again at noon, probably thinks this to be an exaggeration, for his progress is clearly a case of mediation; how should it occur to him that he is constantly falling when he religiously follows his nose!

But in order to make a beginning, let us now assume a daring proposition; let us assume that we know what man is.* Here we have that

[1] Typhon: a monster variously described—most horrifically as having a hundred heads, terrible eyes and fearsome voices.

*It may seem ridiculous to give this proposition a doubtful form by 'assuming' it, for in this theocentric age such matters are of course known to all. Aye, if it were only so well with us! Democritus also knew what man is, for he defines man as follows: 'Man is what we all know', and then goes on to say: 'for we all know what a dog, a horse, a plant is, and so forth; but none of these is a man.' We do not aspire to the malice of Sextus Empiricus, nor have we his wit; for he concludes as we know, from the above definition, and quite correctly, that man is a dog; for man is what we all know, and we

criterion of the Truth, which in the whole course of Greek philosophy was either *sought*, or *doubted*, or *postulated*, or *made fruitful*. Is it not remarkable that the Greeks should have borne us this testimony? And is it not an epitome, as it were, of the significance of Greek culture, an epigram of its own writing, with which it is also better served than with the frequently voluminous disquisitions sometimes devoted to it? Thus the proposition is worth positing, and also for another reason, since we have already explained it in the two preceding chapters;[1] while anyone who explains Socrates differently may well beware lest he fall into the snare of the earlier or later Greek scepticism. For unless we hold fast to the Socratic doctrine of Recollection, and to his principle that every individual man is Man, Sextus Empiricus stands ready to make the transition involved in 'learning' not only difficult but impossible;[2] and Protagoras[3] will begin where Sextus Empiricus leaves off, teaching that man is the measure of all things, in the sense that the individual man is the measure for others, but by no means in the Socratic sense that each man is his own measure, neither more nor less.

So then we know what man is, and this wisdom, which I shall be the last to hold in light esteem, may progressively become richer and more significant, and with it also the Truth. But now the Reason hesitates, just as Socrates did; for the paradoxical passion of the Reason is aroused and seeks a collision; without rightly understanding itself, it is bent upon its own downfall. This is like what happens in connection with the paradox of love. Man lives undisturbed a self-centred life, until there awakens within him the paradox of self-love, in the form of love for another, the object of his longing. (Self-love is the underlying principle, or the principle that is made to lie under, in all love; whence if we conceive a religion of love, this religion need make but one assumption, as epigrammatic as true, and take its realization for granted: namely the condition that man loves himself, in order to command him to love his neighbour as himself.) The lover is so completely transformed by the paradox of love that he scarcely recognizes himself; so say the poets, who are the spokesmen of love, and so say also the lovers themselves, since

all know what a dog is, *ergo*—but let us not be so malicious. Nevertheless, has this question been so thoroughly cleared up in our time that no one need feel uneasy about himself when he is reminded of poor Socrates and his predicament? [Democritus—Greek atomistic philosopher, born about 460 BC.]

[1] See Introductory Note above.

[2] Sextus Empiricus (flourished in the latter half of the 2nd century AD) wrote, among other things, a comprehensive refutation of *mathematikoi*, i.e. teachers of the sciences, including grammar, rhetoric, mathematics, astrology, music, physics, etc. To him is due our fullest surviving expression of Greek scepticism. See n. 1 to p. 385.

[3] Born in the early fifth century BC, Protagoras figures in Plato's dialogue *Protagoras*.

they permit the poets merely to take the words from their lips, but not the passion from their hearts. In like manner the paradoxical passion of the Reason, while as yet a mere presentiment, retroactively affects man and his self-knowledge, so that he who thought to know himself is no longer certain whether he is a more strangely composite animal than Typhon, or if perchance his nature contains a gentler and diviner part. . . .

But what is this unknown something with which the Reason collides when inspired by its paradoxical passion, with the result of unsettling even man's knowledge of himself? It is the Unknown. It is not a human being, in so far as we know what man is; nor is it any other known thing. So let us call this unknown something: *God*. It is nothing more than a name we assign to it. The idea of demonstrating that this unknown something (God) exists, could scarcely suggest itself to the Reason. For if God does not exist it would of course be impossible to prove it; and if he does exist it would be folly to attempt it. For at the very outset, in beginning my proof, I will have presupposed it, not as doubtful but as certain (a presupposition is never doubtful, for the very reason that it is a presupposition), since otherwise I would not begin, readily understanding that the whole would be impossible if he did not exist. But if when I speak of proving God's existence I mean that I purpose to prove that the Unknown, which exists, is God, then I express myself unfortunately. For in that case I do not prove anything, least of all an existence, but merely develop the content of a conception. Generally speaking, it is a difficult matter to prove that anything exists; and what is still worse for the intrepid souls who undertake the venture, the difficulty is such that fame scarcely awaits those who concern themselves with it. The entire demonstration always turns into something very different from what it assumes to be, and becomes an additional development of the consequences that flow from my having assumed that the object in question exists. Thus I always reason from existence, not towards existence, whether I move in the sphere of palpable sensible fact or in the realm of thought. I do not for example prove that a stone exists, but that some existing thing is a stone. The procedure in a court of justice does not prove that a criminal exists, but that the accused, whose existence is given, is a criminal. Whether we call existence an *accessorium* or the eternal *prius*, it is never subject to demonstration. Let us take ample time for consideration. We have no such reason for haste as have those who from concern for themselves or for God or for some other thing, must make haste to get its existence demonstrated. Under such circumstances there may indeed be need for haste, especially if the prover sincerely seeks to appreciate the danger that he himself, or the thing in question, may be non-existent unless the proof is finished;

and does not surreptitiously entertain the thought that it exists whether he succeeds in proving it or not.

If it were proposed to prove Napoleon's existence from Napoleon's deeds, would it not be a most curious proceeding? His existence does indeed explain his deeds, but the deeds do not prove *his* existence, unless I have already understood the word 'his' so as thereby to have assumed his existence. But Napoleon is only an individual, and in so far there exists no absolute relationship between him and his deeds; some other person might have performed the same deeds. Perhaps this is the reason why I cannot pass from the deeds to existence. If I call these deeds the deeds of Napoleon the proof becomes superfluous, since I have already named him; if I ignore this, I can never prove from the deeds that they are Napoleon's, but only in a purely ideal manner that such deeds are the deeds of a great general, and so forth. But between God and his works there exists an absolute relationship; God is not a name but a concept. Is this perhaps the reason that his *essentia involvit existentiam*?* The works of

* So Spinoza, who probes the depths of the God-idea in order to bring existence out of it by way of thought; but not it should be noted as if existence were an accidental circumstance, but rather as if it constituted an essential determination of content. Here lies Spinoza's profundity, but let us examine his reasoning. In *principia philosophiae Cartesianae, pars I, propositio VII, lemma I,* he says: '*quo res sua natura perfectior est, eo maiorem existentiam et magis necessariam involvit; et contra, quo magis necessariam existentiam res sua natura involvit, eo perfectior*' ['The more perfect a thing is in its own nature, the more it involves existence and the more necessary is its existence; conversely, the more a thing in its own nature involves existence, the more perfect it is.']. The more perfect therefore a thing is, the more being it has; the more being it has, the more perfect it is. This is, however, a tautology, which becomes still more evident in a note, *nota II*: '*quod hic non loquimur de pulchritudine et aliis perfectionibus, quas homines ex superstitione et ignorantia perfectiones vocare voluerunt. Sed per perfectionem intelligo tantum realitatem sive esse*' ['But we do not so refer to beauty and other perfections which men out of superstition and ignorance have chosen to call perfections. But instead I understand by perfection only reality or being.']. He explains *perfectio* by *realitas, esse*; so that the more perfect a thing is, the more it is; but its perfection consists in having more *esse* in itself; that is to say, the more a thing is, the more it is. So much for the tautology, but now further. What is lacking here is a distinction between factual being and ideal being. The terminology which permits us to speak of more or less of being, and consequently of degrees of reality or being, is in itself lacking in clearness, and becomes still more confusing when the above distinction is neglected; when, in other words, Spinoza does indeed speak profoundly, but fails first to consider the difficulty. In the case of factual existence it is meaningless to speak of more or less of being. A fly, when it exists, has as much being as God; the stupid remark I here set down has as much factual existence as Spinoza's profundity; for factual existence is subject to the dialectic of Hamlet: to be or not to be. Factual existence is wholly indifferent to any and all variations in essence, and everything that exists participates without petty jealousy in being, and participates in the same degree. Ideally, to be sure, the case is quite different. *But the moment I speak of being in the ideal sense I no longer speak of being, but of essence.* The highest ideality is necessary, and therefore it is. But this its being is identical with its essence; such being does not involve it dialectically in the determination of factual existence, since it is; nor can it be said to have more or less of being in relation to other things. In the old days this used to be expressed, if somewhat imperfectly, by saying that if God is possible, he is *eo ipso* necessary (Leibniz [see above, p. 145.]). Spinoza's principle is thus quite correct and his tautology in order; but it is also certain that he altogether evades the difficulty. For the difficulty is to lay hold of God's factual existence, and to introduce God's ideal essence dialectically into the sphere of factual existence.

God are such that only God can perform them. Just so, but where then are the works of God? The works from which I would deduce his existence are not immediately given. The wisdom of God in nature, his goodness, his wisdom in the governance of the world—are all these manifest, perhaps, upon the very face of things? Are we not here confronted with the most terrible temptations to doubt, and is it not impossible finally to dispose of all these doubts? But from such an order of things I will surely not attempt to prove God's existence; and even if I began I would never finish, and would in addition have to live constantly in suspense, lest something so terrible should suddenly happen that my bit of proof would be demolished. From what works then do I propose to derive the proof? From the works as apprehended through an ideal interpretation, i.e. such as they do not immediately reveal themselves. But in that case it is not from the works that I prove God's existence. I merely develop the ideality I have presupposed, and because of my confidence in *this* I make so bold as to defy all objections, even those that have not yet been made. In beginning my proof I presuppose the ideal interpretation, and also that I will be successful in carrying it through; but what else is this but to presuppose that God exists, so that I really begin by virtue of confidence in him?

And how does God's existence emerge from the proof? Does it follow straightway, without any breach of continuity? Or have we not here an analogy to the behaviour of these toys, the little Cartesian toys? As soon as I let go of the doll it stands on its head. As soon as I let it go—I must therefore let it go. So also with the proof for God's existence. As long as I keep my hold on the proof, i.e. continue to demonstrate, the existence does not come out, if for no other reason than that I am engaged in proving it; but when I let the proof go, the existence is there. But this act of letting go is surely also something; it is indeed a contribution of mine. Must not this also be taken into account, this little moment, brief as it may be?—it need not be long, for it is a *leap*. However brief this moment, if only an instantaneous now, this 'now' must be included in the reckoning. If anyone wishes to have it ignored, I will use it to tell a little anecdote. Chrysippus[1] was experimenting with a sorites[2] to see if he could not bring about a break in quality, either progressively or retrogressively. But Carneades[3] could not get it in his head when the new quality actually emerged. Then Chrysippus told him to try making a little pause in the

[1] Chrysippus of Soli in Cilicia (*c.* 280–204 BC) was an early Stoic philosopher and logician.

[2] A sorites is an extended form of the syllogism, of the form 'All As are Bs; All Bs are Cs; All Cs are Ds; . . . Therefore All As are Ns'.

[3] Carneades (214–129 BC), of Cyrene, a member of the New Academy, was an acute and distinguished critic of Stoicism.

reckoning, and so—so it would be easier to understand. Carneades replied: With the greatest pleasure, please do not hesitate on my account; you may not only pause, but even lie down to sleep, and it will help you just as little; for when you awake we will begin again where you left off. Just so; it boots as little to try to get rid of something by sleeping as to try to come into the posession of something in the same manner.

Whoever therefore attempts to demonstrate the existence of God (except in the sense of clarifying the concept, and without the *reservatio finalis* noted above, that the existence emerges from the demonstration by a leap) proves in lieu thereof something else, something which at times perhaps does not need proof, and in any case needs none better; for the fool says in his heart that there is no God, but whoever says in his heart or to men: Wait just a little and I will prove it—what a rare man of wisdom is he!* If in the moment of beginning his proof it is not absolutely undetermined whether God exists or not, he does not prove it; and if it is thus undetermined in the beginning, he will never come to begin, partly from fear of failure, since God perhaps does not exist, and partly because he has nothing with which to begin.—A project of this kind would scarcely have been undertaken by the ancients. Socrates at least, who is credited with having put forth the physico-teleological proof for God's existence,[1] did not go about it in any such manner. He always presupposes God's existence, and under this presupposition seeks to interpenetrate nature with the idea of purpose. Had he been asked why he pursued this method he would doubtless have explained that he lacked the courage to venture out upon so perilous a voyage of discovery without having made sure of God's existence behind him. At the word of God he casts his net as if to catch the idea of purpose; for nature herself finds many means of frightening the enquirer, and distracts him by many a digression.

The paradoxical passion of the Reason thus comes repeatedly into collision with the Unknown, which does indeed exist, but is unknown, and in so far does not exist. The Reason cannot advance beyond this point, and yet it cannot refrain in its paradoxicalness from arriving at this limit and occupying itself therewith. It will not serve to dismiss its relation to it simply by asserting that the Unknown does not exist, since this itself involves a relationship. But what then is the Unknown, since the designation of it as God merely signifies for us that it is unknown? To say that it is the Unknown because it cannot be known, and even if it were capable of being known, it could not be expressed, does not satisfy the demands of

* What an excellent subject for a comedy of the higher lunacy!

[1] See Xenophon, *Memorabilia* i.4.8.

passion, though it correctly interprets the Unknown as a limit; but a limit is precisely a torment for passion, though it also serves as an incitement. And yet the Reason can come no further, whether it risks an issue *via negationis* or *via eminentiae.*[1]

What then is the Unknown? It is the limit to which the Reason repeatedly comes, and in so far, substituting a static form of conception for the dynamic, it is the different, the absolutely different. But because it is absolutely different, there is no mark by which it could be distinguished. When qualified as an absolutely different it seems on the verge of disclosure, but this is not the case; for the Reason cannot even conceive an absolute unlikeness. The Reason cannot negate itself absolutely, but uses itself for the purpose, and thus conceives only such an unlikeness within itself as it can conceive by means of itself; it cannot absolutely transcend itself, and hence conceives only such a superiority over itself as it can conceive by means of itself. Unless the Unknown (God) remains a mere limiting conception, the single idea of difference will be thrown into a state of confusion, and become many ideas of many differences. The Unknown is then in a condition of dispersion, and the Reason may choose at pleasure from what is at hand and the imagination may suggest (the monstrous, ludicrous, etc.).

But it is impossible to hold fast to a difference of this nature. Every time this is done it is essentially an arbitrary act, and deepest down in the heart of piety lurks the mad caprice which knows that it has itself produced God. If no specific determination of difference can be held fast, because there is no distinguishing mark, like and unlike finally become identified with one another, thus sharing the fate of all such dialectical opposites. The unlikeness clings to the Reason and confounds it, so that the Reason no longer knows itself and quite consistently confuses itself with the unlikeness. On this point paganism has been sufficiently prolific in fantastic inventions. As for the last-named supposition, the self-irony of the Reason, I shall attempt to delineate it merely by a stroke or two, without raising any question of its being historical. There lives an individual whose appearance is precisely like that of other men; he grows up to manhood like others, he marries, he has an occupation by which he earns his livelihood, and he makes provision for the future as befits a man. For though it may be beautiful to live like the birds of the air, it is not lawful, and may lead to the sorriest of consequences: either starvation if one has enough persistence, or dependence on the bounty of others. This man is also God. How do I know? I cannot know it, for in order to know it I would have to know God, and the nature of the difference between God

[1] The Negative and Affirmative ways: see above, p. 51.

and man; and this I cannot know, because the Reason has reduced it to likeness with that from which it was unlike. Thus God becomes the most terrible of deceivers, because the Reason has deceived itself. The Reason has brought God as near as possible, and yet he is as far away as ever.

Now perhaps someone will say: 'You are certainly a crocheteer, as I know very well. But you surely do not believe that I would pay any attention to such a crotchet, so strange and so ridiculous that it has doubtless never occurred to anyone, and above all so absurd that I must exclude from my consciousness everything that I have in it in order to hit upon it.'—And so indeed you must. But do you think yourself warranted in retaining all the presuppositions you have in your consciousness, while pretending to think about your consciousness without presuppositions? Will you deny the consistency of our exposition: that the Reason, in attempting to determine the Unknown as the unlike, at last goes astray, and confounds the unlike with the like? From this there would seem to follow the further consequence, that if man is to receive any true knowledge about the Unknown (God) he must be made to know that it is unlike him, absolutely unlike him. This knowledge the Reason cannot possibly obtain of itself; we have already seen that this would be a self-contradiction. It will therefore have to obtain this knowledge from God. But even if it obtains such knowledge it cannot understand it, and thus is quite unable to possess such knowledge. For how should the Reason be able to understand what is absolutely different from itself? If this is not immediately evident, it will become clearer in the light of the consequences; for if God is absolutely unlike man, then man is absolutely unlike God; but how could the Reason be expected to understand this? Here we seem to be confronted with a paradox. Merely obtain the knowledge that God is unlike him, man needs the help of God; and now he learns that God is absolutely different from himself. But if God and man are absolutely different, this cannot be accounted for on the basis of what man derives from God, for in so far they are akin. Their unlikeness must therefore be explained by what man derives from himself, or by what he has brought upon his own head. But what can this unlikeness be? Aye, what can it be but sin; since the unlikeness, the absolute unlikeness, is something that man has brought upon himself. We have expressed this in the preceding that man was in Error, and had brought this upon his head by his own guilt; and we came to the conclusion, partly in jest and yet also in earnest, that it was too much to expect of man that he should find this out for himself. Now we have again arrived at the same conclusion. The connoisseur in self-knowledge was perplexed over himself to the point of bewilderment when he came to grapple in thought with the unlike; he scarcely knew any longer whether he was a stranger monster than Typhon, or if his nature partook of something divine. What then did he lack? The consciousness of sin, which he indeed could no more teach to another than another could teach it to him, but only God—if God consents to become a Teacher. But this was his purpose, as we have imagined it. In order to be man's Teacher, God proposed to make himself like the individual man, so that he might understand him fully. Thus our paradox is rendered still more appalling, or the same paradox has the double aspect which proclaims it as the Absolute Paradox; negatively by revealing the absolute unlikeness of sin, positively by proposing to do away with the absolute unlikeness in absolute likeness.

But can such a paradox be conceived? Let us not be over-hasty in replying; and since we strive merely to find the answer to a question, and not as those who run a race, it may be well to remember that success is to the accurate rather than to the swift. The Reason will doubtless find it impossible to conceive it, could not of itself have discovered it, and when it hears it announced will not be able to understand it, sensing merely that its downfall is threatened. In so far the Reason will have much to urge against it; and yet we have on the other hand seen that the Reason, in its paradoxical passion, precisely desires its own downfall. But this is what the Paradox also desires, and thus they are at bottom linked in understanding; but this understanding is present only in the moment of passion. Consider the analogy presented by love, though it is not a perfect one. Self-love underlies love; but the paradoxical passion of self-love when at its highest pitch wills precisely its own downfall. This is also what love desires, so that these two are linked in mutual understanding in the passion of the moment, and this passion is love. Why should not the lover find this conceivable? But he who in self-love shrinks from the touch of love can neither understand it nor summon the courage to venture it, since it means his downfall. Such is then the passion of love; self-love is indeed submerged but not annihilated; it is taken captive and become love's *spolia opima*, but may again come to life, and this is love's temptation. So also with the Paradox in its relation to the Reason, only that the passion in this case has another name; or rather, we must seek to find a name for it.

Appendix

THE PARADOX AND THE OFFENDED CONSCIOUSNESS

(*An Acoustic Illusion*)

If the Paradox and the Reason come together in a mutual understanding of their unlikeness their encounter will be happy, like love's understanding, happy in the passion to which we have not yet assigned a name, and will postpone naming until later. If the encounter is not in understanding the relationship becomes unhappy, and this unhappy love of the Reason if I may so call it (which it should be noted is analogous only to that particular form of unhappy love which has its root in misunderstood self-love; no further stretching of the analogy is possible, since accident can play no role in this realm), may be characterized more specifically as *Offence.*

All offence is in its deepest root passive.* In this respect it is like that form of unhappy love to which we have just alluded. Even when such a self-love (and does it not already seem contradictory that love of self should be passive?) announces itself in deeds of audacious achievements, in astounding achievements, it is passive and wounded. It is the pain of its wound which gives it its illusory strength, expressing itself in what looks like self-activity and may easily deceive, since self-love is especially bent on concealing its passivity. Even when it tramples on the object of affection, even when it painfully schools itself to a hardened indifference and tortures itself to show this indifference, even then, even when it abandons itself to a frivolous triumph over its success (this form is the most deceptive of all), even then it is passive. Such is also the case with the offended consciousness. Whatever be its mode of expression, even when it exultantly celebrates the triumph of its unspirituality, it is always passive. Whether the offended individual sits broken-hearted, staring almost like a beggar at the Paradox, paralysed by his suffering, or he sheathes himself in the armour of derision, pointing the arrows of his wit as if from a distance —he is still passive and near at hand. Whether offence came and robbed the offended individual of his last bit of comfort and joy, or made him

* The Danish language correctly calls emotion (Dan. '*Affekten*') 'Sindslidelse' (compare German '*Leiden*schaft'). When we use the word '*Affekt*' we are likely to think more immediately of the convulsive daring which astounds us, and makes us forget that it is a form of passivity. So for example: pride, defiance, etc.

strong—the offended consciousness is nevertheless passive. It has wrestled with the stronger, and its show of strength is like the peculiar agility induced in the bodily sphere by a broken back.

However, it is quite possible to distinguish between an active and a passive form of the offended consciousness, if we take care to remember that the passive form is so far active as not to permit itself wholly to be annihilated (for offence is always an act, never an event); and that the active form is always so weak that it cannot free itself from the cross to which it is nailed, or tear the arrow from out its wound.*

But precisely because offence is thus passive, the discovery, if it be allowable to speak thus, does not derive from the Reason, but from the Paradox. The offended consciousness does not understand itself† but is understood by the Paradox. While therefore the expressions in which offence proclaims itself, of whatever kind they may be, sound as if they came from elsewhere, even from the opposite direction, they are nevertheless echoings of the Paradox. This is what is called an acoustic illusion. But if the Paradox is *index* and *iudex sui et falsi*, the offended consciousness can be taken as an indirect proof of the validity of the Paradox; offence is the mistaken reckoning, the invalid consequence with which the Paradox repels and thrusts aside. The offended individual does not speak from his own resources, but borrows those of the Paradox; just as one who mimics or parodies another does not invent, but merely copies perversely. The more profound the passion with which the offended consciousness (active or passive) expresses itself, the more apparent is it how much it owes to the Paradox. Offence was not discovered by the Reason, far from it, for then the Reason must also have been able to discover the Paradox. No, offence comes into being with the Paradox; it *comes into being*. Here again we have the Moment, on which everything depends. Let us recapitulate. If we do not posit the Moment we return to Socrates; but it was precisely from him that we departed, in order to discover something. If we posit the Moment the Paradox is there; for the Moment is the Paradox in its most abbreviated form. Because of the

* The idiom of the language also supports the view that all offence is passive. We say: 'to be offended', which primarily expresses only the state or condition; but we also say, as identical in meaning with the foregoing: 'to take offence', which expresses a synthesis of active and passive. The Greek word is σκανδαλίζεσθαι. This word comes from σκάνδαλον (offence or stumbling-block), and hence means to take offence, or to collide with something. Here the movement of thought is clearly indicated; it is not that offence provokes the collision, but that it meets with a collision, and hence passively, although so far actively as itself to take offence. Hence the Reason is not the discoverer of offence; for the paradoxical collision which the Reason develops in isolation discovers neither the Paradox nor the reaction of offence.

† In this sense the Socratic principle that sin is ignorance finds justification. Sin does not understand itself in the Truth, but it does not follow that it may not will itself in Error.

Moment the learner is in Error; and man, who had before possessed self-knowledge, now becomes bewildered with respect to himself; instead of self-knowledge he receives the consciousness of sin, and so forth; for as soon as we posit the Moment everything follows of itself.

From the psychological point of view the offended consciousness will display a great variety of nuances within the more active and the more passive forms. To enter into a detailed description of these would not further our present purpose; but it is important to bear fixedly in mind that all offence is in its essence a misunderstanding of the *Moment*, since it is directed against the Paradox, which again is the Moment.

The dialectic of the *Moment* is not difficult. From the Socratic point of view the Moment is invisible and indistinguishable; it is not, it has not been, it will not come. Hence the learner is himself the Truth, and the moment of occasion is but a jest, like a bastard title that does not essentially belong to the book. From this point of view the Moment of decision becomes *folly*; for if a decision in time is postulated, then (by the preceding) the learner is in Error, which is precisely what makes a beginning in the Moment necessary. The reaction of the offended consciousness is to assert that the Moment is folly, and that the Paradox is folly; which is the contention of the Paradox that the Reason is absurd, now reflected back as in an echo from the offended consciousness. Or the Moment is regarded as constantly about to come; it is so regarded, and the Reason holds it as *worthy of regard*; but since the Paradox has made the Reason absurd, the regard of the Reason is no reliable criterion.

The offended consciousness holds aloof from the Paradox, and the reason is: *quia absurdum*. But it was not the Reason that made this discovery; on the contrary it was the Paradox that made the discovery, and now receives this testimony from the offended consciousness. The Reason says that the Paradox is absurd, but this is mere mimicry, since the Paradox is the Paradox, *quia absurdum*. The offended consciousness holds aloof from the Paradox and keeps to the probable, the Paradox being the most improbable of things. Again it is not the Reason that made this discovery; it merely snatches the words from the mouth of the Paradox, strange as this may seem; for the Paradox itself says: Comedies and romances and lies must needs be probable, but why should I be probable? The offended consciousness holds aloof from the Paradox, and what wonder, since the Paradox is the Miracle! This discovery was not made by the Reason; it was the Paradox that placed the Reason on the stool of wonderment and now replies: But why are you so astonished? It is precisely as you say, and the only wonder is that you regard it as an objection; but the truth in the mouth of a hypocrite is dearer to me than if it comes from the lips of an angel or an apostle. When the Reason boasts of its splendours in comparison with the Paradox, which is most wretched and despised, the discovery was not made by the Reason but by the Paradox itself; it is content to leave to the Reason all its splendours, even the splendid sins (*vitia splendida*). When the Reason takes pity on the Paradox, and wishes to help it to an explanation, the Paradox does not indeed acquiesce, but nevertheless finds it quite natural that the Reason should do this; for why do we have our philosophers, if not to make supernatural things trivial and commonplace? When the Reason says that it cannot get the Paradox into its head, it was not the Reason that made the discovery but the Paradox, which is so paradoxical as to declare the Reason a blockhead and a dunce, capable at the most of saying yes and no to the same thing, which is not good divinity. And so always. All that the offended consciousness has to say about the Paradox it has learned from the Paradox, though it would like to pose as the discoverer, making use of an acoustic illusion.

But I think I hear someone say: 'It is really becoming tiresome the way you go on, for now we have the same story over again; not one of the expressions you have put in the mind of the Paradox belongs to you.'—'Why should they belong to me, when they belong to the Paradox?'—'You can spare us your sophistry, you know very well what I mean. These expressions are not yours, nor by you put into the mouth of the Paradox, but are familiar quotations, and everybody knows who the authors are.'—'My friend, your accusation does not grieve me, as you perhaps believe; what you say rather makes me exceedingly glad. For I must admit that I could not repress a shudder when I wrote them down; I scarcely recognized myself, that I who am usually so timid and apprehensive dared say such things. But if the expressions are not by me, perhaps you will explain to whom they belong?'—'Nothing is easier. The first is by Tertullian,[1] the second by Hamann,[2] the third by Hamann, the fourth is by Lactantius[3] and is frequently quoted; the fifth is by Shakespeare, in a comedy called *All's Well that Ends Well*, Act II, Scene iii; the sixth is by Luther and the seventh is a remark by King Lear. You see that I am well informed, and that I have caught you with the goods.'—'Indeed I do

[1] Referring to the phrase *quia absurdum* (*credo quia absurdum*—the popularly quoted paraphrase of Tertullian's remark *prorsus credibile est, quia ineptum est*). Tertullian of Carthage (*c.* 160–*c.* 220) was the first Church Father to write in Latin.

[2] Hamann (1730–88), a German religious writer, emphasized the importance of inner experience, and condemned the rationalism of the Enlightenment.

[3] Lactantius (*c.* 240–*c.* 320), Christian writer and author of the first systematic expression of Christian doctrine in Latin.

perceive it; but will you now tell me whether all these men have not spoken of the relation between some paradox and an offended consciousness, and will you now note that the individuals who spoke thus were not themselves offended, but precisely persons who held to the Paradox; and yet they speak as if they were offended, and offence cannot find a more characteristic expression for itself. Is it not strange that the Paradox should thus as it were take the bread from the mouth of the offended consciousness, reducing it to the practice of an idle and unprofitable art? It seems as curious as if an opponent at a disputation, instead of attacking the author's thesis, defended him in his distraction. Does it not seem so to you? However, one merit unquestionably belongs to the offended consciousness, in that it brings out the unlikeness more clearly; for in that happy passion which we have not yet given a name, the Unlike is on good terms with the Reason. There must be a difference if there is to be a synthesis in some third entity. But here the difference consisted in the fact that the Reason yielded itself while the Paradox bestowed itself, and the understanding is consummated in that happy passion which will doubtless soon find a name; and this is the smallest part of the matter, for even if my happiness does not have a name—when I am but happy, I ask for no more.'

19

MANSEL

on THE LIMITS OF RELIGIOUS THOUGHT

Biographical Note Henry Longueville Mansel, born at Cosgrove in Northamptonshire, in 1820, was educated at Merchant Taylors' School and St John's College, Oxford, taking his degree in 1843. He then taught as a private tutor at Oxford. Ordained deacon in 1844, and priest in 1845. 1855, elected Waynflete Professor of Moral and Metaphysical Philosophy at Oxford. 1858, delivered Bampton Lectures. In 1865 visited Rome, for his health. In 1866, elected Professor of Ecclesiastical History. 1868, appointed Dean of St Paul's. Died in 1871, while on a visit to Cosgrove.

Principal works: *Prolegomena Logica* (1851), *The Limits of Religious Thought* (1858), *The Philosophy of the Conditioned* (1866), and *The Gnostic Heresies of the First and Second Centuries* (posthumous).

Philosophical Note Dean Mansel is chiefly remembered for his Bampton Lectures, in which he tries to trace the limits of religious thought. He was largely influenced in his philosophical views by Sir William Hamilton (1788–1856), the distinguished Scottish philosopher, who denied the possibility of a coherent metaphysical view of the universe, owing to the relative and fragmentary nature of human knowledge, and hence denied that there could be any knowledge of the Absolute. M. went on to apply this principle to theology, and it is noteworthy that the fly-leaf of the Bampton Lectures contains the quotation (from Hamilton): 'No difficulty emerges in theology which had not previously emerged in philosophy.' He argues, briefly that we can know *that* the Infinite exists but not *what* it is. Reasoning will not help to establish any truths about God, and these therefore have to be accepted by revelation. His lectures provoked a certain amount of violent criticism as well as enthusiastic support.

In the first three Lectures M. begins by criticizing both Dogmatism and Rationalism: the former tries to force reason into agreement with revelation, the latter to force revelation into agreement with reason. Both try to produce an exact correspondence between belief and thought, but M. objects that such an attempt is misguided without a prior investigation of the scope of thought: and this in any case will show that all attempts to give a rational account of Christian doctrines are futile. The mind is incapable of judging or criticizing revelation, since to do so it would require a coherent view of the Infinite independent of religion by which to evaluate revelation. In the Second Lecture, M. points out that there are two methods by which a philosophy of religion may be attempted: first the 'Objective' or 'Metaphysical' method, based upon a supposed knowledge of the nature of God and second the 'Subjective' or 'Psychological' method based on a knowledge of the mental faculties of man. He gives reasons for asserting that the former method is useless, in that propositions about the Absolute, the Infinite, the First Cause, all involve contradictions, as do also pantheistic and atheistic theories. In Lecture III he argues that the second method will not help either, for an investigation of human consciousness shows that it cannot conceive the Infinite: for (*a*) it involves discrimination between one object and another: this is limitation, and so there can be no understanding of the Unlimited; (*b*) it involves a distinction between subject and object: but the Absolute is independent of all relation; (*c*) it involves succession in time, but the Infinite is timeless; (*d*) it involves personality, and this is a kind of limitation. Thus both methods of constructing a rational philosophy of religion fail.

Bibliographical Note A useful essay on M. is W. R. Matthews, *The Religious Philosophy of Dean Mansel* (Oxford, 1956). Otherwise, modern discussions of M.'s work are, regrettably, lacking.

THE LIMITS OF RELIGIOUS THOUGHT

The Limits of Religious Thought, Lecture IV

That the Finite cannot comprehend the Infinite is a truth more frequently admitted in theory than applied in practice. It has been expressly asserted by men who, almost in the same breath, have proceeded to lay down canons of criticism, concerning the purpose of Revelation, and the truth or falsehood, importance or insignificance, of particular doctrines, on grounds which are tenable on the supposition of a perfect and intimate knowledge of God's Nature and Counsels. Hence it becomes necessary to bring down the above truth from general to special statements;—to enquire more particularly wherein the limitation of man's faculties consists, and in what manner it exhibits itself in the products of thought. This task I endeavoured to accomplish in my last Lecture. To pursue the conclusion thus obtained to its legitimate consequences in relation to Theology, we must next enquire how the human mind, thus limited, is able to form the idea of a relation between man and God, and what is the nature of that conception of God which arises from the consciousness of this relation. The purpose of our enquiry is to ascertain the limits of religious thought; and, for this purpose, it is necessary to proceed from the limits of thought and of human consciousness in general to those particular forms of consciousness which, in thought or in some other mode, especially constitute the essence of Religion.

Reasonings, probable or demonstrative, in proof of the being and attributes of God, have met with a very different reception at different periods. Elevated at one time, by the injudicious zeal of their advocates, to a certainty and importance to which they have no legitimate claim, at another, by equally extravagant reaction, they have been sacrificed in the mass to some sweeping principle of criticism, or destroyed piecemeal by minute objections in detail. While one school of theologians has endeavoured to raise the whole edifice of the Christian Faith on a basis of metaphysical proof, others have either expressly maintained that the understanding has nothing to do with religious belief, or have indirectly attempted to establish the same conclusion by special refutations of the particular reasonings.

An examination of the actual state of the human mind, as regards religious ideas, will lead us to a conclusion intermediate between these two extremes. On the one hand, it must be allowed that it is not through reasoning that men obtain the first intimation of their relation to the Deity; and that, had they been left to the guidance of their intellectual faculties alone, it is possible that no such intimation might have taken place; or at best, that it would have been but as one guess out of many equally plausible and equally natural. Those who lay exclusive stress on the proof of the existence of God from the marks of design in the world, or from the necessity of supposing a first cause of all phenomena, overlook the fact that man learns to pray before he learns to reason,—that he feels within him the consciousness of a Supreme Being, and the instinct of worship, before he can argue from effects to causes, or estimate the traces of wisdom and benevolence scattered through the creation. But on the other hand, arguments which would be insufficient to create the notion of a Supreme Being in a mind previously destitute of it may have great force and value in enlarging or correcting a notion already existing and in justifying to the reason the unreasoning convictions of the heart. The belief in a God, once given, becomes the nucleus round which subsequent experiences cluster and accumulate; and evidences which would be obscure or ambiguous, if addressed to the reason only, become clear and convincing when interpreted by the light of the religious consciousness.

We may therefore without hesitation accede to the argument of the great Critic of metaphysics,[1] when he tells us that the speculative reason is unable to prove the existence of a Supreme Being, but can only correct our conception of such a Being, supposing it to be already obtained. But at the same time it is necessary to protest against the pernicious extent to which the reaction against the use of reason in theology has in too many instances been carried. When the same critic tells us that we cannot legitimately infer, from the order and visible design in the world, the

[1] I.e. Kant: see pp. 249–50

omnipotence and omniscience of its Creator, because a degree of wisdom and power short of the very highest might possibly be sufficient to produce all the effects which we are able to discern;[1] or when a later writer, following in the same track condemns the argument from final causes, because it represents God exclusively in the aspect of an artist;[2] or when a third writer, of a different school, tells us that the processes of thought have nothing to do with the soul, the organ of religion;[3]—we feel that systems which condemn the use of reasoning in sacred things may be equally one-sided and extravagant as those which assert its supreme authority. Reasoning must not be condemned for failing to accomplish what no possible mode of human consciousness ever does or can accomplish. If consciousness itself is a limitation, if every mode of consciousness is a determination of the mind in one particular manner out of many possible, it follows indeed that the infinite is beyond the reach of man's arguments, but only as it is also beyond the reach of his feelings or volitions. We cannot indeed reason to the existence of an infinite Cause from the presence of finite effects, nor contemplate the infinite in a finite mode of knowledge; but neither can we feel the infinite in the form of a finite affection,[4] nor discern it as the law of a finite action. If our whole consciousness of God is partial and incomplete, composed of various attributes manifested in various relations, why should we condemn the reasoning which represents him in a single aspect, so long as it neither asserts nor implies that that aspect is the only one in which he can be represented? If man is not a creature composed solely of intellect, or solely of feeling, or solely of will, why should any one element of his nature be excluded from participating in the pervading consciousness of him in whom we live and move and have our being? A religion based solely on the reason may starve on barren abstractions, or bewilder itself with inexplicable contradictions; but a religion which repudiates thought to take refuge in feeling abandons itself to the wild follies of fanaticism or the diseased ecstasies of mysticism: while one which acknowledges the practical energies alone may indeed attain to Stoicism, but will fall far short of Christianity. It is our duty indeed to pray with the spirit; but it is no less our duty to pray with the understanding also.

[1] See above, pp. 269–70

[2] Jowett, *Epistles of St Paul*, Vol. ii, p. 406. Jowett argued that the works of nature are quite *unlike* works of art; substantially his point is the same as Hume's (*Dialogues*, Pt. II): 'But surely you will not affirm that the universe bears such a resemblance to a house, that we can with the same certainty infer a similar cause.'

[3] M. criticizes F. W. Newman (1805–97) (John Henry Newman's brother, and Fellow of Balliol) for this view.

[4] 'Affection' here is being used not in its modern and narrower sense, but to mean, roughly, 'emotion' or 'feeling'.

Taking then, as the basis of our enquiry, the admission that the whole consciousness of man, whether in thought, or in feeling, or in volition, is limited in the manner of its operation and in the objects to which it is related, let us endeavour, with regard to the religious consciousness in particular, to separate from each other the complicated threads which, in their united web, constitute the conviction of man's relation to a Supreme Being. In distinguishing, however, one portion of these as forming the origin of this conviction, and another portion as contributing rather to its further development and direction, I must not be understood to maintain or imply that the former could have existed and been recognized, prior to and independently of the co-operation of the latter. Consciousness, in its earliest discernible form, is only possible as the result of a union of the reflective with the intuitive faculties.[1] A state of mind, to be known at all as existing, must be distinguished from other states; and to make this distinction, we must think of it as well as experience it. Without thought as well as sensation there could be no consciousness of the existence of an external world: without thought as well as emotion and volition there could be no consciousness of the moral nature of man. Sensation without thought would at most amount to no more than an indefinite sense of uneasiness or momentary irritation, without any power of discerning in what manner we are affected, or of distinguishing our successive affections from each other. To distinguish, for example, in the visible world, any object from any other, we must be able to refer them to distinct notions; and such reference is an act of thought. The same condition holds good of the religious consciousness also. In whatever mental affection we become conscious of our relation to a Supreme Being, we can discern that consciousness, as such, only by reflecting upon it as conceived under its proper notion. Without this we could not know our religious consciousness to be what it is; and, as the knowledge of a fact of consciousness is identical with its existence, without this the religious consciousness as such could not exist.

But notwithstanding this necessary co-operation of thought in every manifestation of human consciousness, it is not to the reflective faculties that we must look if we would discover the origin of religion. For to the exercise of reflection it is necessary that there should exist an object on which to reflect; and though, in the order of time, the distinct recognition of this object is simultaneous with the act of reflecting upon it, yet, in the order of nature, the latter presupposes the former. Religious thought, if it is to exist at all, can only exist as representative of some fact of religious

[1] 'Intuitive' here is used, as is apparent from what follows, in a general sense: 'intuitions' roughly mean 'experiences' (immediate experiences, about which there may be reflection).

intuition—of some individual state of mind, in which is presented as an immediate fact that relation of man to God, of which man by reflection may become distinctly and definitely conscious.

Two such states may be specified, as dividing between them the rude materials out of which Reflection builds up the edifice of Religious Consciousness. These are the *Feeling of Dependence* and the *Conviction of Moral Obligation.* To these two facts of the inner consciousness may be traced, as to their sources, the two great outward acts by which religion in various forms has been manifested!—*Prayer*, by which they seek to win God's blessing upon the future, and *Expiation*, by which they strive to atone for the offences of the past. The Feeling of Dependence is the instinct which urges us to pray. It is the feeling that our existence and welfare are in the hands of a superior Power;—not of an inexorable Fate or immutable Law, but of a Being having at least so far the attributes of Personality that he can show favour or severity to those dependent upon him, and can be regarded by them with feelings of hope and fear and reverence and gratitude. It is a feeling similar in kind, though higher in degree, to that which is awakened in the mind of the child towards his parent, who is first manifested to his mind as the giver of such things as are needful, and to whom the first language he addresses is that of entreaty. It is the feeling so fully and intensely expressed by the Psalmist: 'Thou art he that took me out of my mother's womb: thou wast my hope, when I hanged yet upon my mother's breasts. I have been left unto thee ever since I was born: thou art my God even from my mother's womb. Be not thou far from me, O Lord; thou art my succour, haste thee to help me. I will declare thy Name unto my brethren: in the midst of the congregation will I praise thee.' With the first development of consciousness, there grows up as a part of it the innate feeling that our life, natural and spiritual, is not in our power to sustain or prolong!—that there is One above us, on whom we are dependent, whose existence we learn and whose presence we realize by the sure instinct of Prayer. We have thus, in the Sense of Dependence, the foundation of one great element of Religion—the Fear of God.

But the mere consciousness of dependence does not of itself exhibit the character of the Being on whom we depend. It is as consistent with superstition as with religion!—with the belief in a malevolent, as in a benevolent, Deity; it is as much called into existence by the severities as by the mercies of God, by the suffering which we are unable to avert as by the benefits which we did not ourselves procure.[1] The Being on whom we depend is, in that single relation, manifested in the infliction of pain as

[1] In a note, M. remarks that this point had been made earlier by Hegel, and quotes the latter's sarcastic assertion that on Schleiermacher's theory a dog is the best Christian.

well as in the bestowal of happiness. But in order to make suffering as well as enjoyment contribute to the religious education of mankind it is necessary that he should be conscious not merely of *suffering*, but of *sin*, that he should look upon pain not merely as *inflicted*, but as *deserved*, and should recognize in its Author the justice that punishes, not merely the anger that harms. In the feeling of dependence we are conscious of the Power of God, but not necessarily of his Goodness. This deficiency, however, is supplied by the other element of religion, the Consciousness of Moral Obligation, carrying with it, as it necessarily does, the Conviction of Sin. It is impossible to establish, as a great modern philosopher has attempted to do, the theory of an absolute Autonomy of the Will, that is to say, of an obligatory law resting on no basis save that of its own imperative character.[1] Considered solely in itself, with no relation to any higher authority, the consciousness of a law of obligation is a fact of our mental constitution and it is no more. The fiction of an absolute law, binding on all rational beings, has only an apparent universality, because we can only conceive other rational beings by identifying their constitution with our own and making human reason the measure and representative of reason in general. Why then has one part of our constitution, merely as such, an imperative authority over the remainder? What right has one portion of the human consciousness to represent itself as *duty* and another merely as *inclination*? There is but one answer possible. The Moral Reason, or Will, or Conscience, of Man—call it by what name we please—can have no authority save as implanted in him by some higher Spiritual Being, as a *Law* emanating from a *Lawgiver*. Man can be a law unto himself only on the supposition that he reflects in himself the Law of God, that he shows, as the Apostle tells us, the works of that law written in his heart.[2] If he is absolutely a law unto himself, his duty and his pleasure are indistinguishable from each other, for he is subject to no one and accountable to no one. Duty, in this case, becomes only a higher kind of pleasure—a balance between the present and the future, between the larger and smaller gratification. We are thus compelled by the consciousness of moral obligation to assume the existence of a moral Deity and to regard the absolute standard of right and wrong as constituted by the nature of that Deity.[3] The conception of this standard, in the human mind, may indeed be faint and fluctuating, and must be imperfect: it may vary

[1] For this theory see Kant, *Metaphysic of Ethics* II. And see above p. 273.

[2] Rom. 2.15.

[3] This view is to be distinguished from one which asserts that the standard is based on an arbitrary fiat of God's Will, and is similar to that held by Ralph Cudworth (1617–88), the Cambridge Platonist, in his *Eternal and Immutable Morality*, Bk I., Ch. 3; Bk IV, Ch. 4. See also n. 1 to p. 442.

with the intellectual and moral culture of the nation or the individual: and in its highest human representation it must fall far short of the reality. But it is present to all mankind as a basis of moral obligation and an inducement to moral progress: it is present in the universal consciousness of sin, in the conviction that we are offenders against God, in the expiatory rites by which, whether inspired by some natural instinct or inherited from some primeval tradition, divers nations have in their various modes striven to atone for their transgressions and to satisfy the wrath of their righteous Judge. However erroneously the particular acts of religious service may have been understood by men, yet, in the universal consciousness of innocence and guilt, of duty and disobedience, of an appeased and offended God, there is exhibited the instinctive confession of all mankind that the moral nature of man, as subject to the law of obligation, reflects and represents in some degree the moral nature of a Deity by whom that obligation is imposed.

But these two elements of the religious consciousness, however real and efficient within their own limits, are subject to the same restrictions which we have before noticed as binding upon consciousness in general. Neither in the feeling of dependence nor in that of obligation can we be directly conscious of the Absolute or the Infinite as such. And it is the more necessary to notice this limitation inasmuch as an opposite theory has been maintained by one whose writings have had perhaps more influence than those of any other man in forming the modern religious philosophy of his own country, and whose views, in all their essential features, have been ably maintained and widely diffused among ourselves. According to Schleiermacher the essence of religion is to be found in a feeling of absolute and entire dependence, in which the mutual action and reaction of subject and object upon each other, which constitutes the ordinary consciousness of mankind, gives way to a sense of utter, passive helplessness —to a consciousness that our entire personal agency is annihilated in the presence of the infinite energy of the Godhead. In our intercourse with the world, he tells us, whether in relation to nature and to human society, the feeling of freedom and that of dependence are always in mutual operation upon each other, sometimes in equilibrium, sometimes with a vast preponderance of the one or the other feeling, but never to the entire exclusion of either. But in our communion with God there is always an accompanying consciousness that the whole activity is absolutely and entirely dependent upon him, that, whatever amount of freedom may be apparent in the individual moments of life, these are but detached and isolated portions of a passively dependent whole.[1] The theory is carried

[1] Schleiermacher, *The Christian Faith*, §4: see above, p. 307.

still further and expressed in more positive terms by an English disciple, who says that 'Although man, while in the midst of finite objects, always feels himself to a certain extent independent and free, yet in the presence of that which is self-existent, infinite and eternal he may feel the sense of freedom utterly pass away and become absorbed in the sense of absolute dependence.' 'Let the relation,' he continues, 'of subject and object in the economy of our emotions become such that the whole independent energy of the former merges in the latter as its prime cause and present sustainer; let the subject become as nothing—not, indeed, from its intrinsic insignificance or incapacity of moral action, but by virtue of the infinity of the object to which it stands consciously opposed: and the feeling of dependence *must* become *absolute*, for all finite power is as *nothing* in relation to the Infinite.'[1]

Of this theory it may be observed, in the first place, that it contemplates God chiefly in the character of an *object of infinite magnitude*. The relations of the object to the subject, in our consciousness of the world and in that of God, differ from each other in degree rather than in kind. The Deity is manifested with no attribute of personality: he is merely the world magnified to infinity, and the feeling of absolute dependence is in fact that of the annihilation of our personal existence in the Infinite Being of the Universe. Of this feeling, the intellectual exponent is pure Pantheism; and the infinite object is but the indefinite abstraction of Being in general, with no distinguishing characteristic to constitute a Deity. For the distinctness of an object of consciousness is in the inverse ratio to the intensity of the passive affection. As the feeling of dependence becomes more powerful, the knowledge of the character of the object on which we depend must necessarily become less and less; for the discernment of any object as such is a state of mental energy and reaction of thought upon that object. Hence the feeling of absolute dependence, supposing it possible, could convey no consciousness of God as God, but merely an indefinite impression of dependence upon something. Towards an object so vague and meaningless, no real religious relation is possible.

In the second place, the consciousness of an absolute dependence in which our activity is annihilated is a contradiction in terms; for consciousness is itself an activity. We can be conscious of a state of mind as such only by attending to it; and attention is in all cases a mode of our active energy. Thus the state of absolute dependence, supposing it to exist at all, could not be distinguished from other states; and as all consciousness is distinction, it could not, by any mode of consciousness, be known to exist.

[1] J. D. Morell (1816–1891), *Philosophy of Religion* (London, 1849), p. 75.

In the third place, the theory is inconsistent with the duty of Prayer. Prayer is essentially a state in which man is in active relation towards God; in which he is intensely conscious of his personal existence and its wants; in which he endeavours by entreaty to prevail with God. Let any one consider for a moment of the strong energy of the language of the Apostles: 'Now I beseech you, brethren, for the Lord Jesus Christ's sake, and for the love of the Spirit, that ye strive together with me in your prayers to God for me:'[1] or the consciousness of a personal need which pervades that Psalm in which David so emphatically declared his dependence upon God: 'My God, my God, look upon me; why hast thou forsaken me, and art so far from my health, and from the words of my complaint? O my God, I cry in the day-time, but thou hearest not; and in the night season also I take no rest:'[2] let him ponder the words of our Lord himself: 'Shall not God avenge his own elect, which cry day and night unto him:'[3]—and then let him say if such language is compatible with the theory which asserts that man's personality is annihilated in his communion with God.

But lastly, there is another fatal objection to the above theory. It makes our moral and religious consciousness subversive of each other and reduces us to the dilemma that either our faith or our practice must be founded on a delusion. The actual relation of man to God is the same, in whatever degree man may be conscious of it. If man's dependence on God is not really destructive of his personal freedom, the religious consciousness, in denying that freedom, is a false consciousness. If, on the contrary, man is in reality passively dependent upon God, the consciousness of moral responsibility, which bears witness to his free agency, is a lying witness. Actually, in the sight of God, we are either totally dependent or partially at least free. And as this condition must be always the same, whether we are conscious of it or not, it follows that, in proportion as one of these modes of consciousness reveals to us the truth, the other must be regarded as testifying to a falsehood.

Nor yet is it possible to find in the consciousness of moral obligation any immediate apprehension of the Absolute and Infinite. For the free agency of man, which in the feeling of dependence is always present as a subordinate element, becomes here the centre and turning-point of the whole. The consciousness of the Infinite is necessarily excluded; first, by the mere existence of a relation between two distinct agents; and secondly, by the conditions under which each must necessarily be conceived in its relation to the other. The moral consciousness of man as subject to law is, by that subjection, both limited and related; and hence it cannot in itself be regarded as a representation of the Infinite. Nor yet can such a representation

[1] Rom. 15.30. [2] Ps. 22.1,2. [3] Luke 18.7.

be furnished by the other term of the relation—that of the Moral Lawgiver, by whom human obligation is enacted. For, in the first place, such a Lawgiver must be conceived as a Person; and the only human conception of Personality is that of limitation. In the second place, the moral consciousness of such a Lawgiver can only be conceived under the form of a variety of attributes; and different attributes are, by that very diversity, conceived as finite. Nay, the very conception of a moral nature is in itself the conception of a limit; for morality is the compliance with a law, and a law, whether imposed from within or from without, can only be conceived to operate by limiting the range of possible actions.

Yet along with all this, though our positive religious consciousness is of the finite only, yet there runs through the whole of that consciousness the accompanying conviction that the Infinite does exist and must exist—though of the manner of that existence we can form no conception—, and that it exists along with the Finite—though we know not how such a coexistence is possible. We cannot be conscious of the Infinite; but we can be and are conscious of the limits of our own powers of thought, and therefore we know that the possibility or impossibility of conception is no test of the possibility or impossibility of existence. We know that, unless we admit the existence of the Infinite, the existence of the Finite is inexplicable and self-contradictory; and yet we know that the conception of the Infinite itself appears to involve contradictions no less inexplicable. In this impotence of Reason, we are compelled to take refuge in Faith, and to believe that an Infinite Being exists, though we know not how, and that he is the same with that Being who is made known in consciousness as our Sustainer and our Lawgiver. For to deny that an Infinite Being exists, because we cannot comprehend the manner of his existence, is of two equally inconceivable alternatives to accept the one which renders that very inconceivability itself inexplicable. If the Finite is the universe of existence, there is no reason why that universe itself should not be as conceivable as the several parts of which it is composed. Whence comes it then that our whole consciousness is compassed about with restrictions which we are ever striving to pass and ever failing in the effort? Whence comes it that the Finite cannot measure the Finite? The very consciousness of our own limitations of thought bears witness to the existence of the Unlimited, who is beyond thought. The shadow of the Infinite still broods over the consciousness of the finite, and we wake up at last from the dream of absolute wisdom to confess 'Surely the Lord is in this place; and I knew it not.'[1]

We are thus compelled to acquiesce in at least one portion of Bacon's

[1] Gen. 28.16.

statement concerning the relation of human knowledge to its object: '*Natura percutit intellectum radio directo; Deus autem, propter medium inaequale,* (*creaturas scilicet*) *radio refracto*'.[1] To have sufficient grounds for believing in God is a very different thing from having sufficient grounds for reasoning about him. The religious sentiment, which compels men to believe in and worship a Supreme Being, is an evidence of his existence but not an exhibition of his nature. It proves *that* God is and makes known to us some of his relations to us; but it does not prove *what* God is in his own Absolute Being. The natural senses, it may be, are diverted and coloured by the medium through which they pass to reach the intellect and present to us, not things in themselves, but things as they appear to us.[2] And this is manifestly the case with the religious consciousness, which can only represent the Infinite God under finite forms. But we are compelled to believe, on the evidence of our senses, that a material world exists, even while we listen to the arguments of the Idealist; and we are compelled, by our religious consciousness, to believe in the existence of a personal God; though the reasonings of the Rationalist, logically followed out, may reduce us to Pantheism or Atheism. But to preserve this belief uninjured, we must acknowledge the true limits of our being: we must not claim for any fact of human consciousness the proud prerogative of revealing God as he is; for thus we throw away the only weapon which can be of avail in resisting the assaults of Scepticism. We must be content to admit, with regard to the internal consciousness of man, the same restrictions which the great philosopher just now quoted has so excellently expressed with reference to the external senses. 'For as all works do shew forth the power and skill of the workman, and not his image; so it is of the works of God, which do shew the omnipotency and wisdom of the maker, but not his image. . . . Wherefore by the contemplation of nature to induce and inforce the acknowledgment of God, and to demonstrate his power, is an excellent argument; . . . but on the other side, out of the contemplation of nature, or ground of human knowledge, to induce any verity or persuasion concerning the points of faith, is in my judgment not safe. . . . For the heathen themselves conclude as much in that excellent and divine fable of the golden chain: That men and gods were not able to draw Jupiter down to earth; but contrariwise, Jupiter was able to draw them up to heaven.'[3]

One feature deserves especial notice, as common to both of those modes

[1] 'Nature penetrates the intellect in a direct ray of light, but God, on account of the disparity of the medium (viz. creatures), does so in a refracted beam' (*De Augmentis Scientiarum*, III.1). For Bacon, see n. 1 to p. 246.

[2] This distinction is Kantian: see *Prolegomena*, Part I, Remark III; and p. 272 above.

[3] *Advancement of Learning*, p. 128, ed. Montague.

of consciousness which primarily exhibit our relation towards God. In both, we are compelled to regard ourselves as *Persons related to a Person.* In the feeling of dependence, however great it may be, the consciousness of *myself*, the dependent element, remains unextinguished; and, indeed, without that element there could be no consciousness of a relation at all. In the sense of moral obligation, I know *myself* as the agent on whom the law is binding: I am free to choose and to act, as a person whose principle of action is in himself. And it is important to observe that it is only through this consciousness of personality that we have any ground of belief in the existence of a God. If we admit the arguments by which this personality is annihilated, whether on the side of Materialism or on that of Pantheism, we cannot escape from the consequence to which those arguments inevitably lead—the annihilation of God himself. If on the other hand the spiritual element within me is merely dependent on the corporeal—if *myself* is a result of my bodily organization and may be resolved into the operation of a system of material agents—why should I suppose it to be otherwise in the great world beyond me? If I, who deem myself a spirit distinct from and superior to matter, am but the accident and the product of that which I seem to rule, why may not all other spiritual existence, if such there be, be dependent upon the constitution of the material universe? Or if, on the other hand, I am not a distinct substance, but a mode of the infinite—a shadow passing over the face of the universe—, what is that universe which you would have me acknowledge as God? It is, says the Pantheist, the One and All. By no means: it is the Many, in which is neither All nor One. You have taught me that within the little world of my own consciousness there is no relation between the one and the many, but that all is transient and accidental alike. If I accept your conclusion, I must extend it to its legitimate consequence. Why should the universe itself contain a principle of unity? why should the Many imply the One? All that I see, all that I know, are isolated and unconnected phenomena; I myself being one of them. Why should the Universe of Being be otherwise? It cannot be All, for its phenomena are infinite and innumerable, and *all* implies unity and completeness. It need not be One, for you have yourself shown me that I am deceived in the only ground which I have for believing that a plurality of modes implies a unity of substance. If there is no Person to pray, if there is no Person to be obedient, what remains but to conclude that he to whom prayer and obedience are due—nay, even the mock-king who usurps his name in the realms of philosophy—is a shadow and a delusion likewise?

The result of the preceding considerations may be summed up as follows. There are two modes in which we may endeavour to contemplate the Deity: the one negative, based on a vain attempt to transcend the conditions of human thought and to expand the religious consciousness to the infinity of its Divine Object: the other positive, which keeps within its proper limits and views the object in a manner accommodated to the finite capacities of the human thinker. The first aspires to behold God in his absolute nature: the second is content to view him in those relations in which he has been pleased to manifest himself to his creatures. The first aims at a *speculative* knowledge of God as he is; but, bound by the conditions of finite thought, even in the attempt to transgress them, obtains nothing more than a tissue of ambitious self-contradictions, which indicate only what he is not. The second, abandoning the speculative knowledge of the infinite, as only possible to the Infinite Intelligence itself, is content with those *regulative* ideas of the Deity, which are sufficient to guide our practice, but not to satisfy our intellect—which tells us not what God is in himself, but how he wills that we should think of him.[1] In renouncing all knowledge of the Absolute, it renounces at the same time all attempts to construct *a priori* schemes of God's Providence as it ought to be: it does not seek to reconcile this or that phenomenon, whether in nature or in revelation, with the absolute attributes of Deity, but confines itself to the actual course of that Providence, as manifested in the world, and seeks no higher internal criterion of the truth of a religion than may be derived from its analogy to other parts of the Divine Government. Guided by this, the only true Philosophy of Religion, man is content to practise where he is unable to speculate. He acts, as one who must give an account of his conduct: he prays, believing that his prayer will be answered. He does not seek to reconcile this belief with any theory of the Infinite, for he does not even know how the Infinite and the Finite can exist together. But he feels that his several duties rest upon the same basis: he knows that if human action is not incompatible with Infinite Power, neither is human worship with Infinite Wisdom and Goodness—though it is not as the Infinite that God reveals himself in his moral government, nor is it as the Infinite that he promises to answer prayer.

'O thou that hearest prayer, unto thee shall all flesh come.'[2] Sacrifice and offering and burnt-offerings and offering for sin, Thou requirest no

[1] The distinction between the speculative and regulative use of the Ideas of pure reason is made by Kant (see p. 249 and n. 3 to p. 260). But K.'s way of applying it is reversed by M.; for K. had argued that the Idea of God cannot be used directly in theoretical enquiries, but has merely a regulative function in guiding enquiry, while M. is saying on the contrary that the true regulative ideas, which are intended to guide our thoughts, are the finite forms under which alone we can think of the infinite God. Briefly: the Infinite, on a Kantian view, has no speculative value, but only regulative; while on M.'s view the finite has no speculative, but only a regulative function (at least within the field of religion).

[2] Ps. 65.2.

more; for he whom these prefigured has offered himself as a sacrifice once for all. But he who fulfilled the sacrifice commanded the prayer and himself taught us how to pray. He tells us that we are dependent upon God for our daily bread, for forgiveness of sins, for deliverance from evil; —and how is that dependence manifested? Not in the annihilation of our personality, for we appeal to him under the tenderest of personal relations as the children of Our Father who is in heaven. Not as passive in contemplation, but as active in service; for we pray 'Thy will be done, as in heaven, so in earth.' In this manifestation of God to man, alike in Consciousness as in Scripture, under finite forms to finite minds, as a Person to a Person, we see the root and foundation of that religious service without which belief is a speculation and worship a delusion, which—whatever would-be philosophical theologians may say to the contrary—is the common bond which unites all men to God. All are God's creatures, bound alike to reverence and obey their Maker. All are God's dependents, bound alike to ask for his sustaining bounties. All are God's rebels, needing daily and hourly to implore his forgiveness for their disobedience. All are God's redeemed, purchased by the blood of Christ, invited to share in the benefits of his passion and intercession. All are brought by one common channel into communion with that God to whom they are related by so many common ties. All are called upon to acknowledge their Maker, their Governor, their Sustainer, their Redeemer; and the means of their acknowledgement is Prayer.

And, apart from the fact of its having been God's good pleasure so to reveal himself, there are manifest, even to human understanding, wise reasons why this course should have been adopted, benevolent ends to be answered by this gracious condescension. We are not called upon to live two distinct lives in this world. It is not required of us that the household of our nature should be divided against itself, that those feelings of love and reverence and gratitude which move us in a lower degree towards our human relatives and friends should be altogether thrown aside and exchanged for some abnormal state of ecstatic contemplation, when we bring our prayers and praises and thanks before the footstool of our Father in heaven. We are none of us able to grasp in speculation the nature of the Infinite and Eternal, but we all live and move among our fellow men, at times needing their assistance, at times soliciting their favour, at times seeking to turn away their anger. We have all, as children, felt the need of the supporting care of parents and guardians: we have all, in the gradual progress of education, required instruction from the wisdom of teachers: we have all offended against our neighbours and known the blessing of forgiveness or the penalty of unappeased anger. We can all, therefore, taught by the inmost consciousness of our human feelings, place ourselves in communion with God, when he manifests himself under human images. 'He that loveth not his brother whom he hath seen,' says the Apostle St John, 'how can he love God whom he hath not seen?'[1] Our heavenly affections must in some measure take their source and their form from our earthly ones: our love towards God, if it is to be love at all, must not be wholly unlike our love towards our neighbour: the motives and influences which prompt us, when we make known our wants and pour forth our supplications to an earthly parent, are graciously permitted by our heavenly Father to be the type and symbol of those by which our intercourse with him is to be regulated—with which he bids us 'come boldly unto the throne of grace, that we may obtain mercy, and find grace to help in time of need'.[2]

So should it be during this transitory life, in which we see through a glass darkly; in which God reveals himself in types and shadows, under human images and attributes, to meet graciously and deal tenderly with the human sympathies of his creatures. And although, even to the sons of God, it doth not yet appear what we shall be when we shall be like him and shall see him as he is; yet, if it be true that our religious duties in this life are a training and preparation for that which is to come, if we are encouraged to look forward to and anticipate that future state, while we are still encompassed with this earthly tabernacle, if we are taught to look, as our great Example, to One who in love and sympathy towards his brethren was Very Man, if we are bidden not to sorrow without hope concerning them which are asleep and are comforted by the promise that the ties of love which are broken on earth shall be united in heaven, we may trust that not wholly alien to such feelings will be our communion with God face to face, when the redeemed of all flesh shall approach once more to him that heareth prayer, no longer in the chamber of private devotion, no longer in the temple of public worship, but in that great City where no temple is 'for the Lord God Almighty and the Lamb are the temple of it'.[3]

Postscript In Lecture V, M. pursues further the distinction he has made between speculative and regulative truth, and argues that the testimony of revelation is plain and intelligible when regarded as regulative, but ultimately incomprehensible to speculation. In particular: 'The true conception of the divine Nature, so far as we are able to receive it, is to be found in those regulative representations which exhibit God under limitations accommodated to the constitution of man; not in the unmeaning abstractions which, aiming at a higher knowledge, distort rather than exhibit the Absolute and the Infinite.' In Lectures VI and VII he

[1] I John 4.20. [2] Heb. 4.16. [3] Rev. 21.22.

attempts to show that the objections brought against revelation on the grounds that it opposed to the speculative reason in man and that it is repugnant to man's moral reason both fail. For first, speculative reasoning necessarily involves contradictions; and such contradictions as it finds in revelation it brings with it. And second, the moral law cannot be conceived as an absolute principle and so cannot be the measure of the Absolute Nature of God. Finally in Lecture VIII, M. tries to give some account of the role of reason in religion: its legitimate function is to judge of a religion in respect of its evidences, as addressed to men, but not in respect of its correspondence with philosophical conceptions of the Absolute Nature of God. Thus there are internal and external evidences of the truth of a revelation. The internal are not as important as some might think, for since we cannot know the absolute character of God, we cannot decisively use the content of revelation as showing that it proceeds from him. All we can say is that the content of revelation is adapted to the wants and circumstances of men—and thus this criterion is negative. It can show that a supposed revelation is *not* from God, rather than that it *is* from God. External evidences, such as miracles and historical events concerning the Founder, provide presumptions in favour of revelation, though man's judgments are fallible. This latter point makes an eclectic Christianity untenable, on the principle that 'exactly in proportion to the strength of the remaining evidence for the divine origin of a religion is the probability that we may be mistaken in supposing this or that portion of its contents may be unworthy of God'. In conclusion M. repeats that the proper province of philosophy is to exhibit the limitations of human thought as incapable of discovering truths about the Infinite. The only guide we have here is revelation, in which God adapts his teaching to our mental constitution.

Mansel's brand of agnosticism regarding the Infinite was carried a step further by Herbert Spencer (see below, n. 1 to p. 392), who had no desire to leave room for revelation: he insisted that ultimate reality is unknowable, but not that this allows us to rely upon faith (see *First Principles*, Ch. IV).

20

JAMES

on RELIGIOUS BELIEF

Biographical Note Elder brother of Henry, the novelist. William was born in 1842 in New York City. Educated at various schools before 1855, when he went with his family to Europe, where he was at schools and colleges in London, Paris, Boulogne and other places. In 1860 the family returned to Newport, R.I., where he unsuccessfully studied art. 1864, entered Harvard Medical School and during his time there he went on a naturalist expedition to the Amazon. Also in 1867 he went to Europe, to Dresden, to study physiology and other subjects. Finally he gained his degree in 1869. A period of ill-health intervened; but in 1872 he was appointed instructor in Harvard College. From 1876 onwards he established the first American laboratory of psychology. In 1897, appointed Professor of Philosophy. In the years 1901–2, delivered the Gifford Lectures in Scotland; and in 1908 the Hibbert Lectures in Oxford. Ill-health caused another trip to England in 1910, in which year, upon his return to the U.S., he died.

Principal works: *Principles of Psychology* (1910); *The Will to Believe* (1897); *Varieties of Religious Experience* (1902); *Pragmatism* (1907); *A Pluralistic Universe* (1908), *Essays in Radical Empiricism* (1912).

Philosophical Note William James, the foremost figure of the philosophical movement known as pragmatism, was influenced in varying ways by Bergson,[1] Mill[2] and C. S. Peirce.[3] Being in origin a psychologist, he was deeply interested in the bearing of psychological studies upon philosophy, and regarded the traditional empiricist account of experience (as being a series of separate impressions or ideas) as erroneous. His concept of a 'stream of consciousness' comes near to that of Bergson, who had argued that the intellect for its own purposes tries to break up the flow of psychic events into discrete entities, and thereby necessarily distorts the nature of consciousness. Thus both traditional empiricism and contemporary rationalism (represented by the Idealists) tend to fit the flux of reality into a straight-jacket of abstractions and misapplied logic. One consequence of this is

[1] (1859–1941), French philosopher, whose interest in evolutionary theory led him to reject the static pictures of reality presented by traditional metaphysicians through their tendency to intellectualize erroneously: his central notion, which he used to illuminate the creativity inherent in the evolutionary process, was that of the *élan vital* or 'life force'.

[2] See above, p. 340.

[3] For a good account of this intricate and original thinker (1839–1914), see W. B. Gallie, *Peirce and Pragmatism* (London, Pelican, 1952).

the doctrine of determinism, which J. strenuously combated as involving that there is no real novelty or life in the cosmos. But, despite his strictures, J. was in many ways close to empiricism, and acknowledges his debt to Mill in his *Pragmatism*. For on his view philosophy must begin with the flux, and the empiricists are nearer to this than the Idealists. J. wished to find an acceptable manner of ruling out the enormous and unverifiable abstractions propounded by the latter kind of metaphysicians; he discovered this in C. S. Peirce's suggestion that the worth of a conception should be judged by the effects it may have that conceivably have practical bearings, though Peirce himself repudiated J.'s formulation of the pragmatic principle, since he had suggested it as a criterion of meaningfulness, while J. used it as a criterion of truth. J. argued that rival metaphysical theories are often empty, simply because it could make no difference in experience or practice which one was to be adopted. (In this, J. foreshadows the Verification Principle.) Nevertheless, not all metaphysics is useless: for some theories, such as that of free will, have an important bearing on what to expect in the future, even if free will and determinism are pragmatically equivalent when describing the past. J.'s conviction that there is spontaneity and freshness in human action was a further motive for rejecting Absolutism, which appears to deny this: hence J. formulated his own position as that of 'radical pluralism'. A crucial issue faced him in this, regarding the nature of relations. Bradley[1] had based his theory of an Absolute principally upon an argument about relations: namely, that whenever (on the basis of experience) we say that A is B, we are landed either with an infinite regress or a contradiction. For A cannot be identical with B, for this destroys the notion of predication (B is no longer *predicated* of A); so that 'A is B' must mean 'A is related to B'. But what does the latter mean? By analogy, 'A is related to the relation between A and B'; and so on *ad infinitum*. Again, if A is supposed to be related to something else, say C, then A as related to B is different from A as related to C. Bradley's conclusion is that there is a contradiction in all experiences, for they imply that two things can be merely 'externally' related. The contradiction can only be resolved when everything is seen as part of a whole, namely the Absolute. J. replied that Bradley's confusion arises only because the concept of A as related to B is different from the concept of A as related to C; but because the concepts are different, this does not show that they cannot apply to the same thing. It is a further instance of the absurdity of identifying concepts with experience—in short, of vicious intellectualism.

J. also rejected Absolutism because it was religiously unsatisfactory. For instance, on Bradley's view, the Absolute is not God, for it is not personal; God is merely an aspect or appearance of the Absolute. But a more serious defect, for J., is that Absolutism implies that evil is a necessary aspect of reality, and no encouragement is offered to improve the world. In line with his pluralism, J. held that God is a finite being combating evil in the world. His interest in religious questions was further expressed in his remarkable *Varieties of Religious Experience*, largely a psychological investigation but issuing in the tentative conclusion that at the outer margin of the subliminal self lies an area where the human being may come in contact with God. J. also argued against 'medical materialism', which seems to suppose that to explain the pathological origin of a state of mind is to remove

[1] F. H. Bradley (1846–1924), the most important philosopher of the Hegelian tradition in England. His position is set out chiefly in his highly original *Appearance and Reality* (1893).

its value. J. saw in the total effect of religious experience its significant fruits.

His essay on 'The Will to Believe' preceded his formulation of pragmatism, but prepares the way for it. Influential and provoking in its day, the essay explores a hitherto unexamined aspect of belief, namely the way in which evidence affects the point of believing something; for failing to make up one's mind, because of lack of conclusive evidence, is equivalent to failing to believe. Pragmatically, we have to decide in advance of perfect evidence. The thesis propounded in the essay foreshadows J.'s defence of theism, which may have to be believed even though thoroughly adequate evidence in its favour is not forthcoming.

Bibliographical Note For J.'s life, see R. B. Perry, *The Thought and Character of William James* (Camb., Mass., 1936). On 'The Will to Believe' see L. T. Hobhouse, 'Faith and the Will to Believe', *Proceedings of the Aristotelian Society*, 1903. More generally, see J. Royce, *William James and Other Essays on the Philosophy of Life* (N.Y., 1912), John Dewey, *Character and Events* (N.Y., 1929), and F. C. S. Schiller, 'William James and Empiricism', *Journal of Philosophy*, 1928. On his views on psychology, see Margaret Knight, *William James* (London, Pelican, 1950).

RELIGIOUS BELIEF

The Will to Believe, §§ I–X

I

Let us give the name of *hypothesis* to anything that may be proposed to our belief; and just as the electricians speak of live and dead wires, let us speak of any hypothesis as either *live* or *dead*. A live hypothesis is one which appeals as a real possibility to him to whom it is proposed. If I ask you to believe in the Mahdi,[1] the notion makes no electric connection with your nature—it refuses to scintillate with any credibility at all. As an hypothesis it is completely dead. To an Arab, however (even if he be not one of the Mahdi's followers), the hypothesis is among the mind's possibilities: it is alive. This shows that deadness and liveness in an hypothesis are not intrinsic properties, but relations to the individual thinker. They are measured by his willingness to act. The maximum of liveness in an hypothesis means willingness to act irrevocably. Practically, that means belief; but there is some believing tendency wherever there is willingness to act at all.

Next, let us call the decision between two hypotheses an *option*. Options may be of several kinds. They may be: 1, *living* or *dead*; 2, *forced* or *avoidable*; 3, *momentous* or *trivial*; and for our purposes we may call an option a *genuine* option when it is of the forced, living and momentous kind.

[1] J. refers to the quasi-Messianic belief that the last Imam or leader of the Sh'īa sect of Islam will return as the Mahdi.

1. A living option is one in which both hypotheses are live ones. If I say to you: 'Be a theosophist or be a Mahommedan', it is probably a dead option, because for you neither hypothesis is likely to be alive. But if I say: 'Be an agnostic or be a Christian', it is otherwise: trained as you are, each hypothesis makes some appeal, however small, to your belief.

2. Next, if I say to you: 'Choose between going out with your umbrella or without it', I do not offer you a genuine option, for it is not forced. You can easily avoid it by not going out at all. Similarly, if I say, 'Either love me or hate me', 'Either call my theory true or call it false', your option is avoidable. You may remain indifferent to me, neither loving nor hating, and you may decline to offer any judgment as to my theory. But if I say, 'Either accept this truth or go without it', I put on you a forced option, for there is no standing place outside of the alternative. Every dilemma based on a complete logical disjunction, with no possibility of not choosing, is an option of this forced kind.

3. Finally, if I were Dr Nansen and proposed to you to join my North Pole expedition, your option would be momentous; for this would probably be your only similar opportunity, and your choice now would either exclude you from the North Pole sort of immortality altogether or put at least the chance of it in your hands. He who refuses to embrace a unique opportunity loses the prize as surely as if he tried and failed. *Per contra*, the option is trivial when the opportunity is not unique, when the stake is insignificant or when the decision is reversible if it later prove unwise. A chemist finds an hypothesis live enough to spend a year in its verification: he believes in it to that extent. But if his experiments prove inconclusive either way, he is quit for his loss of time, no vital harm being done.

It will facilitate our discussion if we keep all these distinctions well in mind.

II

The next matter to consider is the actual psychology of human opinion. When we look at certain facts, it seems as if our passional and volitional nature lay at the root of all our convictions. When we look at others, it seems as if they could do nothing when the intellect had once said its say. Let us take the latter facts up first.

Does it not seem preposterous on the very face of it to talk of our opinions being modifiable at will? Can our will either help or hinder our intellect in its perceptions of truth? Can we, by just willing it, believe that Abraham Lincoln's existence is a myth, and that the portraits of him . . .

are all of someone else? Can we, by an effort of our will, or by any strength of wish that it were true, believe ourselves well and about when we are roaring with rheumatism in bed, or feel certain that the sum of the two one-dollar bills in our pocket must be a hundred dollars? We can *say* any of these things, but we are absolutely impotent to believe them; and of just such things is the whole fabric of the truths that we do believe in made up,—matters of fact, immediate or remote, as Hume said, and relations between ideas, which are either there or not there for us if we see them so, and which if not there cannot be put there by any action of our own.[1]

In Pascal's *Thoughts* there is a celebrated passage known in literature as Pascal's Wager.[2] In it he tries to force us into Christianity by reasoning as if our concern with truth resembled our concern with the stakes in a game of chance. Translated freely, his words are these: You must either believe or not believe that God is—which will you do? Your human reason cannot say. A game is going on between you and the nature of things which at the day of judgment will bring out either heads or tails. Weigh what your gains and your losses would be if you should stake all you have on heads, or God's existence: if you win in such a case, you gain eternal beatitude; if you lose, you lose nothing at all. If there were an infinity of chances, and only one for God in this wager, still you ought to stake your all on God; for though you surely risk a finite loss by this procedure, any finite loss is reasonable, even a certain one is reasonable, if there is but the possibility of infinite gain. Go then, and take holy water, and have masses said; belief will come and stupefy your scruples. . . . Why should you not? At bottom, what have you to lose?

You probably feel that when religious faith expresses itself thus, in the language of the gaming-table, it is put to its last trumps. Surely Pascal's own personal belief in masses and holy water had far other springs; and this celebrated page of his is but an argument for others, a last desperate snatch at a weapon against the hardness of the unbelieving heart. We feel that a faith in masses and holy water adopted wilfully after such a mechanical calculation would lack the inner soul of faith's reality; and if we were ourselves in the place of the Deity, we should probably take particular pleasure in cutting off believers of this pattern from their infinite reward. It is evident that unless there be some pre-existing tendency to believe in masses and holy water, the option offered to the will by Pascal

[1] For Hume, see above, p. 205. Regarding the aspect of Hume's philosophy here alluded to see his *Treatise*, Bk I, Pt III, §3.

[2] *Pensées*, 23. Pascal (1623–62) was in some measure a forerunner of modern Christian Existentialism (see p. 345). For a useful account of this aspect of his thought see David E. Roberts, *Existentialism and Religious Belief* (1957), Ch. I.

is not a living option. Certainly no Turk ever took to masses and holy water on its account; and even to us Protestants these means of salvation seem such foregone impossibilities that Pascal's logic, invoked for them specifically, leaves us unmoved. As well might the Mahdi write to us, saying, 'I am the Expected One whom God has created in his effulgence. You shall be infinitely happy if you confess me; otherwise you shall be cut off from the light of the sun. Weigh, then, your infinite gain if I am genuine against your finite sacrifice if I am not!' His logic would be that of Pascal; but he would vainly use it on us, for the hypothesis he offers us is dead. No tendency to act on it exists in us to any degree.

The talk of believing by our volition seems, then, from one point of view, simply silly. From another point of view, it is worse than silly, it is vile. When one turns to the magnificent evidence of the physical sciences, and sees how it was reared; what thousands of disinterested moral lives of men lie buried in its mere foundations; what patience and postponement, what choking down of preference, what submission to the icy laws of outer fact are wrought into its very stones and mortar; how absolutely impersonal it stands in its vast augustness,—then how besotted and contemptible seems every little sentimentalist who comes blowing his voluntary smoke-wreaths, and pretending to decide things from out of his private dream! Can we wonder if those bred in the rugged and many school of science should feel like spewing such subjectivism out of their mouths? The whole system of loyalties which grow up in the schools of science go dead against its toleration; so that it is only natural that those who have caught the scientific fever should pass over to the opposite extreme, and write sometimes as if the incorruptibly truthful intellect ought positively to prefer bitterness and unacceptableness to the heart in its cup.

> It fortifies my soul to know
> That, though I perish, Truth is so—

sings Clough,[1] while Huxley[2] exclaims: 'My only consolation lies in the reflection that, however bad our posterity may become, so far as they hold by the plain rule of not pretending to believe what they have no reason to believe, because it may be to their advantage so to pretend [the word "pretend" is surely here redundant], they will not have reached the lowest depth of immorality.' And that delicious *enfant*

[1] A. H. Clough (1819–61), English poet.

[2] Thomas Henry Huxley (1825–95), biologist and philosopher, was a vigorous defender of the Theory of Evolution when it first appeared and was the most prominent exponent of Victorian agnosticism (a word which he himself coined). For his final views see *Ethics and Evolution* (1893).

terrible Clifford[1] writes: 'Belief is desecrated when given to unproved and unquestioned statements for the solace and private pleasure of the believer. . . . Who so would deserve well of his fellows in this matter will guard the purity of his belief with a very fanaticism of jealous care, lest at any time it should rest on an unworthy object, and catch a stain which can never be wiped away. . . . If [a] belief has been accepted on insufficient evidence [even though the belief be true, as Clifford on the same page explains] the pleasure is a stolen one. . . . It is sinful because it is stolen in defiance of our duty to mankind. That duty is to guard ourselves from such beliefs as from a pestilence which may shortly master our own body and then spread to the rest of the town. . . . It is wrong always, everywhere, and for everyone, to believe anything upon insufficient evidence.'

III

All this strikes one as healthy, even when expressed, as by Clifford, with somewhat too much of robustious pathos in his voice. Free-will and simple wishing do seem, in the matter of our credences, to be only fifth wheels to the coach. Yet if anyone should thereupon assume that intellectual insight is what remains after wish and will and sentimental preference have taken wing, or that pure reason is what then settles our opinions, he would fly quite as directly in the teeth of the facts.

It is only our already dead hypotheses that our willing nature is unable to bring to life again. But what has made them dead for us is for the most part a previous action of our willing nature of an antagonistic kind. When I say 'willing nature', I do not mean only such deliberate volitions as may have set up habits of belief that we cannot now escape from,—I mean all such factors as fear and hope, prejudice and passion, imitation and partisanship, the circumpressure of our caste and set. As a matter of fact we find ourselves believing, we hardly know how or why. Mr Balfour[2] gives the name of 'authority' to all those influences, born of the intellectual climate, that make hypotheses possible or impossible for us, alive or dead. Here in this room,[3] we all of us believe in molecules and the conservation of energy, in democracy and necessary progress, in Protestant Christianity

[1] W. K. Clifford (1845–79), mathematician, philosopher, defender of Evolutionary Theory against religious critics, and author of works on the philosophy of science, etc. His essay on 'The Ethics of Belief', referred to by J., was published in the *Contemporary Review* (1876) and formed part of Clifford's *Lectures and Essays* (published 1879).

[2] Arthur Balfour (1848–1930), statesman and philosopher, held that all human knowledge ultimately rests on religious faith, which is basically non-rational. His two main works were *A Defence of Philosophic Doubt* (1879) and *Foundations of Belief* (1895).

[3] The present essay was read to the Philosophical Clubs of Yale and Brown Universities.

and the duty of fighting for 'the doctrine of the immortal Monroe', all for no reasons worthy of the name. We see into these matters with no more inner clearness, and probably with much less, than any disbeliever in them might possess. His unconventionality would probably have some grounds to show for its conclusions; but for us, not insight, but the *prestige* of the opinions is what makes the spark shoot from them and light up sleeping magazines of faith. Our reason is quite satisfied, in nine hundred and ninety-nine cases out of every thousand of us, if it can find a few arguments that will do to recite in case our credulity is criticized by someone else. Our faith is faith in someone else's faith, and in the greatest matters this is most the case. Our belief in truth itself, for instance, that there is a truth, and that our minds and it are made for each other,—what is it but a passionate affirmation of desire, in which our social system backs us up? We want to have a truth; we want to believe that our experiments and studies and discussions must put us in a continually better and better position towards it; and on this line we agree to fight out our thinking lives. But if a pyrrhonistic sceptic[1] asks us *how we know* all this, can our logic find a reply? No! Certainly it cannot. It is just one volition against another,—we willing to go in for life upon a trust or assumption which he, for his part, does not care to make.

As a rule we disbelieve all facts and theories for which we have no use. Clifford's cosmic emotions find no use for Christian feelings. Huxley belabours the bishops because there is no use for sacerdotalism in his scheme of life. Newman,[2] on the contrary, goes over to Romanism, and finds all sorts of reasons good for staying there, because a priestly system is for him an organic need and delight. Why do so few 'scientists' even look at the evidence for telepathy, so called? Because they think, as a leading biologist, now dead, once said to me, that even if such a thing were true, scientists ought to band together to keep it suppressed and concealed. It would undo the uniformity of Nature and all sorts of other things without which scientists cannot carry on their pursuits. But if this very man had been shown something which as a scientist he might *do* with telepathy, he might not only have examined the evidence, but even have found it good enough. This very law which the logicians would impose upon us—if I may give the name of logicians to those who would rule out our willing nature here—is based on nothing but their own

[1] 'Pyrrhonistic' from Pyrrho (*c.* 365–275 BC), Greek founder of the school of philosophy known as 'Sceptics', who denied that knowledge of the nature of things is attainable.

[2] John Henry Newman (1801–90) led the Tractarian movement within the Church of England, but was later converted to Roman Catholicism, eventually being made Cardinal. His chief philosophical work is *Grammar of Assent* (1870); other notable writings are *Apologia pro Vita Sua* (1864) and *Idea of a University* (1852).

natural wish to exclude all elements for which they, in their professional quality of logicians, can find no use.

Evidently, then, our non-intellectual nature does influence our convictions. There are passional tendencies and volitions which run before and others which come after belief, and it is only the latter that are too late for the fair; and they are not too late when the previous passional work has been already in their own direction. Pascal's argument, instead of being powerless, then seems a regular clincher, and is the last stroke needed to make our faith in masses and holy water complete. The state of things is evidently far from simple; and pure insight and logic, whatever they might do ideally, are not the only things that really do produce our creeds.

IV

Our next duty, having recognized this mixed-up state of affairs, is to ask whether it be simply reprehensible and pathological, or whether, on the contrary, we must treat it as a normal element in making up our minds. The thesis I defend is, briefly stated, thus: *Our passional nature not only lawfully may, but must, decide an option between propositions, whenever it is a genuine option that cannot by its nature be decided on intellectual grounds; for to say, under such circumstances, 'Do not decide, but leave the question open,' is itself a passional decision,—just like deciding yes or no,—and is attended with the same risk of losing the truth.* The thesis thus abstractly stated will, I trust, soon become quite clear. But I must first indulge in a bit more preliminary work.

V

It will be observed that for the purposes of this discussion we are on 'dogmatic' ground,—ground, I mean, which leaves systematic philosophical scepticism altogether out of account. The postulate that there is truth and that it is the destiny of our minds to attain it, we are deliberately resolving to make, though the sceptic will not make it. We part company with him, therefore, absolutely, at this point. But the faith that truth exists, and that our minds can find it, may be held in two ways. We may talk of the *empiricist* way and of the *absolutist* way of believing in truth. The absolutists say in this matter that we not only can attain to knowing truth, but we can *know when* we have attained to knowing it; while the empiricists think that although we may attain it, we cannot infallibly know when. To *know* is one thing, and to know for certain *that* we know is another. One may hold to the first being possible without the second; hence the empiricists and the absolutists, although neither of them is a sceptic in the usual philosophical sense of the term, show very different degrees of dogmatism in their lives.

If we look at the history of opinions, we see that the empiricist tendency has largely prevailed in science, while in philosophy the absolutist tendency has had everything its own way. The characteristic sort of happiness, indeed, which philosophies yield has mainly consisted in the conviction felt by each successive school or system that by it bottom-certitude had been attained. 'Other philosophies are collections of opinions, mostly false; *my* philosophy gives standing-ground for ever,'—who does not recognize in this the key-note of every system worthy of the name? A system, to be a system at all, must come as a *closed* system, reversible in this or that detail, perchance, but in its essential features never!

Scholastic orthodoxy, to which one must always go when one wishes to find perfectly clear statement, has beautifully elaborated this absolutist conviction in a doctrine which it calls that of 'objective confidence'. If, for example, I am unable to doubt that I now exist before you, that two is less than three, or that if all men are mortal then I am mortal too, it is because these things illumine my intellect irresistibly. The final ground of this objective evidence possessed by certain propositions is the *adaequatio intellectus nostri cum re.*[1] The certitude it brings involves an *aptitudinem ad extorquendum certum assensum*[1] on the part of the part of the truth envisaged, and on the side of the subject a *quietem in cognitione,*[1] when once the object is mentally received, that leaves no possibility of doubt behind; and in the whole transaction nothing operates but the *entitas ipsa*[1] of the object with the *entitas ipsa* of the mind. We slouchy modern thinkers dislike to talk in Latin—indeed, we dislike to talk in set terms at all; but at bottom our own state of mind is very much like this whenever we uncritically abandon ourselves. You believe in objective evidence, and I do. Of some things we feel that we are certain: we know, and we know that we do know. There is something that gives a click inside of us, a bell that strikes twelve, when the hands of our mental clock have swept the dial and meet over the meridian hour. The greatest empiricists among us are empiricists on reflection; when left to their instincts, they dogmatize like infallible people. When the Cliffords tell us how sinful it is to be Christians on such 'insufficient evidence', insufficiency is really the last thing they have in mind. For them the evidence is absolutely sufficient, only it makes

[1] *Adaequatio intellectus nostri cum re*: 'the agreement of our intellect with the thing'; *aptitudinem ad extorquendum certum assensum*: 'tendency to extract certain assent'; *quietem in cognitione*: 'repose in knowing'; and *entitas ipsa*: 'being itself'. On the correspondence theory of truth in medieval thought, see F. C. Copleston, *History of Philosophy*, Vol. ii, pp. 390 ff. and elsewhere.

the other way. They believe so completely in an anti-Christian order of the universe that there is no living option: Christianity is a dead hypothesis.

VI

But now, since we are all such absolutists by instinct, what in our quality of students of philosophy ought we to do about the fact? Shall we espouse and endorse it? Or shall we treat it as a weakness of our nature from which we must free ourselves, if we can?

I sincerely believe that the latter course is the only one we can follow as reflective men. Objective evidence and certitude are doubtless very fine ideals to play with, but where on this moonlit and dream-visited planet are they found? I am, therefore, myself a complete empiricist so far as my theory of human knowledge goes. I live, to be sure, by the practical faith that we must go on experiencing and thinking over our experience, for only thus can our opinions grow more true; but to hold any one of them —I absolutely do not care which—as if it never could be reinterpretable or corrigible, I believe to be a tremendously mistaken attitude, and I think that the whole history of philosophy will bear me out. There is but one indefectibly certain truth, and that is the truth that pyrrhonistic scepticism itself leaves standing,—the truth that the present phenomenon of consciousness exists. That, however, is the bare starting-point of knowledge, the mere admission of a stuff to be philosophized about. The various philosophies are but so many attempts at expressing what this stuff really is. And if we repair to our libraries what disagreement do we discover! Where is a certainly true answer found? Apart from abstract propositions of comparison (such as two and two are the same as four), propositions which tell us nothing by themselves about concrete reality, we find no proposition ever regarded by anyone as evidently certain that has not either been called a falsehood, or at least had its truth sincerely questioned by someone else. The transcending of the axioms of geometry, not in play but in earnest, by certain of our contemporaries (as Zöllner and Charles H. Hinton,[1]) and the rejection of the whole

[1] J. K. F. Zöllner (1834–82), German mathematical physicist; Charles H. Hinton, American mathematician and author of the geometrical fantasy *An Episode of Flatland* (1907). The 'transcending of the axioms of geometry' to which J. refers arises from the discovery of non-Euclidean geometry, the first form of which was published by the Russian mathematician N. Lobachevsky (1793–1856) in 1855. Such a geometry is constructed by replacing Euclid's Axiom of Parallels, and has results different from Euclid's (e.g. the interior angles of a triangle never add up to 180°). Not only does this throw doubt on much previous philosophical thinking about mathematics (as describing ideal entities and representing *a priori* knowledge about the world), but non-Euclidean geometry, originally conceived as an interesting kind of game, has found important applications in modern physics.

Aristotelian logic by the Hegelians,[1] are striking instances in point.

No concrete test of what is really true has ever been agreed upon. Some make the criterion external to the moment of perception, putting it either in revelation, the *consensus gentium*,[2] the instincts of the heart, or the systematized experience of the race. Others make the perceptive moment its own test,—Descartes, for instance, with his clear and distinct ideas guaranteed by the veracity of God[3]; Reid with his 'common-sense';[4] and Kant with his forms of synthetic judgment *a priori*.[5] The inconceivability of the opposite; the capacity to be verified by sense; the possession of a complete organic unity or self-relation, realized when a thing is its own other,[6]—are standards which, in turn, have been used. The much lauded objective evidence is never triumphantly there; it is a mere aspiration or *Grenzbegriff*,[7] making the infinitely remote ideal of our thinking life. To claim that certain truths now possess it is simply to say that when you think them true and they *are* true, then their evidence is objective, otherwise it is not. But practically one's conviction that the evidence one goes by is of the real objective brand, is only one more subjective opinion added to the lot. For what a contradictory array of opinions have objective evidence and absolute certitude been claimed! The world is rational through and through,—its existence is an ultimate brute fact; there is a personal God,—a personal God is inconceivable; there is an extra-mental physical world immediately known,—the mind can only know its own ideas; a moral imperative exists,—obligation is only the resultant of desires; a permanent spiritual principle is in everyone, —there are only shifting states of mind; there is an endless chain of causes,—there is an absolute first cause; an eternal necessity,—a freedom; a purpose,—no purpose; a primal One,—a primal Many; a universal continuity,—an essential discontinuity in things; and infinity,—no infinity. There is this,—there is that; there is indeed nothing which

[1] Hegel's rejection of Aristotelian logic rests on a number of grounds, the main one being that traditional syllogistic logic is merely formal, so that quite different kinds of subject-matter can be treated in this form: but a true syllogism, according to H., must display necessary connections and not merely external connections between the terms of the syllogism. Basically the syllogism is a development showing the interdependence of the universal, the species and the individual. In his use of 'syllogism' H. applies it to every aspect of his system, which has a strong triadic *motif* running through it. See above, p. 295, where he talks of the syllogism implicit in the Trinity.

[2] I.e. the general agreement of mankind, which was supposed to involve a belief in God or gods.

[3] See above, p. 121.

[4] Thomas Reid (1710–96), Scottish philosopher, who used a philosophical appeal to common sense to refute the phenomenalistic theory of Hume (see above, p. 205) in favour of realism (in perception, etc.). See S. A. Grave, *The Scottish Philosophy of Common Sense* (Oxford, 1960).

[5] See above, n. 4 to p. 260.

[6] A reference to Hegelianism: see above, p. 291.

[7] 'Limiting concept'. A reference to Kant's doctrine of Ideas of reason. See above, p. 249.

someone has not thought absolutely true, while his neighbour deemed it absolutely false; and not an absolutist among them seems ever to have considered that the trouble may all the time be essential, and that the intellect, even with truth directly in its grasp, may have no infallible signal for knowing whether it be truth or no. When, indeed, one remembers that the most striking practical application to life of the doctrine of objective certitude has been the conscientious labours of the Holy Office of the Inquisition, one feels less tempted than ever to lend the doctrine a respectful ear.

But please observe, now, that when as empiricists we give up the doctrine of objective certitude, we do not thereby give up the quest or hope of truth itself. We still pin our faith on its existence, and still believe that we gain an ever better position towards it by systematically continuing to roll up experiences and think. Our great difference from the scholastic lies in the way we face. The strength of his system lies in the principles, the origin, the *terminus a quo* of his thought; for us the strength is in the outcome, the upshot, the *terminus ad quem*. Not where it comes from but what it leads to is to decide. It matters not to an empiricist from what quarter an hypothesis may come to him; he may have acquired it by fair means or foul; passion may have whispered or accident may have suggested it; but if the total drift of thinking continues to confirm it, that is what he means by its being true.

VII

One more point, small but important, and our preliminaries are done. There are two ways of looking at our duty in the matter of opinion,—ways entirely different, and yet ways about whose difference the theory of knowledge seems hitherto to have shown very little concern. *We must know the truth*; and *we must avoid error*,—these are our first and great commandments as would-be knowers; but they are not two ways of stating an identical commandment, they are two separable laws. Although it may happen that when we believe the truth A, we escape as an incidental consequence from believing the falsehood B, it hardly ever happens that by merely disbelieving B we necessarily believe A. We may in escaping B fall into believing other falsehoods, C or D, just as bad as B; or we may escape B by not believing anything at all, not even A.

Believe truth! Shun error!—these, we see, are two materially different laws; and by choosing between them we may end by colouring differently our whole intellectual life. We may regard the chase for truth as paramount, and the avoidance of error as secondary; or we may, on the other hand, treat the avoidance of error as more imperative, and let truth take its chance. Clifford, in the instructive passage which I have quoted, exhorts us to the latter course. Believe nothing, he tells us, keep your mind in suspense for ever, rather than by closing it on insufficient evidence incur the awful risk of believing lies. You, on the other hand, may think that the risk of being in error is a very small matter when compared with the blessings of real knowledge, and be ready to be duped many times in your investigation rather than postpone indefinitely the chance of guessing true. I myself find it impossible to go with Clifford. We must remember that these feelings of our duty about either truth or error are in any case only expressions of our passional life. Biologically considered, our minds are as ready to grind out falsehood as veracity, and he who says 'Better go without belief for ever than believe a lie!' merely shows his own preponderant private horror of becoming a dupe. He may be critical of many of his desires and fears, but this fear he slavishly obeys. He cannot imagine anyone questioning its binding force. For my own part, I have also a horror of being duped; but I can believe that worse things than being duped can happen to a man in this world: so Clifford's exhortation has to my ears a thoroughly fantastic sound. It is like a general informing his soldiers that it is better to keep out of battle for ever than to risk a single wound. Not so are victories either over enemies or over nature gained. Our errors are surely not such awfully solemn things. In a world where we are so certain to incur them in spite of all our caution, a certain lightness of heart seems healthier than this excessive nervousness on their behalf. At any rate, it seems the fittest thing for the empiricist philosopher.

VIII

And now, after all this introduction, let us go straight at our question. I have said, and now repeat it, that not only as a matter of fact do we find our passional nature influencing us in our opinions, but that there are some options between opinions in which this influence must be regarded both as an inevitable and as a lawful determinant of our choice.

I fear here that some of you my hearers will begin to scent danger, and lend an inhospitable ear. Two first steps of passion you have indeed had to admit as necessary,—we must think so as to avoid dupery, and we must think so as to gain truth; but the surest path to these ideal consummations, you will probably consider, is from now onwards to take no further passional step.

Well, of course, I agree as far as the facts will allow. Wherever the option between losing truth and gaining it is not momentous, we can throw the chance of *gaining truth* away, and at any rate save ourselves from any chance of *believing falsehood*, by not making up our minds at all till objective evidence has come. In scientific questions, this is almost always the case; and even in human affairs in general the need of acting is seldom so urgent that a false belief to act on is better than no belief at all. Law courts, indeed, have to decide on the best evidence attainable for the moment, because a judge's duty is to make law as well as to ascertain it, and (as a learned judge once said to me) few cases are worth spending much time over: the great thing is to have them decided on *any* acceptable principle, and got out of the way. But in our dealings with objective nature we are obviously recorders, not makers, of the truth; and decisions for the mere sake of deciding promptly and getting on to the next business would be wholly out of place. Throughout the breadth of physical nature facts are what they are quite independently of us, and seldom is there any such hurry about them that the risks of being duped by believing premature theory need be faced. The questions here are always trivial options, the hypotheses are hardly living (at any rate not living for us spectators), the choice between believing truth or falsehood is seldom forced. The attitude of sceptical balance is therefore the absolutely wise one if we would escape mistakes. What difference, indeed, does it make to most of us whether we have or have not a theory of the Röntgen rays, whether we believe or not in mind-stuff, or have a conviction about the causality of conscious states? It makes no difference. Such options are not forced on us. On every account it is better not to make them, but still keep weighing reasons *pro et contra* with an indifferent hand.

I speak, of course, here of the purely judging mind. For purposes of discovery such indifference is to be less highly recommended, and science would be far less advanced than she is if the passionate desires of individuals to get their own faiths confirmed had been kept out of the game. See for example the sagacity which Spencer and Weismann[1] now display. On the other hand, if you want an absolute duffer in an investigation, you must, after all, take the man who has no interest whatever in its results: he is the warranted incapable, the positive fool. The most useful investigator, because the most sensitive observer, is always he whose eager interest in one side of the question is balanced by an equally keen nervousness lest he become deceived. Science has organized this nervousness into

[1] Herbert Spencer (1820–1903), civil engineer and philosopher, was a prominent Victorian agnostic, holding that the Absolute is unknowable: in this he was influenced by Hamilton (see above, p. 361) and philosophically had some affinities with Mansel (see above, p. 377). August Weismann (1834–1914) was a Darwinian biologist, who proposed the hypothesis of the continuity of the germ plasm, and of cell-division, as part of the mechanism of foetal development.

a regular *technique*, her so-called method of verification; and she has fallen so deeply in love with the method that one may even say she has ceased to care for truth by itself at all. It is only truth as technically verified that interests her. The truth of truths might come in merely affirmative form, and she would decline to touch it. Such truth as that, she might repeat with Clifford, would be stolen in defiance of her duty to mankind. Human passions are, however, stronger than technical rules. 'Le cœur a ses raisons,' as Pascal says, 'que le raison ne connaît pas'; and however indifferent to all but the bare rules of the game the umpire, the abstract intellect, may be, the concrete players who furnish him the materials to judge of are usually, each one of them, in love with some pet 'live hypothesis' of his own. Let us agree, however, that wherever there is no forced option, the dispassionately judicial intellect with no pet hypothesis, saving us, as it does, from dupery at any rate, ought to be our ideal.

The question next arises: Are there not somewhere forced options in our speculative questions, and can we (as men who may be interested at least in positively gaining truth as in merely escaping dupery) always wait with impunity till the coercive evidence shall have arrived? It seems *a priori* improbable that the truth should be so nicely adjusted to our needs and powers as that. In the great boarding-house of nature the cakes and butter and the syrup seldom come out so even and leave the plates so clean. Indeed, we should view them with scientific suspicion if they did.

IX

Moral questions immediately present themselves as questions whose solution cannot wait for sensible proof. A moral question is a question not of what sensibly exists, but of what is good, or would be good if it did exist. Science can tell us what exists; but to compare the *worths*, both of what exists and of what does not exist, we must consult not science, but what Pascal calls our heart. Science itself consults her heart when she lays it down that the infinite ascertainment of fact and correction of false belief are the supreme goods for man. Challenge the statement, and science can only repeat it oracularly, or else prove it by showing that such ascertainment and correction bring man all sorts of other goods which man's heart in turn declares. The question of having moral beliefs at all or not having them is decided by our will. Are our moral preferences true or false, or are they only odd biological phenomena, making things good or bad for *us*, but in themselves indifferent? How can your pure intellect decide? If your heart does not *want* a world of moral reality, your head will surely never make you believe in one. Mephistophelian scepticism, indeed, will satisfy the head's play-instincts much better than any rigorous idealism can. Some men (even at the student age) are so naturally cool-hearted that the moralistic hypothesis never has for them any pungent life, and in their supercilious presence the hot young moralist always feels strangely ill at ease. The appearance of knowingness is on their side, of naïveté and gullibility on his. Yet, in the inarticulate heart of him, he clings to it that he is not a dupe, and that there is a realm in which (as Emerson[1] says) all their wit and intellectual superiority is no better than the cunning of a fox. Moral scepticism can no more be refuted or proved by logic than intellectual scepticism can. When we stick to it that there *is* truth (be it of either kind), we do so with our whole nature, and resolve to stand or fall by the results. The sceptic with his whole nature adopts the doubting attitude; but which of us is the wiser, Omniscience alone knows.

Turn now from these wide questions of good to a certain class of questions of fact, questions concerning personal relations, states of mind between one man and another. *Do you like me or not?*—for example. Whether you do or do not depends, in countless instances, on whether I meet you half-way, am willing to assume that you must like me, and show you trust and expectation. The previous faith on my part in your liking's existence is in such cases what makes your liking come. But if I stand aloof and refuse to budge an inch until I have objective evidence, until you shall have done something apt, as the absolutists say, *ad extorquendum assensum meum*, ten to one your liking never comes. How many women's hearts are vanquished by the mere sanguine insistence of some man that they *must* love him! he will not consent to the hypothesis that they cannot. The desire for a certain kind of truth here brings about that special truth's existence; and so it is in innumerable cases of other sorts. Who gains promotions, boons, appointments, but the man in whose life they are seen to play the part of live hypotheses, who discounts them, sacrifices other things for their sake before they have come, and takes risks for them in advance? His faith acts on the powers above him as a claim, and creates his own verification.

A social organism of any sort whatever, large or small, is what it is because each member proceeds to his own duty with a trust that the other members will simultaneously do theirs. Wherever a desired result is achieved by the co-operation of many independent persons, its existence as a fact is a pure consequence of the precursive faith in one another of those immediately concerned. A government, an army, a commercial

[1] 1803–82, American essayist and poet, who stimulated the philosophical movement known as 'Transcendentalism', which was aggressively anti-empiricist.

system, a ship, a college, an athletic team, all exist on this condition, without which not only is nothing achieved, but nothing is even attempted. A whole train of passengers (individually brave enough) will be looted by a few highwaymen, simply because the latter can count on one another, while each passenger fears that if he makes a movement of resistance he will be shot before anyone else backs him up. If we believed that the whole car-full would rise at once with us, we should each severally rise, and train-robbing would never even be attempted. There are, then, cases where a fact cannot come at all unless a preliminary faith exists in its coming. *And where faith in a fact can help create a fact*, that would be an insane logic which would say that faith running ahead of scientific evidence is the 'lowest kind of immorality' into which a thinking being can fall. Yet such is the logic by which our scientific absolutists pretend to regulate our lives!

X

In truths dependent on our personal action, then, faith based on desire is certainly a lawful and possibly an indispensable thing.

But now, it will be said, these are all churlish human cases, and have nothing to do with great cosmical matters, like the question of religious faith. Let us then pass on to that. Religions differ so much in their accidents that in discussing the religious question we must make it very generic and broad. What then do we now mean by the religious hypothesis? Science says things are; morality says some things are better than other things; and religion says essentially two things.

First, she says that the best things are the more eternal things, the overlapping things, the things in the universe that throw the last stone, so to speak, and say the final word. 'Perfection is eternal,'—this phrase of Charles Secrétan[1] seems a good way of putting this first affirmation of religion, an affirmation which obviously cannot yet be verified scientifically at all.

The second affirmation of religion is that we are better off even now if we believe her first affirmation to be true.

Now, let us consider what the logical elements of this situation are *in case the religious hypothesis in both its branches be true*. (Of course we must admit that possibility at the outset. If we are to discuss the question at all, it must involve a living option. If for any of you religion be a hypothesis that cannot, by any living possibility, be true, then you need go no farther. I speak to the 'saving remnant' alone.) So proceeding, we see,

[1] Charles Secrétan, (1815–95), Swiss theologian, strongly influenced by Kant; he stressed the moral content of religion and the vital significance of free will.

first, that religion offers itself as a *momentous* option. We are supposed to gain, even now, by our belief, and to lose by our non-belief, a certain vital good. Secondly, religion is a *forced* option, so far as that good goes. We cannot escape the issue by remaining sceptical and waiting for more light, because although we do avoid error in that way *if religion be untrue*, we lose the good, *if it be true*, just as certainly as if we positively chose to disbelieve. It is as if a man should hesitate indefinitely to ask a certain woman to marry him because he was not perfectly sure that she would prove an angel if he brought her home. Would he not cut himself off from that particular angel-possibility as decisively as if he went and married someone else? Scepticism, then, is not an avoidance of option; it is option of a certain particular kind of risk. *Better risk loss of truth than chance of error*,—that is your faith-vetoer's exact position. He is actively playing his stake as much as the believer is; he is backing the field against the religious hypothesis, just as the believer is backing the religious hypothesis, against the field. To preach scepticism to us as a duty until 'sufficient evidence' for religion be found is tantamount therefore to telling us, when in presence of the religious hypothesis, that to yield to our fear of its being error is better and wiser than to yield to our hope that it may be true. It is not intellect against all passions, then; it is only intellect with one passion laying down its law. And by what, forsooth, is the supreme wisdom of this passion warranted? Dupery for dupery, what proof is there that dupery through hope is so much worse than dupery through fear? I for one can see no proof; and I simply refuse obedience to the scientist's command to imitate his kind of option, in a case where my own stake is important enough to give me the right to choose my own form of risk. If religion be true and the evidence for it be still insufficient, I do not wish, by putting your extinguisher upon my nature (which feels to me as if it had after all some business in this matter), to forfeit my sole chance in life of getting upon the winning side,—that chance depending, of course, on my willingness to run the risk of acting as if my passional need of taking the world religiously might be prophetic and right.

All this is on the supposition that it really may be prophetic and right and that, even to us who are discussing the matter, religion is a live hypothesis which may be true. Now, to most of us religion comes in as a still further way that makes a veto of our active faith even more illogical. The more perfect and more eternal aspect of the universe is represented in our religions as having personal form. The universe is no longer a mere *It* to us, but a *Thou*, if we are religious; and any relation that may be possible from person to person might be possible here. For instance, although in one sense we are passive portions of the universe, in another we were small active centres on our own account. We feel too as if the appeal of religion to us were made to our own active goodwill, as if evidence might be for ever withheld from us unless we met the hypothesis halfway. To take a trivial illustration: just as a man who in a company of gentlemen made no advances, asked a warrant for every concession and believed no one's word without proof, would cut himself off by such churlishness from all the social rewards that a more trusting spirit would earn,—so here one who should shut himself up in snarling logicality and try to make the gods extort his recognition willy-nilly, or not get it at all, might cut himself for ever from his only opportunity of making the gods' acquaintance. This feeling, forced on us we know not whence, that by obstinately believing that there are gods (although not to do so would be so easy both for our logic and our life) we are doing the universe the deepest service we can, seems part of the living essence of the religious hypothesis. If the hypothesis *were* true in all parts, including this one, then pure intellectualism, with its veto on our making willing advances, would be an absurdity; and some participation of our sympathetic nature would be logically required. I therefore, for one, cannot see my way to accepting the agnostic rules for truth-seeking, or wilfully agree to keep my willing nature out of the game. I cannot do so for this plain reason, that a *rule of thinking which would absolutely prevent me from acknowledging certain kinds of truth if those kinds of truth were really there would be an irrational rule.* That for me is the long and the short of the formal logic of the situation, no matter what the kinds of truth might materially be.

I confess I do not see how this logic can be escaped. But sad experience makes me fear that some of you may still shrink from radically saying with me, *in abstracto*, that we have the right to believe at our own risk any hypothesis that is live enough to tempt our will. I suspect, however, that if this is so, it is because you have got away from the abstract logical point of view altogether, and are thinking (perhaps without realizing it) of some particular religious hypothesis which for you is dead. The freedom to 'believe what we will' you apply to the case of some patent superstition; and the faith you think of is the faith defined by the schoolboy when he said, 'Faith is when you believe something that you know ain't true.' I can only repeat that this is misapprehension. *In concreto*, the freedom to believe can only cover living options which the intellect of the individual cannot by itself resolve; and living options never seem absurdities to him who has them to consider. When I look at the religious question as it really puts itself to concrete men, and when I think of all the possibilities which both practically and theoretically it involves, then this command that we should put a stopper on our heart, instincts, and courage, and *wait*

—acting of course meanwhile more or less as if religion were *not* true*—till doomsday, or till such time as our intellect and senses working together may have raked in evidence enough,—this command, I say, seems to me the queerest idol ever manufactured in the philosophic cave. Were we scholastic absolutists there might be more excuse. If we had an infallible intellect with its objective certitudes, we might feel ourselves disloyal to such a perfect organ of knowledge in not trusting to it exclusively, in not waiting for its releasing word. But if we are empiricists, if we believe that no bell tolls to let us know for certain when truth is within our grasp, then it seems a piece of idle fantasticality to preach so solemnly our duty of waiting for the bell. Indeed we *may* wait if we will,—I hope you do not think that I am denying that,—but if we do so we do so at our peril as much as if we believed. In either case we *act*, taking our life in our hands. No one of us ought to issue vetoes to the other, nor should we bandy words of abuse. We ought on the contrary delicately and profoundly to respect another's mental freedom: then only shall we bring about the intellectual republic; then only shall we have that spirit of inner tolerance without which all our outer tolerance is soulless and which is empiricism's glory; then only shall we live and let live, in speculative as well as in practical things.

* Since belief is measured by action, he who forbids us to believe religion to be true necessarily also forbids us to act as we should if we did believe it to be true. The whole defence of religious faith hinges upon action. If the action required or inspired by the religious hypothesis is in no way different from that dictated by the naturalistic hypothesis, then religious faith is a pure superfluity, better pruned away, and controversy about its legitimacy is a piece of idle trifling, unworthy of serious minds. I myself believe, of course, that the religious hypothesis gives to the world an expression which specifically determines our reactions and makes them in a large part unlike what they might be on a purely naturalistic scheme of belief. [The term 'naturalistic' here refers to any theory which describes the universe, or reality, without using any concept such as God, i.e. any concept which represents that which is transcendent and supernatural.]

21

ROYCE

on REASON AND RELIGION

Biographical Note Born in 1855 in Grass Valley, California. Educated at his mother's school and at Lincoln Grammar School in San Francisco; thereafter at the Boys' High School, San Francisco. He entered the recently founded University of California in 1871, where he studied science and literature. He wrote his graduation thesis on the theology of *Prometheus Bound*. In 1876 he was made a Fellow of Johns Hopkins University and wrote a thesis on epistemology. He was instructor in English at the University of California from 1878–82. A visit to William James[1] in 1877 led to his substituting for the latter during James' leave of absence during 1882–3. Thereafter he stayed at Harvard, being appointed professor in 1892 and Alford Professor of Natural Religion, Moral Philosophy and Civil Polity in 1914. After James' death in 1910 he was the leading American philosopher. He died in 1916.

Principal works: *Outlines of Psychology* (1903); *The Religious Aspect of Philosophy* (1885); *The Spirit of Modern Philosophy* (1892); *The World and the Individual* (1900); *The Sources of Religious Insight* (1912); *The Problems of Christianity* (1913).

Philosophical Note R.'s version of Absolute Idealism, elaborated and changed during the course of his philosophical career, begins with an examination of the nature of knowledge, rather than with a direct attempt to portray the structure of reality. The chief problem in this regard is raised by the relation between our ideas (i.e. sensations, etc.) and 'external' reality. An apparent solution is to analyse objects of perception not merely in terms of actual perceptions but also of possible ones. But such possibilities, R. argues, are themselves only ideas—for they are *imagined* events. Thus the prospect of getting 'behind' ideas to a reality with which they correspond is hopeless: like other Idealists, R. held that truth is not a relation of correspondence, but of coherence. An idea is true in so far as it coheres with other ideas. Thus the presupposition that knowledge is knowledge of something inevitably leads to the postulation of an all-embracing and coherent knowledge, an 'absolute experience to which all facts are known'. The conclusion that there is such an absolute experience is strengthened by a consideration of error (R. criticized philosophers for not paying enough attention to this, a neglect partly explicable by the fact that error is difficult to accommodate to Absolute Idealism, for if the Absolute is all-embracing it must include error—and this appears absurd).

[1] See above, p. 378.

By analogy with the correspondence theory of truth, error might be expected to consist in a failure to correspond with reality; but R. replies that an idea must be taken to have a purpose—it is intended to point to something—, so that error consists in failing to attain this purpose. But it can only be known to be an error by reference to a truth it fails to attain. Consequently, error lies in incompleteness, and implies a higher thought. But the possibility of error is infinite, and therefore presupposes an absolute experience which can realize the details of all this infinite error. R. thus brings out the importance (indeed the necessity) of a theory of error for any theory of truth.

Having argued against the thesis of a reality external to ideas, and defined the meaning of an idea as consisting basically in its purpose, R. concludes that the external meaning of an idea lies in its taking its place in a wider plan. And the emphasis on purpose allows R. to combine his Absolutism with a respect for individual persons: each centre of purposes fulfils an essential role, so that the wider purpose embodied in the Absolute in its fullest expression is, on R.'s view, somewhat like the pattern exhibited by a perfect society.

Though not the most famous of his writings on religion, R.'s lectures on *The Sources of Religious Insight* possess a clarity and simplicity which contrasts with the work of most Idealists. In the first Lecture, he draws attention to the religious paradox, namely that the truth about salvation must come from a superhuman source, while nevertheless the individual, in accepting something as revelation, is implying that he has the criteria for judging. Unless we can illuminate the way in which experience gives us an insight, albeit fragmentary, into the higher truth, no external revelation can assist us. R. in turn examines individual and social experience, reason and will as sources of religious insight, and sees in loyalty to a cause the concrete expression of religion which harmonizes the other sources of insight. And because there could be no loyalty in a world devoid of adversity and sorrow, sorrow itself is a further source of insight. The following passage describes the role of reason in providing religious insight.

Bibliographical Note See J. H. Muirhead, *The Platonic Tradition in Anglo-Saxon Philosophy* (London, 1931), J. E. Smith, *Royce's Social Infinite* (N.Y., 1950) and J. H. Cotton, *Royce on the Human Self* (Camb., Mass., 1954). The *Journal of Philosophy* devoted a special issue to Royce in 1956.

REASON AND RELIGION

Sources of Religious Insight, Ch. III

THE OFFICE OF THE REASON

Thus far we have dealt with sources of religious insight which are indispensable, but which confess their own inadequacy so soon as you question them closely. Individual experience can show us, in its moments of wider vision, our ideal, and its times of despair, of aspiration, or of self-examination, our need. But whenever it attempts to acquaint us with the way of salvation, its deliveries are clouded by the mists of private caprice and of personal emotion. Social experience, in its religious aspects, helps the individual to win the wider outlook, helps him also to find his way out of the loneliness of guilt and of failure toward wholeness of life, and promises salvation through love. But, like individual experience, it is beset by what we have called the religious paradox. And it does not solve that paradox. Confessing its own defects, it still undertakes to discern how to overcome them. In so far as it is merely social experience it deals with the world of weak mortals, of futile bickerings, and of love that, in this world, defines but never quite finds its true beloved. By virtue of this transforming love it indeed gives us the hint that our social world may be an apparition of an incarnation of some diviner life than any mortal now experiences. Yet how can mortals thus ignorant pretend to get insight into anything that is divinely exalted?

Thus, both the sources of insight that we have thus far consulted point beyond themselves. Each says, 'If salvation is possible, then human life must be able to come into touch with a life whose meaning is superhuman.' Our question is: 'Is there, indeed, such a divine life?' In order to deal with this question, we have resolved to consult still another source of insight, namely, our Reason. The present lecture must deal with this source of insight.

I

'What does one mean by the Reason?' As I attempt to answer this question, with an especial effort to show the relations of reason and religion, I shall be aided by reminding you at the outset that, at the present time, there is a widespread tendency to discredit the reason as a source of any notable insight into life or into the universe. And this tendency depends upon so defining the business of the reason as sharply to oppose, on the one hand, reason and common-sense experience. That is, some of our recent teachers tell us that the only sort of insight which can be of any use in religion must be won by intuitions and cannot be obtained by what these teachers call the abstract reason. By intuition, at least in the religious field, such men mean some sort of direct feeling of the nature of things, some experience such as the mystics have reported, or such as many religious people, whether technical mystics or not, call illumination through faith. Intuitions of this sort, they say, are our only guides in the religious field. As opposed to such direct apprehension, the use of reason would mean the effort to be guided by formulas, by explicitly stated abstract principles, by processes of inference, by calculations, or by logical demonstrations. James is prominent amongst those who thus oppose the abstract reason to the revelations of intuition;[1] and, especially in his later works, he is never weary of emphasizing the inarticulate character of all our deepest sources of religious insight. When we get true religious insight, so he teaches, we simply feel convinced that these things are so. If we try to give reasons for our beliefs, James holds that the reasons are inapt afterthoughts, the outcome of sophistication, or are at best useful only in putting our convictions into convenient order for purposes of record or of teaching. James's favourite statement of the contrast here in question identified the partisans of reason with the defenders of what he calls 'barren intellectualism'. He maintains that religion is hindered rather than helped by such people. You attain conviction by processes of which the 'barren intellect' can give no adequate account. Conviction, in religious matters, emanates, according to James, from those mysterious depths of the subconscious about which I said something in the last lecture. And convictions thus resulting feel overwhelming to the persons who have them. Such convictions are what many denote by the word 'intuition'. The effort to define abstract principles, as grounds for holding your convictions to be true, constitutes the only effort of the reason in religious matters which James recognizes. According to James, such reasoning processes are inevitably bad. And as a fact, so he insists, nobody seriously believes in God because some theologian or philosopher pretends to have demonstrated his existence. On the contrary, he says, belief in God is intuitive or is nothing of value. And reason is employed in such matters merely because of a frequent overfondness for abstract conceptions, or at best because formulas are useful for the teachers of religious traditions.

Another form of contrast, and one upon which James also often insists, while many other recent writers, whose interests are not those of James, emphasize the same matter, depends upon opposing reason to experience in general, including under the latter term not only the intuitions of the devout, but whatever goes by the name experience in ordinary speech. We see and hear and touch, and by such means get experience. But we make hypotheses and reduce their consequences; we assume premises and demonstrate conclusions; and, according to such writers, what we then do constitutes the typical work of our reason. The characteristic of the reason is that it attempts either to elucidate the meaning of an assertion, or to prove some proposition to be true, without appealing to experience to verify the proposition in question. And such work of the reason, as these writers tell us, is of very limited use, in comparison to the use of our direct experience as a guide. What is found to be true through empirical tests is

[1] See above, p. 379.

rightly tested. What is supposed to be proved true by abstract reasoning is thus at best made dependent for its explicit warrant upon the presupposed truth of the premises used in the reasoning process. Or, as is sometimes said, the reason can discover nothing essentially new. It turns its premises over and over, and gets out of them only what has already been put into them. Experience, on the other hand, is full of countless novelties; for what you can find through observation and experiment depends not upon previous assumptions, but upon the skill and the good fortune of the enquirer, and upon the wealth of life and of the real world.

In brief, for those who look at reason in this way, to use your reason is simply to draw necessary inferences from assumed premises. And no premises, as such writers insist, can warrant any inference except the inference of a conclusion which is already hidden away, so to speak, in the premises themselves. Thus reasoning, as they tell us, is a process which, in the conclusion inferred, merely lets out of the bag the cat which was concealed in that bag, namely, in the premises. Reason, therefore, is indeed (so such writers assert) barren wherever novelty is sought. It is useful only for purposes of formulations, and in certain parts of the abstract sciences, where deduction has a technical place, as a means for preparing the way for experimental tests. In life, experience is the guide to true novelty. And therefore, if religious insight can be attained at all, it must be due not to the reason, but to some sort of religious experience.

Such objections to the use of reason in the religious field depend, as you see, upon identifying the reasoning process with the combination of two well-known mental processes: first, the process of forming and using abstract conceptions; secondly, the process of analysing assertions, or combinations of assertions, to make more explicit what is already contained in their meaning. Our next question may well be this; Is such an account of the work of reason just to the actual usage that common sense is accustomed to make of this familiar name?

II

To this question I must at once answer that we all of us daily use the word reason as the name for a process, or a set of processes which certainly cannot be reduced to the mere power to form and to use abstract ideas, and to analyse the already predetermined meaning of statements. When we speak of an ill-tempered or of a prejudiced man as 'unreasonable', we do not merely mean that he is unable to form or to define abstract ideas, or that he cannot analyse the meaning of his own statements. For sometimes such a man is contentiously thoughtful, and fond of using too many onesided abstractions, and eager to argue altogether too vehemently. No, when we call him unreasonable, we mean that he takes a narrow view of his life, or of his duties, or of the interests of his fellow-men. We mean, in brief, that he lacks vision for the true relations and for the total values of things. When we try to correct this sort of unreasonableness, we do not say to the petulant or to the one-sided man: 'Go to the dictionary, and learn how to define your abstract terms.' Sometimes contentiously prejudiced men are altogether too fond of the dictionary. Nor do we merely urge him to form the habit of analysis. No, we may indeed say to him: 'Be reasonable'; but we mean: 'Take a wider outlook; see things not one at a time, but many at once; be broad; consider more than one side; bring your ideas together; in a word, get insight.' For precisely what I defined in my opening lecture as insight is what we have in mind when in such cases, we counsel a man to be reasonable. So, in such uses of the word reason, reason is not opposed to intuition, as the power to form abstract ideas is supposed by James to be opposed to the power to see things by direct vision. No, reason, in such cases, means simply broader intuition, the sort of seeing that grasps many views in one, that surveys life as it were from above, that sees, as the wanderer views the larger landscape from a mountain top.

When not long since, in a famous decision, the Supreme Court of the United States called attention to what it called 'The rule of reason', and declared its intention to judge the workings of well-known modern business methods by that rule, the court certainly did not mean by 'the rule of reason' the requirement that acts said to be 'in restraint of trade' must be judged merely through a process of forming abstract ideas or of analysing the signification of assertions. No, the court was explicitly opposing certain methods of estimate which it regarded as falsely abstract; and it proposed to substitute for these false abstractions a mode of judging the workings of certain trade combinations which was to involve taking as wide and concrete and practical a view as possible of their total effects. Everybody who read the court's words understood that, in this case, it was precisely the merely abstract conception of something technically defined as a 'restraint of trade' which the court wished, not to make sovereign, but to subordinate to the wider intuition of a fair-minded observer of the whole result, of a given sort of corporate combination. The 'rule of reason' was intended to bring the whole question out of the realm of barren abstractions and of mere analysis, and nearer to the realm where the trained observation of the fair minded man would decide the case—nearer, in fact, to the realm of intuition. Only, the decisive intuition must be something broad, and far-seeing, and synthetic, and fair.

Now I submit that this meaning of the word reason is perfectly familiar to all of you. Reason, from this point of view, is the power to see widely and steadily and connectedly. Its true opponent is not intuition, but whatever makes us narrow in outlook and consequently the prey of our own caprices. The unreasonable person is the person who can see but one thing at a time, when he ought to see two or many things together; who can grasp but one idea, when a synthesis of ideas is required. The reasonable man is capable of synopsis, of viewing both or many sides of a question, of comparing various motives, of taking interest in a totality rather than in a scattered multiplicity.

You may, of course, admit that this use of the word reason is familiar; and still you may say that James's contention is nevertheless sound. For, as you may declare, the real issue is not regarding the meanings that chance to be linked with the word reason, but regarding the relative impotence of that process which James chose to call by this name. As a fact, so you may assert, there exists the familiar process of forming abstract conceptions; and there also exists the process of drawing conclusions through an analysis of what is already contained in the meaning of the assumed premises. Whether or no one calls these two processes, in their usual combination, by the name of reasoning, James is right in saying that abstractions, and that such sorts of purely analytic abstract reasoning as he has in mind, are incapable of giving us religious insight. And both James and the others who oppose reason to concrete experience are right in asserting that you get no novel insight whatever through mere abstractions, or through mere analysis, but are dependent for your advances in knowledge upon experience. Therefore, as you may continue, the issue which James and other empiricists raise must not be evaded by any appeal to vaguer uses of the word reason, whether common sense or the Supreme Court chances to authorize such special forms of expression.

I fully agree to the importance of this comment and of the issue as thus stated. I am ready to consider the issue. But I also insist upon estimating the whole use of reason in its proper context. James, in common with countless other partisans of intuition in religious matters, is fond of insisting that all our nobler intuitions and all our deeper faiths are, in their foundations, inwardly compelling, but inarticulate, and that we degrade them rather than help them when we define their meaning in abstract terms or employ processes of explicit demonstration in their defence. James, in common with many empiricists, also opposes experience in general to all processes of reasoning, and asserts that the latter never teach us anything novel. The issue, fairly viewed, is therefore not a perfectly simple one. It involves the question whether the two modes of getting knowledge between which we are asked to choose are the only modes actually in use. Intuition, and experience in general, are by James and by others sharply contrasted with certain processes of abstraction and of analysis. It is then pointed out that since these latter processes, taken by themselves, never give us any essentially novel insights, you must on the whole cease to use your powers of abstraction and of analysis, except for the mere purpose of record or of teaching, or of some other such technical end—computation, analysis of hypotheses, and the like. You must, at least in religious matters, depend upon the uprushes from your subconscious self or upon whatever else is persuasively inarticulate. In the ultimate, decisions alone can save you. Hereupon the perfectly fair question arises whether the alternatives are thus exhaustively stated. Must one choose between inarticulate faith and barren abstractions? Must one face the alternative: Either intuition without reasoning, or else relatively fruitless analysis without intuition? Perhaps there is a third possibility. Perhaps one may use one's process of abstraction as a sort of preparation for certain articulate and noble intuitions that cannot be approached, by our human sort of consciousness, through any other way. Perhaps analysis is not the whole process which determines demonstrations. Perhaps synthesis—the viewing of many facts or principles or relations in some sort of unity and wholeness—perhaps a synoptic survey of various articulate truths, can lead us to novel insights. In that case inarticulate intuitions and barren abstractions are not the only instruments between which we must choose. For in that case there will be another sort of aid, a more explicit sort of intuition, a more considerate view of our life and its meaning, which we may adopt, and which may lead us to novel results. And these results may be not only articulate but saving.

Or, to state the issue more generally: In seeking for any sort of novel truth, have we only the choice between the experience of the data of sense or of feeling on the one hand and the analysis of abstract ideas and assertions upon the other? May there not be another source of knowledge? May not this source consist in the synthetic view of many facts in their unity—in the grasping of a complex of relations in their total significance? And may not just this be a source of insight which is employed in many of the processes ordinarily known as reasoning processes? May not the formation of abstract ideas, when wisely used, be merely a means of helping us towards an easier view of larger unities of fact than our present sort of human consciousness could grasp except for this auxiliary device? May not analysis be merely an aspect, a part of our live thinking? May not all genuine demonstration involve synthesis as well as analysis, the making of new constructions as well as the dissection of old assertions? If so, then the issue as presented by James and his allies is not rightly stated, because an essential part of its context is neglected. Abstract conceptions are, in fact, in the live and serious work of thought, a mere preparation for intuitions and experiences that lie on higher levels than those which, apart from abstract conceptions, we men can reach. Reasoning processes are fruitful because they involve sorts of experience, forms of intuition, that you cannot reach without them. In brief, reason and experience are not opposed. There is an opposition between inarticulate intuition and articulate insight. There is also an opposition between relatively blind experience of any sort and relatively rational experience. And, in view of such oppositions, it will be perfectly fair to define reason as the power to get articulate insight—insight into wholes rather than fragments. It will also be fair to define the reasoning process as the process of getting connected experience on a large scale.

Whoever views the matter thus will indeed not be forced to be a one-sided partisan of the reasoning process as thus defined. He will, first, fully admit that the formation of abstract ideas is but a means to an end, and that this end is the enlargement of the range of our view of the connections of our experience. He will secondly admit that, as soon as the process of forming abstract ideas is pursued as an end in itself, pedantry and formalism result, whether the topic be one of religion, or of science, or of the world's daily work. He will further agree with James, and with the empiricists generally, that merely analytic reasoning, if such were, in its isolation, a possible thing, would be indeed 'barren intellectualism'. And finally, if he is wise, he will go still further. He will not despise instinct, and feeling, and the movings of faith, and the inarticulate intuitions. For he will know that all these things are human, are indispensable, and are the basis upon which the genuine work of the reason, the wider view of life, must be carried towards its fulfilment. For whoever is to comprehend the unities of life must first live. Whoever is to be best able to survey the landscape from the mountain top must first have wandered in its paths and its byways, and must have grown familiar with its valleys and its recesses. Whoever is to get the mature insight must first have become as a little child.

But whoever, remembering the New Testament word about becoming as a little child, one-sidedly defends the inarticulate intuitions, as the only source of religious insight, should remember also the word of St Paul: 'When I was a child, I spake as a child, I thought as a child, I understood as a child; but when I became a man I put away childish things.'

It is a business of reason not to make naught of the indispensable intuitions of the childlike and of the faithful, but to work towards the insight such that, if we possessed it, we should 'know even as we are known'. That which is weak in this world may indeed confound many who are called wise; but there is no objection to its becoming also truly wise itself. For then it would all the better know why it had been able to confound false wisdom.

III

All such considerations will seem to many of you hopelessly general. You will have missed, thus far in my account, concrete instances to illustrate how what I have now called the reason actually works, how it is related to experience, how it helps us towards the broader view of things, how it makes the connections of life more obvious, how it raises our intuitions to higher levels. And unfortunately, since I have no time to discourse to you upon the science called Logic—the science part of whose proper duty it is to define the nature and the office of what I have now called the reason —I must indeed fail, in this brief summary, to give you any adequate account of what can be accomplished through the appeal to this source of insight. All that I shall try to do, on this occasion, is to mention to you a very few instances, some of them relatively trivial, wherein, through reasoning processes, we actually get these larger intuitions on higher levels, these higher modes of grasping the unity of things. Having thus very imperfectly exemplified what I mean by the synthetic processes of reasoning, I shall be ready barely to suggest to you, as I close, how the reason can be, and is, a source of religious insight.

In some recent logical discussions, and in particular in my colleague Professor Hibben's text-book of logic,[1] there has been used an example, trivial in itself, but in its own way typical—an example which is meant to show how there exists a mental process which is surely worthy of the name reasoning, and which is, nevertheless, no mere process of forming abstract ideas and no mere analysis of the meaning of assumed premises, although, of course, both abstraction and analysis have their subordinate places in this process. The reasoning involved in this example is of the very simplest sort. It is expressed in an old story which many of you will have heard.

According to this story, an aged ecclesiastic, garrulous and reminiscent, was once, in a social company, commenting upon the experience that had come to him in his long and devoted life. Fully meaning to keep sacred the secrets of the confessional, the old man was nevertheless led to say: 'Ah—it is strange, and sometimes terrible, what, in my profession, one may have to face and consider. You must know, my friends, my very first penitent

[1] *Inductive Logic* (N.Y., 1897).

was—a murderer! I was appalled.' The old priest had hardly spoken when the company was joined by an aged and prominent nobleman of the region, whom all present greeted with great respect. Saluting his priestly friend with no little reverence, the nobleman turned to the company and said, with calm unconsciousness: 'You must know, my friends, in my youth I was the very first person whom my honored friend here ever confessed.'

Now observe. The priest had not said who the murderer was. The nobleman in his contribution to the conversation had not confessed to the company the murder. He had not mentioned it in any way. And the priest had scupulously avoided mentioning him. But all present drew at once the reasonable conclusion that, granting the correctness of the two assertions, the nobleman was a murderer. We, of course, must all agree in this conclusion. Now is this conclusion the result of a mere analysis of either of the two assertions made? And does the conclusion merely result from our power to form abstract ideas? Plainly, the conclusion is due to the power of all present to make a synthesis, or, as one sometimes says, to put two and two together. Plainly, whatever abstract ideas are here used, it is not these which constitute the main work of a reasonable being who views the situation in which the nobleman is placed by the whole sense of the conversation. Reason here discovers a novel fact which neither the priest nor the nobleman had stated. This discovery is as much an experience as if it were the observation of an actual killing of one man by another. Only it is the discovery of the relations involved in a synthesis of meanings. This discovery is at once empirical (yes, in the broader sense of the word, intuitive), and it is a discovery of a necessary connection. It is not due to mere analysis. It is not a bit of barren intellectualism. It is not an unpractical comment. It is a discovery that might wreck the nobleman's reputation, and that might more or less indirectly lead to his ultimate conviction upon a capital charge. Now, that is an example, trivial enough if viewed as a mere anecdote, but a typical example, of the synthetic and constructive use of reason as a source of insight.

Let me turn to another also at first sight seemingly trivial case. An English logician, de Morgan,[1] long ago called attention to a form of reasoning which, up to his time, the logicians had unduly neglected. If you assume that 'a horse is an animal', you can reasonably conclude that 'the owner of a horse is the owner of an animal'; that 'whoever loves a horse loves an animal', and so on indefinitely. In brief, as you at once see, from the one assertion, 'A horse is an animal', there rationally follow a

[1] Augustus de Morgan (1806–71), mathematician and one of the pioneers of modern symbolic logic.

limitless number of possible inferences of the form: 'Whatever is in any relation R to a horse is in that same relation R to an animal.' Now you may indeed at first, as I just said, imagine such reasonings to be comparatively trivial. Whether they prove to be so, however, depends wholly upon the objects in question, upon our own interests in these objects, and upon circumstances. They might be vastly important. From the assertion, 'Mr Taft is President of the United States', there follows, by this sort of reasoning, the assertion, 'Whoever is a personal friend of Mr Taft is a personal friend of the President of the United States'. And such a conclusion some people might be very glad to have you draw. So, too, whoever is a member of Mr Taft's family, or household, or club, or of the university whose degrees he holds, or whoever is a fellow townsman, or fellow countryman, or partisan, or opponent, or enemy of Mr Taft, whoever agrees with what he says in his speeches, whoever plays golf with him, or whoever hopes or fears for his re-election, stands in just that relation, whatever it may be, to the President of the United States. And how important such rational inferences might appear for the comprehension of somebody's actual situation and prospects and acts depends upon the persons and the interests that may be in question. To some people just such inferences, at one moment or another, will not seem trivial, will be worth making, and will be anything but feats of barren intellectualism. That they are easy inferences to make is beside the mark. I have no time to ask you here to study with me the harder inferences upon topics that do not concern our main purpose. What I need, however, is to illustrate to you that such reasoning processes go beyond mere analysis, and do involve a rational and articulate intuition of a novel aspect of experience. For I defy you to find by any mere analysis of the assertion, 'Mr Taft is President', the innumerable assertions about friends, about family, about speeches, and policies, and so on, which as a fact rationally follow, in the indicated way, from that first assertion. You find these new results by taking a broader view of the unity of experience. What, then, I need to have you see is that the reason which, even in its lightest deeds, can accomplish such syntheses, and which can lead to such ordered intuitions, and can be the endless source of such novelties, is not merely the reason of whose powers as a source of insight James gives so discouraging a picture.

Having thus barely illustrated the thesis that reason can be both productive of new insight and constructively synthetic in its grasp of wider ranges of experience than we could observe without it, let me add that, in the exact sciences, and in particular in mathematics, the reasoning process, using just such forms of synthesis as I have now illustrated, is constantly leading investigators to the most varied and novel discoveries.

These discoveries are not due to mere analysis. They are reports of facts and the results of synthetic construction. As Mr Charles Peirce[1] loves to point out, the new discoveries made in mathematics, and by purely rational processes, are so numerous that for each year a volume of many hundreds of closely printed pages is needed to give, with strictly technical brevity, even the barest outline of the contents of the papers containing the novel results of that one year's researches. In their union with other sciences, the mathematical researches constantly lead to still vaster ranges of novel discovery. Reason, then, is not merely barren, is not mainly concerned with unproductive analysis, but does enrich our survey of experience, of its unity and of its meaning.

Perhaps some of you may still object that, if I define reason in the terms suggested by these instances, there seems to be danger of making the word 'reason' mean simply the same as the word 'insight'. For insight, as I defined it in my opening lecture, means a coherent view of many facts in some sort of unity. And in this case, as you may now say, why use two words at all? I reply that, in fact, all true insight is, to my mind rational insight, upon one or another level of the development of our power to become rational beings. But you will remember that insight, as I defined it, means knowledge which is intimate and manifold, as well as knowledge which views facts and relations in their unity. The words intuition and experience are often used to lay stress upon that aspect of our insight which either makes it intimate or else brings it into touch with many and various facts. And such usage is convenient. The word reason, as I have just exemplified its more synthetic meaning, calls our attention precisely to that aspect of our better insight which is involved in our power to grasp many facts in their *unity*, to see the coherence, the inter-relationship, the totality of a set of experiences. Now when insight reaches higher levels, these various aspects of our knowledge are never sundered. But as we grow towards higher insight, we know in part and prophesy in part and are childlike in so far as that which is perfect has not yet come.

In these, our imperfect stages of growth, sometimes our knowledge possesses intimacy, but still has to remain content, for the moment, with a more inarticulate grasp of deeper meanings. In such cases James's sort of intuition, or what is often called blind faith, is mainly in question. And this is indeed a stage on the way to insight. We feel unities but do not see them. Sometimes, however, as in much of our ordinary experience, the state of our minds is different; our knowledge revels in, or else contends with, the endless variety and multiplicity of the facts of life, and lacks a grasp of their unity. In that case our insight is often called 'merely

[1] See above, p. 379.

empirical'. We have experience; and so far our knowledge prospers. But we neither feel vaguely nor see clearly the total sense of things. And in such cases our sight is too busy to give us time for higher insight. As the Germans say, we do not see the wood because of the trees.

In a third stage of partial insight we may stand where, for instance, the masters of the exact sciences stand. We then grasp, with clearness, larger unities of controllable experience. We create objects, as the mathematicians create, in an ideal world of our own contemplation; and we then come to see that these ideal creations of ours do, indeed, reveal the eternal truth regarding a world of seemingly impersonal or superpersonal reality. We learn of this reality through the coherent synthesis of our ideal constructions. Our intution is in this case at once empirical, articulate, and such as to survey the broad landscape of the genuine relations of things. But alas! in most such cases our objects, though they are indeed presented to our rational intuition, are often abstract enough in their seeming. They are objects such as numbers, and series, and ordered arrays of highly ideal entities. In such cases the reason does its typical work; but often the objects of our insight fail to meet the more intense needs of life.

Thus, then, inarticulate intuitions, ordinary or sometimes more scientific observations of the details of life, and mathematical reasonings concerning the unity and the connections of highly ideal objects such as numbers, come to stand in our experience as more or less sharply sundered grades of imperfect insight. Thus we naturally come to view the typical achievements of our reason as a thing apart, and the rational or exact sciences as remote both from the intuitive faith of the little ones and from the wealthy experience of the men of common sense and of the men of natural science. As a fact, all these stages of insight are hints of what the Supreme Court meant when it appealed to the 'rule of reason'. True insight, if fulfilled, would be empirical, for it would face facts; intuitive, for it would survey them and grasp them and be intimate with them; rational, for it would view them in their unity.

IV

Our lengthy effort to define the work and the place of the reason has brought us to the threshold of an appreciation of its relation to the religious insight which we are seeking. In looking for salvation, we discover that our task is defined for us by those aspects of individual and social experience upon which our two previous lectures have dwelt. We have learned from the study of these two sorts of experience that, whatever else we need for our salvation, one of our needs is to come into touch with a life that in its unity, in its meaning, in its perfection, is vastly superior to our present human type of life. And so the question has presented itself: Have we any evidence that such a superhuman type of life is a real fact in the world? The mystics, and many of the faithful, answer this question by saying: 'Yes. We have such evidence. It is the assurance that we get through intuition, through feeling, through the light revealed to us in certain moments when thought ceases, and the proud intellect is dumb, and when the divine speaks quite directly to the passive and humbled soul.' Now when we calmly consider the evidence of such moments of inarticulate conviction, they strongly impress upon us what we have called the religious paradox. Faith, and the passive and mysterious intuitions of the devout, seem to depend on first admitting that we are naturally blind and helpless and ignorant, and worthless to know, of ourselves, any saving truth; and upon nevertheless insisting that we are quite capable of one very lofty type of knowledge—that we are capable of knowing God's voice when we hear it . . . of being sure . . . that the divine higher life which seems to speak to us in our moments of intuition is what it declares itself to be. If, then, there is a pride of intellect, does there not seem to be an equal pride of faith, an equal pretentiousness involved in undertaking to judge that certain of our least articulate intuitions are infallible?

Surely here is a genuine problem, and it is a problem for the reason. We know that men differ in faith. We know that one man's intuition regarding the way of salvation may seem to another man to be a mere delusion, a deceitful dream. We know, from the reports of religious experience, that at times even the saints of greatest renown have doubted whether some of their most persuasive visions of the divine were not, after all, due to the cunning deceit of an enemy of souls whom they more or less superstitiously feared. We know that to common sense despite its interest in salvation, the reports of the mystics and of the faithful have often appeared to be but the tale of private and vain imaginings. It is fair to ask what are the criteria whereby the true spiritual gifts, the genuine revelations, are to be distinguished. And this, I insist, is a question for the reason, for that aspect of our nature which has to do with forming estimates of wholes rather than of fragments—estimates of life in its entirety rather than of this or that feeling or moment of ecstasy in its isolation.

If, hereupon, without for the moment attempting to discuss how others, as, for instance, James himself, deal with the problem of the reasonable estimate of the value of our religious intuitions, I sketch for you my own opinion as to how reason does throw light upon the religious paradox, I must again emphasise a matter that I mentioned in my opening lecture and that is much neglected. Religious faith does, indeed, involve a seemingly paradoxical attempt to transcend the admitted ignorance of the needy human being, to admit that of himself this being knows almost nothing about the way of salvation, and nevertheless to insist that he is able to recognize his Deliverer's voice as the voice of a real master of life when he hears that voice, or—apart from metaphor—that he is able to be sure what revelation of a divine life, not his own, is the true one when he happens to get it. But religion is not alone in this paradoxical pride of humility. Science and common sense alike involve a similar admission of the depths of our human fallibility and ignorance, on the one hand, and an analogous assurance that, despite this our fragmentariness of experience, despite our liability to be deceived, we nevertheless can recognize truth when experience once has not wholly verified it, but has sufficiently helped us to get it. For, as individuals, we are constantly confident beyond what our present experience, taken by itself, clearly reveals to us. We, for instance, trust our individual memory in the single case, while admitting its pervasive fallibility in general. We persistently view ourselves as in reasonably close touch with the general and common results of human experience, even at the moment when we have to admit how little we know about the mind or the experience of any one fellow man, even our nearest friend. We say that some of our opinions, for instance, are warranted by the common sense of mankind. That is, we pretend once for all to know a good deal about what the common experience of mankind is. And yet, if we look closer, we see that we do not directly see or experience the genuine inner life of any one of mankind except the private self which each one of us regards as his own, while, if we still further consider the matter, we can readily observe how little each one of us really knows even about himself. When we appeal then to what we call common sense, we pretend to know what it is that, as we say, the mind of mankind finds to be true. But if we are asked to estimate the real state of mind of any individual man, how mysterious that state is! In brief, the paradox of feeling confidence in our own judgment, even while regarding all human opinion as profoundly fallible, is not merely a religious paradox, but also pervades our whole social and personal and even our scientific types of opinion. Not to have what is called a reasonable confidence in our own individual opinions is the mark of a weakling. But usually, if our personal opinions relate to important matters, they bring us into more or less serious conflict with at least some of the opinions of other men. Conflict is one mark that your opinions are worth having. When the conflict arises, we are usually led to consider how fallible other men are. They are fallible, we say, because they are human. How little any poor man knows! Yes, but if this principle holds true, how doubtful are my own opinions! Yet if I fill my mind with that reflection, to the exclusion of all other reasonable considerations, I condemn myself not to mere fallibility, but to certain failure.

The paradox is universal. It pervades all forms and activities of human enquiry. That is the first synthetic observation of the reason, when it surveys the field of human opinion. Everywhere we live by undertaking to transcend in opinion what the evidence before us, at any one moment, directly and infallibly warrants. But is it rational to do this? And if so, *why* is it rational?

The answer is that while there is much irrational presumption and over-confidence in our human world, there is also a perfectly rational principle which warrants certain forms and methods of thus transcending in our opinions the immediately presented evidence of the moment when we judge. This principle is as universal as it is generally neglected. Rightly understood it simply transforms for you your whole view of the real universe in which you live.

An opinion of yours may be true or false. But when you form an opinion, what are you trying to do? You are trying to anticipate, in some fashion, what a wider view, a larger experience of your present situation, a fuller insight into your present ideas, and into what they mean, would show you, if you now had that wider view and larger experience. Such an effort to anticipate what the wider view would even now show, if you were possessed of that view, involves both what are usually called theoretical interests and what pragmatists, such as James himself, have often characterized as practical interests. One can express the matter by saying that you are trying, through your opinions, to predict what a large insight, if it were present to you, would show or would find, that is, would experience. You can also say that you are trying to define what a fuller apprehension and a fairer estimate of your present purposes, and intentions, and interests, and deeds, and of their outcome, and of their place in life, would bring before your vision. In brief (whether you lay more stress upon deeds and their outcome, or upon experiences and their contents), any expression of opinion, made at any time, is an appeal of the self of the moment to the verdict, to the estimate, to the experience of a larger and better informed insight, in the light of which the self of the moment proposes to be judged. The special criteria by which your momentary opinion is tested, at the time when you form that opinion, vary endlessly with your mood and your training and your feelings, and with the topics and tasks in which you happen to be interested. But the universal form in which any opinion comes to your consciousness, and gets its definition for your own mind, is this form of an appeal to an insight that is superior in grasp, in unity, in coherence, in reasonableness to your momentary insight.

Now you can indeed say: 'When I form and express an opinion, I appeal from my present experiences to some wider insight that I view *as if it were* possible. My opinion asserts that *if I were* permitted to see what I just now do not directly experience, I should find the facts to be so and so.' But no such account of the matter is quite complete. Everything that you regard as possible has to be conceived as somehow based upon what you regard as actual. And so, in fact, your opinions are always appeals to some form of wider or larger or deeper or richer insight that, in the act of appealing to it, you regard as a present or as a past or as a future reality—in brief, as a live and perfectly concrete insight to whose verdict you appeal. Philosophers often express this by saying that all opinions are nothing but efforts to formulate the real contents of experience. This view I accept.

So then, as I insist, whatever your opinions, your expression of them is an appeal to some wider insight that you regard as real, and that you view as a live insight which comprehends your ideas, and which sees how they are related to genuine experience. This, I affirm, is the universal form which all opinion takes. A true opinion is true, because in fact it expresses what the wider insight confirms. A false opinion is false, because it is refuted by the light of this same wider view. Apart from such a confirmation or refutation in the light of such a larger view, the very concepts of truth and error, as applied to opinions which are not wholly confirmed or set aside by the instantaneous evidence of the moment when the opinions are formed or uttered, have no meaning. True is the judgment that is confirmed by the larger view to which it appeals. False is the assertion that is not thus confirmed. *Upon such a conception the very ideas of truth and error depend. Without such a conception truth and error have no sense.* If such a conception is not itself a true view of our situation, that is, if there is no wider insight, our opinions have neither truth nor error, and all of them alike are merely meaningless. When you are ignorant, you are ignorant of what the wider view makes clear to its own insight. If you blunder or are deluded, your blunder is due to a defective apprehension which the wider view confirms. And thus, whether you are ignorant or blundering, wise or foolish, whether the truth or the falsity of your present opinion is supposed to be actual, one actuality is equally and rationally presupposed, as the actuality to which all your opinions refer, and in the light of which they possess sense. *This is the actuality of some wider insight with reference to which your own opinion gets its truth or its falsity.*

To this wider insight, to this always presupposed vision of experience as it is, of the facts as they are, you are always appealing. Your every act of assertion displays the genuineness of the appeal and exemplifies the absolute rational necessity of asserting that the appeal is made to an insight that is itself real.

Frequently you do, indeed, call this insight merely the common sense of mankind. But, strange to say, this common sense of mankind is always and inevitably conceived by you in terms that distinguish it from the fleeting momentary views of any or of all merely individual men. Men —if I may judge them by my own case, and by what I hear other men confess—men, when taken merely as individuals, always live from moment to moment in a flickering way, normally confident, indeed, but clearly seeing at any one instant very little at a time. They are narrow in the span of the more direct insight. They grasp data bit by bit, and comprehend, in their instanteous flashes of insight, only little scraps and tiny bundles of ideas. I who now speak to you cannot hold clearly and momentarily before my mind at once even all of the meaning that I try to express in two or three of my successive sentences. I live looking before and after, and pining for what is not, and grasping after unity; and I find each moment crumbling as it flies; and each thought and each sentence of my discourse drops into momentary forgetfulness so soon as I have carefully built up its passing structure. In our life all thus flows. We fly from one flash of insight to another.

But nevertheless our opinions, so we say, reflect sometimes the common sense of mankind. They conform to the verdict of humanity. But who amongst us ever goes beyond thus confidently holding that he reflects the common sense of mankind? Who amongst us personally and individually experiences, at any moment, the confirmation said to be given by the verdict of humanity? The verdict of humanity? What man ever finds immediately presented to his own personal insight that totality of data upon which this verdict is said to depend? The common sense of mankind? What mortal man is there who ever finds incorporated in his flickering, fleeting, crumbling, narrow moments of personal experience the calm and secure insight which this common sense of mankind, or of enlightened mankind, is said to possess?

No, the common sense of mankind, is, for us all, a sort of super-individual insight, to which we appeal without ourselves fully possessing it. This '*common*' sense of mankind is just the sense *which no man of us all ever individually possesses*. For us all it is, indeed, something superhuman. We spend part of our busy little lives in somewhat pretentiously undertaking to report its dicta. But it is simply one of the countless forms in which we conceive the wider insight to be incorporated. *The true rational warrant for this confidence of ours lies in the fact that whatever else is real, some form of such wider insight, some essentially super-individual and superhuman insight is real.* For unless it is real our opinions, including any opinion that we may have that doubts or questions or denies its reality, are all equally meaningless. Thus even when we appeal to common sense we really appeal to a genuine but super-human insight.

Let us not here spend time, however, upon analysing this or that special form in which we are accustomed, for one special purpose or another, to conceive the wider insight. What is clear is that we constantly, and in every opinion, in every confession or ignorance appeal to such an insight. That such an insight is real, must be presupposed even in order to assert that our present opinions are errors. What interests us most at this point is, however, this, that whatever else the whole real universe is, the real universe exists only in case it is the object, and the very being, of such an insight, of such an inclusive experience, of such a view of what is. For, when you hold any opinions whatever about the real world, or about any of its contents, characters, or values, your opinions are either true or false, and are true or false by virtue of their actual conformity to the live insight which experiences what makes them true or false, and which therefore *ipso facto* experiences what the real world is. If there is *no* such world-possessing insight, then, once more, your opinions about the world are neither true nor false. Or, otherwise stated, if there is so such inclusive insight there is no world. To the real world, then, this insight which comprehends the world, and which knows whatever is true to be true, and whatever is false about the world to be false—to the real world this insight, I say, belongs. And the whole world belongs to it and is its object and essence. Whatever is real is real for that insight, and is in its experience, and exists as its possession, and as its well-known and well-comprehended content, and as its image and expression and meaning.

All this I say, as you may note, not because I hold in high esteem any of our private human opinions, but only because, *except in the light of such an all-seeing comprehension of facts as they are, our individual opinions about the world cannot even be false.* For opinion, in all its fleeting blindness and in its human chaos of caprices, is ceaselessly an appeal to the judge, to the seer, to the standard experience, to the knower of facts as they are, to the wider view, to the decisive insight. And opinions about reality in its wholeness, about the world, about the all, are appeals to the all-judging insight, to the all-seeing view, to the knowledge and experience that grasps the totality of facts to the widest outlook, to the deepest insight, to the absolute rational decision. If this be so, then an opinion to the effect that there exists no such widest and deepest insight, and no such final view, is itself just such an appeal to the final insight, simply because it is an opinion about reality. To assert then that there is no largest view, no final insight, no experience that is absolute, is to assert that the largest view observes that there is no largest view, that the final insight sees that there is no such insight, that the ultimate experience is aware that there is no ultimate experience. And such an assertion is indeed a self-contradiction.

This, I assert, is the only rational way of stating the nature of opinion, of truth or error, and consequently of reality. This is the synthesis which reason inevitably accomplishes whenever it rightly views the nature and the implications of even our most flickering and erroneous and uncertain opinions. We can err about what you will. But if we err, we simply come short of the insight to which we are aiming to conform, and in the light of which our ideas get absolutely all of their meaning. In every error, in every blunder, in all our darkness, in all our ignorance, we are still in touch with the eternal insight. We are always seeking to know even as we are known.

I have sought in this sketch to vindicate the general rights of rational insight as against mere momentary or fragmentary intuition. I have also tried to show you what synthesis of reason gives us a genuinely religious insight.

'My first penitent,' said the priest of our story, 'was a murderer.' 'And I,' said the nobleman, 'was this priest's first penitent.'

'I am ignorant of the vast and mysterious real world'—thus says our sense of human fallibility and weakness when we are first awakened to our need of rational guidance. The saying is true. The mystery is appalling. 'I am ignorant of the real world.' Yes; but reason, reflecting upon the nature and the essential meaning of opinion, of truth, of error, and of ignorance, points out to us this thesis; 'That of which I am ignorant is that about which I can err. But error is failure to conform my momentary opinion to the very insight which I mean and to which I am all the while appealing. Error is failure to conform to the inclusive insight which over-arches my errors with the heaven of its rational clearness. Error is failure to grasp the very light which shines in my darkness, even while my darkness comprehends it not. That of which I am ignorant is then essentially the object of a superhuman and divine insight.'

'I am ignorant of the world. To be ignorant is to fail to grasp the object of the all-inclusive and divine insight.' That is the expression of our situation. Reason easily makes the fitting synthesis when it considers the priest and the nobleman. I ask you to make the analogous synthesis regarding the world and the divine insight. This synthesis here takes form in concluding that the world is the object of an all-inclusive and divine insight, which is thus the supreme reality.

I have but sketched for you the contribution of reason to our quest. This contribution will seem to many of you too abstract and too contemplative to meet vital religious needs. In fact, what I have said will mean little to you unless you come to see how it can be translated into an adequate expression in our active life. To this task of such a further interpretation of the mission of the reason as a guide of life my next lecture shall be devoted.

22

OTTO

on RELIGIOUS EXPERIENCE

Biographical Note Otto was born at Peine in Hanover, 1869. After his university training, became *Privatdozent* in Systematic Theology at Göttingen, 1897. 1904, appointed professor there. In 1914, moved to Breslau, where he occupied an official Chair. In 1910 he had set off on a long journey to the East, which helped to give him a deep understanding of non-Christian religions. 1917, appointed to a Chair in Theology at Marburg, where he stayed until his death. In the same year appeared his most famous work, *Das Heilige* (*The Idea of the Holy*). Visited the East again in 1925, and 1927–8. Established a museum for the comparative study of religions at Marburg. Died, March, 1937.

Principal philosophical works: *Das Heilige* (1917), *Religion and Naturalism* (1904), *Mysticism East and West* (1926), *Religious Essays* (1931) and *Philosophy of Religion* (1931).

Philosophical Note O. was not merely an important philosopher of religion, but one of the greatest figures in the comparative study of religions. This background of understanding the phenomena of religion gave his famous *The Idea of the Holy* a freshness and directness often absent from philosophical writings; moreover, it placed discussions of religion in a wider and more realistic context. In philosophy itself, O. was influenced by the Kantian tradition, especially as carried on by Fries,[1] and by Schleiermacher.[2] With the latter, he argued for the autonomy of religion, i.e. it is not to be subsumed under knowledge or practice, as the rationalists and Kant respectively suggested. But from Kant, O. borrowed the notion of an *a priori* category, arguing that the *holy* is such. This category is applicable to reality no less than others such as causality; but does not just have an epistemological function (for Kant, the use of the categories is a condition of gaining knowledge, but does not entail that things in themselves exhibit causality, etc.), but expresses one aspect of reality, as manifesting itself to the religious consciousness. The sense of the sacred or holy forces its special claim upon us just as much as does the moral imperative; and the category of the holy is a universally valid category of meaning and value controlling the religious interpretation of human experience. The holy finds its basic expression in numinous feeling or intuition, and only derivatively through ideas (or ideograms, to use O.'s word).

[1] (1773–1843), German philosopher, who held that self-knowledge is the basis of all other forms of knowledge: *a priori* truth is, basically, discovery by introspection.

[2] See above, pp. 306–7.

Thus theological doctrines are secondary constructions and are not the primary data of religious insight.

Three basic elements in religious experience are distinguished by O.: (1) a certain emotional state, the *sensus numinis*; (2) an autonomous interpretation and valuation of reality through the category of the holy or sacred; (3) an intuitive apprehension of the eternal nature of things, or *divination*. From the Latin *numen*, O. coined the word *numinous* to signify the type of feeling in question, the sense of a *mysterium tremendum et fascinans*, a mysterious something, which is uncanny and Wholly Other, fearful and awe-inspiring, and yet implicit with a strange fascination, holding out a promise of exaltation and bliss (in this last element, O. foreshadows the way in which he tries to fit his account to the experience of mystics or contemplatives). The sense of the numinous is less, according to O., a feeling of absolute dependence (as Schleiermacher had described it) as a sense of creatureliness in which one is set over against the Other. This initial datum of the religious consciousness is expressed symbolically in various ways through ideograms, or conceptual symbols which are used to interpret in a discursive way the various elements of the numinous feeling: these range from the important and rather rudimentary concept of the Wholly Other, through myths (O. was influenced by Plato's use of myths), to theological doctrines.

O.'s emphasis on the 'non-rational' core of religion allows him to illuminate a great many facets of religion as it actually exists in the world often neglected by philosophers, especially in the Kantian and Hegelian traditions, and his descriptive results provide a useful starting-point for the analysis of religious concepts.

Bibliographical Note The following translations of O.'s works have appeared: *The Life and Ministry of Jesus* (Chicago, 1908); *Naturalism and Religion* (London, 1907); *India's Religion of Grace and Christianity* (London, 1930); *The Philosophy of Religion* (trans. of *Kantisch-Fries'sche Religionsphilosophie*) (N.Y., 1931); *The Idea of the Holy* (London, 1923; 5th impression with additions, 1928; Pelican edn, 1959); *Religious Essays* (London, 1931); *Mysticism East and West* (N.Y., 1932); *The Kingdom of God and the Son of Man* (Grand Rapids, Mich., 1938; new and rev. edn, London, 1943); *The Original Gītā* (London, 1939). A good survey of his work is Robert F. Davidson, *Rudolf Otto's Interpretation of Religion* (Princeton, 1947). Also of interest are Rees Griffiths, *God in Idea and Experience* (N.Y., 1931) and John Baillie, *The Interpretation of Religion* (Edinburgh, 1929), which develop and criticize O.'s ideas.

RELIGIOUS EXPERIENCE

The Idea of the Holy, Chs. VI, XI, XII and XIX

THE HOLY AS A CATEGORY OF VALUE

Sin and Atonement

We have already met that strange and profound mental reaction to the numinous which we proposed to call 'creature-feeling' or creature-consciousness, with its concomitant feelings of submergence and prostration and of the diminution of the self into nothingness; bearing always in mind that these expressions do not hit with precision, but merely hint at what is really meant,* inasmuch as this 'diminution of the self', etc., is something very different from the littleness, weakness or dependence of which we may become aware under other conditions than that of numinous feeling. And we had to notice that this experience marks a definite depreciation or dis-valuation of the self in respect, so to speak, of its reality and very existence. We have now to put alongside of this another sort of self-disvaluation, which has long been a matter of common observation, and only needs to be suggested in order to be recognized. 'I am a man of *unclean* lips and dwell among a people of unclean lips.' 'Depart from me, for I am a *sinful* man, O Lord.' So respectively Isaiah and Peter, when the numinous reality encounters them as a present fact of consciousness. In both cases this self-deprecating feeling-response is marked by an immediate, almost instinctive, spontaneity. It is not based on deliberation, nor does it follow any rule, but breaks, as it were, palpitant from the soul—like a direct reflex movement at the stimulation of the numinous. It does not spring from the consciousness of some committed transgression, but rather is an immediate datum given with the feeling of the numen: it proceeds to 'disvalue' together with the self the tribe to which the person belongs and indeed, together with that, all existence in general. Now it is today pretty generally agreed that, all this being the case, these outbursts of feeling are not simply, and probably at first not at all, moral *depreciations*, but belong to a quite special category of valuation and appraisement. The feeling is beyond question not that of the transgression of the moral law, however evident it may be that such a transgression, where it has occurred, will involve it as a consequence: it is the feeling of absolute 'profaneness'.

But what is this? Again something which the 'natural' man cannot, as such, know or even imagine. He, only, who is 'in the Spirit' knows and feels what this 'profaneness' is; but to such an one it comes with piercing acuteness, and is accompanied by the most uncompromising judgment of self-depreciation, a judgment passed, not upon his character, because of individual 'profane' actions of his, but upon his own very existence as creature before that which is supreme above all creatures. And at the same moment he passes upon the numen a judgment of *appreciation* of a unique kind by the category diametrically contrary to 'the profane', the category 'holy', which is proper to the numen alone, but to it in an absolute degree; he says: '*Tu solus sanctus*'. But '*sanctus*' is not merely

* Cf. Hugo of St Victor's words: '*Sumpta sunt vocabula, ut intellegi aliquatenus posset quod comprehendi non poterat.*' ('These words were chosen, that that which could not be comprehended might yet in some measure be understood.') [Hugo of St Victor (*c.* 1096–1141), German theologian and contemplative.]

'perfect' or 'beautiful' or 'sublime' or 'good', though, being like these concepts also a *value*, objective and ultimate, it has a definite, perceptible analogy with them. It is the positive *numinous* value or worth, and to it corresponds on the side of the creature a numinous *disvalue* or 'unworth'.

In every highly-developed religion the appreciation of moral obligation and duty, ranking as a claim of the deity upon man, has been developed side by side with the religious feeling itself. None the less a profoundly humble and heartfelt recognition of 'the holy' may occur in particular experiences without being always or definitely charged or infused with the sense of moral demands. The 'holy' will then be recognized as that which commands our respect, as that whose real value is to be acknowledged inwardly. It is not that the awe of holiness is itself simply 'fear' in face of what is absolutely overpowering, before which there is no alternative to blind, awe-struck obedience. '*Tu solus sanctus*' is rather a paean of *praise*, which, so far from being merely a faltering confession of the divine supremacy, recognizes and extols a value, precious beyond all conceiving. The object of such praise is not simply absolute might, making its claims and compelling their fulfilment, but a might that has at the same time the supremest *right* to make the highest claim to service, and receives praise because it is an absolute sense worthy to be praised. 'Thou art *worthy* to receive praise and honour and power' (Rev. 4.11).

When once it has been grasped that *qādôsh* or *sanctus* is not originally a *moral* category at all, the most obvious rendering of the words is 'transcendent' ('supramundane', *überweltlich*). The one-sided character of this rendering to which we had to take exception has been supplemented by the more detailed exposition of the numinous and its implications. But its most essential defect remains to be noted: 'transcendent' is a purely ontological attribute and not an attribute of *value*; it denotes a character that can, if need be, abash us, but cannot inspire us with *respect*. It might once again, therefore, be an advantage to introduce another term to underline this side of the numinous, and the words *augustus* and σεμνός suggest themselves for the purpose. *Augustus*, 'august', no less than σεμνός, is really appropriate only to numinous objects—to rulers only as offspring or descendants of gods. Then, while σεβαστός[1] indicates the *being* of the numen, σεμνός or *augustus* would refer rather to its supreme worth or *value*, its illustriousness. There will, then, in fact be two values to distinguish in the numen; its 'fascination' (*fascinans*) will be that element in it whereby it is of *subjective* value (= beatitude) to man; but it is 'august' (*augustum*)

[1] In fact, however, the imperial name Augustus was translated into Greek as Σεβαστός. Both σεμνός and σεβαστός derive from the same root (meaning 'to feel awe before', 'to worship'), and mean 'awe-inspiring', 'to be revered'.

in so far as it is recognized as possessing in itself *objective* value that claims our homage.

Mere 'unlawfulness' only becomes 'sin', 'impiety', 'sacrilege', when the character of *numinous unworthiness* or *disvalue* goes on to be transferred to and centred in *moral* delinquency. And only when the mind feels it as 'sin' does the transgression of law become a matter of such dreadful gravity for the conscience, a catastrophe that leads it to despair of its own power. The meaning of 'sin' is not understood by the 'natural', nor even by the merely moral, man; and the theory of certain dogmatists, that the demand of morality as such urged man on to an inner collapse and then obliged him to look around for some deliverance, is palpably incorrect. There are serious-minded men of sincere moral endeavour who cannot understand what such a 'deliverance' or 'redemption' may be, and dismiss it with a shrug of the shoulders. They are aware that they are erring and imperfect men, but they know and put into practice the methods of self-discipline, and so labour onward upon their way with sturdy resolution. The morally robust older rationalism was lacking neither in a sincere and respectful recognition of the moral law nor in honest endeavour to conform to it. It knew well and sternly condemned what was 'wrong', and the aim of its exhortations and instruction was that men should realize better and take more in earnest the facts of moral right and wrong. But no 'downfall' or 'collapse' and no 'need of redemption' came within its scheme, because the objection brought against it by its opponents was in fact just; rationalism lacked understanding of what 'sin' is.[1] Mere morality is not the soil from which grows either the need of 'redemption' and deliverance or the need for that other unique good which is likewise altogether and specifically numinous in character, 'covering' and 'atonement'. There would perhaps be less disputing as to the warrant and value of these latter in Christian doctrine if dogmatic theology itself had not transferred them from their mystical sphere into that of rational ethics and attenuated them into moral concepts. They were thus taken from a sphere where they have an authentic and necessary place to one where their validity is most disputable.

We meet the 'moment' of 'covering' in specially clear form in the religion of Yahweh, in its rites and the emotion they excite; but it is contained also, though more obscurely, in many other religions. It comprises, first, a manifestation of the numinous awe, viz. the feeling that the 'profane' creature cannot forthwith approach the numen, but has need of a covering or shield against the ὀργή[2] of the numen. Such a 'covering' is then a 'consecration', i.e. a procedure that renders the

[1] A footnote is omitted from the text here. [2] 'wrath'.

approacher himself 'numinous', frees him from his 'profane' being, and fits him for intercourse with the numen. The means of 'consecration', however—'means of grace' in the proper sense—are derived from, or conferred and appointed by, the numen itself, which bestows something of its own quality to make man capable of communion with it. And this act is something very different from the 'annulment of mistrust', the phrase in which Ritschl[1] seeks to rationalize these relations between God and man.

'Atonement', following our view, is a 'sheltering' or 'covering', but a profounder form of it. It springs directly from the idea of numinous value or worth and numinous disvalue or unworth as soon as these have been developed. Mere awe, mere need of shelter from the *tremendum*, has here been elevated to the feeling that man in his 'profaneness' is not *worthy* to stand in the presence of the holy one, and that his own entire personal unworthiness might defile even holiness itself. This is obviously the case in the vision of the call of Isaiah; and the same note recurs, less emphatically but quite unmistakably, in the centurion of Capernaum (Luke 7.1–10), and his words: 'I am not worthy that thou shouldest enter under my roof.' Here we have both the light thrill of awe before the *tremendum* of the numen and also, and more especially, the feeling of this unique disvalue or unworth of the profane confronted by the numen, which suggests to the man that even holiness itself may be tainted and tarnished by his presence.

Here, then, comes in the felt necessity and longing for 'atonement', and all the more strongly when the close presence of the numen, intercourse with it, and enduring possession of it, becomes an object of craving, is even desired as the *summum bonum*. It amounts to a longing to transcend this sundering unworthiness, given with the self's existence as 'creature' and profane natural being. It is an element in the religious consciousness, which, so far from vanishing in the measure in which religion is deepened and heightened, grows on the contrary stronger and more marked. Belonging, as it does, wholly to the non-rational side of religion, it may remain latent while, in the course of religious evolution, the rational side at first unfolds and assumes vigorous and definite form; it may retire for a time behind other elements and apparently die away, but only to return more powerfully and insistently than before. And again it may grow to be the sole, one-sided exclusive interest, a cry that drowns all other notes, so that the religious consciousness is distorted and disfigured; as may readily happen where through long periods of time the rational aspects of religion have been fostered unduly and at the cost of the non-rational.

The special character of this consciousness of need for atonement may

[1] Ritschl (1822–89) emphasized the practical and moral side of religion, and interpreted religious beliefs as a system of value-judgments.

perhaps be brought home more clearly by an analogy from our 'natural' emotional life; but at the same time it is important that the religious feeling we are considering should itself be kept distinct from its analogue, as the two are frequently confounded. The analogy is with the feeling arising from moral transgression. There, too, we practise a kind of self-deprecation which is clear and familiar and perfectly intelligible to us, when we esteem ourselves *guilty* of a bad action and the action itself as morally evil. The evil of the action *weighs upon us* and deprives us of our self-respect. We *accuse* ourselves and *remorse* sets in. But alongside this self-depreciation stands a second one, which while it may have reference to the same action as the other yet avails itself of definitely different categories. The same perverse action that before weighed upon us now *pollutes* us; we do not accuse ourselves, we are defiled in our own eyes. And the characteristic form of emotional reaction is no longer remorse but *loathing*. The man feels a need, to express which he has recourse to images of *washing* and cleansing. The two kinds of self-depreciation proceed on parallel lines and may relate to the same action; but none the less it is obvious that they are, inwardly and in their essence, determinately different. Now the second of them has a plain analogy with the need for 'atonement', and so can fairly be drawn upon for its elucidation; while at the same time it is yet nothing more than an analogy from another sphere, viz. that of morality.

No religion has brought the mystery of the need for atonement or expiation to so complete, so profound, or so powerful expression as Christianity. And in this, too, it shows its superiority over others. It is a more perfect religion and more perfectly religion than they, in so far as what is potential in religion in general becomes in Christianity a pure actuality. And the distrust and suspicion which so widely obtains with regard to this mystery is only to be explained from the custom—for which our theoretical cult of homiletics, liturgy, and catechism is largely responsible—of taking into account only the rational side of religion. Yet this atonement mystery is a 'moment' which no Christian teaching that purports to represent the religious experience of the Christian and biblical tradition can afford to surrender. The teacher will have to make explicit, by an analysis of the Christian religious experience, how the 'very numen', by imparting itself to the worshipper, becomes itself the means of 'atonement'. And in this regard it does not matter so very much what the decisions of the commentators are as to what, if anything, St Paul or St Peter wrote on the subject of expiation and atonement, or whether, indeed, there is any 'scriptural authority' for the thing at all. Were there in scripture no word written about it, it might still be written today from our own experience. But it would indeed be extraordinary if it had not long ago been written of. For the God of the New Testament is not less holy than the God of the Old Testament, but more holy. The interval between the creature and him is not diminished but made absolute; the unworthiness of the profane in contrast to him is not extenuated but enhanced. That God none the less admits access to himself and intimacy with himself is not a mere matter of course; it is a grace beyond our power to apprehend, a prodigious paradox. To take this paradox out of Christianity is to make it shallow and superficial beyond recognition. But if this is so, the intuitions concerning, and the need felt for, 'covering' and 'atonement' result immediately. And the divinely appointed means of God's self-revelation, whether experienced and appraised as such—'the Word', 'the Spirit', 'the Person of Christ',—become that to which the man 'flees', in which he finds refuge, and in which he 'hides' himself, in order that, consecrated and cleansed of his 'profaneness' thereby, he may come into the presence of holiness itself.

That these two ideas are viewed with a certain distrust may be traced to two causes. One is, that what is a specifically religious element is distortingly moralized. If we start from mere morality and in relation to a God understood as being the personification of the moral order endowed with love, then all things are wholly inapplicable and a source of genuine difficulty. But we are concerned with *religious* (not merely moral) intuitions, and it is impossible to dispute how right or wrong they are with a man whose interest is wholly in morality and not in religion, and who is therefore quite incapable of appreciating them. Whoever, on the other hand, penetrates to the unique centre of the religious experience, so that it starts awake in his own consciousness, finds that the truth of these intuitions is experienced directly, as soon as he penetrates into their depths.

The other ground of distrust is that usually in our theological systems an attempt is made to develop conceptual *theories* of these ideas, which are all pure intuitions, emotional rather than conceptual in character. They are thus made objects of speculation, and the final outcome is the quasi-mathematical 'doctrine of imputation' and its drastic ascription to the credit of the 'sinner' of the 'merit' of Christ, not to mention the learned enquiry whether this transaction involves an 'analytic' or a 'synthetic' judgment of God.[1]

* * * * * * * * *[2]

Let us look back once more from the point we have reached over the course our enquiry has so far taken. As the sub-title of this book suggests,[3]

[1] See n. 2 to p. 253.

[2] The asterisks are in the original and do not represent an omission.

[3] The sub-title is 'An Inquiry into the non-rational factor in the idea of the divine and its relation to the rational'.

we were to investigate the non-rational element in the idea of the divine. The words 'non-rational' and 'irrational' are today used almost at random. The non-rational is sought over the most widely different regions and writers generally shirk the trouble of putting down precisely what they intend by the term, giving it often the most multifarious meanings or applying it with such vague generality that it admits of the most diverse interpretations. Pure fact in contrast to law, the empirical in contrast to reason, the contingent in contrast to the necessary, the psychological in contrast to transcendental fact, that which is known *a posteriori* in contrast to that which is determinable *a priori*; power, will and arbitrary choice in contrast to reason, knowledge and determination by value; impulse, instinct and the obscure forces of the subconscious in contrast to insight, reflection and intelligible plan; mystical depths and stirrings in the soul, surmise, presentiment, intuition, prophecy and finally the 'occult' powers also; or, in general, the uneasy stress and universal fermentation of the time, with its groping after the thing yet heard or seen in poetry or the plastic arts—all these and more may claim the names 'non-rational', 'irrational', and according to circumstances are extolled or condemned as modern 'irrationalism'. Whoever makes use of the word 'non-rational' today ought to say what he actually means by it. This we did in our introductory chapter. We began with the 'rational' in the idea of God and the divine, meaning by the term that in it which is clearly to be grasped by our power of conceiving, and enters the domain of familiar and definable conceptions. We went on to maintain that beneath this sphere of clarity and lucidity lies a hidden depth, inaccessible to our conceptual thought, which we in so far call the 'non-rational'.

The meaning of the two contrasted terms may be made plainer by an illustration. A deep joy may fill our minds without any clear realization upon our part of its source and the object to which it refers, though some objective reference there must always be. But as attention is directed to it the obscure object becomes clearly identified in precise conceptual terms. Such an object cannot, then, be called, in our sense of the word, 'non-rational'. But it is quite otherwise with religious 'bliss' and its essentially numinous aspect, the *fascinans*. Not the most concentrated attention can elucidate the object to which this state of mind refers, bringing it out of the impenetrable obscurity of feeling into the domain of the conceptual understanding. It remains purely a felt experience, only to be indicated symbolically by 'ideograms'. That is what we mean by saying it is non-rational.

And the same is true of all the moments of the numinous experience. The consciousness of a 'wholly other' evades precise formulation in words, and we have to employ symbolic phrases which seem sometimes sheer paradox, that is, *ir*rational, not merely non-rational, in import. So with religious awe and reverence. In ordinary fear and in moral reverence I can indicate in conceptual terms what it is that I fear or revere; injury, e.g. or ruin in the one case, heroism or strength of character in the other. But the object of *religious* awe or reverence—the *tremendum* and *augustum*, cannot be fully determined conceptually: it is non-rational, as is the beauty of a musical composition, which no less eludes complete conceptual analysis.

Confronted by the fact of the non-rational thus interpreted we cannot be satisfied with a mere bare statement, which would open the door to all the vague and arbitrary phraseology of an emotionalist irrationalism. We are bound to try, by means of the most precise and unambiguous symbolic and figurative terms that we can find, to discriminate the different elements of the experience so far as we can in a way that can claim general validity.

CHAPTER XI

THE TWO PROCESSES OF DEVELOPMENT

This permeation of the rational with the non-rational is to lead, then, to the deepening of our rational conception of God; it must not be the means of blurring or diminishing it. For if (as suggested at the close of the last chapter) the disregard of the numinous elements tends to impoverish religion, it is no less true that 'holiness', 'sanctity', as Christianity intends the words, cannot dispense with the rational, and especially the clear ethical elements of meaning which Protestantism more particularly emphasizes in the idea of God. To get the full meaning of the word 'holy' as we find it used in the New Testament (and religious usage has established it in the New Testament sense to the exclusion of others), we must no longer understand by 'the holy' or 'sacred' the merely numinous in general, nor even the numinous at its own highest development; we must always understand by it the numinous completely permeated and saturated with elements signifying rationality, purpose, personality, morality. It is in this combined meaning that we retain and apply the term 'holy' in our subsequent chapters. But that the course of the historical development may be clearly understood, we venture first to recapitulate our view upon this matter as explicitly as possible.

That which the primitive religious consciousness first apprehends in the form of 'daemonic dread', and which, as it further unfolds, becomes more elevated and ennobled, is in origin not something rational or moral, but something distinct, non-rational, an object to which the mind responds in a unique way with the special feeling-reflexes that have been described. And this element or 'moment' passes in itself through a process of development of its own, quite apart from the other process—which begins at an early stage—by which it is 'rationalized' and 'moralized', i.e. filled with rational and ethical meaning. Taking this non-rational process of development first, we have seen how the 'daemonic dread', after itself passing through various gradations, rises to the level of 'fear of the gods', and thence to 'fear of God'. The *δαιμόνιον* or daemonic power becomes the *θεῖον* or divine power: 'dread' becomes worship; out of a confusion of inchoate emotions and bewildered palpitations of feeling grows '*religio*', and out of 'shudder' a holy awe. The feelings of dependence upon and beatitude in the numen, from being relative, become absolute. The false analogies and fortuitous associations are gradually dispelled or frankly rejected. The numen becomes God and Deity. It is then to God and Deity, as 'numen' rendered absolute, that the attribute denoted by the terms *qādôsh*, *sanctus*, *ἅγιος*, holy, pertains, in the first and directest sense of the words. It is the culmination of a development which works itself out purely in the sphere of the non-rational. This development constitutes the first central fact of religious study, and it is the task of religious history and psychology to trace its course.

Next, secondary and subsidiary to this, is the task of tracing the course of the process of rationalization and moralization *on the basis of* the numinous consciousness. It nearly, if not quite, synchronizes and keeps pace with the stages of the purely numinous development, and, like that, it can be traced in its different gradations in the most widely different regions of religious history. Almost everywhere we find the numinous attracting and appropriating meanings derived from social and individual ideals of obligation, justice and goodness. These become the 'will' of the numen, and the numen their guardian, ordainer and author. More and more these ideas come to enter into the very essence of the numen and charge the term with ethical content. 'Holy' becomes 'good', and 'good' from that very fact in turn becomes 'holy', 'sacrosanct'; until there results a thenceforth indissoluble synthesis of the two elements, and the final outcome is thus the fuller, more complex sense of 'holy', in which it is at once *good and sacrosanct*. The greatest distinction of the religion of the ancient Israel, at least from Amos onwards, is precisely the intimate coalescence of both elements. No God is like the God of Israel: for he is the absolutely Holy One (= perfectly good). And, on the other hand, no law is like Yahweh's Law, for it is not merely good, but at the same time 'holy' (= sacrosanct).

And this process of rationalization and moralization of the numinous, as it grows ever more clear and more potent, is in fact the most essential part of what we call 'the History of Salvation' and prize as the evergrowing self-revelation of the divine. But at the same time it should be clear to us that this process of the 'moralization of the idea of God', often enough represented to us as a principal problem, setting the main line for enquiry into the history of religion, is in no wise a suppression of the numinous or its supersession by something else—which would result not in a God, but a God-substitute—but rather the completion and charging of it with a new content. That is to say, the 'moralization' process assumes the numinous and is only completed upon this as basis.

CHAPTER XII

THE HOLY AS AN *A PRIORI* CATEGORY

It follows from what has been said that the 'holy' in the fullest sense of the word is a combined, complex category, the combining elements being its rational and non-rational components. But in *both*—and the assertion must be strictly maintained against all sensationalism[1] and naturalism[2]—it is a *purely a priori* category.

The rational ideas of absoluteness, completion, necessity and substantiality, and no less so those of the good as an objective value, objectively binding and valid, are not to be 'evolved' from any sort of sense-perception. And the notions of 'epigenesis', 'heterogony',[3] or whatever other expression we may choose to denote our compromise and perplexity, only serve to conceal the problem, the tendency to take refuge in Greek terminology being here, as so often, nothing but an avowal of one's own insufficiency. Rather, seeking to account for the ideas in question, we are referred away from all sense-experience back to an original and underivable capacity of the mind implanted in the 'pure reason' independently of all perception.

But in the case of the non-rational elements of our category of the Holy,

[1] That is, the view that all knowledge is derived from sense-experience (sensations).

[2] In this context, the view that the whole of experience may be accounted for by a method like that of the sciences (here naturalism excludes the supernatural).

[3] Terms borrowed from biological theory, and implying that new characteristics supervene upon the differentiation of structure during embryological development, etc. (as though sense-experience could give rise, through its differentiation, to the experience of the numinous, etc.).

we are referred back to something still deeper than the 'pure reason', at least as this is usually understood, namely, to that which mysticism has rightly named the *fundus animae*, the 'bottom' or 'ground of the soul' (*Seelengrund*).[1] The ideas of the numinous and the feelings that correspond to them are, quite as much as the rational ideas and feelings, absolutely 'pure', and the criteria which Kant suggests for the 'pure' concept and the 'pure' feeling of respect are most precisely applicable to them. In the famous opening words of the *Critique of Pure Reason* he says:

> That all our knowledge begins with experience there can be no doubt. For how is it possible that the faculty of cognition should be awakened into exercise otherwise than by means of objects which affect our senses? . . . But, though all our knowledge begins *with* experience, it by no means follows that all arises *out of* experience.

And, referring to empirical knowledge, he distinguishes that part which we receive through impressions and that which our own faculty of cognition supplies from itself, *sense-impressions giving merely the occasion.*

The numinous is of the latter kind. It issues from the deepest foundation of cognitive apprehension that the soul possesses, and, though it of course comes into being in and amid the sensory data and empirical material of the natural world and cannot anticipate or dispense with those, yet it does not arise *out of* them, but only *by their means*. They are the incitement, the stimulus, and the 'occasion' for the numinous experience to become astir, and, in so doing, to begin—at first with a naïve immediacy of reaction—to be interfused and interwoven with the present world of sensuous experience, until, becoming gradually purer, it disengages itself from this and takes its stand in absolute contrast to it. The proof that in the numinous we have to deal with purely *a priori* cognitive elements is to be reached by introspection and a critical examination of reason such as Kant instituted. We find, that is, involved in the numinous experience, beliefs and feelings qualitatively different from anything that 'natural' sense-perception is capable of giving us. They are themselves not perceptions at all, but peculiar interpretations and valuations, at first of perceptual data, and then—at a higher level—of posited objects and entities, which themselves no longer belong to the perceptual world, but are thought of as supplementing and transcending it. And as they are not themselves sense-perceptions, so neither are they any sort of 'transmutation' of sense-perceptions. The only 'transmutation' possible in respect of sense-perception is the transformation of the intuitively given concrete percept, of whatever sort, into the corresponding concept; there is never any question

[1] See E. Underhill, *Mysticism*, Ch. VII.

of the transformation of *one* class of percepts into a class of entities qualitatively *other*. The facts of the numinous consciousness point therefore—as likewise do also the 'pure concepts of the understanding'[1] of Kant and the ideas and value-judgments of ethics or aesthetics—to a hidden substantive source, from which the religious ideas and feelings are formed, which lies in the mind independently of sense-experience; a 'pure reason' in the profoundest sense, which, because of the 'surpassingness' of its content, must be distinguished from both the pure theoretical and the pure practical reason of Kant, as something yet higher or deeper than they.

The justification of the 'evolutionist' theory of today stands or falls with its claims to 'explain' the phenomenon of religion. That is in truth the real task of the psychology of religion. But in order to explain we must have the data from which an explanation may be forthcoming; out of nothing nothing can be explained. Nature can only be explained by an investigation into the fundamental forces of nature and their laws: it is meaningless to go farther and explain these laws themselves, for in terms of what are they to be explained? But in the domain of spirit the corresponding principle from which an explanation is derived is just the spirit itself, the reasonable spirit of man, with its predispositions, capacities and its own inherent laws. This has to be presupposed: it cannot itself be explained. None can say how mind or spirit 'is made'—though this is in effect just what the theory of epigenesis is fain to attempt. The history of humanity begins with man, and we have to presuppose man as a being analogous to ourselves in natural propensities and capacities. It is a hopeless task to seek to lower ourselves into the mental life of a *pithecanthropus erectus*; and, even if it were not, we should still need to start from man as he is, since we can only interpret the psychical and emotional life of animals regressively by clumsy analogies drawn from the developed human mind. To try, on the other hand, to understand and deduce the human from the sub-human or brute mind is to try to fit the lock to the key instead of *vice versa*; it is to seek to illuminate light by darkness. In the first appearance of conscious life on dead unconscious matter we have a simple, irreducible, inexplicable datum. But that which here appears is already a manifold of qualities, and we can only interpret it as a seed of potentiality, out of which issue continually maturer powers and capacities, as the organization of the body increases in stability and complexity. And the only way we can throw any light upon the whole region of sub-human psychical life is by interpreting it once again as a sort of 'predisposition' at a second remove, i.e. a predisposition to form the predispositions or faculties of the actual

[1] I.e. categories such as causality; see above, p. 421.

developed mind, and standing in relation to this as an embryo to the full-grown organism. But we are not completely in the dark as to the meaning of this word 'predisposition'. For in our own awakening and growth to mental and spiritual maturity we trace in ourselves in some sort the evolution by which the seed develops into the trees—the very opposite of 'transformation' and 'epigenesis' by successive addition.*

We call the source of growth a hidden 'predisposition' of the human spirit, which awakens when aroused by divers excitations. That there are 'predispositions' of this sort in individuals no one can deny who has given serious study to the history of religion. They are seen as propensities, 'predestining' the individual to religion, and they may grow spontaneously to quasi-instinctive presentiments, uneasy seeking and groping, yearning and longing, and become a religious *impulsion*, that only finds peace when it has become clear to itself and attained its goal. From them arise the states of mind of 'prevenient grace', described in masterly fashion by Suso:[1]

> Loving, tender Lord! My mind has from the days of my childhood sought something with an earnest thirst of longing, Lord, and what that is have I not yet perfectly apprehended. Lord, I have now for many a year been in hot pursuit of it, and never yet have I been able to succeed, for I know not aright what it is. And yet it is something that draws my heart and my soul after it, and without which I can never attain full repose. Lord, I was fain in the earliest days of my childhood to seek it among created things, as I saw others before me do. And the more I sought, the less I found it; and the nearer I went, the further I wandered from it. . . . Now my heart rages for it, for fain would I possess it. . . . Woe is me! . . . What is this, or how is it fashioned, that plays within me in such hidden wise?[2]

These are manifestations of a *predisposition* becoming a search and a driving *impulsion*. But here, if nowhere else, the 'fundamental biogenetic law' really does hold good, which uses the stages and phases in the growth

* The physical analogue to these spiritual or mental relationships is the relation of potential to kinetic energy. The assumption of such a relation in the world of mind (i.e. a relation between potential and kinetic mind) is, of course, only to be expected from one who is prepared to accept as the final cause of all mind in the world as a whole the absolute mind as 'pure actuality' whose *ellampatio* or effulgence (in Leibniz's phrase) all other mind is. For all that is potential presupposes an *actual* as the ground of its possibility, as Aristotle long ago showed. But indeed how can we afford to reject such a 'pure actuality'? It is an inconsequent proceeding to postulate actuality, as is done, for a starting point for the physical world, as a system of stored-up energy, whose transference to kinetic energy constitutes the 'rush of worlds and wheel of systems', and yet to reject the analogous assumption in the world of mind and spirit.

[1] Suso (*c.* 1295–1365), the German Dominican mystic, was a follower of Eckhart.

[2] *Works*, ed. Denifle, p. 311.

of the individual to throw light upon the corresponding stages in the growth of the species. The *predisposition* which the human reason brought with it when the species Man entered history became long ago, not merely for individuals but for the species as a whole, a *religious impulsion*, to which incitements from without and pressure from within the mind both contributed. It begins in undirected, groping emotion, a seeking and shaping of representations, and goes on, by a continual onward striving, to generate ideas, till its nature is self-illumined and made clear by an explication of the obscure *a priori* foundation of thought itself, out of which it is generated.* And this emotion, this searching, this generation and explication of ideas, gives the warp of the fabric of religious evolution, whose woof we are to discuss later.[1]

CHAPTER XIX

HISTORY AND THE *A PRIORI* IN RELIGION: SUMMARY AND CONCLUSION

We have considered 'the holy' on the one hand as an *a priori* category of the mind, and on the other hand as manifesting itself in outward appearance. The contrast here intended is exactly the same as the common contrast of inner and outer, general and special revelation. And if we take 'reason' (*ratio*) as an inclusive term for all cognition which arises in the mind from principles native to it, in contrast to those based upon facts of history, then we may say that the distinction between holiness as an *a priori* category and holiness as revealed in outward appearance is much the same as that between 'reason' (in this wide sense) and history.

Every religion which, so far from being a mere faith in traditional authority, springs from personal assurance and inward convincement (i.e. from an inward first-hand cognition of its truth)—as Christianity does in a unique degree—must presuppose principles in the mind enabling it to be independently recognized as true.† But these principles must be *a priori* ones, not to be derived from 'experience' or 'history'. It has little meaning, however edifying it may sound, to say that they are

* The reader may compare what Kant says in his *Lectures on Psychology* (Leipzig ed., 1889, p. 11) of 'the treasure buried in the field of obscure ideas, constituting the deep abyss of human knowledge, which we cannot sound'. This 'deep abyss' is just the *fundus animae* that is aroused in Suso.

[1] O. discusses this in the next selection, Ch. XIX.

† The attestation of such principles is the '*testimonium Spiritus Sancti internum*' of which we have already spoken. And this must clearly be itself immediate and self-warranted, else there would be no need of another 'witness of the Holy Spirit' to attest the truth of the first, and so on *ad infinitum*.

inscribed upon the heart by the pencil of the Holy Spirit 'in history'. For whence comes the assurance that it was the pencil of the 'Holy Spirit' that wrote, and not that of a deceiving spirit of imposture, or of the 'tribal fantasy' of anthropology? Such an assertion is itself a presumption that it is possible to distinguish the signature of the Spirit from others, and thus we have an *a priori* notion of what is of the Spirit independently of history.

And there is a further consideration. There is something presupposed by history as such—not only the history of mind or spirit, with which we are here concerned—which alone makes it history, and that is the existence of a *quale*, something with a potentiality of its own, capable of *becoming*, in the special sense of coming to be that to which it was predisposed and predetermined. An oak-tree can *become*, and thus have a sort of 'history'; whereas a heap of stones cannot. The random addition and subtraction, displacement and rearrangement, of elements in a mere aggregation can certainly be followed in narrative form, but this is not in the deeper sense an historical narrative. We only have the history of a people in proportion as it enters upon its course equipped with an endowment of talents and tendencies; it must already *be something* if it is really to *become* anything. And biography is a lamentable and unreal business in the case of a man who has no real unique potentiality of his own, no special idiosyncrasy, and is therefore a mere point of intersection for various fortuitous causal series, acted upon, as it were, from without. Biography is only a real narration of a real life where, by the interplay of stimulus and experience on the one side and natural endowment on the other, something individual and unique comes into being, which is therefore neither the result of a 'mere self-unfolding' nor yet the sum of mere traces and impressions, written from without from moment to moment upon a *tabula rasa*. In short, to propose a history of mind is to presuppose a mind or spirit determinately qualified; to profess to give a history of religion is to presuppose a spirit specifically qualified for religion.

There are, then, three factors in the process by which religion comes into being in history. First, the interplay of predisposition and stimulus, which in the historical development of man's mind actualizes the potentiality in the former, and at the same time helps to determine its form. Second, the groping recognition, by virtue of this very disposition, of specific portions of history as the manifestation of 'the holy', with consequent modification of the religious experience already attained both in its quality and degree. And third, on the basis of the other two, the achieved fellowship with 'the holy' in knowing, feeling, and willing. Plainly, then, religion is only the offspring of history in so far as history on the one hand develops our disposition for knowing the holy, and on the other is itself repeatedly the manifestation of the holy. 'Natural' religion, in contrast to historical, does not exist, and still less does 'innate' religion.

A priori cognitions are not such as everyone does have—such would be *innate* cognitions—but such as everyone is *capable* of having. The loftier *a priori* cognitions are such as—while everyone is indeed capable of having them—do not, as experience teaches us, occur spontaneously, but rather are 'awakened' through the instrumentality of other more highly endowed natures. In relation to these the universal 'predisposition' is merely a faculty of *receptivity* and a *principle of judgment and acknowledgement*, not a capacity to produce the cognitions in question for oneself independently. This latter capacity is confined to those specially 'endowed'. And this 'endowment' is the universal disposition on a higher level and at a higher power, differing from it in quality as well as in degree. The same thing is very evident in the sphere of art: what appears in the multitude as mere receptiveness, the capacity of response and judgment by trained aesthetic taste, reappears at the level of the *artist* as invention, creation, composition, the original production of genius. This difference of level and power, e.g. in musical composition, seen in the contrast between what is a mere capacity for musical experience and the actual production and revelation of music, is obviously something more than a difference of degree. It is very similar in the domain of the religious consciousness, religious production, and revelation. Here, too, most men have only the 'predisposition', in the sense of a receptiveness and susceptibility to religion and a capacity for freely recognizing and judging religious truth at first hand. The 'Spirit' is only 'universal' in the form of the '*testimonium Spiritus internum*' (and this again only '*ubi ipsi visum fuit*'). The higher stage, not to be derived from the first stage of mere receptivity, is in the sphere of religion *the prophet*. The prophet corresponds in the religious sphere to the creative artist in that of art: he is the man in whom the Spirit shows itself alike as the power to hear the 'voice within' and the power of divination, and in each case appears as a creative force. Yet the prophet does not represent the highest stage. We can think of a third, yet higher, beyond him, a stage of revelation as underivable from that of the prophet as was his from that of common men. We can look, beyond the prophet, to one in whom is found the Spirit in all its plenitude, and who at the same time in his person and in his performance is become most completely the object of divination, in whom Holiness is recognized apparent.

Such a one is more than prophet. He is the Son.

23

COOK WILSON

on THE EXISTENCE OF GOD

Biographical Note Born at Nottingham in 1851, son of a Methodist minister. He was educated at Derby Grammar School and at Balliol College, Oxford, where he obtained first-class honours in classics and mathematics. Was elected a Fellow of Oriel College in 1874, and was subsequently Wykeham Professor of Logic, which chair he held till his death in 1915. He lived at Oxford except for a brief period in Germany, during which he was influenced by Lotze.[1]

Principal works: His writings are collected together in the posthumous *Statement and Inference*, in two volumes, ed. A. S. L. Farquharson (Oxford, 1926).

Philosophical Note C. W. wrote nothing systematic, mainly because of his distaste for the idea of a first principle in philosophy. Like post-Wittgensteinian analytic philosophers, he regarded problems as needing to be solved in a piecemeal and careful fashion; and he foreshadowed later attitudes to language in his view that 'The authority of language is too often forgotten in philosophy, with serious results. Distinctions made or applied in ordinary language are more likely to be right than wrong.' He held firm views on a number of topics, however. He rejected Russell's account of mathematics as deducible from logic, and indeed was opposed to most of the claims made on behalf of modern symbolic logic. At the same time he was a strong opponent of Idealism, holding that knowledge is an immediate and simple apprehension. His conviction that there is a real world of three-dimensional space and time, as conceived by mathematical physics, led him to reject both the above-mentioned views, since in different ways they denied objectivity to mathematics, and he felt that even Kant's position (see above, p. 249), with which he had at one time been in general agreement, was likewise too subjective.

The paper reproduced here contains an important reappraisal of the whole notion of proving God's existence and of the nature of religious experience.

Bibliographical Note See R. Metz, *A Hundred Years of British Philosophy* (London, 1930); R. Robinson, *The Province of Logic: an Interpretation of Cook Wilson's 'Statement and Inference'* (Oxford, 1931); and J. A. Passmore, *A Hundred Years of Philosophy* (London, 1957).

[1] See n. 1 to p. 467.

THE EXISTENCE OF GOD

Statement and Inference, Vol. ii, §§565 ff.

There are subjects which do not appear at first in scientific form, art, morality, religion. In approaching such subjects for the first time it is natural to begin by trying to make proofs, or by criticizing given proofs, without any preliminary consideration of the meaning of proof or of the possible limitation of its province. But such a process may be endless. We may construct and reject proof after proof and yet make no real progress, because we may have presupposed, without distinctly recognizing it, that proof must have a certain form, a form which it happens cannot fit the matter to which we are applying it. The defect therefore will not lie in the particular proofs as such, but in the form of proof in general, and till we recognize this we shall labour in vain.

Or we may have something in our minds which would, whether right or not, prevent our accepting any proof of whatever form.

Or it may and does happen that being already convinced of the conclusion, moral or aesthetic, we admit a faulty proof of it: our interest in the conclusion blinding us to the flaw. This happens even in purely speculative proofs, e.g. even in mathematics.

Or a proof may seem correct and yet it does not quite satisfy us because it does not touch our feelings. Perhaps we are not aware, in our search for scientific completeness of demonstration, that this is the fact and, if we are at all aware, may be afraid to own it, because it seems unscientific. But the demand of our nature remains, and we shall not be satisfied unless we raise the question of the relations of feelings or emotion to truth.

The attempt to vindicate our religious beliefs and, it may be, our moral and aesthetic decisions is often conceived as the attempt to find a 'rational basis' for them.

Now the enquiry after a rational basis for a belief has in its form certain important (if unconscious) presuppositions. We do not seek for something for a thing which it has got already, if we know it: and so also to undertake such a search we must be able to think of the thing, and must have thought of it, as existing without what we seek for it.

Thus it seems as if our question to have any meaning—unless it is to be entirely idle words—must imply that the belief exists somehow already, without the so-called 'rational' basis, and that the search for such a basis is an after-thought or later development. This is a serious implication. It might be considered a concession which imperilled the worth of the belief, and so perhaps be pressed by one side and rejected by the other.

On the other hand, it might be thought to be in the interest of the dignity of the religious consciousness to maintain it: to insist indeed that the belief has a higher basis than reason, or what is usually meant by 'rational', though (it would be said) it cannot disagree without reason, which must confirm it.

We do not ask for a 'rational basis' for a proposition in the exact sciences—e.g. for the Pythagorean discovery of the relation between the sides of a right-angled triangle—because such a proposition has no meaning for us except as resting on a rational basis. Even when a theorem in the sciences is uncertain, e.g. a guess about some cause, it is not natural to put our enquiry into its validity in the form of asking for a 'rational basis'. On the contrary, so far as it exists at all, it has some sort of rational basis; it has been formed somehow on evidence, though the evidence is recognized to be insufficient and the proof but probable. In the case of facts, again, in Nature which we know in some way, but of which we do not know the explanation, when we ask about them, it would be quite unnatural to put our question in the form of asking for a rational basis; we assume as self-evident and without reflection that they have such basis and are members of a rational system.

When we do come to speak in this way, it is because some explanation of the fact has been given which would take it out of a rational system.

For instance, we do not ask for a 'rational' explanation of the cure of diseases by ordinary medicines or surgery, we do not seek to 'rationalize' these. But in the case of faith-healing (in modern times), if scientific people suggest as a true explanation of them that many diseases are really due to hysteria, and are in certain senses apparent rather than real, depend therefore on certain states of the patient's mind, which again can be influenced and changed by the will: this may well be called rationalizing or finding a rational basis for the phenomena. And this would be done in conscious opposition to the 'miraculous' explanation.

It is clear then that when we come to think about the religious consciousness and its beliefs, we have some different attitude from that which we have towards nature and in the sciences, in respect of rationality. But it is not here alone, for in this particular the moral consciousness and, to some extent, the aesthetic consciousness are in the same position.

From one point of view we unhesitatingly speak of all these as rational and even *par excellence* rational. We think that it is only a rational (thinking) consciousness which can be moral, and, more than that, we think that we show our rationality especially in morality. So also we think that it is only a rational consciousness which can be artistic. But in all of them we discern a certain distinction from reason or rationality and even a certain opposition to it. For instance, it is said that Greek philosophers, especially Socrates and Plato, endeavoured to put morality on a rational basis. This implies that morality with its conceptions, judgments, rules and practices, had been existing independently of such a basis.

We must not take this exactly like the relation of our ordinary experience of Nature to the development of the same principle in scientific thinking. For instance, the principles of counting and thinking about distances in space, methodically carried out, become the mathematical sciences. But we don't look at them as the putting of our old experience on a rational basis. It is rather that we know more of the same kind of thing which we knew before. We do not regard the preceding experience as somehow unreasoning and requiring to be justified (if it can stand) by a rational basis; on the contrary, we look upon it as giving the true basis to science itself.

The difference and even opposition shows itself in the study of the subject when the rationalizing attempt has begun. Philosophers assume readily enough that morality is rational just as the ordinary consciousness does when it comes to reflect on the subject. Yet when they come to try to fix the nature of the reason or rationality, to find the place of reason or rational thinking in morality, the attempt has proved to be extremely difficult and there has been no sure unhindered progress from experience to science as in geometry and the natural sciences.

Aristotle struggles vainly with the problem and ends in putting the moral life actually below the speculative on the ground of a certain irrational element in it; a difficulty not to be glossed over by calling this element imperfectly rational rather than irrational.

The living actual moral consciousness, however, protests against such a theoretical position as absurd. We feel indeed that what is noble and dignified and most worth having in life is, on the contrary, above the mere scientific and speculative reason; and so (in modern times) when this consciousness has become more fully aware of its own value we find a different kind of reaction against, or resistance to, 'reason', yet still some reaction.

Thus in modern times, in our English philosophy, after the reason in morality has been represented from the point of view of the knowledge in morality, with great emphasis, as if it were exactly like the scientific and speculative reason and, like that, producing a system of eternal truths,[1]

[1] A reference to Ralph Cudworth (1617–88), the Cambridge Platonist, who elaborated such a view in his *Treatise concerning Eternal and Immutable Morality* (published 1731). See J. A. Passmore, *Ralph Cudworth*, and also A. N. Prior, *Logic and the Basis of Ethics*.

there is a reaction of which the characteristic is a certain repugnance to putting everything in morality under reason. So much so that the very faculty which supplies moral judgments, i.e. moral truth, is not called Reason but Moral sense, with a deliberate and expressed distinction from Reason,* and assimilated to a corresponding faculty in the aesthetic consciousness. And this faculty is considered more valuable to us than our reason, giving us directly what Reason apparently, if perfect, could discover (but only as the result of a long train of argumentation), while such reason as *we* have, from its weakness, will not make the discovery.[1] Besides Reason,[2] as a principle of action, is apparently conceived as only calculating and contriving means to promote our private interest, while the Moral sense is directed to the good of others.

Whatever criticism might be passed on the passages which contain such statements, whatever difficulties or inconsistencies they may involve their author in, the important thing for the present purpose is that the faculty supposed to give us moral judgments is not only distinguished from reason but preferred to it. The same thing holds of the popular associations of the word conscience and finds expression in the philosopher of conscience, Butler.

Without professing to identify Butler's theory with the Moral sense theory, it is enough to notice that, for our purpose and the point of view from which we are regarding moral systems, the conscience theory and the moral sense theory are in essential agreement; there is the same reluctance to make the faculty of moral principles simply reason; the same representation of the moral faculty, i.e. that which gives us moral judgments, as giving us *directly* what our reason, if it could give it at all, could only give as the result of a laborious process: with the further belief that *our* reason cannot give them and that by conscience we feel the force of certain obligations which our reason, conceived as trying to argue from ideas of the good of the world or the happiness of mankind, is not able to recognize. There is the same tendency to make Conscience the higher faculty, it is the 'voice of God in us'.[3]

Another school of thought affirms deliberately that reason can only calculate means for ends given to it, thus admitting that the most

* Hutcheson, *An Inquiry*, Preface, pp. xiv–xv, 'The weakness of our Reason, etc.'. [Thomas Hutcheson (1694–1764), Scottish moral philosopher, mainly known for his ethical writings, in which he emphasized the centrality of what he called the moral sense by which 'we perceive virtue or vice, in ourselves or others'.]

[1] Cf. Butler especially, (*Sermon* v, xii, and xv).

[2] Hutcheson, *An Inquiry*, ii, §1, compared with ii, Introduction.

[3] See Butler, *Sermon* v, p. 49. 'Reason alone, whatever anyone may wish, is not in reality a sufficient motive of virtue in such a creature as man' (Oxford, 1896, Vol. ii, p. 98). Cf. last note to *Sermon* xii. (Ibid., p. 226, note c.)

important thing in moral conduct, the end and motive, is not an affair of reason at all.

About the aesthetic consciousness one or two things seem clear. No artist, and probably no theorist, is likely to admit that mere thinking or reasoning without feeling or emotion could give an aesthetic judgment. There is no science, in the proper sense, of the fine arts. A body of rules like the theory of Music is no exception; there *is* reasoning there, but such as would be admitted in a moral sense or conscience theory of Ethics, the application, that is of given rules; but the rules themselves are the important things.

It is worthy of note that a writer like Hutcheson while speaking sometimes at least in a manner which, if the words were pressed, might imply that in the case of the moral consciousness an absolutely perfect reason could give the moral rules, in the case of the aesthetic consciousness refers its judgement to Taste and Feeling or Sense, and never suggests that *here* a perfect reason might reach the same results; the idea never seems even to occur to him. Further, in his later treatise, *Illustrations upon the Moral Sense*, he maintains outright that Reason does not give us moral judgements, that it cannot originate the moral ends, or any end,[1] in such a way that he seems to deny the possibility for any kind of reason, not merely for ours; this interpretation is confirmed by this that later, speaking of the Divine Consciousness, he says: 'Why may not the Deity have something of a superior Kind, analogous to our *moral Sense*, essential to him?'

In the foregoing remarks two objects have been in view. The first is to remove the unfair prejudice which represents the religious consciousness as if in a unique position of antagonism to reason. The charge against it might be put in the most unfavourable way thus: 'Our reason has a right to call every belief in question, to ask for and criticize the evidence for them. Religious beliefs will not really stand this test. To conceal the weakness Theology tries to avoid the attacks of reason by taking refuge behind mysteries. It assumes a mysterious source of religious truth, Revelation and a mysterious faculty of religious truth, Faith; and, the more effectually to put reason out of court, it insists these are above reason, superior to it and with an authority beyond the canons of reason.'

I have been trying to show that if we look at the thing fairly, we find a very parallel tendency in the moral and aesthetic consciousness. Shortly

[1] Sect. I, ' "does not every *Spectator approve* the Pursuit of publick good more than private?" The Answer is obvious, that he does: but not for any *Reason* or *Truth*, but from a *moral Sense*. . . .' 'Does a Conformity to any Truth make us *approve* an *ultimate End*, previously to any *moral Sense*?' (and Hutcheson maintains that it does not). (Hutcheson, *Illustrations upon the Moral Sense*. See Selby Bigge, *British Moralists*, Vol. i, §§454, 459.)

one may say that in the case of the moral consciousness also we find a faculty assumed to give truths, which is distinguished from reason and considered as even superior to reason. Nor can we say that this is a merely popular and unscientific view, the deliverance of the untrained moral consciousness. On the contrary, we find it in the very philosophic treatment of these subjects itself: undertaken by those who may fairly claim to try to take a thoroughly philosophic view. Nor can it be said that such doctrines belong only to unimportant people not really able thinkers. It is true that philosophy suffers from the fact that it is in a sense every man's subject, and one has to read some queer stuff under that title, but the thinkers in question belong to the strongest and ablest who have written on morals in this or any other country.

The students of philosophy therefore can hardly presume to take the superior attitude towards theology implied in the charge above formulated. We must rather first see that we set our own house in order.

If it be replied that, after all, these faculties of Conscience and Moral sense are aspects of Reason and misunderstood by their advocates and that the kind of reason to which they were opposed was really a kind irrelevant to moral principles, then *prima facie* the same kind of excuse may be made for the religious consciousness.

The second object is to show that the opposition implied in the phrase 'a rational basis for belief in God' was no mere verbal accident, but corresponded to a real opposition, which has made itself felt in other departments of consciousness besides the religious, and that, too, an opposition so far from being destroyed or eliminated by a scientific investigation undertaken by reason in the interests of pure knowledge, that it actually sometimes appears as the result of such an investigation.

To return now to the opposition itself.

It seems that where we can really ask for a rational basis for a thing and the language is really appropriate, we assume that the thing has already a basis which somehow is not rational, or is thought to be something not rational.

Then comes a twofold division.

We may suppose that in truth the thing has only a rational basis, that the other basis given to it is an illusion, and that in seeking for *the* rational basis we are trying to remove this illusion. The Greeks sought, for example, a rational basis for the phenomenon of thunder and lightning, which had been assigned to Jupiter, and supposed they found it in the quenching of fire, and this does away with the non-rational basis.

If the thing which we treat in this way is a belief itself, we essentially alter the character of it, we are explaining the belief to be an illusion and assigning the basis of fact from which it sprang. Thus a rationalistic explanation of the belief in ghosts has been offered that men in a primitive state of half-developed consciousness sometimes confused appearances in dreams with real visions. It must be allowed, however, that in this case we use the phrase 'rational basis' for the phenomenon or fact which is misunderstood rather than for the belief.

The second case would be that in which the thing is supposed to have a basis already; but then it becomes a serious question whether it could have another basis, viz. the rational, at all; especially as we observe that where in moral theory a belief is supposed to have a basis which is not rational in some sense, this view is held on grounds which would make it impossible to have a rational one.

And anyhow, our first business must be to examine into the nature of the basis which the thing or belief is supposed to have already and before our investigation: for that it can have such a basis must be essential to it and, therefore, essential to our understanding of it. In fact the possibility of a 'non-rational' basis will be exactly characteristic of such a belief as compared with those which have a rational basis only; and it is obviously to the distinguishing characteristic that scientific or philosophic investigation must be directed.

What would be the state of mind of one who was really unbiased and looked on it really as an open question, a thing to be proved or disproved?

At all events he will not have any immediate knowledge or conviction, such as his belief that he is warm or cold or uncomfortable, or the question would not be an open one to him. He will regard the opinion so far as it exists as based on some sort of evidence, or on some desire, or on both together; perhaps in some such way as this:

In the earlier stage of the attempt to 'explain' natural phenomena, men naturally prefer what seems most intelligible to themselves and, in a first crude reflection, they think they understand best their own actions; or, rather, this is so natural to them that they don't ever reflect on it, and so their explanation of natural phenomena naturally takes the form of attributing them to a personal agent like themselves.

Inclination as well as reflection contributed to this result, because in any case men would prefer the superior force in nature to be like themselves and especially because, if it were so, they would have a better hope of a comfortable life, and that for two reasons: Such an agent as being a person might be sympathetic with them and inclined to help them, or, if not such but selfish and even malevolent (as they knew persons could be), yet at least accessible and amenable to influence from them if they could contrive to please him, and so better than mere unconscious nature.

Later, even when scientific knowledge has advanced very far and mere superstition became recognized as such, the same influences both in thought and in feeling will operate still, though in a higher form. When the ordinary phenomena of nature have been reduced, with more or less success, to mechanical and non-personal causes, the law of this mechanical nexus will appear as ultimate facts. We do not understand how these ultimate facts came to be there, and the mind tends always to be dissatisfied, whether rightly or not, with the recognition of a mere fact. It will tend therefore to be dissatisfied with mechanical causes.

There will also be a tendency to assign to the highest cause the highest quality; and the more our intelligence grows, the more the mind becomes aware that reason and consciousness have a paramount worth as compared with the unconscious: and so we have a bias towards representing the highest cause as spiritual (especially as it is to be the cause of our own existence as well).

With increasing knowledge men begin to reflect on the adaptation of their own organism to obtain certain ends, which are desirable to them, and the more they know of organic life in general, the more marvellous appears to them the elaborate apparatus by which the ends of organic life are attained; and even to a very superficial knowledge this is seen to be far beyond what men could have thought out for themselves. Such adaptation of means to ends is most easily understood, by the analogy of human action, as the work of a self-conscious spirit conceiving ends and designing and planning accordingly, just as in the more primitive stage the so-called activities of nature are most easily understood on the analogy of human action.

But this time the argument has come to stay, for not only is this the easier explanation, but it is difficult to believe in any other and the difficulty seems to increase and not to diminish with increasing knowledge. We have the celebrated argument from Design which has influenced every period of thought.

Once conceive the highest Cause as spiritual and it is natural to consider him as the perfection or ideal of Spirit, and hence perfect knowledge and goodness are assigned to him. He must then be conceived as author of the moral as well as of the natural order and thus the belief in God has now enlisted on its side all the interest of the moral consciousness.

This might be taken as a sketch of the principal arguments and influences which could and have brought about such a belief in mankind in general apart from a special revelation, whether a fact or not. There are special philosophical and metaphysical arguments as well, but the important fact for us is that the belief is held by the masses of mankind, and it is to this that we have above all to direct our attention: and the mass of mankind is not metaphysical.

The unbiased judge, whom we are imagining, is bound to put the case strongly against the belief, to be very critical about the evidence, and we may suppose he would treat it in some such way as this.

Two different forces contribute to produce the belief. First, there is a rational element in the form of reasoning from evidence, the evidence being from acknowledged fact. Secondly, there is an element which some at least would, when viewed as the origin of a belief, call an irrational element; and, if not so to be called, it is not reasoning from evidence at any rate, it is our *desire*, and this appears as much in the later stage of human culture as in the earlier. We are dissatisfied with mechanism as an ultimate fact because we want the spiritual and conscious to be supreme. The interest of the moral consciousness biases us also, for we are too glad to give it the highest possible sanction. As to the 'rational part':

It has not the completeness of demonstration. There is some probability, perhaps much, in the argument that the existence of spirits depends on a spiritual cause. The argument from Design is also questioned

> (1) as not more than a high probability; (2) the existence of evil and imperfection in general is so much evidence the other way; (3) in modern times the theory of development and evolution explains the apparent adaptation of means to the ends of organic life, without any need of a designing intelligent conscious intelligence: at least some scientific men hold this view, and it is the popular conception of evolution.

The impartial judge might ask therefore whether the great hold the belief has on men's minds is not really due to the strong interest they have in its being true; Wish and Desire, not Reasoning in the sense of reasoning from evidence. He might add that strong desire and hope that a thing should exist, however good it might be in its intention, was certainly no guarantee.

One may venture to think that there may be something beyond and more satisfactory than the defence of or attack upon these arguments, but I want to say a word, before going further, on the argument from Design.

I suspect we won't do it justice, that it has more hold on the mind of those who reject it than they are willing to confess or perhaps are aware of. Probably, when we are first introduced to it, it impresses us very powerfully. When we are more educated and get some idea of science and exact knowledge, it doesn't satisfy the standard of such demonstration as we are familiar with. Besides it has been subjected to severe criticism from the scientific point of view, and so we tend to be afraid of it and regard it as something natural to immature thinking. Perhaps our difficulties are summed up in this, that the very effort to know Nature scientifically presupposes the necessity of everything in nature, and this seems, at first at least, the contradictory of design. But it makes all the difference whether we think in this general abstract way about the argument from design, or whether we are considering some of the actual facts on which the argument itself is founded. We may imagine we have got rid of it as a prejudice or illusion; but if, forgetting our general theories, we are absorbed in the study of the adaptation and harmony of the various parts of a plant or animal to the maintenance of its life and function, is there anyone so adamantine that he can maintain an unemotional contemplative or 'scientific' attitude? Can he help feeling admiration and wonder? Whether it be an illusion or not, the idea of plan and design and choice of means comes on us with irresistible force; we cannot shut it out.

This impression is strengthened and not weakened by the new knowledge gained by modern biology, the gradual development of an organism in successive generations. We see the gradual 'perfecting' of the organism for its functions; it isn't now as though we saw the marvellous adaptation in a given organism and inferred, or could not help thinking of, a designer; it is as if we saw the design or plan in process of being worked out.

But this is not merely the impression of the outsider. This idea of design is actually the clue by which scientific men are constantly working, not only in describing the parts of an animal, but especially the evolution of the organs; for the meaning of the elements in the lower stages is found by them in the higher. Sometimes this comes home to them and they admit its significance.

Secondly, as to the objection derived from evil and imperfection.

First notice that the impression above described is not one which we have before the thought of evil and imperfection occurred to us; it comes over us although we are aware of these things. They are not evidence against design in general. The want of adaptation and fitness in one department does not affect the evidence for it in another, so far as it is evidence, but leaves it untouched. The inference we should rather draw if we confined ourselves to the evidence is one to which our modern habit of thought disinclines us. Helmholtz in his account of the eye[1] takes note of certain optical defects in the crystalline portion, and adds significantly that if such an instrument had been sent to us by an optician we should return it with the request that such defects should be remedied. It is

[1] Helmholtz (1821–94), physiologist and experimental psychologist, who formulated the law of conservation of energy.

directed against the theory of design. But, if so, the inference was not the one which an accurate scientific man should draw. His own description of the structure of the eye gives an instance of that wonderful adaptation, in choice of material and form of organism, which eventually makes us think of a designing intelligence. If we are to argue strictly from such evidence alone with nothing else to go upon, we should infer the plan itself, as much as ever and as clearly and forcibly as ever, but we should infer something which hindered its execution, destroyed it altogether, or made it imperfect. But we have a scruple in drawing such a conclusion, because we think of the designer as also God, and mean an all-wise and all-powerful Spirit who could not make a mistake in plan or be hampered by the necessity in his material in carrying out his plan. But if it is mere design we are thinking of, the natural tendency would be to a dualism, and the tendency is realized in ancient authors like Plato and Aristotle.

As to the objection derived from Evolution.

I doubt whether Evolution as such has added to the objections against design; on the contrary, as I have indicated, if the facts as imperfectly known suggested it, as more perfectly known, they suggest it more strongly. But it tends to suggest the picture of a designing mind working with methods curiously like those of the human mind. It is as if nature made experiments and rejected the less satisfactory, retained the better and even advanced in knowledge and skill. (Many instances, e.g. chrysalis. The outer casing of the chrysalis at one period shows the outlines of limbs and a definite organism, but the interior has nothing to correspond. The case is filled merely with a fluid substance apparently homogeneous. The inference is that a stage between the caterpillar and butterfly has been omitted.)

But the idea of necessity is inherent in Evolution as in all science; the material must be supposed to go through its changes according to fixed laws. What difference does this make? Assuming evidence of plan at all, the difference it would make would be to represent the plan and the gradual working out of it as inhering in the necessity of nature itself and constituting its essence. If we were told that it is a law of all conscious beings to desire to maintain their life, a law in their nature to fear death, we should not think of this as destroying our planning and designing activity in endeavouring to compass such ends.

I have tried to imagine what might be an impartial and unbiased view. But there are many who are not in this condition; what is their attitude to the problem?

Some firmly believe in a divine Spirit and in such a way that the success and failure of what I may call a mere external argument would not really affect their belief, if they would only come to terms with themselves and recognize that this is so. We cannot in a scientific or philosophic interest simply put such out of consideration. They are not men whom we think otherwise irrational, they are to be found among the very wisest. With this kind of belief often goes a dignity and nobleness of character, and, in other spheres of thought, a finer perception of what we admit to be higher; and so there is at least a *prima facie* presumption that their judgment is not wrong in a sphere for which the highest qualities seem necessary. Now if these thinkers engage in a mere speculative argument, it is with little profit either to themselves or others, because they are not really talking of the conception of God as it is for themselves; of the living reality of it in their own minds. In its true reality for them it cannot be seriously considered as a matter of argument. What they ought to do is to try to come to as clear a consciousness as possible of the nature of their conviction: that is the important thing and vital for science and philosophy; this is what they ought to do if they would help in a discussion like this. Perhaps many are deterred by a fear, which they have not fully confessed to themselves, that they may appear irrational. Well, they know well enough that they are not otherwise accounted irrational, perhaps indeed the very opposite. They know there is nothing petty or contemptible in the belief, but that it is confessedly associated at least with what is highest in human nature, and they should not fear to look into their own souls here.

Now some of those who seriously engage in argument are in this case; they are not aware of their true position and that it is their conviction which produces the argument and not the argument their conviction. One observes that sometimes practical theologians will gladly take up some supposed establishment of theism by a philosophical argument. But where do they suppose they themselves were, before they heard of the theory, and what was the meaning of their lives? They possessed something far stronger to them than any such theory and, if they should find a flaw in the philosophical argument after all, they wouldn't admit they now had no ground for the belief.

It is this, whatever it may be, which precedes all such mere theory, which is the valuable thing for them and has been the moving principle of their lives. This is the thing for them and for us to try to understand. Till this is done everything else is lost labour. One sees this sometimes in the greatest philosophers. The arguments by which they seek to recommend some of their most important principles to others are clearly not the process by which they arrived at them themselves, for they are sometimes not only unsatisfactory but fallacious, and if they had not been so convinced of the truth of their conclusion they would have seen that themselves.

Thus Plato and especially Aristotle try to present us with proofs that the rational life is the highest and best: mistaking the nature of proof and not perceiving that what they would prove is the absolute presupposition of any argumentation whatever about the good. The argument as presented in the *Ethics*[1] should take no modern student in. One's first thought when trying to prove anything about God or morality should be—did I really get this conviction myself in this way? Then and then alone do we find the meaning and value of our own thoughts.

I have ventured to suggest above that there might be something better than the attack or defence of the arguments I referred to. It might be inferred that I was prepared at once to suggest some other arguments, perhaps metaphysical ones. But I may repeat that I am concerned with the arguments and considerations that may be supposed to have affected the masses of mankind; for here must lie the secret, and it is here we must look for the inmost reality of the conception or belief. The true business of philosophy seems to be to bring the belief to a consciousness of itself.

It is no use producing philosophic arguments external to this; we should never satisfy ourselves, for we should shirk the thing absolutely necessary for understanding and it would return again upon us as *the* problem. That would be to commit the error so often repeated in so-called 'Moral Philosophy'; to suppose that its function is to find a criterion of goodness, as guide to moral action. If this is taken seriously, men couldn't have known what was good before the criterion had been discovered; they couldn't have lived moral lives. Besides, there is the further difficulty that the 'philosophers' have disagreed about the criterion.

When we do get a philosophic account, then, we must show that it harmonizes with the workings of the unphilosophic consciousness.

About the popular arguments (which I don't believe to be a true expression of the popular consciousness);—we see something can be said for and against, which is enough to show they are not cogent. A simple proof in geometry is cogent and it can't be a matter of debate at all in the proper sense of the term.

Now I want to propose two questions connected with the preliminary considerations about proof with which I began.

Could any proof of such a form be perfect and cogent?

If we had a perfect speculative proof, should we really be satisfied (remembering what the object of the proof is), and would there be nothing wanting?

[1] See *Nicomachean Ethics,* Bk X, Ch. VII.

First, on the form of proof. The form is 'empirical', starting from facts supposed to have the best evidence, viz. direct experience. The special form is 'analogical'. It is manifest that in such a proof we can only have probability and not necessity. To 'empirical' we oppose a proof in which we see the absolute necessity both of the conceptions and of the chain of argument into which they enter.

It may be asked 'why, on this account of the popular reasoning, should we assume it hasn't argued in the necessary and non-empirical form?'

Perhaps the truth is that such a question will not seriously be asked. If there had been reasoning of that kind we should hardly have had such stress laid on the 'design argument', considering the difficulties with which that argument is encumbered. We should certainly have heard much more of the other; and who has heard of it at all? For the moment I will only say that it has not been consciously present to the popular reasoning.

As to the other form of empirical proof, the matured form of it in empirical science; this moves only under certain presuppositions, and it is really the nature of the belief in God to try to get behind these. It is no accident that this method has not been applied; it couldn't be. Could any proof satisfy us, as proof is usually understood—the type of geometrical proof and the proofs in natural science? Perhaps someone may think, IF they could get a proof of the empirical form found in natural science, they would be satisfied. But would they? It is characteristic of the natural sciences, however careful the experiments and observations, that they never see into the nature of necessity, and this is why they never attain mathematical clearness and certainty.

But what of a proof in which we see the necessity? One must question whether a demonstration of such quasi-mathematical form could satisfy us, if we realize what it is we want to prove. In some subjects demonstration of a fact is more valuable knowledge than the direct experience of it. (E.g. eclipse of moon at a certain date, the property of a geometrical figure.) In the case of the geometrical figure we know even more certainly than we could by experience. But in some subjects we have an impulse, which cannot be stilled, for what is called direct knowledge.

If we think of the existence of our friends; it is the 'direct knowledge' which we want: merely inferential knowledge seems a poor affair.[1] To most men it would be as surprising as unwelcome to hear it could not be directly known whether there were such existences as their friends, and that it was only a matter of (probable) empirical argument and inference from facts which are directly known. And even if we convince ourselves on reflection that this is really the case, our actions prove that we have a

[1] See *Statement and Inference*, Part III, §§263–8. Compare Butler, *Sermon* xiv.

confidence in the existence of our friends which can't be derived from an empirical argument (which can never be certain) for a man will risk his life for his friend. We don't want merely inferred friends. Could we possibly be satisfied with an inferred God?

It may be objected: You are only, if right, stating what we earnestly desire. It doesn't follow that we shall get it. It doesn't even follow the desire is a rational one.

It may be answered: the demand for this kind of knowledge is not something of ours outside the conception of God, it lies in the conception itself. We can't think the content of the conception itself. We can't think the content of the conception otherwise; if we do, then we haven't really the conception before us. To substantiate this reply we must think as fully as we can what the content is for the religious consciousness. We can only realize it in certain actual experiences of our own, which we may call religious experiences. Times of great emotion, when, as the saying is, we seem lifted beyond ourselves. Times, it may be, of great trouble; or of great joy. This can't be described in abstract language, any more than we can describe our feelings and attitude in hearing, for instance, a moving piece of music. We have to appeal to the experience of those who have had such feelings. So it is here. In order to understand what the conception of God is for us we must recall such experiences and they must be experiences of our own, not any account of the experience of others.

It might be here objected: The sum is shortly this: (1) You have not rehabilitated after all the argument from design. (2) You admit that an empirical argument such as is used in the natural sciences is not applicable to such a matter and, even if it were, it couldn't be complete in a direction in which we demand completeness. (3) As to a 'demonstrative argument', in which the necessity is understood, you rather imply it doesn't exist yet, and you don't say whether we could have it. But you say that probably even this, if we could have it, wouldn't satisfy us. (4) You indicate that the conception itself demands some direct knowledge—'experience' or something like it.

Now (it may be said) (*a*) this direct knowledge of God, somehow directly in our consciousness, most certainly cannot be had. People know at least what is in their consciousness, and they are not conscious of this; and as you have said of the demonstrative argument, if it existed we should have heard about it;—if this direct consciousness were a fact, the same would be true.

Besides, (*b*) people wouldn't look for a demonstration if they had the direct knowledge, they don't look for a proof of what they are immediately conscious of.

So (it might be urged) the conclusion of the whole matter seems to be this: If the suggestions were right about the different forms of argument, etc., they point to one avenue of knowledge as alone satisfactory; and this avenue is closed. The belief in God, then, would be reduced to a mere hypothesis and an hypothesis which on the one hand your argument cuts off even from the possibility of verification while, in fact, it has serious difficulties to contend with in our experience. It may so far be possibly a true hypothesis, though the demand for direct knowledge is not realizable.

But can even this be allowed? If you put the demand in the conception of God itself, and don't treat it as a mere subjective attitude, is not the case still worse? If the conception demands an impossibility, is it even valid as a conception? If not, it is no use considering whether a real object corresponds to it.

The above objections depend upon the two propositions (*a*) and (*b*).

Let us first notice some facts in the religious consciousness, whether connected with a definite form of religion or not.

We find in the religious consciousness as expressed in its highest and purest form—i.e. not mere rhetoric, for instance—that the direct knowledge of God is regarded not only as a consummation to be desired but certainly to be expected. However, this is not looked on (in such a mood) as a present fact—that we now have this directly in consciousness, but rather as if necessarily in the future. Compare 'but *then* face to face'.

Definitely as this seems to give up any direct knowledge at present, yet there is another tone quite as real. Men speak of God as being everywhere, all-pervading and so necessarily in themselves. They speak accordingly of being in the 'presence of God', and clearly not as a metaphor.

In the religious consciousness, when not so definitely associated with religious forms and expressions, we find the same antithesis. In one frame of mind even to those who have the belief, God seems a long way off—an infinite way, as they would say. He obviously can't be among the objects of the material world. We speak of him as 'behind' it—but as behind an impenetrable veil. In a way it would be a comfort if he only were a long way off in space, but he is 'behind' the infinity of space itself. Even if we say he is *in* the objects which are near enough to us, he seems concealed in them and, necessarily, even more concealed (it seems) than the forces of nature, which in a way are themselves not objects of a direct experience either.

On the other hand we find expressions which imply a consciousness of the nearness of God, of his most absolute closeness. Everyone will recall the lines of Tennyson.[1] Nor can we object that it is poetry and *mere* poetry —for we feel these lines of his express the strongest personal conviction —not a hope, not an inference.

These things are so far no proof—indeed they are antithetical—but they are most important and real elements in experience and may possibly help to a solution. It seems as if our solution ought to find a place for them. They at any rate make us hesitate about accepting the above propositions as so cogent as they claim to be.

Let us now try to face these propositions.

Is it true that we must be aware of what is in our consciousness and actively operating in it? No. Even in the acts of knowing and perceiving there may be something really existing and operating in our minds of which we may not be explicitly aware.

(1) Take first a humble example—the syllogism—'Barbara'.[2] This is a form under which we necessarily think, if we think at all, and all must have it; but it is long before we recognize it. Yet it is real in us because a law according to which our real thought operates. But yet for a time we are unconscious of it. Mill's good village matron, with her daughter Lucy, even believes she hasn't got it and has unfortunately persuaded the philosopher that she hasn't.[3] A little conversation with her, however, would easily bring out the implicit form of the syllogism.

(2) More important for our purpose. Take the familiar topic of Causality. When we speak of what we know directly, of that of which we are conscious, we tend to think of objects of sensuous experience only, feelings of our own, or objects perceived—that is given (as the phrase is) as sensuous perceptions. If we think of these as all the content of consciousness, we shall get into immense difficulty, because there are elements necessary to our experience which can never be objects of perception in the above sense—the ordinary sense. Now we do all tend to make this limitation at first about the nature of that of which we are actually conscious; and it is a principle, too, in philosophy as well as in the untutored consciousness. Thus there was no place in Locke's philosophy for the conception of cause; causality never being an object of such experience as he is thinking of.

[1] 'Speak to him thou, for he hears, and spirit with spirit can meet,
Closer is he than breathing, and nearer than hands and feet.'
From *The Higher Pantheism*.

[2] I.e. of the form 'All M are P; All S are M; therefore All S are P'.

[3] See Mill, *System of Logic*, II, iii. §3; 'It is not only the village matron, who, when called to a consultation upon the case of a neighbour's child, pronounces on the evil and its remedy simply on the recollection and authority of what she accounts the similar case of her Lucy. We all, where we have no definite maxims to steer by, guide ourselves in the same way; and if we have an extensive experience, and retain its impressions strongly, we may acquire in this manner a very considerable power of accurate judgment, which we may be utterly incapable of justifying or of communicating to others.'

But he fails to notice that, because he appreciates the working of the conception and thinks really only of that. Hume's criticism detects this fault. Hume holds the same view of the object in experience and is driven by his logic, in effect, to a denial of the conception of causality altogether; though really he doesn't get this clear, because the conception *is* there and can't be denied away, and consequently he gets into great confusion, sometimes seeming to eliminate the idea altogether, and finally substituting another idea for it, something which it certainly is not.

The fact is, the conception is there and has conditioned the very experience in question. Here it is not merely that we have not become aware of a necessary element in our thinking, but we have actually denied that we have it at all.

(3) And then the most important illustration of all is the notion of our own Self. Following such presuppositions as Hume's, we can predict with certainty what must happen to it. That which itself experiences—experiences these feelings, these perceived objects—cannot possibly itself be one of such objects of experience. It is in a far worse condition than the conception of Causality. And the Self in this philosophy had to go.[1] The very presupposition of experience is condemned by the test of that experience to be non-existent, simply because we can't be aware of ourselves as objects of sensuous experience. Yet that we are conscious of ourselves—though, of course, not in the way of such experience—is the most absolutely certain thing of all. Everyone will recall the words of Descartes.[2]

As to the second proposition, if people have really laboured to disprove that which is most directly present to consciousness, we shall feel no surprise that they should have tried to prove what they have got already. The attempt to derive the law of uniformity of nature by an empirical argument from experience is a notable instance.[3] We have the paradox that a philosophy, whose metaphysic has destroyed the notion of causality altogether, really tried to establish its validity (for science must have it) in the world of experience by an inductive proof. The proof is obviously an utter failure. The thing to be proved is 'tumbling under our feet'[4] all the time, being the very condition of examining scientifically that experience from the examination of which we hope to derive it by scientific examination.

The fact, then, that people have tried to find a proof of God's existence

[1] See *Treatise of Human Nature*, Book I, Part i, Section VI. See also below, p. 464.

[2] See above, p. 107, regarding *Cogito ergo sum*.

[3] Inductive argument (see above, n. 2 to p. 188) seems to involve the presupposition that nature will continue to behave in a uniform way; but the attempt to prove this principle by inductive argument is clearly circular.

[4] A quotation from the *Republic*, 432D.

is so far compatible with his direct presence in their consciousness; and the fact that they think, or some think, they certainly have no direct experience or knowledge of God is compatible with the same hypothesis. And now the facts quoted from the religious experience, oscillating between two extremes—the representation of God as immensely far and unspeakably near—get a new significance and we can hope to explain both sides of the antithesis.

* * * *[1]

Is there any evidence of such a direct experience which we thus ignore?

Let us try to consider again some peculiarities of the religious consciousness. As already said, we ought to try to keep it before us in the most definite and concrete form, recalling in ourselves definite experience and feelings. Though of course we can't attempt to describe it exhaustively, we *can* call attention to some striking features of it. The conception has a certain setting in consciousness and peculiarities which present an analogy to the moral and aesthetic consciousness. I do not now refer to doctrines of revelation and faith as modes of knowledge, because they come from reflection on the conception or belief, but to the active presence and working of the conception in what we may call, all of us, our 'religious experience'. We cannot maintain towards the idea the mere unemotional attitude of the scientific or speculative understanding. We do not think of God, to use popular language, *merely* as the cause of the material world and the power which is always sustaining it; or in more philosophic phrase as the *primum movens*, or, say, as the unity of the material world—i.e. the one reality of which it is all the varied expression, and the true substance, so to say, of which they are the attributes. Nor do we think of God as the basis of the spiritual world, *merely* in the same way as we think of the abstraction of our own selves, or our own self-identity, as the basis of our life manifested in time. But the conception is inseparably connected with certain feelings or emotions.

The one to which I principally want to draw attention is the emotion of reverence. This is not to be confounded with the fear of the superstitious. It is not confined to the lowest or least intellectual, but reaches its completest development in the highest and most cultivated.

Yet, possibly someone might object, this is an utterly wrong method. We want the dry light of science and philosophy; we know that our judgment can be obscured and prevented by feeling; whatever notice the anthropologist must take of such things, it is the very business of the scientific or philosophic investigator to free himself resolutely from their

[1] The asterisks are in the original and do not indicate an omission.

influence. On the contrary, if we imitate scientific procedure, this is exactly what we must not do. With the precept of Bacon and the example of Darwin we must omit none of the facts which we know of, and this fact, that the conception of God can only be realized by us with certain emotions, is not only a very interesting fact but it is an essential characteristic of the conception. If it belongs to the nature of the conception as such that it should produce or be accompanied by such feelings, we must, if we are to understand it, attend to these feelings whether any illusion is connected with them or not.

Let us change the argument to another sphere.

Consider such emotions as are proper to the moral consciousness. Take (e.g.) the emotion of *gratitude*. We have feelings which, as they say, are due to physical causes; they do not originate from any previous thinking of ours, are not excited by conceptions. But there are others which are only possible to a thinking rational consciousness as such. In this sense they are rational, and it is a want of appreciation of the inseparableness of reason and emotion which constitutes the difficulty in moral philosophy of which I spoke at the beginning.

Gratitude belongs to this class of feelings. And it presupposes a good deal of rational activity in consciousness. We are grateful to someone for some good (as we think) done to us.

But what does this presuppose? (1) Not merely our enjoyment of a pleasure, but reflection upon it, distinct thought of it as some good to us. (2) It implies also that we refer it to another as an effect of his causality. Which means again that we have, in some form, conceptions of ourselves as distinct from other selves, also that we have the category of Causality and more especially of the activity of a person as a cause. (3) It implies also that the person, whom we have thought of as a person and a cause, willed and intended the action; otherwise we are not grateful. And further (4) that he is benevolent to us, wishes us well, has done it to please us, and certainly to give us good. The appreciation of these relations between persons perhaps may seem to require considerable rationality; but whether it does or not it must be present or there could be no gratitude.

It may be asked whether this can be true of the consciousness of children. Obviously if they are susceptible of gratitude these elements must be present, or the child could not be grateful; and in actual life we think they are grateful and we certainly treat them as if they regarded the person to whom they are grateful in the way described.

Now here is a feeling whose whole meaning is relative to conceptions and acts of reason, impossible without them; and for it to be possible these relations must be somehow appreciated. But more than this, the feeling itself is inseparable from the act of judgment in which the recipient of the benefit appreciates his true relation to his benefactor. The judgment is not there unless the feeling is there too. We cannot separate the judgment from the act as something in itself speculative and in itself without the emotion. We cannot judge here except emotionally. The same is true of all moral and aesthetic judgments. Reason in them can only manifest itself emotionally.

Now the feeling of gratitude would be admitted as a fact given in experience, and I want now to argue from the facts of experience. In the first place the feeling is obviously only possible for us through the conceptions; if it exists, then, it guarantees the possibility of the conceptions of our thought at least. We must be able to think of ourselves as something more than and different from our feelings and as having the feelings; we must be able to think of another self than our own; we must be able to think of such self as willing and willing us good: and therefore to think of a certain relation between selves. So much for the possibility of the conception.

It may be asked, What of the reality of the object corresponding?

This means now for us: Are they objects of experience? Do we suppose we could communicate by *a priori* teaching to anyone the meaning of the feeling of gratitude? This is no more possible than to explain the meaning of music to one who has not experienced it. He must have really experienced it. He must have an actual self and have distinguished himself from his feelings. He must have had an experience by which he represented a person in such a relation to himself. But now even suppose he was mistaken in attributing goodwill to another person, for that, it may be objected, is but an inference; or that he is mistaken even in supposing another person besides himself, for this again (it may be contended) is but an inference; he hasn't direct experience of the person (it might be said), he really infers him from certain elements in his own experience.

Well, the idea of the goodwill of another person again, even if here mistakenly applied, can only come through some experience of this attitude in ourselves. Goodwill of a person, then, must here be a real experience.

But it may still be pressed that the other person is somebody not in our experience and never can be, and that experience has only guaranteed one person. Let us suppose that this is so, though it seems to me a serious over-statement. Then at least the reality in experience of gratitude guarantees the reality in matter of experience of every element we have said to be presupposed except the last. But as to the last, I at least can't have goodwill towards a person unless I certainly believe he is there.

Let us return to the feeling of reverence with its solemnity and awe. What conception does this presuppose?

In itself it is not fear, love, admiration, respect, but something quite *sui generis*; it is a feeling directed to a spiritual being and presupposes the conception of a spirit.

Can it be directed to a human being? We speak of love and respect and admiration of a human person, and it is true that we speak sometimes of a person of exceptional goodness as revered. But one must contend that this is not right and that we shall detect, on severer analysis, that it is a metaphor of exaggeration, and strictly only implies a high degree of admiration and regard; but we cannot really say we have a feeling of reverence in the presence of such a person; and, if we add the feeling of solemnity which belongs to reverence, it seems still clearer that it is not so.

The feeling, then, seems directed to one spirit and one alone, and only possible for spirit conceived as God.

Again, it is true that we speak of reverence for the moral law; but again I believe no such feeling possible for a mere formula and that, so far as it exists, it is only possible because we think of the moral law as a manifestation of the nature of the Eternal Spirit. Here again the feeling of solemnity seems to help. For those who have such a real experience of reverence and solemnity the existence of this emotion guarantees the possibility of the conceptions, and we retrace the same argument for the reality of the experience as in the case of gratitude. We must affirm, here as there, that we cannot have the conceptions without real experience to correspond. There we admitted, *verbi causa*, the possibility that the assumption of the existence of another person, though grounded on our own experience, might be only an imagination grounded on our own experience of ourselves. But here the feeling *presupposes* the conception of another spirit, whom we must think as not human or like ourselves, or the conception would never give rise to the feeling. Can we resist the conclusion that we must have had experience of the reality of such a being somehow within us?

This argument should have a special claim on a set of thinkers who, from their intellectual bias, may seem to be the most unlikely to admit that there is any sound evidence of belief in God. These are the adepts in the methods of the empirical sciences and the adherents of empirical systems of philosophy. For it is just these who maintain and emphasize the doctrine that we can make no 'idea' ourselves, that the ideas we have are 'ideas' of objects actually experienced, or arbitrary combinations of them by us. In the latter kind, only the combination is supposed to be ours; the elements combined must come from experience.

Have we not here, in what we may call the religious experience, an emotion which absolutely guarantees the existence in us of the idea of a spiritual being transcending everything human, a being which is no combination, arbitrary or otherwise, of the 'idea' of other experienced objects? In the actual emotional experience itself there can be no thought of any arbitrary combination by us of ideas of what is already familiar in experience. Rather something we could not have imagined beforehand, something spiritual which we utterly fail to describe, seems to be present to us without our will or co-operation and, without our will, to fill us with a unique emotion. Is it not certain that the solemn reverent attitude is only possible because we are convinced of the presence of something entirely transcending everything human and all other experience? No one will think it worth while to contend that such feelings could be awakened in us by the contemplation of an hypothetical and problematic combination of our own. When we are not in the actual experience we may have recourse to combinations of ideas from ordinary experience and to analogies from such material. These attempts fail and their failure confirms what has just been maintained, for no combination of objects of ordinary experience, however magnified, can produce the conception of a thing which could affect us with such emotion.

It would seem, then, that the idea of God is one of those ideas which, in accordance with the empirical principle just quoted, must be the ideas of something actually experienced. But the principle itself is not confined to empiricists. Rather the essentials of it (for empiricists understand 'what is given in experience' in too narrow a sense) and all that is necessary for the present application seem necessarily admitted in all philosophy.

But, at the very lowest, we are all entitled to argue that just as the person who has had a real experience of gratitude *must* believe that there is another actual person to whom he is so related that he is grateful to him, so the actual feeling of solemn reverence is only possible because we actually *do* believe in God. So, in such feelings, in the actual experience of reverence and solemnity we are believing (not fancying, not imagining); we *are* believing in God, for it is impossible to have them at all actually except through that belief.

Those who have had such an experience may, at times when it is absent, search for a proof of God's existence and may think they require one. But they are putting a question which could not possibly be a question to them *when* they have such an experience—an experience in which they have been absolutely convinced of the reality which they now seek to establish otherwise. The corrective is to recall such experiences if we can. But that is not easy. There is an analogy in our aesthetic consciousness;

for often we can recall but imperfectly the effect of a piece of music though we are certain the effect was there. Besides, these 'religious' experiences are often, perhaps oftenest, such as have touched us so deeply that we instinctively shrink from trying to reproduce them. They may have been at times of unspeakable sorrow, such as the loss of a friend. Is it not here that the great poet can help us? For he can awaken the mood in us again, and in his imaginary world bring home to us the living experience itself. Poetry does us here a far higher service than philosophy can; yet it needs philosophy to vindicate and complete it. For to turn to poetry in such issues we think of as abandoning the difficulty of reasoning to take refuge in the realm of fancy. This is a great mistake which it is the privilege of philosophy to correct.

But to avoid misunderstanding, something must be added. It is not meant that in what we have called the religious experience a man must say to himself 'Lo, God is here!' or use any ordinary religious formula. It is enough that in such an emotional state he should be convinced of something infinitely beyond himself and all humanity, inspiring him with an emotion which nothing human could inspire—reverent awe. One recalls the fine saying of Tacitus[1] about the religion of the Germans, '*secretum illud quod sola reverentia vident*'.[2]

The feeling, then, points to the reality of the experience. Such a view would throw light upon the antithesis we mentioned. We can see why we can fail to recognize what is in us, and how this which works within us is the original conviction which, under the influence of science, we misunderstand; and that it is really this misunderstanding which made us cast about for arguments such as that from design. But no argument from design, illustrated by examples however wonderful—can have anything like the effect of a single experience of the emotions of reverence and awe. The one is but an argument; the other is a sense of the reality itself and is the only thing that can satisfy us. This need not interfere in the least with anyone's belief in the edifying effect of religious services. These are essentially for those who have already a belief in God. Even the religious exhortation intended for 'conversion' (or whatever it may be called) as a rule assumes that the hearer believes in God. If it is really a question of convincing the hearer of the reality of God, the best chance of the preacher lies in the possibility of awakening in the hearer what has been implicit in some of his own experience. And does not this depend on what is essentially a poetic faculty?

[1] See above, n. 2 to p. 241.

[2] 'That mysterious being which they regard with nothing but reverence.'

24

TENNANT

on THE PROBLEM OF EVIL

Biographical Note Born in Burslem, 1866, son of a wine merchant. Educated in Newcastle, Staffs., and at Cambridge, where he read Natural Sciences. Degree, 1889. Taught for a time; ordained, 1893. Chaplain of Caius College, Cambridge, 1897–99. After a few years in a parish, he returned to Cambridge in 1913 as University Lecturer in the Philosophy of Religion. Elected Fellow of Trinity, 1913. Remained in Cambridge till his death in 1957.

Principal works: *The Origin and Propagation of Sin* (1902), *The Being of God in the Light of Physical Science* (1905), *The Concept of Sin* (1912), *Miracle and its Philosophical Presuppositions* (1925), *Philosophical Theology* (2 vols., 1928, 1930), *The Philosophy of the Sciences* (1932) and *The Nature of Belief* (1943).

Philosophical Note T.'s version of empirical theism is elaborated in the two volumes of his *Philosophical Theology*, from which the passage reproduced below is taken. T. was a careful, learned and acute thinker, but has scarcely found the recognition among theologians and philosophers which he deserves. His philosophical position was empirical, in that he regarded the purely *a priori* method favoured by some philosophers as out of place when we are trying to explain the features of the actual world. But his philosophical method was empirical in a special and further sense. Whereas many philosophers set out to discover the logical presuppositions of knowledge or proceed to a logical analysis of the nature of knowledge without considering the possibility that the nature of our reason itself is contingent upon empirical facts, e.g. the evolutionary process, T. argued that it was necessary to begin with the actual conditions and nature of knowledge: in short, psychology is a necessary preliminary to philosophy. When we adopt this genuinely empirical method, without any metaphysical presuppositions, much of classical 'empiricism' (e.g. Hume's reduction of the self to a series of psychological states) is seen to be wrong. T.'s view is empirical *theism*, in that he held that the conformity to law intrinsic to the world gives a reasonable basis for a theistic explanation, which is the most satisfactory and consonant with the facts. Nevertheless, it is necessary to remove certain obstacles to such an explanation, such as the existence of evil and the present passage shows how T. deals with the problem.

Bibliographical Note An excellent account of T.'s thought is given in C. D. Broad's 'Frederick Robert Tennant' (*Proceedings of the British Academy*, Vol. XLIV, London, 1960), which is reprinted separately.

THE PROBLEM OF EVIL

Philosophical Theology, Vol. ii, part of Ch. VII

The fact that evil exists in the world is a primary datum for the empirical theist, knowable with much more immediacy and certainty than is the being of God. And he cannot approve of either of the chief ways in which pantheists and theists respectively have sought in the past to explain the reality of evil away. He finds no comfort in the supposition that evil is an illusion of finite and temporal experience, an inadequate idea, or an appearance which would dissolve away if only we saw *sub specie aeternitatis*. For, if evil is an illusion, the illusion is an evil; and if no evil would confront timeless vision, it is an evil that we see *sub specie temporis*. The problem of evil is raised by the world as we find it and is not to be solved by diverting attention to other-worldly cognition of a world-order other than the phenomenal and temporal.

Nor, again, can the theist of today resort to the view that evil is unreal or 'non-existent' in the sense of being mere deficiency or negation, having and needing no efficient cause: he possesses psychological knowledge to the contrary. The privation-theory of evil[1] owes its plausibility to the ease with which abstractions can be verbally manipulated. It abstracts moral evil from moral agents, and because the resulting concepts no longer includes subjective activity asserts that it denotes nothing actual or active, substantial or causative. Of course if good were similarly regarded in abstraction from its agents it would likewise be reduced to the unsubstantial. Evil in the abstract is indeed nothing existent, and cannot be said to resist the good; but evil wills none the less resist good wills. St Augustine, in teaching that the evil will or act has no efficient cause, stated that it is due to *not* setting the will upon God; but he overlooked the fact that evil volition also consists in actually setting the will upon something other than God. Thus the positive element in moral evil was suppressed by substituting an abstraction for a concrete fact and by adopting a negative form of words where a positive form is equally called for. Even the will is an abstraction: the only actuality is an agent willing; and he is the efficient cause which the deficiency-theory failed to find because, by a mere verbal device, it had left him out. When St Augustine and other defenders of the privation-theory have sought to present it in such a form as to escape the force of these considerations, they have relied on the special assumptions that only the immutable really exists and that existence and

[1] See n. 1 to p. 152.

goodness are the same. But, as has been observed in previous contexts, the former assumption is baseless and the latter is derived from word-play. Lastly, when the theory identifies moral evil with so-called metaphysical evil, which is but morally neutral finiteness, it obliterates the morality of evil. For these reasons all forms of the theory in question must be discarded as useless for the purpose of theodicy. The error in the theory is nowhere more vicious than in such reasoning as that evil is non-existent, *therefore* God cannot be its cause, or in the ingenious argument (said to emanate from Boethius[1]): there is nothing that the omnipotent God cannot do; he cannot do evil; therefore evil is nothing. At best the privation-theory is a misstatement of such truths as that evil is never an end in itself, nor a power or 'principle' co-ordinate with goodness and absolutely antithetic to it, since moral evil is always choice of a lower good, while physical evil may be instrumental to ethical goodness and may be inevitable in a world which is to be a theatre of moral life. Such facts, it may be observed by the way, preclude the possibility, logically open as long as Actuality[2] is not consulted, that the good in the world is but a necessary condition of the maximum of evil in a worst possible world.

What is meant by the assertion that this world, in spite of its evil, is the best possible needs to be explained, else it may seem to state an absurdity. And explanation may begin with clearing away certain gratuitous errors which have been historically associated with the dictum. It is not necessary to analyse the divine creativity into the actualization of one best world subsequently to the choosing of it, and choice of it subsequently to contemplation of an infinite number of unrealized, purely ideal or possible systems presented to God's thought or imagination. It is not only unnecessary, but also inconsistent in various ways with the requirements of thought and knowledge, so to represent the origination of God's world. God without a world is a superfluous abstraction, and a God who might have 'chosen' a different seminal world from this or different 'primary collocations', would be a different God. The supposed possibilities with which the Creator is alleged to have been confronted are not to be conceived as eternally independent of him; nor are ideas, properly so called, prior to actualities, but are derived from them. Possibility, in the sense that is here relevant, presupposes actuality; and to speak of possible world as prior to an actual world is but to indulge in the reification of abstractions that are meaningless apart from relation to *some* actuality. When possibility rules out not only, e.g. the round square, but also

[1] See above, n. 4 to p. 74.

[2] See *Philosophical Theology*, Vol. i, p. 370. T. uses 'Actuality' to mean transsubjective reality.

non-compossibility with other possibles without one system and with the determinate nature of God, apart from which he is nothing, the supposed infinity of possible worlds vanishes: unrealized possibilities become impossibilities. What is possible for God is not determined by a *prius* of eternal laws, for there can be no such thing, but primarily by his nature and secondarily by that of his one world. As Lotze has shown,[1] empty images or ideas of other possible actualities can only be said to arise with the actual world and its logical and other kinds of order. God and his world are the ground and cause of the distinction between the possible and the impossible, and between the possible and the actual. Having derived the notion of the possible from the actual, the human mind has been apt to invert the order, and to regard the actual as but one case of illimitable possibilities, 'existentially' and logically prior to it. Similarly, when it has not regarded the true and the good as arbitrarily determined by the divine will, it has tended to conceive them as a *prius* which the Creator must recognize, as if he had once been an indeterminate being from whom truth and goodness were not as yet valid. But, once more to quote Lotze, as there is no motion without velocity and direction, on which they can be afterwards imposed, so is there no power that has not some mode of procedure, and no empty capacity which somehow hits upon definite modes of activity. Determinateness excludes what are called possibilities, or other subsequently conceivable modes of action; choice between them, as if none were ruled out by the determinate nature of the Deity, is thus a superfluous supposition. The world is what it is because God is what he is.

That God might have 'chosen' another world than this out of the unlimited sphere of the possible and one in which there was less evil or none at all has sometimes been urged as an objection to ethical theism. To suggest this as a bare possibility is easy. Imaginatively to construct such a possible world is less easy, as is also a demonstration of the alleged possibility. Such initial attempts as are forthcoming are trivial and have been described as specifications for a fool's paradise. Thus it has been surmised that the physical world might have been framed with a view to safeguarding man's physical well-being at every turn. It is a question, however, whether this happy state of things is compatible with the world's being a cosmos, and a further question whether the world would then be instrumental to the realization of moral worth. The particular incompatibilities involved in particular suggestions as to how the elimination of physical and moral evil from a world such as ours might have been effected

[1] Hermann Lotze (1817–81) was Professor of Philosophy at Göttingen and Berlin; he felt that philosophy must be grounded in the natural sciences, and was thus opposed to *a priori* metaphysics.

will be exhibited in due course. At this stage it may but be observed that a world characterized by static perfection is incompatible with a world characterized by evolutionary process, and that ours is of the latter type. This brings us to a remoter problem, of which the problem of evil is an outgrowth, and to the alleged ultimate insolubility of which that of the narrower problem is due. Why God created a world at all is a superfluous problem if by 'God' we primarily mean the world-ground; but why his world is evolutionary rather than already perfected is a question that is perhaps not quite futile, nor so wholly beyond a reasonable answer, in the light of the fundamental tenets of ethical theism, as some would pronounce it to be. A world, as a sphere of existence objective to God, must be composed of finite beings: God cannot create Gods, because 'God' in the theistic sense of the term connotes unoriginateness. And if the world is to realize the good, that being its *raison d'être*, it would seem that it then must be characterized by development or epigenesis.[1] For moral goodness cannot be created as such; it cannot be implanted in any moral agent by an 'almighty' Other. It is the outcome of freedom, and has to be acquired or achieved by creatures. We cannot imagine a living world in which ethical values are to be actualized save as an evolutionary cosmos in which free agents live and learn, make choices and build characters. If there be theists who think otherwise, they must be content to regard the evolutionary character of the world as but part of the ultimate nature of things, and as inexplicable because ultimate. At any rate philosophy must start from what simply is; and it deserves no blame if it modestly withholds enquiry as to how and why things came to be. Theism would only go so far further as to apply its doctrine that God is love which seeks reciprocation.

Apart from all variable and incidental qualities which may belong to love as possessed by mankind, and from such enrichment of the conception of divine love as is supplied by religion, it may be said that love must everywhere and always involve self-imparting and seeking the highest welfare of the beings on whom it is bestowed. In God it must also involve self-limitation in respect of power. Love, in this sense, has always been assigned by theology as what we can only speak of as the 'motive' of God in his volitional creativity. Taking this cardinal doctrine and also the reality of the world's evil for granted, the theist needs to show that in and behind this evil there is a soul of good, or at least to afford reasons for disbelieving that the world, in so far as it is due to God's making and not man's mismaking, contains absolute and superfluous evils. If he can do so, he will not need to seek refuge from an intellectual difficulty

[1] See n. 3 to p. 432.

by merely assuming a wholly incomprehensible divine love, or by faintly trusting the larger hope: his faith will remain reasonable, supported by what passes for knowledge—knowledge which, however, itself ultimately rests on other faith.

Since theism teaches that the world-ground is an ethical Spirit, or that God is love, it must also teach that, in some sense, the world is the 'best possible' of its kind. And it may now be submitted that this implication is defensible, so long as we are consistent and earnest in the use of both the words 'best' and 'possible'.

There is no sense in calling a world a best world unless we specify the *kind* of goodness or worth which that world is said to manifest in the fullest measure. Different values may not be actually compossible, especially if each of them is to be present in its superlative degree; so the notion of a world as the *omnitudo* of values may be as 'impossible' as is the notion of God as the *omnitudo*[1] of all positive attributes. What the theist means by 'best' in this connexion is best in respective of moral worth, or of instrumentality thereto. But those who have allowed themselves to 'charge God foolishly' have substituted for this meaning that of happiest, or sensuously pleasantest. Certainly our world is not, in this sense, the best that we can imagine. Equally certainly, the theist maintains, it was not meant to be. If it were, it would not be truly the best; for we cannot go behind our judgment, rational or non-rational, that the highest value in the hierarchy of values is moral worth, or—what is ultimately the essence of all morality—personal love. The hedonistic theory that pleasure is what gives worth to life, the ultimate good to be striven for, is generally acknowledged to be untenable: at any rate it is out of court for the theist. Happiness may be a constituent element in the highest complex good that we can conceive, and may accompany the attainment of a higher good; but the ultimate standard for the valuation of human life it cannot be. The 'best possible' world, then, or the world that is worthiest of God and moral order, is a theatre of moral life and love. Moral character and moral progress must be its purpose, as the best things which any world can realize. To dispense with them would be, for the Creator, to prefer a worse world. Unalloyed pleasure is condemned by man himself as unworthy to be his 'life's crown'. No pain or want, no effort; no effort, no progress; no progress, no attainment. *Necessity* is the mother of invention; experience is the 'becoming expert *by experiment*': mere happiness would entail stagnation.

Thus we cannot have it both ways: the best world cannot be the most pleasurable; and it cannot lack its crown in moral agents.

[1] That is, the *totality* of values or positive attributes.

The word 'cannot' leads on to a discussion of our second leading term, 'possible': on this occasion in connexion with the notion of divine omnipotence. It has already been found vain to speak of a *prius* of possibilities independent of actualities. It may now be added that, possibilities and impossibilities being once constituted by an actual order, omnipotence cannot be conceived as power or control over the possible and impossible alike, as if both were the same to God. That leads to absurdity. Yet when theism has been rejected on the ground that the evil in the world furnishes an argument against the goodness, or even the existence, of God, it would seem to have been generally assumed that such a being must, by arbitrary exercise of will, be the author of possibility as well as of actuality.

That whatever power may be called omnipotence must be limited by the impossible has been maintained in at least two ways. One of these is to assert that the laws of thought, i.e. the laws of identity, contradiction, etc.,[1] are valid independently of God as well as of the world, and impose themselves upon him as well as upon ourselves with necessity. If this be so, we at once reach a distinction between the possible and the impossible which must be eternally binding upon the Supreme Being. Such a doctrine will not be unacceptable to common sense, but it does not commend itself to all philosophers. It has several times been insisted in this work that the valid, abstracted from that of which it is valid, is a mental figment, not an 'existent' *prius*. And it may be argued that this is so even in the case of the fundamental laws of thought, as well as in that of the empirical laws of Nature. The sum of eternal truths cannot exist, so to say, *in vacuo*, prior both to the things in which they are embodied and to the thinker in whose mind they are ideas, etc. When we speak of God as recognizing truths independent of him, or as establishing truth or validity by fiat, and when we try to conceive of God as able to obliterate the difference between the logically possible and impossible, or to set up that difference as if it once did not exist, we are endeavouring to think of him as a being for whom truth is not yet truth, and therefore as an indeterminate being eventually indistinguishable from nothing.

On the other hand, if the thinker of the eternal truths is determinate, self-consistent, and so forth, with a definite nature and mode of activity, other modes of being and conceivable or possible activities are *ipso facto* precluded. Hence the sum of eternal truths becomes the mode of God's being and activity, and is neither their *prius* nor their product. And this is the better answer to the supposition that the possible is an arbitrary creation of God and that the possible and the impossible are alike to omnipotence. In that God is Love, he is not hate: in that he wills a developing

[1] See above, n. 4 to p. 64.

moral order he is not the creator of a paradise of angels. Possibilities are thus determined by what God is; and God is limited by his very determinateness, not an indeterminate Absolute in whom all differences are lost. Theism has no concern with such an Absolute, and the puzzles set up by the adoption of such a notion constitute no difficulties for theism. Nor is determinateness, or the kind of finiteness which it implies, any derogation from such 'almightiness' as theology can predicate of the Deity without self-stultification.

But, granted that God is a determinate being, restricted to consistency and compatibility in his action, and granted that his world is to be a developing moral order—the highest ideal of a world that we can conceive—then it must follow that there be a possibility and a risk of moral evil in that world. There cannot be moral goodness in a creature such as man without the possibility of his sinning. Without freedom to choose the evil, or the lower good, a man might be a well-behaved puppet or a sentient automaton, but not a moral agent. But the best possible world implies the existence of moral agents; its crown cannot be the puppet or the automaton. Were our conduct determined like the movements of the machinery of a clock, our world might manifest a pre-established harmony[1] and fulfil the purpose of a clock-maker. But it could not fulfil any ideal of its own, and could not have one. Nor could it realize the purpose of a God willing a best possible world. In both these respects a world from which the possibility of moral evil was excluded would be other than a moral order. It is idle, then, wistfully to contemplate the happiness which the world might have known had its creator made us capable only of doing what is right; to profess, like Huxley,[2] our readiness to close with an offer to remove our capacity to do wrong and cause misery; or to indulge the wish that we had been made good at the expense of freedom. There is no moral goodness in a clock, however perfectly it may keep time. Freedom to do good alone, except after suppression of lower motives by moral conflict, is not freedom. Such regrets as these, to which the ablest of men have occasionally allowed themselves to give expression, do but show how hard it is to avoid playing fast and loose with plain words when we would apply logic to a question which excites emotion.

The best world, then, must include free agents, creatures that are in turn 'creators' in the sense that their 'utterances' are not God's positings but their own. And freewill introduces contingencies, new causal series and new possibilities. God stands 'a hand-breadth off' to give his creatures room to act and grow: and here another limitation is involved —the self-limitation of love. The Actual world, including human society

[1] See above, p. 142.

[2] See above, n. 2 to p. 383.

and human achievements, is due to man as well as to God. We are fellow-workers together with God in the actualization of a moral order: otherwise the world were not a moral order at all. For the possibility of moral evil entering into this moral order, God, who foreknew it, is responsible: he permits, so to say, the evil in order that there may be the good. But for the actual emergence of man's moral evil we cannot say that he [God] is responsible: our sin, when 'sin' is strictly and correctly defined, is not God's act but the product of our volition, or devolved freedom. Conceivably moral evil *might* not have emerged, though the basic motivations to it, themselves morally neutral or non-moral, are inevitable consequences of the evolutionary process through which phenomenal man came to be. This vindication of the goodness of God is indeed sometimes alleged to be worthless, on the ground that in creating human wills God created all their volitional issues. But this objection involves the crude notion that a will is a concrete thing, like a machine, instead of a name for an activity, or a trend of activity, of a substantial subject which has nothing in common with a machine. Although, according to theism, God assigned to each soul its specific nature or individuality, determinative of its original responses (when it should become embodied) to primary presentations, and prescribed the scope of certain of its capacities and faculties, this was not to foreordain, as a chain of quasi-mechanical effects, all its future actions, and so to be responsible for its misdeeds. Freewill consists in subjective activities of a plastic person, in directivity of assigned capacities, etc., in choice and transvaluation, in selective distribution of attention such as determines the strength of motives, and so on: doings which are not quasi-mechanical issues of a preformed 'will', on the one hand, nor creative acts of God, on the other hand. Whatever be the beginnings of a man's natural history, his moral history begins with himself. And it begins not in the affective response evoked willy-nilly in a subject of determinate nature, but in the governable responses which a more or less rational being makes to more or less rationally synthesized value-complexes.

Such freewill is the human being's burden at the same time that it is a condition of 'the glorious liberty of the children of God'. And the demand that it should be the one of these things and not the other is but the child's cry for the impossible or self-contradictory. Morality, in an evolved creature such as man, involves the possibility of moral evil and entails conflict and warfare. The objection raised against theism on the score of the prevalence of moral evil is that there is too much of contingency in the world. It will presently appear that the objection raised on the score of the prevalence of physical evil is that there is too much of rigid regularity. As they stand, these objections cancel one another; and the theist's reply to them is that neither the contingency in the human realm nor the uniformity in the physical realm is a superfluity, but both are essential conditions of moral life. Conceivably Nature's regularity and man's waywardness might be tempered by divine intervention; and it is sometimes urged that such intervention ought to be forthcoming if God be both benevolent and omnipotent. Moral evil alone being for the present under consideration, it suffices here to repeat that though safeguards which would make us immune to temptation might secure objective rightness or correctness in conduct, such right-doing would possess no moral worth. They would not secure the morality which, in the last resort, is love—the only real fulfilling of the law—and would not conduce to moral character. Character is made, not born nor given ready-made. The development of morality is naturally not continuous or uninterruptedly progressive; but to coerce it to be so would be to destroy its morality. Suppression of freedom might reduce human suffering, but it would mean surrender of the ideal which the world embodies; and the omnipotence invoked would be inconsistency or indeterminateness such as the idea of God excludes. A world 'in leading-strings' may realize *an* ideal, but can have no ideal that is its own or is moral. To preclude moral evil would be to preclude moral goodness, to do evil, to prefer a worse to a better world.

Thus the difficulties raised by the existence of sin are of an insuperable kind only on one or both of the suppositions (1) that to God there must be no difference between the possible and the impossible, and (2) that the best possible world must be the happiest world and not a moral order. But theism repudiates omnipotence, in this sense, in its characterization of Deity; and it asserts that the instrumentality of the world to the production of a moral order is an expression or revelation of the nature of God, the empirically-suggested world-ground. And if the moral ideal be the best or the highest that a world conceivably can fulfil, the process by which alone it is attainable is also good, despite the evil incidental to it. Theism *requires* that the world be an imperfect or mixed world, in that it takes the purpose of the world to consist in the realization of the highest values by finite and developing creatures, with which an omnipotent establishment of non-moral or static perfection would have nothing in common.

If we suppose the ethical status of man to be less than the whole of the divine purpose, and but a stage to something higher but transcending our power to conceive, the further elements in the world-purpose may condition the evils with which we men are confronted, in respects that are beyond our ken. But, however this may be—and it is practically useless, if theoretically wholesome, to invoke the limitations of our knowledge and the inscrutability of the divine purpose in its fulness—theism is not unable to find a place and a meaning for moral evil in the world of an all-good God, in so far as the world is knowable and its purpose can reasonably be assigned.

Thus far God's purpose has alone been contemplated. And the theodicy which has as yet been constructed in part would not be satisfactory unless man, in struggling through many sins and miseries, could account himself to be striving for his own ideal, as well as fulfilling a divine end. This, however, mankind acknowledges through those who represent it at its best. Indictments of God based on the facts of human sin and suffering seldom imply a denial of the claim of moral values to be the highest in human judgment. We deem the prize worth the cost, and life without moral strife and attainment to be not worth while. If there is no 'peace in ever climbing up the climbing wave', there is zest in warring with evil, and the supreme joys of life are found in love such as is not mere passion. Confronted with the choice between the happy and innocent life of the brute, without thought before and after and pining for what is not, on the one hand, and the life of moral endeavour and spiritual progress, on the other hand, human beings would be practically unanimous in deciding that it is better to have risen above the non-moral level and to have tasted of the tree of knowledge:

> What were life
> Did soul stand still therein, forgot her strife
> Through the ambiguous Present to the goal
> Of some all-reconciling Future?

If the best things we can conceive are bound up with moral character, or rather with personality which includes much more than morality in the barer sense of the word, the best possible world we can conceive is a world which affords opportunity for their attainment. The worser man generally recognizes the supremacy of goodness, while the morally advancing man, from the standpoint he has gained, condemns any other sort of life than that of moral growth as incapable of satisfying his soul's needs, and as unworthy of him as he now is. Had mankind never appeared, had Nature stopped short of her crowning in a rational and moral species, the world's falling short of being a moral order would have remained both unregretted and unapproved. The moral race which has emerged, though born to suffer through its freedom, nevertheless rejoices in living, approves its creator's ideal, accepts the chance of the prize of learning love: at least so long as it can believe the cost to be inevitable and the possibility of moral evil to be not superfluous.

To these qualifying conditions, which have been found to be satisfied, another will be added by those who would regard the divine purpose as finding fulfilment, not in the world-process, but in the far off consummation towards which they believe all creation moves. Reasons have been given for rejecting the notion that evil is absolutely and exclusively evil, ministering to nothing but further evil, never subservient or instrumental to good, and not necessarily or contingently incidental to the actualization of moral good. But some will require theodicy to supply reason for believing that moral evil is not ultimately insuperable, that it will eventually give place to the good, or at least that it is not destined to become supreme over the good so that the world, though a moral order in one sense, would mock our highest moral aspirations. When self-limitation is ascribed to God in place of that omnipotence which is but inconsistency or indeterminateness, such possibilities as these, it is urged, present themselves to be reckoned with. They therefore need to be considered.

Looked at in the abstract, freedom in antithesis to external coercion, and contingency in antithesis to external necessitation, imply the possibility that universal goodness will not be finally realized, and even that moral evil may ever assert and reassert itself until it culminates in moral anarchy. But bare possibilities, like sheer impossibilities, need not be taken too seriously. Probabilities reasonably grounded on experience are another matter; and it is a question whether the theist may not claim that, in so far as the defeat of the divine purpose by man's delegated freedom is concerned, probability favours the view which theism would prefer. Moral advance, in spite of relapses, has undoubtedly marked mankind's history, on the whole, hitherto; and though it cannot be argued from the fact that progress will continue throughout future ages, neither are we at liberty to regard humanity's past progress as a mere accident, or as a state of things which is likely to be permanently reversed. We may reject the view that the contingencies of history are somehow ruled by a dialectic process of which the world-process is a manifestation; we may renounce the Victorian notion of progress as intrinsic and necessarily involved in the world as a whole including man, and regard such optimism as the outcome of a false analogy between spiritual and physical evolution, ignoring human freedom and over-emphasizing the influence of environment; we may refuse to appeal to God's supposed power to subdue all things, including free-will, to himself, so as to conserve the good and exterminate the morally evil; we may deem an inductive inference from the fragment of history up to date to the far future to be absurd; and we may reasonably assume that, in so far as this world is concerned, and while human nature remains essentially what it now is, motivation to evil will never be lacking and sinlessness may never be universal: yet there is good reason to disbelieve in the possibility of evil becoming supreme over good in the world. Man is not merely an organism, and moral evolution is by no means wholly determined by natural heredity and environment. Moreover the environment, in the present case, is partly moral, as is adaptation to it. What is called social heredity is an important factor in moral evolution. And when we contemplate this latter determinant we find that there is something in goodness which promotes its own conservation, and something in evil that promises disruption—if not self-extinction, at least impotence to become supreme. And this is so, contingency and freewill notwithstanding. The wicked are like the troubled sea which cannot rest: the double-minded man is unstable in all his ways. Accordingly, the encroachments of moral evil upon the established good do not become consolidated. Apparent gains are apt to prove vanity, even loss. And it is plain that no universal conspiracy in evil is possible, such as would produce a hell on earth. If that be what is meant by defeat of God's purpose through human freedom, it seems to be precluded by the intrinsic nature of both human goodness and human badness. Evil desires and evil purposes conflict with one another, so that evil as well as goodness resists and thwarts conspiration in evil. On the other hand, conquests in moral goodness and truth, despite their temporary obscuration, when once made are made for ever. The world always has knowledge that it is the better for them. There is a unity of aim, a co-operation in purpose, a solidarity of interest, a growing consensus, among men of goodwill. The moral law, in spite of its continual violation, survives and increases its dominion: the good is self-conservative.

Again, moral evil does not come out of moral goodness, but good does come out of evil and error. Error exposes itself, to the further elucidation and definition of the truth: evil, in its very acquisition, reveals itself to be the lesser good and learns by bitter experience that it is the evil. Nor does each new generation, or each fresh individual, advance *wholly* by first-hand experience, though experimenting for self is a right that never will be renounced, in whatever disasters it may issue. For in human society the social inheritance, or stored experience, counts for much. The higher the moral tone of the many, the more difficult to realize and to entertain become the evil inclinations of the few.

For these reasons, then, it is no flimsy and sentimental optimism, but a reasoned and reasonable expectation, that, as history establishes the fact of moral progress up to date, that progress is not an accident, but will maintain itself. In future ages it may proceed with accelerated speed: for the gains of the good over the evil would seem to be cumulative although evil may ever take new forms. The tendencies inherent in goodness and badness, as such, preclude the possibility that the purpose of a self-limited God, supposing it to include the final victory of goodness over evil, should be defeated by the freedom of his creatures. There is no more reason to believe that moral evil is destined to become supreme than to believe that its possibility, or even its actuality, is incompatible with a moral order such as the 'best possible' world must be.

It is another question whether moral evil is destined, here or hereafter, to become extinct through the response of freewill to fuller light: conceivably, evil may continue everlastingly while unable to become universal and supreme. But this question is not vital for the theodicy of theism such as confesses to limitations besetting its knowledge or probable belief. If natural theology is able to supply reasons for belief in a future life, it is utterly unable to imagine the conditions of such a life or of knowledge accessible to souls that are disembodied or embodied otherwise than they are in this life. It is impossible to foreknow individually, or non-statistically, the issues of the freewill of moral agents in any imaginable circumstances. And theism, while able to adduce reasonable grounds for believing the cosmic process and human history to reveal the purpose of establishing a moral order, in the sense of a theatre for the life of persons possessed of freedom and the moral status, cannot supply similar reasonable grounds for the conjecture that cosmic and human history are but a means, or a stage, towards a future and final consummation in which nothing evil will remain. This is not a necessary corollary of the doctrine that God is a lover of free persons. It is a belief motivated by religious yearning for the fleeing away of all sorrow and sighing and by the ancient predilection for the static and perfected, or for the conception of God as figuratively or literally, all in all. Natural theology, however, cannot make use of either cravings or predilections, and possesses no data for the construction of an eschatology. Theism is not pledged to the doctrine of universal hope, or of the perfecting of every soul, nor to that of the annihilation of the hardened unrighteous, if any such there will be. The possibility of endless warfare against spiritual wickedness in the world to come presents no greater difficulty to theism than does the forthcomingness of moral evil in this present world.

Indeed some theists have gone to the other extreme and have argued that the divine love must ever involve sacrifice and victory, and that the presence of evil is necessary for the continued exercise of the highest love. Just as God is not God without his world, so, it is said, divine love is not divine love without sinning recipients for him to seek and to save. According to this view there is no rest remaining for all the people of God, and no tranquil blessedness for God himself; evil will for ever be in process of being overcome. It is implied that a statically perfect world would be less noble than process towards it, or that progress is not necessarily approach to a realizable goal. Just as we may find satisfaction in conflict and tension, so God may ever rejoice in his own sorrows and find peace in the victory over evil: 'the eternal world contains Gethsemane'. So some have speculated: but in recoil from the old ideas of impassibility and static perfection they have retained somewhat of the rigidity which belonged to ancient thought. It is not necessary to believe that, because the highest kind of good that we know is only realizable in our world through the possibility, if not the actuality, of evil, therefore the continuous presence of evil is essential to the conservation of goodness. Human experience suggests the contrary. There is such a thing as has been called 'the saint's rest'—the relative freedom from moral conflict and from temptation, earned by self-discipline and struggle; and it may have a joy of its own and an interest which does not need the zest of militancy for its maintenance. All morality is not the same morality: there is one goodness of the happy warrior, and another goodness of him who has fought the good fight. And all these kinds of moral state, or of goodness and blessedness, cannot be fully actualized potentialities at once, because some are incompatible with others. It is therefore forbidden for us to postulate that the divine love must ever manifest itself in every specific type; and it is unnecessary to suppose that ethical life is precluded to the Supreme Spirit unless there be for him the possibility of ever sorrowing and striving with sinful souls, or that the existence of evil is an essential condition of the continuing love of God. But, apart from the baselessness of both the kinds of *a priori* speculation that have been considered, the question of the continuance or the self-extinction of moral evil is irrelevant to theodicy.

The problem of evil has thus far been discussed with almost exclusive reference to evil of the moral kind. And the solution that has been presented consists in showing the tenability of the belief that in our developing world all things work together, as a whole, for the highest conceivable good. The possibility of moral evil and the actuality of its consequences are inevitable concomitants of the 'best possible' evolutionary world. It is not maintained that everything is good, or that 'whatever is, is right', or that partial evil is not evil because it is a condition of universal good. Nor is it implied that every particular evil is directly essential to the emergence of some particular good, or that it has a necessary place, like a dissonance in music, in the harmony of the world-process. When it is asserted that all things work together for good, by 'all things' is not meant each and every single thing, but the sum of things regarded as one whole or complex, the universe as a coherent order.

It is by adhering to this general view that the theist can best face the problem presented by the existence of that form of evil for which human freedom is not necessarily, and generally not at all, responsible: the physical evil, or the pain and suffering occasioned by the course of Nature in sentient beings. Indeed any other position than that which has just been summarized seems obviously inadequate as a basis for the explanation of the forthcomingness of physical ills. In order to reconcile the suffering inflicted by the material world upon mankind and other sentient creatures with the goodness and power of the Creator it is both superfluous and insufficient to seek to show that in every particular case pain is essential to some special end, or that in each single instance suffering may fulfil some particular providential purpose. To attempt a theodicy on these lines is as hopeless as it would be today to develop a teleological argument from particular instances of adaptedness, after the manner of Paley.[1] But, as there is a wider teleology than Paley's, so is there a wider theodicy than that which consists in pleading that human and animal pain are sometimes prophylactic—a warning against danger, or that human suffering is sometimes punitive or purgatorial, and thus subservient to benign ends. These assertions are undoubtedly true, and there is no need to belittle their import. But by themselves they will not carry us far towards a theodicy. They but touch the fringe of the problem: or, to change the metaphor, they do not go to the root of the matter. It is useless, again to minimize the pain of the sentient world, or even to reduce our possibly extravagant and unscientific estimate of its intensity, except for the purpose of arguing that, in spite of pain, animal life is probably happy on the whole: otherwise a single pang of useless or superfluous pain is enough to raise our problem. It involves faulty psychology to assert that pain is the necessary background to pleasure; for a lesser pleasure would seem to yield a sufficient contrast to render the enjoyment of intenser pleasure possible. And if pain be sometimes stimulating, educational, preventitive, or remedial, as well as sometimes stunting, crushing and provocative of moral evil, this fact is only significant for an estimate of the worthwhileness of sentient life. The knife may be necessary to cure the disease, but why the necessity of the disease? The escape from mortal danger may require the painful warning, but why the mortal danger? Or, speaking generally, what are we to make of the remoter evil which renders the nearer evil necessary or salutary? The real problem obviously lies further back than these particular and partial solutions reach. It must be shown

[1] William Paley (1743–1805), English theologian, appealed in his *Evidences of Christianity* (1794) and *Natural Theology* (1802) to the signs of teleology in the natural, especially the animal, world—an appeal which, in the manner employed by Paley, fell into disrepute after the publication of the Theory of Evolution.

that pain is either a necessary by-product of an order of things requisite for the emergence of the higher goods, or an essential instrument to organic evolution, or both. Short of this, we cannot refute the charge that the world is a clumsy arrangement or an imperfectly adjusted mechanism.

It can be argued, however, that the former of the foregoing alternatives is applicable in the case of human suffering, while the latter of them can be invoked to meet especially the case of animal pain. The suffering of the lower animals is not merely an accidental superfluity emerging out of the evolutionary process, but is essentially instrumental to organic progress. It renders unnecessary a large amount of inheritance of specialized structure, and so prevents the suppression of plasticity; and as the 'sensitive edge' turned towards danger, or as prophylactic, it is of value for organic progressiveness. Although evil, it is also good for something. Much of human suffering, and many of the outrages of this present life upon our rational prudences and our most sacred affections, on the other hand, seem to be good for nothing, or to be non-essential for the realization of goodness. If a man already has it in him to meet pain with fortitude and patience, he is not necessarily one whit the better man after actually enduring excruciating tortures; and if an all-powerful being 'appointed' him such tortures, merely in order that his fortitude might pass from potentiality to actuality, such a being would be but a super-brute. However, it can be argued that the forthcomingness of our suffering is inevitably incidental to a moral order in a developing world. It issues ultimately out of what is inappropriately called metaphysical evil, or is a necessary outcome of a determinate cosmos of the particular kind that can sustain rational and moral life. The problem which it raises will therefore be solved if it can be maintained that no suffering such as we experience is superfluous to the cosmos as a coherent system and a moral order, however, excessive pain often may be a means to the accomplishment of specific ends such as are attainable by discipline and chastening.

It cannot be too strongly insisted that a world which is to be a moral order must be a physical order characterized by law and regularity. The routine of Nature may be differently described by the spiritualist, the dualist, etc.;[1] but the diversity of these ultimate explanations of law does not affect the present problem. The theist is only concerned to invoke the fact that law-abidingness, on the scale which science is able to assert its subsistence in Nature as already *naturata*,[2] is an essential condition of the

[1] By 'spiritualist', T. means someone who holds the philosophical thesis that the basic stuff of the cosmos is spirit as opposed to matter (the corresponding thesis from that side is materialism). The dualist is one who holds that the cosmos contains both matter and spirit.

[2] T. here uses an expression used by Spinoza; see p. 125.

world being a theatre of moral life. Without such regularity in physical phenomena there would be no probability to guide us, no prediction, no prudence, no accumulation of ordered experience, no pursuit of premeditated ends, no formation of habit, no possibility of character or of culture. Our intellectual faculties could not have developed. And, had they been innate, they would have wasted themselves, as Comte[1] observed, in wild extravagances and sunk rapidly into incurable sloth; while our nobler feelings would have been unable to prevent the ascendancy of the lower instincts, and our active powers would have abandoned themselves to purposeless agitation. All this is obvious; but it has often been ignored in discussion of the problem of physical evil. Nevertheless, Nature's regularity is the key to this problem. Once let it be admitted that, in order to be a theatre for moral life, the world must be largely characterized by uniformity or constancy, and most significant consequences will be seen to follow. It becomes idle to complain, as some writers have done, that the orderliness of the world is too dear at the cost of the suffering and hardship which it entails, and might more or less be dispensed with for the benefit of the sentient and rational beings which people the world. As Hume admitted, if the 'conducting of the world by general laws' were superseded by particular volitions, no man could employ his reason in the conduct of his life. And without rationality, morality is impossible: so, if the moral status of man be the goal of the evolutionary process, the reign of law is a *sine qua non*. It is a condition of the forthcomingness of the highest good, in spite of the fact that it is not an unmixed good but a source of suffering. We cannot have the advantages of a determinate order of things without its logically or its causally necessary disadvantages. Nor can we be evaluating subjects without capacity to feel. The disadvantages, viz. particular ills, need not be regarded, however, as directly willed by God as ends in themselves or as particular means, among other equally possible but painless means, to particular ends. To make use of an ancient distinction, we may say that God wills them consequently, not antecedently.[2] That is to say, they are not desired as such or in themselves, but are only willed because the moral order, which is willed absolutely or antecedently by God, cannot be had without them. Now to will a moral order is to will the best possible world; and it also involves adoption of what we necessarily, if somewhat anthropomorphically, must call a determinate world-plan. Such a determinate method of procedure to realize a definite end in an

[1] Auguste Comte (1798–1857), French philosopher and exponent of 'Positivism'. He not only rejected theological and metaphysical attempts to explain the nature of the world, but sought to replace traditional religion with a positivist (atheistic) cult.

[2] A distinction used by Aquinas: God wills an evil only as a necessary consequence of a greater good, and thus wills it *consequently*. See p. 151.

evolutionary world, however, rules out once and for all any other possible goals and methods. As Dr Martineau[1] has put it, the cosmical equation being defined, only such results as are compatible with the values of its roots can be worked out, and these must be worked out. All determination is negation. If two consequences follow from a system of propositions, or two physical properties are involved in a configuration of particles, we cannot have the one without the other, though the one may be pleasing and beneficial to man and the other may be painful, or in its immediate effects hurtful. And such a result by no means implies lack of benevolence or of power on the part of the Creator, so long as power does not include inconsistency or indeterminateness. It simply bespeaks the inexorableness of logic, the compatibility of things, and the self-consistency of the Supreme Being. That painful events occur in the causal chain is a fact; but, that there could be a determinate evolutionary world of unalloyed comfort, yet adapted by its law-abidingness to the development of rationality and morality, is a proposition the burden of proving which must be allotted to the opponent of theism. One can only add that, in so far as experience in this world enables us to judge, such proof seems impossible. To illustrate what is here meant: if water is to have the various properties in virtue of which it plays its beneficial part in the economy of the physical world and the life of mankind, it cannot at the same time lack its obnoxious capacity to drown us. The specific gravity of water is as much a necessary outcome of its ultimate constitution as its freezing-point, or its thirst-quenching and cleaning functions. There cannot be assigned to any substance an arbitrarily selected group of qualities, from which all that may prove unfortunate to any sentient organism can be eliminated, especially if one organism's meat is to be another's poison, and yet the world, of which that substance forms a part, be a calculable cosmos. Mere determinateness and fixity of nature involve such and such concatenations of qualities and rule out others. Thus physical ills follow with the same necessity as physical goods from the determinate 'world-plan' which secures that the world be a suitable stage for intelligent and ethical life.

And if this be so, the disadvantages which accrue from the determinateness and regularity of the physical world cannot be regarded either as absolute or as superfluous evils. They are not absolute evils because they are parts of an order which subserves the highest good in providing opportunity for moral development. And they are not superfluous ills because they are the necessary outcome of that order. They are collateral effects of what, in itself or as a whole, is good because instrumental to the

[1] James Martineau (1805–1900), philosopher and Unitarian minister. His best-known works are *Types of Ethical Theory* (1885) and *A Study of Religion* (1888).

highest good. They are not good, when good is hedonically defined; but they are good for good, when good is otherwise defined, rather than good for nothing.

As in the case of moral evil, so also in the case of physical evil, appeal has sometimes been made from necessary linkages and conditionings to a supposed possibility of their being over-ridden by divine omnipotence. And as it was found absurd to suppose that God could make developing beings at the same time morally free and temptationless, so it involves absurdity to suppose that the world could be a moral order without being a physical cosmos. To save mankind from the painful consequences which flow from a determinate world-order, such as the earthquake and the pestilence, would involve renunciation of a world order and therefore of a moral order, and the substitution of a chaos of incalculable miracle. Doubtless some directive agency, or the introduction of new streams of causation into the course of Nature, is conceivable without subversion of such regularity as is requisite for human prudence and without the stultification of our science. But the general suspension of painful events, requisite on the vast scale presupposed in the elimination of physical ills, would abolish order and convert a cosmos into an unintelligible chaos in which anything might succeed on anything. We should have to 'renounce reason' if we would thus be 'saved from tears', as Martineau says.

Physical evil, then, must necessarily be. And the goodness of God is vindicated if there be no reason to believe that the world-process involves more misery than Nature's uniformity entails. It is not incumbent on the theist to prove that particular evils are never greater than we judge to be necessary for the production of particular salutary effects: that difficult task confronts only the particular kind of theism which is concerned to dispense with proximate causes and a more or less autonomous world, and regards God as the sole and immediate cause of every natural event, and of every incident in a personal life. According to the theodicy which has here been sketched, it is not necessary to suppose that every specific form of suffering that man undergoes—e.g. the agony of tetanus or of cancer—is antecedently willed by God as a means to some particular end. It can be admitted that excruciating pains are more severe than they need be for evoking virtues such as patience and fortitude, and that to assign them to God's antecedent will would be to attribute devilishness to the Deity. Moreover, the fact that some human beings are born as abortions, as imbecile or insane, seems to be inexplicable on the view that every form of suffering is a particular providence, or an antecedently willed dispensation for educating and spiritually perfecting the person on whom the affliction falls; while to suppose that suffering is inflicted on one person for the spiritual edification of another is again to conceive of God as immoral. But the hardest fact of all for human equanimity, in presence of physical and mental evil, is that the apportionment of suffering among individuals is entirely irreconcilable by us with any divine plan of adjustment of particular afflictions to the particular needs, circumstances and stages of moral development, of individual sufferers. Even more distressing to human thought than the goading intensity of some kinds of pain is the seemingly chaotic distribution of human ills. If we could trace the utility of particular sufferings with their varying degrees of endurableness, or discern any adaptation of pain to the person's sensibility, moral state and need of awakening and chastening, then philosophy might be able to agree with the simple-minded piety which assigns a special purpose to every instance of suffering, and finds therein the visitation or appointment of an all-wise and all-good God. But the wind is not tempered to the shorn lamb; the fiercest trials often overtake those who least need torments to inspire fear, to evoke repentance or to perfect patience, and also those who through no fault of their own lack the mature religious faith and moral experience by which alone they could understand how affliction may be endured for their souls' good. 'All things come alike to all: there is one event to the righteous and to the wicked'—to those who may be enabled, and to those who are unable, to profit by severe trial.

Disastrous as these facts are to the extremer forms of the doctrine of divine immanence in Nature, they are compatible with theism such as allows to the created world somewhat of delegated autonomy. According to the wider theodicy which has here been presented, the human afflictions arising from our relations with the physical world are not willed as such by God at all, or for any purpose. They are rather inevitable, if incidental, accompaniments or by-products of the world-order which, as a whole, and by means of its uniformity, is a pre-requisite of the actualization of the highest good that we can conceive a world as embodying. The world is none the less God's world for its callousness to man; but its autonomy, not the particular incidence of each single ill, is what the religious mind should attribute to his [God's] 'appointment'.

Further, man himself does not deem his suffering to be an excessive price to pay for the dignity of his ethical status, once he recognizes physical evil to be inevitable in a moral world. He is then not compelled to see in his suffering self a mere means either to the perfecting of the race, or to the realization of a divine purpose, or to the manifestation of the 'glory' of God. And this is an important consideration for any theodicy. For man is an end for himself, whatever else he may be. *My* ills can only be justified to *me* if the remoter advantage of there being ill at all be *mine*: not humanity's, or even God's, alone. But in that the remoter advantage is the enjoyment of rational and ethical dignity, the individual man can acquiesce in God's purpose of the world: God's ideal may be his also. It is the assurance that God is fulfilling us individually as well as himself, and fulfilling us for ourselves as well as for himself, that makes human life in this bitter-sweet world endurable by the sensitively and delicately minded, the tender-hearted, believer. It is because a being of the earth, yet so God-like as man, could not be moulded into the image of God *save from within himself*, as a person or free agent, that man can account the payment of the sometimes exorbitant price of the chance of learning love inevitable.

If the doctrine of a future life be a corollary of theism, or an implication of the moral purposiveness and meaning which may reasonably be read into the cosmos, it can be invoked to throw further light on the problem of evil. The balance of felicity and unhappiness in an individual life cannot be struck so long as we confine our thought to experience of the present world alone, if we have reason to believe that the earth is 'no goal, but starting-point for man'. We may then venture to add to our knowledge the faith that 'the sufferings of this present time are not worthy to be compared with the glory that shall be revealed'. Pain is indeed none the less pain, nor any kind of evil the less evil, for that it shall be done away or compensated or because it is a necessary means or by-product. But its hideousness is somewhat transfigured if, besides being involved in the 'best possible' world, it can be seen to have been 'but for a moment' in the time-span of just men made perfect. It is not the reality of evil that is here under consideration, but simply the worthwhileness of this life in which evil has a temporary and necessary place. That should not be estimated by looking only at what may now be seen; but for the idea of compensation hereafter theodicy and theistic religion have no further use. They do not ask us to tolerate the evils of the present world and to abstain from blaming the Creator for them because of a compensation stored up for us in another world: they rather insist that in this life, with all its evils, we may already discern the world-purpose of God to be a reign of love.

This life acquires, indeed, a new aspect if death be but translation to another mansion in the Father's house, and exchange of one kind of service for another. And it is a question whether theism, in asserting the world-ground to be a spirit and the Father of spirits, and in ascribing to the world the role of ministering to rational and moral life, can stop short of adding the doctrine of a future life to its fundamental articles of belief, without stultifying its previously reached interpretation of the world and man. For it would not be a perfectly reasonable world which produced free beings, with Godward aspirations and illimitable ideals, only to cut them off in everlasting death, mocking their hopes and frustrating their purposes. Such spirits, even with their moral status, would after all be pawns, not children of God. Certainly a God who can be worshipped by moral beings must be a respecter of the persons whom he has moulded into his own image. Hence theists generally regard the Supreme Being as a God, not of the dead, but of the living.

There is one particular problem within the larger problem of evil, to which the doctrine of a future life has a special relevance: a problem of the kind indicated by the remark, made at the beginning of this chapter,[1] that explanatory theories are apt to bear within themselves, or to set up, fresh difficulties. If the theistic gospel be the only sufficient interpretation of the intelligibility, orderliness and progressiveness of the world as a whole, it is not unique in respect of explaining without creating new *explicanda*. It does not forthwith brightly illumine every dark recess of the mind of him who would use it as a lantern to his feet. Its very acceptance creates at least one perplexity, not forthcoming for those who reject the theistic interpretation, and necessitates a special theodicy to resolve that perplexity. For it is a difficulty besetting theistic faith that faith itself can be tried; and perhaps many will find here the sharpest edge of the wider problem of evil. God may seem to them to allow so little insight into his dealings with persons, and so little of intelligent—as distinct from purely moral—co-operation with him in working out their individual destiny, that they scarcely dare call him 'Father', though ethical theism requires that they should do so. Their cosmic philosophy appears to collapse in that some of its deduced consequences do not seem to be verified in experience. Moreover, an unwavering faith, a steady and unfaltering sense of the reality of things unseen, is a condition of the peace which alone enables the believer to serve God with a quiet mind, and also of the spiritual zeal and effectiveness of his life. It is the feeling with which the believer regards that life, his alone and his for once alone, that should most strongly evidence his kinship with the Deity; and he should be able to deem the efficacy of his little life-work not indifferent to his God. Should God then try his very faith and so render all that he might build with it precarious? Should the very spring of religious love, the source of the unique beauty and sublimity of character moulded by pure religious sentiment, be capable of being lost, though a man may yearn to retain possession of it above all things else? Duty, service and blamelessness of life are not always easy even when faith is unclouded;

[1] *Philosophical Theology*, Vol. ii, p. 180. The first page and a half of the chapter are not reproduced here.

but that the one bond which links the soul with God should be imperilled by the probationary influences of this life seems at first sight hard to reconcile with the relations which theism asserts to subsist between the soul, the world and God.

We can see that it is of the very nature of faith to provide from within itself for its own trial; for faith is not sight, and whatever truth may be apprehended by faith must be 'deadened of its absolute blaze'. We can also see that a trial of faith is necessitated from without, in that advance in knowledge and in ethical appreciation renders beliefs, which in earlier times were reasonable, no longer tenable. So the difficulty before us narrows down to the old and recurrent question, why, if there is a God whose world-purpose is communion between finite spirits and himself, is faith rather than knowledge vouchsafed to us, or why is not revelation readable by him who runs, with infallible certainty and immediacy?

. . . .

Firstly, it may be suggested that if our wills be ours to make harmonious with the divine will, and the quest for the highest is to be veritably *our* quest and adventure, God must not be too certainly knowable to us, as well as not too active upon us. Otherwise, just as excess of motivation would defeat ethical freedom, so over-abundance of life would preclude that 'groping after God' which is the obverse of revelation to a developing and free agent such as man. The formation (as contrasted with the fruition) of character, and the winning of truth by truth-seeking (as contrasted with the passive imbibing of ready-made infallibilities), require an invisible rather than a visible or demonstrable God, a partial revelation rather than a beatific vision, a divine co-operation rather than a divine overwhelming, the possibility of failure to find rather than the security of essentially non-moral and non-personal success. There must 'needs provision be For keeping the soul's prowess possible'. In other words, the confinement of cognition, as to God and his dealings, or as to our whence and whither, to the form of faith, which is the free soul's venture and cannot be, as ecclesiastical theology has generally taught, an arbitrary gift of God; the consequent possibility of reasonable doubt; the necessity of each soul to fight its way to reasonable belief or conviction compatible with knowledge: these appear to be implications of the purpose of God, and conditions of religious life for creaturely and developing moral personalities. It is from religion, rather than from cosmic philosophy, that we must seek any more light on this matter. And perhaps it begins to appear that these are not discontinuous.

Further, the difficulty presented to theistic faith by the fact that faith is dangerously liable to trial, so long as it does not degenerate into supine credulity, is removed if the belief that this present life is not the whole of life be not faithlessly treated. The momentousness of failure here to achieve our life's ends then becomes relatively insignificant: especially if God cares more for what we are than for what we do. There is such a thing as success in failure. We can attach exaggerated importance, in one sense, to the actual filling of this life with finished products, just as too much importance used to be attached to the particular moral state and the particular contents of an individual's faith at the hour of his passing. It is in harmony with the world-view presented by theism to regard growth towards perfection, whether of character or of faith, rather than attainment of perfectness, as the divine purpose for our earthly life. All aspiration that is here unrealized, all tasks remaining unaccomplished when death cuts us off, all baffled search, honest doubt, and faith that has been shipwrecked while men of goodwill and pure heart have worked in half-light or shadow, may be fulfilled in the life beyond. Bereavement of faith, therefore, like bereavement of friends, is not endless separation, but rather a phase in a process which knows vicissitudes.

Thus the special problem of the temptability of personal faith is to be met in the same way as the larger problem of evil in general. It remains no less a trial to faith that faith necessarily must be tried, just as evil is none the less evil for that it is necessary or that it shall be done away. But if this life is not *all*-important, and if the world-purpose is not consistently ethical unless there is a hereafter, the question why faith that is vital for the fullest life is not immune from trial no longer constitutes a formidable difficulty. The facts which suggest a theistic interpretation of the world also suggest that in this life our seeking rather than our finding is God's purpose for us: question and counter-question, intercourse and dialogue, rather than full light and certain knowledge. The risks attending faith are not fatal, while they are conditions of the ethico-religious status in the life that now is.

INDICES

INDEX OF NAMES

Names of authors cited in the Bibliographical Notes are not included here. Numbers in bold type indicate that the references occur in the Editor's Introductory Notes, etc., or footnotes, though they may also occur in the text on the same page.

Academics, **225, 351**; *see also* Plato
Adam, **141**, 147
Alaric, **31**
Albert the Great, **59**
Alexander of Abonuteichos, **239**
Alexander the Great, **241**
Amos, 431
Anabaptists, **137**
Anaxagoras, **177**
Anaximenes, **65**
Annandale, Marquis of, **205**
Anselm, St, **55-8, 69, 158**
Antigonid dynasty, **241**
Aquinas, St Thomas, **31, 50, 55, 59-61, 70-1**, 147, **151, 180, 307, 332, 481**; *see also* Thomists
Aristotelians, **31, 112, 152, 223, 259, 389**; *see also* Aristotle
Aristotle, **20, 59-60**, 61, **64-5, 68-70, 73-4, 81, 112**, 147, 152, **179, 262**, 292, 450, **452**; *see also* Aristotelians
Arminius, **151**
Asclepius, **239**
Ashley, Lord, *see* Shaftesbury, Earl of
Augustine, St, **31-2**, 32-49, **59, 64, 65, 69**, 79-80, 147, 152, **465**
Augustus Caesar, **424**

Bacon, Francis, **246**, 371, **372**
Balfour, Arthur, **384**
Bampton Lectures, **361**
Barth, Karl, **307**
Bede, the Venerable, **243**
Bentham, Jeremy, **340**
Bergson, Henri, **378**
Berkeley, Bishop, **114, 130, 156-7, 205**
Bhagavad-Gītā, **299**
Boethius, **65, 74, 466**
Boyle Lectures, **195**
Bradley, F. H., **379**
Brown, Thomas, **343**
Brunswick, Duke of, **141**
Buddhism, **88, 298**
Butler, Joseph, **185-6, 443, 453**

Calvinism, **151**
Cambridge Platonists, **367, 442**
Carneades of Cyrene, **351**
Caroline, Queen, **185**
Cartesians, **106, 129, 142, 145, 256**; *see also* Descartes
Cato, **235**
Cebes, **21**, 21-30
Charles I, King, **85**
Cherbury, *see* Herbert of Cherbury, Lord
Christ, **291, 293, 323-4**, 337, **345, 346**, 370, 428, 438
Christine of Sweden, Queen, **185**
Chrysippus of Soli, **351**
Church of England, **385**
Cicero, **212, 225, 238**
Clarke, Samuel, **195**
Clifford, W. K., **384**, 385, 391
Clough, A. H., **383**
Colebrooke, H. T., **300**
Collingwood, R. G., **58**
Comte, Auguste, **481**
Cook Wilson, John, **439**
Copernicus, **105**, 213-15, **249**
Cudworth, Ralph, **367, 442**

Damascene, St John, **63**, 66
Danish Church, **345**
David, 370
Demetrius Poliorketes, **241**
de Morgan, Augustus, **409**
Demosthenes, **238**
de Retz, Cardinal, **242**
Descartes, **57**, **105-7**, **121**, **124-5**, **129**, **133**, **141**, **144**, 145, **158**, **256**, 389, **457**; *see also* Cartesians
Dionysius the Areopagite, *see* Pseudo-Dionysius
Dionysius I of Syracuse, **19**
Dionysius II of Syracuse, **19**
Donatist heresy, **31**
Duns Scotus, **151**
Dutch Reformed Church, **151**

Eckhart, Meister, **435**
Eleatics, **300**; *see also* Parmenides
Elizabeth I, Queen, 245
Emerson, R. W., **394**
Epicureans, **175**, **225**; *see also* Epicurus
Epicurus, **158**, **227**, **277**, 278, 303
Evodius, Bishop, **31**, 31-49
Euclid, 132, **388**

Fermat, **120**, **133**
Fichte, **290-1**
Flavians, **241**
Fries, **421**

Galileo, **105**, **214**, **225**
Gaunilo, **57**
Gifford Lectures, **378**
Gorgons, **347**

Haller, Berchtold, **262**
Hamann, **359**
Hamilton, Sir William, **361**, **392**
Harvey, William, **105**
Hegel, **57**, **290-1**, **346**, **366**, **379**, **389**
Helmholtz, **449**
Heraclitus, **19**
Herbert of Cherbury, Lord, **85-6**, **129**
Herodotus, **243**
Hibben, Professor, **408**
Hiero I of Syracuse, **212**
Hinduism, 298, **299**
Hinton, Charles H., **388**
Hobbes, **176**
Hugo of St Victor, **423**
Hülsemann, **153**
Hume, **160**, **187**, **205-6**, **213**, **248-9**, **341**, 341-2, **382**, **457**, **464**
Hutcheson, Thomas, **443**, **444**
Huxley, T. H., **383**, **471**
Huygens, **141**

Imam, the last, *see* Mahdi
Incas, the, **88**
Indra, 299
Isaiah, 423, 426
Islam, **380**

Jainism, **88**
James I, King, **85**
James, Henry, **378**
James, William, **378-80**, **399**, 401, **402**, 402-3, 405, 407, 410-11
Janssen (father and son), **225**
Jesuits, **180**
Jesus, 52, 370; *see also* Christ
John, St (Apostle), 376
Jowett, Benjamin, **364**
Jupiter, **88**, 445

Kant, **141**, **205**, **213**, **248-50**, **271-3**, **290**, **306**, **340**, **363-4**, **367**, **372**, **374**, **389**, **421**, **433**, 434, 436
Kepler, **105**
Kierkegaard, **345-6**
Kneale, W. C., **58**
Krishna, **299**

Lactantius, **359**
Lanfranc, **55**
Leibniz, **120**, **124**, **133**, **141-2**, **173**, **195**, **248**, **256**, **471**
Leo XIII, Pope, **59**
Lincoln, Abraham, 381
Livy, 216, **241**, 246
Lobachevsky, **388**
Locke, John, **86**, **106**, **114**, **129-30**, **156**, **187**, **192**, **195**, **205**, 456
Lotze, Hermann, **439**, **467**

Lucian, **239, 240**
Lucretius, **158, 224, 243**

Mahābhārata, **299**
Mahdi, **380,** 383
Maimonides, **69, 73, 124**
Mainz, Elector-Archbishop of, **141**
Malcolm, Norman, **58**
Malebranche, **172**
Manicheanism, **31**
Mansel, Dean, **361-2, 376-7**
Marcus Aurelius, **240**
Mariana, **243**
Martineau, James, **482,** 483
Marx, **291**
Mill, James, **340**
Mill, John Stuart, **340, 378, 456**
Milton, John, 227
Mirandola, Pico della, *see* Pico della Mirandola
Mohammed, 282
Monica, St, **31**
Montaigne, **86**
Moore, G. E., **58**
Morell, J. D., **369**
Moses, 133

Nansen, Dr, 381
Napoleon Bonaparte, **306,** 350
Neo-Platonists, **20,** 31-2, **50-1, 179**
Nero, Emperor, **154**
Newman, F. W., **364**
Newman, J. H., **364, 385**
Newton, Isaac, **85, 105, 120, 133, 195, 205**
Noah, 133

Olsen, Regina, **345**
Origen, **188**
Orphism, **30**
Otto, Rudolf, **273, 421-2**

Pachama Viracocha, **88**
Paley, William, **479**
Parmenides, **19;** *see also* Eleatics
Pascal, **382,** 383, 393
Paul, St, **50,** 66
Peirce, C. S., **378, 379, 411**
Pelagianism, **31**
Perkins, William, **151**
Peter, St, 80, 423
Philolaus, **21**
Pico della Mirandola, **179**
Picus, *see* Pico della Mirandola
Plato, **19-21, 31-2, 59, 179, 225, 248,** 292, **348, 422,** 450, 452, **457;** *see also* Academics, Neo-Platonists
Plotinus, **50, 218**
Plutarch, **235, 241,** 243
Poiret, Pierre, **145**
Proclus, **51**
Protagoras, **348**
Pseudo-Dionysius, **50-1,** 74, 75, **178,** 179-80
Puritans, **137, 151**
Pyrrho, **385**
Pythagoras, **19;** *see also* Pythagoreans
Pythagoreans, **35;** *see also* Pythagoras

Reformation, the, **85**
Reid, Thomas, **389**
Rig-Veda, **299**
Ritschl, **426**
Roberval, **120**
Roman Catholicism, **55, 385**
Royce, Josiah, **399-400, 420**
Rūmī, Jalal-ad-dīn, **301**
Russell, Bertrand, **439**
Ryle, Gilbert, **58, 180**

Sāma-Veda, **299**
Śankara, 299
Sanskrit, 300
Schelling, 290
Schlegel, F., 306
Schleiermacher, **273, 306-7, 366, 368, 421**
Scotus, *see* Duns Scotus
Secrétan, Charles, **395**
Seneca, **154**
Sextus Empiricus, **348**
Shaftesbury, Earl of, **129**
Shakespeare, William, 359
Sh'ïa Sect, **380**
Simmias, **21,** 21-30

Simonides of Ceos, **212**
Śiva, 299
Socrates, **19**, 21-30, **346**, 347-55
Sophia Charlotte, Queen of Prussia, **141**
Spencer, Herbert, **377**, **392**
Spinoza, **124-6**, 176, **300**, **480**
St Clair, General, **205**
Stoics, **35**, **50**, **225**, **240**, **274**, **351**
Suarez, **180**
Sufis, **301**
Suso, **435**

Tacitus, 216, **241**, **463**
Talbot, Lord Chancellor, **185**
Taft, President, 410
Tennant, F. R., **464**
Tennyson, Lord, **456**
Tertullian, **359**
Theodoric, Emperor, **74**
Thomists, **260**; *see also* Aquinas
Tillotson, John, **232**
Tractarians, the, **385**

Underhill, Evelyn, **433**

Vasudeva, 300
Vespasian, Emperor, **241**

Weismann, August, **392**
William of Orange, Prince, **85**
Wittgenstein, Ludwig, **439**
Wolff, Christian, **248**, **251**

Xenophon, **352**

Yahweh, 425, 432

Zwingli, **232**
Zöllner, J. K. F., **388**

INDEX OF SUBJECTS

Numbers in bold type indicate that the references occur in the Editor's Introductory Notes, etc., or footnotes, though they may also occur in the text on the same page. The bracketed names show the authors who discuss or hold the topic or thesis in question.

Absolute, the, (Schelling and Hegel) **290-1**; (Royce) **399-400**
creates particulars, (Hegel) **293**
no knowledge of possible, (Hamilton and Mansel) **361**; (Spencer) **377**
is not God, (Bradley) **379**
absolute dependence, (Schleiermacher), **307**, 309, 330; (Mansel) 369; (Otto) **422**
absolute truth, impossibility of, in pragmatism, (Royce) **420**
accident, meaning of term, (Aquinas) **75**; (Descartes) **112**; (Leibniz) **152**
act, *see* actuality
actuality, contrasted with potentiality, (Aristotle) **60, 112**
a relative contrast, (Aristotle) **77**
God's knowledge as pure act, (Aquinas) **180**
nothing moved save by that which is in act, (Aquinas) 68; (Descartes) **117**
affirmative way, (Proclus) **51**; (Pseudo-Dionysius) 51-3, 74-5; (Aquinas) 75; (Kierkegaard) 353
agnosticism, origin of term, **383**
(Berkeley) **158**; (Spencer) **377**
analogy, theory of, (Aquinas) **60, 70-1**; (Suarez) 180
Scholastic meaning of term, (Berkeley) 181
metaphorical and proper, (Berkeley) 181
meaning of term, (Butler) **185**
arguments from, (Hume) 208
see also attribution, equivocal, metaphorical, proportion, proportionality, univocal
analytic, meaning of term, (Kant) **253-4**
opposed to synthetic, (Kant) **254**, 260, **274**
propositions, (Leibniz) **141**
unity, (Kant) 274
anthropomorphism, (Hume) 220, 222
in religious language necessary, (Schleiermacher) 320
antinomy, meaning of term, (Kant) **248-9**
of practical reason, (Kant) 276-7
a posteriori, meaning of term, **86, 207, 266**
argument for God's existence, (Leibniz) 143-4; (Hume) 207
apperception, meaning of term, (Leibniz) **142**

a priori, meaning of term, **86**
knowledge, (Leibniz and Spinoza) **124, 145**; (Wolff) **248**; (Kant) **290**; (Otto) 438
Common Notions as, (Herbert of Cherbury) **86**
concepts, (Kant) **249,** 250; (Fries and Otto) **421**
category, the Holy as, (Otto) 432-8
proof of God's existence, (Leibniz) **145**; (Hume) **208**
see also Ontological Argument
art, its relation to religion, (Hegel) **291,** 295
atheism, placed in the best light, (Hume) 158
(Hegel) 297; (Mansel) **362**
self-contradictory, (Mansel) 372
atomism, (Spinoza) **125**
attribution, analogy of, name for analogy of proportion, (Aquinas) **70**
autonomy, of ethics, (Kant) **272**; (Mill) **340**
of religion, (Schleiermacher and Otto) **273**; (Otto) **422**
axioms, (Spinoza) **125**; (Leibniz) 143
of geometry, (James) 386, **388**

Being, (Parmenides) **19, 300**
being, concept of, (Anselm) **55**
metaphysics as study of, (Aristotle and Aquinas) **60**
convertible with truth, (Aquinas) 61
as non-univocal name of God and creatures, (Aquinas) 74, 180-1
categories of, (Aristotle) **74**
not a real predicate, (Kant) 254
of God, as much as that of an existent fly, (Kierkegaard) 350
see also existence, necessary being
benevolence, (Butler) **185**
Biblical criticism, (Spinoza) **126**
biology, theoretical basis of, (Spinoza) **125**
see also Evolution
blood, circulation of, discovered by Harvey, **104**
bodies, animal, (Descartes) **106, 125**
see also mind

calculus, discovery of, by Newton and Leibniz, **120, 133, 141**
categories, meaning of term, (Aristotle) **74**; (Kant) **249**
causal argument for existence of God, (Descartes) 107-21
causality, (Kant) **434**; (Locke) 456-7; (Hume) 457; (Hegel) **290**
see also cause, causes, induction
cause and effect, simultaneous, (Descartes) **106**
relation between necessary, (Spinoza) **124**
denied, (Hume) **205, 213**
perfections existing in, (Leibniz) **144**
everything contingent has a, (Kant) 258, 260-1
no place in Locke's theory for concept of, (Cook Wilson) 456
see also causes, causality

causes, distinction between four kinds of, (Aristotle) **59**; (Aquinas) 77
primary and secondary, (Aquinas) 77-9
like effects prove like, (Hume) 224
universal relatedness of, (Schleiermacher) 330
discovery of, (Mill) **340-1**
see also efficient cause, final cause, induction, cause, causality
celestial bodies, (Aristotle) **60, 71,** 72; (Hume) 214-15
cogito ergo sum, (Descartes) **107,** 115, 457
commandments of God as summarizing Common Notions, (Herbert of Cherbury) 102-3
duties conceived as, (Kant) 287
Common Notions, (Herbert of Cherbury) **85,** 86 ff.
see also ideas
conatus, concept of, (Spinoza) **125**
concepts, absurdity of identifying experience with, (James) **379**
contradictions implicit in the use of, (Hegel) **291**
analysis of religious, (Otto) **422**
a priori, (Kant) **249,** 250; (Fries and Otto) **421**
see also ideas, Ideas
conscience, (Butler) **185,** 444; (Mansel) 367-8
consciousness of our own existence, indivisible, (Butler) 195
of moral obligation, as argument for God's existence, (Mansel) 367-8
offended, (Kierkegaard) 356-60
objective, (Schleiermacher) 329
human, cannot conceive the Infinite, (Mansel) **362,** 364
religious, (Schleiermacher and Hegel) **366**; (Mansel) 366; (Cook Wilson) 455
stream of, (James) **378**
the Divine, (Hutcheson) 444
creature-, (Otto) **422**
conservation of energy, (Helmholtz) **449**
contradiction, law of, (Aristotle) **64**; (Leibniz) **141,** 143
self-, (Kant) **253**
concept of *noumena* does not involve, (Kant) **272**
implicit in the nature of things, (Hegel) **290-1**
implicit in all statements about the Absolute, etc., (Mansel) **362, 377**
implicit in the notion of relation, (Bradley) **379**
conversion, meaning of term in logic, **61**
Cosmological Argument, (Aquinas) 67-9; (Locke) **130**; (Leibniz) 143-5; (Hume) 228-32; (Kant) **249-50,** 250, 256-63
cosmology, *see* universe
cosmos, *see* universe
creation of universe, whether outside natural order, (Aquinas) 80
and conservation, (Aquinas) 78; (Descartes) **106,** 118
critical, meaning of term, (Kant) **248**

deduction, meaning of term, (Kant) **275**

definition(s), Socrates' search for, **19**
truths by, **58**
causes and effects having the same, (Aquinas) 71
(Leibniz) 143
self-contradictory, (Kant) **253**
Deism, Herbert of Cherbury as 'father' of, **85-6**
Butler's criticisms of, **185-6**
Demiurge, (Plato) **20**; (Plotinus) **50**
demonstration, first principles of, (Aristotle) **64**
see also contradiction, excluded middle, identity
of God's existence, whether possible, (Aquinas) 66-7; (Hume) 229-30; (Cook Wilson) 453-5
of existence not possible, (Kierkegaard) 349
two senses of, 66
no need for, where there is direct knowledge of God, (Cook Wilson) 454
demonstrative evidence distinguished from probable, (Butler) 186
design, argument from, *see* Teleological Argument
determinism, whether compatible with free will, **40-1**; (Spinoza) **125**; (Leibniz) **142**, 148-9; (Kant) **272**
see also free will
Deus sive Natura, (Spinoza) **124-5**
dialectic, concept of, (Plato) **20**, 27-8; (Hegel) **291**, **296**; (Marx) **291**; (Tennant's criticism of) 475
dogmatic, meaning of term, (Kant) **248**
doubt, Descartes' method of, **107**
dualism between mind and body, (Descartes) **106**, **115**; (Leibniz) **142**
duty, contrasted to inclination, **40**; (Kant) 287; (Mansel) 367
dynamics, basic concept of, **142**

efficient causes, argument from nature of, (Aquinas) 68
meaning of term, **59**
emanation, (Plotinus) **50**
eminently, meaning of term, **144**, 180
empiricism, (Locke) **129-30**, 456; (Berkeley) **156**; (Hume) **205**; (rouses Kant) **248**; (in Kant) 258; (Mill) **348**; (Tennant) **464**
agnostic, 158
criticized as giving narrow account of experience, (James) **378**; (Cook Wilson) 462
versus Absolutism, (James) 386-7
enthusiasm, meaning of term, **137**
Locke's distrust of, **130**
reasons for distrust of, (Locke) 136-40
epigenesis, meaning of term, (Otto) **432**; (Tennant) **468**
epistemology, *see* knowledge, theory of
equivocal, meaning of term, **71**; (Aquinas) 73-4
error, Descartes' theory of, **109**
nature of, (Royce) **399-400**

essence(s), as described by definition, (Aquinas) **64**, 65, 72
change of, (Aquinas) 72
God's, (Damascene) 66
does not involve existence, (Kierkegaard) 350; *see also* existence
God as source of, (Leibniz) 144
truth about God not to be found through, (Kierkegaard) **346**
evil, problem of, (Augustine) **31-2**, 465; (Aquinas) 67, 70, 147, 465; (Leibniz) **145-6**, 146-55; (Tennant) 465-88; (Cook Wilson) 448
types of, distinguished, (Tennant) 478-9
and loyalty, (Royce) **420**
as nothing, (Boethius) 466
in Absolutism, (James) **379**
Evolution (theory of), (Huxley) **383**; (Clifford) **384**; (Weismann) **392**; (Bergson) **378**
as argument against Teleological Argument (Cook Wilson) 450
and Paley's teleology, 479
excluded middle, law of, (Aristotle) **64**
existence, not a predicate, **57-8**, **255**; (Kant) 254-6
of God, necessary, (Aquinas) 69; (Spinoza) 126; (Leibniz) 145
inseparable from God's nature, (Descartes) 122
requires cause or reason, (Spinoza) 126; (Leibniz) **141**
capacity for, implies power, (Spinoza) 127-8
of individuals, (Leibniz) **141**
not subject to demonstration, (Kierkegaard) 349
of our friends, our knowledge of the, (Cook Wilson) 435-4; (Berkeley) 154
Existentialism, Schleiermacher and, **307**
(Pascal) **382**
(Kierkegaard) **345-6**
experience, our only guide in reasoning concerning matters of fact, (Hume) 233
too rich for conceptualization, (James) **379**
religious, (Schleiermacher) **306-7**; (Hegel) **366**; (Mansel) 366; (Otto) **421-2**, 422-38; (Cook Wilson) 455
expiation, (Herbert of Cherbury) 93-5; (Otto) 427
extension, identified with matter, (Descartes) **105**, **142**
distinguished from Thought, (Spinoza) **125**
external world, existence of, (Descartes) **107**, **121**; (Berkeley) **156**; (Hume) **205**; (Kant) **272**

faith, that God exists, (Aquinas) 66
presupposes natural knowledge, (Aquinas) 66-7
what is of, cannot be false, (Aquinas) 74-5
uncritical leap of, (Montaigne) **86**
definition of, (Locke) **133**; (schoolboy's) 397
proper matter of, (Locke) 135
and reason, (Locke) 136; (Kierkegaard) 347 ff.

faith, not an independent source of metaphysical truth, (Spinoza) **126**; (Hegel) **291**
depends on a continued miracle, (Hume) 247
rational, (Kant) 285-6
in a fact can help to create it, (James) 395-8
no room for, (Spencer) **377**
whether a mysterious faculty, (Cook Wilson) 444-6
temptability of, (Tennant) 486-8
Fall, the, 147
fallacy of four terms, (Berkeley) **182**
final causes, (Plato) **20**; (Aristotle) **59**; (Leibniz) 144; (Butler) **189**; (Hume) 208-10; (Paley and Tennant) 479
see also Teleological Argument
first efficient cause, *see* God
Five Ways, (Aquinas) **55**, **60**, 67-70; *see* God, Cosmological Argument, Teleological Argument, gradation
form, meaning of term, (Aristotle) **60**
identified with actuality, **112**
simple, God as, (Boethius) 74
Forms, Plato's theory of, **19-20**, 23, 34
Augustine's adaptation of, **31**; (Plotinus) **50**
Aristotle's criticisms, **59**
free will, whether compatible with: God's foreknowledge, (Augustine) **40-1**
determinism, (Leibniz) 149 ff.; (Kant) **248-9**, **271-2**
dependence on God, (Mansel) 370
as producing *summum bonum*, (Kant) 275
vital significance of, (Secrétan) **295**
feeling of freedom, (Schleiermacher) 309; (Mansel) 368
and evil, (Tennant) 475
as fifth wheel of the coach, (James) 384
future life, *see* immortality
future, whether like the past, (Hume) **205**, 233

genus, maximum in any, as cause, (Aquinas) 69
geometry, Greek, **19-20**
analytical, (Descartes) **104**, **133**
and the perception of distance, (Berkeley) 166-7
(Kant) 251-2
non-Euclidean, **388**
God, existence of, whether self-evident, (Aquinas) 63-5
general agreement on, (Herbert of Cherbury) 88-90
necessary, if possible, (Leibniz) **145**, **256**
as a postulate of Pure Practical Reason, (Kant) 284-9
proofs of, (Augustine) **31**; (Anselm) 56-7; (Aquinas) 65-6, *see also* Five Ways; (Descartes) 107-23; (Spinoza) 127; (Leibniz) 143-5; (Berkeley) 158; (Kant) 250-71; (Mill) **341**; (Mansel) 362-3; (Cook Wilson) **439**

see also Ontological Argument, Cosmological Argument, Teleological Argument, gradation, causal argument
meaning of term, (Aquinas) 65, 67; (Descartes) 115; (Hobbes, Spinoza) 175-6
as Truth, (Augustine) 38, 64
existence of not known by us, (Aquinas) 65
as simple form, (Boethius) 74
as final cause, (Aristotle and Aquinas) **60**
as creator and conserver, (Aquinas) 78; (Descartes) **106,** 118; (Schleiermacher) 333
not distinct from created world, (Spinoza) **126**
immanent in Nature, (Tennant) 484
as *Deus sive Natura*, (Spinoza) **124-5**
as perpetual perceiver, (Berkeley) **156**
as primary cause, (Aquinas) 77-8
as first cause, (Schleiermacher) **307;** (Cook Wilson) 458
as source of morality, (Schleiermacher) **307**
as unknown something, (Kierkegaard) 349
as object of infinite magnitude, (Mansel) 369
essence of, unknowable by us, (Aquinas) 65
attributes of, (Herbert of Cherbury) 89-90
names of, (Aquinas) 67; (Herbert of Cherbury) 88
absolute dependence as relation to, (Schleiermacher) 311
fear of, (Mansel) 366; (Otto) 431
dependence on, implies commitment, (Kierkegaard) 349
direct experience of, (Cook Wilson) 458-63
kingdom of, (Kant) 286-7; (Schleiermacher) 334
foreknowledge of, (Augustine) **40, 45,** 46-8; (Aquinas) 79
see also knowledge
Good, the, (Plato) **20;** (Plotinus) **50;** (Pseudo-Dionysius) **51**
goodness, absolute, (Anselm) **55;** (Aquinas) **55**
and badness, as ordinarily understood, repudiated (Spinoza) **125**
summum bonum (Kant) **272;** (Otto) 426
distinction between supreme and perfect, (Kant) 273-4
grace, presupposes nature, (Aquinas) 67
hope of, (Aquinas) 81
(Herbert of Cherbury) 94; (Royce) **420**
gradation of things, argument from, to God's existence, (Anselm) **55;** (Aquinas) 69

happiness, whether it comes by necessity, (Augustine) 46
man's pursuit of, (Aquinas) 65; (Butler) 190; (Kant) 273-4
and morality two elements in *summum bonum*, (Kant) 275
hope of, in religion, (Kant) 288-9
greatest, of greatest number, (Mill) **340**
harmony, soul as, (Simmias) **21**

harmony, pre-established, (Leibniz) **142,** 153
heliocentric theory, (Copernicus) **105**
history, significance of, (Augustine) **31**
  dialectic in, (Hegel and Marx) **291;** (Tennant) 475
holiness, our duty to attain, (Kant) **272,** 283, 286-7
holy, idea of the, (Otto) **421-2**
hypothesis, types of, (James) 380-1

I, meaning of term, (Descartes) **115;** *see also* self
I am who am as name of God, (Aquinas) 67
idea(s), plurality of, about God, (Aquinas) 75
  meaning of term, (Descartes) 109; (Locke) **130;** (Hume) **205;** (Royce) **399**
  innate, (Descartes) 110; (Herbert of Cherbury) *see* Common Notions
  attacked by Locke, **86, 129-30**
  origin of, outside me, doubtful, (Descartes) 110-1
  clear and distinct, as test of truth, (Descartes) 108, 113, **121,** 123, **389**
Idea(s), Plato's theory of, *see* Forms
  meaning of term, (Kant) **249, 262**
  do not stand for anything objective, (Kant) **260**
  of Reason, regulative, (Kant) **290**
  of God, (Kant) **249, 272**
  self-thinking, (Hegel) 304-5
Ideal, meaning of term (Kant) 262
Idealism, *see* Absolute, the
identical, meaning of term, **252**
identity, law of, **64;** (Kant) **274**
  personal, (Butler) 192; (Locke) **192**
ideogram, meaning of term, (Otto) **421-2**
immanentism, (Hegel) **291, 293**
immortality, arguments for, (Plato) **20-1,** 21-30; (Butler) 191-204; (Kant) 281-4
  denial of, in Eighteenth Century, **85**
  and punishment and reward, (Herbert of Cherbury) 95
  North Pole sort of, (James) 381
induction, logic of, **188;** (Bacon) **246;** (Mill) **340-1**
  problem of, (Hume) **205, 457**
  complete, meaning of term, (Mill) **342**
ineffability, of the Godhead, (Plotinus and Pseudo-Dionysius) **50-1**
infinite, idea of the, (Descartes) 116-17
  contrasted with the indefinite, (Descartes) **120**
  flattery of the gods, (Hume) **206**
  cause, cannot be inferred from finite effects, (Mansel) 364
  being, God as, (Kant) 252
  ascending series, argument from the impossibility of, (Kant) **261**
  gain, according to Pascal's wager, 382
  universe as known is not, (Hume) 225

Infinite, coherent view of the, impossible, (Mansel) **361**
infinitesimal, problem of, **120**
initiation ceremonies, Orphic, 30
Intelligence, *see* Nous
intuition, meaning of term, (Mansel) **365**
of religious people, (Royce) 413
numinous, (Otto) **421-2**

knowledge, definition of term, (Locke) **132**
theory of, (Plato) **20;** (Herbert of Cherbury) **85-6;** (Descartes) **107, 113;** (Locke) **129;** (Hume) **205;** (Leibniz and Wolff) **248;** (Tennant) **464**
a priori, (Kant and Hegel) **290**
theoretical, (Kant, Schleiermacher and Otto) **273**
speculative and regulative, of God, (Mansel) 374
through universals, (Hegel) **293**
of timeless truths, (Plato) 19-20; (Leibniz) 143
of God, naturally implanted in all, (Damascene) 63
through his effects, (Aquinas) 67; (Leibniz) 143
intuitive, (Spinoza) **125**
as contrasted with demonstrative and perceptual knowledge, (Locke) **133**
in God, (Aquinas) 180
and self-knowledge, (Fries) **421**
and psychology, (Tennant) **464**

language, perception is like a, (Berkeley) **157-8**
of vision, (Berkeley) 170, 173
use of, as evidence of a person's existence, (Berkeley) 164
religious, (Schleiermacher) 320-8; *see also* analogy
poetic, (Schleiermacher) 322-4
laws of nature, decreed by God, (Descartes) **125**
violation of, (Hume) 236; (Schleiermacher) 335-9; (Mill) 342-4; (Otto) 434
laws of thought, **64;** (Leibniz) **141,** 143; (Kant) **274**
logic, Aristotelian, **259;** (Hegel's rejection of) **389**
modern, (Cook Wilson) **439**
logical possibility, **216** (Kant) 253

matter, (Aristotle), **59**
in physics, (Aquinas) 62
in early Greek philosophy, **65**
cosmos as a plenum filled by, (Descartes) **104-5**
as possibly containing source of order, (Hume) 210
identified with, extension, (Descartes) **105, 142**
potentiality, (Scholastics) **112**
mathematics, as key to reality, (Pythagoras) **19;** (Descartes) **105**
judgments in, (Augustine) **31,** 34-5

mathematics, in astronomy, (Aquinas) 62
as paradigm of knowledge, (Descartes) **106-7**; (Spinoza) **124**; (rationalists) **133**
and primary qualities, (Locke) **130**
and natural sciences, (Kant) **249**
how it applies to world, (Kant) **249**
Russell's view of, (Cook Wilson) **439**
see also geometry
maxim, meaning of term, (Kant) **71**
meaning, theory of, (Plato) **20**
memory and personal identity, (Locke and Berkeley) **192**
see also recollection
metaphor(s), used of God, (Pseudo-Dionysius) 52
analogy of, 181
middle term, meaning of phrase in logic, 67
middle, law of excluded; *see* excluded middle
mind, passivity of, repudiated, (Herbert of Cherbury) **86**
different in kind from body, (Descartes) **106, 115**
not a material mechanism, (Leibniz) **142**
absolute, (Hegel) **290-1**
minute philosophers, meaning of term, **158**
miracles, (Aquinas) **60**, 76-81; (Hume) 232-47; (Schleiermacher) 324-39; (Mill) 341-4; (T. Brown) **343**
etymology of term, 81
monads, conception of, (Leibniz) **142**
moral law, (Kant) **271-2**
autonomous, (Kant) **272**
as determining the will, (Kant) 278
argument from, to law-giver, (Mansel) 367
questions, (James) 393
agents, in other possible worlds, (Tennant) 469
feeling, its relation to the numinous, (Otto) 425
see also morality
morality, whether equivalent to happiness, (Kant) 474
distinguished from legality, (Kant) 279
inspired by God as imaginary ideal, (Mill) **341**
lower than speculation, (Aristotle) 442, 452
see also moral
motion, argument from, to God's existence, (Aquinas) 67-8
rectilinear and circular, (Descartes) **105**
and rest, (Spinoza) **125**
mystic, meaning of term, (Hume) 220
mystical experience, (Plato) **20**; (Plotinus) **50**

natural theology, contrasted with revealed, (Aquinas) **60**
instinct, (Herbert of Cherbury) **86**
naturalism, meaning of term, **398, 432**
(Aristotle's) **61**

nature, as possible first principle, (Aquinas) 67, 70
order of, (Aquinas) 78-80
as teacher, (Descartes) 110-1
light of, (Descartes) **110,** 110-1
as a system of symbolism, (Berkeley) **157**
alternative term for God, (Spinoza) **124-5**
analogy of, (Butler) **185-6,** 194
universal interdependence of, (Schleiermacher) 331
necessitated, (Hegel) **345**
presupposed by knowledge through universals, (Hegel) **293,** 305
routine of, (Tennant) 480
see also laws, of nature
necessary, opposed to contingent, (Leibniz and Spinoza) **124**
what is predetermined is, (Leibniz) 148
judgments, (Kant) 252
being, God as, (Aquinas) 69; (Leibniz) **145**
concept of, (Kant) **250,** 251-2
illusion in all arguments for existence of a, (Kant) 263-6
properties, (Descartes) **112**
see also truths, necessity
necessity, opposed to possibility, (Aquinas) 68-9
natural, (Aquinas) 79
hypothetical and absolute, (Leibniz) 149-50, 155
conditional, (Kant) **265**
of judgments and things, (Kant) 252
idea of, inherent in Evolution, (Cook Wilson) 450
negative way, (Pseudo-Dionysius) **50,** 74, 178-9; (Kierkegaard) 353
non-rational, meaning of term, (Otto) 428-30
notion, Hegel's doctrine of the, **302**
noumena, meaning of term, (Kant) **272**
Nous, (Plotinus) **50**
numbers as ultimate constituents of things, (Pythagoras) **19**
see also mathematics
numinous, meaning of term, (Otto) **421-2**

objective, meaning of term, (Descartes) **112;** (Kant) **260**
consciousness, (Schleiermacher) 329
method, (Mansel) 361-2
evidence, (James) 387
certitude, doctrine of, abandoned, (James) 390
rightness in conduct, (Tennant) 473
occasionalism, **106, 125, 142**
One, the, (Plotinus) **50**
Ontological Argument, (Anselm) **56,** 64, **121;** (Descartes) **57,** 121-3; (Kant) **249,** 250; (Kierkegaard) 350
omnipotence of God, (Kant) **249,** 250, 252; (Boethius) 466; (Leibniz) 146 ff.
limited by determinateness, (Tennant) 470-1

pantheism, (Hegel) 297-304
Hegel's apparent, (Kierkegaard) **345**
self-contradictory, (Mansel) **362,** 372
paradox, absolute, (Kierkegaard) 356-60
the religious, (Royce) **400,** 401
of Christianity, (Otto) 428
perception(s) yields no certain knowledge, (Plato) **20;** (Montaigne) **86;** (Descartes) **106**
as a form of thought, (Descartes) **114**
as source of knowledge, (Locke) **129-30**
esse est percipi, (Berkeley) **156**
meaning of term, (Leibniz) **142**
called impressions, (Hume) **205, 378**
and reality, (Hume) **205**
perfect Being, (Kant) **250**
distinct from supreme, (Kant) 273-4
society, (Royce) **400**
see also perfection, perfections
perfection, of ideas, (Descartes) 113
and existence, (Spinoza) 128, 350; (Descartes) 116-21; (Leibniz) **144;** (Kierkegaard) 350
see also perfect, perfections
perfections, concept of (Aquinas) 69
in God, (Aquinas) **70;** (Kant) 262
all identical, (Aquinas) **72**
in cause and effect, (Descartes) **107;** (Leibniz) **144**
see also perfect, perfection
petitio principii, meaning of term, (Mill) 342
phenomena and *noumena*, (Kant) **272**
physiology, Descartes' views on, **106**
physics, (Descartes) **105-6;** (Newtonian) **85, 105, 195, 205;** (Aristotelian) 62; (Spinoza and Descartes) **125;** (Leibniz) **142**
see also science(s)
piety, its connection with virtue, (Herbert of Cherbury) 91-3
essence of, (Schleiermacher) 307 ff.
polytheism, falsity of, (Herbert of Cherbury) 91-3
virtues of, (Hume) **206**
positivism, (Comte) **481**
potentiality, contrasted with actuality, (Aquinas) **60, 112**
reduction of, to actuality, (Aquinas) 68
pragmatism, (James) **378;** (Royce) **420**
prayer as an active relation to God, (Mansel) 370
privation, meaning of term, (Leibniz) **152;** (Aquinas) 465
probability, in reasoning, (Locke) 135
as a guide to judgment, (Butler) **186**
distinguished from demonstration, (Butler) 186
proof, meaning of term, (Hume) 234
see also God—existence of—proofs of
properties, necessary, (Descartes) **112**

proportion, analogy of, sometimes called attribution, (Aquinas) **70,** 73
proportionality, analogy of, sometimes called proportion, (Aquinas) **70,** 73
propositions, types of (Schleiermacher), 323-8
  see also truths

qualities, primary and secondary, (Descartes) **106, 114;** (Locke) **130**
  distinction criticized by Berkeley, **130, 156**
  occult, (Hume) 223

rationalism, **133, 290, 296, 361**
reality, formal and actual, (Descartes) 112
  or Being, (Parmenides) **19**
  must be rational, (Hegel) 290
  flux of, fitted into straightjacket, (James) **378**
reason, *a priori*, (Hume) 221
  pure theoretical and pure practical, (Kant) 434
  wide sense of, (Otto) 436
  and moral sense, (Hutcheson) **443**
  rule of, (Royce) 404
  and origin, distinguished, (Hume) **206**
recollection, theory of, (Plato) **20,** 21-5
  adapted by Kierkegaard, **346**
relations, (Bradley and James) **379**
religion, Common Notions implicit in, (Herbert of Cherbury) **86**
  origin of, (Hume) **206;** (Otto) 434
  relation to morality, (Kant) 287-9; (Otto) 425
  distinguished from philosophy, (Hegel) **291**
  autonomy of, (Schleiermacher and Otto) **273**
  see also religious
religious ideas, nature of, (Schleiermacher) **307**
  stage of life, (Kierkegaard) **345**
  experience, (James) **380;** (Otto) **421-2;** (Cook Wilson) **439,** 458-63
  concepts, (Otto) **422**
representations, concept of, (Hegel) **291**
revealed theology, contrasted with natural, (Aquinas) **60,** 62
  see also revelation
revelation, necessity of, (Aquinas) 62
  assumptions underlying our notions of, (Herbert of Cherbury) 86-7
  wider sense of term, (Herbert of Cherbury) 101
  criteria of truth of, (Herbert of Cherbury) 100-1; (Locke) **133-4,** 132-6
  reason as natural, (Locke) 137
  analogy of, with nature, (Butler) **185-6**
  essential to notion of religion, (Hegel) 292
  as regulative, (Mansel) **376**

revelation, mind incapable of criticizing, (Mansel) **361**
 and the religious paradox, (Royce) **400**
 see also revealed theology
Romantic movement, the, **306-7, 345**
scepticism, Greek, **348, 385**
 Hume's **205**
science(s), Bacon's view of, **246**
 basis of, undermined by Hume, (Kant) **248**
 presuppositions of, (Kant) **271**
 meaning of term, (Schleiermacher) **324**
 interests of, (Schleiermacher) 339
 deductive and inductive methods in, (Mill) **341**
 and telepathy, (James) 385
 exact, (Cook Wilson) 441
 natural, never see into the nature of necessity, (Cook Wilson) 453
 philosophy must be grounded in, (Lotze) **467**
 see also physics, physiology, Evolution
self, the, (Kant and Hegel) **290**
 had to go, in Hume, (Cook Wilson) 457
 (Hume and Tennant) 464
 see also I, Self, selves
Self, the, *see* Absolute
self-consciousness, three forms of, (Schleiermacher) 313
self-evidence, two kinds of, (Aquinas) 64-5
self-knowledge, (Fries) **421**
self-love, (Butler) **185**
 paradox of, (Kierkegaard) 348, 355
selves, conscious, (Hegel) **293**
 see also self, Self, I
sensationalism, meaning of term, **432**
sense, meaning of term, (Kant) **275**
 inner as opposed to outer, (Kant) 278
soul(s), pre-existence of, (Plato) 25-6
 existence of, (Berkeley) 161-2
 union of, with God, (Malebranche) **172**
 has nothing to do with thought-processes, (F. W. Newman) **364**
 monads as like, (Leibniz) **142**
 see also immortality, World-Soul
spiritualism, meaning of term, (Tennant) **480**
sublunary things, (Aristotle) **60, 71**
 see also celestial bodies
substance(s), hierarchy of, (Aquinas) **60**
 incorporeal, (Boethius) 65
 thinking, (Descartes) **107,** 115
 bodily, (Descartes) 112
 infinite, God as the, (Descartes) 115-16
 single, (Spinoza) **124**
 (Leibniz) 143

as something we know not what, (Locke) **129**
criticized by Berkeley, **156**
sufficient reason, principle of, (Leibniz) **141,** 143
superessences, (Pseudo-Dionysius) **51,** 54
suppositum, meaning of term, (Aquinas) 75
supreme craftsman, *see* Demiurge
syllogism, meaning of term, (Hegel) **295, 389**
Barbara, (Cook Wilson) 456
synthetic, meaning of term, (Kant) **253-4**
a priori judgment, (Kant) **260,** 389
unity, (Kant) **274**

Teleological Argument, (Aquinas) 70; (Hume) 207-32; (Kant) **249,** 250, **266,** 266-71; (Socrates) 352; (Kierkegaard) 352; (Cook Wilson) 447-54; (Tennant) 464
theism, defence of, (James) **380**
see also, God
theology, use of term, (Aristotle) 61
see also revealed theology, natural—theology
time, non-continuity of, (Descartes) **106, 118**
criticism of Kant on, (Hegel) **290**
succession in, (Mansel) 362
transcendental criticism, meaning of term, (Kant) **260**
Transcendentalism, (Emerson) 394
truth, non-privacy of, (Augustine), 33
superior to human mind, (Augustine) 37
convertible with being, (Aquinas) 61
test of, (Descartes) **121;** (James) **379**
utility not a, (Berkeley) 158-9
correspondence theory of, (Herbert of Cherbury) **86;** (empiricists') **124;** (medieval) **387;** (Royce) **399**
coherence theory of, (Spinoza) **124;** (Royce) **399,** 411
ultimate, (Kierkegaard) **346**
is subjectivity, (Kierkegaard) **346**
postulate of the existence of, (James) 386
see also truths
truths, eternal or timeless, (Plato) **19;** (Augustine) **31, 33;** (Leibniz) 143; (Cudworth) **442;** (Tennant) 470
by definition, **58**
contingent, (Leibniz) **142,** 143
of reasoning and of fact, (Leibniz) 143
of fact to be proved by fact, (Berkeley) 160
mathematical, (Descartes) 121
see also truth

universe, Heraclitus' view of, **19;** (Plato) **20**
spherical, (Aristotle) **60**
as a machine, (Deists) **85**
as a plenum, (Descartes) **104-5**

universe, natural constitution of, (Butler) **185**
origin of, (Hume) 211-13
whether eternal, (Hume) **228**; (Kant) **248**
beginning and end of, (Schleiermacher) 333
novelty in, (James) **379**
see also universes
universes, possible, this one best of all, (Leibniz) 145, 153
criticism of this view, (Tennant) 467-8
alternative, (Butler) 191
infinite number of, (Leibniz) 145
univocal, meaning of term **71**
whether terms used about God and creatures are, (Aquinas) 71-2, 74
Utilitarianism, (Butler) **185**; (Bentham and Mill) **340**

Verification Principle, the, **379**
virtue, connected with piety, (Herbert of Cherbury) 91-3
whether equivalent to happiness, (Kant) 474
volitions, connected with judgments, (Descartes) **109**
see also will

wax, argument about the, (Descartes) **114**
will, acts of consequent and antecedent, (Leibniz) 150-1; (Tennant) **481**
see also free will
World-Soul, (Plotinus) **50**